THE LETTERS OF COLE PORTER

Further praise for *The Letters of Cole Porter*:

'An absolute must for any fan of the golden age, musical theatre or the incredible Porter himself.' Matthew Shaftel, editor of *A Cole Porter Companion*

'"Well, did you evah!" Cole Porter's letters are full not just of delightful gossip but of the detail of working on Broadway and in Hollywood during the golden age of the American musical. "What a swell party it is!" – or at least was for Porter moving through high society across several continents. His words read as gloriously as his music sounds.' Tim Carter, author of *Oklahoma! The Making of an American Musical*

'These letters offer fascinating glimpses into some previously unseen corners of the personal and creative lives of one of America's greatest songwriters. Eisen and McHugh provide a gilded frame for the source material in the form of expert glosses and annotations. The result is a new kind of Cole Porter biography.' Jeffrey Magee, author of *Irving Berlin's American Musical Theater*

THE
LETTERS OF
COLE
PORTER

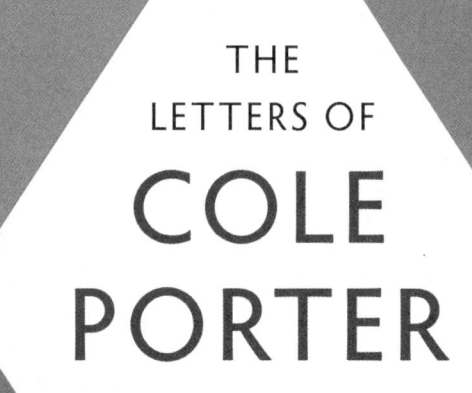

CLIFF EISEN &
DOMINIC McHUGH

YALE UNIVERSITY PRESS
NEW HAVEN AND LONDON

Copyright © 2019 Cliff Eisen and Dominic McHugh

All rights reserved. This book may not be reproduced in whole or in part, in any form (beyond that copying permitted by Sections 107 and 108 of the U.S. Copyright Law and except by reviewers for the public press) without written permission from the publishers.

For information about this and other Yale University Press publications, please contact:
U.S. Office: sales.press@yale.edu   yalebooks.com
Europe Office: sales@yaleup.co.uk   yalebooks.co.uk

Set in Minion Pro by IDSUK (DataConnection) Ltd
Printed in Great Britain by Gomer Press Ltd, Llandysul, Ceredigion, Wales

Library of Congress Control Number: 2019941063

ISBN 978-0-300-21927-2

A catalogue record for this book is available from the British Library.

10 9 8 7 6 5 4 3 2 1

CONTENTS

List of Plates vi
Preface viii
Acknowledgements xii

1 From Peru, Indiana, to Broadway, 1891–1919   1
2 Cole Porter in Europe, 1918–1928   28
3 Porter's Return to the United States, 1928–1937   86
4 Settled – and Injured – in New York, 1937–1944   147
5 A Porter Biopic and Two Flops, 1945–1947   229
6 *Kiss Me, Kate*, 1948   286
7 From *Kiss Me, Kate* to *Out of This World*, 1949–1950   317
8 From Limbo to the Writing of *Can-Can*, 1951–1952   370
9 Two Last Broadway Hits, *Can-Can* and *Silk Stockings*, 1953–1954   429
10 Porter's Last Musicals, 1955–1957   494
11 The Final Years, 1958–1964   583

Endnotes 625
Selected Bibliography 653
Index 654

PLATES

1. Cole Porter, Yale yearbook photograph (1913).
2. Westleigh Farms, Cole Porter's childhood home in Indiana (2011).
3. Cole Porter's World War I draft registration card (5 June 1917). War Department, Office of the Provost Marshal General.
4. Linda Porter, passport photograph (1919).
5. Cole Porter, Linda Porter, Bernard Berenson and Howard Sturges in Venice (c.1923).
6. Gerald Murphy, Ginny Carpenter, Cole Porter and Sara Murphy in Venice (1923).
7. Serge Diaghilev, Boris Kochno, Bronislava Nijinska, Ernest Ansermet and Igor Stravinsky in Monte Carlo (1923). Library of Congress, Music Division, Reproduction number: 200181841.
8. Letter from Cole Porter to Boris Kochno (September 1925). Courtesy of The Cole Porter Musical and Literary Property Trusts.
9. Scene from the original stage production of *Fifty Million Frenchmen* (1929). PHOTOFEST.
10. Irene Bordoni, star of Porter's show *Paris* (1928).
11. Sheet music, 'Love for Sale' from *The New Yorkers* (1930).
12. Production designer Jo Mielziner showing a set for *Jubilee* (1935). PHOTOFEST.
13. Cole Porter composing as he reclines on a couch in the Ritz Hotel during out-of-town tryouts for *Du Barry Was a Lady* (1939). George Karger / Getty Images.
14. Cole and Linda Porter (c.1938). PHOTOFEST.
15. Ethel Merman in the New York production of Cole Porter's *Panama Hattie* (1940). George Karger / Getty Images.

PLATES

16. Sheet music, 'Let's Be Buddies' from *Panama Hattie* (1940).
17. Draft of 'I Am Ashamed that Women Are So Simple' from *Kiss Me, Kate* (1948), Library of Congress. Courtesy of The Cole Porter Musical and Literary Property Trusts.
18. Monty Woolley, publicity photo (1949).
19. Nelson Barclift rehearsing for Irving Berlin's *This is The Army* at Camp Upton (1943). Bettmann / Getty Images.
20. Charlotte Greenwood in Cole Porter's *Out of This World* (1950). PHOTOFEST.
21. Cole Porter and Ed Sullivan on Sullivan's television show, *Toast of the Town* (1953).
22. Cole Porter in an advertisement for Bromo-Seltzer (c.1950).
23. Cole Porter in an advertisement for Rheingold Beer, *Daily News*, New York (18 May 1953).
24. Ann Miller, Cole Porter, producer Jack Cummings and Kathryn Grayson on the set of *Kiss Me Kate* (MGM, 1953). PHOTOFEST.
25. Cole Porter and Jean Howard (1954).
26. Scene from *Silk Stockings* (1955). PHOTOFEST.
27. Cole Porter, music director Andre Previn and producer Jack Cummings working on the film *Kiss Me Kate* (1953). PHOTOFEST.
28. Autograph lyric sheet for *Can-Can* (1953). Courtesy of The Cole Porter Musical and Literary Property Trusts.
29. Sheet music, 'True Love' from *High Society* (1956).
30. Louis Armstrong and Grace Kelly on the set of *High Society* (1956).
31. The last photograph of Cole Porter, New York (1964). PHOTOFEST.

PREFACE

Cole Porter's status as one of the most prolific, enduring and successful American songwriters of the twentieth century, as well as the cultural associations of his extravagant lifestyle and elite social circle, make him a compelling subject for a book focusing on his letters to his friends, family and collaborators, not least because Porter's life and works remain comparatively unexamined. By and large, the closer details of his activities and personality have been overlooked in favour of broad biographical tropes that were established during his lifetime and have been repeated without much refinement or challenge. This is true of even the best authorized and unauthorized biographies: Richard Hubler's *The Cole Porter Story, as Told to Richard G. Hubler* (Cleveland, 1965); George Eells's *The Life that Late He Led: A Biography of Cole Porter* (New York, 1967); Robert Kimball and Brendan Gill's *Cole* (New York, 1971); Charles Schwartz's *Cole Porter: A Biography* (New York, 1977); William McBrien's *Cole Porter: A Definitive Biography* (New York, 1998); and Stephen Citron's *Noel & Cole: The Sophisticates* (New York, 1993).*

Accordingly, in assembling this volume of Cole Porter's correspondence we had specific aims and priorities – as well as several challenges. Our goal was not to write a biography but rather to assemble as much of Porter's extant correspondence as possible, alongside complementary primary sources such as diaries and newspaper articles, and to place the letters in context through a succinct connecting commentary. Fans of Porter's famously witty and wordy songs may be struck by how brief and to the point

---

* Two additional works are fundamental to Porter research and Porter biography: Robert Kimball, *The Complete Lyrics of Cole Porter* (New York, 1983); and Don M. Randel, Matthew Shaftel and Susan Forscher Weiss, eds, *A Cole Porter Companion* (Urbana, IL, 2016).

many of his letters are, and this quality dictated our decision to explain the significance of much of the material. Additionally, part of the challenge was the requirement to guide the reader through the disparate threads of Porter's letters, including business letters to his publishers (such as Max Dreyfus at Chappell), accountant (his cousin Harvey), secretaries (among them Margaret Moore and Madeline P. Smith) and attorneys (John Wharton and Robert Montgomery); working letters about his songs to the book writers of his shows (especially Bella Spewack and Abe Burrows) and arranger (Albert Sirmay); and miscellaneous letters to his fans, actors starring in his musicals (such as Clifton Webb and Ethel Merman), his lovers and his friends. For each of these, but particularly the last two categories, Porter adopts a slightly different tone or diction depending on who he is writing to. For example, his tone of voice in writing to his long-term gay male friends Monty Woolley and Charles Green Shaw is often noticeably exuberant, flirtatious and flamboyant, whereas in writing to his female friends such as Jean Howard he usually adopts a gently charming and affectionate manner. While most of his love letters have apparently not survived, there is a special character to those that have: a particular sincerity and anguish to the sequence of notes (written in French) from Porter to the dancer Boris Kochno in the 1920s, and an almost paternal concern in the letters written to the marine Nelson Barclift in the 1940s.

Even before considering the implications of the facts and details contained in the letters, these nuances speak volumes about Porter's character and offer both the scholar and the general reader new insights into an important historical figure who is at once familiar and yet curiously distant. Of course, the details are where the true surprises lie. For example, we learn that Porter – famously born into a wealthy family and married to a rich divorcee – spent most of his adult life worrying about money, so much so that he often had to weigh up whether the consequently enormous rise in taxes would make it financially crippling to take on certain musical projects. Thus while we might have expected the affluent Porter to have written his songs and musicals without 'needing' the money, in truth the opposite was the case: he sometimes sacrificed his financial stability for his art. The letters also illuminate his relationship with his wife, Linda: he describes falling in love with her during their early acquaintance, and while he openly engaged in sexual relationships with numerous men during his marriage to her, the particular depth of feeling he had for Linda, and his anxiety over the emphysema that threatened her well-being, is striking.

With respect to Porter's professional activities, too, the letters offer perhaps unexpected revelations. Letters to the librettists Bella Spewack and particularly Abe Burrows, on the musicals *Kiss Me, Kate* and *Can-Can*, highlight Porter's concern to collaborate with them on details, rather than expecting Burrows and Spewack simply to slot his songs into their stories. His exchanges with Johnny Green and Saul Chaplin, co-musical directors of the movie *High Society* (1956), similarly show his attention to detail about melody, arrangements and tempi. Twenty years earlier, the extensive diary Porter kept during his experiences writing the movie *Born to Dance* (1936) offers a window into the songwriter's excitement and frustrations on encountering the working practices of Hollywood, so different from those of Broadway. Two other sets of diaries, from the mid-1950s, document the lavish cruises Porter undertook with his friend Jean Howard as a distraction following Linda's death in 1954. And his especially rich correspondence with one of his most loyal friends, Sam Stark, who appears to have retained almost every note or letter he received from Porter, charts the composer's rise and fall during the last two decades of his life. The letters to Stark reflect the years in which Porter went from being one of the most prominent figures in American culture to dying in seclusion in 1964, six years after he had abandoned his work following the amputation of his right leg, finally bringing an end to the constant pain caused by a serious horse-riding accident in 1937. His death is described in detail by his secretary Madeline P. Smith in a poignant letter to Jean Howard that closes the book.

These and many other episodes are brought to life throughout this volume, mostly in Porter's own words. Of course, the content of the book has been dictated by the availability of material. The Cole Porter Trust – which has been extraordinarily supportive of the project – holds a rich selection of material from the mid-1940s to the end of Porter's life, but has only selected earlier material in its possession. At Yale University, the Porter papers include a relatively small selection of letters from across the composer's life, the highlights of which are perhaps the love letters to Kochno and Barclift; even smaller is the Porter collection at the Library of Congress, though it includes useful materials relating to his first attempts at writing musicals and to the later shows *Can-Can* and *Silk Stockings*. The many gaps left by these main collections forced us to work particularly hard in tracking down further materials from the collections of the recipients of Porter's letters, whether from friends (Katharine Hepburn's papers at the Margaret Herrick Library and the Douglas Fairbanks Jr. papers at Boston University) or collaborators (the Arthur Freed and MGM collections at the University of Southern California, the Richard Lewine papers at the New York Public Library and the Bella Spewack papers at Columbia University). (To aid the reader, footnotes indicate important biographical and other factual information; endnotes are used to annotate sources.) Although many gaps nevertheless remain – and readers should not expect a detailed account of every event in Porter's life or analysis of his works – the commentary (understandably more extensive for Porter's earlier years, for which fewer letters are known) uses newspaper reports and other available sources to fill in as far as possible some otherwise unaccounted-for details of Porter's life and times.

Cliff Eisen
Dominic McHugh
2018

ACKNOWLEDGEMENTS

We wish to thank numerous institutions and individuals for their help in the preparations of this volume: James Archer Abbott and Amy Kimball (Evergreen Museum & Library, Johns Hopkins University), Boston University Libraries, James Burrows, Frank Callahan, Jessica Clark (University of Birmingham Library), Christa Cleeton (Seeley G. Mudd Manuscript Library, Princeton University), Columbia University Libraries, Mark Eden Horowitz and Walter Zvonchenko (Library of Congress), Mary Huelsbeck (Wisconsin Historical Society), The Margaret Herrick Library, Juliana Jenkins (Special Collections, UCLA), Diane Mulligan (*The Worcester Review*), The New York Public Library, Patricia Peterleitner (Worcester Academy), Noah Phelps (Sigma Phi Foundation), Hannah Robbins (University of Sheffield), Kate Scott (Indiana Historical Society), Susan Weiss (Johns Hopkins University), Ian Marshall Fisher (Lost Musicals), Geoffrey Block, Michael Feinstein, Anne Kaufman Schneider and the staff of the Arthur Freed and MGM collections at USC, especially Ned Comstock.

We are especially grateful to Lesley Anne Knight, who was a research assistant on this project, and to Nate Sloan, who photographed the Sam Stark collection for us; to Patrizia Rebulla, who helped transcribe Porter's letters to Boris Kochno; to Richard Boursy (Yale University), who made the extensive Yale Porter collection available to us and answered our numerous questions; and above all to Roberta Staats and the Cole Porter Literary and Musical Trusts, without whose generous support and considerable help this volume would not have been possible. Particular thanks are due to Richard Mason for his sensitive and diligent copy-editing; to

ACKNOWLEDGEMENTS

the anonymous readers for their valuable comments; and to the staff of Yale University Press, including Heather McCallum, Robert Baldock, Julian Loose, Marika Lysandrou, Clarissa Sutherland and Rachael Lonsdale.

We are also grateful as ever for the support of our families, including Katy and Sam Eisen, Gilly and Larry McHugh, and Lawrence Broomfield.

CHAPTER ONE

FROM PERU, INDIANA, TO BROADWAY, 1891–1919

'My grandfather,' Cole Porter told Richard Hubler in 1954, '... was a hearty man with a high temper who always considered me extravagant. He used to drive me a couple of miles out into the rolling Indiana countryside and rein in his horse at the top of a rise. He would point with the end of his buggy-whip at a large, rather bleak gray building. "That, Cole," he would say, "is the place you will end up." It was the county poorhouse. I was only eight in those days. Getting home from such a gruesome sightseeing, I would rush to my mother Kate for comfort. She would hug me, saying indignantly, "Cole, don't listen to a thing he says!" '[1]

Porter's brief account is a fair summary of his family's dynamic during his childhood. His grandfather, James Omar Cole (1828–1923), had inherited a considerable real-estate and mining fortune from his father, Albert Cole. According to some sources, James Omar was the richest man in Indiana. A 'tyrant', as Cole Porter later described him,[2] he had firm ideas concerning what his grandson should study and where, and what sort of career he ought to pursue: he wanted him to go to school in Indiana, at a military academy or business school, and possibly to pursue a career in law. James Omar's daughter Kate (1862–1952), Cole Porter's mother, stood up to him at every opportunity, even in her marriage (9 April 1884) to the less well-off Samuel Fenwick Porter (1858–1927), who subsequently went on to become the leading druggist in Porter's home town, Peru. Kate not only wanted her son (born 9 June 1891) to attend an East Coast school, as she had, but also encouraged him to pursue his musical and theatrical interests. These were apparent early on. In 1901 the *Peru Republican* reported that 'Bills are out announcing the appearance of Porter's greatest show on earth which will exhibit in Frank Bearss' yard next Friday. The circus is owned and controlled by Master Cole Porter' and that 'Miss Emma Bearss took her sister Desdemona, and Cole Porter and Kathryn Kenny to Longansport Tuesday afternoon to see Buffalo Bill.'* When Porter was six he studied piano and violin, later travelling on a weekly basis to nearby Marion, Indiana, to take lessons at the Marion Conservatory of Music. Porter's father, Samuel, is a shadowy figure. He appears not to have been involved in the disagreements between Kate and James Omar, but at the same time there are hints in the correspondence between Porter's mother and the headmaster at her son's school, the Worcester Academy, that he was 'disgusted' with Cole.† This animosity was apparently lifelong.

In 1905, Porter enrolled at the Worcester Academy in Worcester, Massachusetts. Founded in 1834 as the Worcester County Manual Labor High School, it was intended, as the original prospectus states, as 'a school for the education of youth in languages, arts and sciences; for promoting habits of industry and economy; and for inculcating the principles of piety and virtue';[3] in 1846 it officially became Worcester Academy.[4] During Porter's time there the principal (1882–1918) was Daniel Webster Abercrombie, who between 1905 and 1909 was in regular correspondence with Porter's mother, Kate.[5] His correspondence details the boy's progress, his health, and above all Abercrombie's affection for Cole:

13 May 1905: Daniel Webster Abercrombie to Kate Porter

My Dear Madam:

As regards music lessons, he could take a lesson a week either on the piano or violin, but it would not be best for him to pursue both at the same time. He would not have time enough for practice, and there would be too great diversion from his regular school work, and too great tax upon his time and strength. There is a school piano available to him for practice but I would

---

* *Peru Republican*, 28 June 1901, 5, and 23 August 1901, 4. Emma Bearss was a member of the prominent Bearss of Peru, a family with close ties to the Coles; her grandfather, Daniel R. Bearss, was married to Cole Porter's maternal great-grandfather's daughter Emma. In 1834, Daniel R. Bearss and Albert Cole were among the first to purchase property on the Peru canal, and Bearss later became a director of the Indianapolis, Peru & Chicago and Wabash Railroads.

† See below, p. 8.

advise him to take the violin as practice on that can be done in his own room; however, we occasionally allow a boy to hire a piano and have it in his room to practice out of study hours. I should be entirely willing to have him do this ... Competent instruction on both piano and violin can be had in Worcester.

19 September 1905: Daniel Webster Abercrombie to Kate Porter

My dear Mrs. Porter:-

I am grateful to you for the kind suggestions of your letter and I shall give them weight and shall try to keep Cole from entangling himself with too many interests.

I saw at once that he was a delicate rather than a robust boy and with that in mind I questioned whether he would be able to stand up under school work and music too, the latter, however, may be a source of recreation to him and so not provide a drain upon his time and strength.

I am delighted with the boy. He seems most ingenious and delightful in spirit and I am sure that we can look forward to only happy relations with him.

15 January 1906: Daniel Webster Abercrombie to Kate Porter

My dear Mrs. Porter:-

I was very much concerned about his physical condition at the end of last term, and he is not today in the condition I wish he were in or he should be in. He has been subject to colds since coming to us, and they wear him down and exhaust him. My heart ached for the little fellow when I saw him starting home Christmas. I wondered if you could feel that we had taken any care of him, and yet I had tried to be unfailing in my observance of his condition and in my advice and help. He is very careless and runs around uncovered, and is careless about his swimming the pool, going out immediately, improperly clothed ... He is interested in his work, studies well for so young a boy, is full of play at the proper time and spirits of the proper sort ... The boys like him. He loves the boys and is fond of them all. He is wise in his companionship, pleasant to everyone and discreet as to whom he admits to the inner circle.

Porter intended to return home for the summer of 1906, but his departure was delayed by a camping accident, as reported in the *Peru Republican*:

**SUSTAINS BROKEN LEG
COLE PORTER MEETS WITH A
DISTRESSING ACCIDENT.
Popular Young Peruvian With a Number
of Classmates on an Excursion
and While Making a Bed in a Hay
Mow Falls Through a Hole.**

Cole Porter's summer of ideal recreation and instruction was brought to a sudden termination last Saturday by a painful though less serious accident than might have been expected from the circumstances.

Cole is a student at Worcester Academy, Massachusetts, and instead of returning home to Peru for the vacation immediately upon the close of school, started with his teacher of athletics and a party of fifteen schoolmates for a yachting cruise along the New England coast, provided with suits of oil skins and all the paraphernalia necessary for learning practical seamanship. Landings have been made for canoeing and camping and all sorts of outing experiences.

The party has been having a wonderful time in the Maine woods and Cole has been writing home that he was developing a prodigious muscle and becoming as strong as Samson.

The boys were having the time of their lives and had established a camp on Bibber's Island in Cascoe Bay, which was poetically christened "Camp Wychmere." From this point, side trips into the wilderness have been made and it was in returning to camp from one of these, a canoeing trip on Lake Sebago, that the larking young men decided to top off their list of unusual doings by sleeping in a hay mow. It was a hilarious experience for the city boys but resulted disastrously for one of their number. The hay slipped with their weight and carried Cole down an opening to the barn floor below, he striking a scaffolding in the fall. A fracture of the leg a few inches above the ankle joint resulted. It was a mercy and a mystery that no more serious injury was received.

He was taken by trolley immediately to a hospital in Portland where medical attention rendered him as comfortable as possible. The broken limb was placed in a plaster cast and Cole himself wrote that he was suffering scarcely at all.

S. F. Porter, his father, upon receiving the news, which came by letter Wednesday, started at once for Portland and will bring his son home to convalesce.[6]

Before his return to Worcester in the autumn, Porter participated in a concert at a local church: 'At five o'clock Sunday evening a vesper service consisting of song and instrumental music was held at the Presbyterian church. In addition to the congregational service a special program was rendered in which Mrs. Anna Constant Shutt, of Washington, D. C., gave a number of organ selections in the exquisite style for which she is noted. Cole Porter played a violin solo with organ accompaniment, a slumber song by Johnson. His management of the violin is a delight. A vocal solo by Mrs. E. H. Griswold, sung splendidly, was an important number on the program.'[7]

Abercrombie's correspondence with Kate Porter resumed the following winter and addressed in particular Cole's relationship with other boys at the school as well as his academic progress:

17 January 1907: Daniel Webster Abercrombie to Kate Porter

My dear Mrs. Porter:

Cole's record is unsatisfactory not because he does not do good work, but because he does not quite do the work that he is competent to do . . . I have talked to him several times last term and this term in regard to doing his best all the time. He always responds to me delightfully. I think he knows my affectionate regard for him and my warm interest in him. I caution him steadily in regard to his associates. He does not go with bad boys but he goes with those considerably older than himself who while they do not exactly pet him yet show their kindness toward him in a marked way. I believe it is better altogether for a boy to associate with his equals in age, as a rule, and I have so told Cole . . . if Cole should identify himself in personal relations with the boys of his own class, and there are some delightful boys in the class and it is a strong class, it would be far better for him, but his cuteness and brightness and versatility commend him to older boys. This is the only undesirable tendency that I see in Cole.

28 March 1907: Daniel Webster Abercrombie to Kate Porter

My dear Mrs. Porter:

That I write is in strictest confidence ... While I feel very kindly toward Karl Mertz, he is not a boy with whom Cole ought to become intimate. His traditions and ideals are far different from Cole's, and from those that Cole has always lived among, and your feeling in regard to Cole's passing his vacation with him at Atlantic City is very wise ... I cannot tell you how deeply I love your son, and how careful I have been to try to pour the good of the school into his life and save him from the objectional [sic] that is found, and must always be found, among boys and among men.

14 April 1908: Harry Ross* to Kate Porter

My dear Mrs. Porter:

We quite agree with you in what you say in a previous letter in regard to our responsibility for keeping Cole at work. He has never fallen low in his work; and our worrying is not at all along that line, but rather that he is inclined to attempt a good many things and is not very strong physically ... I wish you might have seen him in his portrayal of the character "Bob Acres" in the play of the "Rivals"† which the juniors gave last term. It was very finely done and worthy of [a] much more experienced hand in stagecraft. This was one of the things which we allowed him to go into beyond his studies, but that is now past and I think there is nothing special to draw him away this spring term.

Porter was home again in the summer of 1908, at which time Abercrombie wrote to Kate Porter about the coming academic year:

---

* Daniel Webster Abercrombie took a sabbatical leave from July 1907 to June 1908. During that time Harry Ross was acting Principal of Worcester Academy.

† Richard Sheridan's *The Rivals*, a comedy of manners first performed at Covent Garden, London, on 17 January 1775.

20 July 1908: Daniel Webster Abercrombie to Kate Porter

My Dear Mrs. Porter:

    I wish I might see Cole during the summer, and I may find time to write him. I am very deeply interested in his welfare. I want this coming year to be a very different year in his life from last year as regards getting down to his work. He will be in my class for the first time, and I shall try through my contact with him there to inspire him to concentration and to steady purpose in work to use a hunter's phrase, he "scatter his fire". Sociality is such an element of his nature, that proves a weakness to him instead of a strength. He gives too much of his time and self to others, he saves too little for the definite purposes which bring him to school. He is an able boy, who is very popular. Do you think that one may be too popular? Proverbs say that "beware when all men speak well of you". Some of us need have no such caution but Cole should. You cannot doubt the spirit in which I am writing. I know no other way to show my friendship in a boy than by my frankness, though frankness is often misunderstood, even by elder persons than boys, but believe me, that what I have written is from the heart, out of the deep seated purpose to help Cole. I can help him and will if he will allow me to. Please give him my best love.

Intending to apply to Yale University, during the late summer of 1908 Porter – who had failed the Classics portion of the Yale preliminary examinations – received additional tuition in Greek from Alfred E. Dame, a Worcester Academy faculty member. But when he re-took the entrance examination, Porter failed in algebra:

26 September 1908: Daniel Webster Abercrombie to Kate Porter

My dear Mrs. Porter:

    You will be pleased to hear of Cole's success at Yale this last week, though unfortunately he failed in Algebra which last June he passed.

    I think it is a very narrow point of view which they hold at Yale in such matters. A boy who passed Algebra in June ought not to be put to the necessity of another examination in September. If he knew enough Algebra shown by their own test in June, the fair assumption is that he knew enough in September, but according to Yale's cranky ways, the [sic] have conditioned him in Algebra, although they passed him in it last June. I shall write to Yale and try to get the condition removed, though I doubt my success.

One of the more revealing letters in the Abercrombie–Kate Porter correspondence dates from March 1909, Porter's final year at the Worcester Academy. In it, Abercrombie explains a drop in her son's grades – which he attributes to the boy's increasing engagement with his music to the detriment of his other studies – and reacts to what Kate Porter apparently described as the 'disgust' of Porter's father with his son. This letter is one of the few sources to document the antagonism between Cole and his father:

6 March 1909: Daniel Webster Abercrombie to Kate Porter

My dear Mrs. Porter:

Your note is received. Are you not more disappointed than the facts warrant? If you will compare Cole's report for the first half of this term with last terms [sic] record you will find that he has tow [sic] A's and one A- for the first term, which is an advance and that one of his marks namely, his mathematics, has dropped from B- to C so his studies about balance. There is a decline, however, in his deportment from A- to B-. I was not in the Faculty meeting when his name was marked for deportment and on referring to the slips on which the comments of the teachers are preserved, I found an explanation of Cole's deportment mark which is D- these words, 'Irregular, room disorderly, doesn't study alone, Piano in study hours.' From the last words I infer, of course, that he has been playing his piano in study hours. I would say that probably these comments are fully deserved and yet I don't think that you ought to be greatly disappointed, and I certainly don't think there is any justification whatever for his father being disgusted, or suggest bringing him home.

Porter composed a number of songs at Worcester Academy, including 'Fi, Fi, Fifi', 'The Bearded Lady', 'The Tattooed Gentleman' and 'Class Song – 1909', none of which survives.[8] And despite his low grades at times, he had considerable academic success as well. In June 1908 he was awarded the Dexter Prize for excellence in declamation, and in 1909 he was the class valedictorian. Nearly thirty years later, in 1934, a classmate of Porter's, R. P. Robinson, wrote to him with news of their mutual friends and recalled the poem with which Porter had concluded his valedictory address: 'You to the right, and I to the left / For the ways of men must sever. / And it well may be for a day or a night / And it well may be for ever.'*

In June 1909, Porter again failed the Greek section of the entrance examinations to Yale. Two months later, on 20 August, Abercrombie wrote to Edmund Scott, a tutor at Worcester Academy: 'I think I have never had a boy's failure disappoint me more than Cole's. This also to me appears a lack of sincerity and of real work in the boy. I have been greatly distressed in mind ever since hearing of Cole's failure. He has done great discredit to his teaching but he needs a great many hard bumps before good sense will come to him. He ought to have been a great credit to us . . .' It is not out of the question that the experience of his final year at Worcester soured Porter on the Academy. Barely six years later, in February 1916, three years after Porter had graduated from Yale, Abercrombie wrote to Meylert B. Mullin[†]: 'I thank you very much for your kind note which reached me this morning, with its enclosure of the item about Cole Porter. What a genius he has for such work. I haven't laid eyes on Cole since he graduated from school. I think I have not heard from him. His alienation from the school is very sad to me, and without explanation. I don't understand it. It is one of those little tragedies of my life for which I find no explanation and which always bring me real sorrow . . .'[9]

Porter's difficulties with the entrance examinations notwithstanding, he enrolled at Yale in the autumn of 1909, where he majored in English and minored in music. Over the course of four years he took classes in English, French, German, Latin, history, philosophy and biology.[10] Yet much of his time was spent on musical and theatrical activities. He joined the Yale Glee Club, the Whiffenpoofs, a small, a cappella singing group established in 1909,[‡]

---

* Robinson also remembered a debate on 13 March 1909 at which, according to records at Worcester Academy, '[Porter] successfully argued the judge into believing Uncle Sam should not establish a Parcel Post System, chief point being that Uncle Sam could not compete with the Express Companies in handling big parcels.' McBrien, *Cole Porter*, 27.

† Mullin (birth and death dates unknown) was a fellow alumnus of the Worcester Academy.

‡ See Rev. James M. Howard, 'An Authentic Account of the Founding of the Whiffenpoofs' at https://web.archive.org/web/20110718040120/http://www.whiffenpoofs.com/storage/Whiffenpoofs_History.pdf. Porter also regularly attended the 'Pundits', a group organized by William Lyons Phelps, the Lampson Professor of English at Yale, where students were given dinner and lectures on artistic topics. See McBrien, *Cole Porter*, 34.

and was a regular participant in the Yale Dramatic Association, for which he composed two of his earliest shows, *Cora* (1911) and *And the Villain Still Pursued Her* (1912), for both of which only the lyrics survive.* By his own account, Porter also composed more than three hundred songs at Yale,[11] of which only eighteen survive, including 'Bridget McGuire', 'Since Dolly's Come to Town' and 'Antoinette'.[12] His football songs, 'Bingo Eli Yale', 'Bull Dog', 'A Football King' and 'If I Were Only a Football Man', were especially popular. An article in the *New Haven Register* for 12 September 1911 takes special note of them while at the same time promoting a common, if in Porter's case untrue, trope about self-taught 'genius', though perhaps in this instance tongue-in-cheek: '. . . there are several new songs this year and among them two by Cole Porter, of Peru, Indiana, a member of the junior class in the academic department and one of the best entertainers who has ever been at Yale. This year his songs are "Bulldog," and "Eli," and he wrote the music and words . . . Mr. Porter had no musical education but had natural ability along this line. Some of the peculiar and distinctive features of his work have been explained by the fact that he spent several years in the mountains of Roumania, and heard many strange birds while up there.'

In 1912, Porter composed his first surviving show, *The Pot of Gold*, which premiered at the Delta Kappa Epsilon on 26 November 1912. A significant correspondence with the author of the book, Almet F. Jenks Jr. (1892–1966), documents the genesis of the work:

[Summer 1912]: Cole Porter to Almet Jenks[13]

Westleigh on the Mis-sis-sin-e-wa, Peru, Indiana

My Dear Almet:

As for "Manalive," don't you think it offers very little: All talk. I have tried in vain to get "The Dead City" without success. I shall keep on trying but it looks very hopeless.

---

* Kimball, *The Complete Lyrics of Cole Porter*, 11–18. The performance of *And the Villain Still Pursued Her* on 24 April 1912 was noted in *The Yale Literary Magazine* 77 (May 1912), 319: 'Memorabilia Yalensia . . . The Dramatic Association. On April 24th, held its annual smoker at the Lawn Club and presented a burlesque musical comedy, entitled, "And the Villain Still Pursued Her," by T. G. Thomas, 2nd, 1913, with lyrics and music by Cole Porter, 1913.' A later performance was given at the Yale Club in New York on 10 May 1914; see the *Yale Alumni Weekly* 21 (May 1914), 837.

One thing, the idea of Manalive himself might be excellent if applied to Yale. We must have this show such that the audience can comprehend the plot and no drunken DKE crowd would travel to Beacon House.

I do hope you will be obvious and uninteresting. Otherwise we will suffer defeat, for my music was never the result of inspired imagination.

I have written the following songs--

"She was a fair young mermaid"

"I want to be married"

"If I were only a football man"

"My Salvation Army queen"

All I can ask is that you dash off a scenario and send it to me so I can work on opening choruses. Also tell me whom you select for different parts, and I can write fitting songs the more easily.

Don't forget color. We must have lots of that. Be naif and I can join you.

Goodbye.

Devotedly,

Cole

[Summer 1912]: Cole Porter to Almet Jenks

Almet, My Dear:

I am delighted I received a letter from you in which you showed a descent from the ethereal.

As for the title <u>The pot of gold</u> being trite, I think it is truly wonderful. A title is good only when it means nothing until the fall of the final curtain, and you must admit that in this case, the final curtain <u>must fall</u>. As for the caste [sic], it seems rather large, but I suppose you consider it necessary. Of course with so many, rehearsals will be exceedingly difficult. Then, too, a chorus girl is worth more than a small useless part.

I love your two Russian Nihilists. I got the blank after one of the names. Of course, you will be Turnesky in your own inimitable way. I am trying to write a talking mysterioso song for you and your fellow conspirator. As soon as <u>you finish</u> the conversation between the Nihilists on which the plot is formed, write it to me and I will convert it into a <u>recitatif</u>. As a matter of fact I have written your motif already. It combines the splendor of Wagner and the decadence of Strauss.

You speak of three acts. I beg you--Don't! Three would be interminable or choppy. Remember what a change of costume and scene means! It is a terrible thought always, and if possible try to condense your action to 2 acts.

Another thing (Forgive Me) Dink Stover was altogether too short. It gave one sensation but not perception. Please write this play a long one, for we can easily cut parts if we time it and find it soporific. I wish we could make this play a little masterpiece in its own foolish way. Take it horribly seriously, and I will join you. It really is important, for after all it can never happen again.

The minute you finish it send it to me. I have a great deal to do when I return to college, and I must have most of this play in black & white by Oct. 1st.

And another--

"I wonder where my old girl is now"

Write me here until Sept. 6. Then my address will be Shelbourne Farms, Shelbourne, Vermont, care of V. Webb, until Sept. 10. After the wedding at Garrison, the 11th, I go to Humphrey[']s. You will be there too & we can finish things up.

As soon as college opens I shall begin rehearsing songs, & by the second weak [sic] you can begin.

If you have written the opening of the first act, send it at once. Also write me the caste [sic] again, with the names of each member more plainly so I can use them in verses of songs.

You have no idea how delighted I am that you have gone at this play so hard. We ought to open a few eyes.

Goodby, Almet, & thank you.

Devotedly,

Cole

Aug. 234d [!]

[Autumn 1912]: Cole Porter to Almet Jenks

My Dear Almet:

I received the first act, the episode and the note.

Needless to say, I am delighted with the first act. The plot is excellent, the characters delightfully drawn, and most of the lines pertinent and witty.

I have written down the Overture. It begins with the motif—Chlodoswinde's yearning for Larry; then follows the waltz representing her pangs on finding him false, ending in the motif of supreme happiness, which appears again at the end of the play. Following this come's [sic] Larry's love song. Then a thing in 5/4 time introducing the foreign influence on the hotel, modulating into a death march representing the monotony and decadence of the place. This is connected with the opening chorus by a movement which grows more excited as it progresses. The opening chorus is the Rainbow song, which can be sung by guests who depart at the end of it. At this, the bell-boys sing:

"Bellboys"

If you get done soon enough (& by that I don't expect you to tear it off) I can have incidental music, an overture, an entr'acte, combined motifs, melodrama, etc.

Perhaps I sound altogether too serious about it, but I feel that it is up to you to show New Haven a little of that brain. You have no idea how much is expected. You have a reputation.

I have written a song for Anstruther (Arnold) called "My house-boat on the Thames."

"My houseboat on the Thames"

Then a thing which can be stuck in some opening chorus or finale--

"Exercise"

I rather fear for the Episode. It seems to me that it would take nearly as long to prepare this scene as to go at once to the 2nd act, but perhaps I am wrong. However, we can talk that over on returning to college.

Tell me, who do you cast for Penton? Will Jack Blossom be a good Harrison?

I can never thank you enough for accomplishing so much and such good work. Would it be possible to have the second act take place in the lobby also?

Goodbye, Almet. Write me if anything drastic happens.

Devotedly,

Cole

[September 1912]: Cole Porter to Almet Jenks

My Dear Almet:

I received your letter answering in regard to the change of scene and the Episode.

Of course I was delighted to hear from you that the second set doesn't require a switch, and I think your idea of contrast is wonderful. I feel duty bound to tell you how much work I have done because you must believe me enjoying the wilds of Maine. The truth is that I have manuscripted practically all of the first act. Immediately upon reaching New Haven Humphrey [Parsons] is going to try to persuade Dave Smith of the Music School to orchestrate it for about ten instruments.

As for getting together, I wish we could dine someplace Friday night and go through the memebers [sic] of each class and pick out ability. Don't you think we could confine the chorus to bell-boys and feminine guests? I shall leave the caste [sic] almost entirely to you, but of course those who can't sing can't have songs.

You have no idea how grateful I am for your play. I think we ought to get an awful lot of satisfaction in seeing it well done.

I can begin rehearsing songs Monday night, and you ought to begin getting separate parts typewritten as soon as you return.

I have had to insert arrows indicating the approach of certain songs, at which points the conversation must "lead up," but otherwise there are practically no changes.

I am so anxious to see you and talk over the whole thing, having thought of so little else during the past fortnight.

It's a great shame about the Episode, but I really do believe you should disown this attractive child of your brain.

Finish that second act. I can do nothing until you do. You see my only means of making the songs relevant is by writing verses which give the idea of belonging to the person that sings them.

We shall meet very soon, but until then farewell.

Devotedly,

Cole

Sunday. We leave for New Haven tomorrow. Let me know the minute you arrive.

late September, 1912

In 1913 and 1914, even after his graduation, Porter continued to be active at Yale events including, in January 1913, writing and delivering an essay, 'The New Hotel of America', at the Scroll and Key, a 'secret' society founded at Yale in 1842 and consisting of fifteen prominent seniors:*

It seems only fitting when the Taft Hotel is about to celebrate its first birthday to immortalize the celebration by writing an essay on the New Hotel of America.

Of course every town in the country with a sense of decency has a new hotel in these days. You may travel to the little city and look for the shabby hotel whose plush parlors you used to dread, only to find instead a wonderful skyscraper on the main street making all the early Victorian shops about it fairly black with rage.

The minute you arrive, the native who meets you begins booming the hotel to the skies. You are told with hushed awe of the interior decoration, and of the vulgar display of bathrooms. Then after leading up gradually, he ends by giving you the prize package – he mentions the grill – for there is always a grill. This is perhaps the most typical feature of the New Hotel – the grill – a low-ceilinged, rotingly ventilated cellar where the piece de resistance is rarebit, where the vintage is Budweiser all of which is accompanied by an orchestra from Long Branch taking the name of Robert E. Lee in vain.

With the coming of the new type of hotel, we have lost the dear old American plan – the famous gorge – the delight of the really hungry – which required no imagination to satisfy the appetite. Do you remember

---

* Members of the Scroll and Key have included George Shiras (1832–1924, U.S. Supreme Court Justice), Cornelius Vanderbilt III (1873–1942, Brigadier General during World War I), Dean Acheson (1893–1971, Secretary of State under President Harry Truman), Dickinson W. Richards (1895–1973, winner of the Nobel Prize for Physiology or Medicine in 1956), Gilbert Colgate (1899–1965, chairman of what is now Colgate-Palmolive), John Hay Whitney (1904–82, publisher of the *New York Herald Tribune* and from 1957 to 1961 U. S. ambassador to the United Kingdom), the philanthropist Paul Mellon (1907–99), the 1972 Democratic Vice-Presidential candidate Sargent Shriver (1915–2011), John Lindsay (1921–2000, Mayor of New York, 1966–73), Watergate Special Prosecutor Philip B. Heymann (1932–) and A. Bartlett Giamatti (1938–89, commissioner of Major League Baseball, 1989). Many years later, in August 1964, Porter's biographer George Eells wrote to Dean Acheson concerning Porter. Acheson, who for a time had been Porter's room-mate, replied on 8 September: 'I have just seen your letter of August 12 in which you ask for any recollection of Cole Porter's musical promise while we were at Harvard Law School together. So far as I know Cole never studied law at Harvard, but music. A group of Keys men, including Cole, Laurason [sic] Riggs, and myself took a house for the 1915–1916 year at 1 Mercer Circle. Cole and Laurason were writing, "See America First," which opened in Providence and died there.' Yale University, Porter Collection, Box 49, Folder 301.

the days when a heavily betrayed waiter used to place your plate on the table and then encircle it with little bathtubs – the whole giving the impression of a sun surrounded by a myriad of satellites? And will you ever forget the old menu that revelled in its number of vegetables, and gloated over its variety of pie? But those have passed now, and in its stead, we are presented with an aesthetic European plan menu wearing a cover on which is painted a lady in an impossible décolleté gown rising out of a glass of champagne.

But these abuses which beset us are as nothing compared with the architectural evil in the typical New Hotel. And of course, New York is blamed again, when really the whole trouble lies with the owners of the hotels in our little towns. Every little village hotel owner decided to imitate the innocent metropolis to a T. As a result of this we see such a spectacle as the Hotel Taft which completely demoralizes the effect of a New England college campus.

But we rejoice to say that our American taste shows signs of improvement. This is a new era of hotels in America. Perhaps in a few years we shall return as graduates and refer to the dear old days when the Taft stood there.*

A lost and apparently otherwise unknown work by Porter, *The Kaleidoscope*, is documented for 30 April 1913;† on 22 October he sang at the Boston Yale Club[14] and in March 1914 he gave a piano performance at the Waldorf-Astoria for the New York Yale Alumni Dinner.[15] Also in April 1914, Porter and his Yale classmate T. Lawrason Riggs (1888–1943), with whom Porter soon after collaborated on *See America First*, produced *Paranoia, or Chester of the Yale Dramatic Association* at the Hotel Taft in New Haven.[16] And in

---

* The Taft Hotel, opened in New Haven on 1 January 1912 at 265 College Street, beside the Shubert Theatre (where many musicals by Porter and others had out-of-town tryouts), was built on the site of the New Haven House, which had been demolished in 1910. Named after President William Howard Taft, the twelve-storey hotel was at the time the tallest building in the city. It survived until 1973 when it was renovated and reopened, in 1981, as the Taft Apartments. See http://www.patriquinarchitects.com/history-of-the-taft-hotel-in-new-haven-ct/ (accessed 9 August 2018). Kimball and Gill, *Cole*, 21 (facsimile; no source location given).

† *The Yale Literary Magazine* 78 (May, 1912–1913), 377: '*Memorabilia Yalensia. The Yale Dramatic Association* . . . On April 30th, gave its annual smoker play, "The Kaleidoscope," the music and lyrics by Cole Porter, 1913.'

May, at a meeting of the Associated Western Yale Clubs in Cincinnati, Porter and Riggs produced *We're All Dressed Up and We Don't Know Huerto Go*.* The performance was noted in the *Yale Alumni Weekly*: '[T]he Cincinnati convention on Friday and Saturday, May 22 and 23, turned out to be the most interesting one of the most important of the series ... The noise and jollity rose to a crescendo as the committee's stage programme began with coffee. Then followed three hours of very amusing business, in which figured several graduate monologue artists, a Princeton dancing act, and a Mexican play put on by Cole Porter, '13, who was assisted by an all-star cast including Woolley, '11;† Johnfritz Achelis, '13; Laurence Cornwall, '12; and three very delightful undergraduate Dramatic Association actors.'[17]

Several months before *We're All Dressed Up*, on 22 September 1913, Porter had enrolled at the Harvard Law School. One of his assignments – a fictitious brief, whether made up by him or assigned is unknown – describes the following situation:

> Defendant and his friend Brown were standing on a street corner waiting for a car when Brown said to Defendant, "Tell me what you know about the murder in South Boston." Thereupon Defendant spoke the following words intending that only Brown should hear them. "I see from the morning paper that Exum is strongly suspected of the crime. Much evidence tends to show that he is the guilty man, but from the facts stated in the newspaper there is not sufficient evidence to warrant saying he is guilty. Still I would suspect the rascal anyway. My friend Smith says he is guilty and I believe him."
>
> The truth was that there were two morning papers and one of them charged A. B. Exum with the crime and the other the plaintiff. Jones and Brown did not know the plaintiff and both had A. B. Exum in mind. A. B. Exum was in fact guilty. One person in the crowd, waiting for the

---

* Kimball and Gill, *Cole*, 27, cites an undated and unsourced letter by Riggs describing the show's revival at a later meeting of the Associated Western Yale Clubs: 'Apparently we were a success because a few years later the reunion was in Cleveland, and we were again asked to assemble the show ... For this occasion Cole wrote *Cleveland*. He wired the words to us in New York and we learned them on the train. As I remember, there were six or eight pages to the telegram.'

† Porter's lifelong friend, the actor Monty Woolley (1888–1963).

car, overheard the conversation between the defendant and Brown and, having read the paper which charged the plaintiff with the crime, reasonably believed that the plaintiff was the man the defendant was speaking of, but he had been with the plaintiff on the night of the murder and knew in fact that he (the plaintiff) was not guilty.

The plaintiff now sued the defendant for slander. The defendant demurred but was overruled and brings the case upon appeal.[18]

It seems likely, given the names of the plaintiff and defendant, A. B. Exum and X. Y. Jones, as well as the name of the 'lawyer', Coram W. McAfee, C. J., to say nothing of the almost comical scenario, that the entire brief is Porter's work. And it apparently did not bode well for his legal career, which ended in the autumn of 1914 when he transferred to the Harvard School of Music. According to an interview he gave in 1939, 'One day I was at a party and I played a piece I had written and the dean of the Law School said "Porter – don't waste your time – get busy and study music." '[19]

In the spring of 1915, Porter was contacted by the literary and theatrical agent Elizabeth Marbury (1856–1933)* about songs for a show that would eventually become his first Broadway musical, *See America First*. Several telegrams that Porter sent to his mother describe his meetings with Marbury and one, to his grandmother Rachel Cole (see below), may be an attempt, however circuitous, to impress his otherwise sceptical grandfather:

9 April 1915: Cole Porter to Kate Porter[20]

CHECK ARRIVED LAST WEEK[.] THANK YOU[.] GOT OFFER TO WRITE JUNIOR LEAGUE SHOW FOR NEXT YEAR[.] COULD NOT ARRANGE MEETING WITH COMMITTEE UNTIL MONDAY NIGHT[.] WILL COME HOME AS SOON AS POSSIBLE[.] MEETING MISS MARBURY TOMORROW AFTER-NOON[.] LOVE … COLE

---

* Marbury was also the long-time companion of the actress and interior decorator Elsie de Wolfe, later Lady Mendl (1865–1950), who was to become one of Cole and Linda Porter's closest friends.

12 April 1915: Cole Porter to Kate Porter[21]

MARBURY DELIGHTED[.] PRODUCTION ASSURED FOR NEXT YEAR[.] MEETING WEBER AND FIELDS* MANAGER TOMORROW IN REGARD TO INTERPOLATING SEVERAL OF MY OLD SONGS IN THEIR NEW SHOW[.] MEETING JUNIOR LEAGUE COMMITTEE TONIGHT[.] LEAVE FOR HOME TOMORROW AFTER-NOON =COLE

12 May 1915: Elisabeth Marbury to Cole Porter[22]

Dear Mr. Porter,

Will you please meet me, to play over your songs, to-morrow, Tuesday, at 12 o'clock, at "Chez Maurice", Wintergarden Building, Broadway, between 50th and 51st Street.

Sincerely Yours,

[signed:] Elisabeth Marbury

25 May 1915: Cole Porter to Rachel Cole (his grandmother)[23]

JUST RETURNED AFTER SIX DAYS WITH MARBURY. SHOW TO BE PRODUCED IN OCTOBER. TELL GRANDAD LEW FIELDS GAVE ME FIFTY DOLLARS FOR EACH SONG I SOLD HIM AND FOUR CENTS ON EACH COPY.† FOUND YOUR WIRE WAITING. THANK YOU SO MUCH [FOR?] WRITING. COLE

Elizabeth Marbury was as enthusiastic as Porter, arranging for an article about the upcoming show to be published in the *New Haven Register* for 8 June:

Yale Man, Song Writer, Has a Fine Future. "I consider Cole Porter, your Yale graduate, who is now writing his first professional music, the most

---

* Joseph Weber (1867–1942) and Lew Fields (Moses Schoenfeld, 1867–1941) were a popular vaudevillian duo who appeared in numerous Broadway theatres. Fields was the father of Dorothy and Herbert Fields, who together wrote the books for Porter's later musicals *Let's Face It*, *Something for the Boys* and *Mexican Hayride*.

† It is unclear which songs Porter refers to here. The actor and producer Lew Fields later worked with Porter on the *Greenwich Village Follies of 1924*.

promising composer of light opera that I have ever encountered," declared Miss Elizabeth Marbury, the well-known dramatic agent and producer, who was here to witness the first night of Lew Field's [sic] new play for which Mr. Porter has supplied several numbers. Miss Marbury, who is known from coast to coast, and is a recognized authority on matters theatrical, was the one who first induced Mr. Porter, who was graduated from Yale only last year, and is now taking a special musical course at Harvard, to "write for the profession." "It may seem that I am making a large order for the young man," she went on, "but I am convinced that Mr. Porter is the one man of the many who can measure up to the standard set by the late Sir Arthur Sullivan. This looks like a boast, but watch him."[24]

Over the next several months, Porter kept his family informed about the show's progress:

15 December 1915: Cole Porter to Kate Porter[25]

JUST RETURNED FROM NEW YORK[.] UNLESS SOMETHING EXTRAORDINARY HAPPENS SHOW WILL GO INTO REHEARSAL IN A FEW WEEKS PRODUCED BY MARBURY AND MOROSCO[,]* BUT DON'T BE OVER CONFIDENT[.] TELL GRANDAD AND BESSIE[.] TERRIBLYH [sic] SORRY YOU ARE NOT WELL .. COLE PORTER

15 January 1916: Cole Porter to Kate Porter

SHOW GOING BEAUTIFULLY[.] FRIGHTFULLY BUSY[.] WILL WRITE SOON[.] GIVE MY LOVE TO DIXIE AND DOCTOR[.] MISS YOU A LOT[.] GOODBYE[,] COLE.

14 February 1916: Cole Porter to Kate Porter

EVERYTHING GOING BEAUTIFULLY[.] REHEARSING FROM TEN IN MORNING UNTIL TWELVE AT NIGHT[.] TIRED BUT CONTENTED[.] WILL WRITE AT EARLIEST OPPORTUNITY. LOVE TO ALL[,] COLE

---

* Oliver Morosco (1875–1945), theatrical producer and director.

20 February 1916: Cole Porter to Kate Porter

OPEN SCHENECTADY TUESDAY MATINEE[.] PLAY ALBANY THURSDAY FRIDAY SATURDAY NEXT WEEK[,] ROCHESTER FOLLOWING WEEK[.] RETURN TO NEW YORK [sic] AND REHEARSE[.] NEW YORK [sic] OPENING SHOULD BE MARCH FOURTEENTH IF EVERYTHING GOES WELL[.] CAN MAKE NO PREDICTIONS[.] LOVE TO ALL. COLE.

22 February 1916: Cole Porter to Kate Porter

SHOW MOST ENTHUSIASTICALLY RECEIVED[.] HAVE HIGH HOPES FOR BRILLIANT OPENING IN NEW YORK[.] USUAL WORK PREPARATORY TO PREMIERE NOW BEGINNING[.] BIGELOW SCORES TREMENDOUS HIT[.] DONT WORRY[.] LOVE TO ALL... COLE.

The subject of Porter and Riggs's musical was topical in the 1910s in particular: the 'See America First' movement, apparently founded in Salt Lake City in 1906, was taken up by President Taft in 1911, as the *New York Times* reported: 'President Taft today promised a committee appointed by Gov. Crothers of Maryland that he would write a letter indorsing [sic] the "See America first" movement.' A 'See America First' convention was held in Baltimore that same year, and in 1912 the Secretary of the Interior linked the development of national parks to the movement: 'There is no scenery in the Old World grander or more inspiring [than the national parks], and as new roads are built giving easy access to all parts of every park, and inns and lodges are constructed, the American people will gradually learn that the now common phrase, "See America first," has more than a merely patriotic significance.' Less than two months after the opening of *See America First*, a bill was presented to Congress to centralize the administration of the National Park Service.[26] Porter's *See America First*, however, was not long-lived, closing on 8 April after only fifteen performances. The *Evening World* described it as 'an achievement that college boys might have done in the way of entertainment', while the *Evening Sun* called it 'the worst musical comedy in town. Don't see *America First*.'[27] For Riggs, the failure of *See America First* was devastating. Shortly after it closed he wrote, 'I spent the fall of 1915 in Cambridge, working on the book and lyrics of a comic opera, "See America First," with Cole Porter, 1913, who did the music. It was presented in New

York during the winter, but failed dismally. Owing to the fact that the composer and I consented to a complete transformation of the piece to meet the capabilities of its interpreters and the supposed taste of the public, we suffered, in addition to our disappointment, the unsatisfactory feeling that nothing had been proved as to the worth of our efforts. But we are wiser as well as sadder, and for myself I have done with attempts at dramatic composition, so far as I can foresee.'[28] For his part, in a 1953 interview Porter said: 'I'll never forget that night . . . when my first show closed . . . As they dismantled the scenery and trucked it out of the stage alley, I honestly believed I was disgraced for the rest of my life.'[29]

While the 'See America First' movement encouraged both patriotic and aesthetic values, it was also exploited, sometimes in convoluted ways, by American businesses. This may have provided Porter with what was probably his first commercial work and advertising opportunity,* a campaign by the Sherwin-Williams paint company, 'Brighten Up America':

> The February magazines are showing the first ads of the Sherwin-Williams Company's "Brighten Up America" spring campaign. The company was especially fortunate in their selection of a slogan and design, which includes Uncle Sam. They could hardly have chosen an idea for their campaign which is more up-to-the-minute and timely. For many years the Sherwin-Williams Company has used the slogan "Brighten Up," and this year simply tied it up with the word "America" in order to help in the big movement in which all the paint companies are interested to preach to the American people the gospel of the economy of painting. It has been an acknowledged fact that the American people, in spite of their prosperity and expenditure of money, are not spending it to purchase paint for their houses as much as they are for luxuries. They don't think of paint as a necessity or an economy. The Sherwin-Williams "Brighten Up America" campaign is intended to waken the American people to the foolishness of neglecting such an important matter as house painting . . . [A] unique feature of the campaign is a song which the Sherwin-Williams Company is publishing, called "Brighten Up,

---

* Further, see below, pp. 445, 456–7, 482.

America!" The music is by Cole Porter, a graduate of Yale University, who made such a name for himself in writing songs of Old Eli that he is now a professional song writer, having many songs accepted for musical comedies, and his opera, "See America First," was produced on Broadway last winter. This song will be given out by S.-W. agents and dealers and will be featured in some of the spring campaign ads. The agents who are putting on Brighten Up parades will run lantern slides advertising the event the night before in their local movie picture houses. One of the slides will show the words of the "Brighten Up America" song in order to get the audience singing while the pianist plays the tune.[30]

Porter's song – if in fact it was written and published – is apparently lost.[31]

Porter's activities in early 1917 are not well documented, although at least one of his war-related performances was noted in the *New York Times* on 1 February: 'Several Men to Have Wings in Big War Charities Entertainment. The Angel choir which is to take part in the big entertainment for Mrs. Gertrude Atherton's and three other big war charities under the direction of Miss Elsa Maxwell* on Feb. 15 at the Century Theatre is growing ... Miss Laurette Taylor will dance the fox trot with Preston Gibson, and Miss Mimi Scott will sing a song, "I'm Looking for You," with Cole Porter.'[32] Beyond participating in fund-raising events, however, Porter may also have been thinking about volunteering for the war effort, as did many of his Yale classmates, encouraged by an article published in the *Yale Alumni Weekly* the previous autumn: 'Call for American Hospital Workers in France. The demand for workers in connection with the American Ambulance Hospital in France was never greater than at present. Drivers are needed in the Paris service, which is comparatively simple; and also for the field service, which is more serious business. Yale men who care to take on an experience of six months or more in this work may correspond directly with William R. Hereford, Headquarters, American Ambulance, 14 Wall St., New York City. There is also need for hospital orderlies. These men wait on and care for the wounded, serve their meals, lift them, help the convalescents to walk, etc. The need of

---

* Elsa Maxwell (1883–1963) was a professional hostess, gossip columnist and radio host who, to some extent, hitched her star to Porter and to her friendship with him and his wife Linda. In 1957 she published *How to Do It, or The Lively Art of Entertaining*, the title of which is a play on Porter's 'Let's Do It, Let's Fall in Love'.

such workers is so great that the New York office not only pays for board and lodging while in the service, but defrays passage money New York to Paris and return for those who cannot afford to pay their own. In the case of ambulance drivers, the applicant pays his own passage, though board and lodging are provided these when once arrived in France.'[33]

Porter registered for the draft on 5 June 1917 and in July sailed for Europe on the paquebot 'Espagne' to work for the Duryea Relief Organization, which was founded in France in 1914 by the expatriate American writer Nina Larrey Duryea (1874–1951) to aid war survivors and refugees. A programme survives for a concert that Porter gave on board on 17 July, possibly the concert described by one of his shipmates, Albert Le Tarte, who in an article published in the *Brunswick Record* in August 1917 noted that 'a composer [was] with us also, by the name of Cole Porter, who rendered several of his own compositions'.[34] A few months after his arrival in France, Porter himself had an open letter describing his time there published in the *Peru Republican* for 5 October:

Letter from Cole Porter at the Front.

A very interesting letter from Cole Porter, who is personal aid to the president of the Duryea Relief party now at the battle front in France, written to his mother, Mrs. S. F. Porter, of this city, gives interesting and valuable first-hand glimpses of the war and his own work. He gives a description of the latest German infernal machine, the caterpillar, a string of burning torches shot from the ground to hit the French airplanes. We are permitted to copy parts of the letter:

Dear Mother:

An awfully cheery letter arrived from you today (September 4) dated August 13.

Life here continues to offer great surprises. For instance, yesterday I went to inspect the village of Fresnoy. As I was walking along the road of the town I passed the entrance of an abri (shelter in case of air raids). But it looked so much better than most of them that I opened the door to it. I peered down the steps (they are usually about twenty feet below the surface) and there, at the bottom stood a woman of about sixty years smiling up at me. She asked me to come down, which I did, and found an immaculately clean room, a dirt floor swept to a polish, and this was her home. She told me her story – how she was all alone in the world, her husband and her son having been killed, but, until the Boches had come, she had lived in her brick house, on her farm, with thirty cows (she had prizes for cattle on her walls in the cave). Then, the invasion. She fled, but was taken prisoner, sent to Prussia to work, grew ill and was returned to France by way of Switzerland, went back to her home at Fresnoy, found it had completely disappeared, and she happened on this German abri as the only shelter she could find. Of course it was an astounding adventure she'd had, but the amazing part was her gaiety and her charm. I love this French race. They're so attractive, so amusing, so wonderfully brave, and so simple – just like children, all of them. So, we being without a cook, and I being tired of opening canned beans, asked her if she could cook. And she said, "Oh, Monsieur of course I can cook." So I said, "Pack up your things and jump in the motor." So here she is, this extraordinary old sport, living in the house with us, working like a Trojan, and cooking delicious omelettes, rabbit chops and compotes. And she has forgotten her trouble and we've forgotten ours!

Last night being very clear and calm, I went out to the aviation camp with the commandant of this canton, to see a glimpse, at least, of the only attractively exciting side of the whole war. I stood there and saw sixty aeroplanes rise, one by one, and make for St. Quentin. Before each aviator mounted his plane he would come up to his captain, shake his hand, and cry, "Au revoir, mon Capitaine!" and run off to his job. It was very, [sic] touching, mother, to see all this and to know that nearly every night one of these aeroplanes either never returns or else fails and kills its occupants.

A little later we saw three German caterpillars. The caterpillar is the newest German atrocity. It consists of a string of burning torches which is shot from the ground. It rises quickly and if it hits the French aeroplane it wraps itself about it and burns the plane and the accupants [sic] in the air. The French are completely "up in the air" about it. They fear it as nothing else and they can't understand how it is made.

I spent today in Erchen, and tomorrow I go to Amiens. I'm gradually getting awfully well acquainted with this country in the zone-des-armees, and I've worked so hard over my Ford camion that it runs perfectly. I know "Sammie" will be glad to hear that I really am developing into quite a mechanic.

A letter from headquarters today says that the reports from the French officers here in charge were pleased with the thoroughness and the speed of my inspections. I've interviewed over a thousand people and on finishing up here they want me to take charge of an inspection tour in the Vosges Mountains.

Arnold Whitridge* is a captain on Gen. Pershing's† staff. I have seen him.

I am so glad that your garden has been such a success. I can see you eating those delicious things now. Oh, I'd love to run out to Westleigh for about two weeks and then bring you back to France with me. I like my job and my health was never better.

Lots of love to all of you.

Affectionately,

COLE.

Roye-sur-Somme.[35]

It is far from clear what action Porter saw in France, or for that matter what his duties might have been. Although he himself claimed to have been with the French Foreign Legion and to have studied at the École d'Artillerie at Fontainebleau,[36] there is no concrete evidence to back up his assertion. A letter to Monty Woolley from September 1918, however, mentions gas attacks and gas masks:

September 1918: Cole Porter to Monty Woolley[37]

Mont -

Don't waste any time in going to the bank & trying to find out about my finances. I'm worried simply because I can't understand it all.

They shot gas at us this morning + I got panicky. I hate these masks.

Forgive me for writing so often.

<u>Please</u> send me some good books.

I <u>may</u> die - I'm so bored. But <u>don't tell.</u>

---

* Arnold Whitridge (1892–1998) was a fellow student of Porter's at Yale and later a professor of history there; see his obituary in the *New York Times* for 2 February 1989 (https://www.nytimes.com/1989/02/02/obituaries/arnold-whitridge-ex-professor-at-yale-and-an-author-97.html).

† John Joseph ('Black Jack') Pershing (1860–1948) was commander of the American Expeditionary Force on the Western Front, 1917–18.

Porter's reputation for pranks and fabrications somewhat casts at least a shadow of doubt on whether this letter is entirely serious. According to George Eells, an authoritative biographer of Porter's, Monty Woolley, possibly the composer's closest friend, reportedly said that he recalled 'Porter strutting up and down the boulevards in uniforms ranging all the way from a cadet's to a colonel's. Porter . . . had more changes than Maréchal Foch, and wore them with complete disregard of regulation.' Similarly, the annual report for the Yale class of 1913 states that 'Classmate Cole A. Porter has joined the American Aviation Forces in France although nobody seems to know in what capacity.'[38] Nevertheless, Eells quotes an official war record, though without identifying his source: Porter had left the Duryea Relief Organization by January 1918 and was attached to the American Aviation Headquarters on the Avenue de Montaigne in Paris; on 20 April 1918 he enlisted in the 'First Foreign Regiment at the Central Recruiting Office of the Seine, matriculation list no. 12651 – Detailed for pay and rations to the 32nd Field Artillery Regiment – Given the rank of Candidate as a foreigner to take his place August 22, 1918 – Detailed for pay and rations to the 15th Artillery Regiment – Arrived and enrolled in the 1st Battery on September 20, 1918 – Detailed to the Bureau of the Military Attaché of the United States on January 23, 1919 – Discharged on April 17, 1919, by the depot of the 26th Light Infantry Battalion at Vincennes – Stated, at the time, retiring to Paris, 9 Rue Gounod – Stricken from Controls on April 18, 1919.'[39]

CHAPTER TWO

COLE PORTER IN EUROPE, 1918–1928

On 30 January 1918, while still on active duty, Cole Porter attended the wedding of socialites Ethel Harriman and Henry Russell at the Paris Ritz, where he met Linda Lee Thomas (1883–1954), who six years earlier had divorced Edward R. Thomas (1875–1926), owner of the *New York Morning Telegraph*. Two months later, Porter wrote to Monty Woolley, describing his life in Paris and, most significantly (though not without a feint to the contrary), his genuine infatuation with her:

25 March 1918: Cole Porter to Monty Woolley[1]

Monnnnnnnt;

I know you will be happy to hear this: I'm spending most of my evenings with Li'l Ole Marise, dont le pere [sic] est corse et la mere [sic] est corse mais, pour un [sic] raison quelconque, n'est pas corse de [sic] tout.* Its [sic] considered rather dangerous seeing her too often, as her ideas as to finance and the value of a dollar aren't at all clear. Rex Benson† warned me the other day, saying that she'd just been to him to ask that he pay her debts which amount to the tidy little sum of 300,000 francs. But I've explained that I haven't a sou, except for occasional tete-a-tete [sic] dinners and now and then a nice ride in a taxi, so we're very happy in our pastoral way. She's being launched in the haut demi-monde by May Lou, who's beginning to get just a wee bit discouraged, I believe, as things no sooner get on the way, and people are nearly convinced that Marise

---

* 'whose father is Corsican, and whose mother is also Corsican, but for a reason no one knows, isn't Corsican at all'.
† Sir Reginald Lindsay Benson (1889–1968) was a banker and an army officer.

is one of the young intellectuals, when suddenly she gets a relapse and bites some woman she just met, on the arm. We were all in a train of having "an interesting evening" last night at May Lou's-----Mistinguett was there, and Henri Bataille's mistress, Yvonne Dupres [sic], and Charlotte Lyses [sic], Sacha Guitry's former wife,* and we were all talking art and love and drama and no end of difficult things, when Blaaah, enter Marise and falls dead drunk in the fire-place.

I nearly took a flying trip to America, about a week ago, but I've given it up and God knows when I'll hit New York now. I'm going to Spain on the 22nd of April for a month's motor trip with the Duc d'Albe,† my newest best friend. He's got two Rolls and two country places and its [sic] all going to be rather congenial, what with that horrible woman, Linda Thomas going, and several other people that you'd despise. It appears that the motors are meeting us at the frontier, whence we roll to Madrid, where we stay only a few days and make immediately for Seville to see the Fair. He's got a place just outside that is supposed to be fairly beautiful. I don't believe you'd mind him as much as most of the awful acquaintances I've made in France. He looks rather like his cousin, the King,‡ but much better looking. And he's very British, which doesn't usually irritate you, if I remember correctly.

Riggs§ is simply too too. I'm dodging him like a disease during Lent, as he's given up so many things he likes that its [sic] made him mean. The other night I came home and went in my room. And I said "Riggs, it smells bad in my room." And he tottered in, with his rubrics in his hand, looked at me sadly and replied "After all, why shouldn't it?" And yesterday, I said to him "Think of it, in five years, you'll be tied up in a lot of soiled old robes and I'll be happy

---

* Jeanne Florentine Bourgeois (Mistinguett, 1875–1956) was an actress and singer; the actress Yvonne de Bray (1889–1954) was the lover of the dramatist and poet Henry Bataille (1872–1922); the actress Charlotte Lysès (1877–1956) had married the actor, director, screenwriter and playwright Sacha Guitry (Alexandre-Pierre Georges Guitry, 1885–1957) on 14 August 1907. See Olivier Barrot and Raymond Chirat, *Noir et Blanc: 250 acteurs du cinema français 1930-1960* (Paris, 2000), and André Bernard and Alain Paucard, *Sacha Guitry* (Lausanne and Paris, 2002).
† Jacobo Fitz-James Stuart y Falcó, 17th Duke of Alba (1878–1953), was a staunch Spanish Nationalist and after the Spanish Civil War, Franco's ambassador in London.
‡ Alfonso XIII (1886–1941) was King of Spain, 1886–1931.
§ T. Lawrason Riggs was active in the Yale Mobile Hospital during the war and subsequently served as a specialist in foreign languages attached to military intelligence in Paris. Later he attended the Catholic University of America and St Thomas Seminary in Connecticut, and was appointed the first Catholic chaplain at Yale University.

and married." And Riggs said "Well, you may be <u>married</u>." And he came in at dawn, the other morning and woke me up with "You and Willie think you're devoted to each other, but once America goes dry, you won't have a single thing in common." He left last night for Rouen where [he] gets on a mule and rides cross-country with a lot of priests to some shrine. He took my musette with him, leaving at some impossible hour and making the Lasnes give him all sorts of sacred food to take along. I came home, several afternoons ago, and he and a greasy old priest were reading one of those enormous books of his aloud. Really, Lent's never been as hard for me as it has, this time.

Somebody appeared, the other day and had seen you receiving at the Yale Club. But it was Dick Douglas and I decided that, much as I wanted your news, it was asking too much for me to dine with Dick Douglas in order to get it. So I've no idea what you're doing with your life. Please tell your father that I've found a wonderful new perfume called Le Moment Passione, that I've been given a marvelous dressing-gown made of an old Persian material and lined with purple and orange silk, and that, every evening at sun-set, I undress, take a bath in the perfume, put on the dressing gown and read Baudelaire aloud to the concierge's pink young son. It may please him.

Jack Clark's back, after having persuaded his fiancée in the Midi somewhere that it would be much simpler if she married someone else. And I see Bill Tytus a good deal. He's taken an apartment with [Paul Church] Harper and he's violently in love with a Russian woman. He still has la fievre [sic] d'amour which cramps his style toward six every morning. But he's drinking wines sparingly.

With the exception of my occasional soirees [sic] with the half-world, I'm in a complete rut. I lunch and dine with Linda Thomas every day, and between times, call her up on the telephone. She happens to be the most perfect woman in the world and I'm falling so in love with her that I'm attractively triste. It may be merely the Spring, but it looks dangerously like the real thing and I'm quite terrified, for there's nothing like it to kill concentration.

[page cut off here but resumes on next page:]

Please give this letter to Will after you've read it. I've been writing him awful things lately and this is rather chock full of it.

Or, at least it will be when I finish, which may not be for days, as I haven't a damned thing to do, but by hammering away at my Underwood, I give the impression of accomplishing wonders.

Will Stewart* has gone to Constantinople as the aide of an admiral. He left Rome the other day on a sloop, Daisy de Broglie† has gone to Algeria to get her husband's body, and as soon as she gets back to Marseilles, she's giving a big party to celebrate and want wants [sic] us all to come. Sturges‡ is going to America on April 26th and staying the summer. He dreads it awfully. The Grand Duke Alexander§ has taken an apartment just over Toinon, who still cries about Will each time I see her and bores me infinitely. Lucette is still at Biarritz. She has a new lover----an awfully nice beau, parait-il. Maggie has gone away on a motor trip with her lover, Eddie Huffer, and Aliiice [!] has arrived back from Monte Carlo with her lover, after having gained two hundred thousand francs. She intends to spend it on a little diamond. I saw Sydney McCall¶ yesterday, but I saw him first. It appears that [two words unreadable] is at the Ritz. Also, Stanley Spiegelberg.** All of which doesn't excite me very much.

We'll have fun this summer, Monnnnnnnnnnnnt, won't we. I'm coming over to poison Grandfather and then spend the rest of the time with Will. And I promise not to race about AT ALL. We'll just sit around and hash over those attractive days that can never be recalled. Those dear days when we were boys and you were ever so much younger.

---

* William Rhinelander Stewart, Jr. (1888-1945), was a Yale classmate of Porter's. Stewart's father William was socially prominent and active in civic and state affairs, primarily as president of the New York State Board of Charities.

† The socialite Daisy Fellowes (1890-1926), heiress to the Singer sewing-machine fortune, who in 1910 had married Jean Amédée Marie Anatole de Broglie, Prince de Broglie (1886-1918). De Broglie reportedly died of influenza on 20 February while on military duty in Algeria.

‡ Howard Sturges (1884-1955), socialite, was a Yale classmate and lifelong friend of Porter's. Sturges similarly served in Paris during World War I, first at the American Relief Clearing House Headquarters and later with the American Red Cross.

§ Grand Duke Alexander Mikhailovich of Russia (1866-1933) was a brother-in-law of Emperor Nicholas II of Russia.

¶ Sidney McCall (born Mary McNeill, 1865-1954) was a poet and novelist.

** Apparently many of the otherwise unidentified people mentioned in this letter were Porter's Yale classmates. William Griffith Ewing Tytus is pictured, along with Porter, in an undated Yale yearbook: see https://archives.yale.edu/repositories/6/archival_objects/2547003. Tytus, Stanley James Spiegelberg, Richard Alexander Douglas and a Paul Church Harper are listed in the *Catalogue of Yale University 1913-1914* (New Haven, CT, 1913), 744.

Good-bye, WWoolleeyy and write me if you ever have a moment between family rows. Every now and then, your name is mentioned and we all concentrate on how you look. Personally, I remember you perfectly.

Cole Porter

Mar 25

The following December, while en route to Peru, Indiana, to confront his grandfather over the terms of a trust he had created for Cole, Porter met the producer Raymond Hitchcock (1865–1929), who heard him play what at the time was his best-known song, 'An Old-Fashioned Garden'.[2] Hitchcock subsequently engaged Porter to write the score for *Hitchy-Koo of 1919*, which opened at the Liberty Theatre, New York, on 6 October 1919. The *New York Times* for 7 October 1919 reported that: ' "Hitchy-Koo, 1919" is a Hit . . . The music and the lyrics are the work of Cole Porter, who has made a particularly clever job of the lyrics and a good, tinkling one of the music.' Shortly afterwards, on 19 December, Porter married Linda Lee Thomas: 'MRS. LEE THOMAS TO WED. Kentuckian to Marry Cole Porter, Composer, in Paris Today. According to private word from Paris by friends of Mrs. Lee Thomas, formerly the wife of Edward R. Thomas, she is to be married today in that city to Cole Porter, a composer. The couple first met, it is said, last Winter while Mrs. Thomas was in Paris, and Mr. Porter was attached to the American Embassy there . . . Mrs. Thomas was formerly Miss Linda Lee, daughter of William P. Lee, a banker of Louisville, Ky., and was famed for her beauty . . . Mr. Porter is a Yale graduate, and his home is in Peru, Ind. He began composing music and lyrics for operettas and comic operas after his graduation. He wrote the music for "See America First" and also for "Hitchy Koo," for Raymond Hitchcock, last October.'* Around a week later Porter wrote to Monty Woolley about an outing with Linda, including a cryptic reference to 'our song' (that is

---

* *New York Times*, 18 December 1919, 13. Not all of Linda's friends were happy with the match. The art historian Bernard Berenson (1865–1959), a friend and lifelong correspondent of Linda Porter, held out little hope for the marriage. In August 1921, shortly after the Porters' trip to Egypt, he wrote to the well-known art collector Isabella Gardner describing Linda as '. . . a lovely creature, whom both the Duke of Alba and Prince Beauvais were in love with but couldn't marry because she was divorced. She suddenly and to the surprise of everyone married a little musical man from the Middle West 15 [sic] years younger than herself and has nearly worn herself out going his rattling pace ever since. They came to us on their honeymoon, and I saw their future in the blackest terms.' Source: privately owned; see McBrien, *Cole Porter*, 73.

Porter and Woolley's) and a first reference to Sergei Diaghilev's Ballets Russes, which for personal reasons – including Porter's friendship with Diaghilev and his affair with Diaghilev's amanuensis, Boris Kochno – was shortly afterwards to play an important role in his life:

Christmas 1919: Cole Porter to Monty Woolley*

Xmas 1919

I thought of you last night, Mont – t – t. Linda + I had a great big comfortable box at the Opéra for the opening of the Ballet [sic] Russes + you should have been in it. Especially when during the Prince Igor thing, they started [here Porter writes out the first three bars of the dance later made famous as 'Stranger in Paradise'] for it <u>is our</u> tune, isn't it Mon – n – nt! And you'd die at the Boutique, the second one. Its [sic] by far the funniest thing I've seen . . .†

The Porters honeymooned on the Côte d'Azur, the Italian Riviera and Sicily, and travelled frequently during the next several years. In February 1921, while in Egypt,[3] Linda Porter made two short notes on the flyleaf of her copy of Arthur E. P. Weigall's *A Guide to the Antiquities of Upper Egypt* (London, 1913):

28 February 1921, Luxor: Lord Carnarvon and his expert, Howard Carter, are digging at the Valley of the Kings – have discovered nothing so far . . . Visited Winlock working with the Metropolitan near Deir-el-Bahiri.‡

---

* This handwritten note is part of a cache of letters and telegrams from Porter to Monty Woolley, privately owned in Pittsburgh, which featured on an episode of *Antiques Roadshow* (http://www.pbs.org/wgbh/roadshow/season/16/pittsburgh-pa/appraisals/cole-porter-monty-woolley-letters-ca-1940--201106A28/). We have been unable to track down other items in the collection.

† *La Boutique fantasque*, based on music by Gioacchino Rossini, arranged and orchestrated by Ottorino Respighi, had been premiered by the Ballets Russes at the Alhambra Theatre, London, on 5 June 1919.

‡ George Herbert, 5th Earl of Carnarvon (1866–1923), was the financial backer of Howard Carter (1874–1939), who discovered the tomb of Tutankhamun (r. c. 1332–1323 BC) the next year, on 26 November 1922; see T. G. H. James, *Howard Carter. The Path to Tutankhamun* (London, 2012). The Egyptologist Herbert Winlock (1884–1950) headed up the Metropolitan Museum's excavations of the mortuary complex of Mentuhotep II (2010–1998 BC) at Dier-el-Bahari, beginning in 1911; see his *Excavations at Deir el Bahari: 1911–1931* (New York, 1942).

6 March 1921, Tel-el-Amarna: Presented Lord Carnarvon's letter to Mr. Peet who invited us to come over after lunch and see the excavation which he is making for the exploration fund. Had a delightful time. They live in an old house reconstructed by the Germans who were working there after the war. They have uncovered part of the old city. You can see the ground floor of the villas and the plan of gardens, old furnaces, bathroom, etc. – very interesting – they discovered some beautiful old glass (which we didn't see) and some pottery – Are now digging near the Rock Tombs – Mr. Newton, the architect, Mr. Guy and a young photographer whose name I didn't catch.*

The Porters' interest in Luxor in particular may have been piqued by Weigall's description: 'In or near the Valley are the tombs of all the Pharaohs . . . from Amenhotheph Ist to Rameses XIIth, with rare exceptions. The tomb of Tutantkhamen [sic] has not yet been found.' That summer they took a chateau in Antibes, inviting friends and acquaintances to visit them there, among them the Mendls,† Gerald Murphy and Picasso.‡ Some years later Porter wrote to Bella Spewack, author of the book *Kiss Me, Kate*: '. . . we rented the Château de la Garoupe for two summers – 1921 and 1922 – and enjoyed every moment. But in those days we were considered crazy, and it was before the days anyone went to the Riviera in the summer, as the weather was considered too hot.'§

In May 1921, Porter wrote to his friend Monty Woolley, complaining about his silence in a serious but good-natured way:

---

* The location of Linda Porter's copy of *Antiquities of Upper Egypt* is not presently known. A description of it, and a transcription of her notes, is in CPT.

† Elsie de Wolfe (Lady Mendl, 1865–1950) was an actress, interior decorator and author of *The House in Good Taste* (New York, 1913); her husband Sir Charles Mendl (1871–1958) was British press attaché in Paris. A profile of Lady Mendl was published in the *New Yorker* for 15 January 1938; it makes one mention of Porter: 'Her first theatrical coaching was in Paris with Victorien Sardou of the Comédie-Française, and one of her pet friends in the theatre today is Clifton Webb. Jean de Reszke wouldn't believe she couldn't carry a tune till she sang him a hymn to prove it, and Cole Porter and his jazz are now her favored companions.'

‡ The artists Gerald Murphy (1888–1964) and Pablo Picasso (1881–1973). The expatriate Murphy and his wife Sara (Sara Sherman Wiborg, 1883–1975) were close friends of the Porters during the 1920s; in 1923, Murphy collaborated with Porter on the ballet *Within the Quota*.

§ See pp. 388–9.

2 May 1921: Cole Porter to Monty Woolley[4]

Mont -

It has ceased being decent.

I'm very serious. Do you realize that not one word has come from you since December & this is May? And has it entered your great domed head that we are old friends?

This is my final cry for help. And the thing I regret is that even if you continue this conspiracy of silence, I know that the day when we next hit N.Y. I shall be more anxious to see you than anyone else. But, mind you, I resent it. And if ever in the future, we do meet again, once I corner you, I'm going to be so damned remote that you will leave the interview firmly convinced that I had completely forgotten your existence.

I shan't tell you my thoughts as it would obviously bore you. But I do want yours.

So if you've an atom of energy left, won't you sit down + hammer out a letter. It could be done. Won't you contemplate it?

Goodbye Mont-t-t

Co-l-e

The Porters arrived in New York later that year and during their regular stays there during the 1920s, Linda was involved in the art scene and with cultural and philanthropic institutions. In 1920, *Toys and Novelties* reported on an exhibition of Bakst dolls at Knoedler's – an art dealership founded in New York in 1846 – which included 'several portraits, among them one of Mrs. Felix Doubleday and another of Mrs. Cole Porter,'* while the *Annual Report of the American Museum for Natural History* for 1921–3 lists among

---

* *Toys and Novelties* 17 (April 1920), 91. Linda Porter had patronized the Russian-born artist Léon Bakst (Leyb-Khaim Izrailevich Rosenberg, 1866–1924) as early as the mid-1910s; a portrait sketch of her by Bakst, dated 1915, survives at the Evergreen House Foundation, Evergreen Museum & Library, Johns Hopkins University, Baltimore. Linda Porter's patronage lasted until at least 1925 when the *New York Herald Tribune (European Edition)* reported from Paris that 'The exhibition of works of Léon Bakst will terminate in a few days at the Galerie Jean Charpentier, and a group of American friends of the late painter, headed by Mrs. Cole Porter, has made up a purse by which M. Bakst's sixteen-year-old son, who inherits much of his father's talent, will go to the Beaux-Arts. The fortune accumulated by Bakst was exhausted by the support of fourteen Russians, elderly people, after the revolution' (25 November 1925, 2). In Paris, Bakst is also likely to have socialized with the Porters through their mutual acquaintance Diaghilev, for whose Ballets Russes he designed both sets and costumes.

its annual members 'By payment of $10 annually ... Porter, Mrs. Cole.' A headline in the New York Times for 31 December 1922 runs 'SAYS AMERICA FAILS TO APPRECIATE ART' and continues: 'Joseph Pennell, the veteran artist,* yesterday afternoon made a strong plea for greater recognition of modern artists, in an address at the Anderson Galleries. The occasion was the hanging of pictures for the fourth exhibition of the New Society of Artists,† which will have its varnishing day on Tuesday at the Anderson Galleries ... The members of the Varnishing Day Committee are: ... Mrs. Cole Porter.'[5] In January 1923, the New York Times also reported that 'Mrs. W. K. Vanderbilt, Mrs. John W. Garrett and Mrs. Cole Porter are members of the Reception Committee for the lecture of Leon Bakst, in French, at the Plaza on Tuesday morning, Jan. 30, on the art of dress. The proceeds will go to the Brooklyn Music School Settlement.'‡

For his part, Porter appears regularly to have kept in contact with fellow Yalies and in 1922 he wrote songs for a sketch accompanying a Yale alumni production of George Bernard Shaw's *Caesar and Cleopatra*, as the *New York Times* for 21 December, p. 18, reported: 'YALE MEN IN SHAW PLAY ... Bernard Shaw's "Caesar and Cleopatra" is to be presented this evening by the Yale University Dramatic Association at the Heckscher Memorial Theatre. A smoker for the players will follow afterward at the Yale Club, and

---

* Joseph Pennell (1857–1926) was known not only as an artist but also as an author, including a travel book, *The Jew at Home: Impressions of a Summer and Autumn Spent with Him* (New York, 1892). Virulently anti-Semitic, he described German and Russian Jews as 'the most contemptible specimen of humanity in Europe', Polish Jewish towns as 'a hideous nightmare of dirt, disease, and poverty', and he said of Russian Jews that 'They like dirt; they like to herd together in human pigsties' and that 'they like to make money out of the immorality of the Christian. They are simply a race of middlemen and money-changers.'

† Organized in 1918 as American Painters, Sculptors and Gravers, the society was renamed in 1920 as the New Society of Artists; it held exhibitions at the Wildenstein Galleries, 1919 and 1921; the Anderson Galleries, 1922–5; the Grand Central Art Galleries, 1926; the Brooklyn Museum, 1928–9; and the Whitney Museum of American Art, 1932. At various times it was patronized or had associations with Marcel Duchamp, Dashiell Hammett, Georgia O'Keeffe, Leo Stein, Alfred Stieglitz and Virgil Thomson; like the contemporaneous Society of Independent Artists, founded in 1916, its purpose was to mount exhibitions at which all artists were welcome, with neither jury nor prizes. The fourth exhibition of the New Society of Artists took place from 2 to 27 January 1923; a copy of the exhibition catalogue survives in the Seattle Art Museum Libraries. See Joshua C. Taylor, *The Fine Arts in America* (Chicago and London, 1979), 157.

‡ The Brooklyn Music School Settlement was founded in 1909 as an arm of the New York Music School Settlement; see https://www.brooklynmusicschool.org/history-culture-brooklyn-music-school.

a sketch, the book for which was written by George Chappell and the music by Cole Porter, is to be staged by the alumni at the smoker.' In 1925 he contributed to *Out O' Luck*, produced by the Yale University Dramatic Association and directed by Monty Woolley. A review appeared in the *New York Times* on 19 December 1925, p. 15:

> YALE'S 'OUT O' LUCK' IS A WAR COMEDY ... Incidental Songs by Cole Porter Enliven Piece – Will Go on Tour During Holidays. Yale undergraduates reveled in a war play of their own last night, when the Yale University Dramatic Association produced "Out o' Luck," by Tom Cushing, '02, at the Plaza. This play, however, unlike most of those which have been produced since the war, was a comedy, replete with the humor which doughboys can extract from even their most mud-begrimed and outwardly unhappy situations ... There were three songs in the play, "Mademoiselle," sung by Henry C. Potter, '26, who played the hero, "Don Keogh," a wistful lad suffering from the shock of war, "I'm the Hero-ine," sung by John McA. Hoysradt, '36, and "Butterfly," sung by the entire group. The songs were written by Cole Porter, '12.

Only the texts for *Out O' Luck* survive.[6] Porter's songs for the 1922 sketch are apparently otherwise unknown; neither the texts nor music survive.[7] Apart from his musical involvement with fellow Yale alumni, Porter also wrote the bulk of the score of the *Greenwich Village Follies*, which opened at the Sam S. Shubert Theatre, New York, on 16 September. The *New York Times* for 17 September, p. 16, described it as having 'something about it like the sack of Rome; it is like reviewing within the space of thirty minutes a deluge of music, costumes, angels, scenery, food, vivacity and week-end charades'. Porter's songs were not well received and by early 1925, when the show went on tour, most of them had been dropped.[8]

For the most part, however, Porter's musical activities at the end of the 1910s and during the early 1920s were centred in Europe. In late 1919 he may have thought about taking composition lessons with Igor Stravinsky;* on 2 December the painter and musician Paul Thévenaz wrote to Stravinsky in New

---

* Igor Stravinsky (1882–1971) was best known at the time for his ballets *The Firebird* (1910), *Petrushka* (1911) and *The Rite of Spring* (1913), composed for Diaghilev's Ballets Russes.

York: 'In a month or two you will probably receive a visit from Cole Porter, American musician, composer especially of ragtimes. He has a certain talent and wants to study with you. I told him that I was not at all sure that you would accept a pupil. But this could be interesting. He will pay anything you ask. He is a very nice boy, intelligent, gifted, and a multimillionaire.'[9] Negotiations with Porter dragged on for more than two years but nothing came of them. On 18 July 1922, Stravinsky wrote to Winnaretta Singer:* 'I would also like to tell you that mister Cole Porter has abruptly renounced to take lessons with me. When I saw him last, I had a contract that was drawn up and signed by him, accompanied by a letter. He asked me to let him know by lawyer if (and I underline) there <u>was anything in the contract that might not be to my liking</u>. So I did, and offered him a counterproposal, that only included a few precisions to his contract, that had only guaranteed me half of the announced sum. After which his lawyer announced to me the somehow unexpected news of Porter's refusal. Unexpected, because it was Porter himself who urged me to make the changes. I do not hide to you the fact that I feel hurt by his behavior and I regret that he troubled you for nothing.'[10] Also in 1922, on 21 July, while the Porters were in the United States, Linda sent a telegram to her friend Alice Garrett, then at Cannes, asking whether she could rent Garrett's Paris apartment: 'WILL YOU RENT YOUR APARTMENT TO COLE FOR SIX WEEKS SAILING JULY TWENTY SECOND AQ[U]ITANIA TO WRITE REVUE PLEASE WIRELESS HIM YES OR NO LOVE LINDA.'[11] This could refer to *Hitchy-Koo of 1922*, which never made it to New York and closed during its Philadelphia tryout in October, or, since the Porters were on their way to Europe, the 'Ragtime Pipes of Pan' from *Phi-Phi*, a Charles Cochran revue that opened at the London Pavilion Theatre on 16 August.

In the meantime, in May 1920, Porter enrolled at the Schola Cantorum in Paris, where one of his assignments was to orchestrate a Robert Schumann piano sonata.[12] That same year he contributed three numbers to the London musical *A Night Out*, which opened at the Winter Garden Theatre on 18 September,[13] and in 1922 several of his songs appeared in Charles B. Cochran's *Mayfair and Montmartre*. *A Night Out* was well received. *The Times* of London

---

* Winnaretta Singer, Princesse Edmond de Polignac (1865–1943), was heiress to the Singer sewing-machine company. Her marriage to Prince Edmond de Polignac (1834–1901) in 1893 was her second; well known to be lesbian, Singer was also a significant patron of modern composers, including Debussy, Ravel, Milhaud, Poulenc and Kurt Weill.

described it as 'one of the brightest things of its kind which we have had for a long time' and 'the music of Mr. Willie Redstone and the other composers who have lent a hand is dainty.'[14] *Mayfair and Montmartre* fared less well:

> At the beginning of the second part of Mr. C. B. Cochran's new revue *Mayfair and Montmartre*, which was produced at the New Oxford Theatre last night, there was a scene which purported to represent three dramatic critics discussing the first part of the play. They said a good many harsh things about it – intended, of course, to be exceedingly ironical – and finally one of them remarked, "The whole show needs the axe." The scene then ended, amid prolonged applause from the audience. Mr. Cochran was not only courageous to introduce such a *post-mortem* on half of his own production. He also showed a certain amount of perspicacity. Incidentally he has rendered criticism mere plagiarism. If he had held a similar *post-mortem* on the second half he could fairly have introduced some kinder remarks about the production, but by that time a section of the audience had started the work of criticism on its own.
>
> *Mayfair and Montmartre* is not so good as some of its predecessors ... The weakest part of the production lay in the various sketches. Few of them were very amusing, and one called *The Conference Trick*, which represented certain politicians, was in poor taste. It obtained a mixed reception, and should be the first candidate for Mr. Cochran's axe.[15]

The review does not mention Porter or for that matter any of the revue's musical numbers, including songs by Max Darewski, Irving Berlin and George Gershwin.* And there is no evidence that Porter met Gershwin at

---

* Porter's songs included 'Olga (Come Back to the Volga)', 'Cocktail Time' and 'The Blue Boy Blues'. Two other songs, 'The Bandit Band' and 'The Sponge', were copyrighted at the same time and apparently intended for *Mayfair and Montmartre*, although they are not listed in the London opening-night programme; see Kimball, *The Complete Lyrics of Cole Porter*, 132. The child prodigy pianist and composer Max Darewski (1894–1929) composed numerous songs for West End revues and musicals; his songs 'Ting, Ling', 'Versailles', 'Home Once More' and 'I'm Not That Kind of Girl' featured in *Mayfair and Montmartre*. Gershwin's contributions included 'Do It Again', 'My Lady' and 'South Sea Isles'; Berlin's 'Say it With Music' was also included in the show. Piano-vocal scores of several numbers are at the Library of Congress, Music Division, shelfmark M1508 Mayfair and Montmartre. A 1922 British Pathé silent video of some of the song and dance numbers is available at https://www.youtube.com/watch?v=R516rrSQQSo.

this time; as far as is known, Gershwin was not in London for the production. They had, however, met by late 1925 when, according to the *New York Times*, Porter attended a post-concert reception for Gershwin at the home of Jules Glaenzer: 'Mr. and Mrs. Jules Glaenzer gave a reception last night at their home, Sixty-fifth Street and Lexington Avenue, for George Gershwin, whose new piano concerto in F major was presented by the New York Symphony Orchestra at a concert earlier in the evening. The guests included . . . Mr. and Mrs. Walter Damrosch . . . Mr. and Mrs. Theodore Steinway . . . Conde Nast, Noel Coward, Cole Porter and Cyril Maude.'*

The most significant of Porter's large-scale works at this time was the ballet *Within the Quota*, written for Rolf de Maré's Ballets Suédois† as a companion piece to Darius Milhaud's‡ *La Création du Monde*. *Within the Quota* was initially conceived by Porter's friend Gerald Murphy and, according to William McBrien,[16] it was Milhaud who asked Porter – whom he had met at the home of Winnaretta Singer, Princesse de Polignac – to write the ballet. Milhaud's autobiography tells a slightly different story, that it was de Maré who concocted the ballet's plot and commissioned Porter:

> De Maré was to undertake a tour of the United States and wanted to put on an authentic American work, but did not know whom to approach. He was afraid of coming across some composer struggling along in the wake of Debussy, Ravel, or someone composing music *à la Brahms* or *à la Reger*. I had met Cole Porter several times at the house of the Princesse de Polignac. This elegant young American, who always wore a white

---

* *New York Times*, 4 December 1925, 19. Walter Damrosch (1862–1950), at the time conductor of the New York Symphony Orchestra; Theodore Steinway (1883–1957), grandson of Henry E. Steinway, founder of Steinway & Sons pianos, and chairman of the company; Condé Montrose Nast (1873–1942), publisher and founder of the media company named after him; Cyril Maude (1862–1951), English actor.

† The Ballets Suédois, directed by Rolf de Maré (1888–1964), was active from 1920 to 1925; its most important productions included *Les Mariés de la Tour Eiffel* (1921), with a storyline by Jean Cocteau and music by Georges Auric, Arthur Honegger, Darius Milhaud, Francis Poulenc and Germaine Tailleferre; and Milhaud's *La Création du Monde* (1923). See Bengt Nils Richard Häger, *The Swedish Ballet* (New York, 1990), and Nancy Van Norman Baer and Jan Torsten Ahlstrand, *Paris Modern: The Swedish Ballet, 1920–1925* (San Francisco, 1995).

‡ Darius Milhaud (1892–1974) was one of the foremost French composers of the early twentieth century, known in particular for his jazz-influenced music and as a modernist. In 1919 he had composed the influential Brazilian-influenced ballet *Le Boeuf sur le Toit*.

carnation in the buttonhole of his faultless dinner jacket, sang in a low, husky voice songs having just the qualities that de Maré was looking for. I introduced them to each other. De Maré immediately asked him to treat a subject admirably suitable for his music: the arrival of a young Swede in New York. Charles Koechlin undertook to orchestrate his score, which was redolent of the pure spirit of Manhattan, with wistful blues alternating with throbbing ragtime rhythms. This odd partnership between the technician of counterpoint and fugue and the brilliant future "King of Broadway" was an outstanding success. Ferdinand Léger asked an American artist, Gerald Murphy, to paint the scenery, and the skyscrapers of Times Square were seen to rise on the stage of the Théâtre des Champs-Élysées.[17]

Milhaud's account can be faulted on at least one detail: according to the diaries of Charles Koechlin, who in the autumn of 1923 orchestrated *Within the Quota*, Milhaud had previously met Porter at Koechlin's home as early as 5 June 1923 when they had dinner together and, as Koechlin reported, listened to 'Disques Négres'. That same month, Koechlin gave Porter eight orchestration lessons. None of these early meetings, however, concerned *Within the Quota*, which was first mentioned by Porter in a now-lost telegram to Koechlin of 14 September. Further diary entries document Koechlin's work on the ballet:

15 September: Koechlin visits Porter at 13, rue Monsieur.
18–20, 21 and 24–27 September: Koechlin orchestrates *Within the Quota*.
26 September: Porter visits Koechlin at his home at Villers-sur-Mer; they review the orchestration of *Within the Quota*.
28 September and 1 October: Koechlin continues to work on his orchestration.
5 October: In apparent response to an invitation to visit Villers-sur-Mer again, Porter sends Koechlin a (now lost) telegram, apparently in response to an invitation to visit Villers-sur-Mer again; Porter 'ne peut pas venir'.
17 October: Koechlin returns to Paris and reads through Porter's ballet again.

19 October: *Within the Quota* is rehearsed and Koechlin asks Porter for payment for his work.

25 October: Koechlin cashes Cole Porter's cheque for $500, approximately 8,600 Francs.

31 October: Koechlin visits Porter at the Hotel Ritz.

11 December: Koechlin cashes a second cheque from Porter, in the amount of 9,300 Francs.*

Within the Quota premiered on 25 October 1923 at the Théâtre des Champs-Elysées, together with Milhaud's *La Création du Monde*. Milhaud's comment that the event was an 'outstanding success' notwithstanding, the reviews were generally mixed, and mostly negative:

Le Figaro, 27 October 1923
For its first musical event of this year, the Théâtre des Champs-Elysées presented two new ballets, one by MM. Cendrars and Darius Milhaud, the other by Gerald Murphy and Cole Porter. The first has the simple and definitive title, La Création du Monde, the second an English title that the program translated as *l'Immigrant*. These two productions are of the humorous kind, the first infinitely superior to the second ... The second ballet, the ballet-sketch of MM. Murphy and Cole Porter, is entirely different. Here there is no question of style or an attempt to move forward. We go back [instead] several years in the annals of the music hall. We have seen such sketches inserted in innumerable revues, and the music is unfortunately typical of this poor sort of invention. The care with which it was orchestrated by Mr. Koechlin further reveals its weakness [*en révèle davantage l'indigence*] and the grandiloquence of the finale highlights its vulgarity. The music of the finale, however, has the advantage of entering the ear easily ... This was not the usual Swedish ballet performance.

---

* We are indebted to Robert Orledge for these details. On 22 January 1924, Porter sent Koechlin a telegram (also lost) requesting more lessons: he had these on 23, 25 and 29 January and on 1 and 5 February. Further, see Robert Orledge, 'Cole Porter's Ballet *Within the Quota*', *The Yale University Library Gazette* 50/1 (1975), 19–29.

L'Intransigeant, 27 October 1923, p. 4

That as worthy and serious a musician as Mr. Koechlin has granted his patronage – and the most active patronage possible: collaboration – to the score of Mr. Cole Porter, the composer of Within the Quota, cannot be seen merely as a courteous gesture to an American colleague. It must be that Mr. Koechlin, for his part, recognized qualities [in it] other than banal. On a single hearing, and despite the attraction added to it by ingenious orchestral colour, we would be embarrassed if we had to say exactly what these qualities are. Humour? A sense of wit and popular art? A directness without detours or complications? Maybe, and that would be something in itself. If there is more, we will not ask anything more of ourselves than to convince ourselves of it, and in the meantime we are entirely disposed to take Mr. Koechlin at his word.

Le Matin, 29 October, p. 4

More balanced [*pondéré*], but nevertheless very curious, was a ballet-sketch by Gérald Murphy, Within the Quota, comedic and satirical scenes with a score by Cole Porter, a famous jazz composer. The action takes place in America, in front of a giant newspaper page. Typical types of Americans appear: the billionaire, the puritan, the gentleman of colour, the jazzbaby, the cowboy, the queen-of-all-hearts … The public applauded them for their designs and their realizations perfectly adequate to the characters that they embody.

A report published in London was similarly dismissive: 'The other ballet, *Within the Quota*, which might possibly be effective as a scene in a music-hall revue, is a rather poor attempt to do what was done once for all in *Le Boeuf sur le Toit*.'* The expatriate American press, however, was jingoistically favourable:

American Ballet Pleases Gathering At Paris Theatre. Fashionable and artistic Paris made up a brilliant first-night audience, with Americans much in evidence, when the Swedish Ballets yesterday revealed their

---

* *The Times*, 30 October 1923, 10. Milhaud's ballet *Le Boeuf sur le Toit* premiered in February 1920 at the Théâtre des Champs-Elysées, Paris.

new program at the Théâtre des Champs-Elysées in the first of three performances which M. Rolf de Mare, the director, will give here before taking his troupe to America next month. The ballet of the two Americans, Mr. Gerald Murphy and Mr. Cole Porter, the composer, had an undoubted success in the array of new compositions, by some of the best-known modernist composers, which made up the bill.

"Within the Quota" awoke laughter and applause from the audience, in which society and Montmartre were mingled, as it unfolded the story of a Swedish immigrant who lands in America to meet all the glamorous figures of American life which he had imagined, and finds himself separated from them by the sinister figure of prohibition in one form or another.

Mr. Murphy's clever journalistic set brought a hearty laugh as soon as it was revealed and his eccentric costumes had a big effect, and the "intensified jazz" with which Mr. Cole Porter accompanied the dances of the negro, the jazz baby and the millionaires, culminating in a delightful and humorous movie music effect to mark the end of the Swedish boy's search when he meets Mary Pickford amused and highly pleased the audience.[18]

In November, *Within the Quota* moved to New York. The *New York Times* for 23 November 1923, p. 30, noted that, 'Midway in a week's stay here, the Swedish Ballet gave an American novelty in its performance at the Century Theatre last night, one of the latest it had produced in Paris before sailing last month. The piece was its gesture of greeting to America, as it might well have been last Monday, introducing, not Bartholdi's Statue of Liberty, but a Swedish immigrant landing in New York. The ballet sketch "Within the Quota" was by Gerald Murphy, a Yale graduate and son of Patrick Francis Murphy of this city. The descriptive music of a day in harbor and ashore, orchestrated by Charles Koechlin abroad, was sketched originally by Cole Porter, Mr. Murphy's classmate and associate artist now overseas, who wrote a remembered song, "An Old-Fashioned Garden," in one of Raymond Hitchcock's productions of "Hitchy-Koo." '* The more positive response that *Within the Quota* got in New York appears to have enhanced

---

* See above, p. 32.

Porter's reputation in the United States at a time when he was not particularly well known to the public. The next year, the author and music critic Gilbert Seldes wrote in *The Seven Lively Arts*:

> Two composers are possible successors to [Irving] Berlin if he ever chooses to stop. I omit Jerome Kern – a consideration of musical style will indicate why. I am sure of Gershwin and would be more sure of Cole Porter if his astonishing lyrics did not so dazzle me as to make me distrust my estimate of his music ... Banking on Porter is dangerous because essentially he is much more sophisticated in general attitude of mind than any of the others, and although he has written ragtime and patter songs and jazz of exceptional goodness, he has one quality which may bar him forever from the highest place – I mean that he is essentially a parodist. I know of no one else with such a sense for musical styles. A blues, a 1910 rag, a Savoy operetta serio-comic love song, a mother song – he writes them all with a perfect feeling for their musical nature, and almost always with satiric intention, with a touch of parody. It is only the most sophisticated form which is germane to him; in highly complex jazzing he is so much at home, his curiosity is so engaged, he feels the problem so much, that the element of parody diminishes. Yet *The Blue Boy Blues*,* almost as intricate a thing as Berlin ever wrote, with a melody overlaid on a running syncopated comment, has a slight touch of parody in the very excess of its skill. Jazz has always mocked itself a little; it is possible that it will divide and follow two strains – the negro and the intellectual. In the second case Porter will be one of its leaders and Whiteman† will be his orchestra. The song *Soon*,[19] for example, is a deliberate annihilation of the Southern negro sentiment carefully done by

---

* 'The Blue Boy Blues' (1922) satirizes the controversial purchase the previous year by railroad magnate Henry E. Huntington of Thomas Gainsborough's famous *Blue Boy*; see, for example, *Manchester Guardian*, 31 December 1921, 6: 'There are few pictures with which we are more loath to part. The Gainsborough has all the fresh willful loveliness that we like to consider as the signal quality of English art.' Similarly, a certain Basil Thomson wrote to the editor of *The Times* (London) on the 'Loss of a National Asset', arguing that 'Great works of art are among the assets of the nation; they educate the public taste and they attract visitors', before concluding, curiously: 'Moreover, it is probably true that a picture painted in a damp climate suffers when it is kept for years in a dry atmosphere like that of the United States.' *The Times* (London), 23 January 1922, 6.

† Paul Whiteman (1890–1967) was perhaps the best known band leader in the 1920s.

playing Harlem jazz, with a Harlem theme, mercilessly burlesquing the *clichés* of the Southern song – the Swanee-Mammy element* – in favour of a Harlem alley. Porter's parody is almost too facile; *Soon* is an exasperatingly good piece of jazz in itself. He is a tireless experimenter, and the fact that in 1923 others are doing things he tried in 1919, makes me wonder whether his excessive intelligence and sophistication may not be pointing a way which steadier and essentially more *native* jazz writers will presently follow. Native, I mean, to jazz; taking it more seriously. Whether any of them could compose such a ballet as Porter did for the Ballet Suédois is another question.[20]

Shortly after the Paris premiere of *Within the Quota*, the Porters bought a new house in Paris, at 13 rue Monsieur in the 13th arrondissement, close to Les Invalides. Originally built in 1777 by the architect Alexandre Brongniart as a stable and residence for the Comte de Provence, a younger brother of Louis XVI (and from 1814 to 1824 Louis XVII), 13 rue Monsieur was featured in the 25 January 1925 issue of *Vogue* magazine.†

Their purchase of 13 rue Monsieur notwithstanding, the Porters maintained for a short while at least their apartment at the Ritz, as two curious newspaper articles in the *New York Herald Tribune (European Edition)* concerning Porter's apparently abducted dog suggest:

4 January 1924, p. 2
LOST, on the 1st of January, between five and six o'clock in the evening SMALL BLACK AND WHITE CURLY-HAIRED DOG. RED COLLAR, marked JACK HAMLET, 3 RUE DE LA BAUME. Return to MR. COLE PORTER, Hôtel Ritz. WILL RECEIVE LIBERAL REWARD.

5 January 1924, p. 2
CANINE FAVORITE OF STAGE IS LOST. The alleged attempt to kidnap one of the Dolly Sisters recently was closely followed by the

---

* Here Seldes refers to George Gershwin's 1919 'Swanee', which became a hit when it was performed by Al Jolson in his show *Sinbad* (1920).

† The house was put up for sale in 2012 with an asking price of €40 million; see https://www.nytimes.com/2012/09/28/greathomesanddestinations/a-house-in-the-country-without-ever-leaving-central-paris.html (accessed 9 April 2018).

disappearance of another stage star in Paris, when Jack Hamlet vanished in an unexplained manner from the room of Mr. Cole Porter at the Hotel Ritz between five and six o'clock on the afternoon of New Year's Day. No trace of him has been found since, in spite of his conspicuous appearance, for he has black and white curly hair and was wearing a red collar at the time he was missed. He is not a valuable dog, but his owner, the American composer, would like to have him back in memory of days spent together in America.

Mr. Cole Porter, who wrote the music of "Within the Quota," the American immigrant story given in Paris last November by the Swedish Ballets and afterwards taken to America by them, is at work on a new ballet with M. Léon Bakst, the Russian designer, and was planning to put the dog in the show. This is another reason why he needs him back, as well as being sorry to have the dog's stage career in danger of being blasted in the bud. The name, Jack Hamlet, was bestowed upon the future footlight favorite by Mr. John Barrymore, who must have had an idea of the dog's theatrical ambitions. For these reasons the owner is offering a reward to anyone who will restore the fugitive Hamlet to his home and his career.*

In the late spring of 1925 the Porters travelled to North Africa, and in March Porter sent postcards to his friends Monty Woolley and the author and abstract artist Charles Green Shaw:

March 1925: Cole Porter to Monty Woolley[21]

You can't imagine the beauties of the mountains of North Africa – We all wish you were with us to enjoy them.

C –

---

* *New York Herald Tribune (European Edition)*, 4 January 1925, 2, and 5 January 1925, 2. The *Herald Tribune*, the chief newspaper for expatriate Americans on the continent, frequently reported on the Porters' social life. On 2 February 1924, for instance, it noted that 'Lady Michelham has entertained at dinner at the Hotel Ritz, Paris, here guests including: Prince and Prince [sic] Radziwill, Comte and Comtesse Georges de Castellane, Lady Cunard, Lady Cynthia Mosley, Mr. and Mrs. Cole Porter'; on 4 February it reported: 'New of Americans Day by Day. At the dinner-dance at the Hotel Ritz, Paris, last night, Lady Cunard was among those entertaining, having as her guests Grand Duchess Marie, Lady Michelham, Miss Elsa Maxwell, Mr. Cole Porter, Mr. Charles Mendl and Captain Molyneux.'

[?] Spring 1925: Cole Porter to Charles Green Shaw[22]

There are lots of high ceilings in Fez.*

After his return to Europe, in May, Porter sent Shaw a postcard from Cherbourg and Woolley a postcard from Amsterdam, with a picture of the German Kaiser Wilhelm:[23]

2 May 1925: Cole Porter to Charles Green Shaw[24]

Courtney + I send you a great big Rick in your great big behind. C.

15 May 1925: Cole Porter to Monty Woolley[25]

I don't see why you cant [sic] even answer mail on Marshall's Petter [?]. Exactly why cant [sic] you?
   C.

Charles Green Shaw (1892–1974), a Yale classmate of Porter's, had been a close family friend at least since the late 1910s; as early as 1920 Porter's mother wrote to him: 'Dear Charles: You were very good to remember Cole Porter's Mother with a copy of your latest book. I am delighted with it, I think the articles clever . . .'[26] There is little evidence, however, to suggest he and Porter were lovers except perhaps occasionally: although Shaw was homosexual like Porter, the character of Porter's correspondence with him, like his correspondence with Woolley, is intimate, flirtatious, natural, friendly, and seemingly based on a sort of equality of kindred spirits, unlike his serious correspondence with Boris Kochno,† or his earnest and paternal correspondence with Nelson Barclift later. A few of Porter's letters to Shaw are undated but most are written on Parisian stationery or refer to France or Venice. It is likely, then, that the surviving letters largely date from the mid to late 1920s.[27]

---

* A reference to the fact that Shaw was tall. This also explains Porter's later salutations to him as 'Big Boy'.

† See below, pp. 54–71.

[n.d.] Cole Porter to Charles Green Shaw[28]

Big Boy –

But so few letters dernierement. And why!

I saw Duncan Milne + he talks to the Ritz Bar about you. And to so many people!

But much – all the same – I'd like to see your great towering frame crowding a small apartment.

Write to me, Big Boy. Just a Christmas letter, that's all. And tell me all about the way you fellows live, over there.

I miss you a great deal + I beg you to fix your uncle + spend next summer with My Blue-Grass Girl And Me* in Ole' Venezia. Goodbye + forgive if I go away. It's midnight + high time for all good little boys to go up to that wicked hill called Montmartre.

Wednesday

Colole [sic]

[n.d.] Cole Porter to Charles Green Shaw[29]

March

Big Boy –

Write to me. But write to me, Big Boy. I miss you so much. And its [sic] been so long. Wont [sic] you write to me? Wont [sic] you write to me, Big Boy?

inConsOLablE

[n.d.] Cole Porter to Charles Green Shaw[30]

But it doesn't write to me, the Big Boy. And I'm so sad. And I walk along the streets of Paris + people stop + Look at me, simply because I'm muttering "The Big Boy doesn't write to me, The Big Boy doesn't write. The Big Boy doesn't. The Big Boy. doesn---------------'-----------t ---------- wri----------------------te----------------to-----------me-------------.

Policemen have to be called.

C.

---

* A reference to the fact that Linda Porter was born in Virginia.

12 February [no year]: Cole Porter to Charles Green Shaw

IMMENSE MAN,

ONE OF THOSE THINGS HAPPENED TONIGHT THAT COULDN'T POSSIBLY HAPPEN IN NEW YORK. BILL REARDON AND I STARTED FOR THE HILL* AT MIDNIGHT AND AFTER DOING ALL THE OBVIOUS BOITES, LANDED IN A LITTLE SPANISH PLACE WHERE THERE WAS A WOMAN. BUT A WOMAN, CHARLES. SHE WAS FAT AND SIXTY AND AWFUL. BUT OH MY GOD HOW SHE COULD SING A SONG. AND WE SAT THERE FOR HOURS AND DIED OF JOY. BECAUSE SHE WAS ONE OF THOSE THINGS THAT ARRIVE IN ONE'S LIFE EVERY FEW YEARS AND NEVER OFTENER. AND ITS [sic] NOW EXACTLY SIX A.M. AND I HAVE ENGAGED HER TO COME TO THE HOUSE TOMORROW, WHICH IS SUNDAY, AND BRING HER OLD GUITARIST AND HER SON WHO CLAPS HANDS AND SINGS ALL AFTERNOON. AND I'M SIMPLY TRYING TO FILL IN AS MUCH TIME AS POSSIBLE, UNTIL SHE COMES BACK INTO MY LIFE.

OUR TRIP TO TIMBUCTOO FELL THROUGH BECAUSE IT IS NOT ALLOWED. SO WE ARE GOING TO VERSAILLES FOR THE WEEK-END [sic] INSTEAD. AND ITS [sic] MUCH EASIER. AND THEN [HOWARD] STURGES AND I LEAVE FOR ROME ON SATURDAY NEXT TO GO TO A FUNNY PARTY AND AFTERWARDS MOTOR ABOUT SOME OF THE SILLIER HILL TOWNS. THEN LINDA AND I LEAVE FOR SPAIN IN A NEW MOTOR, WHICH IS A RELIEF AS THE OLD MOTOR HAS BEEN COPIED SO OFTEN AND ITS [sic] GOING TO BE GREAT FUN, SPRINGING A NEW BODY ON A LOT OF ANDALUSIANS. ON MAY FIRST, WE START AGAIN FOR A TRIP TO MIDDLE EUROPE, IN A PRIVATE CAR PAID FOR BY A PRIVATE FRIEND OF OURS, IN ORDER TO ENGAGE A TZIGANE ORCHESTRA FOR THE LAST TWO WEEKS OF AUGUST FOR VENICE. AND AFTER ALL THIS IS OVER, WE RETURN TO PARIS TO BUY IMPORTANT PYJAMAS FOR THE LIDO. OTHERWISE, OUR LIFE IS MERE PLEASURE.

YOURS WAS ONE OF THE BEST SHOCKS OF MY LIFE, AND I BEG YOU TO REST UP A WHILE AND DO IT AGAIN. I SUPPOSE YOU HAVEN'T WRITTEN A LETTER LIKE THAT FOR YEARS. AND I SHALL SAVE IT AND PRESENT IT AFTER YOUR DEATH TO GIVE THE WORLD AN EXAMPLE OF MERE STYLE.

---

* Presumably Montmartre.

GOODBYE, CHARLES, AND BLESS YOU FOR NOT FORGETTING THE FACT THAT WE MEN MUST STICK TOGETHER. I DON'T KNOW WHETHER I SENT YOU A CHECK TO HUSH THE RAQUET CLUB OR NOT, BUT I SHALL LOOK IT UP, ONE DAY SOON AND SEND IT TO YOU IN CASE I HAVE BEEN NEGLIGENT ABOUT MONEY MATTERS.

GIVE MY LOVE TO LA DOOMPA* AND HERMIE AND CORTNEY [sic] BURR† AND MONTY [WOOLLEY] AND COVVARUBIAS.‡ AND WANGLE NEXT SUMMER, BECAUSE YOU WOULD LIKE IT IN SPITE OF ALL THE RUMORS. BESIDES WHICH, WE HAVE A LOT OF HIGH CEILINGS.

ITS [sic] SEVEN A.M. AND BED-TIMES [sic].

[handwritten:] Feb. 12   Cole

[n.d.] Cole Porter to Charles Green Shaw, with a postscript by Monty Woolley

BIG BOY !

Monty [Woolley] and [Howard] Sturge[s] and I are all lying here together in my lit d'amour. And in spite of the fact that it is very hot and crowded I miss that great giant body of the boy I love.

Cole

Now that is the letter that Cole just dictated to me for you. Is it by any stretch of the imagination a decent letter? Or isn't that sort of thing prohibited by law from being carried in the mails?

Come over here at once. Don't lag around. Get on a boat immediately and rush over here. You'd love it. Hermie and La Doompa are here and in grand form. Hermie hates everything and everybody. La Doompa is having a marvelous time. I am planning to come back with them, sailing Aug. 11th. Saw a lot of Courtney in Paris, and he may come back with us. MAY. HE MAY COME BACK WITH US, you notice – it is not safe to say anything like that for certain. But it is just possible. Why don't you jump over hr here [sic] for a few weeks and come back with all of us? Is it impossible? We'd all love to have you here so much.

---

* Mrs Herman 'Dumpy' Oelrichs (née Dorothy Haydel, 1891–?) was the wife of Hermann Oelrichs (1891–1948), a businessman and the son of Hermann Oelrichs (1850–1906), American agent of the Norddeutscher Lloyd shipping company.

† Courtney Burr (?–1961), producer, performer and stage manager.

‡ Possibly the Mexican artist and art historian Miguel Covarrubias (also known as José Miguel Covarrubias Duclaud, 1904–57).

Love to Braddie Norman,
MONT
Address:
Cole Porter
Palazzo Rezzonico
Venice.

[n.d.] Cole Porter to Charles Green Shaw

Big Boy –

Linda + I came back via Lyons simply to lunch again at this restaurant. The extraordinary thing is that it has only one menu the whole year round, + you will notice that the lunch menu is practically the same as the dinner menu.

In spite of this, it is always packed because it is inspired food + the Poulet demi-deuil is something we could die for.

Goodbye, Infinite Dimensions – Cole.

1928 or 1929: Cole Porter to Charles Green Shaw[31]

Why?

Porter's last known letter to Shaw was written from his suite at the Waldorf, New York, in May 1959:

19 May 1959: Cole Porter to Charles Green Shaw[32]

Dear Charlie: –

Thank you so much for sending me "Into the Light",* with its frontispiece. It was most thoughtful of you, and I do appreciate it.

Sincerely,
Cole

If you are free on Wednesday, June 3rd, can you dine with me?

---

* Charles Green Shaw's collection of poems, *Into the Light*, was published in New York in 1959.

On 1 August 1925, while the Porters were in Venice, Cole placed an advertisement in the classified section of the *New York Herald Tribune (European Edition)*. Although obscure, it would seem to be an attempt to arrange a clandestine liaison: '**PERSONAL.** WILL SLEEPY HALL please wire his address to Cole Porter, Palazzo Papadopoli, Venice.' The advertisement was repeated in the 2 and 3 August editions of the newspaper.[33] This was during one of several summers in the 1920s when Cole and Linda Porter regularly rented properties in Venice, including the Palazzo Papadopoli in 1924, and the Ca' Rezzonico, fronting on the Grand Canal, from 1925 to 1927. It is not out of the question that it was addressed to Boris Kochno, the amanuensis and lover of the ballet impresario and founder of the Ballets Russes, Sergei Diaghilev (1872–1929).

According to one source, in 1924, Diaghilev and Kochno 'arranged a stage in their garden, backing on to the Grand Canal, making, as a background, three arches covered with greenery, which framed statues borrowed from a museum. The programme consisted of two male variations from *Les Matelots*, the tarantella from *Cimarosiana* and Sokolova's solo, the Rag Mazurka, from *Les Biches*. Boris had to hum *Les Matelots* to Cole Porter, so that he should be able to play it on the piano, for there was no score available.'[34] Porter had almost certainly met Diaghilev, and Kochno as well, by 1923 at the latest, about the time of *Within the Quota*.* Whether they met again in 1924, as Richard Buckle (relying in part on Kochno, see below) states, is otherwise unsubstantiated. In 1925, however, possibly about the time of Porter's 1 August 1925 advertisement in the *New York Herald Tribune*, Kochno became his lover, and a significant, if one-sided, correspondence with Kochno from the autumn of 1925 documents the course of their affair. Although Porter's handwritten letters are mostly undated, their chronology can be reconstructed based on an itinerary of Porter's

---

* In *Diaghilev and the Ballets Russes* (New York, 1973), 222, Kochno writes that, 'One day, Cole Porter invited Diaghilev and me to lunch with George Gershwin, who was passing through Paris and wanted Diaghilev to hear his *Rhapsody in Blue*, which he would have loved to have performed by the Ballets Russes. Diaghilev listened in silence while Gershwin played his score, promised to "think about the question of using it for a ballet", but never gave him an answer.' This anecdote may well be apocryphal and it cannot date from the earlier 1920s as Kochno's placement of it in his narrative suggests: Gershwin did not meet Diaghilev until his trip to Paris in 1928. See William G. Hyland, *George Gershwin* (Westport, CT, 2003), 44, and below, p. 81.

travels that he sent to Kochno and internal references in the letters themselves:*

[?6 September 1925]: Cole Porter to Boris Kochno†

Dimanche matin

<u>2 hres</u>

Boris –

Tu a fait une grande amie aujourdhui – c'etait Linda. Apres que tout la monde etait parti, elle est veneue a ma chamber, me voir – Et elle ne parlait que de Toi – disant que tu avais été charmant, qu'elle te trouvant <u>tres</u> gentile, et que vous aviez rié beaucoup ensemble cet apres midi.

Je mets la troisieme phrase a la fin de la causerie, parce que je crois que ça soit la plus importante, bien que tres peu de gens l'amusent, et que je ne sais pas te dire combine je suis reconnaissant – tu l'as fait. Et cela rend tout tellement plus facile.

Quant a ton depart, j'essaie de me consoler en pensant de ton retour, mais c'est assez difficile. Et la seule chose que je veux vraiment faire, c'est de monter sur la Campanile et announcer a la piazza que je suis amoureux a mourir de quelq'un qui a pris le train de ce soir pour Naples et que je vais le suivre.

Mais, tu sais, Boris, je suis sûr de toi, et... C'etait tellement penible de te voir toujours parmi d'autres personnes, que, peutetre, que nous sommes, un

---

* Porter's letters and telegrams to Kochno survive at (Yale University, Gilmore Library, Cole Porter Collection, MSS 82, Box 67). All are handwritten, and considering Porter's sometimes indecipherable handwriting as well as his less than perfect French, some passages are difficult to transcribe. With this in mind, our translations are both freer and in some respects more polished – in order to convey Porter's sense – than his original French prose.

† ALS. This first letter is difficult to place chronologically. It survives in a folder with an envelope dated 14 September but that date does not fit, either chronologically or with respect to its content, with the letters that follow. See below for a letter that can plausibly be dated 14 September. And if that is the case, then this letter must be from at least a week earlier since it describes not only the time Porter spent with Kochno in Venice but also mentions that Kochno was departing for Naples. That, in turn, makes an earlier date consistent with Porter's letter of 20 September. The most likely Sunday referred to here is 6 September 1925. It is unclear whether by writing '2 o'clock in the morning' he means 2 a.m. following Saturday 5 September – technically Sunday 6 September – or more casually meaning 2 a.m. on the night of 6–7 (Monday) September.

peu plus tranquils ensembles en etant separes pour le moment sachant que, une fois, arrive a Paris, ca va etre si facil de te voir.

Oh, il n'ya pas a dire, Boris, je t'adore a un tel point que je ne pense qu'a toi – je ne vois que toi + je ne reve qu'an moment ou nous serons reunis. Goodnight, darling.

C.

[Sunday morning
<u>2 o'clock</u>
Boris –

You made a great friend today – Linda. After everyone had left, she came to my room to see me and spoke to me only about you – she said you had been charming, that she found you very kind, and that you had laughed a great deal together this afternoon.

I put the third phrase at the end of the list because I believe it is the most important as she finds very few people amuse her and, I do not know how to tell you how grateful I am – you did it. And that makes everything so much easier.

Now that you've left, I'm trying to console myself by thinking of your return, but it's quite difficult. And the only thing that I really want to do, is to climb to the top of the Campanile and announce to the piazza that I'm in love to the point of dying with someone who has taken this evening's train to Naples and that I'm going to follow him.

But you know, Boris, that I am sure about you, and . . . It was hard watching you always among others and perhaps, if we had a little more peaceful time together, this momentary separation [word unreadable]. When I'm back in Paris it will be so easy to see you.

Oh there's nothing to say, Boris, I love you so much that I think only of you – I see only you and I dream only of the moment when we'll be reunited. Goodnight, darling.

C.]

[11 September 1925]: Cole Porter to Boris Kochno

Vendredi soir.

Boris –

On arrive a la fin. Et c'est bien triste.

L'amirail de la flotte americaine qui vient d'arriver m'a telephoné aujourd hui, disant qu'il voudrait bien donner son jazz-band si je voulais arranger une soirée pour les officiers. Mais quant on a asseyé de faire une liste, on a trouvé que toute la jeunesse était partie et qu'il ne restaient que les vielles Mocenigos + Morosinis. Et on a refusé.

Apres quatre jours de sight-seeing a Venice, je vais demain, pour la derniere fois au Lido, pour dire au revoir a la Casa di Sole + au bagnino.

Mon auto est arrivée, ce soir + nous quittons le Paradis mercredi matin pour Ravenne. Mais quand est-ce que je vais te retrouver? Il n'y a pas assez de lettres. Ça je dis froidément. Je suis allé ce soir au Grand Hotel – Niente! Et depuis que tu es parti, il y a six jours, je n'ai q'une seule lettre. Ce n'est pas la peine de me dire que tu n'avais pas le temps, car je sais trop bien que si tu voulais, rien ne serait plus facile. Et je veux souligner le faite que j'en deviens un peu furieux. Tu me manques tellement que je suis un personne tout a fait ratée + si ça continue – ce grand silence – je n'ose pas penser a ce que je pourrais faire. Ah, Boris, ecris moi + dis moi que tu m'aimes comme je t'aime. Tu ne peux pas le dire trop souvent, car tu es tellement loin de moi + j'en suis si malhereux.

C.

[Friday evening.

Boris –

We finally arrived. And it's very sad.

The admiral of the American fleet, who just arrived, telephoned me today and said that he would like his jazz band to play if I wanted to arrange a soiree for the officers. But when we sat down to make a list, we found that all the young people had left and only the old Mocenigos + Morosinis remained. And we refused.

After four days sight-seeing in Venice, I'm going tomorrow to the Lido for the last time, to say goodbye to the Casa di Sole + to the beach.

My car arrived this evening and we are leaving the Paradis on Wednesday morning for Ravenna. But when will I find you again? There are not enough letters. I say that coldly. I went this evening to the Grand Hotel – *Niente!* And since you left, six days ago, I've had only one letter. Don't bother telling me that you haven't had time, because I know perfectly well that if you wanted to, nothing would be easier. And I want to underline the fact that I'm becoming a bit furious about it. I miss you so much that I am falling apart + if this continues – this utter silence – I don't dare think what I could do. Oh, Boris, write me and tell me that you love me as much as I love you. You can't say it too often, because you are so far from me and it makes me so miserable.

C.]

14 [September 1925]: Cole Porter to Boris Kochno

Lundi – 14

Cher Boris –

Mais c'est l'hiver ici, Venice se gele. La piazza est vide. Le Canal' grande n'a plus de chansons. Tout le monde cherche des fourrures + des grogs. Et nous nous regardons un peu confus, sachant bien que nous avons fait une chose très bête – nous sommes resté trop long temps a Venise!

Tante Winne a donné une soirée charmante ce soir – une vieille chanteuse qui a choisi toutes les chansons les plus tristes du monde – Madam Freund. Et Arthur Rubinstein, qui comme toujours a joué assez bien avant le souper, + merveilleusement apres. Mais on sentait que tous les gens pensait [sic] a la fin de leurs vacances + l'atmosphere etait surtout melancolique.

Nous partons – La Princesse Jane, Lady Abdy, Murietta, le gros, Linda + moi, mercredi, pour Ravenne. Murietta a sa voiture + moi, j'ai la mienne... Nous allons tacher a aller a Florence apres quelques jours mais La Princesse tient a arriver a Milan, le 22, alors c'est un peu difficile de savoir comment. Mais Berners sera la a Florence, + je ne sais pas qui d'autre.

Linda a reçu une lettre de Missia, aujourd'hui, disant quelle ne d'embarquait pas, + nous esperons bien qu'on pourra la voir a Florence dans le cas ou nous pourrons y aller.

En tous cas, je vous verrai a Paris vers le premier Octobre. Prevenez moi aussitot que vous arrivez au 13 rue Monsieur.

Au revoir + envoyez moi un mot si vous le temps chez Cook a Florence. Et amitiés a Diagileff + Lifar.

Cole.*

---

* Arthur Rubinstein (1887–1982), pianist; 'the big one' is presumably Charles Green Shaw. Berners is the composer and writer Gerald Hugh Tyrwhitt-Wilson, 14th Baron Berners (1883–1950); Misia is Misia Sert (Maria Zofia Olga Zenajda Godebska, 1872–1950), a pianist and hostess of an artistic salon in Paris. 'Cook' is the Thomas Cook travel agency.

[Monday - 14

Dear Boris –

But it's winter here, Venice is freezing. The piazza is empty. The Grand Canal has no more songs. Everyone is looking for furs and grogs. And we look at each other a little confused, knowing that we did a stupid thing – we stayed too long in Venice!

Aunt Winnie gave a charming soirée this evening – an old singer who chose all the saddest songs in the world – Madam Freund. And Arthur Rubinstein who, as always, played well enough before supper + marvelously afterwards. But we sensed that everyone was thinking about the end of their holidays + the atmosphere was particularly melancholic.

We are leaving – Princess Jane, Lady Abby, Murietta, the big one, Linda + me, Wednesday for Ravenna. Murietta has her car + me, I have mine. We will try to get to Florence after a couple of days but the Princess wants to arrive at Milan the 22nd, so it's hard to know how. But Berners will be at Florence + I don't know who else.

Linda received a letter from Missia [sic] today, saying that she didn't board + we hope we'll be able to see her in Florence if we're able to go there.

In any case, I will see you in Paris about the first of October. Let me know as soon as you arrive at 13 rue Monsieur.

Goodby [sic] + if you have the time send me a note through Cook in Florence. And regards to Diaghilev and Lifar.

Cole.]

[before 16 September 1925]: Cole Porter to Boris Kochno

Boris –
Voila notre programme.
Ravenne – 16
Rimini – 17 Grand Hotel
Perugia – 18 Hotel Brufani
Florence – 20 Hotel d'Italie
Milan – 22   ?
Paris – 25
On se verra a Florence!

[Boris –
Here's our itinerary.
Ravenna – 16
Rimini – 17 Grand Hotel
Perugia – 18 Hotel Brufani
Florence – 20 Hotel d'Italie
Milan – 22   ?
Paris – 25
We'll see each other in Florence!]

[16 September 1925]: Cole Porter to Boris Kochno

Boris – Nous sommes arrivee, ce soir, apres Padova + Ferrara, pour voir ces trésors de Ravenna. Si tu ne les connais pas peut être que nous pourrions y venir, l'été prochain les reparder ensembles. Car, aussitot que je revoyait Sant Apollinaie [sic] Nuovo – (j'étais la il y a deux ans) je me suis demandé mais pourquoi est-ce, que, au lieu de voir ça avec tous ces gens, il n'est pas ici, seul avec moi? Ce'st une ville tout a fait arrangée pour donner des joies? Anoubliables a nous deux. Et, en plus, il faut, tu sais, que ça soit fait notre sejour a Ravenna.

J'ai envoyé Chrichon une lettre a la poste mais il n'y avait rien. Sans doute, tu n'as pas reçu mon programme a temps. Mais j'attends la prochaine avec grand impatience.

Heureusement que j'ai combiné pour etre a Florence, le 20 + 21 – peut etre, le 22. Je suis sûr qu'il sera très difficile de te voir, mais en tout cas, j'aurai le grand luxe de reparder[?] ces beaux yeux dont je rêve, nuit + jour, mon Boris. / Goodnight + n'oublies pas pour un instant que je t'aime.

Ravenna
Mercredi soir
C.

[Boris – We arrived this evening, after Padova + Ferrara, to see the treasures of Ravenna. If you don't know them, perhaps we will go there next summer and see them together. Because as soon as I saw Sant Apollinare Nuovo – (I was there two years ago), I asked myself, why is it that instead of seeing it with all these people, he isn't here, alone with me? This is a city entirely suited to give unforgettable joys to both of us. And besides, you have to, you know, make our stay in Ravenna.

I went to look for a letter at the post office but there was nothing. No doubt you didn't receive my itinerary in time. But I wait for the next with great impatience.

Fortunately I've arranged to be in Florence on the 20th and 21st – perhaps the 22nd. I'm sure it will be very difficult to meet but in any case I will have the great luxury to look at those beautiful eyes of which I dream, night and day, my Boris.

Goodnight + don't forget for an instant that I love you.

Ravenna

Wednesday evening

C.]

[18 September 1925]: Cole Porter to Boris Kochno

Perugia

Vendredi soir – 11 <u>hrs</u>

Boris –

Deux telegrammes – le premier en arrivant le deuxieme en rentrant maintenant. J'ai peur qu'on ne se verra pas a Florence. Et j'en suis desolé. J'avais tout fait pour être là, pendant qu tu y etais. D'abord, on voulait t'éviter, completement. J'avais insisté. Et meme aujordhui, j'ai été très desagreable quant on disait qu'il fallait rester un jour de plus a Perugia + au lieu d'arriver a Florence le 20, d'y arriver le 21. Donc, tout le monde a cedé, + nous partons, apres demain – Dimanche. On arrive le soir a l'hotel d'Italie + on le quitte mardi, ou, au plus tard, mercredi matin. Les dieux nous en veulent + il faut que nous remettions notre rendez-vous jusqu'au premier Octobre. Peut être quelque chose pourrait arriver pour que ça soit changer notre programme. Mais je ne le crois pas.

Et je vois tout en noir + voudrais bien m'en dormir pour les six [dix?] jours suivants.

Au moins, il y a une lettre pour moi a Florence – une lettre de toi, mon Boris. Comme j'ai envie de la toucher.

C.

[Perugia

Friday evening – 11 o'clock

Boris –

Two telegrams – the first already arrived, the second coming now. I'm afraid we will not see each other in Florence. And I'm very sorry about that. I did everything to be there when you are. First, we wanted to avoid you completely. I insisted. And even today I was uncomfortable when it was said you would stay one more day in Perugia + instead of arriving at Florence on the 20th, you would arrive there on the 21st. So everyone gave up + we leave the day after tomorrow – Sunday. We arrive at the Hotel d'Italie in the evening + we leave on Tuesday or, at the latest, Wednesday morning. The gods want us + and we have delayed our appointment until the first of October. Perhaps something could happen to change our programme. But I don't think so.

And everything looks black to me + I would like to sleep for the next six [ten?] days.

At least there is a letter for me in Florence – a letter from you, my Boris. How I long to touch it.

C.]

[20 September 1925]: Cole Porter to Boris Kochno

Dimanche <u>soir</u>

Arrivé ce soir – <u>Une</u> lettre. Mais une lettre tellement difficile a suivie. Il faut numéroter les feuilles. J'ai lutté [?] avec cette lettre pendant une demi-heure. On commençait a Rome le 17, on voyagait subitement a Naples. On se trouvait au 16. On se croyait noyé dans une déclamation de faites. On tournait + on découvrait un [?] Il faut numéroter les feuilles, + ne pas être si russe. Je suis un simple american du middle-west + je ne peux pas te suivre.

Mais la chose qui me rend vraiment <u>rouge</u>, c'est que tu es trop calme. Tu m'écris comme un vieux philosophe, dans cette lettre, + c'est une mentalité de plusieurs jours. Je sais, par ça, que du 16 au 18, tu penses a moi comme quelqu'un de fou qui a besoin d'être endormi. Et cela m'agasse.

Est-ce que je me fais comprendre. Je veux dire que, me voici bouleversé depuis ton arrivé a Venice. Je t'écris des folies? + je n'ai envieé que de t'en ecrire davantage. Et tu me reponds d'une manière si rangée, si reposée que je me demande – mais est-ce qu'il pense que je ne suis qu'un radio qui broadcast ses pensées a tout le monde?

C'est que tu deviens trop récepteur. Et moi j'ai besoin de recevoir un peu de mon coté aussi.

Peut-être que cela t'embête de me dire des choses pareilles, mais c'est ça que je demande de toi. C'est ça dont je rêve. J'ai si faim pour ça – que tu me dis que tu m'aimes + des milliers de fois, pour que je puisse regarder tes paroles écrites dans la nuit quand je souffre pour t'avoir serré contre moi, tes levres? sur le miennes – tes levres que j'embrasse si souvent + si tendrement, mon Boris.

Écris moi, au

Travellers Club.

25 Avenue des Champs-

Elysees.

Je quitte Florence Mercredi pour t'éviter. Il serait facile de l'arranger mais je sais bien qu'il ne faut pas.

Au revoir.

C.*

[Sunday <u>evening</u>

Arrived this evening – <u>A</u> letter. But a letter very difficult to follow. You must number the pages. I fought with this letter for a half hour. It started in Rome on the 17th, suddenly we travelled to Naples where we were on the 16th. We thought ourselves drowned in a recitation of events. We turned [the page] + discovered that they are unnumbered. Don't be so Russian. I'm a simple American from the Midwest and I can't follow you.

What really <u>annoys</u> me, though, is that you are too calm. You write to me in this letter like an old philosopher... I know from this that from the 16th to the 18th you thought of me as a crazy man who needs to be humored. And that annoys me.

---

* A short message from Porter to Kochno apparently dates from a stay in Florence as a reference to the Pitti Palace shows: 'Cher Boris – Linda + moi nous allons a la galerie Pitti ce matin. Apres dejeuner, je rentre a l'hotel pour dormir un peu dans ma chambre #28. Cela sera de 3 a 4 hres. Pour-quoi pas venir me voir la? Cole' ['Dear Boris – Linda and I are going to the Pitti gallery this morning. After lunch, I come back to the hotel to sleep a bit in my room #28. This will be from 3:00 to 4:00. Why not come see me there? Cole']. The contents of the message do not entirely make chronological sense since Porter's letter (of 20 September) implies Kochno was not in Florence and the Porters would have left by the time he arrived. The suggestion in that letter that Kochno write to Porter in Paris is chronologically plausible, since the itinerary suggests he would be returning there on 25 September.

Am I making myself clear? I mean to say, I have been bowled over since your arrival at Venice. I write you trivialities + I only want to write you more. And you answer me so calmly, so dismissively that I ask myself – but does he think that I'm a radio who broadcasts his thoughts to the whole world?

It's because you are too much a taker. And me, I need to get a little on my side too.

Maybe this bothers you to tell me such things but that's what I ask of you. That's what I dream of. I am so hungry for that – that you tell me you love me + thousands of times so I can read the words you have written during the night when I suffer to have your lips against mine – your lips that I have kissed so often + so tenderly, my Boris.

Write to me, at
Travellers Club.
25 Avenue des Champs-
Elysées.

I'm leaving Florence on Wednesday in order to avoid seeing you. It would be easy to arrange but I know now that it shouldn't be.

Goodbye.

C.]

23 September 1925: Cole Porter to Boris Kochno*

RESTONS ICI JUSQU A JEUDI† VENEZ ME CHERCHER QUAND VOUS ARRIVEREZ = COLE

[WE ARE STAYING HERE UNTIL THURSDAY COME LOOK FOR ME WHEN YOU ARRIVE = COLE]

After his return to Paris, Porter continued to write to Kochno:

[probably late September 1925]: Cole Porter to Boris Kochno

Jeudi soir – 2 hrs du matin

---

* Addressed to Kochno at the Hotel Excelsior, Rome, this telegram was re-routed to the Palace Hotel, Naples.

† 24 September.

Mais Boris -

Ca devient difficile. Toute la nuit, je me reveillais, pensant a toi. Et, toute la journee, j'étais a Antwerp meme avant toi, pour voir ton arrivée. Et ce soir, on est venu me demander pourquoi j'avais cet air tellement préoccupé – mais tout ca est très serieux. Je ne le cache plus bien, + si ca continue je serais des vraies betises. Nous sommes allés au theatre, ce soir – + au lieu de voir la piece je voyait toi, mais tout le temps – je n'écoutait rien, j'étais devant toi, tu me souriait, tu me parlait mais c'est de la folie, n'est-ce pas?

Ah Boris comme tu m'as compliqué la vie!

Et comme j'en suis heureux, mon petit.

C.

[Thursday evening – 2 in the morning
But Boris –

It's getting difficult. All night I lay awake, thinking of you. And, all day, I was in Antwerp, even before you, to see you arrive. And tonight, you asked me why I have such preoccupied air – but this is all very serious. I don't hide it well + and if it continues I'd be really foolish. We went to the theatre this evening + and instead of watching the piece I watched you, all the time – I didn't listen to anything, I was before you, you smiled at me, you spoke to me, but it's folly, isn't it?

Ah Boris, how you have complicated my life!

And how happy I am, mon petit.

C.]

[about 15 October 1925]: Cole Porter to Boris Kochno*

Boris –

Ne sois pas si prima donna. Ecris moi, je t'en prie. Je suis a Paris depuis trois semaines – nous allons en Espagne pour Pacque – a Seville pour la Feria – Paris, mois de Mai, + Venise pour Juin–Octobre.

Quel est ton programme?

---

* Since according to this letter (written on stationery of "The Travellers" 25, Avenue des Champs-Elysées) Porter had been back in Paris for three weeks – and because his itinerary suggests he would return on (or about) 25 September – this letter apparently dates from about 15 October.

Ecris-moi – tu es tellement silent + moi, je suis si content d'être rentré + si heureux de redevenir vivant apres ses semaines noires a l'hôpital a New York, + jai envie de te voir. Est-ce possible ou m'as tu oublie?

En tout cas, il faut me dire.

Je t'embrasse

Cole

le 20

[Boris –

Don't be such a prima donna. Write to me. I've been in Paris three weeks – we're going to Spain for Easter – to Sevilla for Feria – Paris the month of May, + Venice for June–October.

What are your plans?

Write to me – you are so silent, + me, I'm content to be back + so happy to return to life after those black weeks in the hospital in New York + anxious to see you. Is that possible or have you forgotten me?

In any case, you should tell me.

I embrace you

Cole

the 20th]

18 October 1925: Cole Porter to Boris Kochno*

N'OUBLIE PAS DE ME PRÉVENIR QUAND TU RENTRAS LINDA SÉRIEUSEMENT MALADE TENDRE

[DON'T FORGET TO LET ME KNOW WHEN YOU RETURN LINDA SERIOUSLY ILL TENDERLY]

---

* Telegram addressed to Kochno at the Hotel de Paris, Montecarlo.

[21 or 28 October 1925]: Cole Porter to Boris Kochno*

Boris –

Tout va si mal que je ne sais pas ou il faut commencer.

D'abord Linda est dans un etat tres serieux. J'ai parlé au medecin, ce matin. Il trouve qu'il vaut mieux que je parte pour l'Amerique pour qu'elle soit plus tranquille ici. J'ai demandé aussi a Linda. Elle insiste que j'y aille. Alors – je pars le quatre + et après le medecin va m'envoyer ses nouvelles tous les jours. Mais, je ne veux pas la quitter pour aller a Londres: Elle est vraiment pitoyable - le poumon gauche est gravement touché + et l'estomac tres gonflé a cause du poumon. Aussi, elle est sie triste, la pauvre + et je serai endessous de tout si je la quittais avant le dernier instant – Je suis sûr que tu comprends, mon ange:

Tu rappelles la tête mysterieuses que j'avais! Alors je me suis couché avec + et pendant trois jours. Je suis sorti pour la premiere fois au-jourd'hui + et je commence a vivre encore une une fois, mais doucement.

Je ne te verrais plus avant mon départ, mon petit. Mais <u>je veux le portrait</u>. Envois-le au bateau La Majestie.

Ne sois pas furieux – tu devrais comprendre + et crois moi quand je te dis je t'aime plus que jamais.

J'ecrirai demain.

Ton

C.

Mercredi nuit.

[Boris –

Everything is going so badly that I don't know where to begin.

Linda's condition is very serious. I spoke with the doctor again this morning. He thinks [literally: finds] that it would be better if I were to leave for the States so that she can get more rest here. I talked to Linda about it, too. She insists that I go. So – I leave on the fourth + afterwards the doctor will send me reports every day. Only I don't want to leave and go to London; she is really in pitiful shape – her left lung is seriously affected and her stomach is very bloated because of her lung. Also, she is very sad, the poor girl + and it would be wrong of me to leave her at the last moment – I'm sure you understand, my angel.

---

* If this letter, and in particular its description of Linda's illness, relates to Porter's telegrams to Kochno of 18 October and 4 November, it must have been written on either Wednesday 21 or 28 October.

You remember the problem I was having with my head! Well I had to go to bed because of it and for three whole days. I went out for the first time today + I'm starting to feel alive once more, but only gradually.

I won't see you again before I leave, my little one. But <u>I want the portrait</u>. Send it to the boat La Majestie.

Don't be furious – you should understand + believe me when I tell you that I love you more than ever.

I will write tomorrow.

Your

C.

Wednesday night.]

4 November 1925: Cole Porter to Boris Kochno*

PARS CE SOIR DE CHERBOURG MON PETIT DÉSOLÉS DE NE PAS T AVOIR VU AVANT D ALLER EN AMERIQUE TENDRESSES = C =

[DEPARTING CHERBOURG THIS EVENING MON PETIT SORRY NOT TO HAVE SEEN YOU BEFORE DEPARTURE FOR AMERICA TENDERLY = C =]

5 November 1925: Cole Porter to Boris Kochno

But I believe that I explained why I can't pass through England profound apologies I embrace you C.

Several other short letters or telegrams to Kochno survive from this time, including invitations to dinner and the cancellation of plans to meet. Two undated letters bear significantly on Porter's feelings for Kochno:

[undated]: Cole Porter to Boris Kochno

Mercredi soir 2.45 AM.

Boris –

Voila la lettre EXPRESSE qui partira a onze hres demain – aujourdhui matin. Fais moi savoir quand elle sera arrivée, parce que ces nouvelles choses m'interesse a mourir!!

---

* Telegram sent from Cherbourg and addressed to Kochno at the Savoy Hotel, London.

Ce-ci – ce'est un mot pour te dire simplement que je viens de te quitter, il y a un quart d'heure, + que tu me manques – mais tanto. Et pour m'excuser si j'éteins la lumiere + te prends dans mes bras + te dis que tu es la seule chose au monde qui m'est chère.

Good night, mon Boris.

C.

[Wednesday evening 2.45 AM.

Boris –

Here is the EXPRESS letter that goes out tomorrow at eleven – that is, this morning. Let me know when it arrives, since these new things interest me to death!!

This – it's just a word simply to tell you that I just left you a quarter of an hour ago + and that I miss you – but *tanto*. And to apologize if I didn't turn off the light + take you in my arms + tell you that you are the only thing in the world that is dear to me.

Goodnight, my Boris.

C.]

[undated]: Cole Porter to Boris Kochno (ALS)

Voila – la lettre officielle – + comme elle est emmerdante [?] mais je ne peux pas la faire. Il est cinq heures du matin. Meme le jour, il m'est presque impossible de faire des phrases [?]. Et meme avant d'oser de te dire la verité, avant de te connaitre, je voulais toujours chasser tout le monde qui etait la et t'annoncer simplement que je t'adorait. Donc tu peux, peut etre, comprendre comme c'est dûr maintenant. Car, j'ai si froid Boris + tu n'es pas la. Et je te veux dans mes bras – mais ici, dans mes bras pour toujours. Pourquoi est-ce que nous sommes si bêtes que tu n'y es pas?

C.

[*Voilà* – the official letter – + as it is [unreadable]. But I can't do it. It's five o'clock in the morning. Even during the day, it's nearly impossible for me to write the words. And even before daring to tell you the truth, before I'd met you, I always wanted to chase away everybody there + tell you that I adored you. So you can, perhaps, understand how hard it is for me now. Because I'm so cold, Boris, + you aren't there. And I want you in my arms – right now in my arms for always. Why are we so foolish that you're not there?

C.]

For his part, Kochno's two surviving accounts of his relationship to Porter are both anodyne and self-serving. The earlier (but undated) appears in a handwritten dictionary, of sorts, of Kochno's friends and acquaintances, which he titled *L'Abecedaire de mes amis*:*

C. for Cole Porter. I met Cole, like some others I came to know in unexpected places and who became my dearest friends – in front of a cabin on the Lido beach in Venice ... One day, an unimportant incident on the beach put me in front of an American speaking fluent French and taking in the sun like all the other lords except for the Princess or Countess San Faustino, who was hidden by her black veils, wearing a cap by Marie Medisi and who, like other people of status stayed in the shadows of the cabins on the Lido ... The American told me his name, which at that time was the same to me as being completely anonymous, and asked if I would have a drink with him that evening in Venice ... P[orter] wanted to talk about my status of secretary of the Ballets Russes, he questioned me about the dance performances and the theatre. His insistence on these subjects made me think that he might be a man of the theatre ... While D[iaghilev] showed me the architecture of palaces, the monuments in the public squares, the frescoes in the churches, and the paintings in the museums, Cole Porter – whose life after the prostrations of an entire day did not begin until the churches and the museums were closed – acquainted me with the sumptuousness of a life like his own that was carried inside of a palace of which, until then, I knew only the facade and the cellars' paths hidden in the shadow of narrow streets by day but illuminated like multicolored lanterns at night ... During these early times with C.P. there was never any conversation about his music ...

The second and apparently later account was published in his *Diaghilev and the Ballets Russes*:

---

* Paris, Archives de l'Opéra, Fonds Kochno, shelfmark 1406, 1–51.

Diaghilev had a horror of jazz. He was a friend of Cole Porter, whose musical comedies were famous, but Diaghilev never talked to him about his music and pretended not to know that this charming, high-living "American in Paris" was a composer. He was aware, however, that with Princess Edmond de Polignac acting as a go-between, Porter had asked Stravinsky to give him lessons in orchestration. Nothing came of it because Stravinsky demanded such an exorbitant fee. Then, in 1927, Diaghilev wrote me from Venice: "Cole is writing a ballet... Danger!"

Shortly before one of my trips to Italy with Diaghilev, Cole Porter gave me a portable phonograph and a collection of dance and jazz records (none of his own composition). Diaghilev immediately replaced this "cabaret repertoire" with recordings of his "gods" – the Italian and Russian opera singers, Tamagno, Caruso, and Chaliapin.

One day, Cole Porter invited Diaghilev and me to lunch with George Gershwin, who was passing through Paris and wanted Diaghilev to hear his *Rhapsody in Blue,* which he would have loved to have performed by the Ballets Russes. Diaghilev listened in silence while Gershwin played his score, promised to "think about the question of using it for a ballet," but never gave him an answer.

Diaghilev was outraged by the jazz invasion of Europe and by its influence on your composers. In 1926, he wrote to me:

Saturday, August 7, 1926

Hôtel des Bains

Lido, Venice

... We have stopped at the Hôtel des Bains because the fracases at the Excelsior make life intolerable. The whole of Venice is up in arms against Cole Porter because of his jazz and his Negroes. He has started an idiotic night club on a boat moored opposite the Salute, and now the Grand Canal is swarming with the very same Negroes who have made us all run away from London and Paris. They are teaching the "Charleston" on the Lido beach! It's dreadful! The gondoliers are threatening to massacre all the elderly American women here. The very fact of their renting the Palazzo Rezzonico is considered characteristic of nouveaux riches. *Cole is greatly changed since his operation; he is thinner and appreciably older-looking.**

---

* Boris Kochno (trans. Adrienne Foulke), *Diaghilev and the Ballets Russes* (New York, 1973), 222.

There are numerous problems with both of these accounts, even leaving aside Kochno's failure to mention that he and Porter were lovers. Unless his description of meeting Porter dates from before 1923, Porter is unlikely to have been an 'anonymous American' if Kochno's own account of a 1924 performance in Venice at the Porters is correct.* It is likely, in any case, that they met in Paris in 1923, since Diaghilev's letter mentioning Porter's ballet – and his familiar reference to Porter as 'Cole' – must date from that year, not 1927, and refer to *Within the Quota*. Porter and Diaghilev, and indeed Kochno, are also known to have socialized, as an undated telegram from Porter to Diaghilev shows:

[undated]: Cole Porter to Sergei Diaghilev[35]

Dear Mr Diaghileff

Would you like to come to dinner Sunday evening at 8½.

We have invited Tante Winne† & I believe she can come.

If it were possible, we would be very happy to have Lifar & Riet. Boris has already accepted...

Sincerely, Cole Porter

It is not true, by Stravinsky's own account, that Porter did not take lessons with him because Stravinsky had quoted an exorbitant fee,‡ nor is it the case that Porter had had a serious operation at that time; this can only be a reference relating to Porter's well-known riding accident of 1937.§ In light of all this, Kochno's accounts can only be considered fabrications.¶

---

* See above, p. 69.

† Winnaretta Singer, Princesse Edmond de Polignac.

‡ See above, pp. 37–8

§ See below, p. 148

¶ It also appears to be the case that while he was involved with Porter in the autumn of 1925, Kochno was also involved with Hermann Oelrichs Jr., a friend of Porter's. On 19 September, at the same time Porter was writing to Kochno, Oelrichs wrote to him (in terms remarkably similar to Porter's), 'I know that I write you too much. But I love you too much, my angel. I think of you too much. I want to see you too much and that is going to end badly. Because you will soon say – Enough! I've had enough.' See James Bone, *The Curse of Beauty: The Scandalous & Tragic Life of Audrey Munson, America's First Supermodel* (New York, 2016), n.p.

In at least one respect, however, Kochno's descriptions may be accurate with respect to Porter's lifestyle in Venice during the mid-1920s. In 1926, while still in Paris, Porter had met the expatriate African-American singer and dancer Ada 'Bricktop' Smith. Porter first appears among her papers in her address book for 1926 – 'Cole Porter / Paris / 13 Rue Monsieur / Grand Hotel / Venice'* – and according to her diary, she first visited Porter at home on 3 May, when she provided liquor, 'extras', received a salary, and gave Charleston lessons. She visited Porter four more times in May and early June and followed him to Venice that summer:

3 May	Bottles	17–85
	Extra	200
	Charleston	200
	Salary	<u>200</u>
		685
	FIRST TIME HOUSE OF Cole Porter	
4 May	Bottles	14–70
	Extra	160
	Charleston	200
	Salary	200
	Charleston Cole Porter	
10 May	Soiree	50
	Charleston	200
	Bottles	13–65
	Salary	<u>200</u>
		965
	Soiree Maxwell Ritz[†] Charleston Cole Porter	
13 May	Bottles	9–45
	Charleston	200
	Salary	<u>200</u>
		445
	Charleston Cole Porter	

---

* New York Public Library, Schomburg Centre, MG 247, Smith, Ada, 1926. McBrien, *Cole Porter*, 108, states that Porter and Bricktop met 'around 1925'. It is more likely to have been only in 1926, given the evidence of Bricktop's diary.

† Presumably the reference here is to a party given by Elsa Maxwell at the Ritz-Carlton.

27 May	Bottles	16–80
	Salary	200
	Charleston	<u>200</u>
		480
	Charleston Cole Porter	
7 June	Soiree	1000
	Cole Porter	2100
	Salary	<u>200</u>
		3300
7 August	6 Oclock	
	Princess	
	San Faustino	
	~~Mr Porter~~	
	~~Boat~~	
28 August	Mr Porter	
	<u>Boat</u>	
	Three times	
	Boat 1.500	
30 August	Mr Porter	
	<u>Palace</u>*	

Two contemporaneous accounts, one undated, the other dated July 1926, describe events put on by the Porters:

> A wave of entertaining has swept over Venice within recent weeks. One of the most elaborate balls was given this week by Mr. and Mrs. Cole Porter in the Rezzonico Palace, the residence occupied by the Robert Brownings on the Grand Canal.† The guests entered from the canal, ascending the steps between gondoliers attired in red and white costumes instead of the usual liveried footmen. Mediaeval torches replaced the usual electric lights.

---

* According to her diary, Bricktop arrived back in Paris two days later, on 1 September. She saw Porter at least twice that autumn, on 3 October and 25 December. See New York Public Library, Schomburg Centre, MG 247, Smith, Ada, 1926.

† During the 1880s, the Ca' Rezzonico was home to the painter Robert Barrett Browning (1849–1912), whose father, the poet Robert Browning (1812–1899), died there on 12 December 1899).

Venice Innovation. July, 1926. Venice. – One of the charms of Venice is that it is never dull. Just when one begins to feel the need of an innovation, out of the hat, like a rabbit, it springs. This time it is out of the heads of four members of the younger set in Venice, Count Andrea Robilant, Marquis di Salina, Baron Franchetti, and Mr. Cole Porter, who are successfully launching the Dance Boat.

A large barge, which has been specially constructed, containing facilities for serving supper, will float out into the lagoon and, on still nights, even into the open sea. A negro jazz orchestra is being brought from Paris to play and there will be dancing.

Invitations have been sent to a number of members of the summer colony, and the subscription list is to be limited to 150 members, with the proceeds going to several Venetian charities.[36]

The negative comments on the 'Dance Boat' in the (probably spurious) letter by Diaghilev have coloured accounts of the Porters' time in Venice, even if numerous other anecdotes confirm that it was at least lavish and extravagant. The composer Richard Rodgers (1902–79), for example, gives this account of meeting Porter in 1926:

As soon as we arrived at the Lido, Larry [Hart] went in search of the nearest bar and I went for a stroll on the beach. Suddenly I heard a friendly English voice calling my name. To my joy it was Noël Coward . . . Noël was in Venice, he told me, visiting an American friend he was sure would love to meet me . . . His name was Cole Porter . . . Promptly at seven-thirty, Porter's private gondola pulled up outside our hotel. Larry and I got in, were wafted down the Grand Canal and deposited in front of an imposing three-story palace. This was the "place" Porter had rented, which we later found out was the celebrated Palazzo Rezzonico, where Robert Browning had died. We were assisted out of the gondola by a liveried footman wearing white gloves, and ushered up a massive stairway, at the top of which stood Noël, Cole and his wife, Linda . . . During the delicious and elegantly served dinner Cole kept peppering me with questions about the Broadway musical theatre, revealing a remarkably keen knowledge of both classical and popular music. Since he impressed me as someone who led a thoroughly indolent, though obviously affluent, life, the sharpness of his observations was unexpected. Unquestionably, he was more than a social butterfly.

After dinner, Rodgers continues, he and Coward and Porter played some of their songs:

> "Why, I asked Cole, was he wasting his time? Why wasn't he writing for Broadway?" To my embarrassment, he told me that he had already written four musical-comedy scores, three of which had even made it to Broadway ... What's more, he said, he had discovered the secret of writing hits. As I breathlessly awaited the magic formula, he leaned over and confided, "I'll write Jewish tunes."*

Many years later, Porter gave a more benign account of his 'night club' in a note to his lawyer John Wharton: 'It is always strange for me how many fables are connected with the facts of anyone's life ... Many biographies speak about me and Linda running a night club in Venice. This must stem from the fact that I had a huge barge converted into a dance floor. I imported a negro band from London and once a week this barge was towed around the lagoons of Venice. The membership consisted of about one hundred of our friends, who paid a certain amount for the privilege of belonging to this club. All the proceeds were given to a local charity. So much for the night club.'[37]

Probably a number of the Porters' evenings were sedate. On 12 August 1925, Duff Cooper, Viscount Norwich, wrote to his wife, Lady Diana Cooper, 'Dinner at the Coles' last night wasn't bad. No charm at all. I played chess with Monty Woolley afterwards, the others went on to the piazza where we joined them later.'†

In addition to running his charity 'Dance Boat', Porter was visited regularly by friends and celebrities; in a letter of 30 June 1953 he recalled a visit by Fanny Brice and his composition of 'Hot House Rose':

---

* Richard Rodgers, *Musical Stages: An Autobiography* (New York, 1975), 87–8. Although self-serving and disingenuous about his embarrassment (it is unlikely Rodgers would not have heard of Porter by that time), Rodgers's account of Porter's lifestyle rings true.

† McBrien, *Cole Porter*, 105. In his *A Durable Fire* (London, 1983), 189, Cooper reproduces a letter from 3 December 1923 describing an earlier meeting with Porter and Irving Berlin: 'Later we went to the Biltmore where Diana and I left our party and joined Cole Porter. There was a good cabaret show there and we went on again to supper with a man called Irving Berlin who writes music. He had a nice flat and gave us eggs and champagne. We had only been drinking whiskey out of flasks hitherto.'

30 June 1953: Cole Porter to George Byron*

Dear George:

HOT HOUSE ROSE. Fanny Brice visited Venice in 1926, when my wife and I were living in the Palazzo Rezzonico. At this time in my life I had given up all hope of ever being successful on Broadway and had taken up painting but Fannie, [sic] whom we grew to know very well, asked me to write a song for her. This was the reason for HOT HOUSE ROSE. When I finished it I invited her to the Rezzonico to hear it and afterwards she always told friends how wonderfully incongruous it was, that I should have demonstrated to her this song about a poor little factory girl as she sat beside me while I sang and played it to her on a grand piano that looked lost in our ballroom, whose walls were entirely decorated by Tiepolo paintings and was so big that if we gave a Ball for less than one thousand people in this room they seemed to be entirely lost. She never sang the song.[38]

Porter travelled to New York in late 1926 – in November he attended a dinner for Lady Mendl† and in December another for Ferenc Molnár‡. After his return to Paris he wrote to his mother with an account of his song 'I'm in Love Again' that does not ring entirely true:

2 February 1927: Cole Porter to Kate Porter[39]

Mammammamma,

I want to tell you a curious story.

Three years ago, when I was writing the *Greenwich Village Follies*, I gave them a tune called *I'm in Love Again*. This tune I had written before and had sung it around Paris, and always with howling success, as the melody was very simple and the sentiment appealed to everyone.

---

* George Byron (birth and death dates unknown) was a singer and the second husband of Eva Kern, Jerome Kern's widow.

† Elsie de Wolfe.

‡ Ferenc Molnár (1878–1952) was a Hungarian author, playwright and stage director. He is known in particular as the author of the 1909 play *Liliom*, the basis for Rodgers and Hammerstein's *Carousel* (1945). For accounts of these two dinners, see the *New York Times* for 17 November 1926, 19, and 19 December 1926, 26.

The great powers of *The Greenwich Village Follies* thought less than nothing of this song, and never would allow it in the show. So it lay in a drawer at Harms, and I thought it was dead for ever. But one thing very funny about that little song, no matter where I traveled to, I'd always hear someone singing it. Last year, in New York, I heard it at Maurice's cabaret. They played it over and over again, simply the one refrain, as no one knew the verse. I went to the band leader and asked him who wrote it, and he said "Oh a Harlem nigger wrote it." Everybody in Paris knows it, and it's almost as well known in London and in Rome. But practically no one knows that I wrote it.

Now, suddenly out of a clear sky, comes a wire from Harms, offering me an excellent royalty to publish this song and do everything they can to make a big hit out of it. And I have sent them a verse and a second refrain, and its [sic] coming out immediately as a popular song. As Harms usually only publish songs in productions, and never launch a song unless they make a big hit of it, I shall be surprised if I dont [sic] make a lot of money out of it.

Dont [sic] you think its [sic] a funny story, that poor little deserted song suddenly landing on her feet.

I've no news except that I'm as happy as a lark, and so is Linda. We are staying here until the last week in March, when we leap in the motor and go all over Spain, ending up at Seville, at the Albas, for an Easter house-party. The Prince of Wales* is going too, and it will be very gay.

I have written a lot of new songs, and I believe excellent ones, which I am going to send to Harms, and I hope they will publish them. Also, I have just finished two more paintings on glass of Spanish bullfights, and now I'm doing a big one of a beautiful nude lady, sailing away from New York in a balloon.

Paris is empty and charming. We have had beautiful spring weather, and the Bois is crowded.

I can't thank you enough for your Christmas check. You were very sweet to send it to me, and I had a grand time spending it on totally useless things.

Goodbye and lots of love from us both. Linda said you were the gayest person she saw in New York, and that after being with you, everyone else seemed dead. And Weston said "Oh sir, you have no idea how chic Mrs. Porter looked in New York."

---

* Edward Albert, later Edward VIII and, after his abdication, the Duke of Windsor.

Give my love to Sammie, my papa, and to Bessie and Dixie. I'd love to see you so much. Do you want me to come over in the spring and bring you to Venice? Think that over.

Cole, February 2, 1927

This letter – the original of which has not been traced – is not without at least one problem: Porter is incorrect in stating that 'I'm in Love Again' was not given as part of the *Greenwich Village Follies*,[40] and apparently it was published as early as 1925, not in 1927 as Porter says it would be.

One notable event in the Porters' social life in 1927 was the opening in mid-May of the Hotel les Ambassadeurs, for which Porter would write a revue in 1928:

PARIS SURRENDERS TO OUTDOOR LIFE. Ambassadeurs Has Gala Opening. Dining and entertainment in the Champs Elysées are nearer the Place de la Concorde than in pre-Bonaparte days, when the Bal Diable was a long-famous establishment at the point where the Rue Marbeuf now intersects the great thoroughfare. Here Charles Dickens once had his Paris home. A notable event of the week was the gala opening of the Hotel les Ambassadeurs, where dinner was accompanied by a high-powered cabaret performance, with intervals for the guests to take a fling with Terpsichore. Prince George of England* was the guest of Prince and Princess Jean de Faucigny-Lucinge.† Prince and Princess Viggo of Denmark, the latter Miss Eleanor Green of New York before her marriage,‡ were among the dancers ... Among the thousand diners were Sir Charles and Lady Mendl, the latter Elsie de Wolfe; Miss Eleonora Sears of Boston,§ Mr. and Mrs. Cole Porter ... [41]

---

* George Edward Alexander Edmund, Duke of Kent (1902–42).

† The French aristocrat Prince Jean-Louis de Faucigny-Lucinge (1904–92), a descendant of Louis IX, and his wife Mary Lilian Matilda, Baroness d'Erlanger (1901–45), whom he married in November 1923.

‡ Prince Viggo, Count of Rosenborg (1893–1970) and his wife, the former Eleanor Margaret Green (1895–1966), whom he married in June 1924. Because Viggo married without permission of the Danish king (at the time, Christian X), he renounced his place in the Danish line of succession.

§ Eleanora Randolph Sears (1881–1968) was a tennis player. Sears won the U.S. National Championship in 1911 and the three consecutive years 1915–17.

Linda Porter's position in Paris society was also noted by Helen Josephy and Mary Margaret McBride in their *Paris Is a Woman's Town*: 'Women who dare to wear clothes that are strikingly individual and about three seasons ahead of the style trend naturally gravitate toward Louise-boulanger* . . . Bright modern color contrasts and combinations of marvelous materials are . . . characteristic of this house which is patronized by Mrs. Michael Arlen;† Madame Agnès,‡ Parisian modiste and one of the best-dressed women in Europe; Mrs. Cole Porter, society leader and wife of the song writer; and Mrs. Wellington Koo,§ wife of the Chinese ex-ambassador to England.'[42]

In early 1928, Porter returned to New York, to work on his show *Paris*, at which time he wrote to his cousin and financial manager, Harvey Cole. This note is among the earliest surviving letters to document Porter's lifelong concern with managing his income, whether through money earned from his shows, disbursements from the family businesses, or gifts (and eventually the estate) from his mother:

9 February [1928]: Cole Porter to Harvey Cole[43]

DEAR HARVEY,

I HAVE JUST BEEN FIGURING OUT MY FINANCIAL STATUS WITH MY MOTHER AND FIND THAT IN ORDER TO LEAVE NEW YORK, -- I SAIL ON MARCH SIXTH, I MUST HAVE THREE THOUSAND FIVE HUNDRED DOLLARS BEYOND MY REGULAR ALLOWANCE. AND SO I AM WRITING TO YOU TO FIND OUT WHETHER YOU COULD GET HOLD OF IT FOR

---

* Louiseboulanger, a fashionable salon opened in 1927 by Louise Melenot (1878–1972) and her husband, Louis Boulanger (birth and death dates unknown).

† Probably Countess Atalanta Mercati (1903–64), who in 1928 had married the author Michael Arlen (1895–1956); see *New Yorker*, 26 May 1928, 61: 'Perhaps the best European theatre has been observed in Michael Arlen's wedding to Countess Atalanta Mercati, at Cannes. The Baron, as his British friends always roguishly call him, was wed in an orthodox service: he was married, that is to say, wearing a gold crown lined with baby blue. The gifts included a diamond bracelet which, after all, will last forever, and a handsome cheque from the bride's angry and absent father.'

‡ Madame Agnès (birth and death dates unknown) was a hat designer popular from the late 1920s to the 1940s; she had a shop on the Rue Saint-Honoré.

§ Oei Hui-lan (1899–1992) was the third wife of the Chinese statesman and diplomat Vi Kyuin Wellington Koo (1888–1985).

ME, PERHAPS BY MAKING ONLY A PARTIAL PAYMENT ON MY PRESENT INDEBTEDNESS AT THE FIRST NATIONAL, OR MAYBE BY FINDING SOMETHING THAT YOU COULD SELL.

BEGINNING MARCH SEVENTH, I WILL BE RECEIVING A WEEKLY ROYALTY OF ABOUT $150 ON THE PRODUCTION RIGHTS OF MY NEW SHOW.* THIS SHOW WILL RUN UNTIL THE FIRST OF MAY, CLOSE FOR THE SUMMER, AND OPEN IN NEW YORK IN THE EARLY AUTUMN FOR A WINTER'S RUN. THE SHOW IS A HIT AND I CANT [sic] SEE HOW ANYTHING CAN STOP IT. THIS MONEY COULD BE APPLIED ON MY INDEBTEDNESS, IF YOU WISH.

IN ANY CASE, WRITE ME AS SOON AS POSSIBLE, AS I WANT TO LEAVE NEW YORK, CLEAN.

MY BEST REGARDS TO YOU AND MILDRED,

SINCERELY YOURS

[signed:] Cole†

Paris opened at the Music Box Theatre, New York, on October 1928. The *New York Times* reported that: 'Irene Bordoni,‡ the fascinating Bordoni of feathers and gorgeous costumes, of rolling eyes and French accent – in short, Irene Bordoni – came back to town at the Music Box last night as the star of an entertainment called "Paris." . . . Miss Bordoni sang four songs in the traditional Bordoni manner – and three of the four were of the sort that might be called grand. Nor can it be mere coincidence that these

---

* *Paris*, which opened at the Music Box Theatre, New York, on 8 October 1928 and ran for 195 performances. Out-of-town tryouts, the source of the income mentioned by Porter in his letter, began considerably earlier, at Nixon's Apollo Theatre, Atlantic City, on 6 February 1928. Before its New York opening, *Paris* was also performed in Philadelphia, Boston and Washington D.C.

† Harvey Cole wrote back on 11 February, detailing Porter's financial obligations and noting that 'Matters in West Virginia are looking no better and it will apparently be all we can do to make the regular distributions', a reference to the family business concerns generally. He concluded by writing, 'I am delighted to hear that your new show is going so well. I had already heard the news from Aunt Bessie. I feel sure that you are coming into your own and am more pleased than I can tell you.' On 15 February, Porter signed a promissory note, borrowing $3,500 from the First National Bank of Peru, Indiana, due on 14 January 1928; it was paid on 22 June 1928. Source: Yale University, Gilmore Library, Cole Porter Collection MSS 82, Box 49, folder 299.

‡ Irène Bordoni (1885–1953) was an actress and the star of *Paris*.

three were written by Cole Porter.'* The *New Yorker* was 'ecstatic' about Porter's songs:

> I'm a little hampered in writing a review of "Paris," by Martin Brown, at the Music Box, because directly behind me sat a lady and gentleman, both wits. The lady wit was upset before the curtain rose because the program threatened three renditions of an E. Ray Goetz song called "The Land of Going to Be." Her companion thought it was a misprint for "The Land of Going to Bed." As the evening wore on and Irene Bordoni obliged with the selection six times, the pair grew what you might call almost bitter ... When it came to Cole Porter's songs, however, I cared for no one's opinion but my own, an ecstatic one. "Babes in the Wood," "Don't Look at Me That Way," and "Let's Fall in Love" are up to Mr. Porter's best, and there is no better. No one else now writing words and music knows so exactly the delicate balance between sense, rhyme, and tune. His rare and satisfactory talent makes other lyrists [sic] sound as though they'd written their words for a steam whistle.[44]

On 15 April 1928, the *New York Times* reported that:

> PARIS LIFE IS QUIET DURING HALF-SEASON ... The opening of the classic races at Longchamps was marked by Ralph Strassburger† giving a big dinner party in a private salon at the Ritz, when the entertainers were two Southern girls, the Misses Lamkin and Ward, who made a big hit at Palm Beach with the latest jazz and plantation songs and who are now capturing Paris ... The following night there was another big dinner with the American composer, George Gershwin, whose

---

* *New York Times*, 9 October 1928, 27. Bordoni's songs included 'Don't Look at Me that Way' and the duet, 'Let's Do It, Let's Fall in Love'. According to Kimball, *The Complete Lyrics of Cole Porter*, 103–4, 'Quelque-Chose' was introduced by Bordoni during the show's tryouts but was dropped before the New York opening; similarly, 'Which?' was probably written for Bordoni but is not listed in any playbills. This accounting does not square with the *New York Times* review and remains unresolved.

† Ralph B. Strassburger (1883–1959) was a businessman and racehorse owner and breeder. He was married to May Bourne, a daughter of Frederick Gilbert Bourne, president of the Singer Sewing Machine Company, and may as a result have been acquainted with Porter through members of the Singer family, including Winnaretta Singer and Daisy Fellowes.

ingenious modern compositions have delighted Parisians, giving them a taste for more American music. Among the guests were Grand Duke Dimitri and his American wife, the Princess Ilyinski, formerly Audrey Emery;* also Cole Porter, who added to the jazz feast by playing his own compositions; Mrs. Porter and Prince and Princess Obolensky, formerly Alice Astor, who has just returned from London, where her mother, Lady Ribblesdale, underwent an operation.† The Duchess of Sutherland,‡ the Grand Duchess Marie of Russia§ and Michael Arlen were also present.[45]

But while Paris life may have been quiet for the high-society set, it was a busy time for Porter who on 10 May opened a new show, *La Revue des Ambassadeurs*, at the Ambassadeurs Café.¶ The background to this production – essentially American, not French – was described in the *New York Times* for 19 February:

When Latin temperament meets American efficiency in the theatre, a revue is often produced. That, at least, is the experience of William Morris Jr., who meets at least one foreign "buyer" each month. His latest experience was with Edmond Sayag, a revue producer of Paris, who spent one week in America and then went cheerfully home with a show packed under his arm. For during M. Sayag's short visit at the William

---

* Grand Duke Dmitri Pavlovich Romanovski (1891–1942) had been exiled from Russia for his involvement in the murder of Grigori Rasputin in 1916; he married the Cincinnati real-estate heiress Audrey Emery (1904–71) in 1926.

† Prince Serge Obolensky (1890–1978) and Ava Alice Muriel Astor (1902–56), a daughter of John Jacob Astor IV. They had married in 1924. The Obolensky family fled Russia in 1917 during the Russian Revolution. Alice Astor's mother, Ava Lowle Willing (1868–1958), was the first wife of John Jacob Astor IV.

‡ Eileen Sutherland-Leveson-Gower (1891–1943). She married George Sutherland-Leveson-Gower, Marquess of Stafford (1888–1963), in 1912; he succeeded his father as the 5th Duke of Sutherland in 1913.

§ Grand Duchess Maria Pavlovna of Russia (1890–1958).

¶ In the programme, the revue is titled *Troisième Ambassadeurs – Show of 1928*, but in the printed book of lyrics, *In the Old Days and Today*; see Kimball, *The Complete Lyrics of Cole Porter*, 90. For many years, the orchestral parts for *La Revue des Ambassadeurs* were considered lost; only an incomplete piano-vocal score, published in Paris by Salabert in 1928, survived. The orchestral parts were rediscovered in 2014; see https://www.nytimes.com/2014/06/23/arts/music/cole-porters-lost-show-unearthed.html.

Morris offices contracts were signed for a group of American performers, headed by Buster West and Clifton Webb,* to appear in Paris this Spring in an American revue which will be known as "Vingt-huit" ...

M. Sayag's entrance into the William Morris offices caused one of those emergency conferences which enlist every nerve and all the nerve of a booking-office system. First of all, M. Sayag wanted the best dancing chorus obtainable, and believed that this detail could be accomplished with no more difficulty than the pushing of a button. After all, he had to hurry back to Paris. So, magically, within twenty-four hours sixteen dancing girls had received his approbation. Concurrently, the jazz bands were signed without even one saxophonist going into a decline.

These details completed, M. Sayag announced that he would have specialty dancers. There are specialty dancers and specialty dancers, but it was evident he wanted the latter. Long-distance calls, telegrams and shouting brought contracts from Myrio, Deshe and Barte, Dario and Irene, and Bud and Jack Pearson of "Take the Air." The nucleus for "Vingt-huit" now safely in his pocket, the visitor then declared that he wanted a dancing star. Whereupon William Grady, who up to this time had merely taken a supervisor's part in the proceedings, sought out on the telephone Buster West, who had left town some time ago with the "Scandals."† To make a long story suspenseless, it may be disclosed that Mr. West was located and said "yes" from somewhere in a telephone booth.

Two hours before M. Sayag's boat sailed, Mr. Grady, still surviving, announced that he had secured Clifton Webb of "She's My Baby."‡ Bobby Connelly was contracted to direct the dances and Cole Porter to do the music and lyrics. Everyone sighed, shook hands and M. Sayag smilingly boarded the Paris.

---

* Buster West (1901–66) was a dancer and actor; he performed 'Baby Let's Dance' and 'Fountain of Youth' in *La Revue des Ambassadeurs*. Clifton Webb (1889–1966) was an actor, singer and dancer. A long-time friend of Porter, Webb had known the composer at least since the mid-1910s, when he appeared in Porter's *See America First*. He later appeared in *You Never Know* (1937). Webb joined the cast of *La Revue des Ambassadeurs* several weeks into the show's run; see below, pp. 84–5, and for *You Never Know*, pp. 153–6.

† Between 1919 and 1929, with the exception of 1928, the producer George Wight mounted an annual revue, *Scandals*, in New York.

‡ Richard Rodgers and Lorenz Hart's *She's My Baby* ran for seventy-one performances at the Globe Theatre, New York, between 3 January and 3 March 1928.

For the information of those who want to know what all the excitement was about, it can be stated that "Vingt-huit" will open at the Ambassadeurs, Paris, on May 15 and that the entire troupe will sail April 15 – excepting Mr. Webb, who will depart at a later date. After Paris the revue will be presented in London. It will then be seen in America – or, at all events, that is the plan.[46]

A review was published in *L'Intransigeant* for 21 May 1928:

We have all seen, if not in real life then at least at the cinema, a sumptuous "night club" near Broadway, with pretty girls who deploy their graces in plain sight of the spectators. Thanks to Edmond Sayag, we get a similar sensation and spectacle without crossing the Atlantic. We should add that pretty girls are not the only attraction of this essentially American revue. First and foremost is Buster West, because he is absolutely the dominant personality of the evening: this devil of a man, who in profile looks like Charlie Chaplin – but without his legendary mustache – manages the most unexpected comic effects from the flexibility and virtuosity of his truly amazing legs. He is an artist of quality, and well supported by the Nesbit brothers, full of brilliance, too; the trio Myrio, Desha and Barte, very remarkable; the three Eddies; Evelyn Hoey, that pretty mayflower, and the girls, brunettes or blondes, all equally charming. The whole world revolves around them. The sets by MM. Marcel and Andre Boil have a share in the very successful creation of an atmosphere of freshness, liveliness and youth. As for the principal, Vanimator ... it's really Waring's Pennsylvanians Orchestra who perform – and with what fantasy! – the lively and sentimental music of Mr. Cole Porter.[47]

A review in the *New York Herald Tribune (European Edition)* adds further details:

Leading off is the "Touring Car" filled with wide-eyed sightseers and with Eleanor Shaler wittily pointing out the wonder of Gay Paree to the rich American, Jack Pearson. Then come bouncing down the two comedian-dancers, John and Buster West, a pair of wonders ... The song and dance scene "Blue Hour" is sung by Morton Downy while Myria, Desha and Barte dance in dazzling fashion, yet another interpretation of

Gershwin's "Blue Rhapsody" [sic]. The dancing of this trio, particularly the whirling through the air by Desha, is a revelation of the show. There follows "An Old Fashioned Girl," with Mary Leigh as the shy little crinoline maid, and Basil Howes as the attentive swain, and "Baby, Let's Dance," a comedic episode, again with Buster West, two pleasing numbers. Frances Gershwin, with her famous composer brother coming from his table to accompany her, made a very happy hit in her song and dance, "Maroc Garden." The clever Nesbit Brothers, and a nimble trio of colored dancing jesters, the Three Eddies, made a hit with last year's "Black Birds"' when Florence Mills charmed Paris with her delightful personality. Katheryn Ray, Carter Wardell, the Pearson Brothers and many more things go on, and for the dancing intermission the Waring Pennsylvanians are there to keep the revels up.[48]

Clifton Webb joined the cast during the run of the show and Porter wrote to him from Lyon with a new song and a rude suggestion:

16 June 1928: Cole Porter to Clifton Webb[49]

Dear Clifton –

I am sending you the refrain of your song. You should have a copy made by Olivier, chez Durand, music shop, Place de la Madeleine. He is the head copyist there. Keep one copy for rehearsal + give the other to Tom Waring* + get him into doing it for his band. I will send the verse + the lyric as soon as finished.

Also tell Leteutre, Sayap's [sic] secretary, to put this on the program – this title Maid of Mystery. And when you have done all these things, take your finger and stick it up your ass.

My address is Chateau de Gourdon, Gourdon-par-le-Bar, Alpes Maritimes.
Goodbye + love to all my playthings.
Cole.
Saturday morning.

---

* Presumably the bandleader Fred Waring (1900–84), who featured in *La Revue des Ambassadeurs*.

CHAPTER THREE

PORTER'S RETURN TO THE UNITED STATES, 1928–1937

Shortly after the opening of *La Revue des Ambassadeurs*, Cole Porter wrote to his cousin and financial manager Harvey Cole, concerned – as he so often was – about money:

29 May [1928]: Cole Porter to Harvey Cole[1]

Dear Harvey,

Thank you for the weekly reports on royalties. I notice that at the end of the Philadelphia run, they dwindled considerably, but a wire came after the Boston opening, saying that the show was a big hit there, so that they should go better now.[*] Also, the Gilbert Miller Office[†] writes that we have The Music Box Theatre for the New York run, which will have a gross of $3000 per week.

After this, I have a choice of two musical comedies, one with Gilbert Miller, another with Schwab and Mandel, and I shall do the one with the better book.[‡] This will keep me busy until Christmas.

Cochran, the London manager,[§] came over last week to ask me to do the next Pavilion show there, following the Noel Coward revue, running there

---

[*] In Philadelphia, *Paris* was first given on 13 February; it opened in Boston on 7 May.

[†] Gilbert Heron Miller (1884–1969) was a theatrical producer. Among other works he produced Somerset Maugham's *The Constant Wife* (1927), Laurence Housman's *Victoria Regina* (1938), T. S. Eliot's *The Cocktail Party* (1951) and Dylan Thomas's *Under Milk Wood* (1957); see the obituary in the *New York Times*, 3 January 1969, 1 and 24.

[‡] Neither of these appears to have materialized.

[§] Charles B. Cochran (1872–1951) was a producer, director and impresario. A frequent collaborator with Noël Coward, Cochran produced *Wake Up and Dream* and, later, *Nymph Errant* (1933), and the London production of *Anything Goes* (1935).

now. An American edition of this show is opening in New York, in October, but the original company will stay in London and close around February. Cochran's idea is for a new revue to go in there on March 1st.* I signed to do this at $500 per week salary for the run. An average run at The Pavilion is six months. So this show should net me $12000 apart from song sales.

The Ambassadeurs show here is a great success. But I only got $2000 for it. They cant [sic] pay money in France. But I did it because I wanted to be busy here. I have signed to do it again, next May, for $4000.

I write you all these details because I want to borrow $10000 from The First National, in case there is no distribution. I need $3000, July 1st, $3000 on August 1st, and $4000 on September 1st. We want to go to Venice on June 15th and stay until late August, then sail for the Bordoni opening. I cant [sic] swing Venice on my allowance. But its [sic] the only place where I can rest, and I need a rest badly. You may think it silly of me to continue going to Venice, when I cant [sic] afford it. But with all the work I have, I shall be averaging at least $25000 a year earnings from now on, and our house in Venice is the thing I like most in the world, and the place itself irons me out as nothing else.

I talked to my mother about all this, before I sailed. So I wish you would show her this letter and ask her advice. If the bank refuse to give you $10000, then get as much as you can, and I will try to borrow elsewhere. But I dont [sic] see why they should refuse if I promise to continue giving them my Bordoni royalties for the run of the show plus whatever part of all other royalties they want of my other shows until the whole thing has been paid off. Please do your best to fix this for me, Harvey, and wire me the answer.

Give my love to Mildred. I hope you are well and happy.

Yours,

[signed:] Cole

May 29.

[handwritten:] Paris

About the same time, *Vanity Fair* wrote that: 'Until recently a resident of Paris and well known in the song world there, Cole Porter has come back to

---

* *Wake Up and Dream* had a tryout in Manchester, beginning 5 March 1929, and opened in London, at the London Pavilion, on 27 March. Noël Coward's revue, *This Year of Grace*, played at the London Pavilion from 22 March 1928. In New York, *This Year of Grace* played at the Selwyn Theatre from 7 November 1928 to 23 March 1929.

New York's celebrated Tin Pan Alley as a full-fledged professional composer and lyricist.[2] Though nominally still based in Europe, Porter had, in fact, more or less taken up full-time writing for New York* even if his next show was already in the works for London. Probably in late 1928, Charles Cochran engaged him for *Wake Up and Dream*, which opened at the London Palladium on 27 March 1929 and in New York later that year, on 30 December at the Selwyn Theater. Richard Watts Jr. reviewed the show in the *New York Herald Tribune*: 'The much-heralded London revue called "Wake Up and Dream" arrived at the Selwyn Theater last night, considerably assisted by Jack Buchanan, Tilly Losch and the lady who must go through life known as Raquel Muller's sister,[†] and by that grand song, "What Is This Thing Called Love" . . . A number of us who have admired the lyrics of Mr. Cole Porter and had wished that he would write a whole score without demonstrating his passion for zoology had our wish last night, but it hardly can be said that we were altogether satisfied. There is not one reference in "Wake Up and Dream" to the sex habits of the beaver and the gnu, but, on the other hand, there is little of the brilliant style to be found in his better songs. The familiar "What Is This Thing Called Love" is charming in every way, but the rest of the score, as well as the remaining lyrics, seemed last night interesting but less than striking.'[‡]

Watts's comment about Porter's 'passion for zoology' was a reference to the review he wrote of Porter's *Fifty Million Frenchmen*, which had opened at the Lyric Theatre, New York, on 27 November 1929, a month before *Wake*

---

* With the exceptions of 1931 and 1933, Porter produced at least one new Broadway show every year between 1929 and 1936 and music for four films between 1929 and 1937: *Fifty Million Frenchmen* (1929), *The New Yorkers* (1930), *Gay Divorce* (1932), *Anything Goes* (1934), *Jubilee* (1935), *Red, Hot and Blue!* (1936), and the films *The Battle of Paris* (1929), *Adios Argentina* (1934–5 but not produced), *Born to Dance* (1936) and *Rosalie* (1937).

† The producer, director and dancer Jack Buchanan (1891–1957), together with dancer Tillie Losch (1903–75), choreographed *Wake Up and Dream*. 'Raquel Muller's sister' is unidentified.

‡ *New York Herald Tribune*, 31 December 1929, 24. The zoological theme, as well as the critics' high regard for 'What is This Thing Called Love?', also figures in a review of *Wake Up and Dream* published in *Time Magazine* for 13 January 1930: 'Charles B. Cochran, the British Ziegfeld, is quite as resourceful as his U. S. composer. The music, for instance, which accompanies his latest revue is by a trio consisting of Johann Sebastian Bach, Maurice Ravel and that infectious zoologist, Cole ("Let's Do It") Porter who used to lead the Yale Glee Club . . . Cole Porter fulfills the duty of popular composers to provide at least one haunting ballad per show. Its name: "What is This Thing Called Love?"'

Up and Dream, and in particular to the song 'Let's Do It, Let's Fall in Love': 'Mr. Cole Porter continued his studies in natural history during the course of "Fifty Million Frenchmen," which had its premiere last night. The lyrics he devised for the new musical comedy once more discussed learnedly and wittily the sex habits of the beaver, oyster, armadillo, gnu, aardvark and kindred exhibits in zoology and proved again that their author is the most definitely individual and completely brilliant current deviser of song words, but it also made some of us wish that Mr. Porter wouldn't pound at one theme so constantly. The lyrics of "Fifty Million Frenchmen" are assuredly the most delightful in town, but you are inclined to wish, even while admiring them, that their inventor would forget for a moment or two his interest in the animal kingdom.'[3]

Linda Porter, for her part, was occupied in 1929 with renovations to their Paris home at 13 rue Monsieur, and in particular a renovation of Porter's music room, which resulted in a lawsuit by the decorator Armand-Albert Rateau,[*] and a countersuit by Linda Porter as the *New York Herald Tribune (European Edition)* reported:

> Mrs. Cole Porter, wife of an American composer, won an important step in the lawsuit involving her music room in her home at 13 rue Monsieur yesterday when the Court of Appeals of the Seine decided for her and against the artist-decorator who designed the room for her.
>
> Mrs. Porter was sued in April by M. A. A. Rateau, who told the lower court that he had consented to do the work for a reduced amount of $10,000 with the understanding that Mrs. Porter's music room would be a sort of show room for him and that she would agree to show the room to her friends and his customers.
>
> On April 30, M. Rateau asked for the appointment of an expert to appraise his work, claiming that Mrs. Porter had not allowed him to use the room, and the lower court appointed M. Masson, an expert.

---

[*] Armand-Albert Rateau (1882–1938) was a furniture maker and interior designer. See Frank Olivier Vial and François Rateau, *Armand-Albert Rateau: Un Baroque chez les modernes* (Paris, 1992). A 1925 notice concerning Rateau's work notes: 'The art of M. Rateau, decorator, is in not indiscriminately mixing modes, masculine and feminine, styles, sources, flowers, and scrollwork. He creates, but he creates by seeking moderation rather than lavishness or frivolity.' Jared Goss, *French Art Deco* (New York, 2014), 178.

"Although the expert knew I was working on this appeal, which, if granted, would have made his work useless," said Me. Courtois yesterday, "he insisted upon visiting Mrs. Porter's house, and on two occasions, June 27 and July 4, forced the door of the house, in the presence of me and the commissaire of police, in order to view the music room."

Yesterday's order of the Court of Appeal set aside the lower court's appointment of the expert, saying that the decorator had merely alleged and offered no proof of an "agreement" between himself and Mrs. Porter, and that since he had already been paid $10,000, he seemed to have no case.

It is understood however, that the decorator has started another suit in the Civil Tribunal of the Seine, which is now being met with a counter suit by Mrs. Porter.[4]

The matter remained unresolved until 1932, at which time Linda Porter won a definitive judgement:

Mrs. Cole Porter Wins Verdict in Suit Over $10,000 Music Room

More than five years of controversy involving the $10,000 music room in the Paris home of Mr. and Mrs. Cole Porter, socially-prominent Americans, is apparently at an end following a decision by the first chamber of the Seine civil tribunal rejecting damage claims brought by A. A. Ratteau, interior decorator.

M. Ratteau held that Mrs. Porter never has paid him the full sum agreed upon between them for installation of a music room in the Porter house, at 13 rue Monsieur. Also, he told the court, Mrs. Porter failed to keep her promise that she would permit the decorator to bring his clients to view the expensive work, for which Mrs. Porter paid him $10,000.

Asking 1,000,000fr. damages, M. Ratteau also requested authority to remove the woodwork he had installed in the room. After hearing a plea by Me. Lucien Courtois, of the Paris bar, for Mrs. Porter, the court ordered the suit dismissed. Its judgment climaxes a series of suits brought by M. Ratteau and a counter suit by Mrs. Porter which resulted from the original disagreement five years ago.[5]

At the end of 1929, Porter was once again concerned about his finances, and, as his income increased commensurate with his professional success, his tax liability in particular:

29 October [1929]: Cole Porter to Harvey Cole[6]

Dear Harvey –
    Will you please get in touch with
    Curtis Brown
    6 Henrietta St.
    Covent Garden
    London
    Who were my agents, when I did <u>Wake Up + Dream</u>* in London + try to settle this English tax question.
    Naturally, I don't want to pay it.
    Best regards to you both.
    Cole

On 1 January 1930, Porter, Linda and 'Dumpy' Oelrichs left New York for a six-month cruise to Venice, by way of Hollywood, Hawaii, China and Japan.[7] Shortly after they left, on 14 January, Linda Porter sent a telegram to Monty Woolley: 'GOODBYE PROFESSOR[.] I THINK WE WILL MISS YOU[.] MUCH LOVE=LINDA.'[8] For his part, Porter was engaged during the trip with work on *The New Yorkers*, which had its premiere at B. S. Moss's Broadway Theatre, New York, on 8 December 1930, and ran for 168 performances. The *New York Times* was lavish in its praise of Jimmy Durante's performance but less enthusiastic with respect to Porter's lyrics and music: 'Most of Cole Porter's tunes and rhymes hold well to the average of song-and-dance scores, patiently reminding you once that "Love can make you happy; love can make you blue." But for "The Great Indoors," celebrating the luxury of week-ends immune from fresh-air poisoning, he has done original

---

* Porter's publisher Harms, New York, representing Chappell & Co., London, wrote to Harvey Cole on 7 March 1930 that Porter had been paid $1,000 on 5 April 1929, $1,000 on 8 March 1929 (paid in London), and $2,500 on 12 June 1929. http://www.lionheartautographs.com/autograph/19790-PORTER,-COLE-Composer-Cole-Porter-Writing-About-Tax-Issues-on-Black-Tuesday-1929.

research; and his two male college songs, one for the students at Sing Sing, have something refreshing to say.'[9] The *New York Herald Tribune* described it as 'hard, pretty and cynical' and said of Porter's music: 'Among the more or less fragrant songs of "The New Yorkers" are "Say It With Gin" and "I'm Getting Myself Ready for You"; in both of which Mr. Porter satirically hymns the insect aspirations of some of the inhabitants of and visitors to this seductive island. A frightened vocalist, Miss Kathryn Crawford, sings a threnody entitled "Love for Sale" in which she impersonates a lily of the gutters, vending her charms in trembling accents, accompanied by a trio of melancholy female crooners. When and if we ever get a censorship, I will give odds that it will frown upon such an honest thing.'*

In 1931, Porter's income was given a further boost when he joined ASCAP, the performing rights organization that negotiated and collected licensing fees on behalf of composers and performers. His agent, Richard Madden,[†] wrote to him on 10 April of that year: 'I know you will be pleased to know that I have received your first royalty check from the American Society of Composers for $100, which they call "First royalty payment of 1931," as per the memorandum herewith that accompanied it. This amount will, of course be deposited to your account the same as play royalty and you will be advised accordingly. I think you will find this to be a particularly easy source of revenue and it is only a pity that for these past years you have not been a member of this Society. I feel like congratulating myself for putting you into it, as it is a revenue that you are justly entitled to and that you are going to enjoy to the full extent from now on, inasmuch as I advised you in another letter, you are to be in Class A, which means the largest

---

* *New York Herald Tribune*, 9 December 1930, 20. Shortly after the opening of *The New Yorkers*, the Porters attended a party hosted by Elsa Maxwell that was typical of the festive soirées in Porter's social set. See *Time Magazine* for 22 December 1930: 'Elsa Maxwell, rich California socialite who lives in Paris and entertains amusingly on her visits to Manhattan, gave her annual Manhattan costume ball. The invitations bade 350 guests come dressed as their "opposites." Miss Maxwell rigged herself in pantaloons and high stiff collar as Herbert Hoover . . . Dancer Adele Astaire thought she was the opposite of an angel. Lady Ribblesdale went as Charlie Chaplin, Banker Mortimer Schiff as Oscar Wilde. Two socialite matrons chose to dress as "Ladies of the Temperance Union." Composer Cole Porter went as an oldtime footballer, his wife as a housemaid. Princess Hohenlohe-Schillingsfurst wore the robes of a nun.'

† Richard J. Madden (birth and death dates unknown) was Cole Porter's agent; the Richard J. Madden Play Company was based at 33 West 42nd Street, New York.

possible revenue for the use of your songs. Incidentally, I think you can thank Ray Hubbell and Gene Buck* for their particularly fine interest on your behalf in seeing that you have been put in the Preferred Class.'[10] But this, and the failure of *Fifty Million Frenchmen* in London,† only served to exacerbate Porter's tax problems:

31 March 1931: Cole Porter to Harvey Cole[11]

Dear Harvey,

I received the terrible news about my income tax and I suggest the following:

As my trip around the world last year was done with the purpose of studying Oriental music I should think you would be able to get a reduction from that angle.

The trip cost me $18000. I went to New York to start work on the "New Yorkers" in July. From then on I lived practically all the time at the Ritz Hotel in New York. I should ask Madden to go to the Ritz and find out how much I spent during the 5 ½ months I was there. Besides my expenses at the hotel, restaurants, motors, etc., cost me about $300 a week. Also my steamship passage to New York and back cost me $1600.

Linda says that nothing can be taken off from my income tax due to our living in Paris as the house is in her name, but if you want to be sure about this, write to her new lawyer, Frank L. Polk Esq.

Best regards to you and Mildred,

[signed:] Cole

Cole Porter

---

* John Ray Hubbell (1879–1954) was a songwriter; Edward Eugene Buck (1885–1957) was a lyricist and sheet-music illustrator.

† See the *Manchester Guardian*, 7 October 1931, 5: ' "Fifty Million Frenchmen," the revue which is now running at the Palace Theatre, Manchester, will be taken off by the producers, the Daniel Mayer Company, at the end of this week. The original production cost is said to have been £10,000, and the weekly running expenses £1,250. It was felt that the revue had not met with a sufficient share of success ... The decision to end "Fifty Million Frenchmen" marks one of the most expensive theatrical failures of recent years.'

5 October 1931: Cole Porter to Harvey Cole[12]

New York City, Oct. 5th, 1931

DEAR HARVEY,

I FORGOT TO WARN YOU TO HOLD OFF BEGINNING TO PAY ON THAT LAST NOTE. IT IS TRUE THAT I EXPECTED TO HAVE MONEY COMING IN AT ONCE. BUT ALAS FIFTY MILLION FRENCHMEN IS A FAILURE IN ENGLAND. WHAT'S WORSE, WE HAVE HAD SUCH DIFFICULTIES CASTING MY NEW SHOW* HERE, THAT WE CANT [sic] POSSIBLY OPEN ON THE ROAD UNTIL THE END OF NOVEMBER. ALL OF WHICH MEANS THAT I HAVEN'T A RED CENT AND NEED BADLY THE LAST DISTRIBUTION, AND THE NEXT TWO. WILL YOU SEE WHAT YOU CAN DO ABOUT THIS. IT WAS STUPID OF ME TO HAVE FORGOTTEN ABOUT THOSE PAYMENTS, AND I APOLOGIZE FOR PUTTING YOU TO THIS TROUBLE.

YOURS SINCERELY

[signed:] Cole

Porter's 1932 show, *Gay Divorce*, starring Fred Astaire, opened at the Ethel Barrymore Theatre, New York, on 29 November. The *New York Times* wrote:

All the entrepreneurs of "Gay Divorce," which was mounted at the Ethel Barrymore last evening, have gone to considerable pains to produce a clever musical comedy. In the stellar role they have cast Fred Astaire, who can dance the crisp idioms of the modish toe-and-heel fandango. The music and the lyrics are the work of Cole Porter, whose facetious grace is already familiar . . . Mr. Porter's tunes and lyrics have the proper dash and breeding. For the amusingly venomous Luella Gear he has written a sardonic number entitled "I Still Love the Red, White and Blue," and a politely coarse ballad mischievously entitled "Mr. and Mrs. Fitch." "You're in Love" and "Night and Day" pay their gentlemanly respects to romance. One might be more fervent about Mr. Porter's score if he had good voices

---

* *Nymph Errant*.

to sing it. But Mr. Astaire and Miss Luce,* being singers only by necessity, make the chief song numbers of "Gay Divorce" perfunctory items.[13]

The *Times*'s only cursory mention of 'Night and Day' notwithstanding, the song became one of Porter's biggest hits. On 2 February 1933 his editor and arranger at Chappell, Albert Sirmay,† wrote to him: 'My dear Cole, It gives me great satisfaction, that the victory which I predicted for your music, didn't fail to come. That goes especially for "Night and Day", which can be heard all over New York, on the air and otherwise. I think this is the finest and most artistic song, which has been written for many years. In the meantime I saw "Gay Divorce". It was a delightful evening. That's about all I wanted to tell you. I envy you for your Rue Monsieur. But come back soon! With kindest thoughts, Yours Albert Szirmai.'[14] And on 3 July, Irving Berlin‡ wrote to Porter: 'Dear Cole: I am mad about NIGHT AND DAY, and I think it is your high spot. You probably know it is being played all over, and all the orchestra leaders think it is the best tune of the year -- and I agree with them. Really, Cole, it is great and I could not resist the temptation of writing you about it. Love from us to you and Linda. As ever, Irving.'[15]

The second of Porter's shows for London during the early 1930s was a Gertrude Lawrence vehicle, *Nymph Errant*, based on a novel by James Laver, a Keeper at the Victoria and Albert Museum. The story revolves around the attempts of its lead, Evangeline Edwards, to lose her virginity. Shortly before it opened in Manchester on 11 September 1933, Cochran wrote to Porter: 'I want to express to you my eternal gratitude. You have been a tower of strength not only in your own department but with valuable suggestions to the good of every department.'[16] The show was positively reviewed in the *Manchester Guardian* for 29 September – 'Mr. Cole Porter's lyrics and music have a

---

* Claire Luce (1903–89), who took the role of Mimi in *Gay Divorce*.

† Albert Sirmay (Szirmai, 1880–1967) was a composer and music editor. The Hungarian Sirmay emigrated to the United States in 1923. Music director for Chappell Music, he edited the works of Jerome Kern, Richard Rodgers and George Gershwin, in addition to Porter. Throughout Porter's career, he played a crucial role in arranging the composer's works for publication and offering the composer advice. In 1965 he discovered 100 unpublished Porter songs at Porter's Waldorf suite. See *New York Times*, 5 May 1965, 1 and 52.

‡ Irving Berlin (1888–1989) was the pre-eminent American songwriter and lyricist for most of the twentieth century.

light and varied wit . . .'[17] – and after it premiered at the Adelphi Theatre, London, on 6 October, *The Times* reported that, 'Gertrude Lawrence makes her effects without a superflous [sic] word or gesture, and she rarely lets a clumsily written piece of dialogue tempt her to leave the plane of artificiality on which the play must stay if it is to live. Her love song to the doctor who persistently regards her as a mere patient,* and the whimsical regret with which she surrounds her heroic rescuer's lyrical praise of her mother are, perhaps, the most delightful things of the evening. But her performance – which is nearly always a matter of making bricks without straw, is a continual delight . . . Mr. Cole Porter's lyrics are pointed, and the music has style.'[18]

Shortly before the London opening of *Nymph Errant*, Porter wrote to his cousin Harvey Cole, again about financial matters, noting the relatively unsuccessful run of *Gay Divorce* in New York:

16 May 1933: Cole Porter to Harvey Cole[19]

Dear Harvey,

Your letter of the 29th April received. Our secretary in Paris wrote you about my 1932 expenses. If you never received the letter, let me know and we will do it all again.

My new show goes into rehearsal on August 1st in London and opens there September 15th.† The Gay Divorce opens there also in September.‡ I hope to make some money on the latter in England as against the U.S.A. where everyone connected with it had to take a 50% cut to keep it alive.

---

* 'The Physician'.

† *Nymph Errant* was first performed on 6 October 1933.

‡ *Gay Divorce* did not open in London until 2 November 1933, when it played for 180 performances at the Palace Theatre. *The Times* for 3 November 1933, 12, reported that: 'The piece itself is an odd entertainment. It sets a collusive divorce to music, the tuneful music of Mr. Cole Porter, giving us a heroine who contrives to arrive at her inevitable misunderstanding with the hero by mistaking him for the professional co-respondent she has engaged. Odd this romance may be, but from it spring several taking songs, notably one called "Night and Day," much pleasant scenery, and a ravishing display of frocks.'

I shall come back in October to start work on a new show and will see you then.

Our best regards to you and Mildred.

Yours

[signed:] Cole

Whatever 'new show' Porter had in mind at the time apparently never materialized. By all accounts his next show, *Anything Goes*, was not conceived until 1934. Originally planned by Guy Bolton and P. G. Wodehouse as a comedy about gamblers and a shipwreck, the real-life fire aboard the USS *Morro Castle*, an ocean liner plying the route between New York and Havana that cost thirty-seven lives,[20] caused the producers to take on Howard Lindsay and Russel Crouse* to recast the plot as a romantic comedy, albeit still set on an ocean liner and with a prominent role for a comic gangster, Moonface Martin.† *Anything Goes* opened at the Alvin Theatre, New York, on 21 November 1934, running for 420 performances. *Time Magazine* was somewhat offhand in its praise for the show – '[Porter's] score for Anything Goes, while it does not include a melody as sensational as his "Night & Day" for last year's Gay Divorce, is as good as the best any of his peers are turning out'[21] – while the *New York Times* called it a 'thundering good musical show . . . hilarious and dynamic entertainment' and Porter's score, 'dashing . . . with impish lyrics' and 'exultant tunes'. 'You're the Top' is described as 'one of the most congenial songs Mr. Porter has written.'[22] The *New York Herald Tribune* wrote:

---

* Russel Crouse (1893–1966) was a playwright and librettist; Howard Lindsay (1889–1968) was a theatrical producer, director and playwright. Crouse and Lindsay later worked with Porter on *Red, Hot and Blue!* (1936).

† See *New York Times*, 12 September 1934, 26: '**Ship Fire Prompts Play Change**. In order to permit the rewriting of certain scenes which treat in a farcical manner of a shipboard disaster in midocean, Vinton Freedly announced yesterday that he had postponed the scheduled presentation of a new musical play by Guy Bolton, P. G. Wodehouse and Cole Porter from November until December. In view of the Morro Castle disaster the producer considered such material would be in bad taste'. Porter later told Richard Hubler (possibly apocryphally) that, however indirectly, the *Morro Castle* disaster gave rise to the show's name. While the script was being rewritten, '[William] Gaxton, coming to the theatre for rehearsal a week before the show opened, plaintively demanded of the stage-doorman: "What are we going to call this musical hash, anyway?" The doorman shrugged, grinned, and said: "Well, you know, Mr. Gaxton, anything goes."' See 'How to Beget a Musical Comedy by Cole Porter as told to Richard G. Hubler', Stanford University, Cole Porter Collection, shelfmark FE209, 2–9, Manuscripts, 3.

... when a play contains not only Mr. [Victor] Moore but Miss Ethel Merman* and William Gaxton,[†] it joins the sparse ranks of the blessed and becomes, in its way, a public benefaction. You may think this to be enough encomium for the new opera at the Alvin. After all it is only some expansive frivoling set to music and with the usual obligato of dancing boys and girls. There are nevertheless additional felicities in "Anything Goes," almost breath-taking in their splendor. No less a minstrel than Cole Porter, a pet son of the Orpheus family, is the composer of the songs, sentimental and ribald, in a hymnal fully up to his standard.[23]

Anything Goes was produced in London less than a year later, at the Palace Theatre on 14 June 1935. Among other revisions to the lyrics, P. G. Wodehouse wrote several new lyrics for 'You're the Top'. As a lyric sheet for the two songs shows, these changes were approved by Porter, who in a few instances added lines of his own or rewrote some of the words:[‡]

'You're the Top!': Text Changes for the London Production (extract)

Porter's original	London text (changes by Wodehouse in italics)
Refrain 2	**Refrain 2**
You're the top!	You're the top!
You're Mahatma Ghandi.	You're Mahatma Ghandi.
You're the top!	You're the top!

---

* The actress and singer Ethel Merman (Ethel Agnes Zimmermann, 1908–84) took the role of Reno Sweeney in *Anything Goes*. In 1936, Merman played Nails O'Reilly Duquesne in Porter's *Red, Hot and Blue!* and together with Bob Hope premiered 'It's De-Lovely'. She later appeared in *Du Barry Was a Lady* (1939) and *Panama Hattie* (1940).

† William Gaxton (1893–1963), actor and singer. Gaxton took the lead role, Billy Crocker, in *Anything Goes*.

‡ Not in Kimball, *The Complete Lyrics of Cole Porter*. Cochran sent the lyrics to Porter on 3 July, as well as a report on the show's takings: 'Business is much better than anything in Town, but not entirely satisfactory. We are nearly, but not quite, selling out every night at full price. We sell out the back seats at cheaper prices and our gallery is not nearly full ... People tell me it is because the weather is hot, but I never allow alibis. I prefer to think that it is because Reno is not perfect, and that if I can get her played perfectly we shall sell out for a year.' CPT, Correspondence 1935.

You're Napoleon brandy.
You're the purple light of a summer night in Spain
You're the National Galr'ry,
You're Garbo's sal'ry,
You're cellophane.
You're sublime,
You're a turkey dinner,
You're the time
Of the Derby winner.
I'm a toy balloon that is fated soon to pop,
But if, baby, I'm the bottom
You're the top.

REFRAIN 4
You're the top!
You're an Arrow collar.
You're the top!
You're a Coolidge dollar.
You're the nimble tread of the feet of Fred Astaire,
You're an O'Neill drama,
You're Whistler's mama,
You're Camembert.
You're a rose,
You're Inferno's Dante,
You're the nose
On the great Durante.
I'm just in the way, as the French would say "de trop,"
But if, baby, I'm the bottom
You're the top.

You're Napoleon brandy.
You're the purple light of a summer night in Spain
You're the National Galr'ry,
You're Garbo's sal'ry,
You're cellophane.
You're the grace
Of the Brontasaurus
You're the pace
Of a Cochran chorus
I'm a toy balloon that is fated soon to pop,
But if, baby, I'm the bottom
You're the top.

REFRAIN 4
You're the top –
You're a dress by Patou
You're the top –
You're an Epstein statoo
You're the nimble tread – of the feet of – Fred Astaire
You're a Mussolini
You're Mrs. Sweeney
You're Camembert
You're the fun –
Of a film by Arliss
You're the sun –
On the Crystal Parliss
I'm a lazy lout – that's just about to stop*
But if – Baby – I'm the bottom
You're the top.

---

* This line by Porter replaces 'I'm just in the way, as the French would say "de trop"' which in the London version was moved to Refrain 3. In the original, it occurs in Refrain 5.

Similar adjustments were made to 'Anything Goes', although in this instance the changes seem radically to change the meaning of the song. Whereas Porter's original is an exercise in relatively harmless wordplay, Wodehouse's rewriting is a diatribe against the pursuit of money at all costs. Furthermore, in one noteworthy change reflecting different social sensibilities, where Wodehouse in the third refrain writes 'When ladies fair who seek affection / Prefer coons of dark complexion', Porter has circled 'coons' and in the margin replaced it with 'gents'.

'Anything Goes': Text Changes for the London Production (extract)

Porter's original	London text (changes by Wodehouse in italics)
REFRAIN 2	**REFRAIN 2**
When Missus Ned McLean (God bless her)	*When maiden aunts can freely chuckle*
Can get Russian reds to "yes" her,	*At tales much too near the knuckle*
Then I suppose	*The facts disclose*
Anything goes.	Anything goes.
When Rockefeller still can hoard en-	*When in the House our Legislators*
Ough money to let Max Gordon	*Are calling each other, "Traitors"*
Produce his shows,	*And "So and So's"*
Anything goes.	Anything goes.
The world has gone mad today,	*The world's in a state today*
And good's bad today	*Like Billingsgate today*
And black's white today,	*We are each today*
And day's night today	*For free speech today*
And that gent today	*Nothing's blue today*
You gave a cent today	*Or taboo today*
Once had several châteaux.	*Or meets with scandalized "Oh"*
When folks who still can ride in jitneys	*But while we hope for days more sunny*
Find out Vanderbilts and Whitneys	*The Government gets our money*
Lack baby clo'es	*'Cause Neville knows*
Anything goes.	Anything goes.

REFRAIN 3

If Sam Goldwyn can with great conviction
Instruct Anna Sten in diction,
Then Anna shows
Anything goes.
When you hear that Lady Mendl standing up
Now turns a handspring landing up-
On her toes,
Anything goes.
Just think of those shocks you've got
And those knocks you've got
And those blues you've got
From that news you've got
And those pains you've got
(If any brains you've got)
From those little radios.
So Missus R., with all her trimmin's,
Can broadcast a bed from Simmons
'Cause Franklin knows
Anything goes.

When Grandmammas, whose age is eighty
In night clubs are getting matey
With gigolos
Anything goes.
When mothers pack and leave poor father
Because they decide they'd rather
Be tennis pros.
Anything goes.
The world has gone mad today
And good's bad today
And black's white today
And day's night today
In Colney Hatch today
We ought to snatch today
A little rest and repose
When ladies fair who seek affection
Prefer coons* of dark complexion
As Romeos.
Anything goes.

REFRAIN 4 (London only: P. G. Wodehouse)

The dogs chase fleas
The bees chase honey
And we all are chasing money
And when it shows
Anything goes.
The Duke who owns a mounted castle
Takes lodgers and makes a parcel

---

* Crossed out by Porter and replaced with 'gents'.

Because he knows
Anything goes.
It's grab and smash today
We want cash today
Get rich quick today
That's the trick today
And the Great today
Don't hesitate today
But keep right on their toes
And lend their names, if paid to do it
To anyone's soap or suet
Or baby clo's
Anything goes.

Until about 1935, when Porter and Moss Hart* set out on a round-the-world cruise, during which they wrote *Jubilee*, the scant surviving correspondence deals mostly, though not exclusively, with financial matters. On 30 October 1934, Harvey Cole wrote to Porter: 'I am sorry that I made the loan for $6,000.00 instead of $5,000. The mistake was mine . . . I am glad to learn that the show is doing well.'[24] Porter replied on 1 November:

1 November 1934: Cole Porter to Harvey Cole[25]

Dear Harvey:

It is alright about the $6,000 loan, instead of $5,000. I shall hang on to the extra one thousand dollars, as I am a little bit poor for the next weeks, after which the money will roll in and I shall then be able to pay off the debt.

Please apply the Hartwell bonds on my note, and I heartily approve of the charge that you have made for your services.

With best regards to Mildred and to you,

Cole, [signed:] Cole

---

* Moss Hart (1904–61) was a playwright and theatre director. Hart had earlier collaborated with Irving Berlin on *Face The Music* (1932) and *As Thousands Cheer* (1933).

Both at this time and later, Porter was frequently linked with projects that either he dismissed out of hand, that never materialized, were composed by others, or were just fantasies in the minds of producers and performers. On 19 May 1933 the *New York World-Telegram* reported: 'Dwight Deere Wiman and Tom Weatherly* bought the dramatic rights to "She Loves Me Not," Edward Hope's new novel, yesterday. This one ran as a serial in the Saturday Evening Post, and the Messers. W. and W. want to convert it into a comedy with incidental songs, for which purpose they will probably consult with Cole Porter, their favourite composer.' It is not known whether Porter was, in fact, approached to write *She Loves Me Not*; in the end, Lindsay's play was produced with songs by Arthur Schwartz and Edward Heyman, opening at the 46th Street Theatre on 20 November 1933.

In December 1934, Porter wrote again to Clifton Webb, and in January 1935 to Sarah Scott, whom he had known in Worcester:

15 December 1934: Cole Porter to Clifton Webb

Dear Cliff:

I can imagine nothing more awful than writing songs for you for your next picture.† Moss Hart and I are leaving on a beautiful boat called the "Franconia", January 12th, and are going around this funny world of ours.‡

I am very sorry to hear that your health is not good, but I believe that when you get out in the high spots of the M-G-M studio, everything will be well. It seems to me that it is pretty affected of you not being in New York. The parties are great and they need you. Last night even Frances§ threw a

---

* Dwight Deere Wiman (1895–1951) was an actor, playwright, director and Broadway producer. Tom Weatherly (1899–1982), producer and publicity agent. Weatherly had co-produced Porter's 1932 show *Gay Divorce*. Edward Hope (1896–1958), writer. Hope's 1933 novel *She Loves Me Not* was the basis for the 1934 Paramount film, starring Bing Crosby, of the same name.

† Clifton Webb had appeared in *The Heart of a Siren* (Associated Pictures Productions, 1925) and the short *The Still Alarm* (Vitaphone Corporation, 1930), but did not appear in another picture until *Laura* (Twentieth Century Fox, 1944).

‡ See below, p. 106.

§ Possibly the singer and actor Frances Langford (1913–2005). Concerning her role in *Born to Dance*, see below, pp. 123–5, 128.

good one. As for the Maxwell party in honor of none other than myself,* it made history. Laura Corrigan† is a tremendous event in town. In fact, she has arrived to such an extent that she won't meet Barbara Mdivani.‡ The farewells for Neysa§ were endless, and finally finished at the George Kaufman's,¶ which was one of the greatest parties I have been to for years. But everybody cried in corners because you were not there.

I hope you will be great in pictures. I arrive back in New York at the end of May and then make for Hollywood for three months to be with Walter Wanger.** If things don't work out, I shall be in New York.

Blessings on you my boy, and please don't marry Gloria Swanson.††

Love.

[signed:] Cole

---

* The party Elsa Maxwell gave in Porter's honour was on 9 December; see *New York Times*, 9 December 1934, 91: 'Miss Elsa Maxwell will give a supper dance this evening in the starlight roof garden of the Waldorf-Astoria to celebrate the birthday of Cole Porter, the composer. The affair will be called the Turkish ball and guests have been requested to come in costume.'

† Laura Mae Corrigan (1879–1948) was a socialite; see Siân Evans, *Queen Bees: Six Brilliant and Extraordinary Society Hostesses between the Wars* (London, 2016).

‡ Barbara Hutton (1912–79) was a socialite and heiress to the Woolworth fortune. She had married Alexis Mdivani (1905–35), a self-styled Georgian prince, in 1933; they divorced in 1935. She subsequently married six times between 1935 and 1966.

§ Probably Neysa McMein (1889–1949), an artist best known for her magazine covers including *McCall's*, *National Geographic*, *Woman's Home Companion*, *Collier's* and *Photoplay*; she also created the official portrait of fictional homemaker Betty Crocker for General Mills. See Brian Gallagher, *Anything Goes: The Jazz Age Adventures of Neysa McMein and Her Extravagant Circle of Friends* (New York, 1987).

¶ George S. Kaufman (1889–1961) was a playwright, theatre director and drama critic. Together with Leueen MacGrath and Abe Burrows, he wrote the book for Porter's *Silk Stockings* (1955).

** Walter Wanger (1894–1968) was a film producer. Wanger earlier contracted Porter to compose two songs for the 1929 film *The Battle of Paris* (Paramount Pictures), 'Here Comes the Bandwagon' and 'They All Fall in Love'.

†† Gloria Swanson (1899–1983) was an actress. Porter's comment is possibly made in jest, a reference to Swanson's six short-lived marriages: among them, she was married to the actor Wallace Beery from 1916 to 1918; to Herbert K. Somborn, president of the Equity Pictures Corporation, from 1919 to 1925; and to Henri, Marquis de la Falaise de la Coudraye, a French aristocrat, from 1925 to 1930.

10 January 1935: Cole Porter to Sarah Scott,* Worcester, MA[26]

Dear Mrs. Scott:

Your charming letter arrived this morning, and made me very happy indeed to realize that one can have such loyal friends. We are off tomorrow night.[27] We are excited because our trip takes us to all the crazy places in the world, names that I dreamed about since I was a child, the Fiji islands, Zanzibar and Madagascar – just think of it.

I arrive back in New York the first of June and shall be here all summer. In case you ever come to town, please take the trouble to telephone me, as I should so love to see you again.

My best regards to your daughters, and thank you so much for writing me.

Sincerely yours,

[signed:] Cole Porter

The trip Porter mentioned to both Webb and Sarah Scott was a South Seas voyage with Moss Hart, Howard Sturges, Monty Woolley and Billy Powell,† one purpose of which was to write the show *Jubilee*. They set out on 12 January and during the trip Hart kept a diary that includes a number of references specific to Porter and their musical interests. En route, Porter wrote again to Clifton Webb and to 'Dumpy' Oelrichs:

14 January [probably] 1935: Cole Porter to Clifton Webb[28]

Cute Clifton

To have sent me the prison book, which I leapt on + finished the first day out. It was excellent + I thank thee.

We are all a little dazed. The boat is a joy, there never was such balmy weather + our little gang is so happy together. Linda + I have committee meetings + beam at our leaving such amusing friends.

---

* Sarah Scott (1866–1962) was active at several clubs in Worcester, including the Worcester Women's Club and the Hall Club. She wrote a profile of Porter that was published in the April 1931 issue of the *Worcester Academy Bulletin*, 45–7.

† William Powell (1892–1984) was an actor. Powell appeared in more than ninety films and is best known for his appearance in the 'Thin Man' series (*The Thin Man*, 1934; *After the Thin Man*, 1936; *Another Thin Man*, 1939; *Shadow of the Thin Man*, 1941; *The Thin Man Goes Home*, 1944; and *Song of the Thin Man*, 1947).

Goodbye. I'll keep you posted on our career. Give my love to the great Mabel,* + bless you for <u>ze</u> book.

Devotedly Cole.

Moss Hart's diary

En route from Panama Canal to Los Angeles: 'There is time to work – to swim – to read – to talk – to laze away an hour in a deck chair or at the pool; and in consequence, we are working well and without strain or tenseness. Cole Porter writes his music and I write my play with no fear of what the critical fraternity will say to-morrow morning – we have only ourselves to please . . . ' [p. 11]

Samoa: 'It was in Samoa, incidentally, that we were treated to a spectacle I shall long remember. We were the guests of the Boys' School – and a school of some two hundred sons of native chiefs from the outlying islands, and I never shall forget the sight of these magnificent specimens of young Samoan manhood or the organ-like quality of their voices. They sang for us in a setting of near-primitive beauty, and as we had just come from Robert Louis Stevenson's house, they sang for us his "Requiem," which they had set to their own music. There is no describing those voices. We were all, I imagine, more moved than we cared to admit. So much so that Cole Porter arranged to go back and have them sing again in the afternoon . . .' [p. 25]

Kalabahi: 'It is going to amuse me some night next winter to stand in the back of the Music Box Theatre and watch the curtain fall on the first act of a certain musical comedy as yet untitled. For the words "End of Act I" were scrawled across the page as we saw the last of New Guinea, and I shall watch the beginning of Act II long after it has lost its first, fine, careless rapture for the reason that Act II was begun the morning of the day we landed in Kalabahi. Two pretty strange places to see the birth of a Broadway musical comedy . . . Here, too, the natives had been singing and dancing for two days prior to our arrival, but there was neither joy nor passion in it. Their dance was an angry stamping of the earth they found so hard a master, and their song was a wail of agony rising at times

---

* Possibly the singer Mabel Mercer (1900–84), who was a frequent performer at Chez Bricktop in the 1920s and might have become acquainted with Porter there.

PORTER'S RETURN TO THE UNITED STATES, 1928-1937

to a sob. It was the song of a people whose life was filled with an unceasing fear of devils and evil spirits, whose race was dying out and whose years were spent in a sullen acceptance of an unending, useless toil. If you had not realized it before, you were now brought up sharp against the realization that you were, indeed, a long, long way from Tipperary.' [pp. 33–4 and 40]

Bali: 'We saw some superb dances, and when we asked, with bated breath, who the chief dancer was, we were told that he or she was just a fisherman in from his work or a girl from a neighboring village. There were no prima donnas here – no regal outbursts of artistic temperament. If a man or woman could dance magnificently it was expected that they would do so for the pleasure of their fellow townsmen and for the sheer joy of dancing. The most astonishing dancers of them all, however, are the children. They are instructed in the art of the dance from the age of two years and perform only until they are twelve. The curious thing is to see these little girls dressed in their beautiful costumes dance with the fervor and passion of an old-world courtesan – face, arms, body and sensuous, insidious mass of movement, and immediately, the dance finished, become little girls of nine again . . . All dances and native plays are accompanied by appropriate music on the gamelan, an orchestra made up of gongs of various sizes, xylophones, drums, flutes and other similar instruments. The accompaniments to the various dances are well known to the people, each character in each of his moods having his own characteristic music. You hear the gamelan playing all day and night. It is a soft, strange music that plays all day and all night. You go to sleep with it. It rings in your ears long after you have left.' [pp. 43–5]

10 April [1935]: Cole Porter to Mrs Herman ('Dumpy') Oelrichs[29]

April 10th, evening, bound for Zanzibar.

Dumpy Darling -

I'm so tired, on this fabulous trip of saying "If only La Dumpa were here", so I shan't mention it, but you've no idea how much you have been missed.

All the news about the Beard* is grand. He has become entirely Arcadian. He is up for his swim every morning at seven – sometimes at six – he eats very little, he drinks at most, three cocktails before dinner & nothing else, during the day, he is usually in bed by 9.30 – but never later than 10.30, & due to his constant swimming, sun-bathing & ascetic life, he has become very handsome, & all the photographers fight for his profile. Also, his future has been temporarily fixed, for Moss has asked him to direct the book of our show,† & as Moss & I seem to have complete control, I don't believe this will <u>not</u> work out.

Suddenly, yesterday, our show looked nearly finished. I still have much more to do than has Moss, but if it were necessary, we could go into rehearsal tomorrow, especially as Monty has been in at all our discussions & could take a company over immediately.

Moss, by the way, is an angel from Heaven & we all love him dearly. In fact, everybody <u>loves</u> every<u>body</u> else & its [sic] all rather sickening.

I leave you now. I've got to be cute in the morning as we all are being received by His Black Highness, the Sultan of Zanzibar.‡

Give my love to that Hermie & tell him that today at noon we were Lat. obd. 4043E.

Goodbye & great love to you

[signed:] Cole.

Linda has a hate on Weston.

In addition to his New York and London shows of the early 1930s, Porter also started writing for films. The first was *The Battle of Paris* (Paramount, released 30 November 1929), for which Porter wrote two songs, 'Here Comes the Bandwagon' and 'They All Fall in Love', while the film *Adios Argentina*, on which Porter worked in late 1934 and early 1935, was never produced. Both *Born to Dance* (MGM, 1936), an Eleanor Powell and James Stewart vehicle, and *Rosalie* (MGM, 1937), with Nelson Eddy and Eleanor Powell, made it to release. As Porter noted in a letter to Harvey Cole, in mid-1935 he was not only financially well-off due to the success of *Anything Goes*, but had received the first instalment of his pay for *Born to Dance*:

---

* Monty Woolley.
† *Jubilee*, which opened at the Imperial Theatre, New York, on 12 October 1935.
‡ Sheikh Sir Khalifa II bin Harub Al-Said, Khalifa bin Harub, Sultan of Zanzibar, 1911–60.

3 July 1935: Cole Porter to Harvey Cole[30]

Dear Harvey:

Dick Madden suggests that instead of letting that money lie around in the bank in Indiana, that you invest it in something and make a little profit for me. I have enough money here, what with "ANYTHING GOES" running through the summer in New York, and having opened with great success in London, to live on royalties.*

The first installment of Paramount money† arrived – $10,000. When the next and last installment arrives, then we can talk annuity. As I wrote you, I have a man here who is interested in arranging it, but you may think this unnecessary and that you could do it all yourself. Please advise me about this.

Best regards to you both.

[signed:] Cole‡

The success of Porter's early 1930s shows, and *Anything Goes* in particular, led *Theatre World* to dub him the 'ace' composer and lyricist of the day in an interview published in September 1935:

> "They used to regard me as a dilettante ... and refused to believe that best-sellers could possibly emanate from a young man well-endowed with the world's goods. Luckily my first number, 'Old-Fashioned Garden,' sold two million copies, after which the denizens of Tin-Pan Alley stopped talking about the 'millionaire playboy!'
>
> "I usually work after midnight, so that my studios in Paris and Nice are sound-proof. But I sometimes compose at other times, and am quite liable to wander off to a piano while my guests go into dinner, and then appear later in the evening with a completed number. 'Miss Otis Regrets' was written at a party just as a joke, but it caught on and people started

---

* *Anything Goes* had opened at the Palace Theatre, London, on 14 June 1935.

† For *Born to Dance*.

‡ Harvey Cole replied on 5 July 1935: 'I will be glad to invest the surplus funds, although I hardly know what to put it into. The return on Government securities is practically nothing and I think they are likely to decline in value. Nearly everything else is more or less speculative. If you know of anything you would like to have I will be glad to arrange for it. With reference to the annuity, I think it would be just as well to let the man in New York arrange for it, as I am not much of an expert along this line. I am delighted to know that "Anything Goes" is still going so well.' Yale University, Gilmore Library, Cole Porter Collection MSS 82, Box 49, folder 299.

to talk about it. They were singing and playing it in New York before it was published."

... Like many American revue writers, he starts at the end and works backwards. That is to say, he first finds his "kick" and builds up to it. This, incidentally is why American lyrics and sketches usually have more point than their English counterparts. His latest sensation, "You're the Top," was composed with the idea of providing a number to be sung in front of the curtain while the necessary costume changes were made...

Talking of Cole Porter's work, Fred Astaire once told me that his favourite melody was "Night and Day," to which he danced his famous routine for nearly 1,000 performances over here and in the States. "People often ask me if I am not tired of hearing this number," he [Astaire] said. "But I can honestly say that I never grow weary of it. There is such inspiration to be derived from it and it is my first choice of all the songs I have sung in musical productions."[31]

In December, Porter, with Linda, went to Hollywood to work on *Born to Dance*. While he was there, he kept an extensive journal, documenting in detail his meetings with MGM:

Born to Dance diary, 20 December 1935–9 June 1936
FRIDAY, DECEMBER 20, 1935

Went to Sam Katz's* office. He could not have been more charming and told me that unlike other productions on the MGM lot, my picture would not be the result of havoc, as most of them are. After having explained that he had engaged Jack McGowan and Sidney Silvers[†] to construct the book of my picture, he called them in and they told me the idea of their story.

---

* Sam Katz (1892–1969) was a producer.

† Jack McGowan (1894–1977) was a writer. In addition to *Born to Dance*, his credits include *Girl Crazy* (RKO, 1932), *Broadway Melody of 1936* (MGM, 1935), *Broadway Melody of 1938* (MGM, 1937), *Babes in Arms* (MGM, 1939), *Broadway Melody of 1940* (MGM, 1940) and *Lady Be Good* (MGM, 1941). Sidney Silvers (1901–76) was an actor and writer. He appeared in several Broadway shows in the late 1920s and made his film debut in *The Show of Shows* (The Vitaphone Corporation, now Warner Bros., 1929); Silvers both contributed to the script of *Born to Dance* and played the role of 'Gunny' Saks.

The idea was based on the recent escapade of Jack Barrymore and Elaine Barrie.* Sam Katz explained that what they wanted to do was to have Clark Gable play the Jack Barrymore part, and Jean Harlow the Elaine Barrie part.† I held out for more singers in the principal leads, and they finally decided that if the girl playing the love interest opposite Gable could sing, the trio would be a very strong box office draw.

When the conference was. over, Sam Katz said "Come back in a few weeks." I left, feeling that once we started, all would be peaceful.

MONDAY, JANUARY 6, 1936

Dined with Sam Katz in the commissary on the MGM lot. Present: Sid Silvers, Jack McGowan, and a new author named Hatch (Hatch evidently is a magazine writer, and has moments of being a complete Englishman, and other moments of being a middle-Westerner), Mr. Pye (Sam explained that Pye was an excellent art director on the lot and had a great many fine ideas for staging concerted numbers), another gentleman whose name I did not catch, but obviously an assistant of Sam Katz, and Alex Aarons, whom I had known in New York, but who now is also working for Katz.‡

---

* John Barrymore (1882–1942) was an actor, the actress Elaine Barrie (1915–2003) was his fourth wife. The 'recent escapade' of Barrymore and Barrie was their affair, which led to Barrymore's divorce from Dolores Costello. A lengthy account of the divorce proceedings was published in the *New York Times* for 10 October 1935: 'WIFE DIVORCES JOHN BARRYMORE. Former Dolores Costello, Charging Desertion, Gets Children and $163,000 in Securities.' Also see Elaine Barrie's obituary in the *New York Times* for 4 March 2003: '... As a Hunter College student of 19, she wrote an adoring letter to Barrymore, then 53 and hospitalized in Manhattan. He phoned her, they had a pleasant talk and he invited her to visit him. There was a most meaningful kiss in his hospital room. They almost immediately became known to the public by the Shakespearean names they had bestowed on each other, Ariel and Caliban, from "The Tempest." There was a mysterious voyage on Barrymore's yacht, a cross-country chase (with her pursuing him), an elopement and tender reconciliations after spectacular quarrels.

† Clark Gable (1901–60) had acted with Barrymore in *Night Flight* (MGM, 1933); Jean Harlow (1911–37) had acted with Gable in *Red Dust* (MGM, 1932) and with John Barrymore in *Dinner at Eight* (MGM, 1933).

‡ Erich S. Hatch (1901–73) was a writer. His novel *1101 Park Avenue* (New York, 1935) was the basis for the film *My Man Godfrey* (Universal Pictures, 1936). The Broadway producer Alex A. Aarons (1890–1943) was from 1927 co-owner, with Vinton Freedley, of the Alvin Theatre (now The Neil Simon Theatre). In Hollywood he was a production assistant for *Broadway Melody of 1936* (MGM, 1935). Merrill Pye (1891–1963) was art director at MGM from the mid-1920s and the first resident designer of musicals, beginning with *Broadway Melody of 1929*. See Michael L. Stephens, *Art Directors in Cinema: A Worldwide Biographical Dictionary* (London, 2008), 251.

After dinner we went to Sam Katz's office for a conference. Immediately I was told that all ideas of the original story, and of having Clark Gable and Jean Harlow, had been discarded. Sam held forth that it was dangerous to have two principal leads who could not sing, play in a musical, and suggested that whatever story we decided upon should be done by singing and dancing people. I remarked that this had been my contention when the first conference took place, but that they had persuaded me that the box-office draw of two such great stars as Gable and Harlow would give the picture importance, which would make up for their not singing. So I found myself holding up for their ideas at the first conference, and they holding up for mine at this second conference. Soon it became evident that the authors had no story in mind at all. Someone suggested why not do a musical of "If I Had a Million",* but Sam did not like the idea, as he wanted a boy and girl love story running through a revue. It was suggested that no audience would pull for a boy and girl if they were consistently being interrupted by a large concerted dance routine. So this was discarded.

The next suggestion was that we do a story based upon the sightseeing automobile, which shows the homes of the movie stars in Hollywood. This in order to utilize all the stars on the lot.

Then someone said, "I have a great idea for the beginning of a picture. Why not show in an opening chorus a long line of people waiting to see the body of a dead movie actor, and then take up the separate lives of the people who are waiting in line." This was met with great enthusiasm for a few minutes, and then suddenly the whole crowd turned on the suggestion.

Several other suggestions were presented. Finally Jack McGowan said to me, "Cole, why don't you write an opening chorus, and it may be we can get a story from that?" By this time I felt as if I were attending a performance of "Once In a Lifetime", or "Boy Meets Girl",† but I was not

---

* A 1932 Paramount anthology film based on the narrative conceit of a wealthy businessman who leaves his money to eight strangers.

† *Once in a Lifetime*, a 1932 Universal Pictures film in which three vaudeville performers, whose acts have been cancelled due to the success of *The Jazz Singer*, head to Hollywood to break into the film business. *Boy Meets Girl*, a 1935 Broadway comedy by Sam and Bella Spewack (later the book writers for Porter's *Kiss Me, Kate*), was the basis in 1938 for a Warner Bros. film of the same name, starring James Cagney and Pat O'Brien.

upset, on account of the numerous warnings I had received from others who had come to Hollywood.

Then, one by one each of the people at the conference took me in the other room, patted me on the back and told me not to worry. As a parting shot, Sam Katz said to the authors, "Try to think of a story within a reasonable time, and when you get it, let Cole know." The authors then gaily suggested to Sam Katz that they all have a vacation in the desert, and he said, "Yes, boys, by all means."

Then Sam Katz drew me aside and said, "Now, Cole, don't worry about authors, because I can spend $200,000 on authors in order to give you the right script. Goodbye, Cole, come back in a few weeks."

This was the end of the conference.

MONDAY, JANUARY 13, 1936

Present: Eric Hatch
                Alexander Aarons
                Jack Cummings.*

They came to the house for lunch, as a result of having called me up and told me that at last they had a great idea for my picture.

On arrival, Jack Cummings took me aside and told me that McGowan and Silvers had been thrown out of the picture, as they were exhausted from just having finished "Broadway Melody."

Jack Cummings is to be the producer of my picture, and he is another member of "The Family." "The Family" means that he is related to Louis B. Mayer,[†] as is practically every other person you meet on the Metro lot.

The idea of the picture was this – a boy and a girl on newspaper syndicates try separately to win the Pulitzer Prize for the best-written newspaper story of the year. They are in love, but in competition, and finally together write a story which wins the Prize.

Cummings suggested that we show relief maps of two hemispheres, and that, say, we were going to cover a story in Tibet, an electric line

---

* Jack Cummings (1900–89) was a film producer and director; he was married to Betty Kern, daughter of Jerome Kern. Cummings later produced the film version of *Kiss Me, Kate*; see below, p. 454.

† Louis B. Mayer (1884–1957), one of the twentieth century's pre-eminent film producers, co-founder with Marcus Loew of Metro-Goldwyn-Mayer (MGM) in 1924.

would take us from the newspaper office across America, over the Pacific into a certain spot in the Himalayas. This method of presenting sketches to be used throughout the picture.

As it was explained to me, I liked it much better than anything that had been suggested so far, and we parted very exhilarated.

I immediately got to work on an opening number and finished it.

TUESDAY, JANUARY 14, 1936

Sam Katz telephoned me and asked me to be at his house at 2:00 P.M. for a conference. I went there and found Cummings, McGowan and Silvers. Before we started, Sam drew me aside and told me that Hatch had been thrown out of the picture. He then announced to us all that he had just had a meeting with Louis B. Mayer, and that Mayer definitely wanted my picture to be a revue, in order to utilize all of the stars on the lot. Then there was a long discussion as to whether or not to use "As Thousands Cheer", which Metro owns.* Once more they all suggested to me that I write a new "Man Bites Dog", which was the opening sketch in the stage production of "As Thousands Cheer." I killed this as soon as possible, knowing I could not possibly top Irving's number.

By this time all thought of "As Thousands Cheer" had disappeared, and Sam said, "I don't think we should use 'As Thousands Cheer' at all. I think we should make this the 'Metro Revue,' and all we need is a central idea to start it off.["]

Silvers, thinking of the days when he used to be a stooge for Phil Baker in vaudeville,† suggested we open by showing him in the box of a theater watching a stage performance. No one liked this idea, and for half an hour there was complete havoc. Then I suggested that it might be interesting to base our Revue on the different sections of a newspaper.‡ If this device were taken, all we would have to do would be to plant the

---

* *As Thousands Cheer*, revue, book by Moss Hart, music and lyrics by Irving Berlin. Premiered at the Music Box Theatre, New York, on 30 September 1933, the show ran for 400 performances until 8 September 1934.

† Phil Baker (1896–1963) was a comedian. Baker and Sid Silvers were a vaudeville act from about 1919 to 1928, after which Baker pursued a solo career.

‡ This is not much different from the plot device for *As Thousands Cheer*, sketches loosely based on then-current news items and the affairs of the rich and famous. It was not adopted for what eventually became *Born to Dance*.

newspaper in the beginning, then turn the pages to find our different sketches. They all leaped at this, as if I had suddenly discovered radium, and Sam suggested that after such a great idea I should go to the desert and take three weeks rest. Silvers and McGowan then asked if they could go too. So for a few minutes it looked as if I were going to the desert alone with two maniacs. I insisted that we begin work on this Revue immediately, and here in Hollywood, as time was flying, so it was decided that tomorrow Silvers and McGowan come to the house at 2 p.m., and we talk all afternoon – every afternoon. They wanted to come in the morning at 11 and remain all day, but I firmly announced it was too long a session for me, and that I did my best work alone.

That was the end of this conference.

***

On arriving home, Alexander Aarons called me up and I told him what had taken place. He said that within a few days I should go myself to Sam Katz and tell him that it is impossible to work with McGowan and Silvers.

We shall see.

WEDNESDAY, JANUARY 15, 1936

Present: Jack McGowan
             Sid Silvers.

They appeared immediately after lunch and announced that, after thinking the matter over, they did not like the Revue being based upon the different sections of a newspaper. They began to discuss the Eric Hatch idea of the boy and girl rivalry on a newspaper, and decided they did not like that either. Then McGowan suggested we do a picture based upon the pursuit of John Barrymore by Elaine Barrie, and give up all idea of writing a Revue, but instead do a straight musical story.

I suggested that Sam Katz's reason for wanting me to do a revue was to utilize all the stars on the lot. Then Silvers asked me, "Do you want to do a Revue?" I said, "No, I don't believe I do, unless we can find a revolutionary idea, but I have great respect for Sam Katz, and as long as he clings to a Revue so much, I want to give him a few days before I tell him definitely that nobody has been able to present an idea good enough to warrant doing one." At this Silvers and McGowan yelled with joy, and said, "We don't want to do a Revue either and we had hoped you would say yesterday that you didn't, when we all met."

McGowan went on to explain that before my arrival at the conference yesterday, Sam Katz told them that what he would like to do, would be to throw out Freed and Brown, the songwriters of the next BROADWAY MELODY,* and give me the score, but that he could not do it because it would break their hearts.

There was a period of silence, during which McGowan read the New Yorker, and Sid Silvers began nursing a large whisky and soda. Suddenly McGowan leaped to his feet and cried "I have a great idea." The only reason Katz doesn't want to throw Freed and Brown out of the BROADWAY MELODY is, because they did the first BROADWAY MELODY, but if we change the title of the second BROADWAY MELODY to something else and write a new Broadway Melody for them, they cannot complain. Silvers thought this was the greatest idea that McGowan ever had, and suggested that they both rush to the office and tell Katz, but I persuaded them not to do this, but instead bring me the script tomorrow and let me see whether or not I like it, before speaking about this violent change in plans.

So, they left feeling that everything had been solved, and we are meeting again tomorrow.

THURSDAY, JANUARY 16, 1936
Present: Sid Silvers
            Jack McGowan.

Arrived 3 p.m. I asked them whether or not they had found, overnight, any idea for a Revue, and both of them confessed that they had been so drunk that they had not thought of pictures since they left the house yesterday.

Then I asked whether they still liked the idea of changing the title of the new BROADWAY MELODY, and giving me the script. They both

---

* *Broadway Melody of 1938* (MGM, 1937), with music and lyrics by Nacio Herb Brown (1896–1964) and Arthur Freed (1894–1973). Brown, who mostly wrote individual songs (often uncredited) for films during the 1930s, is best remembered for 'Singin' in the Rain', which was featured in *The Hollywood Revue of 1929* (MGM, 1929); Freed had written the lyrics, and Brown the music, for *Broadway Melody of 1936* (MGM, 1935).

decided it would be impossible to make this suggestion, on account of the danger of breaking Freed and Brown's hearts. So they told me the complete story of BROADWAY MELODY, which took about an hour. McGowan then brought up a play that he had written in New York last year for Harry Richman called Say When,* and asked me whether I would like to use it. I could not remember it well, after so long a time, so he told me the story of "Say When".† I asked whether Metro owned this, and he said "no, but he thought if I asked for it they would buy it from him."

By this time we realized it was entirely useless that we ever meet again, and I made an appointment with them to go to Sam Katz's office tomorrow and tell him the way we feel about his Revue. On the way out they both asked me to come to their office about half an hour before the appointment so that we could all say the same thing.

Then they said "Goodnight."

FRIDAY, JANUARY 17, 1936

Went to the office of Jack McGowan and Sid Silvers at 11:30, and they were both in a state of jitters, and also rather terrified at the idea of announcing to Sam Katz that we did not want to do a Revue, but I told them not to worry, that I thought I could explain our reasons without upsetting him too much.

So at 12:00 we went to the office of Sam Katz. In came Jack Cummings, who had obviously been ordered to listen in. I explained to Sam that after a great deal of conversation amongst us about some angle for a revue, we could get no further, because in our hearts none of us wanted to do a revue, and that the boys had contributed nothing to me and I had contributed nothing to them. I told him I felt guilty accepting so large an amount of money per week and not being able to work on something about which I was enthusiastic. Told him what I could do well would be a Cinderella story on a low-comedy premise, with Eleanor

---

* Musical comedy, book by Jack McGowan, lyrics by Ted Koehler, and music by Ray Henderson. *Say When* had a short run of seventy-six performances at the Imperial Theatre, New York, from 8 November 1934 to 12 January 1935.

† The plot of *Say When* revolves around two vaudevillians who fall in love with two girls from Long Island high society; see Brooks Atkinson's review in the *New York Times*, 9 November 1934, 24.

Powell* in mind. I could see that he was very disappointed, but was somewhat assuaged by my suggestion, in that it included the person of all who he is trying to make an important star – Eleanor Powell. So he very nicely said, "Then boys, we will give up all idea of a Revue, and all you have to do is find what Cole is looking for." McGowan suggested a musical, based upon a six-day bicycle race. Silvers did not like this, and thought a radio story would show off Powell to her greatest tap-dancing ability.

"Say When" was brought up again, but it obviously could not do anything for Powell, so this was discarded.

Suddenly Silvers thought of a musical play that he, McGowan and Buddy De Sylva† had worked on four years ago, about two sailors and the hostess of a lonely-hearts club. McGowan brought up the objection that De Sylva would probably have to be paid about $5000 for his rights in the property, but Sam waved that aside saying, "Oh, that's all right, boys; don't let that stop you." As they explained it, it sounded amusing and a good vehicle for Powell. Sam was obviously pleased.

Just then the telephone rang and it was Max Gordon on the wire, speaking from Philadelphia about the terrible sketches in the new Follies.‡ Sam and Max talked a long time about this, then I was called to the telephone, and a great deal of conversation went on as to whether I was having a good time in California. I told Max I was.

During the telephone call, Sam must have found time to think, because the minute it was over, he said, "Now boys, I like this idea for your picture very much, but why couldn't you lay it in Honolulu instead of New York?" The boys explained to him that this was impossible. So he

---

* Eleanor Powell (1912–82) was a dancer and actor. Well known for her solo tap-dance numbers, Powell, who took the role of Nora Paige in *Born to Dance*, also appeared in Porter's musical films *Rosalie* (MGM, 1937) and *Broadway Melody of 1940* (MGM, 1940).

† 'George Gard Buddy' DeSylva (1895–1950) was a songwriter, film producer and, together with Johnny Mercer and Glenn Wallichs, founder of Capitol Records. DeSylva was involved in the production of at least twenty Broadway shows between 1919 and 1932, including George Gershwin's *La La Lucille* (1919) and *George White's Scandals* (1922–6). His credits as a film producer included the early Shirley Temple films *The Little Colonel* and *The Littlest Rebel* (both Fox, 1935) and *Captain January* and *Poor Little Rich Girl* (both Fox, 1936).

‡ *Ziegfeld Follies of 1936* (Winter Garden Theatre, New York, 30 January–9 May and 14 September–19 December 1936), with music by Vernon Duke and lyrics by Ira Gershwin.

said, "Well, anyway, give me one character and one scene that I have always clung to: the character, a female wharf rat who can sing torch songs; and the scene, two battleships, one full of boys and one full of girls, to be used as a setting for a comedy lead-up to an important march song.["] This did not seem to upset anybody, and as I left, Sam said to McGowan and Silvers, "You boys go away now and try to bring me back an idea in two weeks."

That was the end of this conference.

****

On the way home in the motor, I figured out, by computing the salaries of the writers engaged on this picture so far, that it had cost MGM $29,000 to decide not to do a Revue.

TUESDAY, JANUARY 21, 1936

Jack McGowan telephoned. I asked him whether they had gone away and he said no, because Sid Silvers was ill, and he wanted to make an appointment with me to go to see Sam Katz to find out "where we were at," that he and Sid Silvers were to see Buddy De Sylva to find out whether Buddy would sell his rights to this idea for a picture for $5000.00. He replied that he had just talked to Buddy, but Buddy wouldn't sell for less than $12,000.00. $12,000.00 seemed to me very expensive.

2:00 p.m.

Sam Katz telephoned me to say that he had arranged for the release of Laura Hope Crews for the Boland part in "Jubilee."* I said, "Sam, how about my picture?", and he said, "Don't worry, my boy, we will find an idea in a few weeks. In the meantime, take advantage of California and get a lot of health."

THURSDAY, JANUARY 23[, 1936]

Sam Katz telephoned, saying, "Cole, I have great news for you. I bought the idea for that picture from Buddy De Sylva and it only cost me $17,000.00." That was all.

---

* Laura Hope Crews (1879–1942) and Mary Boland (1882–1965) were stage and, later, film actresses.

TUESDAY, JANUARY 28[, 1936]

I came in and found that Jack Cummings had telephoned, so I gave him a ring and asked what he wanted. He replied, "I only telephoned to find out how you liked California." I said "How about my picture?", and his reply was, "I don't know anything about your picture, I just got back from Palm Springs, I've been there for the last ten days, why don't you go there?" Then he rang off.

WEDNESDAY, JANUARY 29[, 1936]

I found a message to call up Jack McGowan. I called him and asked why he had telephoned. He said "I just wanted to call you up to tell you not to be discouraged, and to say that if you wanted Sid or me to see you, we could come over anytime and say 'hello.'" I said "Have you worked out any story yet?" He replied "No, nothing yet." So I told him that it might be better that we not meet until they had found at least some outline of a story. This seemed to delight him and he rang off.

FRIDAY, JANUARY 31, 1936

Sam Katz telephoned and said, "Have you seen the boys lately?" I said "No, Sam, I haven't, but I talked to McGowan on the telephone and asked him whether he and Sid Silvers had as yet found a story, and he said, 'No, they had not.'" I suggested that we not meet again until they had.

This pleased Sam very much and he said "That's absolutely right, Cole, it would only be confusing to you, so just let them alone until they find a story, and in the meantime have a good time and get the benefits of California. Goodbye."

WEDNESDAY, FEBRUARY 12th, 1936

Sam Katz telephoned and said "How are you, Cole, and do you still like California?" I told him I did, and then he added, "I think the boys have really gone to work and they might have something for you by the end of the week. Goodbye, Cole."

FRIDAY, FEBRUARY 14th[, 1936]

Sam Katz telephoned again to say that McGowan and Silvers wanted to meet me sometime on Monday, so we made an appointment for 2:30 next Monday, February 17th.

MONDAY, FEBRUARY 17th, 1936
CONFERENCE IN OFFICE OF MR. SAM KATZ

PRESENT: Sam Katz, Jack Cummings, Jack McGowan and Max Gordon* listening in. (Max Gordon is being paid $2500 per week for 12 weeks to listen in at conferences.)

Once we were settled in our very comfortable chairs, Sam said to Jack McGowan, "Now, Jack, tell Cole the story you worked out." Then Jack began, "Well, we open our picture with a shot of the New York harbor, where three sailors (Allan Jones, Sid Silvers and Buddy Ebsen†) are being given an important letter by the captain of their boat, to deliver to an admiral in Washington." Then he stopped a moment and said, "Hell, Sam, that's all wrong." And Sam said, "Yes, that isn't the opening that you told me the other day, at all." There was a short silence until Jack said, "I'm sorry, Cole, but I can't remember any of it. Sid is in bed with the flu and you'll have to wait until he gets out, and then we'll tell you the story."

So Sam suggested that Jack McGowan give me a list of the characters they plan to have in this picture. As the list progressed, I was suddenly very surprised to hear that there would be a troupe of Japanese acrobats in the Lonely Hearts Club, but as the scene of acrobats with Silvers was described it sounded very funny. Sam didn't laugh with the rest of us, and I couldn't understand why, until he said, "Jack, you can't make those acrobats Japanese, on account of the danger of political trouble, make them 'Arabs.'" Jack said, "Sam, they're supposed to be spies." To which Sam retorted, "Then make them 'Arab' spies."‡

When we had discussed the characters a bit, Sam said to me "Now, Cole, my boy, Sid will be out of the hospital by the end of the week, and

---

* Max Gordon (1892–1978) was a theatre and later film producer. His early theatrical successes included the original stage version of *The Jazz Singer* (Fulton Theatre and Cort Theatre, New York, 14 September 1925), *The Band Wagon* (New Amsterdam Theatre, 6 March 1931), and Jerome Kern's *Roberta* (New Amsterdam Theatre, 18 November 1933). Gordon is mentioned in Porter's song, 'Anything Goes': 'When Rockefeller still can hoard en- / Ough money to let Max Gordon / Produce his shows, / Anything goes.'

† The dancer and actor Buddy Ebsen (1908–2003) had appeared with Eleanor Powell in *Broadway Melody of 1936* (MGM, 1935); in *Born to Dance* he took the role of 'Mush' Tracy. The actor Allan Jones (1907–92), who appeared in the Marx Brothers' *A Night at the Opera* (MGM, 1935) and *Show Boat* (Universal, 1936), did not, finally, appear in *Born to Dance*; see below.

‡ In the film as it was released there are neither Japanese nor Arab acrobat spies.

I will give you a ring and you can talk with him before we go away." I said, "Sam, what do you mean, 'go away'?" He replied, "Well, I am taking the boys and their wives, on Saturday, for a little trip to Panama. We will get back about the tenth of March and by that time I think we ought to have an outline of the story."

Jack McGowan had been very silent during the last few moments, and suddenly he leaped to his feet saying, "I have a great idea. Instead of making them sailors on a battleship, why not make them sailors on a submarine?" This caused great enthusiasm, especially as we had all been secretly thinking that this picture was going to be singularly reminiscent of "FOLLOW THE FLEET",* but Sam didn't like this idea at all, and he said, "You know, Max, I always wanted to have a scene showing two battleships, one covered with boys and one covered with girls." Jack Cummings immediately stifled him by saying, "Sam, we can get just as good an effect if you have those three sailors on a submarine, because we can get the entire Atlantic fleet to put on a parade for us and have the submarine at the tail end of it." This calmed Sam, and, from now on, it's agreed that the three sailors will be "three sailors on a submarine."

That was the end of the conference.

TUESDAY, MARCH 3, 1936

The following radio was forwarded from Sam Katz's secretary to me:

"Advise Cole Porter our story line complete. Stop. Our opening song must approximate traditional stirring navy song to be sung by male chorus in beginning and reprise for final.† Stop. Cole Porter can begin working on this now and try to have same ready for us on our return. Regards."

TUESDAY, MARCH 10, 1936

Arthur Lyons telephoned saying: RKO wanted to borrow me from MGM and start me working within two weeks on the next Fred Astaire

---

* *Follow the Fleet* (RKO, 1936), in which a sailor (Fred Astaire) attempts to rekindle a romance with the woman he loves (Ginger Rogers) while on liberty in San Francisco.

† 'Rolling Home'.

picture,* and asked if I was interested. Of course, I was interested, and when about ten minutes later Sam Katz telephoned and said, "Hurry out to the studio, I want to read you the story we have for you", I was very downhearted, thinking that I had to throw up a great job for a mediocre picture. But once I arrived in his office and sat with Max Gordon and Jack Cummings, as Sam read the scenario and a great deal of the dialogue of the picture which McGowan and Silvers are writing for me, all qualms left and I realized that I had fallen on a wonderful film.

When it was over, I played the opening number (which he had wirelessed me about) and they were so delighted with it they all kissed me. Then I played another number which I had just finished, "It's De-Lovely", and they were equally enthusiastic about it and spotted it immediately in the story.*

We went into details about what I would have to write, and in checking up on the musical numbers, I found that there will be a total of seven (7) numbers at most, three (3) of which I have written.

*This was later thrown out.†

TUESDAY, MARCH 10, 1936

We discussed casting, and I heard to my great joy that the picture will be played by Allan Jones opposite Eleanor Powell, Sid Silvers opposite Una Merkel, Buddy Ebsen opposite Judy Garland, and Frances Langford to play the jilted society girl.‡

At the end of the conference, Sam said to me, "You will notice there is no mention of one battleship covered with boys and another battleship

---

* Astaire's next film turned out to be the George and Ira Gershwin *Shall We Dance* (Paramount, 1937). At this time, March 1936, Astaire's two 1936 RKO films, *Follow the Fleet* and *Swing Time*, had either already been released (*Follow the Fleet* on 20 February) or were already in production (*Swing Time* was released on 12 October).

† 'It's De-Lovely' was not used in *Born to Dance* but appeared in *Red, Hot and Blue!* (1936). 'Which I had just finished' suggests that 'It's De-Lovely' was composed – or that Porter at the time gave the impression it was composed – about March 1936, which contradicts two other accounts he gave of the song's origin, or at least the origin of its title. See pp. 238–9 for alternative explanations of its genesis.

‡ The part of Ted Barker, intended for Allan Jones, was taken by James Stewart (1908–97). The actress Una Merkel (1903–86) played the role of Jenny Saks, and the part intended for the actress and singer Judy Garland (1922–69), 'Peppy' Turner, was given to Frances Langford. The role of the 'jilted society girl', Lucy James, intended for Langford, was taken by the actress Virginia Bruce (1910–82).

covered with girls, but Jack McGowan and Sid Silvers are doing their best to work it in."

THURSDAY, MARCH 12th, 1936

Conference in the office of Sam Katz. Present: Sam Katz, Jack McGowan, Sid Silvers, Jack Cummings.

McGowan read aloud the outline of the story and the dialogue that they had finished so far, and once more I was convinced that they have presented me with a great picture.

I played them all the numbers which I had finished, including a new one that I wrote last night for Frances Langford. It's called "Goodbye, Little Dream, Goodbye." This number seemed to have much greater success than I could have ever expected. They sang it over and over again, and at the finish Sam Katz said to me, "You know, Cole, that song is beautiful, it's – why it's Jewish."

FRIDAY, MARCH 13th, 1936

As the result of "Goodbye, Little Dream, Goodbye", Major Zanft* asked me to come to see him at his office. He told me that people in the Katz unit had dined last night with the powers at Paramount and they raved so over this new song that Paramount had asked him to offer me $50,000. for two months' work on the next Crosby picture.[†] I refused, first, because it was a Crosby picture; second, because the locale was Hawaii, and third, on account of the California tax law.[‡]

Arthur Lyons called me up to tell me about the excitement "Goodbye, Little Dream, Goodbye"* had caused on the MGM lot, and added that the Katz outfit had hinted to him that they would like to have me back

---

* John Zanft (1883–1960) was a veteran of World War I who was given the honorary title Major for arranging troop entertainments during World War II. Zanft later wrote a theatrical column under the name 'John Zan' and was vice-president of the Fox Theatre Corporation.

† What eventually was *Waikiki Wedding* (Paramount, 1937). By this time, Crosby's last film of 1936, *Pennies from Heaven* (Major Pictures Corp.), would already have been in production.

‡ Prior to 1930, changes in California's tax structure addressed inequalities in tax rates, rather than state revenue; these were changed during the Depression to make up for shortfalls in revenue; see https://www.boe.ca.gov/info/pub216/revenue_crisis.html (accessed 19 April 2018).

next year for the same length of time, but for $100,000, instead of the paltry $75,000 that I am struggling along with now.

This was later thrown out.

MONDAY, MARCH 16th, 1936

Conference in the office of Mr. Sam Katz. Present: Sam Katz, Jack McGowan and Sid Silvers.

I arrived to find Jack and Sid very excited over having thought of a title for our picture, to wit: "GREAT GUNS." I didn't like it, nor did Sam, especially, but the boys were so enthusiastic that we let them rave on.

They also had an idea that the reprise of the opening song of the picture should be used as the entrance for Langford, which would mean throwing out "Rolling Home." I said nothing about this, but after they left I told Sam I was going to fight them on it.

THURSDAY, MARCH 19th, 1936

Conference in office of Mr. Sam Katz. Present: Sam Katz, Max Gordon, Jack Cummings, Jack McGowan, Sid Silvers.

McGowan read aloud a lot of new dialogue, and it was grand. Then I played them a Honky-Tonk-Waltz-Clog, "Hey, Babe, Hey", and it was a thundering success.

Then Sam led in a tubercular-snore specialist, called Robert Wildhack,† who proceeded to amuse us a great deal with a new routine showing the different ways of saying "yes".

Then a boy of sixteen was led in, a waif from West Virginia, who performed on the harmonica, and gave one of the greatest performances I had ever heard, especially when he used his nose instead of his mouth. After the two performers had left, Sam explained that he was using them in the boys' next picture and wanted me to hear them.

We all parted very exuberant.

---

* 'Goodbye, Little Dream, Goodbye' was not finally used in *Born to Dance*. Porter considered it for the stage show *Red, Hot and Blue!* and it was included in the Boston tryout (October 1936), but then dropped from the production as too sombre for an opening number; see Kimball, *The Complete Lyrics of Cole Porter*, 202.

† Robert Wildhack (1881–1940) was an actor. He started in vaudeville delivering monologues and appeared as 'The Snorer' in *Broadway Melody of 1936* (MGM, 1935).

TUESDAY, MARCH 31st, 1936
CONFERENCE IN OFFICE OF MR. SAM KATZ

Present: Sam Katz and Max Gordon.

I played them a new rhythm song which I had just finished for Eleanor Powell called "RAP TAP ON WOOD."

Sam Katz was so pleased with it that he began talking to me about planning from now on to come back every year on January 1 and work for him until June 1, and he added "Next January will be especially interesting for you, because that is when we are going to shoot your present picture." This scared me a little bit, knowing as I do so well how quickly songs date.

Also on 31 March, during his stay in Hollywood, Porter wrote to Monty Woolley, congratulating him on his success in Rodgers and Hart's *On Your Toes*:

31 March 1936: Cole Porter to Monty Woolley[32]

Beardie –

The notices arrived from the Boston papers, & how grand they were. And today – Variety, + I cried. And the show* sounds so attractive + I'm so happy for you. And bless that dear Dwight [Deere Wiman] for realizing what the rest of us only feared, that, from your cradle you were destined to be a magnificent ham.

We are proud of you + the wire I sent you about Marie Dressler is barely an exaggeration.

Linda talks of you all day long. I think the thing that has impressed her most is that you had a manicure. She said to me tonight "You know, in time, he might even eat fruit."

But there's no kidding about all this. You have landed + beautifully + I only beg you to behave + not vomit on Luella.†

You might even give her my love.

Goodnight, Edgar

Potah

He continued his diary on 2 April 1936:

---

* *On Your Toes* subsequently opened in New York on 11 April. Woolley played the part of Sergei Alexandrovitch.

† Possibly the screenwriter and movie columnist Louella Parsons (1881–1972).

THURSDAY, APRIL 2nd, 1936
CONFERENCE IN OFFICE OF MR. SAM KATZ

Present: Sam Katz, Max Gordon,
           Jack Cummings, Jack McGowan
           Sid Silvers.

I played the authors "RAP TAP ON WOOD", and they were delighted with it. So that means another number in the bag.

Then McGowan read aloud the love scene leading up to what I thought would be "I'VE GOT YOU UNDER MY SKIN", but as he read it, I realized that this song would be entirely unfitting.* So I left, promising to write another one.

MONDAY, APRIL 13th, 1936
CONFERENCE IN OFFICE OF MR. SAM KATZ

Present: Sam Katz and Max Gordon.

I took in a number on which I had been working very hard for the past week, called "WHO BUT YOU", and played it for them. Even as I was playing, they walked away from the piano and looked out the window, and at the finish of it they told me it was absolutely no good.†

Then the authors came in and read me some new material, which was excellent. Sam suggested that I play them the number that I had brought in, but I refused, as I knew there was no chance of its going over his head. So we discussed putting back "I'VE GOT YOU UNDER MY SKIN". They all decided they wanted that song, but when I left I knew it was wrong, and much too romantic a number for this character to sing.

TUESDAY, APRIL 14th, 1936
Conference in office of Mr. Sam Katz

Present: Sam Katz, Max Gordon, Jack McGowan, Sid Silvers, Jack Cummings and Seymour Felix (Dance Director)‡

---

* It did, however, become part of a later scene, sung by Virginia Bruce.

† Porter later considered using 'Who But You?' in *Red, Hot and Blue!*, although it was eventually dropped from that show as well.

‡ Seymour Felix (1892–1961) was a director and choreographer active on Broadway in the 1920s and in Hollywood from 1933.

I played them a song which I had resurrected and rewritten last night, called "EASY TO LOVE".* The response was instantaneous. They all grabbed the lyric and began singing it, and even called in the stenographers to hear it, their enthusiasm was so great. When the singing was finally over, Seymour Felix got on his knees in front of Sam, Katz and said, "Oh, please Mr. Katz, let me stage that song when the picture is shot."!

So left once again very happy.

MONDAY, APRIL 20th, 1936
CONFERENCE IN OFFICE OF SAM KATZ
Present: Sam Katz   Jack McGowan
             Sid Silvers   Jack Cummings

I took in "I'VE GOT YOU UNDER MY SKIN" and they all liked it very much. Sam Katz asked me to get hold of Frances Langford at once and coach her for the song so she could come out and demonstrate it as soon as she was ready.

WEDNESDAY, APRIL 22nd, 1936
CONFERENCE IN OFFICE OF SAM KATZ
Present: Sam Katz, Sid Silvers, Jack McGowan, Jack Cummings, Roy Del Ruth (who is to direct the picture).†

McGowan read the entire script, and I played all the numbers finished up to date. Del Ruth, who is supposed to be a very taciturn person, was most enthusiastic and told us he thought we had a great picture.

FRIDAY, APRIL 24th, 1936
CONFERENCE IN OFFICE OF SAM KATZ
Present: Sam Katz, Sid Silvers, Jack McGowan and Jack Cummings.

I took in the verse to "EASY TO LOVE" and they seemed to feel that it would fit perfectly.

Then the discussion began as to who would play the lead, as Allan Jones had just opened in the Show Boat‡ and is so bad that Sam Katz doesn't want him any more.

---

* First written for *Anything Goes* (1934) but revised for *Born to Dance*.
† Roy del Ruth (1893–1961) was a writer and director.
‡ *Show Boat* (Universal Pictures), with Allan Jones taking the role of Gaylord Ravenal, opened on 17 May 1936.

PORTER'S RETURN TO THE UNITED STATES, 1928-1937

After I returned home, I began thinking about James Stewart* as a possibility for the male lead. I talked to Sam Katz about this on the telephone and he thought the idea was most interesting, if Stewart could sing. The next day Stewart came over to the house and I heard him sing. He sings far from well, although he has nice notes in his voice, but he could play the part perfectly.

MONDAY, MAY 11th, 1936
CONFERENCE IN OFFICE OF SAM KATZ

Present: Sam Katz, Jack McGowan, Sid Silvers, Jack Cummings, Roy Del Ruth, Seymour Felix, and a strange man, whose name I did not get.

Frances Langford came in with her manager, and sang the concerted number which I had just finished, "LOVE ME, LOVE MY PEKINESE" and "I'VE GOT YOU UNDER MY SKIN".

The concerted number was received with great enthusiasm, and as for "I'VE GOT YOU UNDER MY SKIN", as sung by Miss Langford, it was what is called in Hollywood "colossal".

Then Sam said, "Now, Cole, I want you to write a SKATING WALTZ. We haven't enough beauty in this picture and I want to sign Sonja Henie[†] for an Ice Ballet." I said, "But, Sam, where can you put it?" He replied, "Well, instead of taking the male lead and the Broadway star to a nightclub, we will take them to a skating rink. The only difficulty about the whole thing is that Henie wants too much money, she wants $100,000, and we only want to give her $50,000." I said "Sam, how long will the sequence take?" He said, "Oh, two minutes."

I left this conference, feeling very happy about the picture but definitely worried as to Sonja Henie and the SKATING WALTZ.

WEDNESDAY, MAY 13th, 1936

Sam Katz telephoned me to say that Del Ruth had been to see him and wanted me to throw out the opening to the picture, "ROLLING HOME". Sam asked me to think this over and let him know.

---

[*] The Hollywood star James ('Jimmy') Stewart, who took the role of the male lead, Ted Barker.
[†] Sonja Henie (1912–69) was a Norwegian figure skater and actress. She won the Olympic gold medal in skating in 1928, 1932 and 1936; signed by Twentieth Century Fox in 1936, she debuted later that year in *One in a Million*. She did not appear in *Born to Dance*.

FRIDAY, MAY 15th, 1936

Jack Cummings and Sid Silvers came to the house. They looked rather embarrassed, and I knew there was bad news in store for me. The bad news WAS that they had all met and decided my opening was no good. After questioning them a little bit I found out WHY they found it no good, and saw an easy solution to adapt it to all their wishes, so the opening stays in.*

SATURDAY, MAY 16th, 1936

Sam Katz telephoned me saying "Cole, I have a great script for next year when you come back to me. It is by Bill McGuire, who wrote The Great Ziegfeld, and it is a wonderful story."† Then he began to describe the story, and it became more and more complicated, and when he finished I had no idea whether it was good or not. But it was nice to know that Sam was thinking seriously of the future.

SUNDAY, MAY 17th, 1936

Sam Katz telephoned – said he had Al Newman for my orchestra director, and Eddie Powell to make the orchestral arrangements.‡ This is a great break for me, as they are the two best men in their lines in Hollywood.

I had been worrying ever since a few days ago about Sonja Henie and the SKATING WALTZ, so I asked Sam the news, and he said, "No, Cole, that's out, she won't come down on her price."

---

* It is not known what Cummings and Silvers felt was wrong with Porter's opening, or what changes Porter made to it. It remained in the film.

† William Anthony McGuire (1881–1940). *The Great Ziegfeld* – which earned McGuire an Oscar nomination for best writing, original story – was released by MGM in 1936.

‡ Alfred Newman (1901–70) was one of Hollywood's best-known composers and arrangers. Newman was nominated for forty-five Oscars during his career and won nine, for *The Hurricane* (The Samuel Goldwyn Company, 1937), *Alexander's Ragtime Band* (Twentieth Century Fox, 1938), *Tin Pan Alley* (Twentieth Century Fox, 1940), *Mother Wore Tights* (Twentieth Century Fox, 1947), *With a Song in My Heart* (Twentieth Century Fox, 1952), *Call Me Madam* (Twentieth Century Fox, 1953), *Love is a Many-Splendored Thing* (Twentieth Century Fox, 1955), *The King and I* (Twentieth Century Fox, 1956) and *Camelot* (Warner Brothers, 1967). Edward B. Powell (1909–84) was a composer and orchestrator. Powell, who most often worked with Newman, is credited on more than 375 films including Charlie Chaplin's *Modern Times* (Charles Chaplin Productions, 1936), *All About Eve* (Twentieth Century Fox, 1950), *Miracle on 34th Street* (Twentieth Century Fox, 1947), and *The King and I* (Twentieth Century Fox, 1956). Newman was the musical director for *Born to Dance* and Powell the orchestrator.

PORTER'S RETURN TO THE UNITED STATES, 1928–1937

TUESDAY, MAY 19th, 1936

Present: Jack Cummings, Roger Edens,* Eddie Powell, Al Newman, Sid Silvers, and the head of the Music Department (whose name I do not know).

They all came to the house. I plied them with whiskies and sodas, and then played the entire score. Even if the score had been awful, none of them would have known it, as they all felt so well, but they left saying it was the greatest thing they had heard in years.

WEDNESDAY, MAY 20th, 1936
CONFERENCE IN ROGER EDENS'S OFFICE

Present: Sam Katz, Seymour Felix, Mr. Pye (the art director), Sid Silvers, Jack McGowan, Roy Del Ruth, Al Newman, Eddie Powell, Commander Haislett [sic],† Virginia Bruce.

Virginia Bruce gave us an audition of "I'VE GOT YOU UNDER MY SKIN" and "LOVE ME, LOVE MY PEKINESE". She sang them very well indeed and, after she had left, they definitely decided to throw out Frances Langford and use Bruce instead.

Then I played the finale to them,

"SWINGIN' THE JINX AWAY"

and it went with a bang. So my troubles are nearly over.

Just as I was leaving, somebody came in and said, "Sonja is making her tests," so I said "Sam, are you going to use Sonja Henie after all?" He said, "Well, Cole, we haven't quite decided yet, but if her tests are good, I think we will take her, although I still think $100,000 is too much money." So I shall have to begin thinking about that SKATING WALTZ again.

Then Sam took me to his office and gave me the McGuire script, about which he telephoned me a few days ago. I left the studio very happy

---

* Roger Edens (1905–70) was a composer, arranger and producer. He shared Academy Awards for best score for *Easter Parade* (MGM, 1948, with Johnny Green), *On the Town* (MGM, 1949, with Lennie Hayton) and *Annie Get Your Gun* (1950, with Adolph Deutsch). Edens made the musical arrangements for *Born to Dance*.

† Harvey S. Haislip USN (retired) (1889–1978) was marine advisor for *Born to Dance*; the author of several U.S. Navy sea adventure novels, Haislip was awarded the Distinguished Service Medal for his duty as commanding officer of the USS *Stewart* during World War I.

about the picture, as the enthusiasm from everybody is so great. They start shooting on June 15* and it is practically sure that they have the Pacific fleet. Del Ruth says the picture should be ready for release on October first.†

TUESDAY, MAY 26th, 1936

Sam Katz called me to the telephone while I was in the midst of an excellent egg, and said "Cole, can you take a great shock?" My reply was a groan, and then he said, "Your Finale 'Swingin' The Jinx Away' is out." When I recovered sufficiently to speak I said, "Sam, I know this is wrong," and he said "Everybody has decided the lyric is wrong and the tune hasn't enough drive", so I gave him a "Goodbye" and hung up the telephone. I called Sid Silvers and Jack McGowan immediately and they were outraged. It seems that all this developed from Mr. Del Ruth and Mr. Seymour Felix having planned elaborate production effects on the water, which they felt could not follow my number, even if the tune were any good, and they had decided it was not. One of the details of the production was to be a fleet of motorboats covered with girls.

I called up Sam Katz in the evening and told him I still felt that my tune was right, and that my lyric was right, in that it established the swing as a National institution, and that if he would only arrange for a curtain back of the singer this number, showing the capitol of Washington, those concerned with the production of it could go anywhere afterwards, as long as it was America. Also pointed out that the song would have value on account of the elections next autumn. By this time Sam completely agreed with me regarding the lyric, but still thought the tune was not any good. So, I called up Silvers and McGowan again and told them what had happened. They recounted their interview with Sam Katz in the afternoon. It seems that Del Ruth and Felix had turned him to such an extent against the finale that he was not at all sure that any of my

---

* According to *Variety*, 15 July 1936, *Born to Dance* did not go into production until the week of 7 July: 'Hollywood, July 14. Metro's "Born to Dance" went into production last week after long rehearsal of a flash number "I'm Nuts About You" . . .'

† *Born to Dance* was released on 27 November.

tunes were any good, or that I had ever written a good tune. So they had to get up and give an audition and sing every hit I have had since I started writing.

WEDNESDAY, MAY 27th, 1936

Jack Cummings telephoned me and asked if I would come out to the studio and discuss the Finale with them all. I refused, saying that as far as I was concerned the Finale was the best I could possibly do, and that furthermore it seemed very topsy-turvy that a director and a dance director should dictate to me what I should write, and pointed out that if this occurred in the Theatre and the director and the dance director announced that they could not produce a number which I had written, we always got a new Director and a new Dance Director. Then I rang off.

In the evening Linda and I dined with Sam Katz at his house. It was a very pleasant dinner with excellent Chinese food, followed by beautiful singing by Igor Gorin.* There was no mention made of the Finale until we left, and then Sam came out to the car with me and said "Well, Cole, old boy, you were right; I had two piano arrangements made of your Finale, and after hearing it several times, I think the lyric is not only right, but you have written a great tune, so your worries are over." But in the meantime, I called up Arthur Lyons† and told him to cancel any arrangements with Sam Katz about making my contracts for next year. We shall not go into that until all my work has been accepted and approved on this present job.

FRIDAY, MAY 29th, 1936

Miss Moore‡ telephoned me at the swimming pool to say that Jack Cummings wanted me to come out and discuss the Finale with Del Ruth

---

* Charles Igor Gorin (Ignatz Greenberg, 1904–82) was a singer and music teacher. Trained as an opera singer, Gorin was cantor at the Leopoldstrasse Synagogue in Vienna; he fled Austria for the United States in 1933. A frequent performer on radio and, later, television, Gorin appeared as Nicki Papaloopas in *Broadway Melody of 1938* (MGM, 1937).

† Arthur Lyons (1906–93) was Cole Porter's agent in Hollywood. His other clients included Jack Benny, Joan Crawford, Lucille Ball, Ray Milland, Hedy Lamarr, Jerome Kern and Eugene O'Neill.

‡ Cole Porter's secretary.

and Eddie Powell. So I called up Jack and said "Has Del Ruth teamed Eleanor Powell with him against me on my finale?" and he replied "Well, he is very set against it and Eleanor says she can't dance to it." I made an appointment to go out to the studio at 4 in the afternoon.

Then I began telephoning. First I telephoned to Roger Edens and to Eddie Powell, and asked them to be there. Then I telephoned to Silvers and asked him if he could possibly go to the studio quickly and persuade Edens to get busy with Eleanor Powell and try to work out some routine for the number. At four o'clock I arrived at Sam Katz's office, and he took me for a long walk to a large rehearsal hall, where I found Del Ruth, Seymour Felix, Sid Silvers, Roger Edens, Eddie Powell, Finston* (head of the Music Department at MGM), Eleanor Powell, her mother and an upright piano. When I came in I realized there was battle in the air. Then Sam said "Now, Cole, my boy, Roy Del Ruth will tell you what he thinks of the finale." Everybody became very silent and Del Ruth began. He said, "This is not personal at all, but I definitely do not like your Finale. I think it is a great let-down after your other numbers and will ruin the picture. It seems to me the lyric is entirely wrong, and as far as the tune goes, it reminds me of everything I have ever heard since I was a small boy. I had hoped so much that you would write a hit song that had the brilliance of BROADWAY RHYTHM, our great number in BROADWAY MELODY."† When he had finished I said "I understand your point of view perfectly, but I disagree with you in every way. I think my lyric is excellent and applies completely. As to the tune, you tell me it reminds you of everything you've ever heard since you were a little boy, which is exactly what I wanted to do. For weeks, I studied all of the American folk-songs and tried to write a melody which would be essentially American, not fashionable jazz, but a spirited folk-song, such as the ARKANSAS

---

* Nat W. Finston (1895–1979) was a composer, conductor, producer and chairman of the Academy of Motion Picture Arts and Sciences, 1938–44. Finston was head music director for Paramount and MGM from 1928 to 1945.

† 'Broadway Rhythm', composed by Herb Brown, and performed by Frances Langford, Buddy Ebsen and Eleanor Powell, for *Broadway Melody of 1936* (MGM, 1935).

TRAVELER."* Then I asked Eddie Powell what he thought of the number in regard to its orchestration, and he said "Well, as far as I go, it's a great chance for me, because it is obviously written for orchestration and military band, and I can easily make it much more brilliant than I made 'Broadway Rhythm' last year, because it lends itself to scoring."

Then Finston got on his feet and said "Mr. Del Ruth, I am sure you are wrong about this number. You say it won't be a 'hit song'. I will bet you on the other hand that the orchestras throughout the country will take up this song to such an extent that you will curse Cole Porter for having written it."

At this moment Eleanor Powell stood up and said "Nobody has asked my opinion, but the number suits me perfectly. In fact, I already have a routine which I would like to show you." At which she took the middle of the floor, her accompanist went to the piano and she proceeded to do one of the most exciting dances I have ever seen in my life. When this was over, Sam Katz said "Well, Cole, my boy, I guess you were right, if the number suits our star, and Eddie Powell says he can arrange it even better than 'BROADWAY RHYTHM', I think there should be no more discussion about it, so the number is definitely in."

Then Seymour Felix took the floor and he said "But, Mr. Katz, how am I going to bring on my motor boats filled with girls after that lyric." Sam completely lost his temper and said "I don't want your motor boats filled with girls. I want this number to lead up to our star, and if you want to use girls, the only way I will allow it is if you can shoot them out of cannons. And by the way, that would be a swell effect."

But Felix was not to be "downed". He said "But the number is corny. I have always hated that old-fashioned one-step rhythm and you are going to kill your picture if you leave it in." Then Sam exploded, and by the time he finished, there was very little left of Mr. Seymour Felix.

When I realized that the battle was over and that there was nothing more to discuss, I said "goodnight" to everybody. When I shook hands with Del Ruth he smiled and said "Well, Cole, thanks for everything."

---

* Song by Sanford C. Faulkner (1806–74), the official state song of Arkansas from 1949 to 1963. 'The Arkansas Traveller' appeared frequently in animated cartoons of the 1930s and 1940s, including *Merrie Melodies* and *Looney Tunes*.

Then Sam stood up and addressed everybody, saying "Ladies and Gentlemen: The discussion is over, the Number is set for the Finale, and we are going to have a swell picture. It is going to be a million dollar picture, maybe it will cost a million and a half," and he beamed with satisfaction.

When I got home I telephoned Sam Katz and said "Sam, is this settled definitely or not, because it's very worrying when people change their minds as often as they have about this Number." He said "Cole, my boy, just put it all out of your mind, the number is definitely in and there will be no more discussion about it." Then I said "But, I am still worried about Felix. Felix dislikes it so much that I'm afraid he won't do a good job on it." To which Sam replied "Don't you worry, Cole, my boy, I already have another dance director in mind. I'm sick of Mr. Felix and I've practically decided to get rid of him."*

TUESDAY, JUNE 2nd, 1936

Sam Katz telephoned and said "Cole, will you do me a favor?", and I said, "Probably, what is it?", and he said "Will you come out and play and sing your score to Louis B. Mayer and Thalberg† tomorrow afternoon?" I said "Why?" and he answered, "Well, Cole, my boy, after all, they are slightly interested." So I agreed to do it, however, with dread.

WEDNESDAY, JUNE 3rd, 1936

After a stiff whisky and soda, and my arms full of books which Miss Moore had prepared, containing the lyrics in the order which they come in the picture, I left for the studio. A few minutes later I was in Louis B. Mayer's office. He was there, also Sam Katz, Jack Cummings, Roger Edens, Sid Silvers, Mrs. Koverman, (L. B's secretary and an angel), Eleanor Powell and Virginia Bruce. Suddenly the door opened and in crept Thalberg, looking more dead than alive, and obviously angry at being disturbed to hear this score. I passed out the lyric books and began.

---

* The dance ensembles in *Born to Dance* were directed by Dave Gould (1899–1969).
† Irving Thalberg (1899–1936) was a prominent Hollywood producer. Together with Louis B. Mayer he was instrumental in the founding of Metro-Goldwyn-Mayer, where he was head of production from 1925.

By the time "ROLLING HOME" was over, I realized that the atmosphere was friendly. When I finished "Hey, Babe, Hey", there was wild applause and L. B. began jumping around the room whispering to people. I attacked "ENTRANCE OF LUCY JAMES" next, and it was during this that Thalberg suddenly became a different person and began smiling. Then the door opened and in walked Eddie Mannix (General Manager of MGM),* and L. B. said "Cole, you've got to repeat 'Hey, Babe, Hey' for Eddie," which I did, and they all sang it. From then on it was clear sailing and the moment I finished the Finale, Thalberg leaped out of his seat, rushed over to me, grabbed my hand and said "I want to congratulate you for a magnificent job, I think it's one of the finest scores I have ever heard." He was followed by L. B., who came up and put his arms around me and said "Cole, how about coming into the next room and signing your contract for next year," to which I replied, "No, L. B., I don't understand money matters." Then Mrs. Koverman said "Gentlemen, I think this is worth a celebration, what do you all want to drink?" So we ordered big whiskies and sodas, and everybody stood around the piano and sang the entire score again. It was completely jubilant.

Then L. B. addressed the house and said "Now, Sam, this material is so fine that I don't want you to take any chances with it. I want every lyric heard, and in order to assure that, I want you to make 'rushes' of these numbers and then show them in theaters as 'shorts' to find out whether the audiences can understand every word. And another thing, this Finale is so brilliant, that I want you to go to town and spend $250,000 on that Number alone." When everybody had hugged and kissed everybody else, I went over to Sam Katz's office with Jack Cummings, to see the model for the LONELY HEARTS CLUB and the drawings for the FINALE. The model for the LONELY HEARTS CLUB was so beautiful that I wanted to join the club at once. As for the FINALE, it's staggering.

While this was going on, more whiskies and sodas were brought in for everybody and I motored home, exhausted and just a little bit tight.

On arriving home I found that the minute I left L. B.'s office, he telephoned to Arthur Lyons to come to the studio and arrange my contract for next year.

---

* Edgar Joseph Mannix (1891–1963) was a studio executive at MGM known as 'The Fixer'.

<u>TUESDAY, JUNE 9th, 1936</u>

I signed for $90,000 for one picture* beginning December 1, 1936.†

Born to Dance was released on 27 November 1936 and was both a critical and financial success. The *New York Times* wrote that, 'If, in this necessarily fragmentary discussion of Metro-Goldwyn-Mayer's 'Born to Dance' as it came yesterday to the Capitol, some feature is overlooked, some item of comedy or mimicry unmentioned, it will not be because of a lack of enthusiasm. It will be because the producers have crammed the film so full of pleasantry and gayety, as a setting for Eleanor Powell's exquisitely tapped-out rhythms, that it leaves one ga-ga for a time ... No fewer than seven Cole Porter compositions, most of them destined to a good measure of the ephemeral fame of modern song hits, punctuate the proceedings. According to this reviewer's eagerly attuned ear, "I've Got You Under My Skin," "Easy to Love" and "Hey Babe Hey" are due for top billing on the subway song sheets, while "Rap-Tap-Tap on Wood" and "Swinging the Jinx Away" should be items of importance for the swing set. "Rolling Home" is something choice for roysterers ...' *Variety* described the film as 'corking entertainment, more nearly approaching the revue type than most musical films, despite the presence of a "book". It is out of the ordinary both in that respect and because of its exceptional production merit. And it's box office. Cast is youthful, sight stuff is lavish, the specialties are meritorious, and as for songs, the picture is positively filthy with them. Cole Porter included at least two hits among the seven numbers delivered.'[33] The Orpheum, an RKO theatre in Denver, reported 'continuous packing them in' (*Variety*, 2 December 1936), and in New York, where *Born to Dance* showed at the Capitol Theatre, 'Musical may be held back a bit by shopping and weather but at $53,000 on the first week, it is still a bangup first in this week's N.Y. Handicap. Plans holdover until Christmas.'[34]

---

* *Rosalie* (MGM, 1937), another Eleanor Powell vehicle.

† Shortly after the conclusion of these meetings, reports circulated that Porter intended to travel from Chicago to Ontario to see the Dionne Quintuplets (born 28 May 1934); see the *New York Evening Journal* for 16 June 1936: 'Cole Porter is the most excited man around these days. He leaves from Chicago almost immediately by motor, with a letter of introduction to Dr. Dafoe, who is going to introduce him to the Dionne Quintuplets, and he is going to write a song about them.' There is no evidence that the trip took place or that he wrote a song about them.

In his *Born to Dance* diary entry for 21 January, Porter mentioned the 'Boland part', the role of the Queen that Mary Boland took in his Broadway show with Moss Hart, *Jubilee*, which opened at the Imperial Theatre, New York, on 12 October 1935. The *New York Times* was generally lavish in its praise, even suggesting that some of the songs in the show had been inspired by Porter's and Hart's South Seas cruise: 'As thousands cheer,* Jubilee has finally hung its hat in the Imperial Theatre, where it had a tumultuous première Saturday evening. It is a rapturous masquerade ... There is, perhaps, a hint of distant splendors in some of Mr. Porter's tunes and in one Eastern dance, "Begin the Beguine" ... ["Jubilee"] is an aristocrat of American festivals to music. It is the dome of many-colored glass that Broadway artisans know how to stretch above the raw materials of entertainment ... Last year Mr. Porter wrote a brisker score† than the one the Franconia brought home as cargo. But the music for "Jubilee" is jaunty, versatile and imaginative ...'[35]

Porter's 1936 show, *Red, Hot and Blue!*, reunited many of the principals from *Anything Goes*, including producer Vinton Freedley, the authors Lindsay and Crouse, and Ethel Merman in the starring role, 'Nails' O'Reilly Duquesne. It had been mooted at least since the spring of 1935 when Freedley had signed Merman to the lead, but it was not written for almost a year and only opened at the Alvin Theatre, New York, on 19 October 1936. The *New York Herald Tribune* gave the show a positive review, perceptively noting, as well, that good performances make a significant difference to the success of a show:

> With two such heart-warming performers [as Ethel Merman and Jimmy Durante] properly cast and with a score by Mr. Porter, even if it is in his second-best vein, a musical comedy has a beautiful head start to success. Since Mr. Durante has never been funnier and Miss Merman sings as alluringly as ever, it is safe to set down "Red, Hot and Blue" as a triumph ... It is always a pleasure to listen to Mr. Porter's music, and the only critical problem arises from deciding whether one of his numbers belongs in his first or second flight. The confession must be made that,

---

* A reference to Irving Berlin's 1933 revue, *As Thousands Cheer*.
† *Anything Goes*.

upon first hearing, the suspicion arises that the score of "Red, Hot and Blue" is in the second category. Miss Merman, however, invariably fools one. When she sings a number you are immediately forced into the conviction that it is a masterpiece. It is only as an afterthought that you begin to realize that it may have been merely a pretty good piece, raised into the major leagues by Miss Merman's exciting rendition. At least it is safe to say that "Down in the Depths on the 90th Floor" is almost as good as Miss Merman makes it sound, which is a great tribute to it. The Durante song about the skipper from Heaven* is a comic masterpiece, as I think I have suggested, and the lyrics of "Ridin' High" are in Mr. Porter's best topical manner.[36]

The critic in *Time Magazine* was less positive: 'This first brand-new star to rise in Broadway's 1936–37 musicomedy firmament was judged by most observers to be of the second magnitude . . . Also second-best in the opinion of most listeners is the score Cole Porter has composed for his 12th musical show. Victim of his own previous high standards, composer Porter will doubtless have the misfortune of hearing Red, Hot and Blue's comic number, "It's De-Love-ly," unfavorably compared with "A Picture Of Me Without You" which he wrote last year for Jubilee, and his current torch song, "Down in the Depths, On the 90th Floor," rated way below his "I Get a Kick Out of You" in *Anything Goes*.'[37]

Shortly after the opening of *Red, Hot and Blue!*, Porter wrote to an unidentified correspondent concerning the addition to the show of 'Down in the Depths' during the tryout in Boston, a story he returned to in a piece he wrote for the *New York Times*, 'Notes on the Morning After an Opening Night':

24 October 1936: Cole Porter and unidentified correspondent[38]

Just last week while the new show was playing in Boston,† we all decided another song should be added. It had to be done in a hurry, of course, but I

---

* 'A Little Skipper from Heaven Above'.

† *Red, Hot and Blue!* had a tryout at the Colonial Theatre, Boston, beginning 7 October 1936. The added song was 'Down in the Depths' (originally 'On the 90th Floor'), which replaced 'Goodbye, Little Dream, Goodbye'. Kimball, *The Complete Lyrics of Cole Porter*, 206.

didn't have any difficulty, as I knew the situation in the show perfectly. I got my song in mind Tuesday, worked on it that night and Wednesday, and it was in the show, orchestrated and sung by Ethel Merman on Thursday night [October 15, 1936].

8 November 1936: "Notes on the Morning After an Opening Night" by Cole Porter

Am I made wrong?

While Russel Crouse was pacing back and forth in the lounge of the Alvin Theatre during the opening performance of "Red, Hot and Blue!"* giving a perfect take-off on all of the ten million ghosts, and Howard Lindsay was somewhere on his New Jersey estate getting quarter-hourly reports from his wife, I was in as good a seat as the management would give me, and, flanked by Mary Pickford and Merle Oberon,† was having a swell time watching the actors. Russel claims this is being as indecent as the bridegroom who has a good time at his own wedding.

The morning after an opening of one of my own shows is more or less the same as any other morning – except that I sleep much later. In the case of "Red, Hot and Blue!" I broke my record by exactly ten minutes.

The reason for my behaviour isn't that I'm confident of the play's success or that I'm totally without nerves. I'll put up my nerves against the best of them. But, for some reason, the moment the curtain rises on opening night, I say to myself: "There she goes," and I've bid goodbye to my baby.

***

During the months of preparation the piece itself becomes something of a person to me – not always a nice person, perhaps, but at least some one that I've grown fond of. The minute it is exposed to its premiere audience, however, I feel that it's no longer mine. It belongs to the performers. And I become just another $8.80 customer. That is why I take my friends along and make a night of it afterward.

---

* *Red, Hot and Blue!* premiered at the Alvin Theatre, New York, on 19 October 1936.
† Mary Pickford (Gladys Louise Smith, 1892–1979) and Merle Oberon (Estelle Merle O'Brien Thompson, 1911–79) were prominent Hollywood actresses.

The morning after is still a hangover of the holiday mood. One of the luxuries is to wake up to an inspired breakfast and then hunt for the notices. It is a pleasant feeling, this sensation of laziness which dictates that the entire day be dedicated to comfortable indolence, and nothing else but.

***

At any rate, there was I, my breakfast done and the notices half finished, when the telephone rang. It was Vinton Freedley,* the girl at the desk announced: would I talk to him? I hesitated a moment. Whenever a producer calls up a song writer it always means trouble. And this was my day of rest. However, I weakened. I steeled myself for the inevitable barrage and decided to take the call.

"Hello, Cole, this is Vinton talking. How are you feeling?"

"I'm feeling fine. How are you feeling?"

"I'm feeling fine too."

And he hung up.

Considerate fellow, Vinton, when you get down to it.

Pleasantly relieved, I settled back to the notices again.

The telephone rang once more. "Ethel Merman," the girl at the desk announced.

I wasn't sure what to do. I love Ethel. I hope it will not be considered ungracious of me, in the face of the other very talented artists who have sung my songs and helped them along to popularity, to confess that I'd rather write for Ethel than any one else in the world. Every composer has his favorite, and she is mine. Her voice, to me, is thrilling. She has the finest enunciation of any American singer I know. She has a sense of rhythm which few can equal. And her feeling for comedy is so intuitive that she can get every value out of a line without ever overstressing a single inference. And she is so damned apt.

***

We decided in Boston one day that her first number in the show, whatever its melodic qualities might be, was too somber to start things

---

* Vincent Freedley (1890–1943) was a theatre and television producer; he produced four shows by Porter: *Anything Goes* (1934), *Red, Hot and Blue!* (1936), *Leave it to Me!* (1938) and *Let's Face It!* (1941).

off, and it became advisable to replace it. So that same afternoon I locked myself in my room and emerged the following morning with "Down in the Depths, on the Ninetieth Floor". The song was scored in the afternoon and that evening Ethel sang it in the show.* And sang it beautifully. One thinks of these things, on the morning after an opening, with affection and gratitude. For, after all is said and done, a song writer is very much at the mercy of his interpreters, and it adds greatly to his sense of comfort to know that numbers are in capable hands.

These thoughts ran through my mind and still I hesitated, for usually when Ethel phones one it is to suggest changes in her songs, and this was one morning when I did not feel like doing anything of the kind.

However, I took the call.

"Hello, Cole. This is Ethel talking. How are you feeling?"

"I'm feeling fine. How are you feeling?"

"I'm feeling fine too."

And she hung up.

***

Cheerfully I returned to the notices. But again the phone interrupted, and this time it was Henry Spitzer† of Chappell's. Henry is my music publisher. I like him very much in spite of the fact that he often talks business. Right now I did not feel like being bothered with details pertaining to restricting numbers on the radio, additional arrangements, foreign rights, special licenses and the like.

However, I had taken the other calls. I might just as well take his too.

"Hello, Cole. This is Henry talking. How are you feeling?"

"I'm feeling fine. How are you feeling?"

"I'm feeling fine too."

And he hung up. A pal to the end.

A couple of minutes later Jimmy Durante‡ was on the phone. Jimmy had been after me to write him a song which he could sing with the girls in the show. Writing for Jimmy is not easy. It isn't the range of his voice,

---

* See above, pp. 140–1.

† Henry Spitzer (?1897/8–1952) was a music publisher; he committed suicide in 1952 (see *The Billboard*, 4 October 1952, 49).

‡ Jimmy Durante (James Francis Durante, 1893–1980) was a comedian and singer.

which is usually the major problem when turning out numbers for other performers, but rather catching that certain something which goes into the making of the Durante personality. The man who cleans up my apartment had several extra basketfuls of paper to cart out during the days I was fashioning "Little Skipper From Heaven Above" for Jimmy. But I took the call.

"Hello, Cole. This is Jimmy talking. How are you feeling?"

"I'm feeling fine. How are you feeling?"

"I'm feeling fine too."

And that was that.

By this time I was more or less finished with the notices. They ran according to form. I was considering the prospect of going back to bed when the telephone rang once more.

It was the press agent of the show.

"Hello," I said, beating him to the punch, "I'm feeling fine."

"That's fine, because then you'll be able to do a piece about it."

P.S. He was feeling fine too.

In December, Porter wrote to Monty Woolley, mentioning his next assignment, the MGM film *Rosalie*, which would be released the following year, on 24 December 1937.

18 December 1936: Cole Porter to Monty Woolley[39]

Dear Beardie:

I enclose $100, which you will please spend on that sack suit you have been crying about. If you can't get anything magnificent for $100, let me know and I will supply the deficit.

It was very nice to get your drunken telegram this morning and to realize that you haven't improved in the least.

For a few days The Oregon Mist got us down and the streets were so flooded that it was worth your life to venture out, but once more The Usual Weather has descended upon us and we are basking naked in the sun again.

I got my assignment to do "ROSALIE",* the day after I arrived, which pleased me mightily, but when I called up Sam Katz a week later and told him that I had written the Title Song, he replied "Oh, Cole, don't hurry about this, just get a good rest and enjoy California." So I have had to call off all work, lest they lose respect for me.

Linda decided that we should not have any Christmas at all this year, consequently she's very busy every day ordering Christmas trees, turkeys and geese for a bang-up Christmas Eve party. It's going to be one of those evenings where everybody gives a present to everybody else and it's going to cost us all a hell of a lot of money by the time they get out of the house.

[signed:] Cole

Two days later, an interview with Porter was published in the *New York Herald Tribune*. Unlike many interviews that merely skim the surface of Porter's career and works, this one credibly describes his working method and his use of rhyming dictionaries:

Cole Porter, who according to his own admission, gets his inspiration from night clubs, never leaves them until 3 or 4 o'clock in the morning.

"Recently," he says, "I visited a night club six times to get a feeling of swing in the new tunes played there. I go to the theater constantly to keep in touch with popular musical taste. My interest in composition is modern, of course, but I like going back to the classics. I am especially interested in providing dance forms that haven't been used recently. In 'Born to Dance,' for instance, I used an old-fashioned hornpipe, and in 'Red, Hot and Blue' the Szardas.

"In every show I always try to use my favorite tempo, one seldom used in America – the paso doble – or three-two time, a lively tempo."

So that his lyrics may be up to the minute in timeliness, he continually searches for that elusive topical idiom. He must know the newest wisecracks and clichés, so that his song lyrics appeal to every type of society – the younger set, the man-about-town, the first-nighters, Broadway, the racetrack, the prize ring and the roulette table.

---

* MGM, released 24 December 1937 and starring Nelson Eddy and Eleanor Powell.

Wherever Porter goes he is always busy on scores and lyrics. He works from 11 in the morning until 4 officially, and after that keeps at the job, making mental notes in transit – in automobiles, in trains and airplanes.

"In writing a song," he says, "I start with a title first. From this title I work out the psychology of the tune. Next I write the lyric backward, and in this way build it up to a climax. In the lyric I work first for the climax, and if I can't find a good climactic line I throw out the tune."

Porter's comments on rhyming are informative.

"I consult rhyme dictionaries. I swear by them. For long, easy rhymes I use Andrew Loring's Lexicon. Other books I have in constant use are Roget's 'Thesaurus,' an atlas, Fowler's 'Modern English Usage' and a dictionary.*

"I have learned the map through my lyrics, for the backgrounds of pictures and places forces me to learn a great deal about geography. Motion pictures are more difficult to write for than the stage. I must deliver my tunes in a shorter time. I have only seven numbers in pictures, but twenty-one in an ordinary show."[40]

---

* Several of Porter's (mostly later) dictionaries survive at UCLA, Special Collections, Collection Number 316. These include: Maximilian Delphinius Berlitz, *Deuxième Livre pour L'Enseignement des Langues Modernes, Partie Française pour Adultes, Novelle Éditions, Revue et Complètement Remaniée* (New York, 1950); Maximilian Delphinius Berlitz, *Los Verbos, Aprendidos por la Conversación* (New York, c.1943); Maximilian Dephinius Berlitz, *Libro Italiano, Nuova Edizione Reveduta ed Ampliata* (New York, 1953); Gaston Benedict, *Metodo Directo Progresivo, Español, Primer Libro* (Los Angeles, n.d., copyright 1942); and Gaston Benedict, *Metodo Directo Progresivo, Español, Segundo Libro* (Los Angeles, n.d., copyright 1931).

CHAPTER FOUR

SETTLED – AND INJURED – IN NEW YORK, 1937–1944

Porter spent part of 1937 in New York and California, and part of the year in Paris. He was in New York at the start of the year when Irving Berlin sent him the score of his new, as yet unreleased film, *On the Avenue*,* and a few months later, when Porter was in Beverly Hills, he wrote a letter of recommendation to the Broadway producer Dwight Deere Wiman (of Porter's *Gay Divorce*) on behalf of the aspiring composer Brooks Bowman:†

7 January 1937: Cole Porter to Irving Berlin[1]

YOUR AVENUE SCORE JUST ARRIVED STOP WE HAVE BEEN PLAYING IT ALL EVENING AND ITS [sic] VERY GREAT STOP MANY THANKS SORRY YOU HAVE THE FLU AND LOVE YOU BOTH FROM US ALL=COLE.

24 May 1937: Cole Porter to Dwight Deere Wiman[2]

Dear Dwight:

This is to present to you a very talented young man, Brooks Bowman. He wrote the great Princeton Triangle Show two years ago and, not only his lyrics, but his music is very interesting. I know it will be worth your while to listen to him.

Best regards and love from us both to you and Steven.

Yours,

[signed:] Cole Porter

---

* The film was released by Twentieth Century-Fox on 12 February 1937.

† Brooks Bowman (1913–37). His 1934 Princeton Triangle Club show, *Stags at Bay*, included his best-known song, 'East of the Sun (and West of the Moon)'. He died in a car accident on 17 October 1937, barely five months after Porter wrote his letter of recommendation.

While he was in Paris, Porter's shows proved a summer success in the New York area – an aspect of his career and finances that is little documented: the *New York Times* reported on performances of *Gay Divorce* in July and August, at Jones Beach Stadium for a crowd of 8,000, and at Randalls Island Stadium for a crowd of 10,000, at which another 4,000 had to be turned away.[3] He returned to New York on the *Normandie* on 30 September 1937, intending to sign a contract for a new show with the Shubert Organization. Two shows were under consideration: *Greek to Me*, which was abandoned early on,* and *You Never Know*, which premiered at the Winter Garden Theatre, New York, on 21 September 1938. Porter had travelled with the Scottish actor Jack Buchanan (1891–1957); other travellers on board included Hedy Lamarr.†

In October, Porter accepted an invitation from Countess di Zoppola‡ to spend some time at her house in Mill Neck, New York. On 24 October, while riding on the property, Porter's horse shied, threw him, and fell on his legs, both of which suffered compound fractures. He was operated on at a hospital in Glen Cove and then moved to Doctors Hospital in Manhattan, where he underwent a second surgery in late November. Two letters to Monty Woolley, from November and December 1937, show Porter's

---

* According to McBrien, *Cole Porter*, 215, *Greek to Me* was abandoned in February 1938. A report in the *New York Times* for 9 November 1937, however, suggests it may have been dropped several months earlier: 'Lee Shubert, by the way, no longer has an option on "Greek to You," although Clifton Webb still likes the leading role and wants to play it . . . Russel Crouse and Howard Lindsay, who were to have assembled a book from an original story by Lowell Brentano and William Jourdan Rapp, have been too busy on "Hooray for What!" And Cole Porter, who was slated to supply the songs, is recuperating from an accident.' For *You Never Know*, see p. 153.

† *New York Times*, 1 October 1937, 18: 'The French liner Normandie brought among her passengers yesterday an unusually large complement of actors, actresses, singers and others of the entertainment world. Miss Hedy Kiesler, Viennese actress and star of the Czechoslovak film "Ecstasy" which was temporarily banned in the United States several years ago on indecency charges, was one. Miss Kiesler, who will be known henceforth as Miss Hedy Lamarr, signed a contract during the voyage with Louis B. Mayer of Metro-Goldwyn-Mayer . . . Jack Buchanan, English musical comedy and film actor, arrived on the liner to appear with Evelyn Laye and Adele Dixon in the new Howard Dietz-Arthur Schwartz musical show, "Between the Devil." He traveled with Cole Porter, who came here to sign a contract with Lee Shubert to do a musical show.'

‡ Edith Mortimer (birth and death dates unknown), who had married the Italian aviator Count Mario di Zoppola in 1919; they divorced in Reno, Nevada, in 1929; see the *New York Times* for 5 February 1929, 22.

determination to carry on normally, but at the same time, the extent to which he suffered:

23 November 1937: Cole Porter to Monty Woolley[4]

Dear Mr. Woolley:

I am sending you a book which you will, I think, eat up, called THE GOLDEN SOVEREIGN, which is a sequel to Victoria Regina.* Naturally, Rigger [T. Lawrason Riggs] brought it to me. He came down the other day with a satchel full of presents and they were touching.

First, A bouquet of Christmas roses from his garden in New Haven,
Second, A hunter and a deer from Sweden, made out of pipe cleaners,
Third, A bottle of Coty's Eau de Cologne[†]
Fourth, Two books,
Fifth, A Bottle of Muscatel

He was so grand and so funny, and I resent the fact that I see him so little these days.

When I get a little bit better I shall write you the scientific details of my fractures. I have picked up a lot of new medical words which I throw around with great effect, and I am sure you will be impressed.

Linda arrived last night and from all I hear, was met by an entire male chorus. She and Katie[‡] came out to see me today with that old [Howard] Sturge[s], and they all looked very fit. Naturally Linda brought me a very beautiful new gold cigarette case.

The town buzzes with your success, in fact, people talk about you too much and I do my best to head them all off and on to fresher subjects. Of course, all the figures have been distorted so, by the Elsas of life, that you are now making just a little bit more than Clark Gable. I don't know

---

* Laurence Housman, *The Golden Sovereign* (New York, 1937), a collection of plays set during the reign of Queen Victoria. Its prequel, Housman's *Victoria Regina* (London, 1936 but written in 1934), had its premiere in London on 21 June 1937.

† Coty, Inc. was founded in Paris by the Corsican-born Joseph Marie François Spoturno in 1904; it was among the first firms to market perfumes to the general public, rather than as an exclusive luxury item. Coty was purchased by Pfizer in 1963 and by Joh. A. Benckiser GmbH in 1992.

‡ Porter's mother, Kate Porter.

whether Lennie* wrote you the Robert Rubin story or not, but just in case he didn't, here it goes: Lennie saw him at one of those theatrical parties that Lennie goes to, the other night, and said "Mr. Rubin, how do you like your new acquisition?" to which Mr. Rubin responded "What new acquisition?" and Mr. Hanna replied "Why Monty Woolley". Then Mr. Rubin said "Oh! Mr. Hanna, we all know we've got something there and Monty Woolley is going to go very far."

Goodbye and thank you so much for those frequent and excellent letters, they do me a great good. Goodbye, and bless you.

[added by hand:] As you know, I think I had your little malady† in 1928 but only discovered I was ill when it had already reached the advanced secondary stage. My only advice is <u>never</u> but <u>NEVER</u> miss a treatment. You will be tempted to as you will always feel so well. I also drank profusely all during my illness & it seemed to do no harm.

I'll write again soon.

Love

C

2 December 1937: Cole Porter to Monty Woolley[5]

Dear Monty:

Stop writing pages about your damned lip and then saying it must be a bore to sit around patiently while my bones knit.

If I had merely broken my legs, I'd have no complaints to make. But, although the left leg got a compound fracture, (that means that the bones went through the skin and were exposed to the air), the right leg was mashed to such a pulp from below the knee to the ankle that a great many of the nerves were injured, one of them very seriously and most of the pain has come from there.

From the second day it was obvious that the toes of my right leg were without sensation. And after a few more days, the excruciating pains, as if

---

* Leonard Colton Hanna Jr. (1889–1957) was a close friend of Porter's at Yale and later director of Hanna Mining, an iron-ore processing company in Cleveland, Ohio.

† Here Porter possibly refers to a sexually transmitted disease.

from burns, began. It was explained that these were <u>blebs</u> forming. It seems that blebs always form after injury to nerve tissue. Isn't that a nasty word, bleb? And a bleb is a hemispheric ulcer about an inch in diameter. The pain grew so much worse that the doctors decided that the cast must be removed and a coffin-like box be put in its place so that the blebs could be treated with Amartan. Amartan is the stuff they used for the burnt passengers of the Hindenburg.

When the cast was removed I shall never forget the first sight of my leg. I asked, "What is that jelly its [sic] covered with?" and the reply was, "That's not jelly, that's blebs." It was hard to believe for the whole leg looked like a flowing mass of lava and it sorta made me sick.

Then I began to find out that large areas of my leg felt like some one [sic] else's leg and thats [sic] when the trouble began. For in tracing the different nerves during the Amartan treatment, it was discovered that the anterior papliteal [sic] nerve seemed to be totally dead. As you know, the sciatic nerve goes down the back of the thing. Then one branch of it comes forward to a point just below the knee and runs from there on down the front of the leg and over the instep to the toes. This branch is the anterior papliteal [sic].

The Amartan treatment dried up some of the blebs but not all, so that quite a few of them had to be cut off, which didn't add to my comfort. In the meantime was starting the cruelest blow of all. All the minute off-shoots from the old papliteal [sic] began to struggle for existence again, causing curious pressures and pains that felt the very lightning bolts. Also the craziest illusions, some of which I wrote down as the doctors wanted them for data. I'm enclosing a few of them and you can believe them or not.

Porter's letter goes on to describe the effect on him of various drugs – 'Morphine simply made me want to give parties and did nothing toward diminishing the pain. Hyoscine drove me crazy, Nembutal ... induced nothing but drowsiness. Then they hit on Dilaudid ... it's a mixture of morphine with a lot of other nice drugs ... I have had a shot of it every four hours for the last month and it has saved my life ...' – and at the request of his doctors he wrote 'A Few Illusions Caused by An Injured Anterior Popliteal Nerve', detailing some of his deliriums while medicated:

I'm a toe dancer, but a toe dancer who dances only on the toes of his right foot. The music in the orchestra pit is charming and it's very pleasant hopping around and around to that gay tinkling strain. But after a while, I realize that my toes are tired, and, risking the reprimand of the ballet master, I decide to drop to the ball of my foot and give them a rest. But, lo and behold, try as I may, I cannot do it, for my ballet slipper has been made in such a way that I must stay on the tip of my toes. So, long after the curtain has gone down, the music has stopped and I'm alone in the theatre, I watch the sad show I make as I go on and on, doomed forever to hop around on those poor tilted toes. It's a relief to wake up and be no longer a toe dancer. But it's an awful bore to have this tremendous new pressure on the sole of my foot, which forces it up with such incredible insistence that I feel, as if, at any moment, the tendons of my ankle would break. Gradually I get used to this, however, as it continues pushing and pushing, but I must say I become rather discouraged when late at night I look at my toes to find that they are as far away as they ever were from the shin bone.

The toes on my right foot are having a delightful time under the covers; they are tapping up and down on the cast and then resting from their exertions by stretching, and stretching so completely that each is separate from the other. This is such a pleasant feeling that it seems too good to be true. So I pull up the covers. It is *not* true.

My right leg stretches, slanting upwards before me, like the side of the hill, the summit of which is my toes. From the ankle down – and approaching me – any number of small, finely, sharply-toothed rakes are at work. Each one has about the same routine. For instance, the rake that has been allotted to the inside of my leg begins at the ankle, proceeding slowly toward the knee, and digs as deeply as it can into my skin, at times much deeper than at others, and consequently varying in its painfulness. It goes slowly on in this manner until it reaches a point just a little short of the knee, then retraces its tracks until it finds the spot where it was able to penetrate the most, at which point it settles down to dig to its heart's delight. The same procedure takes place over the entire leg and continues until I yell for a hypo.

The toes on my right foot are tapping against the cast again and once more stretching happily in the morning sun – that is, until I look at them and find that they aren't. A little later the rakes go to work, but for some reason they have reversed their procedure and instead of beginning at the ankle and digging toward the knee, they start just below the fracture and wind up at the toes. Those that mount the sole of the foot have great difficulty digging under the nails of the smaller toes, which are so close to the skin, but they finally succeed and the result is a most interesting new form of torture. In the late afternoon I notice that the right foot is doing its best to fit into a show that is much too short for it, but it persists and persists until someone inserts, inside the cast, a jagged glass shoehorn that extends from the inner heel all the way around to the little toe, but it is sadly ineffective and only adds to the confusion.

Even after a shot of Dilaudid has started to calm everything down, and the jagged glass shoehorn has changed into a rough stone shoehorn, it is obvious that the foot will never fit into that shoe . . .[6]

Although Porter had been working on *You Never Know* – or what might have been *You Never Know* or *Greek to Me* – since at least October 1937 (a surviving sketch of the text for 'At Long Last Love' is written on S. S. *Normandie* stationery),[7] he did not sign a contract for the show until 31 December 1937, at which time it was still titled *Bei Kerzenlicht* (*By Candlelight*) after the German property on which it was based.* In light of Porter's recent accident, the contract included a special provision: 'It is explicitly understood that in view of the partial physical disability of the Composer, of which the Manager is completely informed, the Composer shall not be required to be present at each and every rehearsal. It is the Composer's intention, however, to exercise every effort to be present whenever it is essential and definitely necessary.'[8]

Porter apparently made good progress with the show, writing to J. J. Shubert on 1 March 1938:†

---

* *You Never Know* is based in the first instance on Siegfried Geyer's three-act play, *Kleine Komödie*, first produced in Vienna in 1927. It was subsequently adapted for the English-language stage by P. G. Wodehouse and ran for 128 performances at the Empire Theatre, New York, between September 1929 and January 1930. In 1933, the play was produced as a film, *By Candlelight*, and in 1937 – the immediate antecedent of *You Never Know* – in a musical version by Robert Katscher, premiering at the Deutsches Volkstheater on 30 April. Katscher, who fled Austria in 1938, was peripherally involved in *You Never Know*. Negotiations between J. J. Shubert and Porter pre-date by some weeks the signing of a contract: a draft agreement between them is dated 7 December (SOA, Solo Series, Box 10, folder 5).

† Jacob J. Shubert (1879–1963) was a pre-eminent theatre owner and producer. For the Shubert family generally, see Foster Hirsch, *The Boys from Syracuse* (Carbondale, IL, 1998).

1 March 1938: Cole Porter, telegram to J. J. Shubert[9]

Many thanks for having arranged the orchestra reading today. I know that you will agree with me that Spialeg* [sic] has done a great job. All my gratitude to you and warm regards. Cole Porter.

And his work on the musical, according to a letter Linda Porter wrote to her friend Bernard Berenson on 18 March, was what Porter claimed saved his life: 'This has been a <u>dreadful</u> winter! Cole is out of hospital + always an uncertainty about his right leg which was so badly smashed that the doctors could not decide whether or not the nerve was severed, – in which case he would have been lame for life. Finally, a month ago, his right leg was operated. The nerve, thank God! in tatters, but still intact . . . The left leg (double fracture) is healed – he is free from cast on this leg so can hobble about in his rooms at the Waldorf on crutches . . . has written a new score for "By Candlelight" which, incidentally, is a great success . . . He says this work saved his life for it makes him forget his pain.'[10]

Shortly afterwards, *You Never Know* ran into difficulties, including a contractual dispute between the Shuberts and Robert Katscher, the composer of *Bei Kerzenlicht,* and his Viennese publisher, Georg Marten, and in April the writer George Abbott† was called in to revise the seemingly unsuccessful book, possibly at Porter's request.‡ Premiered on 21 September 1938 at the Winter Garden Theatre, New York, *You Never Know* was among the least

---

* Hans Spialek (1894–1983) was a composer and orchestrator. Born in Vienna and a Russian prisoner of war after World War I, Spialek emigrated to the United States in 1924 where he joined the staff of Chappell Music. He orchestrated several shows for Porter, including *Fifty Million Frenchmen* (1929), *The New Yorkers* (1930), *Gay Divorce* (1932), *Anything Goes* (1934), *Panama Hattie* (1940) and *Something for the Boys* (1943).

† George Abbott (1887–1995) was a theatre and screen writer, director and producer. During his lengthy career, Abbott won two Tony Awards for best musical (*The Pajama Game* and *Damn Yankees,* 1955 and 1956, respectively) and the Pulitzer Prize for drama (*Fiorello!,* 1960). He was nominated for an Academy Award for writing *All Quiet on the Western Front* (1930), based on the 1928 novel by Erich Maria Remarque.

‡ On 28 April, J. J. Shubert wrote to the show's director, Rowland Leigh (1902–63), that 'Cole Porter had George Abbott see You Never Know in Pittsburg [sic]'. Source: SOA, Solo Series, Box 10, folder 5. The *New York Times* for 26 April reported that 'George Abbott went to Pittsburgh to see last Saturday's two performances [of *You Never Know*] – this as a favor to his friend, Cole Porter, composer of the show'.

successful of Porter's shows, running for only seventy-eight performances. *Theatre Arts Monthly* for 22 November reported that '[*You Never Know*] finally came to the Winter Garden flourishing a comet's tail of stars and displaying enough credit lines to fill two pages of the program. With Cole Porter, Clifton Webb, Lupe Velez, Libby Holman and the rest, something should have happened. It didn't. As an intimate revue it might have passed, but it dies under the weight of musical comedy routine and the size of the theatre.' The *New Yorker* noted Clifton Webb's 'stylish dancing' but added that 'Cole Porter's music and lyrics only occasionally suggest that intricate and fascinating gift.' And writing in the *New York Times*, Brooks Atkinson dismissed most of the score with the off-hand remark, 'There is one of his patter serenades "Alpha to Omega," that is gay and clever, and some of the rest of them may, as Mark Twain said of classical music, be better than they sounded.'* Ironically, while the show was still in tryouts, M. Clifford Townsend, Governor of Indiana from 1937 to 1941, wrote to Porter on 16 April 1938 to invite him to a 'Cole Porter Day' on 23 May at Peru, citing *You Never Know* in his proclamation, as 'Mr. Porter's latest and most successful musical'. Porter replied:

19 April 1938: Cole Porter to M. Clifford Townsend[11]

My dear Governor:

I am indeed very deeply touched by your letter of the 16th inst. informing me of the plans of the citizens of Indiana, presumably initiated by you, whereby my family and I will be so signally honored on May 23rd.

Although I live by the employment of words (and a little music) I now find them very inadequate to express my real gratitude, and that of my family, in accepting this most extraordinary honor. The one little fly in the ointment is that the slow progress I am making in recovering from an accident, will prevent me from being physically present. It is gratifying, however, to

---

* Wolcott Gibbs, 'Words and Sad Music', *New Yorker*, 1 October 1938, 30; Brooks Atkinson, 'Clifton Webb, Lupe Velez and Libby Holman Appearing in a Cole Porter Musical', *New York Times*, 22 September 1938. Further, see Cliff Eisen, '*You Never Know*: Anatomy of a Flop', in Don M. Randel, Matthew Shaftel and Susan Forscher Weiss, eds, *A Cole Porter Companion* (Urbana, IL, 2016), 242–60.

feel that the one who can most completely represent me, my mother, will doubtless suffer the embarrassment of such rare riches that I myself would like to enjoy.

Living so long in a world of make-believe, where a kind of transitory tribute is paid one for his so-called good deeds by way of entertainment, makes me further realize that the testimonial you and my good citizen neighbors are planning is after all the one recognition that is worth while.

With genuine gratitude and assurances of my very sincerest regards, believe me,

Most cordially yours,

[unsigned]

P.S. Would it be possible for me to possess the original (or a duplicate for framing) of your proclamation. I'd love to have it prominently hung in my work shop.

Linda Porter wrote to Bernard Berenson, reporting on Porter's health: 'With constant care he will make a complete recovery ... He is as gay as a lark ... & is now writing a second score.'[12] That second score was *Leave it to Me!*, which Porter had started as early as April 1938, and that had its New Haven tryout beginning 13 October and its Boston tryout beginning 17 October. On 25 October, Linda Porter wrote to Jean Howard: 'Coley is in Boston with his new show Leave it to Me which opens Nov. 2nd in N.Y. He comes home, I hope, on Thursday. The show has had excellent notices. I saw it in New Haven before any cuts were made and it was very amusing (but too long) and the score lovely. Victor Moore as the American ambassador in Russia is irresistible. The Spewacks* wrote the book. You know how well they write. Pray for our success!! Heaven knows what our future plans are – I don't – or whether we will come to California. Cole is not signed up.'[13]

Leave it to Me! opened at the Imperial Theatre, New York, on 9 November 1938, and unlike *You Never Know*, was well received: Arthur Pollock wrote

---

* Bella Spewack (1899–1990) and her husband Sam Spewack (1899–1971) were both writers. *Leave it to Me!* was their first collaboration with Porter; more famously, they wrote the book for *Kiss Me, Kate*.

in the *Brooklyn Daily Eagle* for 10 November 1938 that 'Vinton Freedley knows how to do it! Take "Leave It to Me!" the musical comedy he presented with all its luminous charms, robust fun and a singularly agile beauty at the Imperial Theater last night. It has everything . . . [Cole Porter's] songs and lyrics are among his best, sounding newer and neater than any he has done in several years.' *Leave it to Me!* included two stars making their Broadway debuts, Gene Kelly and Mary Martin. Ten years later, Porter recalled his first 'discovery' of Mary Martin, who subsequently starred in Kurt Weill's *One Touch of Venus* (1943), and Rodgers and Hammerstein's *South Pacific* (1949) and *The Sound of Music* (1959).

8 October 1949: Cole Porter to Stanley Musgrove*

Dear Stannie:

Your story about Mary Martin and "My Heart Belongs to Daddy" is so inexact that I must tell you the truth.

We had engaged June Knight for the part which later Mary played, but June found a Texas millionaire and decided that he was more interesting than her career for the time being, so we were completely up a tree at the last moment. Suddenly an agent called up and said he had a girl which might interest me. I asked him to bring her to my room at the Waldorf where she proceeded to give such a good audition that I called up the producer and told him, -- "This is the girl. Don't look any further." He rushed over to my room and she repeated her audition, after which we signed her up immediately for a very small sum. Mary had just come from Los Angeles where she had sung and was a complete failure.

When <u>Leave Her To Me</u>[!] [sic] opened in New Haven, as I was ill, Linda telephoned immediately after the performance saying, "Your star is not Sophie Tucker but it is that little girl called Mary Martin who stopped the show with 'My Heart Belongs to Daddy.'"

All my best.

[unsigned]

---

* CPT, Correspondence 1949. Stanley Musgrove (1925–86), writer, director and publicist. He is best known for his publicity work for Mae West. See his obituary in the *Los Angeles Times*, 19 March 1986.

Leave it to Me! ran for 291 performances, closing on 15 July 1939. During its run, Porter travelled early in 1939 to Cuba with his valet Paul Sylvain and a friend, Ray Kelly,* and to Peru with Kelly, Sylvain and Howard Sturges.[14] Shortly after his return, in an interview published in the *New York Herald Tribune,* Porter made some unexpected comments about 'hit songs' – in particular an assertion that a show should have only one hit song – and dropped a hint concerning his Republican-leaning politics:

> ... to Cole Porter, the ranking creator of smart and glittering theatre lyrics of his time, more than one hit song to a show is no less than a calamity, a misfortune of major proportions, but one which strikes without warning and can be foretold by no barometer of public taste yet invented.
>
> "One really big hit song is all any show should have," says Mr. Porter, "and I wish I could find some way to spread out successful lyrics to cover a number of productions. Four or five songs which catch the public fancy and become widely known tend to dissipate and diffuse their own successful effect. We find that if they have been released to bands and over the radio audiences feel that they are familiar with the entire score and are bored or disappointed accordingly, whereas if only one song stands out, even if they have heard it repeatedly before, they look forward to it with pleasure and anticipation. But the thing that baffles song writers, producers and musical directors is that nobody – and I say this quite unqualifiedly – nobody can, with any degree of consistent accuracy, tell what is going to catch the public ear and be a hit song. I certainly can't and for that reason some of my shows have been awash with hit songs and lyrics I should far have preferred to distribute over two or three productions."
>
> ... "The policies of a Democratic administration, hurricanes and other acts of God are supposed to be unpredictable," he says, "but they are as regular as the stars in their courses compared to the progress of a popular song. You remember, for example, 'Begin the Begin' [sic] in

---

* Ray C. Kelly (birth and death dates unknown), a sailor on one of the passenger liners the Porters used to travel between Europe and the United States, apparently met Cole Porter in 1932 and subsequently remained an intimate friend. See McBrien, *Cole Porter*, 145.

'Jubilee' four seasons ago? Well, that had a moderate success at the time along with 'Me and Marie' and 'Nice Municipal Park,' but it didn't achieve a vast national vogue because we didn't release 'Jubilee's' music to the radio at the time. Now, however, a band somewhere, I forget where, has revived the song with a swing treatment, Artie Shaw made a swing record of it, it has passed through the swing stage and has reverted to its original scoring as a rhumba, with the result that during the run of 'Jubilee' 'Begin the Beguin' [sic] wasn't a tenth the hit it is at this very moment. There was a four-year delay before it became really big-time stuff."*

... "To show that you never can tell about hits in advance take 'My Heart Belongs to Daddy,' which I wrote for 'Leave It to Me.' I had, as a matter of fact, hoped there might be the makings of hit songs in 'I Want to Go Back to Old Topeka,' 'Tomorrow,' and 'Most Gentlemen Don't Like Love,' but 'Daddy' was just written in as a spot song with no particular relation to the book of the show, and I said to myself that it was just one of those things. Not at all: along comes Mary Martin and over night the dingus becomes better known than the name of the show in which it is sung.

"It takes, according to my experience anything up to two months to discover whether a song is a real wow or just a flash in the pan. With my stuff particularly, people have to hear it several times before they can discover whether or not it is really attractive to them. It took all of three months to find out that 'Night and Day' was getting anywhere. 'Gay Divorce' opened the first of December, 1932, and I wasn't sure until the end of February the next year that I had anything authentically profitable on my hands."

... "My great professional tragedy is that I have to be a book hunter," Mr. Porter says. "Look at such happy scoundrels as Rogers [sic] and Hart. They know how to write their own books."†

---

* See *Variety*, 15 February 1939: ' "Begin the Beguine," four years old, by Cole Porter, and out of a more or less flop musical show, is ... being replugged, this time as a pop, chiefly on the strength of the impetus lent it by Artie Shaw's recording.'

† *New York Herald Tribune*, 2 April 1939, E1-2. Porter's comments about the uncertainty of writing a hit notwithstanding, he is quoted on the dust jacket of Bruce Abner and Robert Silver's *How to Write and Sell a Song Hit* (New York, 1939, and advertised as 'Inside information on titling, composition, lyric writing and song marketing by two experts') as saying, 'At last would-be song writers have a bible.'

At the end of the article, the author, Lucius Beebe, mentions Porter's prospects for the 1939–40 season: a show for Vinton Freedley, a Buddy DeSylva and Herbert Fields musical for Mae West,* a late autumn show for Moss Hart and George Kaufman† or, if these fell through, a film for MGM, the script of which was apparently already written. The MGM film was *Broadway Melody of 1939* – a Fred Astaire-Eleanor Powell vehicle – which because of production delays was not released until the next February, renamed as *Broadway Melody of 1940*. The Buddy DeSylva project, if in fact this was what Porter had in mind, was *Du Barry Was a Lady*, which opened at the 46th Street Theatre on 6 December 1939. The reviews were lukewarm, especially with respect to Porter's score, although there was universal praise for the show's star, Ethel Merman, and one of Porter's songs, 'Do I Love You?' The *New York Herald Tribune* wrote that:

> It is a strange thing to say of so bright and dashing a show as "Du Barry Was a Lady" that there is something nostalgic about it, but the quality is present and it is one of the virtues of the new musical comedy. In its glitter and expansiveness and toughness, in its hard-boiled gayety and its unashamed low-comedy laughter, it is the type of Broadway girl-and-music entertainment that used to prosper in the vicinity of Forty-second Street in the palmy days of prohibition and now is seen so rarely... It is, of course, Miss Merman and Mr. Lahr who make "Du Barry Was a Lady" the good fun that it is. Since Cole Porter's songs for Miss Merman are not quite as effective as usual, this most dashing of our lady comics must rely chiefly on that air of hearty good-fellowship that is so winning a part of her... As for Mr. Porter's score, I must say again that I do not think it is one of his best, but it contains one of the nicest songs of the year in "Do I Love You?' and is generally serviceable.[15]

The *New York Times* review was similar:

---

* Mary Jane ('Mae') West (1893–1980) was a well-known actress and sex symbol.

† The playwright and producer George S. Kaufman (1889–1961) had previously written the books for George Gershwin's *Strike Up the Band* (1930) and *Of Thee I Sing* (1931), and Arthur Schwartz's *The Band Wagon* (1931).

SETTLED – AND INJURED – IN NEW YORK, 1937–1944

According to the title, "Du Barry Was a Lady." As a matter of fact she is Ethel Merman, which is more to the point, and Louis is Bert Lahr, which puts us all one up on history. For the musical show in which they are appearing is burlesque in gorgeous finery, with a lively score by Cole Porter ... Miss Merman is the perfect musical comedy minstrel ... Give her a roguish bit of bawdiness like "Give Him the Ooo-La-La," with a good tune and shoddy lyrics, and she can set a hoop-skirt swaying like a one-woman chorus. Give her a modern ballad like "Katie Went to Haiti" and she can set it on fire. Mr. Porter's ideas are a little skimpy this time, and never more so microscopic than in "But in the Morning, No!" ... As the music-maker Mr. Porter has written a number of accomplished tunes in the modern idiom and one excellent romantic song, "Do I Love You?" but the lyrics are no more inspired than the book; they treat all humor as middling.[16]

In light of the political situation in Europe, the Porters in 1939 gave up their Paris home at 13 rue Monsieur, relocating to New York. And in January 1940, together with friends, they travelled to the South Seas via Cuba and the Panama Canal aboard the Swedish liner *Kunsholm*.[17] Linda Porter wrote to Jean Howard on 19 January: 'We are off on our cruise tomorrow morning at the crack of dawn – & you don't know how glad I am to go and *how* I look forward to being *lazy* – I shall probably return looking much like Elsa Maxwell in size. Len Hanna, Bill Powell, Roger Stearns, Winsor French,* S[turges], and I: Doesn't that sound nice? We will be gone seven weeks, returning to the Waldorf Mch. 15th – so please delay your trip East until then.'[18] In April, shortly after their return Linda Porter wrote to Bernard Berenson of her bronchial problems and her desire to live in the country where she could 'walk and live in fresh air for a change ... New York is no place to live.'[19] To that end, while Porter was in Los Angeles, she went house hunting in Massachusetts, where she rented, and eventually bought, Buxton Hill, in Williamstown. She wrote to Jean Howard on 12 September: 'This house is *MINE* – isn't that wonderful? I got it for nothing, & pray God! I won't spend a fortune doing it over. I want *so many things*: a guest house, a swimming pool, a new garage (the Barn) & lots of gardens. If I go bankrupt, you might buy it!! ... Cole is splendidly well. *Very* busy.'[20]

---

* Len Hanna's companion.

The show Porter was working on at the time, *Panama Hattie*, had tryouts in New Haven beginning on 3 October and Boston beginning on 8 October. On 12 October, Linda Porter wrote to Jean Howard: 'Saturday. I just got back from Cole's Boston opening – *Panama Hattie* is a HIT. Do come out for the opening & bring that nice Charlie* . . . I *think* I sign the papers on Monday for the house. It has been held up because the title was not clear. But I have it, really, & will go to Williamstown directly when everything is settled.'[21] About the same time, Porter wrote to his cousin Omar, also expressing enthusiasm for the show:

29 October 1940: Cole Porter to Omar Cole[22]

Dear Omar:

Katie† gave me those two beautiful photographs of your Big Horn adventure. They are wonderful and I am having one of them framed.

We have great excitement here, what with the show‡ opening tomorrow night. It looks as if it would be good.

All my love to everybody out there and thanks for the swell pictures.

Best to you and to Josephine,

[signed:] Cole

Panama Hattie opened at the 46th Street Theatre, New York, on 30 October 1940 and the reviews were consistently positive. The *New York Herald Tribune* wrote, 'Here is Broadway girl-and-music saturnalia at its peak, humorous, tuneful, hard-boiled, sentimental, rapidly paced and handsome, filled with good low comedians and beautiful girls . . . Mr. Porter's score . . . is filled with any number of excellent songs', while the *New York Sun* described it as 'a particularly luxurious musical comedy'. According to Brooks Atkinson, writing in the *New York Times*, 'Everything is in order in "Panama Hattie," which opened at the Forty-sixth Street last evening. Cole Porter wrote the music and lyrics in his pithiest style, and Ethel Merman

---

* Charles Feldman (1905–68) was a Hollywood attorney and film producer. At the time he was married to Jean Howard.

† Porter's mother.

‡ *Panama Hattie*.

sings them like a high-compression engine.'[23] Perhaps in response to the show's success, Margaret Case Harriman published a profile of Porter in the 23 November 1940 issue of the *New Yorker* that, in addition to recapitulating his career, includes a description of his working methods and preferred working environment:

> Cole Porter produces this sentimental dynamite methodically, working with charts. The charts, occupying the top of his piano along with a litter of cigarette cartons, throat tablets, and Kleenex, indicate the musical plan of whatever show he is working on and help him to pace the show by writing a comedy number after a romantic song, a fast number after a slow one. Porter's headquarters in New York is a three-room suite on the forty-first floor of the Waldorf Towers – a kind of streamlined Mecca where a tide of agents, actors, arrangers, managers, and fascinated friends is regulated, but seldom stemmed, by Miss Margaret Moore, Porter's secretary, and by his valet. Miss Moore's telephone rings constantly with urgent messages from Elsa Maxwell, William Rhinelander Stewart, Clifton Webb, and other of the boss's cronies, all of whom must communicate with him through his secretary. Porter has not answered a telephone in years. The living room, where he works, has, besides the piano, a radio phonograph so huge that Porter, who is not very tall, has to stand on his toes to see the machinery in the top of it. A card table holding bottles, glasses, and a cocktail-shaker stands in one corner of the room, and some two hundred phonograph records are stacked indiscriminately on a long table against one wall. Behind the records is a row of dictionaries: English, French, and Spanish, two or three rhyming dictionaries, a medical dictionary, and a thin book called "Words, Ancient and Modern."
>
> ... Unlike songwriters who compose over a piano keyboard, Porter stays away from the piano until he has written the words and music of a song in his head and has put them down on paper. Then he plays it and sings it, making changes. He plays cheerfully, with a rhythmic shrug of his right shoulder that suggests at times a hot "I'm Just Wild About Harry" piano player, at other times a simple, ineffable delight in his own work. He has different ways of singing, too. If he is pleased with a lyric, he sings it with a relish that is handsome to see, throwing his head back

and closing his eyes. If he is not yet sure about it, he leans forward tensely and listens to each word as it comes out of him. His singing voice is high, true, and slightly metallic, and his own comment on it is brief. "I sing unpleasantly," he says. Nearly all of Porter's most successful songs have been written to fit the personality or the vocal tricks of the star who is engaged to sing them. He wrote "Night and Day," in "Gay Divorce," to fit Fred Astaire's voice, which has a small range and sounds best on a certain few notes. He wrote "I Get a Kick Out of You" for Ethel Merman, in "Anything Goes," when he discovered that her best notes are A-flat, B-flat, and C-natural, and that she has an engaging manner of throwing herself away in the last few bars of a song. Porter long ago abandoned the songwriters' tradition that a popular number should have a sixteen-bar verse and a thirty-two-bar chorus; some of his songs have had a thirty-two-bar verse and a sixty-four-bar chorus. He likes to add a few extra bars, or "tag," to a Merman chorus, holding some of the notes twice as long as usual, because he knows that Miss Merman can deliberately flat a long note and make it sound brassy and fine, and that she can work up to an exciting finish with a few unexpected bars. He tries, too, to put the words "very" and "terrific" in the lyrics he writes for Miss Merman; no one, he says, can sing these words as she can. The verse of "It Ain't Etiquette," sung by Bert Lahr in the Porter show "Du Barry Was a Lady," ends with the phrase "Now, for ninstance, Snooks." Porter feels that syllables like those were obviously created so that Lahr could spray them at an audience.*

---

* Margaret Case Harriman, 'Words and Music', *New Yorker*, 23 November 1940. Reprinted in Margaret Case Harriman, "The Wise Live Yesterday: COLE PORTER". *Take Them Up Tenderly: A Collection of Profiles* (New York: Alfred A. Knopf, 1945), 135–49. The curious phrase 'for ninstance' is explained by Harriman: 'Porter will tell you, with a reminiscent grin, that the source of "for ninstance" is a story about Miss Peggy Hopkins Joyce that entertained certain Americans in France a few years ago. Miss Joyce, who had arrived in Monte Carlo in one of her statelier moods, confided to a friend a few days later that she had simply decided to *leave*, because Monte Carlo was full of such *dreadful* people that season. When the friend protested mildly that a good many attractive people seemed to be around, Peggy drew herself up and loftily inquired, "For ninstance, whom?" Porter treasures things like that, sometimes for years.' For a detailed account of Porter's and other Broadway composers' compositional methods, see Dominic McHugh, 'I'll Never Know Exactly Who Did What: Broadway Composers as Musical Collaborators', *Journal of the American Musicological Society* 68/3 (2015), 605–52.

In December, Porter and Howard Sturges travelled to South America, as Linda Porter wrote to Jean Howard: 'Cole and Sturges are in Lima, Peru, having a wonderful time. They fly back to Peru, Indiana the 23rd when we all spend Xmas together.'[24] And in the late spring of 1941 Porter was in Hollywood, working on the Fred Astaire-Rita Hayworth vehicle, *You'll Never Get Rich*, which was released by Columbia Pictures on 25 September. During the summer he worked on *Let's Face It!*; the songs appear to have been nearly completed by late August, at which time Porter wrote to the show's producer, Vinton Freedley, who had earlier produced *Anything Goes* (1934) and *Red, Hot and Blue!* (1936):

22 August 1941: Cole Porter to Vinton Freedley[25]

Dear Mr. Freedley:

After having been here with me three weeks, Dr. Albert Sirmay finished yesterday. We have written out and sent to New York the following numbers:

(1) OPENING SCENE 1, ACT 1
(2) A LADY NEEDS A REST
(3) JERRY, MY SOLDIER BOY
(4) LET'S FACE IT
(5) FARMING
(6) EV'RYTHING I LOVE
(7) ACE IN THE HOLE
(8) YOU IRRITATE ME SO
(9) BABY GAMES
(10) Reprise of EV'RYTHING I LOVE (in Miss Walsh's key)
(11) RUB YOUR LAMP
(12) I HATE YOU, DARLING (Miss Walsh's torch)
(13) LET'S NOT TALK ABOUT LOVE
(14) A LITTLE RUMBA NUMBA

I have finished, but not yet written out, Eve Arden's solo, entitled PETS.

I still have to write the number at the end of Scene 1, Act 2, for Jean and Muriel with the ensemble. Actually I have a number for this spot, but I don't like it enough and I want to do better.

I also have to write the introduction to Danny's specialty just before the final curtain,* but otherwise I am practically all set for rehearsal.

Best

[signed:] Cole

Let's Face It! opened at the Imperial Theatre, New York, on 29 October 1941, and ran for 547 performances. John Anderson wrote in the *New York Journal-American*: 'In the face of "Let's Face It" Vinton Freedley's new musical production at the Imperial last night, let us release all the unshed adjectives that have been held back in a stingy season, let us toss up the verbal banners, slap our grateful sides, already aching with laughter and cry "Hurrah" if not "Bravissimo." Danny Kaye is terrific. Exclamation point. Cole Porter's songs are delightful. Ditto! The production is brilliant.' And Brooks Atkinson reported in the *New York Times*: 'Let's face the facts of "Let's Face It!" which was staged at the Imperial last evening. It is a wonderfully joyous musical show . . . Cole Porter has shaken some good tunes and rhymes out of his sophisticated jukebox . . . "Jerry, My Soldier Boy" is resounding band music. "You Irritate Me" is "You're the Tops" [sic] turned upside down. In "Farming" Mr. Porter shakes a wry stick at the sport of smart people. "Let's Not Talk About Love" restores the patter song to its ancient eminence as a test of memory and wind.'[26]

As Christmas 1941 approached, Linda reported to Jean Howard that Porter was 'splendid – he is out every night – theatres music etc. – in spite of a cast which must weigh a *ton*'.[27] And on 3 January 1942 she sent a telegram to Monty Woolley congratulating him on his appearance in the soon-to-be-released *The Man Who Came to Dinner* (Warner Bros., 1942) – 'PERFECTLY DELIGHTED WITH YOUR GREAT SUCCESS. HAVE NEVER READ SUCH NOTICES. LOVE HAPPY NEW YEAR=LINDA'[28] – while Porter sent a telegram to Johnny Mercer† congratulating him on his song 'Arthur Murray Taught Me Dancing in a Hurry' from *The Fleet's In* (Paramount, 1941):

---

* Eve Arden's solo, 'Pets', and the ensemble number with Muriel and Jean, 'Revenge', were both dropped during rehearsals. Danny Kaye's speciality number, 'Melody in Four F', was composed by Sylvia Fine and Max Liebman; it was dropped late in the run of the show, when José Ferrer replaced Kaye, and was replaced by 'It Ain't Etiquette' from *Du Barry Was a Lady* (1939).

† Johnny Mercer (1909–76) was a songwriter and singer.

9 February 1942: Cole Porter to Johnny Mercer[29]

DEAR JOHNNY. YOUR LYRIC ABOUT ARTHUR MURRAY IS A JOY[.] PLEASE WRITE MUCH MORE AND MUCH OFTENER[.] BEST REGARDS= COLE PORTER.

About this time Porter became acquainted with the dancer and choreographer Nelson Barclift (1917–93), with whom he had a relationship for several years. A corporal in the U.S. Army, Barclift's earliest dancing credits included *The Eternal Road* (1937), *Right This Way* (1938) and Kurt Weill's *Lady in the Dark* (1941); he later choreographed Irving Berlin's *This is the Army* (1942) and the Orson Welles–Cole Porter extravaganza *Around the World* (1946).

19–20 March 1942: Cole Porter to Nelson Barclift[30]

Thursday–Friday 3AM
    Mar 19–20 1942

Do you realize, Barclift, that yesterday was St. Joseph's day & that today is St. Cuthbert's day. I haven't much use for St. Joseph as he resented being called the husband of the <u>Virgin Mary</u> & you know what <u>she</u> produced. But St. Cuthbert was a straight guy & I'm so glad it's Friday instead of Thursday.

My hut* is becoming habitable. Even that nasty guest room is being de-decoraterized & by the time you get here, you can sleep in it without waking up with ribbons in your hair. The West Point program arrived <u>with</u> photograph. Naturally I was proud of your build-up but until I saw that picture of you, I never realized that you were that old Russian dike who used to sing in Paris with a guitar. Her name was – I thing [sic] – <u>Stroeva</u>.† Ask Sturge [Howard Sturges].

Also tell Sturge you want to meet Jean Feldman [Howard]. She will be in N.Y.C. on Monday next, St. Victoria's day. I've told her that you're my Passing

---

* Porter's cottage in Williamstown, on the grounds of Buxton Hill.

† The Russian singer Dora Stroëva (1889–1979) had appeared in Irving Berlin's 1923 revue *The Music Box* and sang on the animated short, *Alexander's Ragtime Band* (Fleisher Studios, 1931).

Fancy so if you suddenly fly out the window she will probably fly with you. But don't miss her. She's one of America's Great Women. Don't bring up Sylvia* as she hates Sylvia's guts & its [sic] so sad because poor little Sylvia is all alone in the world whilst Jeannie has a nice alive husband & infinite Texas relatives.

I have the damnedest [sic] record on that Capehart.† It's called <u>In The Village</u>. It was written by <u>Ippolitow-Iwanow</u>‡ [sic] & he should be ashamed of himself. <u>But</u> I'm in my sitting-room & that Capehart is in the bar. Also the record is on the <u>Repeat</u>. How does one <u>deal</u> with such crises?!?

Call up Ben, please. <u>And</u> Ollie.§ They love you dearly but don't know how to get hold of you. Ben's telephone number is Plaza 3-0041. Ollie is El dorado 5-3871 [this practically never works, but try from year to year.] It would make me worry less about you if I knew you were in occasional touch with them because they are the only two people in N.Y.C. [excepting always Sturges] who are <u>good</u>.

'Way out here, one gets that wicked city idea about New York & all those purlieus. Have <u>you</u> been in a purlieu, tonight? Confess. Say "Guilty." But do write me soon that you reported it all to Ben & Ollie for, for some intangible reason, they cleanse the impurity out of all they touch. And they touch <u>plenty</u>.

It's bed-time now. The ole open-fire is a-fadin'. 'Cross the cotton-fields, the darkeys are singin' their lullabyes. Night's a-fallin', sugah. – So sweet dreams, puss.¶

Your Chum & <u>Still</u> Your Fan [in spite of that scarf around your neck, Babushka]

---

* Sylvia Ashley (1904–97) was an English-born model, actress and socialite. Porter's 'poor little Sylvia is all alone in the world' probably refers to the fact she was at the time Douglas Fairbanks Sr.'s widow (they were married from 7 March 1936 until Fairbanks's death on 12 December 1939). She was subsequently married to Edward Stanley, 6th Baron Stanley of Alderley (1944–8), and to Clark Gable (1949–52).

† Capehart, a luxury home phonograph popular during the 1930s and 1940s; see Robert W. Baumbach, *The Incomparable Capehart* (New York, 2005).

‡ Mikhail Ippolitov-Ivanov (1859–1935) was a Russian composer and conductor.

§ Oliver Jennings was an heir to the Standard Oil fortune (founded by Oliver Burr Jennings, 1865–1936) and the partner of Ben-Hur Baz.

¶ These lines appear to be Porter's parody of a number of traditional songs concerning African-Americans, among them Stephen Foster's *My Old Kentucky Home*.

Albert.
> Barclift, – Barclift,
> I just heard a meadow-lark lift
> Her voice and sing a song in praise of thee,
>   So Barclift, – Barclift
> I, a glass of Cutty Sark lift
> And drink to the meadow-lark
> not thee
> C.

In March 1942, Porter signed a contract to compose seven songs for Gregory Ratoff's* film *Something to Shout About* (at the time of the contract called *Wintergarden*), and on 27 June a contract for two additional songs. *Something to Shout About* was released on 25 February 1943; Porter's 'You'd Be So Nice to Come Home To', written for the film, was nominated for, but did not win, an Academy Award. Porter mentioned his work on the film in a letter to Barclift:

1 June 1942: Cole Porter to Nelson Barclift[31]

June 1st 2. A. M. after a dull dinner, but a long one

Barclift –

All your news is grand & thank you for the Berlin numbers.† It seems to me that the Sleep number is even better than the Canteen but I'm old enough never to know.

I haven't written you lately because my Ratoff job is so crazy that it has nearly got me down. And yesterday, Arthur Lyons‡ called up to say that M.G.M. had a stint for me, that being to write new songs for Du Barry,§ but that they had offered so much that if I accepted the offer, my income tax for

---

* Gregory Ratoff (1897–1960) was a producer, director and actor.

† Irving Berlin's *This is the Army* (1942), which Barclift choreographed.

‡ Arthur Lyons, Porter's agent in Hollywood.

§ *Du Barry Was a Lady*, first produced on stage at the 46th Street Theatre, New York, on 6 December 1938, was released in a film version by MGM in 1943. Starring Lucille Ball, Red Skelton and Gene Kelly, it tells the story of a night-club coatroom attendant who dreams he is King Louis XV, courting Madame Du Barry, who became the king's last lover and was executed in Paris in 1793 during the Reign of Terror.

1942 would be so big that I'd starve. He's trying to wangle a new deal but the rub about M.G.M. is that they won't make those nice contracts that spread over the years, such as my present one.

Forgive all this about Ole Cole & believe the fact that I'm much more interested in anything that concerns you.

So perhaps it's better that you telephone me, any Sunday, reversing charges, around seven o'clock, your time.

You tell me that you think of me a hundred times a day. I like that. But I like more that whether I think of you or not you are always here.

I can't worry with you about your present opus.* Berlin won't make a fool of you. And if by some chance, he should, you can always come back to the shelter of Hedges Place.†

I say good night to you now. If you have time, call up Linda at Williamstown,‡ Mass (there are infinite Williamstowns) and if you've got any spare days, ask her to ask you up. The reason I mention this is because I love you so much & I know that the more you know her, the happier you will be.

I said good night to you before. But I repeat, with a reat-pleat and a rough-cull that everything that you do is my twenty-four-hour-a-day delight.

Good morning, Edgar. And bless you for being alive.

Mrs. Harrington-Carrington.

C.

---

* Irving Berlin's *This is the Army*. Laurence Bergreen, in his biography of Irving Berlin, reports that about this time the composer Harry Warren made negative comments about Berlin during the Allied bombing of Germany, including 'They bombed the wrong Berlin.' He further reports that Porter came to Irving Berlin's defence writing to Berlin: 'I can't understand all this resentment to my old friend, "The Little Gray Mouse." It seems to me that he has every right to go to the limits toward publishing the music of his Army show as every cent earned will help us win the war. If I had my way he would have been given the Congressional Medal because . . . he is the greatest song-writer of all time – and I don't mean Stephen Foster. It's really distressing in these days of so much trouble to know that envy still runs rampant even on that supposed lane Tin Pan Alley. I'm sure you will agree about this, dear little mouse. Love – Rat Porter'. See Laurence Bergreen, *As Thousands Cheer: The Life of Irving Berlin* (New York, 1990), 418. No source is given for Porter's letter.

† Presumably Porter's house on Hedges Place in West Hollywood. It was listed for sale in 2014 for $11.5 million; see the advertisement in the *Los Angeles Times* for 20 October 2014; http://www.latimes.com/business/realestate/hot-property/la-fi-hotprop-cole-porter-20141029-story.html

‡ The Porters' home in Williamstown, Massachusetts.

In the summer of 1942, on 23 July, Porter sent a telegram to Ethel Merman, congratulating her on the birth of her daughter Ethel[32] – 'DEAR ETHEL CONGRATULATIONS ON YOUR NEW SUPER PRODUCTION WHAT IS HER VOCAL RANGE LOVE = COLE'[33] – and he wrote to the dancer William Skipper*:

29 July 1942: Cole Porter to William Skipper[34]

Dear little Skipper:

Forgive me for not answering your letter sooner. I must blame it on my studio.

Freddie Nay and Lew Kesler are both here and they tell me you were wonderful in "Star and Garter".†

They also tell me that Aunt Sam‡ just got you and that you are going to be one of our superior sailors. Please keep me posted as to your address, as I don't want you to get lost in the crowd.

I have no news except that I shall be back in New York again on September first, and if you are anywhere near, please telephone me.

Goodbye, dear Skipper, and the best of luck.

Love,

[signed:] Cole

Throughout his career, Porter was concerned to protect what he saw as essential to his songs, their harmonies and in particular his melodies. He was also concerned that poor performances would be detrimental to his songs' successes, writing to Harry Goetz, production manager at Columbia Pictures, in the summer of 1942:

---

* William Skipper (1915–87) was a dancer and choreographer. He appeared in Porter's Panama Hattie (1940), served in the Coast Guard as a Lt. Commander during World War II, and returned to Broadway in 1946 when he was cast as the juvenile lead in Irving Berlin's Annie Get Your Gun.

† Lew Kesler Jr. (1905–81) was a choreographer; Fred Nay (1911–93) was an actor and stage manager. The musical revue Star and Garter ran at the Music Box Theatre, New York, from 24 June 1942 to 4 December 1943.

‡ That is, 'Uncle Sam'.

4 September 1942: Cole Porter to Harry Goetz[35]

Will you please insist with me that Hal McIntyre's Victor record of "You'd be so nice to come home to" not be released. It will do the tune great harm as the melody and harmonies are completely distorted.* Best regards,

Cole

The previous January, Porter – with financial backing from Len Hanna, Dwight Wiman, Mrs Paul Mellon and others – had opened the 1-2-3 Club at 123 East 54th Street: 'Roger Stearns plays the piano and other people play gin rummy in this big, low-ceilinged, softly lighted room.'[36] It was also, apparently, a safe meeting place for Porter and other homosexuals. On 14 September 1942, Porter invited Barclift to meet him there:

14 September 1942: Cole Porter to Nelson Barclift[37]

COME TO "123" TONITE = COLE.

In October and November, Porter wrote again to William Skipper:

4 October 1942: Cole Porter to William Skipper[38]

Skipper –

Your letter arrived. I can't tell you how happy I am that, at long last, you have discovered the whimsies of old New Orleans. For years I have been told about the charm of this hot-bed of vice but when I was there as a child, I was at a definite disadvantage.

The New York news is not so hot. I saw two musicals in Boston – <u>Count Me In</u> and <u>Beat The Band</u>. Bob Alton's work in <u>Count Me In</u> was swell and Lichine, who did the dances for <u>Beat The Band</u> delivered <u>once</u> in a number

---

* Hal McIntyre (1914–59) was a saxophonist. McIntyre and his orchestra recorded 'You'd Be So Nice to Come Home To' for Victor on 22 July 1942 but the recording was not released; see Brian Rust, *The American Dance Band Discography 1917–1942. Volume 2: Arthur Lange to Bob Zurke* (New York, 1975), 1,224.

called The Steam Is On The Beam, but otherwise his work was unbelievably old hat.

My show is temporarily off because Freedley has suddenly decided that he doesn't like the book.

But why do we even mention such trivial matters? There you are, in the wilds of New Orleans + here am I, in the Berkshires, just about to milk a cow.

Goodnight, dear Skipper. My love to your Ma when you write her. Address me always – Waldorf – Love – Cole

9 November 1942: Cole Porter to William Skipper[39]

Dear Skipper:

Lew's address is – 155 East 48th Street, New York City. Freddie Nay* is in California. He can be reached at 1746 Van Ness Avenue, Hollywood, California. He has had constant work since he arrived there about four months ago, and I do not believe he will come East for a long time.

Between each picture, Tito† threatens to hit New York again, but he makes such good money while he has worked that it seems unlikely we shall see him again here. I doubt also if he will be drafted, as he is an alien.

No moew [sic] news now, but if you get a telephone call from me in New Orleans one day, don't be surprised as I might go to California after a stop-over at the St. Charles Hotel,

Love,

[signed:] Cole

In late 1942, Porter was approached by Warner Brothers to write a musical film, *Mississippi Belle*. Although Porter did not sign a contract until 28 December, a letter of 4 November to him from the film's producer,

---

* Frederic Nay (1911–93) was a bit actor and ensemble player on Broadway and in Hollywood, chiefly during the 1930s and 1940s. He appeared in Porter's *Jubilee* (1935), *Panama Hattie* (1940) and *Let's Face It!* (1941).

† The dancer Tito Reynaldo (birth and death dates unknown); he had appeared in Porter's *Du Barry Was a Lady* (1939).

Benjamin Glazer,* shows that work on the film had started sometime earlier. Glazer reported to Porter that he considered the story difficulties with the film 'to be solved at last', and suggested a musical number based on an eighteenth-century story he had recently come across:

> Back in 1730 there was published a musical composition which purported to be the last Will and Testament of a Mr. Matthew Abby who died at Cambridge in a very advanced age after having for a great number of years "served the College in quality of Bedmaker and Sweeper" in which he left to his wife his whole estate: "To my dear wife, / My joy and life, / I freely now do give her / My whole estate, / With all my plate, / Being just about to leave her." For some seven stanzas he enumerates his possessions, and touchingly concludes: "This is my store, / I have no more, / I heartily do give it, / My years are spun, / My days are done, / And so I think to leave it." Perhaps this delightful composition turned up among the research material you have gathered. If not, I will be glad to mail you a photostatic copy from here. What we had in mind was melody and verse of yours along somewhat similar lines. Our heroine's father, you will remember, was a roaring, fighting, singing Mick, who died when she was young, and left his all to the Bishop in trust for her. If such a man had made a will it might easily have been a musical one, in which rather than enumerate the items of his bequest, he chose to give her salty advice as to how to live her life, what manner of man to choose, and what to avoid. He could have written it in many moods and many strains, and Caitlin would sing it all her life. In fact, practically nothing could happen to her in which her father's Will his wisdom had not anticipated.[40]

Porter replied on 18 November, alluding to his upcoming show *Something for the Boys*:

---

* Benjamin Glazer (1887–1956) was a screenwriter, producer and founding member of the Academy of Motion Picture Arts and Sciences; he won Oscars for his writing for *Seventh Heaven* (1927) and *Arise, My Love* (1941).

18 November 1942: Cole Porter to Barney Glazer, Warner Bros[41]

Dear Barney Glazer:

By all means send me a photostat of the poem that you have discovered. It sounds delightful and twisting it, as you suggest, it would certainly be an excellent theme song for Caitlin.

We went into rehearsal on the Michael Todd* show yesterday so I have been very busy, but I can't wait to clear this up and work on the picture, as it douns [sic! sounds] interesting.

All my best regards, and thank you very much.

Sincerely yours,

[unsigned]

At the start of 1943, Porter's semi-patriotic *Something for the Boys* premiered at the Alvin Theatre, New York, on 7 January and ran for 422 performances. With a book by Herbert and Dorothy Fields,† and starring Ethel Merman, *Something for the Boys* was a critical success. The plot concerns a defence worker, a carnival pitchman and a burlesque queen who transform a Texas ranch into a boarding house for soldiers' wives. Lewis Nichols wrote in the *New York Times*, 'All season long the world has yearned hopefully for a big, fast, glittering musical comedy. It has it now, for last evening the fabulous Mike Todd brought in "Something for the Boys," and as it danced its way across the stage of the Alvin is [sic] quite clearly was not only something pretty wonderful for the boys, but something for the girls as well. For Cole Porter has taken tunes from his topmost drawer, Herbert and Dorothy Fields have written words that are better than most, Hassard Short‡ has directed in his usual impeccable manner and Ethel Merman gives a performance that suggests all Merman performances before last night were

---

* The theatre-owner and producer Michael Todd (Avrom Hirsch Goldbogen, 1909–58). He produced Porter's *Something for the Boys*.

† Herbert Fields (1897–1958) and his sister Dorothy (1905–74) were librettists, screenwriters and – in Dorothy's case in particular – songwriters. They had already collaborated with Porter on *Fifty Million Frenchmen* (1929), *The New Yorkers* (1930), *Du Barry Was a Lady* (1939), *Panama Hattie* (1940) and *Let's Face It!* (1941).

‡ Hubert Edward Hassard ('Bobby') Short (1877–1956) was an actor and the director of more than fifty Broadway or West End shows including Arthur Schwartz's *The Band Wagon* (1931), Irving Berlin's *As Thousands Cheer* (1933) and Porter's *Jubilee* (1935), *Something for the Boys* (1943) and *Mexican Hayride* (1944).

simply practice.'* In mid-January, Porter travelled to California to work on *Mississippi Belle*; he wrote a newsy letter to William Skipper and continued his correspondence with Barney Glazer. Although no song along the lines suggested by Glazer in his letter of 4 November 1942 was written for the film, for others, as Porter wrote in several subsequent letters, he relied extensively on previously published historical American, English and Irish texts:

21 January 1943: Cole Porter to William Skipper[42]

Dear Skipper:

I told Dr. Sirmay of Chappell's to send you the music of "JOIN THE NAVY" from Panama Hattie. Have you received it? Miss Moore will send you the complete lyrics as soon as the box in which they are hiding, is unpacked. I hope they will reach you in time to be useful.

I just arrived on the coast to be here six months, doing a picture for Warner's and a very interesting picture too, as it's all about the Erie Canal, Mississippi River and New Orleans, in the period from 1840 to 1860.[†] I have a lot of research work to do, but it's so interesting and the story is so good that I'm all excited.

Our little show SOMETHING FOR THE BOYS looks like about the biggest hit I ever had. We were awfully lucky in New York to have the usual dead-pans practically sitting on the edges of their seats, so anxious were they for a big stinkin' musical.

I saw Jack Riley[‡] last night and I'm going to the Philharmonic with Freddie Nay[§] tonight. Freddie has landed completely on his feet, he has a xis [sic]

---

* *New York Times*, 8 January 1943.

† *Mississippi Belle*.

‡ Jack Riley (birth and death dates unknown) was an actor; he featured as a bit performer in six Broadway shows between 1938 and 1942, including Porter's *Panama Hattie* (1940) and *Let's Face It!* (1941).

§ In early 1943 Nay was taken on for a bit part in the Bob Hope-Betty Hutton film comedy *Let's Face It!* (based on the show but without Porter's songs).

months contract at Paramount at $100.00 a week. Betty Grable* has decided she can't go anywhere without him, so his life is just one beautiful bed of roses.

Left Lew† in fine form, he is playing the piano in the pit of SOMETHING FOR THE BOYS, and he also gets program credit for having staged several of the comedy numbers. Jack Cole‡ did a wonderful job with the dancing boys and girls and received outstanding notices in every newspaper.

Let me know about "JOIN THE NAVY", and blessings on thee.

Write me when you have time.

[signed:] Cole

20 April 1943: Cole Porter to Benjamin Glazer[43]

Dear Barney:

For your information the following is a list of my sources for certain lyrics:

(1) <u>AMO AMAS</u>

Adapted from a late 18th Century drinking song entitled "AMO AMAS". I found the original lyric on page 261 in "Early Songs of Uncle Sam" by George Stuyvesant Jackson, published by Bruce, Humphries, Inc., Boston, Mass.

(2) <u>BROTH OF A BOY</u>

The lyrics are adapted from the lyrics of a song entitled "LULLABY" on page 107 of the Volume "SONGS OF ERIN" published by Boosey & Company, London.

(3) <u>THE GREEN HILLS OF COUNTY MAYO</u>

The melody of this is adapted from the melody of "DOBBINS' FLOWERY VALE" a traditional Irish air which I found in "Irish Country Songs", Second volume, published by Boosey & Co., London, edited by Herbert Hughes.

---

* Betty Grable (1916–73), actress and one of the leading Hollywood stars of the 1930s and 1940s. Grable appeared on Broadway only twice: she took the part of Alice Barton in Porter's *Du Barry Was a Lady* (1939), and from 12 June to 5 November 1967 she appeared as Mrs Dolly Gallagher Levi in *Hello, Dolly!*.

† Lew Kessler (birth and death dates unknown) was a musician and choreographer.

‡ Jack Cole (1914–74) was a choreographer.

The rest of the lyrics and melodies are, as far as I know, original, with the exception of scattered couplets which I have taken for MAMIE MAGDALIN and the LOADING SONG. These I found in "American Ballads and Folk Songs" by John A. Lomax and Alan Lomax, published by The MacMillan Company, New York. According to the compilers of this book, all of these couplets are without authors.*

Forgive my not having shown you any more material lately, but Bill Ellfeldt[†] and I are still very busy putting new numbers down and I shall call you shortly.

Your sincerely,

[signed:] Cole Porter

5 May 1943: Cole Porter to Benjamin Glazer[44]

Dear Barney:

For your files, my song, "WHO'LL BID?" is adapted from the FEMALE AUCTIONEER, page 58, in the book AMERICANS AND THEIR SONGS by Frank Luther, published by Harper Brothers.[‡]

Sincerely,

Cole

24 May 1943: Cole Porter to Robert Buckner[45]

Dear Mr. Buckner:

RE: MISSISSIPPI BELLE

If in Scene 40, you find that you need two numbers instead of 1, I suggest that in addition to AMO AMAS, that you commence the scene with either GAUDEAMUS, on page 141 in the Harvard Song Book, published by the

---

* Porter's sources were: George Stuyvesant Jackson, ed., *Early Songs of Uncle Sam* (Boston, 1933); Herbert Hughes, ed., *Irish Country Songs* (London, 1909); John A. and Alan Lomax, *American Ballads and Folk Songs* (New York, 1934); and Charles Villiers Stanford, arr., *Songs of Erin* (London, 1901).

† William Ellfeldt (1906–77) played the uncredited role of the piano player in the film *Confidential Agent* (Warner Brothers, 1945).

‡ Frank Luther, *Americans and their Songs* (New York, 1942).

Harvard Glee Club, Cambridge, Massachusetts, 1922, or <u>INTEGER VITAE</u> on page 163 in the same Harvard Song Book.
 Sincerely yours,
 [unsigned]

About this time, Jack Warner had the idea to produce a biopic of Porter's life that was eventually released in 1946 as *Night and Day*, starring Cary Grant as Cole Porter and Alexis Smith as Linda Porter. Warner met with Porter, probably in the second week of May 1943, and subsequently sent him a telegram on 15 May: 'Dear Cole: After our very lovely luncheon talk the other day I was sure that we would be able to get together and quickly close the deal on the screening of your life, using your great numbers and three or four new ones for what I am sure would make a great film. But the terms that are being outlined by Arthur Lyons . . . are so tough that I am sure it was not your intention to set it up on such a prohibitive plane. Therefore I think you should talk this over with Arthur* and tell him to bring it down to a realm of possibility as we want to go ahead to make what I know will be one of the most important pictures and a great tribute to yourself and your fine spirit.'[46] Porter's telegram of 17 May suggests that negotiations concerning the film had already started:

17 May 1943: Cole Porter to Jack Warner[47]

DEAR JACK IN REPLY TO YOUR WIRE THE "TOUGH TERMS" WHICH YOU SPEAK OF ARE NOT "TOUGH TERMS" INAUGURATED BY ARTHUR LYONS BUT ARE TERMS WHICH I HAVE DISCUSSED WITH HIM AND ARE THE ONLY TERMS IN WHICH I AM INTERESTED. I AM NOT IN A POSITION TO NEGOTIATE FOR THE RIGHTS OF A PICTURE OSTENSIBLY ABOUT MY LIFE AND USING MY SONGS AND SOME NEW SONGS FOR ANYTHING LESS THAN THE TERMS WHICH I HAVE DISCUSSED STOP I AM EXTREMELY FLATTERED THAT YOU ARE INTERESTED IN SUCH A PROPOSITION BUT AT THE SAME TIME I DO NOT WANT TO DISPOSE OF MY LIFES [sic] WORK UNLESS IT CAN BRING ME AT LEAST THE AMOUNT OF SECURITY THAT IS ESTABLISHED IN THE DEAL LYONS HAS SUBMITTED. I DO NOT LIKE TO BE IN THE POSITION OF PUTTING A

---

* Arthur Lyons.

PRICE ON MY HEAD WHICH SAYS IT IS WORTH A FIGURE WHICH CAN BE ARGUED ABOUT BUT THERE ARE PRECEDENTS IN FORMER PICTURES OF THIS TYPE WHICH INDICATE A STANDARD OF VALUE AND I THEREFORE DO NOT THINK THAT THE TERMS ARTHUR LYONS QUOTED ARE EXHORBITANT [sic]. MY BEST TO YOU BOTH=COLE PORTER.

In June, Porter received a mug as a present from Lauren Bacall – a sign of his increasing intimacy with the Hollywood crowd – and shortly afterwards, on 18 July, while he was travelling in Mexico, he sent a postcard to Sam Stark, co-owner of the jewellery shops located in the I. Magnin stores, a recent friend who from this time on was a regular correspondent of Porter's.* Coincidentally, the same month he signed the contract for his next Broadway musical, *Mexican Hayride*. The show is only occasionally alluded to in his surviving correspondence. Instead, it was his work with Warner Brothers – on *Mississippi Belle* and *Night and Day* (which at the time was tentatively titled *Cavalcade*) – that was the chief concern of his correspondence for the next several years, both with the studio and with his lovers and his friends, foremost among them Stark.

10 June 1943: Cole Porter to Lauren Bacall[†]

Dear Betty:

Thank you again for the super mug. You were sweet to think of me, and I love you dearly.

[signed:] Ole Cole

---

* See McBrien, *Cole Porter*, 256. According to McBrien, Stark later married Harriette, the daughter of the Mafia boss in Kansas City. I. Magnin was a luxury department store founded in San Francisco in 1876; during the early years of the twentieth century, I. Magnin opened shops in several luxury hotels throughout California. See Devin Thomas Frick, *I. Magnin & Co: A California Legacy* (Garden Grove, CA, 2000).

† Lauren Bacall (Betty Joan Perske, 1924–2014), one of Hollywood's greatest stars and winner of an Academy of Motion Picture Arts and Sciences honorary award in 2009. She is, perhaps, best known for her films with Humphrey Bogart, *To Have and Have Not* (1944), *The Big Sleep* (1946), *Dark Passage* (1947) and *Key Largo* (1948); on Broadway she won Tony Awards for *Applause* (1970) and *Woman of the Year* (1981). Source: Boston University, Howard Gottlieb Archival Research Center, Lauren Bacall Papers, B.9 Scrapbook Vol. I. Bacall's scrapbook also includes a photograph of Porter inscribed to her: 'For Betty The Great from her old pal Cole.'

18 July 1943: Cole Porter to Sam Stark[48]

Dear Sam –

This is just one great laugh after another + the only blot is the absence of our beloved Sam.

I miss you awfully + I love you deeply – Cole

14 [August] 1943: Cole Porter to Sam Stark[49]

Sat. 14, 43 Williamstown

Sam,

You are a lamb to have sent me all those films! And your letters have been so swell. Why are you tellement good to me? I don't get it. It couldn't be – but Sam, I'm so old. So Sam, let's drop it – that is, all but my gratitude which is vast.

This place is Heaven-in-the-mountains + the peace + privacy of it, not to mention the comfort <u>and</u> the food – well, my pretty, you'd approve. Lytell [sic] and Helen Hull* are here too + Hubert Le Jeune but they are in the main house + as I breakfast here in Ze Cottage + never lunch, we only meet at dinner. Which is a blessing as Porter is at work and <u>hard</u>, writing a show[†] so that he can afford to open Camp Cole again in January.

Please tell all this to dear little Roger as I know how he resents getting letters. Tell him also that the carload of Chiclets arrived for which I bless him. Don't mention the fact, however, that he wrote to me saying he was sending me <u>Choclits</u>!

I enclose a clipping for Paul[‡] from Lew.

Thank that old miner, Jim Shields[§] for the postcard from Morelia which I could read and warn Willie that Linda is coming out to visit me

---

* Helen Huntington Hull (1893–1976) was a socialite and arts patron; she served at various times on the board of directors of the New York City Ballet, the Metropolitan Opera, the New York Philharmonic and Lincoln Center. In 1941 she divorced her first husband, William Vincent Astor (1891–1959), a son of John Jacob Astor IV (1864–1912), and married Lytle Hull (1882–1958), a real-estate broker.

† Probably *Mexican Hayride*, which opened at the Winter Garden Theatre, New York, on 28 January 1944 and ran for 481 performances.

‡ Paul Armstrong according to annotations by Stark on other letters sent to him by Porter.

§ The partner of William Haines; other details are unknown.

next spring so for Christ's sake, will he please plan to whip up that damned pergola.

Goodnight Sam + my great love to you + all that gang that I miss but oh so much.

Cole

Also, tell Roger that Linda is in top form + calls all the flowers by their Latin names. And I forgot, give Paul a beega Keess.

9 June 1943: Cole Porter to Sam Stark[50]

Sam –

It's 4 A.M + I'm slightly plastered but you must know that my big event of 1943 was the Great Gertzen.*

As for the gifts, Number One, Number Two <u>and</u> Number Three, they merely make me repeat the fact that

<u>Cole</u> <u>Loves</u> <u>Sam</u>!

Isn't it curious how quickly one moves[†]

In the summer of 1943, Cole and Howard Sturges travelled to Mexico. Shortly after his return both he and Linda wrote to Jean Howard:

15 August 1943: Cole Porter to Jean Howard[51]

Dear Jeannie –

This is everything that's wonderful – Linda is in top form and the place is all in technicolor. I miss you lots and love you more.

My love to Charlie et pour La Ess,‡ a beega goose.

Your slave –

Cole.

---

* Stark had changed his name from Gertzen.

† This sentence is written vertically up the left side of the letter, with an arrow pointing to the Waldorf logo.

‡ Sylvia Ashley.

18 August 1943: Linda Porter to Jean Howard[52]

Is Ess still with you? ... She does, as you say, make a house come alive. Cole has that same wonderful quality! ... Cole & [Howard] Sturges came up for a long weekend after they *finally* got back from Mexico where they spent a very exciting two weeks. Coley looked well, but tired. No wonder! They missed plane connections in Brownsville, Texas & lost days on the return trip! I have turned Buxton Hill over to Coley and he invites whom he pleases for weekends. Last week we were entirely alone as he wanted to work but this Friday he is bringing [Howard] Sturges & Ollie Jennings ... I wish you were here, Jeannie, to see the changes I have made in the garden & grounds – the place is beginning to look RIGHT. Should you come to N.Y. before I close the house you must come up & see for yourself. I never think about the house – only about the shrubs & flowers and I do without clothes to buy them. Coley has been an angel & helped me out just as I was getting into debt. That was heaven.

During the first week of August, Porter sent Sam Stark a collection of English and American short stories:

3 August 1943: Cole Porter to Sam Stark[53]

Dear Sam:

A book entitled MODERN ENGLISH & AMERICAN LITERATURE, by Somerset Maugham,* will arrive shortly for you. I highly recommend it as being beautifully edited.

There are two stories especially that I want you to read, the first is THE FOG HORN by Gertrude Atherton, the second is ROMAN FEVER by Edith Wharton.

---

* W. Somerset Maugham's Introduction to *Modern English and American Literature* (New York, 1943).

Thank you for your nice wire, and please take goo [sic] care of that little pal, as he is very delicate.

I shall write you shortly.

Love,

[signed:] Cole

And Porter's agent, Arthur Lyons, concluded the deal with Warner Bros. for *Night and Day*; Jack Warner telegrammed Porter on 7 August: 'DEAR COLE: HAVE JUST CULMINATED THE DEAL WITH ARTHUR LYONS FOR THE STORY OF YOUR MOST WONDERFUL LIFE. AM POSITIVE WE HERE AT THE STUDIO WITH YOUR AID WILL MAKE A PICTURE WE WILL ALL BE PROUD OF.'[54] Porter replied by telegram on 9 August:

9 August 1943: Cole Porter to Jack Warner[55]

DEAR JACK. I AM DELIGHTED TO HEAR THAT DEAL HAS BEEN SET AND I AM SURE WE CAN MAKE A SWELL PICTURE. LOVE TO ANNIE AND YOU. COLE

Negotiations concerning *Night and Day* – continued through the summer. Jack Warner dealt primarily with Arthur Lyons, but on 14 August wrote to Porter directly in an attempt to secure publishing rights for new numbers in the film: 'I have been talking to Arthur Lyons about the additional new numbers to be written for the picture . . . we are very anxious to have our own music company publish these numbers, the same as we do with the rest of our pictures . . . I realize that you have an understanding with Chappell and Max Dreyfus, but I think this picture is a little different and that our music company should handle the publishing of these few numbers . . . I am writing directly to you because I think it is a question that you will have to answer, as you are the only one to determine who should publish the music.'[56] In the event, no new numbers were composed for *Night and Day*.

That summer, Porter and his friend Howard Sturges had travelled to Mexico for two weeks and, though tired upon their return, enjoyed a visit at Buxton Hill from friends such as Nelson Barclift and Ollie Jennings. Porter mentioned his visitors in a postcard to Sam Stark of

27 August. And he was increasingly impatient for a contract to be signed with MGM:

27 August 1943: Cole Porter to Sam Stark[57]

Dear Sam –

Thank heaven Daisy + her pals are safe. Barclift + Artie + Sturges are here with us. Barclift + Artie go to England in a month to play London for 12 weeks, then the provinces, then etc. My love to you + all your wicked gang.

C.

13 September 1943: Cole Porter to Arthur Lyons[58]

WHAT IS THE REASON FOR DELAY IN SUBMITTING TO ME WARNER BROTHERS CONTRACT FOR CAVALCADE. I SUPPOSED ALL DETAILS HAD BEEN WORKED OUT. IS THERE ANYTHING OF IMPORTANCE HOLDING IT UP. PLEASE ADVISE ME. COLE

Porter finally signed a contract with Warner Bros. on 29 December 1943[59] and during the autumn of that year, and well into 1944, he wrote frequently to Sam Stark and occasionally to Monty Woolley:

14 September 1943: Cole Porter to Sam Stark[60]

Sammie –

Extraordinary postcards continue to arrive from you for which I am always grateful. But where in hell do they come from? Have you a secret cave somewhere? I don't get it.

Tell Roger that I dined with Louisa Wednesday night, in her apartment. Ernest was there and Alex and all the dogs <u>and</u> great quantities of wonderful champagne. Of course, he has the news of Nonny's 8 ½ pound boy.

Please congratulate Paul on his acceptance of the jalopy. I received word from Bill Gray that the transfer had been arranged + I'm so grateful to Paul that, at last, he came off his high horse.*

---

* According to marginal notations, Louisa Wannamaker and Paul Armstrong, details concerning whom, as well as Bill Gray, are unknown.

To get back to Topic A. I'm really at work.* Therefore, I make very little sense. This may account for the fact that I lost your letter, giving me the dates of your visit to N.Y.C. So please write or wire all details, once more. Give me time to get you seats for Oklahoma.† Also let me know when or if I can steal you for a week-end here. In any case, give me the data as to when I can see you. If I could see you all the time + throw you a ball, every night, that would make me happiest but I know that you + Allen‡ will be in New York together + naturally will prefer to remain, more or less, unmolested. But it would be le grand luxe to steal you away from time to time, without destroying your binge.

My love to my favorite firm, Haines§ + Fickeisen + my blessings upon you, dear Sam. You might also embrace Rodger + Laverne for me.

Goodnight –

Your devoted

Ole Cole.

26 November 1943: Cole Porter to Monty Woolley[61]

Dear Mr. Woolley:

That word "ferocitrocities" is truly wonderful and I am going to do my best to use it in a lyric.

Thank you very much indeed.

Love,

[signed:] Cole

---

* Presumably Porter refers here to *Mexican Hayride*.

† Rodgers and Hammerstein's *Oklahoma!* had opened at the St James Theatre, New York, on 31 March 1943.

‡ Allen Walker (dates unknown) was Sam Stark's partner, and co-owner with Stark of the jewellery counters in the I. Magnin department stores.

§ William Haines (1900–73) was an actor. He owned the house at 416 North Rockingham, Hollywood, that Porter rented beginning in 1943. Haines was blacklisted in 1934 for refusing to conceal his homosexuality through a marriage of convenience. He subsequently had a successful career as an interior designer. See McBrien, *Cole Porter*, 267–8.

29 November 1943: Cole Porter to Sam Stark[62]

Dear Sam:

It seems incredible that I haven't thanked you for your beautiful ink drawing, which every one has admired so much, and which is my constant joy. It's really a masterpiece. As a matter of fact, there is one item in that drawing that I take rather seriously. I refer to the suggestion of having Bill Haines tear down that God damn pergola and sending Grant's tomb out instead.* I remember years ago in Paris, Clarence Mackey's mother, who was used to getting what she wanted, tried to persuade the city of Paris to let her illuminate the Arc de Triomphe for a party which she was giving in her house on the Place de l'Etoile. When they refused she said "Well, would you then consider selling it?"† I shall certainly approach Mayor LaGuardia‡ and let you know the results immediately.

My love to you and to dear little Paul,§ and the three rats.

The show¶ is seething in rehearsals and I'm no way near finished.

Ole lonesome

[signed:] Cole

4 December 1943: Cole Porter to Sam Stark[63]

Dear Sam:

Could I have the negative of the photograph of myself with the turban on by my work bench, also the negative of Roger in his tan and white jacket, sitting in one of those long green canvas back chairs? I need them badly.**

Love,

[signed:] Cole

---

* Stark's drawing appears not to survive; Porter's allusions are therefore unexplained.

† Katherine Mackey (née Duer, 1880–1930) was the wife of the financier Clarence Hungerford Mackay (1874–1938); they married in 1898 and had a daughter, Ellin (who in 1926 married Irving Berlin) and two sons, John and Clarence.

‡ Fiorello H. LaGuardia (1882–1947) was mayor of New York, 1934–45.

§ Paul Armstrong.

¶ *Mexican Hayride*, which opened at the Winter Garden Theatre, New York, on 28 January 1944.

** These two photographs appear to be lost.

Mexican Hayride's Boston tryout opened on 29 December 1943 and Porter wrote to Sam Stark twice at the start of January 1944, mentioning not only the show, but also concerns with his tax liability:

4 January 1944: Cole Porter to Sam Stark[64]

Dictated in Boston

Dear Sam:

Thank you and little Paul so much for my opening night wire. This show has in it 45 minutes of unadulterated boredom, which we are now trying to eliminate. This 45 minutes of unadulterated boredom still exists after we have cut out 20 minutes of the show, so you can see what a job we have ahead of us. The only really great thing about the opus is its production, which is out of this world, but after all it would show us up quite an awful lot if we had the show billed as

"Scenery and costumes in Mexican Hayride"

so we are really hard at work.

I just heard from Mrs. Pearman* that Paul had to go back to the hospital for another sinus operation. Please let me know about this <u>at once</u>.

I am going to see my lawyer when I get back to New York to find out whether I can afford to do another picture beside the Warner Bros. NIGHT AND DAY. I am in a curious quandary. I have been notified that my March taxes will be so big that it leaves me with no money to live on, therefore, it would be nice to have money coming in from another picture, but if I take this second picture, then the income tax would be so big that I won't even have enough money to pay for a roof over my head, and I may let you know this has worked out from my new address

"A tree in the park"

Goodbye and again many thanks for the wire, and love to all those charming people,

Devotedly,

[signed:] Cole

---

* Apparently the mother of Porter's friend, Michael Pearman, about whom little is known. See McBrien, *Cole Porter*, 153–5.

14 January [1944]:* Cole Porter to Sam Stark[65]

Waldorf – Jan 14th 4 A.M.

Sam – I opened your Christmas present only last night when I flew down from Boston for a three days release. And oh what a beautiful present it is + I thank you so much. Curiously enough, I have never owned a Saint Christopher medal before + suddenly, to have one, at last, gives me a great kick.

When I arrived, last eve, I left a message for little Roger[†] to call me. He did at 1 A. M. He is ill again + he hawks when he talks. He tells me he is willing to stay until my little show opens – Jan. 27th[‡] – but once that is over he must return to his canary.

I am here really to find out what I can live on except money. My lawyer + my tax man meet me today. Mr. Morgenthau[§] wants $90,000 bucks from me on March 15th for my first quarter + it's a bit too much. If this can't be readjusted I shan't arrive in California until April when they start shooting the Warner Bros. Night + Day. In the meantime I can stay in my cottage in Williamstown which I shouldn't mind at all. But perhaps a rabbit can be pulled out of a hat in which case I shall be there much sooner, for which I pray.

Tell Willie Haines to fix the Mezas as he sees fit, also the other picture with the bad frame.

I think of little Paul all the time + that damned sinus. Please keep me posted about him constantly.

That thing called Mexican Hayride still stinks but luckily we finally got the Winter Garden in N.Y. + many shows that stink run on + on when they play at the Winter Garden on account of the side-walk business.

---

* Although no year is given, the reference to *Mexican Hayride* dates this letter to 1944.
† According an annotation on this letter, Roger Armstrong.
‡ *Mexican Hayride* opened on 28 January.
§ Henry Morgenthau Jr. (1891–1967) was Secretary of the Treasury, 1934–45, during the administration of Franklin D. Roosevelt.

I sent you my pet book - <u>Goodnight, Sweet Prince</u>.* In Boston, I read it every moment I could find. It seems to me to be all that's delightful.

And so, good morrow, Sam. If you see Eddie Davis,† ask him to telephone me collect. I shall be at the Ritz-Carlton in Boston from Monday, Jan. 17th until Thursday, Jan. 20th. From then on, this Waldorf.

And again, dear Sam, I thank you for my beautiful key-ring.

Tell [Jimmie] Shields that I saw something he would appreciate in Boston, – such a charming steeple of an old Pilgrim church.

Love

Cole

Shortly before the opening of *Mexican Hayride* on 28 January, Jack Warner had written to Porter that he had assigned composer Arthur Schwartz to produce *Mississippi Belle* and that Schwartz 'plus a great cast should make, ultimately, a fine film'.[66] Porter replied on 24 January:

24 January 1944: Cole Porter to Jack Warner[67]

Dear Jack: I forgot to tell you I am delighted that Arthur Schwartz is going to produce Mississippi Belle. Best, Cole

And he wrote twice to Sam Stark, including a brief mention of *Mexican Hayride*:

27 January 1944: Cole Porter to Sam Stark[68]

Dear Sammy:

That beautiful box of Marrons‡ arrived and I am saving them for a festive evening.

---

* Possibly Gene Fowler, *Good Night Sweet Prince: The Life and Times of John Barrymore* (New York, 1943).

† The actor and writer Eddie Davis (1907–58) had recently appeared on Broadway in *George White's Scandals* (1939), with music by Sammy Fain, and the Al Jolson-produced musical comedy *Hold on to Your Hats* (1940), with a book by Guy Bolton, music by Burton Lane and lyrics by E. Y. (Yip) Harburg.

‡ Marrons glacés.

Please keep the night of February 24th open. Also warn Willie Haines and little Jimmie Shields and, of course, Paul.

Dinner at 8 p.m. at Perino's.*

Love,

[signed:] Cole

29 January 1944: Cole Porter to Sam Stark[69]

THE HAYRIDE OPENED LAST NIGHT AND EVERYTHING IS QUITE OKAY. LOVE=COLE

Mexican Hayride had a lukewarm reception, which perhaps explains Porter's laconic 'quite okay'. Writing in the *New York Herald Tribune*, Howard Barnes claimed 'It is fortunate for "Mexican Hayride" that Bobby Clark[†] and Cole Porter are in there pitching. The former is at his antic best, while the celebrated song-writer backs him up with two or three elegant ballads. Otherwise the new Winter Garden offering is a big, brash and generally undistinguished extravaganza.'[70] The *New York Times* wrote that '... the new musical swings right along in the cheerful tradition [of Broadway comedy], not brilliant, perhaps, but good ... Of Mr. Porter's score, the best number bears the title almost startling in its forthrightness, "I Love You" ... "What a Crazy Way to Spend Sunday," "Carlotta" and "Abracadabra" also are good; the lyrics on the whole do not have the composer's usual convolution of tongue-twisting words.'[71]

In early February, Hal Wallis, production manager at Warner Brothers,[‡] sent Porter a working script for *Night and Day*, which Porter acknowledged

---

* A restaurant at 3927 Wilshire Boulevard, opened in 1932 by Alexander Perino and patronized by the Hollywood elite; see Joseph Temple, '7 Famous L. A. Restaurants', http://blog.iwfs.org/2014/09/7-famous-l-a-restaurants-from-the-studio-era/, and Hadley Meares, 'The Michelangelo of the Menu: Alexander Perino's rules of Fine Dining', https://www.kcet.org/food/the-michelangelo-of-the-menu-alexander-perinos-rules-of-fine-dining (both accessed 20 January 2018).

† Bobby Clark (1888–1960) was a comedian, writer and director; he took the starring role, Joe Bascom (alias Humphrey Fish), in *Mexican Hayride*.

‡ Harold ('Hal') B. Wallis (born Aaron Blum Wolowicz, 1898–1986) was a film producer. His film credits for Warner included *The Adventures of Robin Hood* (1938), with Errol Flynn, and *Casablanca* (1942), with Humphrey Bogart. Wallis left Warner Bros. later in 1944; *Night and Day* was produced by Arthur Schwartz.

on 17 February; later the same day Porter apparently received a telegram from Cary Grant, the preferred actor to play Porter in the film, which he then passed on to Wallis:

17 February 1944: Cole Porter to Hal Wallis[72]

Night and Day script just arrived. Will read it on train. Sorry to miss you when you come here. Best, Cole Porter.

17 February 1944: Cole Porter to Hal Wallis[73]

Dear Hal. Following wire just arrived: "Dear Cole, desire assure you of no intention offend by not answering your letter as I immediately contacted Warner with object reading script of Night and Day then meeting with my manager to discuss possibility of making picture so could write you more fully rather than answer merely expressing wish to comply your flattering suggestion that I play the role. However script did not reach me until last week although previous commitments now make my availability doubtful. I thought you might like knowing that I consider it one of the finest scripts I've read, but then its [sic] about one of the finest people I've known. Roger Davis said you arrive here soon so perhaps we may meet and I can explain my contractual obligations. Meanwhile love Barbara and me, Cary Grant".

Hope to heaven you can wangle this. Will arrive next Thursday and will telephone you. All my best Cole Porter

And his correspondence with Nelson Barclift continued:

14 March 1944: Cole Porter to Nelson Barclift[74]

Barclift –

Your letter dated Mar. 5th arrived today.

Well, it's just like the good-old days. The great Etienne suddenly ups & leaves me without giving notice & John* has become so fresh that I have to

---

* Presumably two of Porter's valets.

SETTLED – AND INJURED – IN NEW YORK, 1937–1944

fire him. This leaves me with Eric, a German Swiss who was Etienne's assistant to take over. He is good but not brilliant. My cook is Jean Gabin's* former valet & I have an old housemaid who works well. Her name is <u>Mishy</u>. I asked her where she got her name & she answered "All I know is that <u>my</u> name is <u>Mishy</u> & my sister's name is <u>Tishy</u>."

The Sundays are booming again but we eat in the new room now - the <u>solarium</u>. [Howard] Sturge[s] is with me & what a joy. I'm doing a re-write of <u>Mississippi Belle</u>. My producer is Arthur Schwartz & he's grand news. He just finished <u>Cover Girl</u>[†] & everybody went wild at its press preview. Linda arrives the 27th to stay a month. She will occupy the Barclift room, Weston living in Miss Moore's former. Miss M. is due for a shock when she hits town, April 1st. She has been moved downstairs to the Capehart room & she wont [sic] like it.

... Lil Paul lives in the Long Beach hospital where he has had 3 operations for sinus. He is there under observation but curiously enough is allowed to come to L.A. every night. Annie just had her portrait painted by Dali.

30 March 1944: Cole Porter to Nelson Barclift[75]

Dear Barclift:

From now on you will receive the THEATRE CRITICS REVIEWS – I had your APO number wrong. I haven't time to write you now as we are throwing a slight party tonight. The new sun room is but something to dream about. Everybody looks at it and falls in a heap, with the exception of Elsie [de Wolfe], who being a decorator herself, looked at it and said simply "What a nice sun room!"

Linda arrived and is living in your room. We moved out the bed near the garden and whipped up one of those dressing tables that ladies like, so she

---

* Jean Gabin (Jean-Alexis Moncorgé, 1904–76) was a French actor famous in particular for his roles in *La bandera* (1935), *Pépé le Moko* (1937), *La Grande Illusion* (1937) and *The Human Beast* (1938). He left France for Hollywood in 1940, where he remained until 1944. Porter probably met Gabin at the premiere of *Something for the Boys*, which Gabin attended in the company of Marlene Dietrich, with whom he was having an affair.

† *Cover Girl* (Columbia Pictures, 1944), starring Rita Hayworth and Gene Kelly. The plot revolves around Rusty Parker, whose romance with her dancing mentor is threatened when she becomes a celebrated cover girl.

is in complete comfort. There's only one fly in the ointment, she prefers a bath-tub to a shower. Weston is in the room Miss Moore* used as an office last year. She prefers a shower to a bath-tub, so they spend their time running into each other, trading bath rooms.

Etienne has ceased to exist. California got him after a few days here and he left giving me only one day's notice. He did not even say "goodbye" to me. He has become a Captain in a restaurant where he makes fabulous money, so here is to his happy future.

[Howard] Sturge[s] left last week for a dude ranch in Arizona. He will drive the cows crazy for about three weeks and return here to live at the Roosevelt with the Beard.† By that I mean that he will live in the same hotel with the Beard.

Sunday luncheons boom again. The two bluejays are still about the pool. Little Paul is still in the hospital with those unending headaches. He is, for some reason, under observation. Practically everyone I know, who has been released from the army forces, is due to sinus trouble. Little Paul has had three very painful operations for sinus and still they won't let him go. Roy Cromwell‡ was thrown out on account of sinus and is back at his pretty little house on the hill. You probably remember that his nose was getting flatter and flatter, due to their having taken out the central cartilage. He has had a new cartilage put in, he is very handsome and the effect of the nose upon him is something terrific. He is the charming, delightful fellow that we first knew out here.

Annie finally decided that her bedroom had to be done by Bill Haines, so that is now under process now [sic]. Her daughter, Joy, has suddenly switched from the age of 13 to 19 and goes out to all of the parties, looking, I must say, very beautiful. I must say also that Annie looks about 21. Jean and Charlie have gone to New York in regard to his picture "FOLLOW THE BOYS".§ We saw a press pre-view the other night. It looks like a great money-maker and it's <u>very bad.</u>

---

* Margaret Moore, Porter's secretary.

† Monty Woolley.

‡ The actor Richard (Roy) Cromwell (LeRoy Melvin Radabaugh, 1910–60) was best known for his role in the Oscar-nominated *The Lives of a Bengal Lancer* (Paramount Pictures, 1935) for which he received co-star billing with Gary Cooper; he was married to Angela Lansbury from 1944 to 1945.

§ *Follow the Boys* was released by Universal Pictures in 1944.

SETTLED – AND INJURED – IN NEW YORK, 1937-1944

Sylvia and her new husband, Ed Stanley of Alderley,* arrive today to stay with Norma, and what with parties being given for them and the parties being given for Linda, the near future looks like just your dish. Joan Fontaine and Brian Aherne are splitting up.† Merle fell in love with her camera man and decided to throw Alex out, but Alex was so kind about it that she is sticking.‡ Kay is in the Aleutians drinking up all of the soldiers [sic] whisky rations.

Mike Todd is here arranging a picture deal for "MEXICAN HAYRIDE". I shall be delighted if it fell through as that sale will merely make us all so much poorer.§

Moss Hart wants to do a musical with me, if he can get an idea. In the meantime the Fields have whipped up something about the 1890's, in New York and are sending me the story. Also, Louis Shurr has an outline of a story for Gaxton and Moore, written by Gaxton. The thing that throws me off about this last item is that Gaxton refers to himself as "a handsome young journalist"[.]

The "HAYRIDE" continues to rough it on $46,000 a week at the Winter Garden, and SOMETHING FOR THE BOYS is breaking the records in Chicago. Blondell leaves THE BOYS this week - the show moves to Detroit next week, headed by Joy Hodges.¶ It remains to be seen whether THE BOYS is star-proof or not.** It may still continue to draw as "the sticks" are all so pleased about the production itself. Before it left for the road, Todd had

---

* Edward John Stanley, 6th Baron Sheffield, 6th Baron Stanley of Alderley and 5th Baron Eddisbury (1907–71) was a British peer. He was married to Sylvia Ashley from 1944 to 1948.

† The actress Joan Fontaine (1917–2013); she was married to the actor Brian Aherne (1902–86) from 1939 to 1945.

‡ Merle Oberon was married to the film producer and director Alexander Korda (1893–1956) from 1939 to 1945.

§ The theatre and film producer Mike Todd (1909–58) is best known for *Around the World in 80 Days* (United Artists, 1956) and as Elizabeth Taylor's third husband. Todd produced Porter's musicals *Something for the Boys* (1943) and *Mexican Hayride* (1944). The film version of *Mexican Hayride* (Universal), produced by Robert Arthur (1909–86), was released in 1948. Porter's suggestion that a film version of *Mexican Hayride* would 'make us all so much poorer' refers to the increased tax liability it would create.

¶ Joan Blondell (1906–79) was an actress; Joy Hodges (1915–2003) was a singer and actress. *Something for the Boys* had closed in New York on 8 January 1944.

** Presumably a reference to the fact that the lead in New York was Ethel Merman.

completely new sets and costumes made so that it hasn't that bedraggled look of most road shows.

[Charlie] Chaplin seems to be putting it all over Joan Barry, which pleases everybody out here. The low-down is that the whole thing was started by Col. McCormick in Chicago who decided to te[s]t Chaplin for having spoken in favor of Russia at Madison Square Garden and also in San Francisco.*

Don't miss "THE MIRACLE OF MORGAN'S CREEK". It's the most brilliant picture I have seen in years.†

I can't go on writing as that nasty governess is beating that awful child next door again.

We all miss you and Artie and love you dearly.

Your old pal,

[signed:] Cole

Mississippi Belle continued to pose problems for both Porter and MGM. Porter disagreed with Arthur Schwartz's intention to replace some of his songs, both for dramatic and exploitation reasons:

14 April 1944: Cole Porter to Arthur Lyons[76]

Dear Arthur:

---

* See the *New York Times* for 5 April 1944, 1: 'CHAPLIN ACQUITTED IN MANN ACT CASE. With lips trembling as he clutched at the knot of his necktie, an emotion-choked Charlie Chaplin tonight heard himself acquitted of Mann Act charges . . . The jury of seven women and five men cleared the world-famed comedian of Government charges that he transported his former protégé, 24-year-old Joan Barry, to New York City and back in October, 1942, for immoral purposes.' The Mann Act of 1910 – also known as the White-Slave Traffic Act – made it a felony 'to knowingly transport or cause to be transported, or aid or assist in obtaining transportation for, or in transporting, in interstate or foreign commerce, or in any Territory or in the District of Columbia, any woman or girl for the purpose of prostitution or debauchery, or for any other immoral purpose, or with the intent and purpose to induce, entice, or compel such woman or girl to become a prostitute or to give herself up to debauchery, or to engage in any other immoral practice.' See http://legisworks.org/sal/36/stats/STATUTE-36-Pg825a.pdf.

† *The Miracle of Morgan's Creek* (Paramount, released 1944), comedy directed by Preston Sturges, with Eddie Bracken and Betty Hutton, in which a small-town girl wakes up after a sending-off party for the troops and finds herself married and pregnant, but has no memory of her husband's identity. The film was nominated for an Oscar for original screenplay, and for best director (Preston Sturges) by the New York Film Critics Circle Awards.

MISSISSIPPI BELLE

Mr. Arthur Schwartz cuts out "I'M NOT MYSELF AT ALL", because it is essentially an Irish song. I agree this should be cut out.

He cuts out "WHO'LL BID?" because he doesn't like it, and says it no longer fits the script, and that the number is not strong enough. I do not agree with him, and feel that the script could easily be fixed so that this song would fit in the picture.

He cuts out "SCHOOL, SCHOOL, SCHOOL, HEAVEN BLESSED SCHOOL" and substitutes a song in the public domain. I still feel that this song belongs in the score.

He cuts out "MY BROTH OF A BOY" because of its Irish feeling, but I still think that it should be retained in the score, because it is sung by an Irish character, which character Mr. Schwartz is retaining.

He cuts out "AMO AMAS" which I feel is more effective for the spot than the comedy song which he suggests.

He cuts out "WHEN YOU AND I WERE STRANGERS" saying it is too Irish. I maintain that it is not in the least Irish and still feel with Chappell & Company that it is my No. 1 song in the score.

He tells me that it is doubtful whether he will use "MISSISSIPPI BELLE" at all and doesn't know as yet whether "MARY MAGDALIN" can remain until the script progresses. I maintain the "MARY MAGDALIN" is a very strong production number for the picture.

He leaves me with "KATHLEEN" which has commercical value, [and] "WHEN A WOMAN'S IN LOVE," although he is not sure of this yet. I think "WHEN A WOMAN'S IN LOVE" has a lot of commercial value and belongs in the score.

He leaves in "THE GREEN HILLS OF COUNTY MAYO", "HIP, HIP, HOORAY FOR ANDY JACKSON" and the "LOADING SONG", none of which have any value, except as atmosphere in the full score.

I feel that the five new numbers that he has suggested, added to the five numbers which he retains from the original score, will not add up into as good a score as the original score which was approved by Warner Bros.

In late April, Schwartz wrote to Porter again, sending additional material for *Mississippi Belle,* noting that 'papers are being drawn on the release of the song EXPERIMENT,* which I am crazy about', and reporting that negotiations had started with Cary Grant for his appearance in *Night and Day*.[77] A little more than a month later, on 8 June, Porter had a telegram from Billy Rose, who had approached him the previous February to write songs for his upcoming spectacular, *Seven Lively Arts*: '... I HOPE YOU CAN OVERCOME THE COMPLICATIONS YOU REFER TO[.] I THINK THE SEVEN LIVELY ARTS IS THE FIRST SHOW IN MANY YEARS WORTHY OF YOUR TALENTS AND I AM NOT KIDDING ABOUT THAT TALENT STUFF.'[78]

As a letter to Nelson Barclift shows, Porter had initially turned Rose down, but by 10 June he had relented:

15 June [1944]: Cole Porter to Nelson Barclift[79]

Thursday June 15.

Dear Barclift –

I leave June 30 for N.Y. to start work on the Billy Rose review <u>The Seven Lively Arts</u> which goes into rehearsal Oct 1st. He offered me this job last February but I threw it down as it included several ballets & a 20 minute symphonic piece to be played on stage <u>plus</u> 10 songs. I would have leapt at it but he wouldn't give me 6 months to do it after this <u>Mississippi Belle</u> rewrite. I was practically set on a Bing Crosby job when Rose telephoned me last Friday & offered me the job again but without the ballets & the symphonic bit. So I'm doing it after he agreed to put all rehearsals from September 1st to October 1st. It sounds very exciting & I need mental excitement. You know that it will re-open the Ziegfeld theatre in December. Bobby Short is staging it all. Bel Geddes does the sets.† Aaron Copland or someone equally interesting will do the ballets & the on-stage orchestral job,‡ [Alicia] Markova & [Anton] Dolin are engaged, Bert Lahr for comedy sketches, Rose promises me top singers – he says he has found a great new girl, – a young Merman,

---

* 'Experiment' had originally been written for *Nymph Errant* (1933).
† Norman Bel Geddes (1893–1955) was a theatrical designer and industrial engineer.
‡ Aaron Copland (1900–90) was one of the most prominent American composers of the twentieth century. In the event, the ballet was composed by Igor Stravinsky (1882–1971).

also he will give me a top juvenile etc. etc.* I believe he will. In any case it sounds like a lot of fun. I haven't done a revue for years & it's a pleasant change.

Your life in that fascinating country sounds delightful – or is that the wrong word? I beg you as it [sic] did in my note the other day, see every sight you can. It may be difficult now but do it. It will color your whole life & make you happier later on.

If you have hardships & become homesick, think of one major hardship that people like myself have. I'm so sick of having wonderful kids like yourself saying goodbye & disappearing for so long and feeling so damned inadequate to help get them back home again to their families & their friends. Every Sunday lunch here now is a farewell party & in spite of the laughs, the under-current is sad as hell.

Goodbye Barclift. Tell that Artie how great he is & how super great you are. I enclose a clipping & a few photographs.

Best – Love from Linda* and C.

*Linda sent it from the Berkshires.

Billy Rose continued to correspond with Porter concerning arrangements for *Seven Lively Arts*; in a telegram of 27 June he asked Porter whether Alexander Smallens would be a satisfactory conductor and informed him that Robert Russell Bennett would probably be available to orchestrate the songs.† Porter replied by telegram on 29 June:

---

* Alicia Markova (1910–2004) and Anton Dolin (1904–83) were dancers. The comedian Bert Lahr (1895–1967), best known for his role as the Cowardly Lion in *The Wizard of Oz*, had played in Porter's *Du Barry Was a Lady* (1939). Rose's promise of a young Ethel Merman was not quite fulfilled: in the event, Beatrice Lillie (1894–1989) took the female lead, a possibility raised by Rose in a telegram to Porter of 27 June (CPT, Correspondence 1944).

† Alexander Smallens (1889–1972) was a conductor. The orchestrator Robert Russell Bennett (1894–1981) was assisted by the orchestrators Hans Spialek (1894–1983) and Ted Royal (1904–81). Spialek had earlier orchestrated, or contributed to the orchestrations of, Porter's *The New Yorkers* (1930), *Gay Divorce* (1932), *Anything Goes* (1934), *Du Barry Was a Lady* (1939), *Panama Hattie* (1940), *Let's Face It!* (1941) and *Something for the Boys* (1943); Royal had worked on *Du Barry Was a Lady*, *Let's Face It!*, *Something for the Boys* and *Mexican Hayride* (1944). Some scores of Royal's and Spialek's orchestrations survive in NYPL, in the Billy Rose Theatre Division.

29 June 1944: Cole Porter to Billy Rose[80]

WOULD BE DELIGHTED TO HAVE ALEXANDER SMALLENS. PLEASE COUNT ME OUT FOR CBS ORCHESTRA REHEARSAL JULY FIFTH. ARRIVE WALDORF ON JULY SIXTH AND FROM THEN ON WILL BE ENTIRELY AT YOUR DISPOSAL. AM PRAYING THAT YOU GET BEA LILLIE. HAVE BEEN PUTTING PRESSURE ON FANNIE* AND SHE BECOMES MORE AND MORE ENTHUSIASTIC. IF SHE KNEW YOU HAD BEA LILLIE I THINK SHE WOULD LEAP AT IT. WOULD MUCH RATHER HAVE RUSSELL BENNETT THAN ANY ONE ELSE. LET ME TALK TO YOU ABOUT [ANTONY] TUDOR AS CHOREOGRAPHER WHEN I SEE YOU. JUST SPOKE TO BUDDY [DE SYLVA] AGAIN. HE FINDS THAT DUBOIS HAS ASSIGNMENT FOR A PICTURE FOLLOWING THE ONE HE IS NOW MAKING, BUT BUDDY IS DOING HIS BEST TO GET DUBOIS OUT OF IT SO THAT YOU CAN HAVE HIM. HE WILL LET ME KNOW BEFORE TOMORROW NIGHT.† ALL MY BEST COLE

In the midst of his work on *Seven Lively Arts* Porter continued to correspond with Arthur Schwartz concerning both *Mississippi Belle* and *Night and Day*:

15 July 1944: Cole Porter to Arthur Schwartz[81]

Dear Arthur:

I immediately got busy about the transcription of I'm Dining With Elsa.‡ Unluckily, it was not taken off the air by Frank Black's outfit, but Eddie Wolpin

---

* Presumably the singer, actress and comedian Fanny Brice (1891–1951).

† Raul Pène Du Bois (1912–85) was a designer. His previous designing credits included the *Ziegfeld Follies* of 1934 and 1936 as well as Rodgers and Hart's *Jumbo* (1935). For Porter, he designed *Leave it to Me!* (1938), *Du Barry Was a Lady* (1939) and *Panama Hattie* (1940); in subsequent years he worked on Kurt Weill's *The Firebrand of Florence* (1945) and Leonard Bernstein's *Wonderful Town* (1953). He did not, finally, work on *Seven Lively Arts*. The singer and comedian Beatrice Lillie (1894–1989) was the star of the show, although according to *Variety*, 1 November 1934, 2, she signed on without knowing much about it: 'The English comedienne . . . [c]laims she agreed to do the musical without knowing what the show was about, "but with Cole Porter and Moss Hart doing it," she said, "I thought I'd kinda leave it to them."'

‡ A song composed in the 1920s as a birthday present for Elsa Maxwell; only the text survives. See Kimball, *The Complete Lyrics of Cole Porter*, 138.

thinks there is a possibility of tracking it down by asking other people connected with the broadcast.* In case this fails and you still want it, I can make a lead-sheet for you and send it out.

I shall be very happy indeed to get the revised version of Mississippi Belle.

Regarding the Night and Day picture, I agree with you completely about throwing the hospital out of the frame and if you can't find a decent substitute, to throw the frame out altogether. I like the idea very much of starting the picture with Cole as an undergraduate at Yale. The more I think of the childhood sequences on the farm, the more I dislike them.†

I talked to Jack Warner and congratulated him on the idea of putting Monty Woolley in the Night and Day picture, and he seemed very sanguine about getting him. Since coming East, I find that The Beard is being sought after by several Broadway producers for winter productions. I know of one which, if it goes through, would make it impossible for Monty to appear in the picture, so I hope you can settle this as soon as possible.‡

The Billy Rose show sounds very exciting and he has so many ideas definitely mapped out that I'm already hard at work and having a wonderful time. Bea§ is signed, but for some reason, there is great difficulty about getting her over. Billy has at least appealed to Max Beaverbrook¶ who thinks he can wangle it. A buzz bomb hit the Panama Hattie Theater in London and nearly destroyed it. Luckily, it was between performances, so no one was killed.**

All my best,
Sincerely,
[unsigned]

---

* Frank Black (1894–1968) was a bandleader; Eddie Wolpin (1908–89) was general manager of Famous Music, the Paramount Pictures publishing division.

† These scenes did not, finally, appear in the film.

‡ In the event, no other role came through and Woolley appeared as himself in *Night and Day*.

§ Beatrice Lillie, who took the female lead in *Seven Lively Arts*; at the time, she was working in London.

¶ Max Aitken, 1st Baron Beaverbrook (1879–1964), Canadian-British business tycoon and prominent figure in British society.

** *Panama Hattie* had opened at the Piccadilly Theatre on 4 November 1943.

Porter also reported on *Seven Lively Arts* to Sam Stark, writing the same day to William Skipper as well:

4 August 1944: Cole Porter to Sam Stark[82]

Dear Sam:

Your letter of August 1st arrived and made me very happy.

The Billy Rose show* progresses nicely. We have auditions every Wednesday night as we are looking for seven kids, six girls and one boy and each one of them with an outstanding personality and voice. The result of this instead of being discouraging is extraordinary. There is so much talent in this country that it makes you want to sit back and gloat. We have found one girl called Mary Roach† who has the looks and personality of a young Mary Pickford. She has a lovely, though not big voice, but it is highly schooled <u>and</u> she can dance. There are others that have walked in about which we are not sure, but all of them wreak [sic] of talent and ambition. As I sit there I feel very proud of my own country.

Sturge leaves with me today for Williamstown for the usual Friday to Tuesday week-end. How he bears up during this terrible heat I cannot understand, as he still spends Tuesday, Wednesday and Thursday night way down deep in the Pennsylvania station where the temperature averages 110.‡

Do not mention it to Linda, but she is not very well and I am worried about her. She seems to be so tired all the time and this in spite of the fact that she lives the quietest of lives and the climate up there agrees with her perfectly. Len Hanna is staying with her now and that's a man you must meet. I shall fix it the next time you come East. Please arrange the next time you

---

* *Seven Lively Arts*.

† Mary La Roche (1920–99) was a singer and actress. In addition to *Seven Lively Arts*, her Broadway credits included several Gilbert and Sullivan operettas, *The Pajama Game* (1954), *Mame* (1966) and the 1980 revival of *The Music Man*; she worked in several films, including *Gidget* (1959) and *Bye Bye Birdie* (1963), and on television.

‡ A reference to the U.S.O. canteen at Pennsylvania Station, New York. The U.S.O. (United Service Organization), a non-profit NGO founded in 1941 to provide live entertainment to U.S. military troops and their families, not only mounted performances for military personnel in the field, but also established clubs and canteens for servicemen and servicewomen in several U.S. cities.

come East not to fail to give Williamstown some of your free days. I think you will like it.

I am delighted to hear that Jimmie [Shields] is doing so well. [Bill] Haines sat down and wrote me a telegram about him which relieved my worries a lot. If I had only known in time that he was going to be operated upon, I would have forwarded some kind of jewelry to be put into him instead of the hernia. I am sure that if he were lined with gold he would never be ill again. When my grandfather was 75 years old and about to die, we shipped him to the Mayo Brothers.* They took out all of his fleshy tubes and substituted copper. The result was that he lived until he was 95. But of course Jimmie could not rough it on copper. Tell him that the Duc† is making me a flamboyant cigarette case to replace the lost "ROSALIE" etui. I got the insurance on it and am adding a bit of dough that I have saved in my "piggy bank".

Thank little Paul [Armstrong] for the batteries which came as a God-send. I shall write him as soon as possible.

Love from us all and blessings on Thee, dear Sam.

[signed:] Cole

4 August 1944: Cole Porter to William Skipper[83]

Dear Skipper:

It was very nice to receive your letter of August 2nd. I am delighted to hear that you will be on leave within a short time. My program is as follows: I hit New York every Tuesday at 5 p.m. and return to Williamstown every Friday at 1:30 p.m. I am always free Tuesday and Thursday nights but never Wednesday night, as Billy Rose and I have auditions then at the Alvin Theatre. During the day I am always with Dr. Sirmay of Chappells and could not even see God if he called. So please make your plans accordingly and decide how often you are going to have dinner with me.

---

* The non-profit clinical and medical research Mayo Clinic in Rochester, Minnesota.
† According to a marginal note, 'Verdura', Fulco Santostefano della Cerda, Duke of Verdura and Marquis of Murata la Cerda (1898–1978), an influential Italian jeweller; apparently Porter arranged Verdura's introduction to Coco Chanel.

Linda speaks of you constantly and still has, I think, a rather indecent passion for you.

Goodbye my child and don't forget to write again,

Your old pal

[signed:] Cole

An undated letter from Porter to Sam Stark in the Cole Porter collection at Stanford University is filed with letters from the summer of 1943 but apparently – based on Porter's reference to Yamanaka & Company – more properly belongs in 1944:

[1944]: Cole Porter to Sam Stark*

Lamb Samb –

I should not worry you with this item what with Italy being invaded et. cet. But this is a serious crisis. I showed Fulco the beautiful bottle-opener that Charlie Tate, out-of-you, gave me + at once he cried "Santa Maria, what a great idea for Xmas presents. I can put a few bits of gold in them and make a fortune!" It was too late to tell him that I had brought a dozen of them east with practically the same idea as far as Noël [Coward] went. He did however get the name of the firm out of me so in case he was sober enough to remember it + writes to you on this subject, you are at least warned.

The Duca, Natasha Wilson + Nicky de Quinsbourg [Guinsbourg?] are here for the week-end. But they are staying in the château, <u>not</u> in la petite chaumière.† Not that I don't love them but oh how the French does fly! and one tires of that constant <u>merde</u> instead of good old fashioned shit.

Tell Paul [Armstrong] that John‡ is slightly shocked that he has to have all of the tires re-capped or re-taped or re-decorated before he will accept that

---

* Although this letter is undated, both its contents and its preservation between Porter's postcard of 18 July and his letter of 14 August in Stark's apparently chronological collection, suggest it was written about this time.

† That is, in the main house at Buxton Hill, not Porter's 'No Trespassing'.

‡ Porter's chauffeur.

car. John says that all that was done just before he, John, left. But whatever it is, have somebody pay for it quick, quick + send me the bill. I can't write a new show and at the same time feel that my beloved Paul is starving because he must use up all his income to re-do tires before he can face that elderly Phaeton.

I talked to Li'l Roger [Davis] on the telephone + he sounded surprisingly normal. Tell him that Bobbie Raison* called up today + as a consequence he is coming to N.Y.C. to spend the week-end of September 18th with me. I have to stay in N.Y.C. because of auditions + now that I have kicked Miss Moore out of my back room, he will be très comfortable. Barclift has been occupying that back-room over every week-end + it must be a lucky room for each time he emerges from it in the morning, he is wearing a new ring. The only bore connected with these rings is that most of them are too big + Miss Moore spends much too much time at Cartier's having them re-fitted for Barclift's little finger.

I can't talk to you about this Williamstown place. You will have to come here to give me the words. For everything about it is so beautiful + so bang-up. And the bang-up part of it is all due to the wonderful Linda. You must arrange your next visit to include these remote Berkshires for it's all that's pleasant + peaceful + Perino.

As for [William] and [unreadable] Fickheisen, ask them to spread the moth-balls, but well, around Rockingham.†

I arrived in N.Y.C. to find that Dobbs had packed all my trunks – and there were plenty – without the moth treatment – I mean the trunks had been left at the Waldorf before I went to Calif. – and all my old pet complets had been eaten to death.

Goodnight. Thank you for the post-cards, especially for that lovely old photo of our child.

---

* Robert Raison (birth and death dates unknown) was an actor and intimate friend of Porter's.

† Porter's residence in Los Angeles, which he rented from actor-turned-decorator William Haines. *Vogue* published a description of part of the house in its 1 September 1945 issue: 'One room is really a garden *sous cloche* – the once open terrace glassed in, and with Mexican colours, raw pink and green. Thick green string rugs are planted like grass on the flagstone floor ... The second room is fresh as an outdoor pavilion, has fruit chintz, Chinese porcelains, a watery expanse of mirrored wall, a light-struck bar built across one window. Under the piano the rug is patched, worn thin by Porter's feet.' Also see McBrien, *Cole Porter*, 269.

Tell Willie [Haines] – or rather, <u>ask</u> him to try the Japanese screen that I bought at Yamanaka* for a nickel. I think it is swell but if it destroys the room, to hell with it. Yamanaka has been taken over by the government – <u>that is</u>, the U.S.A. Linda tipped me off on this + the treasure for sale for practically nonsence [sic] that might interest Mr. Haines, Inc. Yamanaka has Chinese loot too.

Take Jimmie [Shields] into some secluded corner + talk to him about rare perfumes, soaps + cigarette-cases. Find out what he needs most + report.

I said goodnight to you pages ago + this is the finale. I love you so much, dear Sam.

Good morning

Cwole [sic]

Among the songs Porter was composing at this time for *Seven Lively Arts* was 'Wow-Ooh-Wolf!'; in a letter of 15 August 1944, Billy Rose suggested a number of possible 'wolf lines' to Porter, more punch-lines to jokes than song lyrics, including 'The only difference between a Hollywood wolf and a Broadway wolf is 3000 miles', 'He's A W O L . . . A Wolf on the Loose', 'The wolves in my hotel are so old, they hire the bell-hops to howl for them', 'A mink in the closet usually means a wolf at the door' and 'He's a wolf in cheap clothing.'[84] Arthur Schwartz reported that filming of *Night and Day* would probably start in the autumn and that he was trying to finalize the dialogue for *Mississippi Belle*; the problem with starting to shoot, he said, was that 'Technicolor commitments are very hard to get.'[85] A few days later he wrote to ask Porter, with respect to casting *Night and Day*, to approach '. . . the many stars who are indebted to you because of your great contribution to their success [who] would surely be more receptive if approached by you

---

* Yamanaka & Company was an Asian art firm founded by Yamanaka Sadajiro (1865–1936) in New York in 1895. In addition to locations in Boston (from 1899) and London (from 1900), it had agents in Paris (from 1905), an office in Beijing (from 1917) and a branch in Chicago (from 1928). Its inventory was confiscated in 1944 by the U.S. Office of Alien Property Custodian, according to the Yasuhashi Harumichi family papers at the Frick Collection, New York. According to a letter from Porter's lawyers Paul, Weiss, Rifkind, Wharton & Garrison of 16 April 1965, the screen Porter purchased was left to Sam Stark. Source: Stanford University, Cole Porter Collection, shelfmark FE209, folder 1–25, Correspondence: 1965.

rather than the studio.' These included Fred Astaire, Mary Martin, Danny Kaye, Sophie Tucker, Betty Hutton, Jimmy Durante, Bert Lahr and Irene Dunne; Schwartz added that 'If Fred Astaire or Mary Martin, or both let us say, should tell you they would be delighted to oblige, were it not for their picture contracts, we on this end would then try to arrange with Metro and Paramount respectively.'[86] Porter followed up on Schwartz's request in early September, writing to Danny Kaye:

6 September 1944: Cole Porter to Danny Kaye[87]

Dear Danny:

You probably know that Warner Brothers is doing a supposed biography of me called NIGHT AND DAY.

Would you consider appearing in this picture, singing either FARMING or LET'S NOT TALK ABOUT LOVE? I should certainly appreciate it a great deal if you would. If you would consider this, then Arthur Schwartz would talk money to your agent. I imagine they will start shooting this picture in December.

Goodbye, dear Danny, and all my best to you and Sylvia [Fine],
That old*
[unsigned]

Mike Curtiz,† who was to direct *Night and Day*, sent Porter a telegram on 28 August, responding to an apparently lost telegram of Porter's – 'I JUST RECEIVED YOUR WIRE AND HASTEN TO TELL YOU HOW DELIGHTED I AM TO BE THE DIRECTOR OF NIGHT AND DAY[.] BY NATURE I AM VERY CRITICAL AND SKEPTICAL ABOUT STORY PROBLEMS UNTIL THEY ARE COMPLETELY LICKED[,] ESPECIALLY BIOGRAPHICAL

---

* On 16 September, Porter wrote similar letters to Betty Hutton, Jimmy Durante and Sophie Tucker; Tucker responded by telegram on 19 September 1944: 'HAPPY TO SING FOR MY FAVORITE COMPOSER STOP HOW ABOUT MOST GENTLEMEN DON'T LIKE LOVE[?] SHOULD BE OUTSTANDING HIT IF DONE WITH FIVE BEAUTIFUL DAUGHTERS[.] HAVE YOUR MAN CONTACT NED DOBSON[,] WILLAM MORRIS AGENCY HERE[.] LOVE=SOPHIE'. CPT, Correspondence 1944.

† The film director Michael Curtiz (1886–1962) is best known, perhaps, for *Casablanca* (1942).

STORIES[.] BUT THINGS HAVE FALLEN INTO PLACE FOR US IN THE LAST TEN DAYS OF CONFERENCES WITH THE WRITERS AND ARTHUR SCHWARTZ AND I AM NOW CONVINCED THAT WE ARE WELL ON THE WAY TO CONSTRUCT A STORY WITH GREAT WARMTH AND ORIGINALITY AS WELL AS HUMAN CHARACTERIZATION[.] I ALWAYS HAVE FELT THAT WITH THE FABULOUS STORE HOUSE OF MUSICAL MATERIAL IN YOUR CATALOG TO WORK WITH WE COULD MAKE AN ENTERTAINMENT[,] BUT NOT UNTIL THIS PAST WEEK HAVE I FELT THAT IN ADDITION TO THAT WE COULD CONTRIBUTE A GREAT HUMAN AMERICAN STORY' – and Porter wrote to Jack Warner, seemingly anxious to get on with the production:

29 August 1944: Cole Porter to Jack Warner[88]

Dear Jack:

I just heard from Arthur Schwartz and I can't tell you how happy I am that Mike Curtiz will direct Night and Day. How soon will it be ready for production? I want to arrange my dates. Love to you and Annie.

Cole

As the movie began to take shape, Arthur Schwartz wrote concerning some possible changes to the lyrics of 'In the Still of the Night':

. . . at the moment I want to tell you about a lyric problem. We are planning to use the song "In The Still Of The Night" twice in the picture. The second time will be deep in the story and with a production. We propose to use it for the first time in a scene in a church in Peru, Indiana. Cole has come home from Yale for the Christmas Holiday and the family has donated a beautiful organ to the church. It is Sunday morning and Cole is at the organ. A choir of twenty or thirty boys is singing the melody of "In The Still Of The Night", and during its rendition we cut to Cole's mother and grandfather sitting proudly below. My immediate question is: Would you consider re-writing the lyrics of the song to make it suitable for a rather Hymnal interpretation, still keeping the title? The melody is as beautiful and pure as any piece of church music I know, and if you agree to make the lyric change, Curtiz and I guarantee to you a scene of overpowering beauty which will add to the story immeasurably. Following the church scene there are several others in and around Cole's home and at the end of the Indiana sequence Cole has told his grandfather that he has definitely decided against a legal career because he wants to pursue his music. Cole's mother, who has been his champion all along, approves of his decision. We see that she is greatly influenced by the deep impression the song in the church has made upon her.[89]

Porter replied on 6 September:

6 September 1944: Cole Porter to Arthur Schwartz[90]

Dear Arthur:

I have thought seriously about changing the lyric of IN THE STILL OF THE NIGHT to make it fit a hymnal interpretation. I don't like the idea at all. I think the present lyric makes it a good romantic song, but that a lyric which would make it suitable to be sung in a church would make it a much too saccharine bit of religious material. Perhaps you could get some one else to write this lyric, some one who had not had previous association with the song. Of course, I should want to approve of this lyric were it done. Of one thing I am sure and that is I could not do it.

It makes me very unhappy also to hear that you brought back that Peru, Indiana business into the picture. I thought you had definitely thrown that out, of which I highly approved. If all of this Peru stuff is back in the picture, I want to read every line of it as the last version would have been extremely embarrassing had it been retained and I don't want in any way to upset my family.

The Billy Rose show* is a fascinating job but oh so tough. I have written two numbers for Bea Lillie and one for Bert Lahr. I have three more to do for them, besides any number of others. Billy Rose, however, is a great relief after Mike Todd† as he is an excellent editor and a very constructive one.

---

* *Seven Lively Arts.*
† A reference to Porter's dissatisfaction with Todd's direction of *Mexican Hayride*.

Your music is played so much on the air that it seems to me it is wicked for you not to compose more.

All my best

[unsigned]

1 September 1944: Cole Porter to Sam Stark[91]

Dear Sam:

How nice you were to send the three cups and saucers, one for Linda, one for Sturges and one for me. We look forward to them on our toes.

The glue certainly did arrive and Linda spent the whole week-end restoring her albums. Bless you for it. I realize what a tough request that was as they tell me that it is the essence of rubber.

Have you a photograph of the Eugene Berman picture?* If so, kindly forward it to me.

I can't write you any more as I am now having my hair-cut while a doctor sticks a needle in my behind.

Love,

[signed:] Cole

dictated August 31st

The Hays Code† posed problems for *Night and Day*. On 6 September 1944, Arthur Schwartz wrote to ask for any additional lyrics Porter might have written for 'Me and Marie' and 'I'm Getting Myself Ready For You' – he anticipated problems with the line ending 'when first you see me in my so to speak'. 'Love For Sale' – controversial when it was first performed in *The New Yorkers* (1930) for its portrayal of prostitution – was a particular

---

* Eugène Berman (1899–1972) was a Russian painter and theatre and opera designer.

† The Motion Picture Production Code – commonly known as the Hays Office or Hays Code after William H. Hays (1879–1954), the first president of the Motion Picture Producers and Distributors of America (1922–45) – established and enforced guidelines that governed acceptable or unacceptable content and language for motion pictures produced by major studios for public audiences in the United States. It was adopted in 1930 and replaced in 1968 by a rating system developed by the MPPDA's successor, the Motion Picture Association of America. For a copy of the code, including changes made to it during the 1940s and 1950s, see http://productioncode.dhwritings.com/multipleframes_productioncode.php.

concern and in the absence of a 'cleaned-up' radio version, Schwartz suggested using the song instrumentally. Porter replied on 8 September, addressing Schwartz's concerns about several specific songs:

8 September 1944: Cole Porter to Arthur Schwartz[92]

Dear Arthur:

I'm just off to the country where I can be reached from Friday evening at 7 p.m. and Tuesday up to 11:00 a.m. My telephone number is Williamstown, Massachusetts 742.

In answer to your two letters of September 6th. I have already written to Danny Kaye but have had no reply.*

I have left word for Mary Martin to call me in the country.

I will do my best to get hold of Betty Hutton next week. I shall attack Fred Astaire the moment he returns from abroad.

Miss Moore is tracking down "I NEVER REALIZED". It was published in England and until I made a row about it, was published as having been written by Melville Gideon, who had appropriated it.†

Miss Moore will send you the patter of ME AND MARIE.‡

Regarding I'M GETTING MYSELF READY FOR YOU§ and the line ending with "When first you see me in my so-to-speak" there was never a radio version, or a second version for the stage. I hope you're not using that old dud tune.

Miss Moore will send you complete lyrics of "LET'S NOT TALK ABOUT LOVE".¶

---

* In the end, Danny Kaye did not appear in *Night and Day*.

† 'I Never Realized' was sung in the London production of *The Eclipse*, which played at the Garrick Theatre from November 1919; the show was apparently inspired by a solar eclipse on 29 May 1919, during which '. . . the British astronomer Arthur Eddington ascertained that the light rays from distant stars had been wrenched off their paths by the gravitational field of the sun. That affirmed the prediction of Einstein's theory of general relativity, ascribing gravity to a warp in the geometry of space-time, that gravity could bend light beams.' See *New York Times*, 31 July 2017. 'I Never Realized' was subsequently incorporated into the New York run of *Buddies*, which played at the Selwyn Theatre from 27 October 1919–12 June 1920; the song was published in 1921. Melville Gideon (1884–1933) was a composer and performer.

‡ From *Jubilee* (1935).

§ From *The New Yorkers* (1930).

¶ From *Let's Face It!* (1941).

Regarding LOVE FOR SALE,* I never wrote a radio version. Lately, however, June Knight had some one write for her a new lyric and she sings it on the slightest provocation in the camps. The title is BONDS FOR SALE. Miss Moore will also send you complete lyrics for

LET'S DO IT
YOU'RE THE TOP
FRIENDSHIP
MY HEART BELONGS TO DADDY†

Regarding the Beard, I talked to him last night. He is most anxious to be in our picture.‡ His contract with Fox calls for ten weeks beginning October 10. He asked whether it would not be possible for you to shoot all of his scenes together in the latter part of your shooting, in which case he will be free.

If this is not possible, he will be willing to work at night. Therefore, you can have him if you want him.

The Billy Rose show§ is my pet in years. What a man!

All my best, dear Arthur,

Sincerely yours,

[signed:] Cole

P.S. Mr. Miles White¶ is very anxious to do the NIGHT AND DAY costumes. Could you let me know as soon as possible whether you would like him or not and I will let him know.

Schwartz's reply of 12 September is revealing of both the casting and legal arrangements that had to be made for the film: 'Cary [Grant] looks practically certain . . . As to Monty [Woolley], I think that dates can be arranged so that he can do both his picture at Fox, and ours. . . . I consider Fred [Astaire] most important of all . . . One of our clearance problems may be Ethel Merman. In spite of the fact that she has been so closely identified with your

---

* From *The New Yorkers* (1930).

† 'Let's Do It' from *Paris* (1928); 'You're the Top' from *Anything Goes* (1934); 'Friendship' from *Du Barry Was a Lady* (1939); and 'My Heart Belongs to Daddy' from *Leave it to Me!* (1938).

‡ Monty Woolley, who appeared in *Night and Day* and sang 'Miss Otis Regrets'.

§ *Seven Lively Arts*.

¶ The costume designer Miles White (1914–2000) was not hired for *Night and Day*. His main Broadway costume design credits were for Rodgers and Hammerstein's *Oklahoma!* (1943) and *Carousel* (1945).

shows, I don't think it would be practical to have her appear in the picture. I say practical, first, because Ethel is going to open in a show very soon,* and won't be available; and, secondly, if she were available, she photographs pretty badly.' There was also, Schwartz noted, a potential legal problem since if Merman was represented as singing a song in any particular show, Warner would have to get her consent to be 'impersonated' by someone else. '. . . One way out, of course, would be to have those songs that she introduced sung in night clubs or at parties and thereby not be legally involved . . . One more clearance problem, and I'm through for the day: If we are to make "production use" (as distinguished from "incidental" or "visual-vocal") of any songs belonging to stage properties, we must get the consent of your book collaborators and stage producers . . . I wonder about Vinton Freedley† since I recall some reports of differences between you and him.'[93]

About this time, Porter also wrote letters to Jean Howard and to Sam Stark, before returning to his correspondence with Arthur Schwartz concerning *Night and Day*:

8 September 1944: Cole Porter to Jean Howard[94]

Dear Bob-Cat:

Your beautiful photograph arrived. Certainly it's by far the best you have ever had taken. I have substituted it for the one that you gave me and you have no idea how much people admire it.

I'm way over my head on the Billy Rose show, but liking the job a great deal. I shan't ask you when you are coming to New York as I know perfectly well that none of your plans ever materialize.

Sturge and I go every Friday to Williamstown and return every Tuesday. Now and then he is untrue to us and can't resist Newport and Narragansett. He still works in the bowels of Pennsylvania Station and how he survives I don't know, as he gives large fashionable luncheons every day at the Colony.

---

* *Sadie Thompson*, by Vernon Duke. Merman withdrew from the show in September 1944, some two months before its opening at the Alvin Theatre on 16 November 1944. She did not appear in *Night and Day*.

† It is unclear what 'differences' Schwartz alludes to, although in the context it apparently relates to 'My Heart Belongs to Daddy' and the unsold picture rights for *Leave it to Me!* (1938), which Freedley had produced.

Linda is in wonderful form in spite of almost constant butler trouble. The last one who left said "I'm giving you notice, Madam. I'm tired of the mountains and want to work on the seashore from now on for several months."

Bea Lillie arrives September 10th and we go into rehearsal October 2nd.

I can't tell you how much I miss your beautiful face. Give my love to that big Swede* and ask her whether she ever received a book from me, or not. You might add that it's the custom in this country to acknowledge gifts.

A big kiss from

Cole

14 September 1944: Cole Porter to Sam Stark[95]

LINDA IS VERY WELL INDEED AN[D] I AM NOT AT ALL XUSY [sic] SO CAN YOU CHANGE YOUR PLANS AND STAY UP IN THE COUNTRY UNTIL TUESDAY WHEN I USUALLY COME DOWN? IF THIS TAKES UP TOO MUCH OF YOUR TIME OKAY BUT THE LONGER YOU STAY WITH US UP THERE THE HAPPIER WE SHALL BE. PLEASE LET ME KNOW AT ONCE ON ACCOUNT OF DIFFICULTY GETTING RESERVATIONS LOVE=COLE

20 September 1944: Cole Porter to Arthur Schwartz[96]

Dear Arthur:

I am sending you a copy of "I NEVER REALIZED".

I wrote only the refrain but I wrote both the words and music of the refrain. The verse must have been written by Melville Gideon.†

All my best,

Sincerely,

[signed:] Cole

[typed note at bottom dated 9/30/44:] gave Mr. Schwartz a new refrain, dictated by Mr. CP-while Mr. S. in 41-E.‡

---

* The actress Greta Garbo (1905–90).

† See above, p. 211.

‡ 'I Never Realized', finally, was not included in *Night and Day*. Porter's new refrain does not survive.

Shortly afterwards, on 23 September, Jack Warner sent a telegram alerting Porter to an impending visit to New York by Mike Curtiz and Arthur Schwartz: 'DEAR COLE. MIKE CURTIZ [AND] ARTHUR SCHWARTZ WILL ARRIVE NEW YORK ON MONDAY OR TUESDAY FOR CONFERENCES WITH YOU . . . IT WILL GIVE US ALL A CHANCE TO GET THE ULTIMATE OUT OF A GREAT STORY OF WHAT I CONSIDER A VERY IMPORTANT AMERICAN GUY.' A note typed at the bottom of this telegram, almost certainly by his secretary, Margaret Moore, records that 'Mr Porter wired "Dear Jack – Your swell wire received. I shall be here to cooperate in every way. My love to you both[.] Cole"'.[97]

2 October 1944: Cole Porter to Hal Wallis[98]

Dear Hal:

In regard to the portable piano which goes all through the early part of NIGHT AND DAY, I happened to run across Charlie Munn last night. It was he who gave it to me as I was sailing in 1916. It is officially called a Pianotina. It's really a Zitherharp with a piano keyboard, and was made to order for Charles A. Munn, by Lyon & Healy of Chicago. He is one of the owners of Lyon & Healy, in case you want a duplicate or a model of the original.*

It was awfully nice seeing you in New York and I am sure that under your guidance things will work out beautifilly [sic].

All my best,
Sincerely yours,
[unsigned]

About this time, William Skipper apparently wrote to Linda Porter, to enquire about Cole, and she answered him on 7 October: 'You are very sweet to worry about Cole – you know, when he is busy with a song he is thinking the <u>whole time</u> about music and lyrics to the exclusion of everything + everybody, which <u>does</u> change him from his usual gay charming self. His health is excellent . . .'[99] And Porter himself wrote to Jean Howard – apparently he was keen to meet up with Greta Garbo.

---

* Lyon & Healy, founded in Chicago in 1864, is a manufacturer of harps and other instruments.

9 October 1944: Cole Porter to Jean Howard[100]

DEAR LITTLE JEANIE, WHERE IN NEW YORK CAN I TRACK DOWN THAT BEAUTIFUL SWEDE BE A GOOD GIRL[.] LOVE=
COLE

Although *Night and Day* took up much of Porter's time in the autumn of 1944, the opening of *Seven Lively Arts* was approaching and the choice of music director, Maurice Abravanel,* was apparently questioned by Igor Stravinsky, whose *Scènes de ballet* was also written for the show. Porter wrote to Catherine d'Erlanger† with information about Abravanel to be passed on to the composer:

13 October 1944: Cole Porter to Baroness Catherine d'Erlanger[101]

Dear Catherine:

Thank you so much for your note. Please give the following information to Igor Stravinsky regarding the orchestra director for THE SEVEN LIVELY ARTS:

<u>EUROPEAN</u>

1930–1932	Berlin State Opera Unter den Linden
1932–	Grand Opera Paris (Don Giovanni)
1932–33	Sala Pleyel Symphony Concert
1933–	Musical director with Balanchine's British Opera Co.-Australia, (Sydney and Melbourne)

<u>BROADWAY PRODUCTIONS & OPERA</u>

Once conducted 7 operas in 9 days at Metropolitan

METROPOLITAN OPERA - - - -   1936–1938

---

* Maurice Abravanel (1903–93) was a conductor. After several appointments in Germany, Abravanel relocated to Paris in 1933; he subsequently performed in Australia, at the Metropolitan Opera, New York, in 1936, and from 1946 as director of the Utah State Symphony Orchestra. On Broadway he was particularly important as the conductor of Kurt Weill's *Knickerbocker Holiday* (1938), *Lady in the Dark* (1941), *One Touch of Venus* (1943), *The Firebrand of Florence* (1945) and *Street Scene* (1947).

† Marie Rose Antoinette Catherine de Robert d'Aqueria de Rochegude, Baroness d'Erlanger (1874–1959) was a society hostess and arts patron; she was married to the merchant banker Baron Emile Beaumont d'Erlanger (1866–1939).

CHICAGO OPERA -------	1940
KNICKERBOCKER HOLIDAY --	1938–1939
LADY IN THE DARK ------	1940–1943
ONE TOUCH OF VENUS ----	1943–1944

I think we are very lucky to have him.
All my love,
[unsigned]

Not only was Stravinsky apparently unacquainted with Maurice Abravanel – who in the end did conduct *Seven Lively Arts* – but from Billy Rose's point of view, there were also problems with both the length and scoring of his ballet. In asking Stravinsky to pare down his orchestration in order to reduce production costs, Rose may also inadvertently have antagonized Stravinsky by noting the scoring of Porter's songs; possibly Stravinsky recalled his unsatisfactory encounter with Porter in the early 1920s: 'Except for your composition,' Rose wrote, 'there is nothing in the Cole Porter score that requires a forty-piece orchestra. Robert Russell Bennett assures me he can reorchestrate the Porter music very effectively for twenty-eight men. This will mean a saving to me of $60,000 on the year. As a practical man of the theatre I hope you can appreciate my problem and reorchestrate your composition for this smaller number of men. Otherwise I would have no choice but to replace it with other music. I would very much like to retain it and if you are willing to do this will wire you the new instrumentation.' A compromise was reached by eliminating the tuba, one of the trombones and seven strings.* Two weeks later Porter again took up his correspondence with Arthur Schwartz concerning the casting for *Night and Day*:

25 October 1944: Cole Porter to Arthur Schwartz[102]

Dear Arthur:

When Fred Astaire returned from Europe, I talked to him regarding the NIGHT AND DAY picture. He wants to do it just as much as we want him to do

---

* For a more detailed account of Stravinsky's *Scènes de ballet*, see Stephen Walsh, *Stravinsky. The Second Exile: France and America, 1934–1971* (New York, 2006), 163–6; for Billy Rose's letter to Stravinsky, see ibid, 165.

it. I told him to take the angle at Metro that they MUST allow him to do it. The only thing that he asks is that you arrange time with him between pictures. Until I spoke to him, he thought he would have to run through the whole picture, so he was greatly relieved when I told him it was only for the song and dance. I think he intends to get Louise Bremner [sic].* I should talk to him but not on the basis that he is SURE. Simply say how happy I am that there is a good chance of his doing it, and that I would never get over it if he didn't do it, to think my having written the song for him† and he having had such great success with it.

How about that transcription of the "Wrong syllable" song?‡ I've waited with frency [sic] to get it.

Goodbye, dear Arthur, and love from 41-E.§ Your old friend

One letter concerning *Seven Lively Arts* provides insight into an aspect of performance practice in Porter's music that is otherwise not well documented – tempo:

6 November 1944: Cole Porter to Jack Donohue¶

Dear Jack:

To lessen the difficulty of your understanding the master work which you will receive tomorrow, entitled "OPENING ACT 1 SCENE 1", the following layout may be of help to you. In the first place it's all in galop tempo. Played in its proper tempo the whole thing should last for one minute and 36 seconds, not including the introduction which comes before rise of curtain. Therefore, each 16 bars equals 12 seconds.

---

* Here Porter means Lucille Bremer (1917–96), one of the dancing girls in *Panama Hattie*. She starred with Fred Astaire in the film *Yolanda and the Thief* (MGM, 1945) and *Ziegfeld Follies* (MGM, started 1944 but not released until 1946).

† Astaire had introduced the song 'Night and Day' in Porter's 1932 *Gay Divorce*.

‡ A telegram of 27 October, from Arthur Schwartz to Porter, identifies this as Frank Loesser's 'Sing a Tropical Song', composed for the film *Her Lucky Night* (1944): 'I thought by this time Frankie Loesser surely had sent you the transcription on [sic] his calypso song. He may have had some difficulty getting it, or the birth of his child a couple of weeks ago may have possibly put him on a long jag of celebration. When I told him you wanted the number, he was so thrilled I am sure he will get it for you.' (CPT, Correspondence 1944).

§ Porter's suite at the Waldorf, New York.

¶ CPT, Correspondence 1944 (copy). Jack Donohue (1908–84), director, performer and choreographer. Donohue was responsible for the musical staging in *Seven Lively Arts*.

LAYOUT OF OPENING ACT I, SCENE I

PART A
    SECTION I   16 bars
    SECTION II   16 bars (middle)
    SECTION III   8 bars (reprise of last 8 bars of Section I)

PART B
    TRIO – 32 bars written in 16 bars. hurdy-gurdy effect (waltz & galop tempi)

PART C
    SECTION I   8 bars (with reprise of Section III of Part A)
    SECTION II   16 bars – Coda

I can't tell you how happy we all are with your swell work.
Best,
[unsigned]

Porter's comment, 'TRIO – 32 bars written in 16 bars', is explained by the conductor's score for the number:[103] whereas the rest of the movement is written in 2/4 time, the trio is notated in 4/4 time. Accordingly, the 16 bars of the trio are the equivalent of 32 bars in the rest of the Introduction. Porter's comment that the whole should last for one minute and thirty-six seconds means that the tempo must be a crotchet = 60.

The Porters' considerable involvement with modern art, already apparent in the 1920s, is further documented in the 1940s through Cole's interest in the works of Grandma Moses (Anna Mary Robertson, 1860–1961). An undated letter from her to Porter records the sale of twelve paintings: 'Eagle Bridge Dec 7. Mr Cole Porter Dear Sir, am shipping out the twelve paintings. Now if there are some that you do not like ship them back. COD. They are $7.00 each. Thanks for the order, pleas [sic] remember me to Mrs Cole Porter … Yours in haste Moses'.[104] And in November 1944 Porter purchased two other pictures from Grandma Moses, as a receipt dated 6 November shows:

    EagleBridge, Nov. 6./44
        Mr Cote [sic] Porter Dear Sir,
        am ship[p]ing out your two paintings in the morning.

They are [:] Cambridge valley in winter	$ 50,
Over the river to Grandmas [sic] house	$ 65,

	115

I will try to get some of your Christmas paintings done if not all, will send on what I have in time,
> with best wishes,
> mother moses[105]

The *New York Times* took special notice of one of these pictures, *Cambridge Valley in Winter*, in an article dated 16 January 1949: 'Cole Porter is a trim, slight man, groomed with subdued, elegant taste. The only bright touch in his get-up when he was visited a few days ago in his apartment on the forty-first floor of the Waldorf Towers was a white carnation. The most colorful thing in the room was a big painting by Grandma Moses, full of her naively gay whites and blues, which hung in a place of honor over the piano'*. Porter was offered another seven paintings in late November, including *Catching a Turkey*, *That Is a Fine Turkey*, *The Old Bake Oven* and *Catch Him Rover*.†

In November, Porter wrote to Stanley Musgrove, far more intimately than he had in his letter the previous month concerning 'My Heart Belongs to Daddy':

19 November 1944: Cole Porter to Stanley Musgrove[106]

My dear Stan

If you have in mind anyone who needs cheer & charm & the warmth of a thinking full heart, write to this person. Your letter arrived & put me on the top of all the hills of Elysium. No matter the topography yours was my first

---

* *Cambridge Valley in Winter*, from Cole Porter's estate, was later auctioned by Sotheby's; see http://www.sothebys.com/en/auctions/ecatalogue/2011/american-paintings-n08751/lot.121.html.

† For Grandma Moses's letter to Porter, see Ira & Larry Goldberg Auctioneers, sale 6, lot 797. The provenance of another Moses picture, *Sugaring Off*, can also be traced to Porter, who subsequently gave it to Cy Feuer; see https://www.christies.com/lotfinder/Lot/anna-mary-robertson-grandma-moses-1860-1961-4816730-details.aspx.

letter since many a moon. In answer to your question about the gentlemen present when we dined at Le Pavillon the elder was Ollie Jennings.* He was several years after me at Yale. He is embarrassingly rich but does so much good with his money that his inherited wealth is no weapon for Mr. Browder.† The other one was Benhur Baz. His first name is the result of his papa reading the original Wallace novel & falling in love with the title. Ben is a Mexican. All his family are artists & Ben is a fine painter in oil & tempera & I believe he will go far...

Linda isn't well at all but I told her about your letter & she sends her love to you with mine.

Arrange to go to Havana. It is delightful.

My show opens in Philadelphia on Nov. 24th.‡ I shall be there at the Hotel Barclay until Sat. Dec. 2nd.

Please write me a list of articles that I can send you. This will give me great joy.

So good night, Stan and bless you for the letter.

Your devoted

C.

As Porter noted, the Philadelphia tryout of *Seven Lively Arts* opened on 24 November 1944. Shortly afterwards, Porter wrote to Monty Woolley:

29 November 1944: Cole Porter to Monty Woolley[107]

Dear Beard:

Your wire dated November 25th, just arrived. I have studied its contents for hours but I don't get it. I thought Tennyson said that years ago.

---

* Le Pavillon opened in 1941 at 5 East 55th Street; at the time it was considered the finest French restaurant in the United States. Le Pavillon closed in 1971.

† Possibly Earl Russell Browder (1891–1973), general secretary of the Communist Party of the United States, 1932–47.

‡ *Seven Lively Arts*.

I know you will be very bored to hear that I have a colossal hit on my hands called SEVEN LIVELY ARTS. I stuck your name in one of the lyrics last night just to keep your memory alive.*

Love,

[signed:] Cole

While Porter may have wanted to give Monty Woolley a bit of publicity, he was also concerned with (and sometimes piqued by) how he was himself billed. On 29 November, Porter's agent, Richard Madden, wrote to him: 'I quote below copy of a wire received last night from Billy Rose. "With everybody on edge and slug nutty for loss of sleep I doubt advisability of revamping house boards for the few remaining days but of course will if Cole insists but it would be smoother my way. It will be handled in New York precisely in conformity your telegram. Regards Billy Rose." This is in reply to one from me to him, in which I insisted upon giving you single line precedence over [the director, Hassard] Short on House Board signs and also insisted that you approve the billing for the New York publicity before it is set up. Are you willing to allow present billing to stand for these few days or possibly aggravate billing at this time, considering your general relations with him?'[108] A note typed at the bottom of this letter reads: 'Dec. 1/44 called Mr. Madden – Miss Rubin ans. Told her C.P. read letter and gave it to me – he said "Mr. M. could have telephoned me this." Porter also wrote to Jean Howard on 29 November:

29 November 1944: Cole Porter to Jean Howard[109]

Dear Jeanie:

Thank you so much for the wire regarding the broadcast and the opening.

The show is wonderful and I have never had such a nice experience in the theatre as with the curious little Billy Rose. He tops any producer that I have ever worked with.

I am so sorry you won't be here for that little opening in New York.

---

* In 'Dainty, Quainty Me': 'When anyone mentions Martha Raye, Carmen Miranda, / Lana Turner, Anita Louise, Joan Davis, Betty Hutton, / Gregory Ratoff, Red Skelton, Monty Woolley, Don Ameche, / Jack Oakie, Sir Cedric Hardwicke and other stars of the cinema, / I have to take an inema.'

In the meantime don't forget that I love you dearly and miss you between every minute.

Your old sweetheart

[signed:] Cole

Throughout his career, Porter was frequently asked about the origins of his songs and for the most part he was diligent in answering questions about them. A letter he wrote to Louis Walters, the owner of a nightclub in New York, is typical:

30 November 1944: Cole Porter to Louis Walters*

Dear Lou Walters:

In regard to THE LAZIEST GIRL IN TOWN, I wrote only one verse and one refrain. Nothing happened to this song for a long time and then somebody began singing it in Harlem where many more lyrics were written. I can't suggest to you who would know about this.

I am sorry not to be of more help to you.

Sincerely yours,† [unsigned]

Even before *Seven Lively Arts* opened in New York on 7 December, Porter's editor at Chappell Music, Albert Sirmay, wrote to congratulate him:

To-day is again a day of pride and glory for you and I can't let it go without saying a few words to you. First of all I want to say how happy I feel about you. In your new show you are giving again a most delightful evidence of your great talent. Instead of declining, your imagination, the freshness of your ideas and your skill both as a composer and lyricist are all on the increase. I myself have a personal affair with your song "Every time". It chokes me whenever I hear it, it moves me to tears. This song is one of the

---

* CPT, Correspondence 1944. Louis Edward Walters (1896–1977) founded the Latin Quarter nightclub at 1580 Broadway in 1942.

† According to Kimball, *The Complete Lyrics of Cole Porter*, 140–1, 'The Laziest Girl in Town' was published in June 1927 and probably written for a summer show at Edmond Sayag's Ambassadeurs Café. Other details are unknown. The song was made famous by Marlene Dietrich in Alfred Hitchcock's *Stage Fright* (1950).

greatest songs you ever wrote. It is a dythiramb [sic] to love, a hymn to youth, a heavenly beautiful song. It is not less a gem than any immortal song of a Schubert or Schuman [sic]. Contemporaries usually fail to recognize real values. I don't care what critics may say, this song is a classic and will live forever as many others of your songs. Well, my dear Cole, I am immensely happy about you. I don't need to tell you how much I like you. After all these years of my close association with you you should know about it. I not only like you, but I have also the highest respect for your wonderful character, your highly cultured spirit, which all make you a unique personality. You may not be the Beethoven of America, but you are the Cole Porter of America. And that's just enough.[110]

The critics, however, did not agree. The *New York Times* for 8 December 1944, for instance, reported that: 'Cole Porter has written the music for the show, and the tunes definitely are not his best. Probably the nearest approach to the old Porter style – he will regret having written all those good ones in former years – is "Ev'ry Time We Say Goodbye". Porter mentioned the negative reviews in letters to Jean Howard (notwithstanding his earlier comment to her that 'the show is wonderful') and Arthur Schwartz:

12 December 1944: Cole Porter to Jean Howard[111]

Dear Jean:

Your beautiful answer to the Moses picture arrived.

You ask me how I ever guessed you wanted one and my answer is: that for five months you hinted for one every time I saw you, as you coyly lowered your eyes and twisted your pretty foot in my little Brentwood garden. I didn't have time to reframe it, but I'm sure that you will have some brilliant idea.

The opening was SOMETHING. It's not fashionable to like "DON'T FENCE ME IN," but I suppose that old Texas blood of yours comes forth and you accept it.

As usual, the Press tried to run me out of town but I know that the last one is the best job I have done for years, so I am not depressed.*

---

* It is likely that these two paragraphs refer to two different works: 'Don't Fence Me In', originally written for *Adios, Argentina*, was subsequently used in the film *Hollywood Canteen*, released in December 1944. The bad reviews Porter mentions refer to *Seven Lively Arts*.

We see Michael constantly and he is a joy.

Lots of love to you, dear Jeannie,

[signed:] Cole

14 December 1944: Cole Porter to Arthur Schwartz[112]

Dear Arthur:

The press gave me bad notices on "The Seven Lively Arts". I am accustomed to them through the years but Billy Rose and Max Dreyfus* are both highly incensed.

Billy Rose wants to run a big ad in the papers, after the numbers get started on the air and on recordings; this ad quoting the critics on my back shows to prove how little the critics know a good song, when they hear one.

You have all my scrap books and I know you are a busy man but can you get someone to go through them and collect all the bad notices, especially from well known critics of today. For instance, I remember some critic saying, in regard to "Night and Day", that it was a weak copy of my good song, "What Is This Thing Called Love", also Robert Benchley in The New Yorker, speaking of "Begin The Beguine", wondered why such a big production had been built around such a commonplace song.† Another thing that always has happened is – "Cole Porter is not up to his usual standard."

If you can collect this list for me, I would be glad to pay whoever does the dirty work but I need it badly.

In the meantime, our little opus has sold out for 15 weeks and this, in spite of bad press on my numbers.

All my best.

As ever,

CP/R Dictated by Mr. Cole Porter over the telephone.

---

* Max Dreyfus (1874-1964) was a music publisher. He owned Chappell Music, which published *Seven Lively Arts*, among other Porter shows.

† Possibly Porter's memory failed him here. Robert Benchley's review of *Jubilee* in the *New Yorker* for 19 October 1935, 32–4, does not mention 'Begin the Beguine'. Although he suggests Porter's lyrics are too subtle – 'The lyrics which Mr. Cole Porter has devised, with an eye to pleasing perhaps eighteen people, are negligible in market value' – he nevertheless said of the show '. . . Messrs. Moss Hart, Cole Porter, Hassard Short, Max Gordon, and (everybody's sweetheart) Sam Harris have a show in "Jubilee!" which is heart-warming and beautiful, and I hope that it runs forever, because it is so nice.'

23 December 1944: Cole Porter to Arthur Schwartz[113]

Dear Arthur:

Thank you for your special delivery letter with the bad notices included. I am sorry but your friend, Mr. Herman Lissauer,* has not been thorough enough, but I beg you say nothing about this to him. I distinctly remember the Bob Benchley notice in the New Yorker, in which he wondered why so great a production was built around such an inferior tune as BEGIN THE BEGUINE, but four years later when the tune became popular, Bob Benchley and I met and he apologized for his notice, in his charming way.

Also I remember reading a notice regarding NIGHT AND DAY, as being an inferior attempt to copy WHAT IS THIS THING CALLED LOVE. I saw this clipping in one of the scrap books just before I sent them to you, and they are both most important for Billy Rose.

Also there are many notices saying 'Cole Porter not up to his usual standard', which Mr. Lassauer [sic] hasn't found. Perhaps it would be better to give this job to some dirty lawyer.

All my best wishes for the New Year and thanks for the effort. What can I send as a present to Mr. Lissauer, as I am very grateful for what he has done?

Sincerely,

[unsigned]

Porter's letter was a response to Arthur Schwartz's of 18 December, in which he recalls a bad notice of his own and his resolve to write a response. Schwartz continued with news of progress on *Night and Day*: 'Cary Grant and Monty Woolley have both signed their contracts. Mary Martin's agent believes Paramount will allow her to do DADDY, but this deal still has to be worked out. I have been working on Arthur Freed about Fred Astaire, and I think we'll get him. There is this hitch about Fred: as anxious as he is to appear in the picture, he will not do so unless it is in technicolor because he has now seen himself in a couple of color epics and will never do black and white again. Jack Warner has not yet assured me that we will get color . . . The script is through one complete draft and revisions are now being made to get it into reasonable length.'[114]

---

* Herman Lissauer (1892–1957) was a researcher at MGM.

In the midst of work on *Night and Day*, and just after Christmas 1944, Warner Bros. received notice of a lawsuit by Ira Arnstein claiming that Porter's songs were plagiarized. Warner Brothers wrote to Porter to alert him on 27 December:

> Dear Mr. Porter: A constant litigant in the United States Courts named Ira Arnstein has written a letter to this company addressed to the attention of the legal department, another letter to Mr. Harry M. Warner, president, and a third letter to Mr. Arthur Schwartz in all of which he claims that certain of your songs are a plagiarism of compositions of his. The letters are accompanied by various manuscripts and printed pages of Arnstein's music together with diagrams pointing out the claims of Arnstein. While far from a musical expert myself I am sufficiently qualified to venture the opinion that these claims are absolutely ridiculous. On the other hand if Arnstein follows his usual course he can become an awful nuisance. It is for the foregoing reason that we are advising you of these claims so that you and we may take necessary protective measures either independently or otherwise as may be advisable. It is my suggestion that you appoint a time for me to come to see you with all the material Arnstein has furnished so that you may be fully advised as to the nature of Arnstein's claims.[115]

Ira Arnstein (birth and death dates unknown) was famous for instigating lawsuits against other composers, claiming plagiarism: in 1936 he filed suit against the Edward Marks Publishing Company, and in 1939 against the composer Joe Burke (1884–1950).* In his suit against Porter, which came before the courts in 1946, he alleged not only that Porter had stolen his music – specifically he claimed that 'Don't Fence Me In', 'Begin the Beguine', 'I Love You', 'Night and Day' and 'You'd Be So Nice to Come Home To' were plagiarized – but also that Porter's employees had broken into his apartment, although he was unable to substantiate this claim. Porter subsequently filed a motion for summary judgement and the case was dismissed. On appeal, Judge Jerome Frank overturned the lower court's ruling and in doing so established two tests

---

* See Gary Rosen, *Unfair to Genius: The Strange and Litigious Career of Ira B. Arnstein* (Oxford, 2012).

for copyright infringement that became a landmark ruling: the first was to establish that a defendant in fact made use of a plaintiff's copyrighted work, the determination of which relied at least in part on expert opinion; the second was that the determination of appropriation depended not on expert witnesses but on whether or not the intended audience found a substantial similarity between the works – put otherwise, an expert determination of use of copyright material did not settle a case but resulted in a jury trial.*

---

* For the text of Judge Frank's ruling, see https://law.justia.com/cases/federal/appellate-courts/F2/154/464/1478575/.

CHAPTER FIVE

A PORTER BIOPIC AND TWO FLOPS, 1945–1947

At the start of 1945, Porter's surviving correspondence mostly concerned the song 'Don't Fence Me In' – originally written in 1934 for the unproduced film musical *Adios, Argentina* but subsequently used by Warner Bros. in their 1944 *Hollywood Canteen* – and progress on the film *Night and Day*:

4 January 1945: Cole Porter to Jack Warner[1]

Dear Jack:

Your very nice letter of December 30th arrived. After bothering you about the billing on DON'T FENCE ME IN, all billing about this song has entirely disappeared, so I evidently made my objections too late. Perhaps, however, this can be taken care of in the rest of the country, or abroad when the picture is shown. I know nothing about these matters and I shant [sic] bother you further.

Everything sounds grand about NIGHT AND DAY and my last little prayer each night is that you can wangle a techni-color equipment for it.

It made me extremely happy to read that you are looking around for an assignment for me at Warner Brothers. I would so much rather work there than anywhere else, Jack. Certainly your studio has treated me beautifully in the past and I feel sort of at home there, what with you at the head of it all.

My love to you and that lovely Annie, and may your 1945 be something out of this world.

Best,

[unsigned]

4 January 1945: Cole Porter to Jack Warner[2]

Dear Jack:

In my letter written this morning, I forgot to tell you that Mr. Herman Starr's* secretary, Miss Whittaker, called my secretary, Miss Margaret Moore, to say that I had talked with her about the publicity on the song
DON'T FENCE ME IN
and that Mr. Starr said this is entirely up to the Warner Bros. Publicity Department and suggested that I talk with you regarding it.

Later I talked to Herman Starr himself and he told me he had called up your Publicity Department, who told him the publicity had all been set and it was too late to change it.

I realize that this was entirely true, but do hope that you can do something about the publicity in other citiws [sic] and in other countries, when the picture is shown.

My best,

[unsigned]

Porter had good reason to be interested in the billing, and consequently the exploitation, of 'Don't Fence Me In'. Although the specific upshot of this episode is not known, Porter evidently benefited from it over the next several weeks: on 31 January, *Variety* reported that 'Cole Porter's "Don't Fence Me In" slid over the 1,000,000 mark in sheet [music] sales within the past couple of days, the first song to do that since "White Christmas"† and the second since 1929. With the million-mark passed, the song so far has given no indication of slackening and total sale of around 1,250,000 is forecast ... An unusual type of tune for Porter, "Fence" piled up its sales in a comparatively short time. It was started about three months ago.'[3]

5 January 1945: Cole Porter to Arthur Schwartz[4]

Dear Arthur:

Thank you so much for the material regarding the bad notices.‡ I appre-

---

* Herman Starr (1899–1965) was president of the Music Publishers Holding Corporation and an important figure at ASCAP; see his obituary in *Billboard*, 16 January 1965, 1 and 10.
† By Irving Berlin, written in 1941.
‡ For *Seven Lively Arts*.

ciate deeply all the work you have done for me.

Charles Hoffman* has arrived with the new script [for *Night and Day*] and is sending it to me. Unluckily at the present moment I am not able to see any one, but perhaps before he leaves I shall be able to see him.

All my best. I'm so happy that you liked the Ma Moses picture.†

Sincerely,

[unsigned]

As is the case with all celebrities, rumours abounded about both Porter's health and his work. Although she apparently did not write about Porter in early 1945, gossip columnist Hedda Hopper‡ – or at least Porter heard it was her – reported several misleading facts that Porter felt compelled to correct:

16 January 1945: Cole Porter to Hedda Hopper[5]

DEAR HEDDA. SOMEBODY GAVE YOU AN AWFUL LOT OF WRONG DOPE. I AM NOT OUT OF THE HOSPITAL. I AM NOT GOING FOR A WEEK WITH LINDA TO OUR UPSTATE HOME. I DO NOT RETURN TO HOLLYWOOD IN MARCH. JACK WARNER DID NOT BEG ME TO DO ANOTHER PICTURE. I BEGGED HIM. LOVE TO YOU AND YOUR HAT=COLE

Hopper was not the only one spreading rumours. Less than a month later, on 14 February, Jack Warner wrote to Porter: 'The statement by Dan Walker§ that we are giving up your picture *Night and Day* because of lack of drama, comes under the heading of the statement by that great American

---

* Charles Hoffman (1911–72), film and television writer and producer; his credits include the 1960s television shows *Batman* and *The Green Hornet*.

† Concerning Porter's purchase of numerous pictures by Grandma Moses, see above pp. 219–20.

‡ The gossip columnist Hedda Hopper (Elda Furry, 1885–1966), who was also famous for her elaborate hats.

§ Danton Walker (1899–1960), a writer and producer at MGM and a Broadway columnist.

who said "The story of my demise is greatly exaggerated."* We are starting picture April 30th. It will be in technicolor† and more enthused about it than ever.' The same day that Porter wrote to Hopper, he continued his correspondence concerning *Night and Day*:

16 January 1945: Cole Porter to Arthur Schwartz[6]

Dear Arthur:

I enclose a letter from Babe Pearce. He used to be Bob Alton's assistant. Later Fred Astaire found him so excellent in dance routines that he had Babe help him on all his own dances.‡ He is an excellent man and I highly recommend him.

Have written to him that I had sent this letter to you for attention.

All my best,

[unsigned]

Porter had another stint at the Doctors Hospital in January 1945, writing to Sam Stark at the end of the month:

29 January 1945: Cole Porter to Sam Stark[7]

1/['30' struck through and replaced above with:] 29/45 Docs Hosp.

---

* CPT, Correspondence 1945. The 'great American' is Mark Twain. The facts surrounding this familiar quote are more mundane. On 28 May 1897 the editors of the *New York Journal* wrote to their English editor, Frank Marshall White, concerning rumours that Twain was on his deathbed. White contacted Twain, who wrote to him: 'I can understand perfectly how the report of my illness got about, I have even heard on good authority that I was dead. James Ross Clemens, a cousin of mine, was seriously ill two or three weeks ago in London, but is well now. The report of my illness grew out of his illness. The report of my death was an exaggeration.'

† Jack Warner had explained in an earlier letter of 30 December 1944 that due to the war, technicolor was not always available to the studios: 'Everything is really on the upbeat on NIGHT AND DAY. Cary Grant and Monty are all set and the balance will be an important cast. I am trying to see if we can get technicolor camera equipment on this picture. Owing to the war, technicolor equipment is quite limited, but I am doing all I can to secure it for NIGHT AND DAY.' CPT, Correspondence 1944.

‡ Bernard (Babe) Pearce (birth and death dates unknown) was a choreographer and dancer; he had worked with Fred Astaire on the film *Holiday Inn* (1942). Robert Alton (1906–57), choreographer and dancer; he was later the dance director for the film *The Pirate* (1948), for which Porter wrote the music.

Dear Sam – Enclosed 400 bucks to pay for diverse items. If this is not enough, demand mo'. If too much, credit me it. Leave Hosp tomorrow (30th)
All's well.
As ever
(Ah loves yuh)
Cole Enema Potah

Linda Porter reported to William Skipper on 27 February: 'Cole is back after his second trip to the hospital when they kept him for 10 days: – he "overdid" [it?] at the Waldorf. Saw too many people, answered too many phone calls etc etc – it was difficult to keep him quiet. He is far better, much less nervous and his leg is healing beautifully.'[8] In the meantime, Arthur Schwartz, who was producing *Night and Day*, wrote to Porter concerning some delays and concerns Warner Bros. had with respect to the film:

> It's been a long time since I've written to you, and I hope you'll forgive me. We've been having some difficulties, but they are practically all straightened out now. The main one was that the budget for the script you read was astronomical, and all of us were disturbed. Production costs these days are simply unbelievable, as you'll realize when I tell you that the figure given us as an estimate for total cost was somewhere above $3,500,000.00, <u>without</u> Technicolor.
>
> We have made some cuts in the script and score, and especially in the number of sets, and a revised budget is now being prepared. It should be ready in a few days.
>
> At a long meeting last week, Jack Warner finally gave in to Curtiz and myself on Technicolor. We will have it. That is, unless Cary Grant refuses to give us a postponement of about four or five weeks to get the Technicolor cameras which are not available for the original date we planned. We are working on Cary and his agent now and feel practically certain Cary will go along with us. At this same meeting, Warner said he would allow us a budget of $2,800,000.00, which is, by a wide margin, the largest budget for any picture ever made at this studio.
>
> I confess I'm a little frightened at making so costly a picture, because if we get released in a particularly bad time for business, we may just about break even. But even if we fortify ourselves with a perfect script,

and all of the name personalities we are trying to sign, this is the kind of picture that should gross at least $5,000,000.00, domestically. That is, with business conditions around the country being normal, or slightly inflated, as now.

I am giving you all these figures in strictest confidence, Cole. You know how studios feel about having picture costs known by anybody. The fact that Warner is willing to go so far in expenditure assures another important thing: exhaustive exploitation when we get released.

Now that Technicolor seems assured, I am following up on Fred Astaire and Danny Kaye. I just spoke [to] Leland Hayward* a moment ago and he will help us set up the Astaire commitment. I called New York yesterday and spoke to Lou Mandel, the personal representative and lawyer for Danny Kaye,† to see if he could get Goldwyn to allow Danny to do the number without considering it the equivalent of Danny's outside picture commitment. Do you possibly stand strongly enough with Goldwyn to go to bat for us if he turns it down?

The Mary Martin commitment seems fairly certain now because of her new arrangement with Paramount.‡

For the part of Carol, we have some hope of getting Ann Sheridan (with a dubbed voice). If she doesn't want to play this small part, we would then go for Frances Langford or Ginny Simms, both of whom want the part very much.§

For the part of Gracie, we like Jane Wyman, who has a very good comedy sense and whose voice could be dubbed as well.¶

---

* The theatrical agent and producer Leland Hayward (1902–71) was Fred Astaire's agent.

† Danny Kaye (1911–87) was an actor, singer and comedian; in the end, Kaye did not appear in *Night and Day*.

‡ Mary Martin played herself in *Night and Day,* singing 'My Heart Belongs to Daddy' from Porter's *Leave it to Me!* (1938).

§ The actress Ann Sheridan (1915–67) had recently appeared in *They Drive by Night* (1942), with George Raft and Humphrey Bogart; *The Man Who Came to Dinner* (1942) with Bette Davis and Monty Woolley; and *Kings Row* (1942), with Ronald Reagan. Frances Langford (1913–2005) had appeared in Porter's *Born to Dance* (1936) and with James Cagney in *Yankee Doodle Dandy* (1942). Eventually the part of Carol went to the actress Ginny Simms (1915–94).

¶ The actress Jane Wyman (1917–2007) played Gracie Harris in *Night and Day*. Because she sang 'Let's Do It, Let's Fall in Love', she effectively filled the role of Irène Bordoni.

A PORTER BIOPIC AND TWO FLOPS, 1945–1947

I still haven't got a Gabrielle. The one who comes closest is a girl I haven't seen, but who is in your show, "Mexican Hayride." What do you think of Luba Malina? Her still photographs look very good, and I have a couple of home recordings of her voice, which is not bad. People who have seen the show tell me that she is inclined to get too broad.* I would take your opinion as a pretty good conclusion on whether she could do our part.[9]

A few days later, on 17 February, Schwartz wrote to Porter asking him to put 'pressure' on Danny Kaye to sign on to the film. According to a note at the bottom of this telegram, Porter called Schwartz to discuss the matter, adding that in future all telephone calls would be 'charges reversed', as they were otherwise too expensive.[10]

Rumours about Porter's authorship of 'Don't Fence Me In' also surfaced about this time:

23 March 1945: Cole Porter to Sam Stark[11]

Dear Sam:

I am feeling much better which is very dull news. I enclose a clipping from VARIETY which I thought might interest you.

The charminh [sic] group picture arrived and I believe I thanked you for it, but I don't think you look thin at all. Seriously why don't you settle down and try to get that great bulk off you before I arrive. All it takes is just a little will power.

That's all, Mr. Gertzen. Goodbye and lot of love from Linda and me,

[signed:] Cole

P.S.

Regarding the article, you may not have heard that Winchell[†] wrote in his column that I had bought the entire song of DONT [sic] FENCE ME IN from Bob Fletcher. Later, Kate Smith made a broadcast in praise of the

---

* Luba Malina (1909–82) was an actress. Although Porter rejected her for the part of Gabrielle (see below, letter of 28 March 1945), she nevertheless later appeared in the film version of *Mexican Hayride* (1948). In *Night and Day*, the part of Gabrielle was taken by the actress Eve Arden (1908–90).

† Walter Winchell (1897–72) was a gossip columnist and radio broadcaster.

song and presented me with a watch. Winchell said that Fletcher had written to Kate Smith saying that if he could not have the money that I made on the song, that at least he deserved the watch. I got lawyers in and tracked the story down. Kate Smith never received a letter from Fletcher asking for the watch. On the other hand Fletcher has been charming about the whole matter. The man who gave Winchell the information which he published is ... Curley Harris, a man who works for United Artists in New York and to whom Winchell pays $60.00 a week for dirt. This is the end of my story.*

[signed:] C

The article referred to by Porter – an explanation of the circumstances surrounding the writing of 'Don't Fence Me In' and a defence of Porter – had been published in *Variety* the week before:

> A compounding of misinformation has made the trade wonder what there is to the report that Cole Porter bought "Don't Fence Me In" for $150. Adding some slight weight to the erroneous published statement is the fact that the cowboy song supposedly sounds so foreign to what is accepted to be Porter's sophisticated songwriting style. All Porter did in 1934, was to buy the rights to a verse by a Montana farmer, titled "Don't Fence Me In," strictly at the behest of film producer Lou Brock. This was when Brock had Porter under contract to write a score for "Adios Argentina," which he (Brock) later sold to 20th Century Fox but which the latter never produced. The Montanan, Fletcher by name, had mailed in this poem to Brock, who felt it had the germ for a song. Porter agreed and they paid $150 for the verses. As Herman Starr, head of the Warner Bros. music publishing interests put it, "No question but that Cole got the title from Fletcher and thus was inspired to the 'flavor' of the song, but 'Don't Fence Me In' is of course 100% original in melody with Porter, as is the lyric. It's true, however, that he not only got the title from Fletcher but also used a couple of his lines, but that's nothing startling. Many a songwriter gets titles from books, plays, films, current

---

* See p. 225 above.

phrases, anything of the moment. The only difference is that Porter paid for it."[12]

The fabricated flap over the origins of 'Don't Fence Me In' is symptomatic of a public interest concerning the source of Porter's words and music more generally. Among numerous letters Porter wrote concerning his sources, his account of 'Begin the Beguine' is typical:

23 March 1945: Cole Porter to Frank O. Colby[13]

Dear Mr. Colby:

In answer to your very nice letter of March 14th, this is what I know about the word BEGUINE as I used it in my song BEGIN THE BEGUINE.*

I was living in Paris at the time and somebody suggested that I go to see the Black Martiniquois, many of whom lived in Paris, do their native dance called The Beguine, in a remote night club on the left bank of the Seine. This I did quickly and I was very much taken by the rhythm of the dance, the rhythm was practically that of the already popular rumba but much faster. The moment I saw it I thought of BEGIN THE BEGUINE as a good title for a song and put it away in a notebook, adding a memorandum as to its rhythm and tempo.

About ten years later while going around the world we stopped at an island in the Lesser Sunda Islands, to the west of New Guinea, at a place called "Kalabashi" [sic]. My spelling of Kalabahi is entirely phonetic. A native dance was started for us, the melody of the first four bars of which was to become my song.†

I looked through my notebook, and found again, after ten years, my old title BEGIN THE BEGUINE. For some reason the melody that I heard and the phrase that I had written down seemed to marry. I developed the whole song from that.

---

* From Porter's show *Jubilee* (1935).

† For a brief account of Porter's time in Kalabahi, see the entry in Moss Hart's diary, above, pp. 106–7.

Later on in a French dictionary I found that the word "BEGUINE" meant nun.* How the nun ever became the dance I cannot explain, but I believe that this completely covers what you asked for.

Sincerely
COLE PORTER

Although Porter's memory of 'Begin the Beguine' seems to be confirmed by Moss Hart's diary, in other instances he may have misremembered or slightly fabricated the facts surrounding the origins of some of his songs. The following May, Porter wrote to Abel Green:

25 May 1945: Cole Porter to Abel Green[14]

Dear Abel:

In response to your letter of May 17th, I can cite the following occurrence:

In 1935 when my wife and I and Monty Woolley were approaching the harbor of Rio de Janeiro, by boat, it was dawn. My wife and I had risen especially for the event, but Mr. Woolley had stayed up all night to see it and during the night had enjoyed a few whiskys and sodas.

As we stood on the bow of the boat, my exclamation was – "It's delightful!". My wife followed with – "It's delicious!". And Monty, in his happy state, cried – "It's de-lovely!". This last exclamation gave me the title for the song which was an outstanding hit of the next show that I did.

I hope this is the sort of thing you meant.

All my best.

Sincerely yours,
Cole Porter

Porter gave more or less the same account to Richard Hubler in 1954,[15] but Robert Kimball reports a different version of this story, also deriving from Porter: 'I took a world tour a couple of years ago, and I was in Java with Monty Woolley and Moss Hart. We'd just been served that famous Eastern fruit – the mangosteen – and were all enjoying it mightily ... Moss Hart

---

* In fact, the word 'beguine' derives from the Latin *beguina*, meaning 'a member of a women's spiritual order professing poverty and self-denial, founded c.1180 in Liege in the Low Countries'. Beguine as a dance derives from the colloquial French *béguin* meaning 'an infatuation' and before that a nun's headdress. https://www.etymonline.com/word/beguine (accessed 2 August 2018).

said, "It's delightful!" I chimed in with "It's delicious". And Monty Woolley said, "It's de-lovely!" and there's the title of the song.'[16]

Night and Day, and in particular its casting, continued to be the main topic of Porter's correspondence through the spring of 1945:

28 March 1945: Cole Porter to Arthur Schwartz[17]

Dear Arthur:

My underground spies tell me that in spite of what I said to you, you have talent scouts watching Luba Malina with an eye to casting her in the Bordoni part. Once more may I assure you that she stinks.*

Another girl came to my mind who, they tell me, is charming. Her name is Yvette and you probably have heard her on the air.† It seems that she has looks and might fill the bill, so switch your scout, please and give her a "going over".‡

I read in Dorothy Killgallen, or it may have been Danton Walker,§ that you were leaving Warner Bros. in disgust, so I know it's not true and that everything is okay.

I still arrive May 2nd.

All my best, dear Arthur,

Sincerely,

[unsigned]

Arthur Schwartz's next letter to Porter, in which he returns to the topic of Luba Malina and other issues related to *Night and Day*, is revealing of some important aspects of the production, including Cary Grant's piano playing, and of the ways piano scores of Porter's songs were made accessible to the public:

---

* For Luba Malina, see above, p. 235. The singer Irène Bordoni (1885–1953) had starred in Porter's *Paris* (1928).

† Possibly the actress and singer Yvette (birth and death dates unknown), who appeared in episodes of *The Morey Amsterdam Show* (1948), *Cavalcade of Stars* (1949) and *Star of the Family* (1950).

‡ In the end, Bordoni was not represented in *Night and Day* and her best-known song, 'Let's Do It', was given in the film to the fictional Gracie Harris and situated as belonging to Porter's 1916 show, *See America First*.

§ Dorothy Kilgallen (1913–65) was a Broadway columnist; her 'The Voice of Broadway', which started in 1938, was syndicated in nearly 150 newspapers.

Your "underground spies" must consist of agents for Luba Malina. After our talk on the phone about her, I dropped any idea of using the girl. There is some possibility of our getting Hildegarde,* although the conditions may be too tough.

We have seen tests of Yvette, and I have heard her on the air a good deal. I was for her many months ago, but [Michael] Curtiz thought she was an empty personality. However, we still have a hold on her, and, if no one better shows up, we will probably use her.

I am not leaving Warner Brothers in disgust. Everything is swell except that the strike leaves us without costume and set designers, and until they return we cannot actually start production. I am told that there is hope of a settlement, or a switch of unions, which will bring the men back to work at any moment now, but my own opinion is that it will take some time.†

I have been in touch with Cary [Grant] very frequently, and the other day he came in to demonstrate his piano virtuosity. It's remarkable that he can play so well. He had studied the published piano part of all the songs he will be seen doing, and plays all the notes as they are written. Since those piano parts are childishly simple in most cases – a device of Sirmay to sell more copies to the public – what I'm doing now is to have some slightly fuller piano parts made so that when Cary's hands are shown, he will be constantly doing something interesting.

The moment we know our definite production date, we can sign a good many of the specialty people I have been in touch with, and of course I'll keep you posted closely. The leading candidate for the part of Carol, which, as you know, is a small part, but loaded with songs, is Ginny Simms. We all seem to feel she's the best-looking of the prominent singers, although she's not exactly Hedy Lamarr.

---

* Hildegarde (Hildegarde Loretta Sell, 1906–2005) was an actress and singer commonly known as 'The Incomparable Hildegarde'. She did not appear in *Night and Day*.

† In March 1945 more than 10,000 members of the Conference of Studio Unions, representing the rank-and-file studio workers, including carpenters and electricians, went on strike against studio labour practices. The strike lasted thirteen months; see Brett L. Abrams, 'The First Hollywood Blacklist: The Major Studios Deal with the Conference of Studio Unions, 1941–47', *Southern California Quarterly* 77/3 (1995), 215–53.

A PORTER BIOPIC AND TWO FLOPS, 1945–1947

In May, Porter wrote again to Nelson Barclift, gossipy and flirty letters of a sort he often wrote to his lovers – different in tone from those he wrote to old friends like Gerald Murphy:

8–9 May [1945]: Cole Porter to Nelson Barclift[18]

May 8–9

2.30 A.M.

Nelson –

I only wish you could be here tomorrow night because Norma is bringing her ski-instructor boyfriend. She says she found him at Sun Valley but I'm still betting that she took him out of a tree. He's <u>awful</u> + behaves like a bad waiter. His name is Marty Aerongé. And Norma is so embarrassing about him. She said the other day, for instance, "I used to be Canadian but I'm Free French now!" She shouldn't say such things, should she.

Otherwise, tomorrow night, it's <u>just us</u> – Sylvia, Vera, Jean Feldman, the wicked old baroness, Benita, Pat Boyer, Annie Warner, Anita Loos, Fanny Brice, John Conle Rosebud (Vera's Jewish boy – he's awful cute in a big way), Cukor, Reggie Gardner, Roger, Sturge, Eddie Goulding, Haines, Jimmie Shields, Michael Chaplin, Ernst Lubitsch + Old Albert.* I'm putting half of them out-doors for dinner as we're having those summer nights now. But I'm sorta depressed that Ma Honey won't be present to supervise everybody's good time.

But you <u>will</u> be, next year. I spent the evening with Eric Remarque.† He's locked up every night after 8 P.M. at the Beverly Wilshire so we went over to see him tonight. He thinks the Germans will crack + soon. In fact he talked very convincingly + I'm suddenly bucked up + reeking of optimism.

But it's bed time [sic] my C[ute].L[ittle]. Nose so goodnight. I miss you like hell.

---

* Sylvia Ashley was an actress and socialite; Jean Feldman (Jean Howard); the 'wicked old baroness' is Catherine d'Erlanger; Pat Boyer (1899–1978) was the wife of actor Charles Boyer; Annie Warner; Anita Loos; Fanny Brice; George Cukor (1899–1983) was a film director; Reggie Gardner (1903–80) was an actor; Roger Stearns; Eddie Goulding; William Haines; Howard Sturges; Jimmie Shields; Michael Chaplin; Ernst Lubitsch (1892–1947), film director.

† Erich Maria Remarque's works were banned by the Nazis in 1933; in 1939 he emigrated to the United States.

Please, in spite of the fact that you are merely a frivolous moth, don't forget me entirely. I realize I date. I know that my trimmings are tarnished. I admit that I'm poor. But be kind, Nelson to someone who really is true-blue.

Albert*

By the way, what colour is true-blue.

17 May 1945: Porter to Gerald Murphy[19]

Dear Gerald:

The delightful book on clouds arrived. I already had a book on clouds which I tried to study in Williamstown, but it was so difficult. The book you sent me is exactly what I wanted and I am having a lot of fun with it.

The belt made out of Lillian Russell's garters† has completely re-established me socially in Hollywood. Everybody wants to see me simply in order to see the belt, and I am having a hell of a time. Please congratulate Mr. Dickinson again for his masterpiece.

I shan't bother you by mentioning California weather, but I must say that it is [sic] made me feel like a new man.

Good-bye, dear Gerald – and great love to Sarah and her husband.

Your old college chum,

COLE

(Dictated, but not read)

In May, Porter had a fourth operation on his legs, which he described in detail in his next letter to Barclift:

---

* Porter's signing off as Albert, his middle name, is possibly a sign of his intimacy with Barclift.

† Lillian Russell (1861–1922), actress and singer. According to an article in the *New Yorker* (Geoffrey Hellman, 'Corsets De Luxe'), 'The first gartered corset was made for Lillian Russell, who was so enchanted with it she became a regular customer, later ordering from Mme. Binner the most expensive corset ever made. It cost thirty-nine hundred dollars – fourteen hundred dollars for the corset proper and twenty-five hundred dollars for the garters, which had diamond buckles.' See Lillian Ross, ed., *The Fun of It: Stories from The Talk of the Town* (New York, n.d.), n.p.

21 May 1945: Cole Porter to Nelson Barclift[20]

Dear Barclift:

Your letter arrived May 3rd and it was a joy to hear from you again after so many months. Please tell Artie not to be upset by the Sophie Tucker book* arriving in sections of 16 and in duplicate. The only idea was to get them to him very quickly and in case of any section being lost the duplicate might arrive safely. It had no importance at all except that I am so tired of hearing from people who receive books months and months after I have sent them.

I suppose people always say that operations are successful. On my left leg, Moorehead† first had to break both bones again, take out the jagged ends, splice the tendon of achilles and then further up on the tibia cut eight inches of bone to the marrow out and graft it over the fracture. He didn't want to do it as he was so afraid there were still streptococci in the fracture, but I insisted because I was so tired of hanging on to people. Luckily, he didn't find streptococci, but staphlococci, which are much less dangerous germs. So I didn't die at all. Then he operated on the right heel in order to get the scar tissue out of it, so that I could once more, after seven and a half years, lie on a bed without putting my heel over the edge; it was so painful when it touched even a sheet, as the scar tissue pressed upon the heel bone. The first operation on this wasn't a success and he had to do it again. While this was going on I had two nervous breakdowns and lost 25 pounds which I am still regaining. I arrived here more or less of a wreck, but within two weeks I feel like a different person. I walk on crutches, short distances, but the wheel-chair is used a great deal. The pain in the left leg is hard to take, but it will gradually disappear within a year, he promises me. And that's the last story of my legs for the moment. You ask me how many more operations are necessary. I can't tell you yet as I am not at all sure that the last three were really successful. It will take time to know. If this work doesn't have to be done again, I still have two operations ahead, but I can name my date for them which I should think would be in about two years.

---

* Sophie Tucker (1887–1966) was a singer and actress. Porter refers to Tucker's autobiography, *Some of These Days* (Garden City, 1945).

† John J. Moorehead was one of Porter's surgeons. The same year Moorehead published a book, *Clinical Traumatic Surgery* (Philadelphia and London, 1945).

Why do you start me on stories about these legs? I have never talked so much about them in my life, as I am now. They don't depress me in the least, luckily, as my ultimate aim is to win the 100 yard dash and anything that will go toward their getting better is exactly what I want.

I didn't receive your letter telling me of John's meeting with Bob Lynn, the former vet of Lido Beach. Please write me this news again.*

"Night and Day" starts shooting the first week in June. I got everything I asked for including Cary Grant and technicolor. Last week I okayed Alexis Smith for the "Linda" part. Henry Stephenson plays my grand-dad, temporarily dropping his British accent.† They have five mothers picked out for me and any number of fathers, and I shall go to the Warner lot soon to take my pick.‡ Monty [Woolley] also is signed to play himself and he runs all through the picture. He gloats now because he has been under salary already for six weeks at $6,500 a week. What is more this money all stays in his bank because, according to his contract with Darryl,§ he has the right to do one outside picture a year. The shooting will take about six months so figure out what "The Beard's" income tax will be. The last script that I saw was very good. Mike Curtiz, who will direct, and Arthur Schwartz, who will produce, are coming out to see me this week with the final script. It took any number of authors and any number of scripts before I gave my okay, as there was [sic] too many gloomy moments. At present it is rather light except for the wonderful love story of Cole and Linda. I believe the music will be beautifully presented, so I am really not worried. We also have Fred Astaire to do the "Night and Day" song and dance¶ and several other personalities will appear only in spots.

I am delighted to hear that "Don't Fence Me In" is doing well with the natives, but I resent getting word from a friend of mine that the Japs sing it too.

---

* John and Bob Lynn are unidentified.

† The Canadian-born Alexis Smith (1921–93) played the part of Linda Lee Porter. Henry Stephenson (1871–1956) took the role of Omar Cole.

‡ The role of Porter's mother, Kate, was taken by Selena Royle (1904–83). The character Samuel Fenwick Porter, Cole Porter's father, ultimately did not appear in the film.

§ Darryl F. Zanuck (1902–79) was a film producer and co-founder, with Joseph Schenck (1878–1971), of 20th Century Pictures (distributed by United Artists). From the late 1920s until 1933, Zanuck worked for Warner Bros., as a writer and, from 1931, head of production.

¶ Fred Astaire did not, finally, appear in *Night and Day*.

Jeannie* is not having a baby. On the other hand she is very busy learning how to be a professional photographer. She attends a school downtown, goes to work at nine every morning and often doesn't return until eleven at night. She has been working consistently and has now reached "Color Photography". She looks more beautiful than ever, although, unluckily, I see her only on Saturday nights when there is a party or now and then during the week when she gets off work early and comes here to dine with Sturge and me.

Please tell your friend, Stuart Churchill, the vocalist with Fred Waring, that I believe it unwise that he sing the first "<u>Just One of Those Things</u>".† It would make a great row between Chappell's and Harms, and I should probably end up in jail.

The Warners have never been happier. As for Joy, she went to New York and had her nose bobbed. The result is that she is one of the prettiest girls in town and last month married a Navy man, Lieutenant Orr, who seems like an awfully nice chap. I don't know whether Shirley Temple‡ is engaged or not, as I don't know Shirley Temple.

I missed seeing Irving§ when he was here, but people who did, say that he is very worried about the world indeed. I know nothing of your T.I.T.A. plans from this end, but I do hope they will let you all continue at least until the end of the war, instead of putting guns on your shoulders.

Thank you very much for the pictures, but I couldn't recognize anybody in them. Of course, I am certain that you are in all of them, but you must have changed radically.

If you are burned at Gilbert Miller for doing a musical version of "The Swan",¶ because you had worked on the same thing for so long, you can

---

* Jean Howard.

† Fred Waring (1900–84) was a band leader; Stuart Churchill (1903–2000) was his vocalist. The 'first' 'Just One of Those Things' was written for *The New Yorkers* (1930) and although it was dropped during the Philadelphia tryouts, it was published in November of that year by Warner Bros.; the well-known 'Just One of Those Things' was written for *Jubilee* (1935) and published in October 1935, also by Warner Bros.

‡ The actress and singer Shirley Temple (1928–2014). On 19 September 1945, at the age of seventeen, she married John Agar (1921–2002), an Army Air Corps sergeant and member of a prominent Chicago meat-packing family.

§ Presumably Irving Berlin.

¶ Gilbert Miller (1884–1969) was a theatrical producer; he produced Ferenc Molnár's stage play *The Swan* in New York during the 1922–3 season. A musical version was never produced although a film version, with Grace Kelly, Alec Guinness and Louis Jourdan, was released by Paramount Pictures in 1956.

imagine the heat of my burn when you write me that a song of yours entitled "You Forgot To Tell Me That You Love Me" is about to be published. I have had this title in my title book for years. How dare you tread upon my source of revenue!

Please tell Artie that I shan't send him further books unless he wants that one he read in Williamstown.

Dick Clayton's address is:
COM. SEEVE. PAC. ADM.
c/o Fleet Post Office
San Francisco, Calif.

I was delighted to read that you are working very hard and have completed a play. As for your missing all your friends here, you have no idea of how often they all ask me about you.

The Sunday lunches are exactly as they have always been. Roger still sits at the end of the table, with a clown hat on, and throws everybody into the aisles.

Sturges stays on with me until July 1st. In the meantime, Bob Bray of Peleliu* is at this moment flying back to be here for six months and I hope awfully that he can spend most of his time in the house with me. [Len] Hanna took a house not far from me for two months and only left today. Harry Krebs is staying with me on his furlough. He certainly is a problem child as I take him everywhere and unless people make a great row over him he spits at them. But it is great fun having him and I shall hate to see him leave.

Linda has been having one of those terrible colds again and, in spite of the fact that everything is open at Williamstown, she has to stay in bed for another two weeks at the Waldorf before she can risk making the trip. Poor darling – it is pitiful, the unending recurrence of these terrible colds. Thank God for the Sulphas.† If it weren't for them she wouldn't be alive today, as the scars in her lungs have gradually become bigger and it is practically impossible for her to throw off any infection. Please write her at Williamstown when you have time and ask Artie to write also. She loves you both dearly and it would buck her up.

---

* The actor Robert Bray (1917–83) was a member of the U.S. military during World War II. He is particularly known for his roles in television and Hollywood B-Westerns, including *The Lone Ranger* and *Stagecoach West*.

† A derivative of sulphanilic acid, use to treat streptococcal infections.

So good-bye, Sargeant Barclift. I should be here probably until October. I have three offers,* but nothing can be set until after this strike† is over. I shall not do an autumn show, but have already been accosted for several productions for the spring.

Your old pay [sic]

Cole

[signed:] Cole

In June Porter wrote to Barclift about the time he spent with Cary Grant, and problems with *Mississippi Belle*:

5 June 1945: Porter to Nelson Barclift[21]

Barclift –

The enclosed snapshot will show you that "plus ca [sic] change, plus c'est la meme [sic] chose."‡

But during the week, life is entirely different. We dine at home nearly every night. We never go to restaurants. We never go to night-clubs. For Saturday lunch there is a gang here always, a combination of the east & the west, nicely mixed & then Sunday, the ole time stuff.

My hours will shock you. I rise at nine, breakfast by the pool at nine thirty. My trainer whom I brought west appears at eleven. There are infinite exercises & an interminable massage. Freedom comes at three P.M. & a secretary at four who stays an hour. Miss M.§ is not allowed to come west but in spite of letters she wines [sic] that she must come "to clear up her files."

The strike continues so I see no picture work. I have no longer any ideas as to a N.Y. show even for the spring of '46. The income tax when you work is too big to cope with. Believe it or not, my first quarter was $140,000 & my second, $100,000.

I shall do my best for Deseterins Liguit. [?] Thanks a lot for wishing me a happy birthday. If you knew <u>how</u> happy it will be, you would do your best to

---

* One of these offers may have been Orson Welles's *Around the World*; see below, pp. 251–60.

† See above, p. 240.

‡ The photograph sent by Porter is apparently lost.

§ Porter's secretary, Margaret Moore.

bitch it. Night & Day starts shooting next week. I see a good deal of Cary [Grant]. He is nice but he studies me too much & it embarrasses me.

Mississi-pee-pee Belle is still on the shelf. Annie W.[arner] has a beautiful young lover but she hides him. Merle & Lucian [sic] Ballard* are merely waiting for Korda† to arrive in two weeks to sign a little paper. Then they go to work. Lucian [sic] is nice too but dull. In fact, everybody is nice including Sturge who sends you his love.

I send you my respects. Go further west & invade Bali. That is where you will be re-born.

A big kiss for Artie – Cole

Shooting on *Night and Day* began in mid-June. On 13 July, Arthur Schwartz wrote to Porter, sending him the latest version of the script, informing him that the first thirty pages had been shot, and in particular alerting him to some changes in the lyrics to his songs demanded by the Hays Office. Censorship of Porter's lyrics was a problem throughout his career:‡

> BLOW, GABRIEL, BLOW: You understand, I think, that the word 'hell' is included on the list of forbidden words and phrases which has been adopted by the Association, and, consequently, it will be necessary for you to change this word in this lyric.
> I GET A KICK OUT OF YOU: Political Censor Boards everywhere will delete the word 'cocaine'.
> ME AND MARIE: Please eliminate the underlined portion of the following lines: 'Me and my Marie <u>proceed to raise the dickens</u> by the old seaside.'
> MY HEART BELONGS TO DADDY: In the second refrain, please eliminate the underlined portion of the following line, 'I never dream of <u>making the team</u>.'

---

* Merle Oberon and her husband at the time, cinematographer Lucien Ballard (1908–88).
† Alexander Korda (1893–1956) was a Hungarian-born film producer; his credits include the Orson Welles vehicle, *The Third Man* (1949).
‡ See above, p. 210.

Porter made several handwritten notations on this letter. In the left margin, beside 'BLOW, GABRIEL, BLOW' he wrote: 'I was wrong. / Gabriel wrong / mighty wrong / etc. – so long.' Underneath 'cocaine' he wrote 'Some go for perfume from Spain', and under 'making the team', 'coaching'. But, in fact, few of the suggested replacement lyrics were used, in part because two of the songs – 'Blow, Gabriel, Blow' and 'Me and Marie' – were not used in the film, and in the case of 'My Heart Belongs to Daddy', because the portion of the text in which the 'offending' words occur was not included. In 'I Get a Kick Out of You', the line 'Some get a kick from cocaine' was replaced with 'Some go for perfume from Spain' (as Porter had written), followed, in both cases, by 'I'm sure that if I took even one sniff'. In his next letter to Schwartz, Porter suggests a change to the unused 'Me and Marie':

4 August 1945: Cole Porter to Arthur Schwartz[22]

Dear Arthur:

Will you be very kind and send me several stills of Selena Royle? My mother clamors for them. (Third request).

Forgive me for being a pest.

The following is a suggestion for a lyric to replace the present one in "Me And Marie".

And until the sun begins to beckon
We go on and on a-neckin' and a-neckin'.*

Sincerely,
COLE

Porter was apparently in frequent contact with Irving Berlin around this time – in August, Berlin sent a pre-release copy of one of his new songs and throughout his career Porter appears to have been closer to Berlin than any other songwriter – and in September he wrote an encouraging note to William Skipper, whose career was floundering:

---

* Kimball, *The Complete Lyrics of Cole Porter*, 194, does not mention these lines. They were intended to replace 'For when once we get the proper settin' / We being a-pettin' and go on a-pettin''.

21 August 1945: Cole Porter to Irving Berlin[23]

Dear Irving:

"You Keep Coming Back Like a Song"* arrived. It's great Berlin.
Thanks a lot for your thoughtfulness.
Your pal,
COLE

24 September 1945: Cole Porter to William Skipper[24]

Dear Skipper:

Your note arrived. I understand exactly how you feel, my boy, but please don't be discouraged. You have far too much talent not to be recognized and soon. I believe your state of mind is the usual post-war depression that every G.I. has and has had after every war. So please cheer up.

I shall call you soon. In the meantime, my blessings upon thee.
Your old friend,
Cole

Night and Day was finished in November 1945, and on 20 November, Jack Warner sent Porter a (self-)congratulatory telegram: 'DEAR COLE. HAVE FINALLY COMPLETED PICTURE. GOING ON RECORD WITH YOU HAVE MOST IMPORTANT MUSICAL EVER PRODUCED. THIS NOT MERELY WORDS BUT REALLY A FACT. WILL TAKE SEVERAL WEEKS BEFORE SCORING COMPLETED BUT WHEN YOU SEE THE FILM I KNOW YOU ARE GOING TO BE EXTREMELY HAPPY AS I AM. EVERYBODY DESERVES PLENTY OF KUDOS FOR THE GREAT WORK DONE ARRIVING NY AROUND DECEMBER FIRST. STAYING AT TOWERS WILL SEE YOU THEN. LOVE FROM ANNIE [AND] MYSELF=JACK'.[25]

---

* Berlin's 'You Keep Coming Back Like a Song' was written for the film *Blue Skies*, released by Paramount Pictures on 16 October 1946; introduced by Bing Crosby, the song was nominated for, but did not win, the Oscar for best song.

20 November 1945: Cole Porter to Jack Warner[26]

Delighted with your enthusiastic wire. When do you think I should come West to look at it? Very anxious to see it. My love to Annie and to you.

Cole

Although in his letter of 5 June to Nelson Barclift, Porter said he 'no longer [had] any ideas as to a N.Y. show even for the spring of '46', by the summer he had started working with Orson Welles on a musical adaptation of *Around the World in Eighty Days*, as Welles himself recounted in an article in the *New York Herald Tribune*.* Probably they met again at the end of November, as a 26 November telegram from Welles to Porter suggests: 'DEAREST COLE: I SHOULD BE ON MY WAY EAST IN A COUPLE OF DAYS. FONDEST ORSON.'[27] *Around the World* came to the stage on 31 May 1946.† In the meantime, Porter wrote in late December 1945 to Jack Warner – 'Wasn't it a nice Christmas'?[28] – and to Sam Stark, with New Year's wishes:

30 December 1945: Cole Porter to Sam Stark[29]

Sam –

This is a note to wish you the happiest so far of all your New Years.

I wish you were with us. [Howard] Sturge[s] + I spent the entire day reading <u>Snowbound</u> aloud.‡ You have never seen nature turning on the snow better than she has for the last 24 hours.

Perhaps however it is just as well that you weren't here. For you would have been outdoors all days on your snow-shoes making a snow-man + throwing snow-<u>balls</u> + that would have embarrassed us.

I forgot to thank you for the collapsible camp-stools. They arrived + charmed the populace. Linda keeps the green one permanently in her green sitting-room + puts extra men on it.

---

* Helen Ormsbee, 'Welles Like Phileas Fogg in Overcoming Obstacles', *New York Herald Tribune*, 16 June 1946, D1: 'Cole Porter and I blocked out the plan for the script and music for this show last August [1945] in Hollywood.'

† See below, p. 259.

‡ The narrative poem *Snow-Bound: A Winter Idyl* by John Greenleaf Whittier, first published in 1865.

But this is merely a note so I must say goodbye ere it become a god-damned bore.

Again, my sweet Sam, a magnificent 1946 + thanks an awful lot for garnishing so beautifully my 1945.

Your slave –

Cole

In early January, Porter read an article in the *New York Sun* about a vote in Town Line, New York, a hamlet about fourteen miles east of Buffalo, 'the last remnant of the Confederacy': 'Town Line, Last Stronghold of the Confederacy, Votes Jan. 24 on Return to the Union . . . Since Dade County, Ga., and Vicksburg, Miss., voted to return to the Union of July 4 last, it is believed that Town Line, N. Y., is the last bit of confederacy left in the United States. Just why Town Line ever lined up with the Confederates is now obscure, but the records show that the hamlet voted 85 to 40 to secede from the Union back in 1861.'* Porter sent Sam Stark a copy of the article and wrote to him on 9 January:

9 January 1946: Cole Porter to Sam Stark[30]

Dear Sammy:

Don't you think this extraordinary? How do these people ever hold out for the Confederacy, especially during the Civil War, surrounded as they were by the enemy? This article has worried Monty [Woolley] and me to such an extent that he called up Harold Ross[†] and asked him to send a special man up there to get all the data about it for an article in The New Yorker. Ross seemed very interested. I enclose the article because it all seems to be your kind of dish.

Your great heavy joke about becoming so thin, was finally discovered when I talked to Robert[‡] on Tuesday. What with a letter from him telling me about you having become a mere wraith, and one from Bobby Raison with

---

* *New York Sun*, 7 January 1946, 46.

† Harold Wallace Ross (1892–1951) was a journalist and co-founder, in 1925, of the *New Yorker*.

‡ Probably Robert Bray.

the same news, Linda and I began to be very worried about you, decided you were taking Thyroid and were on the point of writing you a very severe letter, when Robert suddenly let the cat out of the bag. He does say, however, that you are not nearly as – shall I say – fat as you were.

Orson [Welles] and I really are at it now and starting to cast.* After everything looked completely off, Mike Todd† suddenly gave in to all the clauses in my contract. We have to open the show cold‡ in New York, due to all the mechanical devices necessary for this production. There will be at least 32 scenes - - and an <u>aerial ballet</u> to close the first act.

Please reserve April for this and no fooling.

Lots of love from us and my best to Allen [Walker],

[signed:] Cole

About this time, Porter appears to have been feeling healthier than he had for a while. On 14 January, Linda wrote to Sam Stark about the time she spent with him, driving around Massachusetts, and on 15 January, Porter's secretary Margaret Moore wrote to Stark that 'Mr. Porter seems to be better now than he has been for the past eight years'.[31] Porter himself wrote to Stark again on 18 January:

18 January 1946: Cole Porter to Sam Stark[32]

New York, January 18, 1946

Dear Sam:

This is one of those "pest" requests. My sister-in-law has an ill husband§ and she wants to take him somewhere for a re-build. She asked for information

---

* *Around the World.*

† For Mike Todd, theatrical producer, see p. 195.

‡ That is, without any out-of-town tryouts. In the event, *Around the World* had a tryout in Boston, opening there on 28 April 1946.

§ Presumably Porter refers here to the husband of one of Linda Porter's sisters. According to her obituary in the *New York Times* of 21 May 1954, 28, these were a Mrs William Wallace of Nantucket, Massachusetts and her half-sister, a Mrs Lee Abbell of Covington, Kentucky.

concerning LaQuinta.* I know nothing about it. Could you find this out for me? Have they bungalows, how much do they cost and is the food edible? Also can one rent an automobile there so that the two of them can tour southern California?

I suppose the best thing for you to do would be simply to ask a few friends and then request the present manager of hotels to send me a letter with all the details.

Forgive this bother to you.

Love,

[signed:] Cole

As was the case throughout his career, Porter was regularly sent books, scripts or plot synopses to read. One such request gives some insight into his notion that the plot of a successful musical comedy always included some element of suspense:

22 January 1946: Cole Porter to Mrs John Shelton[33]

Dear Honoria:

I was delighted to get your letter and to read your synopsis. Unluckily I was not born a critic, but this is my opinion; it seems to me that you have a very good basis for a ballet but not for a musical comedy. I do not believe there is enough story for a musical comedy, as you have no suspense whatever. Even though most people do not realize it, no musical comedy is a success unless its book has a solid story with suspense.

Take this advice for what it is worth, which is practically nothing, but I have done my best.

My love to you,

[signed:] Cole

Night and Day, in the meantime, had its first preview at the Warner Brothers Beverly Hills Theatre on 11 February; the next day Jack Warner sent another congratulatory telegram to Porter: 'DEAR COLE: HAD

---

* La Quinta, a resort town in southern California. Probably Porter refers specifically to the La Quinta Resort and Club that opened in 1926.

A PORTER BIOPIC AND TWO FLOPS, 1945–1947

SNEAK PREVIEW LAST NIGHT AT OUR BEVERLY HILLS THEATRE. AS YOU KNOW MAJORITY OF AUDIENCE PROFESSIONAL PEOPLE. REACTION WAS EVERYTHING ONE WOULD DESIRE. WE HAVE AN IMPORTANT FILM AND ONE I KNOW YOU WILL BE VERY PROUD OF AND ALSO A SUCCESS WHICH I KNOW IS WHAT COUNTS. ANN SENDS HER LOVE. EVERY GOOD WISH=JACK.'[34]

Porter wrote back:

12 February 1946: Cole Porter to Jack Warner[35]

Delighted with the beautiful news. When do you expect to send a print East? All my best,
   Cole

Slightly later, after he had heard parts of the film's soundtrack, Porter was particularly complimentary about the song arrangements:

19 April 1946: Cole Porter to Ray Heindorf*

Dear Ray: Herman Starr sent me pressings of some of the proofs from Night and Day. Your arrangements are magnificent. Don't forget that you promised me three complete sets of all music including what has been cut out. I shall appear on June first and menace you till I get these. All my gratitude,
   COLE PORTER

At the start of April 1946, Porter had signed a contract with Orson Welles's Mercury Enterprises for *Around the World*, based on Jules Verne's 1873 novel, *Around the World in Eighty Days*. The terms included a $5,000 advance for Porter against a 5 per cent interest in the show; film rights (50 per cent each to Porter and Welles); and subsidiary rights (25 per cent each to Porter and Welles). The film contract, between Porter and Welles

---

* CPT, Correspondence 1946 (transcription of a telegram). Ray Heindorf (1908–80), composer and arranger; he conducted and arranged the production numbers for *Night and Day*.

on the one hand, and London Film Productions on the other, was signed on 25 April.[36] Among the provisions in it is one that is true of Porter's contracts generally and that gives further and more detailed insight into what he considered to be essential to his music: 'The purchaser shall have the right in every instance to orchestrate and arrange said musical compositions so long as no substantial change is made in their basic melody'. In short, Porter understood the 'basic melody' to be the most distinctive aspect (together with the words) of his songs; this was especially the case with respect to film scores, which often used orchestrations radically different from those used in stage productions. There were also, as usual, rumours, including one that Porter and Orson Welles had had a falling out. Hedda Hopper, who earlier had misrepresented Porter's relationship with Jack Warner, also apparently reported problems between Porter and Welles, which prompted another telegram from the composer:

15 February 1946: Cole Porter to Hedda Hopper[37]

HEDDA DARLING. YOUR SOURCE ABOUT ORSON AND ME QUITE WRONG. WE ARE GETTING ALONG FAMOUSLY AND THE SHOW IS PRACTICALLY IN REHEARSAL. I DONT [sic] COME OUT TO METRO UNTIL IT HAS BEEN PRODUCED. LOVE AND KISSES=COLE

The Boston tryout for *Around the World* opened on 28 April to mostly negative reviews. The *Daily Boston Globe* for 29 April, for instance, described it as 'indeed a Welles production, vast, occasionally brilliant, sometimes dull and confused, satirical and compounded of many elements ... "Around the World" was postponed from Friday night, and it might just as well have been put off until tonight. The show is about 90 percent settings and production and things kept going wrong Saturday night in what must have been a phenomenally rough performance ... Mr. Porter's melodic invention has resulted in only two really striking songs, "Look What I Found," "Should I Tell You I Love You"; a bright little circus march and a comic number, "Missus Aoda." '[38] Possibly Porter himself was concerned about the success of the show, since in an interview on the day of the opening he seems both to distance it from his previous works and to claim some affection for it:

Cole Porter Would Rather Write Crazy Shows Than Gay Musicals . . .
"Now I am planning to associate myself with the crazy and unusual productions of the theatre – the kind of thing one dreams about but never quite dares to attempt. I shall never follow a pattern again – which means I shan't write the kind of musical show I have been doing for so long.

"Frankly, it's because I am bored. I want to do something different."

. . . "This is a drama – with music, too," says Porter, as he sits at a scenic rehearsal. Several whistles and a strange contraption which sounds like a Fourth of July "cannon" suddenly shriek with deafening results.

"Just to get the audience in a proper mood to appreciate your music," grins Welles.

"My music will be louder and noisier," boasts Porter, who doesn't mean a word of it. He says that he hopes the public will like best his "Should I Tell You I Love You," which is sung in an Indian jungle setting . . . "My last songs are always my favorites," he says with the pride of a father of new-born triplets."[39]

One review galled Porter in particular and in a letter to Sam Stark he explained why he thought the review was negative, indulging in conspiracy theory:

30 April 1946: Cole Porter to Sam Stark[40]

Dear Sam:

We had to open last Saturday night although totally unprepared because the show cost so much money that there was none left unless we opened.

You will notice that the review in THE RECORD is by far the worst. This is because it is a Hearst paper and after Orson made the picture CITIZEN KANE,* Hearst gave an order that for the rest of Orson's life, his name should never be mentioned and that anything that he did should be

---

* Orson Welles's *Citizen Kane* was widely seen as a negative biography, at least in part, of newspaper magnate William Randolph Hearst, who, after the film's release, prohibited its mention in any of his newspapers.

condemned to hell. I am not a bit depressed about these notices, as I think we have a show.

Love,

[signed:] Cole

Porter gave Stark more details in a letter the next week:

4 May 1946: Cole Porter to Sam Stark[41]

Dear Little Sammie:

I have neglected you shamefully, but many troubles have been mine. At the present moment I count on arriving on the Constellation May 31st., 11:45 PACIFIC STANDARD TIME, and if you have daylight time – (12:45 at night). It looks as if Robert Bray* will be in Mexico on location, so you will probably have to meet me, or if this is inconvenient, hire a chauffeur and a car to meet me.

Will you also rent a good car for me without chaffeur [sic]. I shall need it until my Buick arrives on the coast, which will probably be two or three weeks after I do.

I can't give you any news on the show† yet, as in Boston we are the prey of drunken stage hands and drunken electricians – even when they are sober. Most of them are 90 years old. They all hate the show because there are so many changes, scenes and light changes and they are used to nice comfortable operas in which there are only two sets and no changes of lighting whatsoever.

We open in New Haven next Tuesday night, or at the latest next Wednesday night, after which we shall know more, what with a new gang of mechanics.‡

Orson has been a tower of strength and the most considerate producer I have ever met. The whole company loves him and rightfully so, because he never loses his temper, or his power to surmount almost impossible difficul-

---

* According to a marginal note, Robert Bray (1917–83), the television and film actor.
† *Around the World*.
‡ *Around the World* opened at the Shubert Theatre, New Haven, on Tuesday 7 May.

ties. So if the show flops I shall at least have had a great experience with a wonderful guy.

Linda, [Howard] Sturge[s] and I saw the NIGHT AND DAY picture last night – and it is a dream. I know you will like it.

It will be so nice to see your slender svelte form again. Please don't make too many engagements as I want to wreck most of your evenings.

Love from your devoted

[signed:] Cole*

Around the World opened at the Mercury Theatre, New York, on 31 May and fared no better than it had in Boston. The *New York Times* for 1 June reported that 'Cole Porter has written an inferior score', the *Newark Evening News* for the same date said that 'Once again the Adelphi Theater is the dispirited scene of some extremely painful and inept globe-trotting set to music with a dire what-you-may-call-it known as "Around the World" blasting away in a tasteless, amateurish fashion', and the *New York Morning Telegraph* for 3 June lamented that 'Mr. Welles manhandled the Jules Verne novel, with insipid contributions from Cole Porter.' A few reviews gave grudging approval to some of Porter's songs: the *Brooklyn Eagle* wrote that 'Cole Porter wrote the music, a pretty good song here and there, nothing very lovely, nothing as beguiling as is to be expected of Cole Porter', while according to the *New York Journal American*, 'The music, by Cole Porter, is friendly and familiar, especially "Should I Tell You I Love You." '

As Porter noted in his letter to Sam Stark, he had finally seen *Night and Day* on 3 May. He wrote to congratulate the producer, Michael Curtiz, three days later:

---

* In a letter of 10 April, Porter's secretary Margaret Moore suggested to Stark he travel east for the opening of *Around the World*. And in a letter of 18 April she wrote to him again including details on how Porter himself sometimes secured tickets for shows: 'I'm delight to get theatre tickets for you – but I sincerely hope you will approve of my method for getting good seats for GLASS MENAGERIE. This is still a very popular show and hard to get good seats for evening, so I had to get them through Mr. Porter's special man here – George Solotaire, 160 W. 44th St., though the price is very high. Whenever Mr. and Mrs. Porter cannot get good seats for any show, they always call upon this man – and as you well know, many times Mr. Porter wants tickets for shows on such short notice.' Source: Stanford University, Cole Porter Collection, shelfmark FE209, Correspondence: 1946 (TLS on Waldorf stationery).

6 May 1946: Cole Porter to Michael Curtiz[42]

Beloved Mike. Linda and I saw Night and Day picture Friday night and you have our eternal gratitude for treating us so beautifully. What a great director you are and how lucky we were to have been put in your hands. Love,
    Cole.

The same day, Porter also wrote to several of the actors in *Night and Day*, thanking them for their performances, including Alexis Smith, who took the role of Linda Porter, and Ginny Simms, who took the role of Carole Hill.* Porter wrote to Smith, 'We saw the NIGHT AND DAY picture last Friday night and what pleased us most was your wonderful performance as Linda. As my Linda said to me about your Linda, as we left the picture, "How lucky I am to be shown on the screen as such an enchanting girl" . . .' and to Ginny Simms, 'I saw the NIGHT AND DAY picture last Friday night and I can never tell you how happy you made me by the way you sang my songs.'[43] A few weeks later he sent a telegram to Arthur Schwartz:

28 May 1946: Cole Porter to Arthur Schwartz[44]

DEAR ARTHUR I SAW A SHOWING OF NIGHT AND DAY AND I COULD NOT HAVE HAD A BETTER PRODUCER. LOOK FORWARD TO SEEING YOU AND HEARING YOUR NEW SCORE† WHEN I HIT THE COAST. ALL MY BEST. COLE.

Early in May, Porter wrote again to Barclift:

---

* Carole Hill is a fictitious character invented to compensate for some stars who could or did not appear in the film. As Carole, Ginny Simms sang 'What is This Thing Called Love' (*Wake Up and Dream*, 1929), 'I've Got You Under My Skin' (*Born to Dance*, 1936), 'Just One of Those Things' (*Jubilee*, 1935), 'You're the Top' with Cary Grant (*Anything Goes*, 1934) and 'I Get a Kick Out of You' (*Anything Goes*, 1934).

† Possibly Schwartz's music for *The Time, the Place and the Girl*, released by Warner Bros. on 28 December 1946, or his Broadway show *Park Avenue*, which had a short run of seventy-two performances at the Shubert Theatre, New York, from 4 November 1946 to 4 January 1947.

A PORTER BIOPIC AND TWO FLOPS, 1945–1947

6–7 May [1946]:* Cole Porter to Nelson Barclift

2 A M on

May 6–7

Glitter-boy –

One of those quiet Monday nights. Sturge & I were dining at Chassin's [sic].† Jimmie Shields & Roger Davis joined up ... Vera was at the next table – we told her our plans – so she brought her boy-friend. So we all spent the evening on Sylvia [Ashley]'s boat, drinking Black Velvet & zee wheeskey [!] et soda. [Howard] Sturge[s] found his way into Sylvia's fur safe & suddenly appeared with all of them on, including the god-damnedest little mull you've ever seen. I examined Douglas' [Fairbanks, Jr.] mink-lined over-coat on the Q.T. as Sylvia had mentioned it & (dare I say?) with an idea of selling it. But it's a dud. The collar is Astrachan & the stuff of the coat is a restrained dark-blue tweed but oh my God, that mink lining! Its [sic] lemon-colored alley-cat. So even if the whole ensemble ... were a foot & a half longer, I shouldn't allow you to be seen in it as it's Hollywood trash. Therefore, my pretty, no mink lined coat yet. Chin up but until I meet some richer widow, no mink-lined over-coats a-tall.

Two of your letters tottered in – one written Thursday – the first, in fact & all the time me sitting on the mail-box waiting for the news of your opus at the opera.‡ Thank God, it was good. And even if you didn't get top-billing in Variety, it all counts a great deal & the recognition of it will come as surely as ours did before when the critics kicked us around for so long simply because we were raising hell on the Continent.

Please go out of your way to be nice to Linda. She likes you an awful lot already & I want you to be friends, not only for her sake but even more, for yours. All you have to do is to call her up from time to time & go to see her around the six oclocks. [sic] Do that for me.

And now good night Nelson. I actually miss you in spite of the fact that I realize perfectly that you are incapable of love, affection, loyalty, sentiment or friendship.

---

* This letter probably dates from 1946 since there is otherwise no Monday 6 May during the period 1941–7 when Porter was corresponding with Barclift.

† Chasen's, a trendy restaurant at 9039 Beverly Boulevard, Los Angeles; opened in 1936, it closed in 1995.

‡ Porter's reference here is obscure.

Why should I suddenly throw away so much writing-paper? Could it be "My Cute Little Nose?" For Christ's sake don't have it altered!

Love

C

... P.S. Sturge isn't leaving here for months!

A few days later, he gave the bandleader Paul Whiteman an account of the song 'Rosalie' (*Rosalie*, 1937), which Whiteman was performing at the time:

9 May 1946: Cole Porter to Paul Whiteman*

Dear Paul:

This is the only story I have about the song *Rosalie*:

In 1937 I was writing a picture for M-G-M called *Rosalie* and it was very important that the title song be good. I wrote six before I handed one in, but I was very proud of No. 6. Louis B. Mayer asked me to play the score for him and when I finished he said to me, "I like everything in the score except that song *Rosalie*. It's too high-brow. Forget you are writing for Nelson Eddy[†] and simply give us a good popular song." So I took *Rosalie* No. 6 home and in hate wrote *Rosalie* No. 7. Louis B. Mayer was delighted with it, but I still resented my No. 6 having been thrown out, which to one seemed so much better.

Six months later when the song became a hit, I saw Irving Berlin and he congratulated me on it. I said to him "Thanks a lot, but I wrote that song in hate and I still hate it." To which Irving replied, "Listen, kid, take my advice, never hate a song that has sold a half million copies."

This is the only story I have about *Rosalie*. I am delighted you are playing it and shall listen in with great interest.

Your old friend,

Cole Porter

---

[*] Paul Whiteman (1890–1967) was one of the foremost bandleaders of the time. The original of this letter has not been traced; it is reproduced in facsimile in Kimball and Gill, *Cole*, 147.

[†] The actor Nelson Eddy (1901–67) was the lead, Dick Thorpe, in *Rosalie*, a story about a West Point cadet who falls in love with a girl who turns out to be a European princess. Whiteman recorded 'Rosalie' on his album, *The Night I Played 666 Fifth Avenue* (Grand Award Record Corp., 1959).

In the meantime, Linda wrote to Jean Howard to tell her of their plans and mentioning Porter's upcoming trip to Hollywood: 'I am off to Williamstown early Wednesday morning for the Spring planting, and hope to see all the apple trees in full bloom! I return on Sunday to spend the rest of the month in N.Y. with Cole. He leaves May 31st for Hollywood, and June 1st Weston and I motor to Buxton Hill for four solid months, where I hope to regain my strength.'[45] About the same time, Porter sent a telegram to Sam Stark, alerting him to his arrival in California:

30 May 1946: Cole Porter to Sam Stark[46]

STILL ARRIVING TOMORROW FRIDAY NIGHT BY CONSTELLATION UNLESS ROBERT* TELEPHONES YOU OTHERWISE WILL YOU MEET ME. ALSO CAN YOU HAVE MASSEUR FOR ME AT NOON SATURDAY LOVE=COLE.

Porter had travelled to California to work on songs for the MGM film *The Pirate*. Apparently he composed six songs in about a month, but four of them disappointed the producer, Arthur Freed, who asked for rewrites and otherwise truncated some numbers.[†] Porter later complained to Sam Stark in a telegram:

[n.d.]. Cole Porter to Sam Stark[47]

DEAR SAM AND STAN [MUSGROVE] I ALSO SAW PIRATE NITE BEFORE LAST I AGREE WITH YOU THAT [IT] IS A HIT BUT LOVE OF MY LIFE HAS BEEN CUT TO A MERE REPRISE WHICH DOES IRREPARABLE HARM TO SCORE AND TO ME OTHERWISE EVERYTHING FINE=COLE.

---

* Probably Robert Bray.
† Earl J. Hess and Pratibha A. Dabholkar, *The Cinematic Voyage of the Pirate: Kelly, Garland, and Minnelli at Work* (Columbia, MO, 2014), 72–3 and 232.

In the meantime, *Around the World* closed on 29 July 1946 after only seventy-five performances, excepting *See America First*, the least for any show Porter was involved with.*

29 July 1946: Cole Porter to Orson Welles[48]

DEAR ORSON[,] YOUR TRAGIC NEWS ARRIVED THIS MORNING STOP ALL MY SYMPATHY GOES OUT TO YOU FOR YOU HAVE MADE MORE THAN HUMAN EFFORTS TO KEEP OUR POOR LITTLE SHOW RUNNING SO LONG[.] YOUR DEVOTED=COLE.

Night and Day was released on 3 August, only a few days after *Around the World* closed. Although a commercial success – *Night and Day* was tied for fourteenth on a list of the top-grossing films of 1946[†] – the film received mixed reviews, notwithstanding the enthusiasm of Porter, Jack Warner and the public. To be sure, *Variety* described it as 'a smash. It will mop up from New England to New Zealand. It has everything', anticipating its financial success.[49] And the *New York Herald Tribune* wrote that:

> Cole Porter ... has been accorded a splendidly restrained accolade for his more or less memorable tunes and words ... "Night and Day" weaves a casual biography around its subject, depending more on music and authenticity than big dramatic punches ... [Cary Grant] is almost arrogant enough to look like a Yale man, and he pretends to play the piano with remarkable deception. [Monty Woolley] is as arrogant as any Yale professor who made good in the outside world, and he quips a quip better than ever ... No end of credit must go to Michael Curtiz for his restrained direction of a tale which might have been a caricature of the

---

* See *New York Times*, 30 July 1946, 32: 'The Orson Welles-Cole Porter production, "Around the World," will terminate its career at the Adelphi Theatre after Saturday night's performance it was announced yesterday. The musical extravaganza, staged and adapted by Mr. Welles from Jules Verne's "Around the World in Eighty Days," opened at the tail-end of last season receiving a rather cool reception from a majority of the drama reviewers. The attraction, however, staged an uphill fight until recently, when Mr. Welles decided to call it quits because of poor business.'

† See *Variety*, 8 January 1947, 8. *Night and Day* grossed four million dollars; the top-grossing film, *The Bells of St. Mary's*, brought in eight million dollars.

Era of Wonderful Nonsense. He has inserted a few sequences of hullabaloo which are likely to look corny to a new generation, but let me assure the kids that they are muted rather than overdrawn. In short "Night and Day" is a gala tune-fest, sticking to the creations of a popular song-writer rather than the birth-pains attending them.[50]

John McCarten, however, writing in the *New Yorker*, dismissed the film as a travesty:

Fairly early in "Night and Day," there is a scene in which we discover Cary Grant sitting moodily at a grand piano in a room not much smaller than Carnegie Hall and designed to represent a nook in an Indiana homestead. Rolling his eyes around this plushy interior, Mr. Grant presently lets his glance rest on an elegant grandfather's clock. "Loike," he says in an accent that sounds singularly remote from the Middle West, "the tick, tick, tock of the stitely clock," and before you know it, he has put together the words and music of Cole Porter's most popular song. Mr. Grant, in passing himself off as Cole Porter, labors under an almost unbearable series of handicaps. Although he is getting on in years now, he is compelled by the script to depict the composer in his early days, as a Yale undergraduate even more bouncy than most, and to indulge in such painful juvenile activities as leading a chorus through that song about Eli Yale and a bulldog. Apart from having to attend college at an age when most Yale men would be working for the Luce publications, Mr. Grant is forced to break into song every now and then, which is rather too bad, since his voice, though resonant, is no more mellifluous than the average subway guard's. Like most actors confronted with the problem of portraying a composer at work, he doesn't try to show how the muse is wooed but shows instead how she may be knocked down, jumped on, and tossed over the piano like an afghan.

I know nothing about Cole Porter except that he has written some damned good songs, but I very much doubt that his life has been as exceedingly dull as it is made out to be in "Night and Day." According to the plot, Mr. Porter started out with thousands of dollars and a talent for writing music, and wound up with millions of dollars and his talent unimpaired. The fact that his legs were injured in an accident is hardly as dramatic as Beethoven's deafness, but the Warner Brothers seem to think it is. I never expected to see another biographical film quite as dismal as the one the Brothers produced about George Gershwin,* but this hash of Mr. Porter's career makes the Gershwin epic seem, in retrospect, a dazzler. Still, the picture offers a lot of Cole Porter music, and no matter what Hollywood may have done to Mr. Porter's life, his songs are always good listening.[51]

In late September, Porter did a radio interview with Louella Parsons, the script of which survives among Sam Stark's papers. Among other songs, it discusses 'Night and Day'. More importantly, perhaps, it shows how scripted Porter's interviews could be and the extent to which he personally intervened – the script as it survives includes 'stage directions' in Porter's hand:

PORTER: That's my trouble. I don't know how to write songs that people like immediately. I wrote "Night and Day" in 1932 for a Fred Astaire show. I had a terrible time getting Fred to sing it – and as for Monty Wooley [sic] . . .

PARSONS: WHAT'S HE [struck through by Porter and replaced with 'Monty'] GOT TO DO WITH IT?

PORTER: Monty was the first person to dislike it. One day I was working on it, at the piano, while Monty was reading a book. He finally glanced at me and said, "You certainly don't think that tune will be a hit! I advise you to give it up." [struck through by Porter and replaced with 'Give it up.']

PARSONS: COLE, THE WORLD'S MIGHTY GLAD YOU DIDN'T. IT'S A CLASSIC NOW.

PORTER: Oh [added by Porter above: (Laugh)], I never give up Louella.

In early November 1946, Porter wrote to Jack Warner and Ray Heindorf, to thank them for recordings of *Night and Day*:

---

* *Rhapsody in Blue* (Warner Bros., 1945).

8 November 1946: Cole Porter to Jack Warner[52]

Dear Jack:

The recordings of "Night and Day" arrived, and when I asked to pay for them I was told they were a present from you. I deeply appreciate this.

Sam Gertzen [Stark] and I will be in Hot Springs in about ten days. I shall telephone you before arriving in the hope that you are there and can persuade the manager to give us rooms.

In the meantime, don't forget my gratitude.

Best,

[unsigned]

8 November 1946: Cole Porter to Ray Heindorf[53]

Dear Ray:

The wonderful recordings arrived and I thank you very much.

I wrote Jack Warner thanking him.

Best luck to you.

Sincerely,

Cole Porter

About the same time, Porter asked his cousin and accountant Harvey Cole for financial information relative to his dealings with his landlord, possibly in connection with a lawsuit he was considering concerning the lease of Haines's house at 416 Rockland Ave. in Los Angeles.*

26 November 1946: Cole Porter to Harvey Cole[54]

Dear Harvey:

Will you get for me from the Wabash Valley Trust Company all cancelled checks made out to either

William Haines

---

* See p. 285.

or

Williams, [sic] Haines, Inc.

from January 1, 1943 on, and send them to Miss Moore, 41-E Waldorf Towers.

Best regards,

[signed:] Cole

Surviving letters from early 1947 are mostly addressed to Sam Stark:

3 January 1947: Cole Porter to Sam Stark[55]

Dear Scamp That You Are:

What a wicked little boy you were to send me those three wonderful books. You should save your earnings for more serious matters and not waste them on me. I'm enjoying them, however, an awful lot.

New York misses you. Your letter about your Christmas party was very welcome.

My new Cadillac has arrived and it looks like a very big jewel. Don't forget when I start my trek back to California, you are coming East to motor back with me in the old Chrysler.

Lots of love from us both,

[signed:] Cole

6 January 1947: Cole Porter to Sam Stark[56]

Sam – I'm so ill. I have what scientists call <u>The Common Cold</u> but if this is common, how much do I sympathize with the human race! I don't go in for colds, even aristocratic colds. So to be sunk to such depths by a vulgar <u>common</u> cold, all I can ask is "What next?"

You might like it here, with us. We go out. People ask us to dinner + we accept. This is all so new to me after so . . . [a page missing here]

. . . enough. Even if I came back to the coast where my heart is, this urge to work would still – but enough of my lament. And how are you, you naughty boy? And what are <u>your</u> troubles?

[Howard] Sturge[s] left today to stay in Palm Beach with Consuelo Balsan.* He prefers deaf duchesses for some reason + Consuelo is the deafest of them all. Elsa† telephoned yesterday from Cannes to say it was so cold there that she and Annie Warner‡ were ski-ing today to Monte Carlo. Jean, la Feldman came in to call. She looked better than anyone had ever looked. She is up to no good but I couldn't find out which gender of "no-good" it was. Millicent Hearst§ gave a great brawl last night for all the visiting British stage stars. After dinner, Bea Lillie sang the funniest song I have heard in years called "Maud – let's admit it, you're rotten to the core"!¶

I could go on + on but I'm very ill + en plus, I have no work. What I have, however, is Hope so don't worry about me.

It was nice taking up your time.

Please give my best wishes to John who sent me such a nice Christmas wire + to Stanislas [Stanley Musgrove] who wrote me a wonderful letter.

And if you see the young man** who works for that clip-joint at the Bel Air Hotel give him a big goose de ma part. I'm afraid he wouldn't respond to an ordinary one.

And goodnight, Mr Stark.

Your admirer

Cole.

And Allan's [sic, Allen Walker] admirer, aussi!

---

* Consuelo Vanderbilt Balsan (née Vanderbilt, 1877–1964) was a daughter of the railroad magnate William Kissam Vanderbilt. She married her first husband, Charles Spencer-Churchill, 9th Duke of Marlborough, on 6 November 1895; they separated in 1906 and divorced in 1921. On 4 July 1921 she married a French pilot, Lieutenant Colonel Jacques Balsan (1868–1965). See Amanda Mackenzie Stuart, *Consuelo and Alva Vanderbilt: The Story of a Daughter and Mother in the Gilded Age* (New York, 2005).

† Elsa Maxwell.

‡ Wife of movie mogul Jack Warner.

§ Millicent Veronica Hearst (1882–1974) was the wife of media tycoon William Randolph Hearst (1863–1951).

¶ For a recording by Beatrice Lillie, see https://www.youtube.com/watch?v=XB-kZN9Bc28.

** A note by Sam Stark in the margin identifies the 'young man' as Robert Raison.

8 January 1947: Cole Porter to Sam Stark[57]

Stark – I ordered for you today the album of Finian's Rainbow.* Mine came yesterday + I have played it without cessation ever since. This seems to me the most attractive music + lyrics since Oklahoma[†] so when it arrives don't throw it at someone you dislike.

The show opens Friday night, next. It has been enchanting Philadelphia for the last two weeks. What's more, it has been knocking all the Broadway ticket brokers for triple loops. Therefore I was so happy to hear that Linda and I were invited "By The Producer" to sit in the first row for the premiere for free! We accepted quick quick + you can't imagine what finery we are both whipping up.

The doctor came today to look at my "Common" cold + decided I wouldn't die. Thank God I won't die below my station!

I enclose a letter from [Nelson] Barclift. I don't believe this letter about Mr. Fly. Do you? All this worries me. I'm so afraid that Barclift through merely knowing Fly will end up in a major jail.

Goodbye, Butterfly + my best to Allan [sic, Allen Walker]

Your pal –

Porter

13 January 1947: Cole Porter to Sam Stark[58]

Dear Mr. Gertzen [Stark]:

I can't send you sheet music of the Bea Lillie song because it is private material. Nor can I send you a recording of "See that you're born in Texas" as a recording was never made.[‡] Nor can I give you the moon.

Love,

[signed:] Cole

---

* 'Yip' Harburg and Burton Lane's *Finian's Rainbow* opened at the 46th Street Theatre, New York, on 10 January 1947. The original cast recording was released by Columbia Records.

† Rodgers and Hammerstein's *Oklahoma!* was first given at the St James Theatre, New York, on 31 March 1943.

‡ From *Something for the Boys* (1943). A 1943 radio cast recording, including the chorus 'See That You're Born in Texas', was released on AEI (B00000N5G) in 1995; see https://www.youtube.com/watch?v=LheZnhLm9Ig.

A PORTER BIOPIC AND TWO FLOPS, 1945–1947

Having already heard the recording, Porter on 13 January finally saw Yip Harburg and Burton Lane's *Finian's Rainbow*, which had opened at the 46th Street Theatre on 10 January:

13 January 1947: Cole Porter to E. Y. ('Yip') Harburg[59]

Dear Yip:

You gave us a wonderful night in the theatre last Friday night* with your delightful book and lyrics and this is a mere note to congratulate you and to thank you for allowing the public to appreciate your great talent.

And thanks also for the NIGHT AND DAY plug.

Sincerely,

[signed:] Cole Porter

15 January 1947: Cole Porter to Sam Stark[60]

Sam – In my frantic desire to keep up with the Gertzen set, I have been reading Steve Canyon.† But Steve must improve an awful lot or the next time you see me I shall look like one of Bobbie Raison's old zoot suits, that is, from your prejudiced eyes.

I saw Tito [Reynaldo] tonight. He was at 1-2-3 at the next table to me. When I greeted him he was very-far-away. But I paid no attention as I like him so much.

Linda + I go out quite a lot. I think I told you this. And it's sort of a nice contrast to the years when, on account of my conspicuous legs, we couldn't. But we do it very carefully + between each evening with the "gratin," we dine simply at the Old Pav. with a buddy or two. To finish this week, we Windsor it‡ on Sunday night. Then on Monday, our private little polar expedition takes off. Max + Helene§ in my Cadillac + Linda + I in hers. The objective is my

---

* *Finian's Rainbow.*

† A comic strip by artist and author Milton Caniff (1907–88), named after the eponymous adventurer; it ran from 13 January 1947 to 4 June 1988.

‡ Possibly a reference to Edward VII (1894–1972, after his abdication Duke of Windsor) and his wife Wallis Simpson (1896–1986)

§ Porter's valet and Linda's maid.

cottage at Williamstown. There we will dig in for a week. According to all the weathermen we can be sure of constant Ma Moses landscapes.* Also I have moved all my recordings up there so Linda will hear all the music from Bach to Berlin. And the great thing about Linda is that she will like it.

Pep is very hurt that Judy didn't even acknowledge his present to her.† Everytime a letter arrives from you, he grabs it from me ravenously, ever hoping for even one little word. But no, – silence.

Gossip – I saw Vincent Astor‡ + Alice + David Bouverie§ last night. Alice + David looked very happy. Vincent is so upset that Minnie has left him that he has lost his voice. When he whispered this to me, I told him I liked his new voice better. The inner sanctum low-down is that Minnie who went to the coast with Annabella (but I don't believe this is a lesbian tie-up) is so fed up with Vincent's drunkenness that she may never come back. The crazy angle about it all is that Vincent went to cry on his first wife's shoulder (Mrs. Lytle Hull) + Helen Hull is doing all she can by telephone to persuade Minnie to come back to the family hearth. What's more, Helen says that Minnie has behaved outrageously! Work this out. And tell only Kitty.¶

Goodnight, Stark. I miss you – my best to Allan [sic, Allen Walker] + to John + to Stanislaus.

Your fan

Cole

---

* Presumably Porter means it will be snowy; cf. Grandma Moses's *Cambridge Valley in Winter* above, p. 220.

† Porter's dog Pep and Stark's dog Judy.

‡ William Vincent Astor (1891–1959), businessman, philanthropist and a son of the businessman and investor John Jacob Astor IV (1864–1912). He married Helen Dinsmore Huntington, well known to be lesbian, on 30 April 1914. They divorced in 1940, and in 1941 Helen married the real-estate broker Lytle Hull. Vincent subsequently married Mary Benedict Cushing ('Minni'); they divorced in 1953.

§ Ava Alice Muriel Astor (1902–56), a daughter of John Jacob Astor IV, married her fourth husband, David Pleydell-Bouverie (1911–94) on 27 March 1940. She had previously been married to the Russian artistocrat Sergei Platonovich Obolensky; Raimund von Hofmannsthal, a son of the Austrian writer Hugo von Hofmannsthal; and the English journalist Philip John Ryves Harding.

¶ Possibly Kitty Miller (1891–1979), a New York socialite and the eldest daughter of financier Jules Bache (1861–1944).

22 January 1947: Cole Porter to Sam Stark[61]

Jan 22 '47. Night + 10° below zero.

Sambambino –

Miss Moore telephoned today that a letter addressed to Mr. Pep Porter had arrived at the Waldorf, forwarded from here which is Williamstown. This, despite warning the P.O. here that this would be my address until Saturday next. She is forwarding it back. How exhausting it is, the white collar!

As I wrote Robert earlier, Linda + I went for a spin this afternoon in my new Cadillac. Pep drove. And a spin it was indeed. For the roads are completely covered in ice. The more important roads have a slight gravel surface furnished by the State of Massachusetts but <u>our</u> road, i.e. the one from our little home to the village, is a good stand-in for the Cresta Run.* Such fun!

Goodbye, Stark. If they were only non-meltable, I would enclose such attractive icicles. One of them is hanging from my nose. The other? – but you couldn't take it.

Good hunting to Bobbie [Raison] + Catharine [d'Erlanger]. And happy semesters to John + Stanislaus. To Allan [sic], my best + to you, my scamp, a terrific kick in the ass.

Always your serf
Cole

25 January 1947: Cole Porter to Sam Stark[62]

Saturday night.

Sam The Wham!

Thank you for your letter of Jan 18th with all it's [sic] news.

I'm so fresh from Berks. That all I can tell you is that Harry [Krebs] + I dined au Pavillon tonight. Gilbert + Kitty Miller were opposite. You know that Kitty was Jules Bache's daughter. She had a sister, Hazel, who's [sic] <u>2nd</u> husband was Freddie Beckman. Hazel died last week + left her entire estate

---

* An ice skeleton-racing and toboggan track in St Moritz, Switzerland.

to her children by her 1st marriage except for her life insurance, 100 grand which she left to Freddie. Who can live on 100 grand? Ask Bill [Haines] + Jimmie [Shields] about them. They entertained us all when we were in Mexico.

Freddie B., before he married Hazel – now, get me straight, not Allan's [sic, Allen Walker] Kitty's sister – was kept by a series of lonely, rich gentlemen, one of whom was Mr L[en] C Hanna + Freddie was so good at "collecting things" that by the time Mr Hanna threw him out, Mr. Beckman had added quite a lot of objets d'art to his collection.

So the biggest question in NYC today is "who will keep Freddie Beckman next?"

Louella Parsons [sic] news about Dorothy Frasso + the Villa Madama is very incorrect. Dorothy sold it years ago to Mussolini.* All she has left is a small cottage on the place where Carlo (that was her husband) was allowed to live, after the sale + it's a moot point whether she has any right to this cottage or not. She is also trying to get all the lire that she was paid, out of Italy. If she does, she is a fool because, as you know, a lira isn't worth –

But why do I write you all this? I came back to find a most puzzling letter from Col. Bill Shinley. But never a word from [Robert] Raisin [sic]. What have I done? I wrote him such a nice wholesome note.

A postcard arrived from you + John + Stanislaus + it was cheering to realize that all you kids still remembered me.

Pep† was definitely embarrassed to receive Judy's illiterate letter. I don't believe he had ever associated with bitches like that before. Even by mail. I admit he has been too sheltered what with Helene + Weston to "maid" him, Max to valet him, Paul + Ernest to take him driving + Linda and me to clean up his shit.

---

* The Villa Madama, west of Rome on Monte Mario, was commissioned by Cardinal Giulio de' Medici in 1518, based on a design by Raphael. It was sold to Mussolini in 1941 by the then-owner, Carlo, Count Dentice di Frasso, and his wife Dorothy Cadwell Taylor. The heiress Dorothy Taylor (1888–1954) had first married the British aviator Claude Grahame-White in 1912 but divorced him in 1916 after she inherited nearly twelve million dollars; she married Count Carlo Dentice di Frasso (1876–death date unknown), son of Count Ernesto Dentice, 7th Prince of Frasso, in 1923. Frasso is a commune about 40 kilometres northeast of Naples.

† Porter's dog.

Goodnight, Stark. My best to Allan, + to John + Stanley my respects + to you, my old-fashioned devotion.

Cole.

2 February 1947: Cole Porter to Sam Stark[63]

Sunday night Feb 2nd 47

Stark, The Lark!

First, to correct certain errata:

1) Dorothy Frasso doesn't maintain that she still owns a <u>cottage</u> on the Villa Madama acreage. It is a far bigger item, the <u>stables</u>.
2) I saw Gilbert Miller. Hazel didn't leave poor Freddie Beckman $100 000 in life insurance. She left him a million in life <u>insurance</u>. Now we're talkin'...

Tell Bobbie Raizon [sic, Raison] that I can't remember ever having written him a letter even one with "foreign" words in it. By the way, what are "foreign" words? "Foreign" to what?

The book <u>Scientists Against Time</u>* isn't so damned profound. It is at times too technical for my purely academic education but otherwise it's a lot of nice clean fun. Please delve.

<u>Finian's Rainbow</u> has been sent by <u>Liberty</u>. The delay was due to a slip – my slip. There have been distractions and unpleasant distractions.

The memorial service for Grace Moore† at the Rockefeller church on Riverside Drive was beautiful + mostly arranged by Clifton Webb. Have you ever seen the interior of that church? It is incredibly fine!

I envy you, your trip to Ense[?] with John + Stanislascovitch.‡ That is one of my pet spots + what a spot it must have been with such delightful pets.

This is called answering a letter. I'm in a bad mood. I want to come west so god-damned much but on account of good reasons it can't be done yet. Linda is a joy + our jaunts to Williamstown are idyllic but they can't be staged

---

* James Phinney Baxter III, *Scientists Against Time* (Boston, 1946), won the 1947 Pulitzer Prize for history.
† Grace Moore (1898–1947), operatic soprano and actress.
‡ Stanley Musgrove.

often enough or for a long enough time. We are off again Wednesday for a five days respite . . .

Paul [Sylvain, Porter's chauffeur] is nearly well again but Miss Moore has a skin disease due to wearing a black slip. The dye was defective. She appeared Monday painted clown-white. She is still in bed, where I sent her quick [?]. Her whole body is painted clown-white now, she tells me. I don't know whether her doctors are the Ringling Brothers* or not.

[Howard] Sturges, The Tea-Cup Rattler arrives from Palm Beach tomorrow.

Tidbits for Kitty [Miller?]: Bill Paley is wooing (+ apparently successfully) the divorced Mrs. Stanley Mortimer.† He is the owner of the Columbia Broadcasting Company. She is one of the three Cushing sisters. The other two are 1) Mrs Vincent (Minnie) Astor + 2) Mrs Jock Whitney (the former Betsy Roosevelt.)‡ In the meantime, Clare Boothe Luce§ is hitting the hay with Jock. She gives as her reason that she wants to make Jock more politically minded.

That's all, Sammy. My best to Allen [Walker] + John + Stannie [Musgrove], my blessings.

As for you, Mr Gertzen, I'm still your vassal

Cole

15 February 1947: Cole Porter to Sam Stark[64]

Saturday Feb 15, '47

And you, my poppet! How are you?

---

* The seven brothers of the Ringling family who in 1906 purchased Barnum & Bailey Ltd and in 1919 merged their circuses as Ringling Bros. and Barnum & Bailey Circus.

† William S. Paley (1901–90) was the founder of CBS; he married the socialite Barbara Cushing Mortimer (1915–78) on 28 July 1947.

‡ Mary Benedict Cushing (1906–78) was the second wife of Vincent Astor. Betsy Cushing (1909–98) had married James Roosevelt II (1907–91), the eldest son of Franklin D. Roosevelt (at the time Governor of New York), in June 1930. She divorced Roosevelt in 1940 and on 1 March 1942 married the millionaire John Hay Whitney (1904–82).

§ Clare Boothe Luce (1903–87) was an author and diplomat. She was married to Henry R. Luce (1898–1967), the magazine magnate whose stable of publications included *Time*, *Life*, *Fortune* and *Sports Illustrated*.

I have no news apart from the fact that I am slowly planning to turn on New York like a snake toward the 23rd of March + head west either by motor or by boat. Would that divert you too much from your endless orgies, caro mio?

Keep this strictly subcutaneous but ponder there on. I shall look up the boat question quick, quick.

Linda + I motor back to Winchellville* tomorrow. Pep [Porter's dog] was embarrassed to get that book, "More Please"† from Judy [Stark's dog] but he was charming about it. He gave it to a cur in the village. He is sending Judy a book that he just finished. Read it to her aloud. I'm sure she could never read it herself.

I gloated when you told me that you had invited Robert to dine with you with Stan + John. Or was it Robert who told me? In any case, I know you all had a lot of fun + it was grand of you to do that, Sambambino.

That's enough now. So goodnight.

Your fan

Cole

[Added in margin to left:] My best to Allen [Walker].

Work on *The Pirate* continued through early 1947, when Porter corresponded with the composer Roger Edens,‡ who was responsible for some of the uncredited music in the film, about 'Niña' and 'Mack the Black' in particular:

18 February 1947: Cole Porter to Roger Edens[65]

Dear Roger:

A spy of mine met some one who had been to your house and you played some transcriptions from THE PIRATE. He spoke especially of LOVE

---

* That is, New York; the reference is to Walter Winchell.

† Unidentified. No book with the title *More Please* appears to have been published about this time.

‡ Roger Edens (1905–70) was a composer and lyricist at MGM.

OF MY LIFE. If this rumor is correct, and if you could spare a few extra transcriptions, I should be so grateful to receive them here at the Waldorf.

All my best,
Sincerely yours,
[signed:] Cole

26 [February 1947]: Cole Porter to Roger Edens

NINA. NINA. NINA. FASCINATION NINA. WHAT A LOVELY CHILD: NINA. YOU ENCHANT ME NINA. YOU'RE SO SWEET. I MEAN YUH. FAIRLY DRIVE ME WILD COLE.

27 February 1947: Cole Porter to Roger Edens

IN NINA. CHANGE LINE YOU BROKE MY HEART EITHER TO YOU STOPPED MY HEART OR YOU HIT MY HEART* COLE.

4 March 1947: Cole Porter to Roger Edens[66]

Dear Roger:

The record of MACK THE BLACK arrived and has me in a dither. Also the sheet music of MACK THE BLACK parts 1 and 2, my original song of MACK THE BLACK and the new arrangement of LOVE OF MY LIFE. It seems to me that this last arrangement is beautiful and I am very grateful to you.

Will you kindly tell all of this to Miss Lela Simone?†

All my best,
[signed:] Cole

---

* The final text read '. . . you hit my heart'. Porter's apparent original version, '. . . you broke my heart' is not noted in Kimball, *The Complete Lyrics of Cole Porter*, 382.

† Lela Simone (1907–91) was a solo pianist with the MGM studio orchestra, part-time from 1937 and full-time from 1939; she had emigrated from Germany in 1933. As part of Arthur Freed's team at MGM she also worked as a vocal coach, piano instructor and music editor; her last work for MGM was on *Gigi* in 1958.

In late March, Porter wrote to Mrs Arthur Reis, executive chair of the League of Composers, that he was about to leave for Hollywood for 'the preparation of a new musical play in the films',[67] presumably *The Pirate*. And as a result, he could not accept an invitation from Irving Berlin to a dinner for Sophie Tucker. After his time in Hollywood, Porter toured the American Southwest, including Tombstone, the Grand Canyon, San Antonio and the Alamo and sent a postcard to Monty Woolley:

1 [or 19] April 1947: Cole Porter to Irving Berlin[68]

VERY SORRY CANNOT ATTEND SOPHIE TUCKER DINNER ON MAY FOURTH AS WILL STILL BE IN LOS ANGELES=COLE PORTER

19 April 1947: Cole Porter to Monty Woolley

April 1947

I arrive April 28. Telephone when you can spare a dime
C. P.

Shortly after his return to New York, Porter made a quick trip to Peru, Indiana, to see his mother, who was unwell.* While there, he sent Roger Edens another telegram concerning 'Niña':

8 May 1947: Cole Porter to Roger Edens

NINA / NINA NINA NINA / YOU'RE THE PRIZE GARDENIA / OF THE SPANISH MAIN. / NINA / WHILE MY THEME SONG I SING / DON'T BE SO ENTICING / OR I'LL GO INSANE. / NINA – TILL ALAS I GAZED IN YOUR EYES. / NINA I WAS MENTALLY FINE / BUT SINCE I'VE SEEN YUH / NINA NINA NINA / I'LL BE HAVING SCHIZOPHRENIA / TILL I MAKE YOU MINE / STOP ADDRESS ME WALDORF NEW YORK CITY FROM MONDAY ON UNTIL THEN PERU INDIANA BEST COLE

---

* Porter sent a telegram to Sam Stark on 19 July to tell him 'MY MA IS BETTER'. Stanford University, Cole Porter Collection, shelfmark FE209.

The line given here by Porter, 'While my theme song I sing', does not appear in the published text.*

Boris Kochno, Porter's lover in the 1920s, apparently returned to New York in May 1947, although it is unlikely that he saw Porter, as a note dated 29 May to him from Linda Porter suggests: 'Dear Boris: I am so glad that you are returning to New York in October; – do phone me as soon as you arrive, for by that time I shall probably be back from the country. Cole is in Hollywood – I go tomorrow to my house at Williamstown, thank Heaven!'[69] In August, Porter wrote to Monty Wolley:

28 August 1947: Cole Porter to Monty Woolley[70]

Beard –

I hear it was a horror[†] + I'm so damned sorry.

I fly eastward slowly, stopping off for a few days in Indiana. My ma isn't nearly well enough. Then I hit Williamstown whence I shall call you. Linda isn't nearly well enough either. I'm well enough.

Sam [Goldwyn] called yesterday morning at 9.30 asking me to the studio to see all of your scenes from <u>The B's Wife</u> at 12.30 noon.[‡] I was wakened at noon + couldn't make it. Sam raves over your work. He always says "He's so warm, so warm."

At Junior Fairbanks,[§] night before last, I heard Sam say to Charley Schwartz who had just arrived from N.Y. "Hello Charley. Since the last time I saw you, we've passed a lot of water under the bridge!" I heard this.

Goodnight, Li'l Beardy. I think of you. A kiss for Cary [Grant].

Cole

Although it was not released until 11 June 1948, *The Pirate* was largely finished by September 1947:

---

* Kimball, *The Complete Lyrics of Cole Porter*, 382.

† Porter's reference is obscure.

‡ *The Bishop's Wife* (The Samuel Goldwyn Company, 1947), starring Cary Grant as an angel who helps a bishop build a new cathedral and repair his marriage. Monty Woolley played the role of Professor Wutheridge.

§ Douglas Fairbanks Jr.

A PORTER BIOPIC AND TWO FLOPS, 1945–1947

26 September 1947: Cole Porter to Arthur Freed[71]

Dear Arthur:

The records arrived and I thank you very much. I shall not open them until I go to New York as I am afraid that some injury might come to them before I have processed records made.

Have you previewed <u>The Pirate</u> yet? All my best to you, dear Arthur.

Sincerely yours,

[signed, but not in CP's hand:] Cole

To some extent the filming was at times acrimonious. An assistant director's report from 13 May 1947 states that Judy Garland – who took the starring role of Manuela – and Porter argued about how to pronounce the word 'caviar', Porter apparently wanting it as three distinct syllables. Similarly, Garland apparently did not like 'Be A Clown'.* The movie was panned when it was released in 1948 and Porter later said that, taken together, *Around the World* and *The Pirate* were serious blows to his professional standing: 'The failure of the travelogue idea in Eighty Days Around the World [sic] - - which closed in eighty days - - was so resounding that my own reputation took a fall. It was not improved by my down-beat score for The Pirate, a $5,000,000 motion picture that failed to get back even the cost of the emulsion for developing the negative. My agent told me: "No one wants you Cole. They think your tunes are old-fashioned."'[72]

For reasons that are not known, the subject of *Born to Dance* came up in Porter's correspondence with Sam Stark, and in October 1947 Porter sent him the diary he had kept of his meetings at MGM in 1935:

16 October 1947: Cole Porter to Sam Stark[73]

Mr. Sam Stark
　　1014 N. Doheny Drive
　　Los Angeles, California

Dear Sam:

I am sending you under separate cover a copy of the diary I made while I was writing <u>Born to Dance</u>.† Every word of it is entirely true and therefore

---

* Earl J. Hess and Pratibha A. Dabholkar, *The Cinematic Voyage of the Pirate*, 101 and 115.
† See pp. 110–38.

highly indiscreet, so I beg you show it to practically no one except, of course, to Allen [Walker] and Stanny [Musgrove].

Last Thursday I had Paul [Sylvain] take a bottle of toilet water called Molinard* to the drug store here to be sent to you. This is one of two bottles that [Howard] Sturges brought me from Paris and as there was so much he gave me permission to send you half of the supply. You may like it.

Love,

[signed:] Cole

About this time, Porter became involved in a charity fronted by Douglas Fairbanks Jr., 'Share Through Care':

GIFT TO ELIZABETH WILL HELP BRITISH. Douglas Fairbanks, Jr., Announces Share Through Care Project New York, Sept. 23 – The Share Through Care Committee headed by Douglas Fairbanks, Jr., at a press conference today launched its initial project, the Princess Elizabeth Wedding Gift, in a country-wide campaign to aid the British people through Care's special food package ... The Share Through Care committee originated, Fairbanks said, by a small group who wished to do what they could to alleviate suffering in Europe. The committee is a permanent organization to send packages to the needy in 15 European countries. The Princess Elizabeth wedding gift† is the group's first undertaking but projects for other countries are underway, Fairbanks added.[74]

Porter was in touch with Douglas Fairbanks Jr. about the charity in October (and with Fairbanks's wife, Mary Lee) and shortly afterwards apparently solicited a donation from Sam Stark.

---

* Manufacturer of perfumes (*créateur parfumeur*), founded in 1849 in Grasse, France.

† Elizabeth II had announced her engagement to Philip Mountbatten, Prince Philip of Greece and Denmark (subsequently the Duke of Edinburgh), on 9 July 1947. They were married on 20 November 1947.

28 October 1947: Cole Porter to Douglas Fairbanks, Jr.[75]

Dear Junior: –

First, let me repeat my wire to you, saying how happy we were to receive your news of Melissa.*

Second, I am working hard on your SHARE THROUGH CARE and have, so far, written to 25 people asking for their help, beside helping a bit on my own.

Third, Linda and I have a request to make: The Duke and Duchess of Montoro† will arrive in Los Angeles in about ten days. Linda and I decided that the nicest people to be nice to them would be you and Mary Lee, Phyllis [Astaire] and Fred [Astaire] and Merle [Oberon] and Lucien [Ballard]. We feel very responsible for them as "Tana" is Linda's god-child. I hope you can find time to do this for us.

You will find them everything delightful, and she is so pretty. They will be in Los Angeles about five days and, like all the rest of the world, hunger to meet film stars and see pictures being made.

I know you must be tired of these requests, but this couple is so enchanting that I know you will not feel that they are a weight on your hands.

Lots of love to Mary Lee, and again my congratulations to you both.

Your devoted

[signed:] Cole

29 October 1947: Cole Porter to Mary Lee Fairbanks[76]

Dear Mary Lee –

I wrote Douglas yesterday telling him that Linda was Tana de Montoro's god-mother. I made a mistake. Linda is not her god-mother at all!

Love to you, dear Mary Lee. You were sweet to remember to wire me about Melissa.

Love + blessings

Cole

---

* Fairbanks had married Mary Lee Hartford on 22 April 1939; Melissa was their third daughter.

† Maria del Rosario Cayetana Fitz-James Stuart y Silva, 18th Duchess of Alba (1926–2014) and Don Luis Martínez de Irujo y Artázcoz (1919–72). They had married on 12 October 1947.

11 November 1947: Cole Porter to Sam Stark

Dear Sam: –

Thanks a lot for your SHARE THROUGH CARE cheque.

I am returning your letter from Saint-Quentin. Your whole record shows that my original name for you, "Saint Sam", was correct.

Love from us both,
COLE

Porter had several (now lost) letters from Stark shortly afterwards and wrote back to him on 17 December and again on 30 December:

17 December 1947: Cole Porter to Sam Stark[77]

Dear Sam: –

A series of letters arrived from you, with clippings etc. included, for which I thank you: (1) the picture of Gene Kelly and Judy Garland dressed as clowns;* (2) the clipping about Pouilly Fuissé (misspelled by Miss Maxwell); (3) the letter from Demetrious. Never back a show. (4) The picture of the Palazzo Barbaro.† This was the first palace we had in Venice. We took it in 1923 for one season . . .

There is a sudden shaft of light from Hollywood from a man called Sperling,‡ who has a unit at Warner Bros. He wants me to do a musical and he and Lyons§ have nearly come to terms. This might work out.¶

---

* A reference to the scene in *The Pirate* during which Kelly and Garland, dressed as clowns, sing 'Be a Clown'.

† The Palazzo Barbaro was one of a pair of adjoining palaces in the San Marco district of Venice, fronting on the Grand Canal.

‡ Milton Sperling (1912–88), screenwriter and film producer; he owned an independent production unit – an administrative organization hired by major studios to finance and release, but not film, pictures – at Warner Bros., United States Pictures. He did not, in the end, produce a Porter musical.

§ Arthur Lyons.

¶ Apparently nothing came of the proposal.

[Howard] Sturges and I were very surprised, as we sat Sunday in front of the open fire in Williamstown, to hear Louella Parsons broadcast about my lawsuit against Bill Haines.* How Jimmy Shields must have boiled!

I shall write you at length when my news is better but, so far, it has all been bad and sad.

Love from us both,

[signed:] Cole

30 December 1947: Cole Porter to Sam Stark[78]

Dear Sam: –

I was outraged to receive the Concert Companion.† Of course, this is my favorite type of book, and I shall use it constantly. But you had already sent me a most beautiful Christmas present in the form of a file – so I resent this shower of gifts, in spite of the fact that I thank you from the bottom of my heart.

I also received the wonderful notice from Time on "It Had To Be You". This is, by far, the funniest notice I have ever read.

Lots of love from us both, and again, my gratitude,

Your devoted

[signed:] Cole

---

* Porter's suit concerned his continuing residence at 416 N. Rockingham, which Porter claimed Haines had agreed to renew; apparently the suit was successful. See McBrien, *Cole Porter*, 302.

† Robert Bagar and Louis Biancolli, *The Concert Companion: A Comprehensive Guide to Symphonic Music* (New York and London, 1947).

CHAPTER SIX

KISS ME, KATE, 1948

Although his inner circle was not large, Porter's correspondence with his closest friends seems to reveal a more genuine identity than the relatively neutral personality he projects in many of his other communications. The second of the following two letters to Sam Stark, by now one of his most intimate acquaintances, is particularly notable for its frank references to Porter's homosexuality. He begins by teasing Stark sympathetically about an illness he had contracted, which is perhaps what encouraged Porter to be a little more sincere in this letter. Later, he refers to a lover (Michael Pearman) and mentions Gore Vidal's gay novel *The City and the Pillar* (1948). Here is confirmation, if it were needed, that although Porter kept this part of his life private, he was sexually active, promiscuous, and apparently not particularly repressed about his sexuality. The letter also gives Stark an update on Porter's health at the time – treatments on his right leg to delay the need for an operation:

13 January 1948: Cole Porter to Sam Stark[1]

Dear Sam: –

I am sending you, under separate cover, a book which you lent me. It has been standing in a bookcase in Williamstown just above a radiator, so it is rather badly warped. Please sit on it for a while and I am sure it will resume its normal lines.

I am also sending a program of Allegro.* I may have sent you one of these before.

---

* Rodgers and Hammerstein's third Broadway musical, *Allegro*, opened on 10 October 1947.

I also received the bank statement from Stark, Morgan Harjes et Cie.* I had no idea that your banking firm had so many branches around the world. Naturally, I regret a great deal that you can no longer handle my account, due to lack of funds. But, perhaps I can find a few dollars later on to put me in good standing again. There was a postscript on this statement from one of your tellers, and he signed it simply "Robert".† Who, pray, could this be?

That's all.

Love,

[signed:] Cole.[2]

21 January 1948: Cole Porter to Sam Stark[3]

Samb, the Lamb –

How could you contract Virus X?‡ You, playing in the purity of your garden! I thought only Jewish agents had it. I hope that by now you are back in your pristine form. It is difficult to think of you riddled with disease.

Michael P.§ went to W'mst'n¶ with me for the last weekend. He was charming in spite of the fact that he insisted upon playing all my bad recordings instead of all my good ones. But there is really a delightful gent. A weekend in that minute cottage is a sure test.

Telephone to Stannie** + tell him – shush – that Sylvia†† dined with us tonight. She said that she had practically never seen Gable‡‡ because as a result of his having neuritis, his dentist had removed all of his teeth + that he was hiding in the valley until the new sets arrived. I hesitated to wire this news.

---

* Morgan Harjes & Co. was a Paris-based investment bank founded in 1868 by John H. Harjes.

† Robert Bray.

‡ A severe outbreak of influenza, reported in *The Stanford Daily*: https://stanforddailyarchive.com/cgi-bin/stanford?a=d&d=stanford19480109-01.2.5 (accessed 11 September 2018).

§ Michael Pearman, a friend of the Porters from the mid-1930s.

¶ Williamstown.

** Perhaps Lord Stanley, Sylvia Stanley Alderley's ex-husband, though references to 'Stannie' in Porter's letters to Stark normally relate to Stanley Musgrove.

†† The actress, model and socialite Sylvia Stanley Alderley, Lady Ashley, widow of Douglas Fairbanks Sr. (1904–77).

‡‡ Presumably the movie star Clark Gable.

I am going through treatments of my right leg, 3 times a week, Tuesday, Wednesday + Thursday mornings. They are so painful that they often make me pass out. But the blessing of them is that they may make an operation at least temporarily unnecessary.

It suddenly looks as if I might have a Broadway show.* I shall know more shortly + will send on the news. If it happens, this will be wonderful indeed for I long for work . . .

I air mailed The City + The Pillar.† Then I picked up an old letter from Bobby Raison recommending it to me so it must be old West Coast news by now. I think this book is extraordinary. Certainly the author knows his subject + he writes well.

Goodnight, dear Sammy. I am awfully sorry that you have been ill. Buck up quick quick + write me that you are blooming again.

Goodnight. My love to Allen [Walker].

Your

Cole.

Aside from the reference to his sex life, Porter also alludes for the first time to the musical that would prove to be his biggest success on Broadway: *Kiss Me, Kate*.‡

Business also continued to be on Porter's mind. His financial status was as precarious as ever, and he never seemed to catch up on his expenditures, not least because of his multiple extravagant residences. The following letter to his cousin Harvey, who was still running his affairs in Indiana, shows how he was now relying on his mother – always referred to as Katy – to maintain his lifestyle. He asks Harvey to organize the payment for James Omar Cole, Porter's cousin, who was running the farm for her:

---

* *Kiss Me, Kate*.

† *The City and the Pillar* was Gore Vidal's third novel, published on 10 January 1948.

‡ On 27 January 1948, Porter also sent an impatient telegram to Stark: 'WHY DONT YOU ANSWER QUICK MY LONG LETTER OR TELEPHONE REVERSE CHARGES=COLE.' Stanford University, Cole Porter Collection, shelfmark FE209, Correspondence: 1948 (TLS on Waldorf stationery), 1–6.

17 February 1948: Cole Porter to Harvey Cole[4]

Dear Harvey: –

Did you and Omar ever come to an agreement as to the amount Omar should be paid per year by Katy for running her farm? As I told you when I was in Indiana, he should be paid from June 1947, when he took over.

All my best to you and Mildred.

Sincerely,

[signed:] Cole

His next letter to Harvey (not reproduced here) reaffirms the sense of Porter's need for money, as he asks how much he could expect to receive every month from his mother's trust.[5] Then in the following letter, Porter is more explicit as to the reasons for his financial anxiety. The tax* he owed as a result of the film *Night and Day* was considerable – $100,000 – and he only had about a third of that amount in hand to deal with it. The letter also highlights his mother's active role in keeping Porter afloat, to her own financial detriment. Porter seems to be acutely aware of this:

2 March 1948: Cole Porter to Harvey Cole[6]

Dear Harvey: –

I wrote to Katy, telling her that Omar would accept nothing for his services. I also wrote to Omar, telling him that although we would rather have it otherwise, as long as he insisted on accepting nothing, I could at least tell him how very grateful both Katy and I were.

Katy doesn't like this arrangement at all. She insists that he be paid. So, perhaps the following would be the only solution: Could you find out in some way what the usual amount would be for what Omar is doing for us? If so, then perhaps she could give him that amount as a Christmas present each year, which he cannot very well refuse. Will you please look into this matter?

I received your information regarding the money that Katy gave me in 1947 being considered as a gift and not as a loan. My tax man, Pinto, thought

---

* Porter's worries about tax continued throughout his adulthood; see various letters in Chapters 4 and 5 where he expresses concern on the topic.

it would save her money if it were considered a loan, in which case if it were not repaid, it would be an asset to her estate upon her death. But if you prefer it the other way, that is perfectly O.K. with me. The only thing that worries me, really, is about 1948, as she is continueing [sic] to help me until I recover.

You remember that, on top of the loan which you made for me, I shall have to pay the Government an extra $100,000 in taxes, when the Bank of America loan is paid, on the <u>Night and Day</u> film. So far, the payment of this loan has been put off until May of this year. Arthur Lyons, my agent on the Coast, hopes to continue to put off the payment of this loan until I have sufficient funds to pay the tax on it. So far, I have only $35,000 toward this amount. So you can see how much further help I shall need. And if Katy continues to give me this help, as she insists upon doing, it will make her gift tax a considerable sum from now on, unless the whole amount is treated as a loan.

Please give me your judgement [sic] on all this.

Sincerely,

[signed:] Cole

In reply to the last letter, Harvey Cole not only reaffirms Kate Porter's insistence that the money she sent Porter be regarded as a gift that need not be repaid, he also outlines a plan to reduce the amount of taxes Porter owed. The singer Al Jolson* had been the subject of an enormously successful biopic, *The Jolson Story*, in 1946. Cole reveals that Jolson was trying to avoid paying income tax on the film and suggests that Porter might do the same with *Night and Day* if Jolson were successful:

4 March 1948: Harvey Cole to Cole Porter[7]

Dear Cole:

I have your letter dated March 2, 1948. Regardless of what Mr. Pinto said, there is not the slightest question but that the amounts given by Katy to you in 1947 should be treated as a gift and a gift tax return filed. The gift tax will amount to $952.34. Of course, if he is considering only the taxes which she

---

* Al Jolson (1886–1950), a prolific actor and singer, perhaps best remembered for his appearance in the early talking film *The Jazz Singer* (1927).

will have to pay in her lifetime, he is probably right in that treating the transaction as a loan this amount would be saved. However, if it is treated as a loan and repaid to her or her estate after her death, the assets of her estate will be increased by $50,000.00, all of which would be subject to the estate tax at the highest rates which will be applicable to her estate. If it should be so treated, the increased federal estate taxes would amount to $17,500.00 without taking into consideration increased state inheritance taxes.

Moreover, she insists that it was a gift and she does not expect it to be repaid.

I have prepared a gift tax return for her which she is signing and mailing to the Collector, together with her check for the amount of the tax. I enclose herewith two copies of a donee's return, which please sign and mail to the Collector of Internal Revenue, Indianapolis, Indiana. This should be done prior to March 15. Other gifts which your mother may make to you during the year year 1948 will require the payment of a substantially greater gift tax than that which is imposed upon the 1947 gifts. This is true both because she has used her entire exemption of $30,000.00 for 1947 and also because the additional gifts will be taxed at a higher rate. This, however, cannot be avoided, and the tax will still be substantially below that which is applicable to the estate tax after her death. You understand that if these transactions are treated as loans, the amount of the loans must be considered as a part of her estate for the purpose of determining the estate tax.

I talked to M. S. Cassen, the tax man who looks after the J. C. Cole estate returns, today. He told me that he was informed that Al Jolson was taking the position that the proceeds of the moving picture about his life, I believe "The Al Jolson Story," constituted a capital gain, taxable only at the rate of 25% instead of ordinary income taxable at the income tax rates. His theory is that he has sold a capital asset which he can never dispose of again, namely, the storey [sic] of his life. It might pay for you to look into this and see whether or not he gets by with it, and whether you could use a similar plan on "Night and Day."

I will make some investigation and advise you as to the charge customarily made for looking after farms such as your mother's.

Yours very truly,
[unsigned]

Much as his financial situation was vexing, Porter could take comfort in a new project on the horizon. Although he did not know it at the time, *Kiss Me, Kate* would become the most successful and enduring musical of his career. An article in the *New York Times* broke the news: 'Last night John C. Wilson signed contracts under which he will stage and supervise a new musical, which Cole Porter and Bella Spewack are writing. As yet untitled, the production is based on an idea supplied by Lemuel Ayers* and Arnold Saint Subber,† who will serve as sponsors of the venture. Reticent about the details of the forthcoming show, which is slated for next fall, Miss Spewack conceded, however, that Mr. Porter's material – i.e. the music and lyrics – is excellent. Miss Spewack, of course, will provide the book.'[8] *Kiss Me, Kate* would mark a change of direction for Porter, largely because it was not written around the talents of a specific star, unlike (for example) the Ethel Merman shows.‡ Nevertheless, it also highlighted a familiar form: the backstage musical. The show depicts the on- and offstage exploits between a divorced couple, the actors Fred Graham and Lilli Vanessi, as they appear in a musical version of Shakespeare's *The Taming of the Shrew*. It was the first of a series of book musicals in which Porter's name would be far bigger than that of the performers, to be followed in the 1950s by *Out of This World* (1950), *Can-Can* (1953) and *Silk Stockings* (1955). As Porter remarked in the next letter to Sam Stark, the new project had great potential:

9 March 1948: Cole Porter to Sam Stark[9]

Dear Sammy: –

I am sending you, under separate cover, photographs taken by the great Michael Pearman, of my cottage and the main house – taken last month.

You can see from these how hard it has been surviving this terrible winter!!!

---

* Lemuel Ayers (1915–55), a prominent set designer of major Broadway (e.g. *Oklahoma!*, 1943) and Hollywood (*Meet Me in St Louis*, 1944) musicals. He also designed *Kiss Me, Kate*.

† Arnold Saint Subber (1918–94), producer of numerous Broadway productions. He was especially successful, later in his career, in producing seven of Neil Simon's plays.

‡ *Anything Goes*, *Red, Hot and Blue!*, *Du Barry Was a Lady*, *Panama Hattie* and *Something for the Boys*.

What does Klinsor's [sic] Magic Garden* mean?

It looks as if I should come West some time in April, to stay the summer and work on my new show. I have persuaded Bella Spewack to come out there too, so that we can finish the Opus in the balm of California. It looks like a very good show indeed.

We both send love to our Sammy,

[signed:] Cole.

P.S. – I am also sending you a menu, from the Pavillon,† of a little dinner that [Howard] Sturg[es] gave the other night; to show how meagre our rations are here in New York.

The *New York Times* revealed more information about *Kiss Me, Kate* within days of the announcement:

> Although nothing is signed, Jarmila Novotna‡ of the Metropolitan Opera and José Ferrer§ are being spoken of as the leads in that untitled Cole Porter-Bella Spewack musical. The grapevine reports that Miss Novotna (she's no stranger to the Broadway stage having appeared four years ago in "Helen Goes to Troy")¶ recently heard the music and is said to have expressed her whole-hearted approval over Mr. Porter's collection of sharps and flats ... Supposedly a secret, the plot is based on "The Taming of the Shrew" and stems from an idea of Lemuel Ayers and Arnold Saint Subber, who will produce it next season under John C. Wilson's supervision. It isn't a feat of the imagination to deduce that Miss Novotna would be the Katherine and Mr. Ferrer the Petruchio.[10]

---

* Presumably a reference to Richard Wagner's *Parsifal*.

† The high-class French restaurant at the Ritz Tower Hotel in New York that the Porters regularly frequented.

‡ Jarmila Novotna (1907–94), a Czech soprano who was a star at the Metropolitan Opera in New York in the 1940s and 1950s.

§ José Ferrer (1912–92), a prolific Puerto Rican actor, director and producer. He later won an Academy Award for *Cyrano de Bergerac* (1950).

¶ An English-language version of Jacques Offenbach's *La belle Hélène* ran at the Alvin Theatre on Broadway with Novotna in the title role, from 24 April to 15 July 1944.

As well as starting to work on *Kiss Me, Kate*, Porter continued to keep up to date with his friends. In the following two letters to Stark, he discusses Robert Bray, the possibility of renting a new house, the purchase of a new car (because his valet-chauffeur was angry with him for cancelling a trip to Europe), and a planned visit to his mother's house in Indiana. Mention is also made of Bella Spewack's intended visit to Los Angeles to work on the new show. Although she is credited as co-author of the book with her husband Sam, Bella seems to have been the main author:

11 March 1948: Cole Porter to Sam Stark[11]

Dear Sammy: –

A letter from Robert [Bray][12] arrived yesterday, telling me that his option at RKA* hadbeen [sic] taken up for another year, with a raise. If you see him, please tell him how delighted I am that he has persisted so hard in his work, and that his efforts have been rewarded.

Love,

[signed:] Cole

16 March 1948: Cole Porter to Sam Stark[13]

Dear Sam: –

I have your letters of March 0, March 1, March 11 and March 12. This is the first time I have ever received a letter postmarked "March 0", and I thank you very much.

In reply to your letter of March 0, I was delighted to get the story of the Bluie [sic, Robert] Raisin.

As for the epistle of March 1st, I am most embarrassed not to have known about Klingsor's Magic Garden.†

Now we go on to the letter of March 11: Dick Cromwell‡ wrote me and offered me his house, unfurnished, for $40,000, which of course I refused. I

---

* Perhaps a theatrical or film agency, as Bray was an actor.
† A reference back to Porter's letter of 9 March.
‡ Presumably the actor Richard Cromwell (1910–60), who appeared in major films such as *Jezebel* (1938) and *Young Mr. Lincoln* (1939).

hope Sam Shedinger[14] stays long enough in New York so that I can see him but, as usual, I leave for Williamstown on Friday the 19th and shan't be back until the evening of Monday, the 22nd.

If you are irritated by mislaying your glasses, take my advice and buy a pair for every spot where you usually sit. This will solve all your troubles.

In this letter you enclose a note from Robert [Bray]. As I told you, I am delighted that his option was taken up and I hope you have delivered him this message...

Finally, we come to the letter of March 12th, and this is the reply: I was shocked by the champagne that Allan [sic, Allen Walker] served with the dinner he gave. Very few bottles of 1928 champagne are good any more; and as for 1921, it is so old and flat that people with country places only give it to the pigs.

These are my plans: My apartment here is being sublet for at least six weeks from April 1st on, which means that I move to [Howard] Sturges' apartment, as Sturges sails next Tuesday for Paris. I believe I can settle everything here within the first two weeks of April. Then I shall go to Indiana to stay with my Ma, after which I shall fly to Los Angeles. We begin work on my show; Bella Spewack is coming out there also to work with me; and it looks as if I should remain there for at least four months.

During the summer, I want to look for a new house which I can rent, beginning either the summer of 1949 or of 1950. This depends on the outcome of the Haines battle.* I am broken-hearted that I couldn't buy the Haines house, but after conferring with infinite lawyers and tax experts, I hadto [sic] give the whole thing up.

I bought a new 1948 convertible Cadillac today, and Paul† will motor out in it. It isn't nearly as pretty as the 1947 model, but I had to get it to please Paul, as he was so unhappy that I gave up plans for our going to Europe for the summer.

That's about all my news, Mr. Stark. Lots of love from us,
Your devoted
[signed:] Cole.

---

* See above, p. 285.
† Note by Stark: 'Sylvain his chauffeur-valet'.

P.S. – Please write me many, many more letters. They are the only stars in my sky.

The main contracts for *Kiss Me, Kate* were signed on 29 March. Porter's agreement with producers Saint Subber and Lemuel Ayers required that he deliver the score by 18 October for a 15 December premiere. His royalty was 5% of the gross; for the sale of the motion picture rights, 30% would go to Porter, 30% to Bella Spewack and 40% to the management.[15] A rider of 17 June stipulated that the selection of the orchestra, choral conductor and dance editor must have the written approval of the composer; that the orchestra must be at least twenty-eight (except with permission); that the choice of scenic designer and costume designer would be only with approval of the author; that Lemuel Ayers is approved as scenic and costume director; and that John C. Wilson is to be engaged as manager 'to direct and stage the play' and 'to completely and solely supervise, both financially and artistically, the production and operation of the play'.[16] These contractual obligations demonstrate Porter's right to be involved with all aspects of his musicals, at least at this point in his career: along with Bella Spewack, he had creative oversight of the original production.*

Writing to Sam Stark on 30 March, Porter revealed that Linda had been ill (with the flu)† but that he still intended to fly to Los Angeles to work on *Kiss Me, Kate*:

30 March 1948: Cole Porter to Sam Stark[17]

Dear Thin Sam: –

I saw John Smithson last night, and he told me that you were as slender as a pine. I have still to see this. I put John in the hands of Harry Krebs, as I was leaving for Williamstown. Harry took him to several cocktail parties and he made a great success. He definitely belongs now to the Tauch set. In fact, he

---

* A further contract held at the Cole Porter Trust reveals an agreement between Bella Spewack and Porter to write the work, which is 'suggested by THE TAMING OF THE SHREW'. It is unclear why this further agreement (dated 2 April 1948) was necessary.

† McBrien, *Cole Porter*, 311, cites a letter from Linda Porter to Bernard Berenson detailing the nature of the illness: '[I] picked up a virus "Flu" germ & I spent three weeks in bed. I am up for the first time today – a bit shaky.'

has moved in and has a room in Ed Tauch's* apartment house. The reason I saw him was because I went to a dinner given in honour of Ollie Jennings, who has not died at all. He sails on Friday to scatter his great-aunt's ashes over Lyons, France.

I received such a nice letter from Robert.† He says that everything is going fine, that he is with the children all the time and with his mother and father. Does this mean that things are not going well with his wife and that he was not able, after all, to get his house back?

My present plans are to leave New York toward the end of April, staying a week with my mother on the farm, and then fly to the Coast. I may, however, be delayed on account of my show.

Linda has been seriously ill, but at last is recovering beautifully. We both send you lots of love,

[signed:] Cole

In the event, his own health caused a delay. Ongoing treatments to his right leg left him in enormous pain and his trip west was postponed until May:

13 April 1948: Cole Porter to Sam Stark[18]

Dear Sam: –

It looks as if I should hit the coast on May 6th or 7th, and I shouldn't be angry at being met at all. I shall let you know definitely as soon as I get my plane reservations...

Linda is very much better; and my right leg is slightly better, but it has been a horror for the last two weeks.

Love from Park Avenue & 60th Street.

Your old friend

[signed:] Cole

Further treatments to his right leg and further pain led to the trip being put back even further to the middle of May:

---

* An architect by profession, Ed Tauch was a friend and lover of Porter's from the mid-1930s. See McBrien, *Cole Porter*, 154–5.

† Probably Robert Bray.

28 April 1948: Cole Porter to Sam Stark[19]

Dear Sam: –

Thank you for your letter of April 23rd.

I have put off my departure on account of my leg, which has been bad. The result is that I intend to arrive now at Los Angeles on May 17th. I shall keep you posted as this date is entirely dependent upon my leg.

Love,

[signed] Cole

P. S. – The Vert'es* book, which will arrive shortly, is really a present from Linda – and a second hand [sic] present. A Parisian banker sent it to Linda when she was ill, and you will notice that it is autographed by Vert'es. If you don't like it, throw it in the ocean.[20]

By May, Porter and Spewack were making significant progress with *Kiss Me, Kate*. The *New York Times* speculated that Alfred Drake, who starred in the original production of Rodgers and Hammerstein's *Oklahoma!* on Broadway in 1943, was lined up to be the male lead: 'Mr. Drake . . . has been approached to appear in the musical on which Cole Porter and Bella Spewack are working for next season . . . That Mr. Drake has a contract until 1949 with "Joy to the World" and that his preference is for straight roles doesn't deter anyone on Broadway, where Cassandra and Pollyanna sit side by side.'[21]

In the next letter to Stark, Porter reveals that he had already completed most of the score for *Kiss Me, Kate* by early May, confirming that casting did not inspire the composition of this score. Although some of these songs were discarded before the show reached Broadway, it is an interesting insight into Porter's productivity that he managed to write sixteen songs within about two or so months. And although he jokingly writes to Stark that 'most of the music is so simple that it sounds as if it had been written by an idiot child', the quality and stylistic range of Porter's songs for *Kate* are unusual, proving that his health wasn't an insurmountable obstacle to his creativity, notwithstanding his comments in this letter:

---

* Possibly a reference to the French costume designer Marcel Vertès, who went on to win two Academy Awards (Best Costume Design and Best Art Direction) for *Moulin Rouge* (1952).

4 May 1948: Cole Porter to Sam Stark[22]

Dear Sam: –

Linda and I were fascinated by the clippings about the Baroness.* Thank you a lot. Also, thank you for enclosing Robert [Bray]'s note and the article about his beard.

Yesterday, I had a blood transfusion, and I feel like a boxer. But now that it is nearly over, I must admit that this leg business has been going on for nearly six weeks, and for the last three weeks, it has been complete agony, as an ulcer and an abscess, due to the bump that Peppy [Porter's dog] gave me when he ran the length of the hall and jumped on me in his charming enthusiasm, appeared close together and just over a large nerve center. This started all the nerves in my leg raising terrific hell, and the pain has been so great that drugs had practically no effect. Also, due to the bump, a part of my shin bone was exposed and the surface was cracked. The skin around this exposed bone is gradually re-covering it, and will, within a few weeks, cover it entirely. But I have learned my lesson and from now on, will always wear a guard on my right leg. Enough of this.

I believe I am now set for the trip to the Coast. I leave here on Friday, May 14th, and stay the night in Chicago. I have given up going to Indiana because the Doctor thinks it would be too much for me. Therefor [sic], I have asked my mother to come up to Chicago and be with me while I am there.

I leave Chicago Saturday, May 15th, at 3:50 P.M. Chicago time (Daylight Saving) via TWA Constellation, Flight No. 95, and arrive in Los Angeles same day, at 9:10 P.M., California time (Daylight Saving) – Los Angeles airport.

Do you think you could still meet me and come back to Brentwood for the night and perhaps even stay over Sunday with me?

The servants are being notified, so that Max will be at the Airport to take care of my luggage – so please don't arrive in a Bekins van.

My show is very exciting. I have already written sixteen songs and only have about five more to do. I believe you will like this score as most of the music is so simple that it sounds as if it had been written by an idiot child.

---

* Catherine d'Erlanger.

Linda is on the crest of the wave, and it is such a joy to see her bouncing around again.

Great love from us both,

[signed:] Cole

In the event, Porter arrived in Los Angeles on Friday 14 May for his trip, and was met by Stark.* On 20 May, MGM's *The Pirate* was released at the Radio City Music Hall.[23] Consistent with other reviewers, Thomas Pryor's round-up in the *New York Times* of the week's new films described it in mixed terms as 'a big, colorful show which moves haltingly at times but is rescued by the dazzling terpsichorean acrobatics provided by Gene Kelly. Judy Garland gives capable assistance, and the Cole Porter score is lively'.[24]

Over the summer, *Kiss Me, Kate* became the main focus of Porter's activities. A gossip column in the *New York Times* on 23 May noted that 'The usual reliable source says that besides Alfred Drake, Marion Bell[†] and Carol Bruce[‡] are contenders for roles in the Cole Porter-Bella Spewack musical, "Kiss Me, Kate."'[25] A few days later, a further *Times* column announced that 'a telephoning reporter caught Alfred Drake yesterday in the act of reading the script [to Lerner and Weill's *Love Life*]. Attach no significance to that, for Mr. Drake reads a lot of scripts. Another now under his consideration is the Cole Porter-Bella Spewack musical, "Kiss Me Kate."'[26]

Alongside the casting decisions, there was tension in the background regarding authorship of the book. Sam and Bella Spewack had long functioned as a team in their work for theatre and film, including the movies *My Favorite Wife* (1940) and *Week-end at the Waldorf* (1945). They had previously collaborated with Porter on *Leave it to Me!*, but Bella worked alone with Porter in the early stages of *Kiss Me, Kate*. The following telegram sees Porter trying to bring Sam into the project officially, apparently as a reflection of the unofficial guidance he was already giving:

---

* On 8 May 1948, Madeline P. Smith wrote to Stark: 'Mr Porter will now arrive in Los Angeles on Friday, May 14th, instead of Saturday, May 15th – at 9:10 P.M. Los Angeles time.' Stanford University, Cole Porter Collection, shelfmark FE209, Correspondence: 1948 (TLS on Waldorf stationery), 1–6.

† Marion Bell (1919–97) was an actress, best known for her appearance in the original production of Lerner and Loewe's *Brigadoon*. She was briefly married to the lyricist Alan Jay Lerner.

‡ Carol Bruce (1919–2007) appeared in numerous Broadway productions, including the 1946 revival of *Show Boat*.

16 June 1948: Cole Porter to Sam Spewack[27]

BELLA WRITES ME THAT YOU DON'T WANT TO TAKE ANY CREDIT FOR THE BOOK. I BEG YOU TO RECONSIDER THIS DUE TO ALL THE CONTRIBUTIONS YOU HAVE MADE. ALSO IT WILL MAKE OUR PUBLIC MUCH HAPPIER TO READ QUOTE BOOK BY SAM AND BELLA SPEWACK UNQUOTE WILL YOU DO THIS GREAT FAVOR FOR ME ALL MY BEST REGARDS DEAR SAM = COLE=

But it was many months before Sam became the official co-author of the book of *Kiss Me, Kate*. The following letter reveals the truth about the casting situation: contrary to the claims in the *New York Times*, there were no candidates for Fred/Petruchio and the main possibilities for Kate/Lilli were two relative unknowns, Ruth Warrick and Patricia Morison, as well as the operatic soprano Dorothy Kirsten. Porter's preference is clear from the message to Spewack, which also mentions the director John (Jack) C. Wilson:

16 June 1948: Cole Porter to Bella Spewack[28]

Bella, Bellissima!

If Jack Wilson has not read you my reply regarding book changes, please ask him to do so.

There are two girls here working like maniacs for the Kate part, 1) Ruth Warwick* [sic] & 2) Patricia Morison.† I don't believe Warwick [sic] can sing the part even if she studies all summer because singing is not her vocation. She is an amateur when she sings. <u>But</u> she is lovely & could undoubtably [sic] act the part beautifully. She is a young, not too young, Ruth Chatterton.‡

Pat Morison is, to me, a much more interesting possibility. Apart from her voice which is a high mezzo, she looks like Lynn Fontanne & Kate. As I wired Jack [Wilson], she is working with Constance Collier on the Kate part. I feel strongly that this is our girl. So much so that I believe we might over night, create a great new star.

---

* Ruth Warrick (1916–2005) was an American singer and actress who appeared in the film *Citizen Kane* (1941) and the TV show *All My Children* (1970–2005).

† Patricia Morison (1915–2018) was a prolific stage actress whose credits included *Kiss, Me Kate* on Broadway, in London and in two television productions.

‡ Ruth Chatterton (1892–1961) was an American film and stage actress, best known for appearing in the film *Dodsworth* (1936).

I can picture you putting your hat over your face & squirming in despair as I write you this but this Morison girl is the one. There is also a girl called Adele Robbins for the Lois-Bianca part who has the bounce which you require but she has very little experience. She is, however, worth seeing.

So I suggest that you fly out rather soon and examine these three girls. <u>And</u> with Jack.

As far as the Fred-Petruchio part goes, there isn't even an applicant.

In case Jack has not told you, I have written a sock song for the two gangsters.* I indicated that they could sing this song for their exit on page 2-6-29 of your book. But now, on further consideration, I think it might ruin the rest of the scene. So I suggest that they enter after the scene is finished, in front of the curtain & sing it just before we go into the final <u>Shrew</u> scene.

Also I have made a song out of the latter part of Kate's final speech beginning with "I am ashamed that women are so simple." (She can slide into this.) I have altered the beautiful words slightly but you will approve when you hear the song. This leads at once into a lively finale. You should write me always when there are book complications. In that way it will be easier for me to back you for I have great respect for your great talent and experience.

Dorothy Kirsten† came out here yesterday. I agree with all of you that she could never play the part. On top of this, the only two songs that interested her were 1) <u>Were Thine That Special Face</u> and 2) <u>I Am Ashamed</u>. She was right. The other numbers for the part are musical comedy in spite of the colaratura [sic] passages in the first act finale & the 2nd act <u>Shrew</u> finale which can be adjusted to the girl we pick.

My love to you, dearest Bella & to your Sam.

Your devoted

Cole

Aside from the comments on the casting ideas and the progress of songs such as 'Brush Up Your Shakespeare' and 'I Am Ashamed That Women Are So Simple', of note in this letter is Porter's encouragement that Spewack write to him with any 'book complications'. Porter was aware of a potential

---

* 'Brush Up Your Shakespeare'.
† Dorothy Kirsten (1910–92) was one of America's most popular operatic sopranos.

conflict with Wilson and seems keen in this letter to maintain a strong collaboration with his fellow writer.

In fact, that sentiment was to come into play immediately, as Porter sent Spewack a copy of the following letter he wrote to Wilson about proposed changes to the book:

16 June 1948: Copy (sent to Bella Spewack) of a letter from Cole Porter to John C. Wilson[29]

Dear Bella:

The following is a copy of the letter I sent to Jack Wilson regarding changes in the script:

"First, in regard to revisions of the first act. I have studied them very carefully and this is my decision. I think all sensible revisions that are made for economy's sake are excellent. As to cutting out Bella's scenes, where Kate is dressed as a boy, I think this is a good idea if you won't lose a lot of comedy by doing so and also if it won't mean that <u>Were Thine That Special Face</u> will be kicked around in different bad spots in the second act and finally cut out of the show, as most people think this is the best number in the show.

With regard to the second act, I can't, for the life of me, figure out how I can make a number out of the "This is the moon if I say it is the moon" scene. If you all insist that I attempt this I must have explicit instructions. How much of the scene do you want incorporated in the number? Do you want the number to be literally Shakespeare's words or do you want me to alter them for the sake of rhyme etc.? Personally, I much prefer Bella's first scene in the second act, where Petruchio appears before the curtain and tells the audience that Kate is not able to ride the mule to incorporating the original Shakespeare singing, and if you think it could be strong enough to go in next to closing I don't agree with you.

Also, I have already taken care of that next to closing spot. I had been looking for that spot for weeks, as I always have had one of those low comedy numbers in practically all my shows, just before the final scene. The number I have written should be sung by the two gunmen just before their final exit, on page 29 of Bella's original second act.

The number is titled <u>Brush up your Shakespeare</u>. It's [sic] music is reminiscent of East Side, West Side, i.e., the typical Bowery song of the 1900's, and I firmly believe it will tie up the show into a beautiful knot. The lyrics are a series of gags and I am almost sure that it will be a show-stopper and everyone that I have played it to is crazy about it.

No doubt Bella will kill herself when she hears that I have written a number for the gangsters, but it is the type of song that any two vaudeville mugs could put over."

Love,

Cole

He wrote again the following day, in the form of a telegram, assuring Spewack of his support for her work:

[17 June 1948]: Cole Porter to Bella Spewack[30]

DEAR BELLA. I WROTE YOU LAST NIGHT ASKING YOU TO LOOK AT LETTER WHICH I WROTE TO JACK WILSON REGARDING BOOK CHANGES. ON SECOND CONSIDERATION I AM MAILING YOU A COPY OF THAT LETTER TODAY SO YOU WONT [SIC] HAVE TO ASK JACK FOR IT. YOUR LETTER ARRIVED THIS MORNING. I SHALL LOOK UP MARACCI* AT ONCE. PAT MORISON IS STUDYING KATE PART WITH CONSTANCE COLLIER. I CANNOT TELL YOU HOW DELIGHTED I AM THAT YOU ARE COMING OUT HERE JULY FIRST[.] STICK TO YOUR GUNS ABOUT YOUR WONDERFUL BOOK AND I SHALL ALWAYS BACK YOU[.] GREAT LOVE = COLE

Porter refers in the telegram to the English stage and screen actress Constance Collier (1878–1955), who appeared in the films *Stage Door* (1937) and *Rope* (1948). Collier had become a noted voice coach in the early sound era of Hollywood, and Morison (Porter's first choice for the role of Lilli/Kate) went for lessons to prepare for the role. Porter reported to Bella Spewack in a telegram:

---

* Carmelita Maracci (1908–87) was a celebrated dancer and choreographer, known for her fusion of ballet and Spanish dance techniques. She worked for a range of companies, including American Ballet Theatre.

19 June 1948: Cole Porter to Bella Spewack[31]

CONSTANCE COLLIER THINKS YOUR SCRIPT IS ONE OF THE FINEST SHE HAS SEEN IN YEARS[.] SHE SAYS IT IS A MASTERFUL JOB[.] I AM QUOTING HER LITERALLY[.] SHOW THIS WIRE TO THE BOYS[.] LOVE = COLE

A few days later, Porter wired Spewack again:[32]

24 June 1948: Cole Porter to Bella Spewack[33]

I SUGGEST THAT YOU DELAY YOUR VISIT HERE[.] WRITING YOU DETAILS ON SATURDAY[.] LOVE = COLE

The reason may have been connected with an important backer's audition for the musical, which took place that weekend, according to the *New York Times*: 'The Cullmans (Howard and Marguerite),* whose interest in a new show invariably coincides with success for the theatrical venture, are backing their high opinion of "Kiss Me Kate," the forthcoming Cole Porter-Bella Spewack musical, to the extent of $15,000. The Broadway "angels" appraised the musical as [sic] its first audition held over the weekend. Rehearsals are scheduled to start on Sept. 15 under the directorial supervision of John C. Wilson. Lemuel Ayers, co-producer of the entertainment with Arnold Saint Subber, is providing the scenery and costumes. Robert Russell Bennett will do the orchestrations. A choreographer has still to be signed. The guess is that "Kate" will be arriving in New York in November.'[34]

Work on *Kiss Me, Kate* continued over the summer. Two curious reports in the *New York Times* in late July even suggested that Porter had moved on to thinking about his next project. On 17 July an article claimed that 'Cole Porter and Douglas Fairbanks Jr. have been working quietly for the last month on an

---

* Marguerite and Howard Cullman, who married in 1935, were well-known investors in Broadway shows. The hits they put money into include *Oklahoma!*, *Carousel*, *Brigadoon*, *South Pacific*, *Annie Get Your Gun* and *Fiddler on the Roof*. See Marguerite's obituary at the *New York Times* from 27 July 1999: https://www.nytimes.com/1999/07/27/theater/marguerite-w-cullman-94-an-investor-in-broadway-hits.html (accessed 9 June 2018).

idea for a musical with a modern setting which they hope to have in shape for the cameras sometime next year. The only details available now are that Fairbanks will play one of the starring roles, that the photography will be in Technicolor and that the production will be made independently by the Fairbanks Company.'[35] A week later, the *New York Times* revealed more details:

> The news that Douglas Fairbanks Jr. is planning to star in a musical most likely came as a surprise to constant moviegoers . . . The actor cleared that up the other day, however, by flatly stating that he did not consider himself either a singer or a dancer. At the moment all he and Cole Porter, who will write the score, have is "an amusing idea, with a certain amount of fantasy, which can be told nicely in terms of a musical" . . . They are keeping the plot secret until it is all worked out lest someone else walk off with it, but Mr. Fairbanks elaborated to this extent: "In my role the action will be done almost like a dance, or perhaps I might even say vice versa. The songs will develop from the story and what their exact number will be we don't know yet. But," he added, "there won't be any elaborate production numbers. This will be a musical done strictly in movie terms, and we believe we've really got something different." Plans are to start production after the first of the year under the banner of the Fairbanks company.[36]

However, the project never came into being and Porter, still in California,* focused on *Kiss Me, Kate* once more. By the middle of August, Harold Lang† had been hired to play Bill/Lucentio, but the show still lacked a choreographer.‡ The final choice, Hanya Holm,§ was approached by Saint Subber on

---

* The *New York Times* reported on 16 August that Porter 'isn't due back from the Coast until early next month' and that this meant the opening of *Kiss Me, Kate* would be delayed until 'early next year'. See Sam Zolotow, 'Lunts Alter Plan for Comedy's Bow', *New York Times*, 16 August 1948, 11.

† Harold Lang (1920–85) was a popular Broadway dancer in the 1940s, appearing in several musicals before *Kiss Me, Kate*. He later starred as Joey in the landmark 1952 revival of Rodgers and Hart's *Pal Joey*.

‡ 'Mr. Porter, now on the West Coast, is expected in New York early next month when production activities will start in earnest', *New York Times*, 21 August 1948, 9.

§ Hanya Holm (1893–1992) was one of the most prolific and respected choreographers of the twentieth century, both in the ballet and Broadway spheres. Her later Broadway credits included *My Fair Lady* (1956) and *Camelot* (1960).

30 August, and she appears to have accepted quickly, signing her contract on 30 September.[37]

In early September, Porter went on a long motor trip with Robert Bray from Los Angeles to North Dakota and Chicago. The next three letters to Stark reveal details of that trip, the planned production schedule for *Kiss Me, Kate*, and disagreements with Bill Haines over the rental of his house at 416 North Rockingham, where Porter lived in California from 1943 onwards:

8 September 1948: Cole Porter to Sam Stark[38]

Dear Sammie: –

First, let me tell you again what a blessing those two thermoses were on the trip. They saved our lives many times.

Second, I must thank you for the delightful bottles of wine that you put in the basket for us. They always came in most handy.

Third, my gratitude for the book-bag.

The whole trip was a howling success, and I was very sad when it suddenly finished in Chicago. Robert will tell you all about it when he returns. By the way, I gave him the book-bag with the key to it and thermos case to return to you.

These are the plans: We go into rehearsal on November 1st, and open in Boston during the first week in December. We play there for three weeks and possibly another week in Philadelphia; and then open in New York. So reserve your Christmas holidays.

Whatever happened to Bobby?*

Love,

[signed:] Cole

29 September 1948: Cole Porter to Sam Stark[39]

Dear Sammie: –

I settled the case with Haines† out of court, at the following figures: I have the house definitely until October of 1952, plus three yearly options after

---

* Presumably, Robert Raison.
† Bill Haines, the owner of 416 North Rockingham.

that date; but, during these three optional years, Haines has the right to sell the house, in which case I would have to leave within two months. I am also paying $1750.00 towards his lawyer's fees.

I am delighted that this matter is settled and feel very happy that I am sure of at least four years more in that pet house of mine.

The bad news about Kitty* breaking her hip, added to the serious illness† that you have had, is really too much, and I am so sorry for both you and Allen.

My show‡ goes into rehearsal on November 1st. We move to Boston on November 28th, open in Boston on December 2nd. We play there until Christmas night and then open in New York on December 30th. This is one day earlier than I predicted we would open when the first talks about the show began in March – so you owe me a pat on the back for being a good guesser.

Little Bobbie§ has left Heller's employment and has the choice of two jobs, beginning next week. I don't believe he knows how much these jobs will pay yet. I also don't believe that he likes New York very much, and I shouldn't be at all surprised if he returned to California, although that has not entered his head yet. He has had an awful time trying to find a room in which to live without spending every cent that he has made. He finally doubled up with a young man called Swope, but he is living in discomfort and has a rather sad expression on his face constantly. He goes with me to Williamstown on Friday for the week-end, and Harry [Krebs] joins us on Saturday.

Linda is in grand form but, alas, my mother is not. She hadn't written me for so long that I telephoned her today, and she has been ill in bed for the last week, with very exaggerated colitis. She said on the 'phone: "I am such a bother to other people that I really ought to shoot myself – but that would mean another scandal in the family."

When you feel well enough to write, do so. Robert [Bray] will probably call you soon. He tried to get the Laguna house last week but there was no answer.

Lots of love to you, dear Sammy, and to Allen. I do hope that from now on you will all have continued better news.

[signed:] Cole.

---

* A relative of Stark's partner Allen Walker.
† Marginal note by Sam Stark: 'asthma'.
‡ *Kiss Me, Kate*.
§ Annotation by Stark: 'Raison'.

29 September 1948: Cole Porter to Sam Stark[40]

Dear Sam,

After writing to you today the details of my settlement with Haines about the Rockingham house, Bill O'Connor* suddenly called up from the coast saying that Haines had changed his mind and would not settle with me on the terms about which I wrote you unless I would pay the fifteen per cent difference in rent from Oct. 1, 1946 until Oct. 1, 1948. Bill refused absolutely and said he would not settle under these new terms and that unless Haines would stick to his verbal agreement, he, Bill, would fight this case to the Supreme Court of the United States which would take at least a period of five years. Haines is thinking it over.

I simply wanted to keep you posted.

This letter has been typed by none other than little Bobby Raison.

Love,

[signed:] Cole

On 2 October, the *New York Times* reported that Lisa Kirk,[†] who had made her Broadway debut the previous year in Rodgers and Hammerstein's *Allegro* (in which she sang 'The Gentleman is a Dope' to acclaim), would play one of the lead roles in *Kiss Me, Kate*. Despite the fact that Holm had already signed to create the dances for the production, the article continued: 'Although rehearsals of the show are scheduled to get under way on Nov. 1, a choreographer is still lacking. The sponsors are hopeful, however, of settling that matter next week. The Messrs. Ayers and Subber also must find an actress for the title part. Thus far only Alfred Drake and Harold Lang, the young dancing star of last season's "Look, Ma, I'm Dancin'!", are certain for the company. Present plans call for a New York opening on Dec. 29.'[41] In fact, Holm had agreed to be the choreographer in September (as noted above) and a letter in her papers from 5 October shows that she wanted to engage Ray Harrison as her assistant; the *New York Times* was not always up to speed on what was going on behind the scenes.[42]

The following day, Porter wrote to Stark from New York:

---

* Porter's lawyer or other legal representative.

† Lisa Kirk (1925–90) was a celebrated actress who mainly played soubrette roles such as Bianca in *Kiss Me, Kate*.

6 October 1948: Cole Porter to Sam Stark[43]

Dear Sammie: –

Your letter, dated "Friday", arrived. What smart writing paper! Is it yours, or does it come from the Carmelita Hotel?

I am so glad to hear that you are feeling much better. As for your suggestion that you might go to Arizona, Linda had already talked to me last week, asking me to find out whether you would consider going to Arizona for a while with her during the winter. She doesn't want to go to Tucson; she wants to go to a Dude Ranch, and I think [Howard] Sturges knows of an excellent one. I imagine she would like to go for January and February, or perhaps for February and March. In the old days Sturges always went with her but he has become such an international butterfly that you can't pin him down any more to one spot. Also, he has discovered Palm Beach. Think this over before you give me an absolute negative reply.

I can't tell you about Heaven on Earth,* because it folded before I saw it. Edward, My Son,† however, is wonderful. I went to the opening; it was one of those great electric nights like the night of the opening of A Street Car [sic] Named Desire.‡ Tomorrow night I go to the opening of the Kurt Weill show, Love Life.§ There are excellent reports on this show from Boston, and it looks like a winner.

That is all my news for now, dear Sam. Please take excellent care of yourself, and write when you have time.

Love,

[signed:] Cole.

Among Holm's papers is an announcement of an audition for backers on 7 October, which provides numerous details of the costs and current state of

---

* *Heaven on Earth*, a musical comedy by Jay Gorney, with book and lyrics by Barry Trivers and directed by John Murray Anderson, opened at the New Century Theatre, New York, on 16 September 1948 and closed after only twelve performances, on 25 September.

† *Edward, My Son*, a play by Robert Morley and Noel Langley, directed by Peter Ashmore and produced by Gilbert Miller and Henry Sherek, ran for 260 performances at the Martin Beck Theatre, New York, between 30 September 1948 and 14 May 1949.

‡ Tennessee Williams's *A Streetcar Named Desire* had opened at the Ethel Barrymore Theatre, New York, on 3 December 1947.

§ Kurt Weill's vaudeville *Love Life*, with book and lyrics by Alan Jay Lerner, opened at the 46th Street Theatre, New York, on 7 October 1948.

the casting for the show, a list of songs in the score, and budget issues. Excerpts from the document[44] include:

> AUDITION – At the audition Mr Wilson will tell the story of KISS ME KATE, [sic] which is based on TAMING OF THE SHREW by William Shakespeare, and describe some of the dialogue. He will present Alfred Drake who will play the leading role and Lisa Kirk who plays the second female leading role. They will sing the songs in the score such as ANOTHER OPENING, ANOTHER SHOW, WUNDERBAR, IT WAS GREAT FUN THE FIRST TIME, WHY CAN'T YOU BEHAVE, SO IN LOVE WITH YOU AM I, WE OPEN IN VENICE, TOM, DICK AND HARRY, I'VE COME TO WIVE IT WEALTHILY IN PADUA, TOO DARN HOT, WHERE IS THE LIFE THAT LATE I LED, BUT I'M ALWAYS TRUE TO YOU (DARLIN' IN MY OWN FASHION) etc., etc. Mr Joseph Moon will accompany at the piano.
>
> [...]
>
> FINANCING: Cost of the production is budgeted at $180,000 and weekly profit, based on $40,000 weekly gross, is estimated at $9,400. This profit will first be used to repay subscribers who put up $180,000. Accordingly, on the estimates, subscribers should be paid out in approximately 20 weeks. Thereafter, this profit will be divided equally between subscribers and producers. Thus, on the estimates, for every week the show runs to a full house after 20 weeks, when the original subscriptions are repaid, approximately $5000 will be paid to subscribers in proportion to their subscriptions, or approximately 2.8% weekly return. [...]

PRODUCTION BUDGET		WEEKLY PROFIT ESTIMATE	
Scenery	$36,550	Weekly Gross	$40,000
Properties	$15,000		
Electrical Equip.	$5,600	Theater Rent	$12,000
Costumes	$35,500	Royalties	$4,000
Rehearsal Expense	$24,500	Salaries	$11,600
Sundries	$16,000	Advertising	$1,350
Orchestrations	$9,500	Sundries	$1,650
Deposits & Adv.	$20,000		$30,600
	$162,550	Weekly profit	$9,400

Although money still had to be raised, the production was well underway by the second week of October. Telegrams from Saint Subber in the Hanya Holm papers show that the first call for singers and dancers was 14 October and auditions for 'special singers and dancers – the ones I have a list for' were set for a day later.[45] On 16 October, the *New York Times* announced that Patricia Morison was about to sign her contract to play Lilli in the show.[46] With the word out that *Kiss Me, Kate* was soon to appear, various parties came forward to offer themselves or their friends to work on the production. The following letter from Porter to the American conductor Robert Shaw (1916–99) gives an example:

18 October 1948: Cole Porter to Robert Shaw[47]

Dear Bob: –

Thank you very much for the letter regarding Mr. Maurise [sic] Levine.* I am sorry, but I have already engaged Pem [sic] Davenport† to do the choral work for our new show.

I can't tell you how much I have enjoyed your broadcasts.

All my best,

[signed:] Cole Porter

Confidence in the new show was high. A report in the *New York Times* on 28 October revealed that Saint Subber and Ayers thought the production was so advanced that it was unnecessary to spend more than two and a half weeks on the road, so the New Haven tryout had been cancelled.[48] Porter wrote to Stark to encourage him to attend the opening in Philadelphia:

---

* Maurice Levine (1918–97) was a prolific conductor and musical director, for example of the original production of Weill's *Lost in the Stars* (1949). He was best known for curating the *Lyrics and Lyricists* series at the 92nd St Y in New York.

† Pembroke Davenport (1911–85) conducted Porter's *Seven Lively Arts*, *Kiss Me, Kate* and *Out of This World*.

10 November 1948: Cole Porter to Sam Stark[49]

Dear Sam: –

I haven't time to write to you now. Are you coming East to go with us to the opening of <u>Kiss Me Kate</u> December 30th? You must let me know at once.

Love,

[signed:] Cole.

22 November 1948: Cole Porter to Sam Stark[50]

Dear Sam: –

I received your very nice letter of Nov. 17th. Please forgive me if I can't answer you now, as I am too damned busy.

I think it is a wicked shame that you can't come to the opening. The house will seem empty without you.

Love,

[signed:] Cole

Optimism seemed justified when, on 23 November, the *New York Times* announced a change of venue and pre-opening sales: 'Contracts were signed yesterday for "Kiss Me, Kate," to make its Broadway debut at the [New] Century Theatre on Dec. 30. The Cole Porter-Bella Spewack musical, written around Shakespeare's "The Taming of the Shrew," already has amassed $150,000 in advance sales, thanks to about thirty-five theatre parties. For a while the Broadhurst had been mentioned as a possible show case for the attraction, but the producers decided on the Century because of its larger seating capacity.'[51] (The Broadhurst's capacity is roughly 1,150 seats versus the New Century's 1,700.) The show opened on 2 December at the Shubert Theatre in Philadelphia. Porter's telegram report to Stark was plain:

3 December 1948: Cole Porter to Sam Stark[52]

SMASH=

COLE=

Five days later, he wrote again to Stark to relay the news that Linda's health was once more in decline:

8 December 1948: Cole Porter to Sam Stark[53]

Dear Sam: –

I rolled on the floor at your clipping about the debutante and Beethoven's piano.

On top of my wonderful show news, I have terrible news about Linda. Night before last she got congestion of the lungs – nearly died during the night. Since then, she is being kept alive by oxygen. Se [sic] is very seriously ill.

Love,

[signed:] Cole

Two days later, the immediate panic over her health was over and Porter was able to make plans for Christmas. *Kiss Me, Kate* was set to open on Broadway on 30 December and he intended to gather many of his closest friends around him:

10 December 1948: Cole Porter to Sam Stark[54]

LINDA AND I WILL BE HERE AT THE WALDORF ON CHRISTMAS DAY AND WE HAVE OUR CHRISTMAS TREE PARTY ON CHRISTMAS NIGHT AT [HOWARD] STURGES APARTMENT[.] LINDA IS SUDDENLY OUT OF DANGER[.] LOVE FROM US BOTH= COLE.

13 December 1948: Cole Porter to Sam Stark[55]

Dear Sam: –

I have seats for you, Robert [Bray], Sturge [Howard Sturges] and myself for the night of Wednesday, Dec. 29th, for <u>Edward, My Son</u>. I hope you approve of this. If you don't, let me know and I will get seats for something else – but, to me, this is by far the best show of the season.

I received your letter of Dec. 9th with the details of your arrival and departure, for which I thank you.

I wrote a few days ago that Linda was much better, but she seems to have had a relapse, and yesterday was a terrible day. I went up to see her this morning and she is much better. She had a fairly good night and today, for the first time, talks in her normal voice. She said to me this morning, with that great calm of her's, [sic], "This is the first day that I think I will live."

Love,

[signed:] Cole

P.S. – Thanks a lot for the charming letter from Sam, the second.*

A week before Christmas, Porter wrote to Jean Howard about a mutual acquaintance and also updated her on Linda's health and the triumphant Philadelphia tryout of *Kiss Me, Kate*:

17 December 1948: Cole Porter to Jean Howard[56]

Dear Jeannie: –

Michael [Pearson] tells me that you have become a friend of Leslie Bradley and his wife. Probably Leslie doesn't want his beginnings known, but for several years he was my valet, and an excellent one. Then he went to the Riviera on vacation and came back from it looking like Adonis, and left me to go into pictures in England. It makes me very happy to know that he has done so well, as he is one of the nicest people I ever knew. Give him my best, and lots of love to you and Slim.†

[signed:] Cole

P.S. My new show opened in Philadelphia and is the biggest hit of my life. But all the fun has been spoiled as, immediately after the opening, Linda contracted pneumonia and is living at the Doctors Hospital in an oxygen tent. She is better, however, and will definitely recover.

Among Stark's papers is an invitation dated 22 December 1948 from Sophie and Van Schley (identities unknown) to Mr and Mrs Cole Porter to a party after the opening of *Kiss Me, Kate*, on which Stark noted: 'Sam Stark attended also'.[57] On opening night Alfred Drake, who was playing Fred/Petruchio, wrote a good luck message to Porter, though he noted it was probably not needed: 'It has been a great pleasure. It will be a great pleasure. Thank you

---

* Stark's annotation: Sam Stark Shebinger.

† Slim Aarons (1916–2006), a celebrated American photographer famous for photographing celebrities.

for writing such a wonderful score. Thank you for writing such wonderful songs for me. Thank you for your many kindnesses. I can think of no other production wherein I have been the recipient of so much consideration and thoughtfulness – so much of it from you ... There's no need to wish you luck.'[58] Drake's prediction came true the following day when the unanimously positive reviews declared the show a hit. Brooks Atkinson in the *New York Times* was especially full of praise for Porter's achievement: 'Cole Porter has written his best score in years, together with witty lyrics,' he declared. The review continued:

> Occasionally by some baffling miracle, everything seems to drop gracefully into its appointed place, in the composition of a song show, and that is the case here ...
>
> The Italian setting has practical advantage. It gives Mr. Porter an opportunity to poke beyond Tin Pan Alley into a romantic mood. Without losing his sense of humor, he has written a remarkable melodious score with an occasional suggestion of Puccini, who was a good composer, too. Mr. Porter has always enjoyed the luxury of rowdy tunes, and he has scribbled a few for the current festival – "Another Op'nin, Another Show," "We Open in Venice," "Too Darn Hot" and "Brush Up Your Shakespeare," which is fresh out of the honky-tonks. All his lyrics are literate, and as usual some of them would shock the editorial staff of The Police Gazette.
>
> But the interesting thing about the new score is the enthusiasm Mr. Porter has for romantic melodies indigenous to the soft climate of the Mediterranean. Although "Wunderbar" is probably a little north of the Mediterranean Sea, the warm breezes flow through it; and "So In Love Am I" has a very florid temperature, indeed.*

---

* Brooks Atkinson, 'At the Theatre', *New York Times*, 31 December 1948. https://archive.nytimes.com/www.nytimes.com/books/98/11/29/specials/porter-kate.html (accessed 9 June 2018).

CHAPTER SEVEN

FROM *KISS ME, KATE* TO *OUT OF THIS WORLD*, 1949–1950

Porter's popularity and fame were renewed in the New Year, following the opening of *Kiss Me, Kate*. Typical of the acclaim he received was a telegram from Irving Berlin: '... ELLIN* AND I SAW "KISS ME KATE" LAST NIGHT AND THOUGHT IT WAS SWELL[.] CONGRATULATIONS ON A WONDERFUL JOB AND A SMASH[.] LETS [sic] SEE YOU SOON SO I CAN TELL YOU IN PERSON WHAT I THINK OF THE MANY HIGHSPOTS[.] LOVE=IRVING.'[1] Porter's position in the public eye had never been stronger. On 16 January, the *New York Times* ran a profile headed: 'Cole Porter is "The Top" Again: After five years in which his tunes seemed less popular, he has come back with "Kiss Me, Kate".' The article contains a brief interview:

> "I don't know how my music gets that way," he said the other day. "I simply can't analyze it. I can analyze the music of others. The word for Dick Rodgers' melodies, I think, is holy. For Jerome Kern, sentimental. For Irving Berlin, simplicity. For my own, I don't know."
>
> His interest in the musical side of his work has grown. He summed up his current attitude in this way:
>
> "I enjoyed writing the songs of 'Kiss Me, Kate.' I think the show has more music in it than any I have ever done. I liked what Irving Berlin had done with 'Annie Get Your Gun.'† His having so much music in it made

---

* Berlin's wife, Mary Ellin Berlin (1903–88).

† Berlin's *Annie Get Your Gun* opened on 16 May 1946 and ran for 1,147 performances – by far Berlin's biggest commercial and critical success. Many of Berlin's other shows were revues (*Face the Music*, *As Thousands Cheer*), but *Annie* was a book musical, rich with plot-led numbers.

me feel like trying a similar thing. In the old days I would tinker with a tune to make it fit a lyric; I don't think I would now. I also liked writing for people with real voices like Alfred Drake and Patricia Morison. I want to do more shows like this one." [. . .]

Since he is soft-spoken and has a sense of proportion, Mr. Porter is not sore at the critics, but he thinks that most dramatic reviewers should not write about music. As evidence, he offers: "My good friend, George Jean Nathan,* knows it's 'The Star-Spangled Banner' only when he sees people standing up." When I asked Mr. Porter whether he wanted these views to appear in print, he replied with a deadpan blandness that did not conceal the light in his eyes. "Only if you mention Nathan by name." [. . .]

Know what happened to "Begin the Beguine" when it was part of the score of "Jubilee," produced in 1935? Nothing. It died. Some years later a swing recording by Artie Shaw became the rage. "The song got so popular," Mr. Porter remarks wryly, "that performers eventually got around to doing it the way I wrote it."[2]

Porter was also on the cover of *Time* magazine on 31 January 1949, further evidence of his cultural status at that moment. But as he revealed in the following letter to Bella Spewack, his success was tempered by personal problems:

12 January 1949: Cole Porter to Bella Spewack[3]

Dear Bella: –

Your letter of January 10th arrived. I am awfully sorry about that card being missing.

Why are you in the hospital? Saint Subber† assures me that you aren't ill. Is it a rest? Or are you ill?

Linda is still in the hospital but seems to be better. The terrible agony that she went through spoiled all the joy of Kiss Me, Kate.

Love,

[signed:] Cole

---

* George Jean Nathan (1882–1958) was a prominent drama critic and the inspiration for the character Addison De Witt in *All About Eve* (1950).
† The producer of *Kiss Me, Kate*.

FROM *KISS ME, KATE* TO *OUT OF THIS WORLD*, 1949–1950

A week later, he was able to report more positively to Sam Stark on Linda's health, as well as the recording of the original cast album of *Kiss Me, Kate*, which had only been lightly censored due to Porter's racy lyrics:

19 January 1949: Cole Porter to Sam Stark[4]

Dear Little Sam: –

I have neglected you lately for the Columbia Recording Company, which is making the album of twelve sides of the Kiss Me, Kate score. They will be twelve-inch records, and everything in the show except the First Act Finale* is being recorded with the stage lyrics.

Linda is definitely off for Tucson on Friday, February 28th, with [Howard] Sturges, her maid, her nurse, and Gracie.† And I expect to fly to my little home in Brentwood very shortly afterward.

That's all,

[signed:] Cole

One of Stark's passions was his collection of theatre memorabilia, which explains why so much of his correspondence with Porter has survived. The next two letters are Porter's response to Stark's impatient request for copies of the sheet music from *Kiss Me, Kate* for his collection and his sharp rebuttal of Stark's apparent claim that the sheet music for 'Too Darn Hot' did not match what was heard in the show:

20 January 1949: Cole Porter to Sam Stark[5]

Dear Sam:

Stop being so impatient about getting the numbers from Kiss Me, Kate. You will receive them as soon as they are published, and before the general public gets them. If you can hold your horses a bit, you will receive a total of fifteen numbers.

Call up Bobby Raison for all my news. It will save me so much time and there aren't enough hours in the day to attend to my work here.

That's all,

[signed:] Cole

---

* The finale of the first act contained the word 'bastard'.
† Gracie was Linda Porter's dog.

10 February 1949: Cole Porter to Sam Stark[6]

Dear Sam:

Under separate cover I am returning the copy you sent me of TOO DARN HOT. If you knew music you would realize there is no mistake in this copy.

Thank you very much for sending me the clippings. I died at the idea of a show being called "The Life of Cole Porter". I have forwarded these clippings to Linda.

Best from Tully* and me.

[signed:] Cole

Porter had little time to write to Stark because success had brought with it responsibilities, such as overseeing the cast album and publication of the sheet music mentioned in the letters above. But he had also moved on to write the score of his next show, according to *Time* magazine, which 'Subber and Ayers plan for next fall'; it would eventually become *Out of This World* (1950). Furthermore, the article notes that he was about to leave for Hollywood 'to help cast a second company of *Kiss Me, Kate*, which may turn out to be the biggest smash of his career'.[7] The following letter to Stark confirms his plans to travel:

27 January 1949: Cole Porter to Sam Stark[8]

Dear Sam: –

I arrive Tuesday night in Los Angeles. Robert† is meeting me.
Can you spend the week-end of Friday, Feb. 4th with me?
Please telephone me on Wednesday afternoon (Feb. 2nd).
Love,
[signed:] Cole

The Porters' ongoing concerns over Linda's health may have been behind the decision for her to draw up her will, which she signed on 24 January; she

---

* Margaret Egan, Porter's West Coast secretary.
† Probably Robert Raison.

FROM *KISS ME, KATE* TO *OUT OF THIS WORLD*, 1949–1950

essentially left everything to Cole.[9] Whether or not by coincidence, a day later (25 January) Porter removed his collection of twenty-one gold cigarette cases from The Fifth Avenue Bank Safe Deposit Vaults, Inc., at 530 Fifth Avenue. These cases were specially commissioned by Linda for the opening night of each of his musicals, as well as a couple that were Christmas presents.* The following letter from Cole to Linda highlights the tenderness between them at this time:

5 February 1949: Cole Porter to Linda Porter[10]

Dearest Linda,

I was very surprised, and so pleased to get your letter written on two postcards this morning. It also made me happy to read I should not worry about you, because until this note from you I did worry.

Please let me know, through [Howard] Sturge[s], when you want me to come over. I am keeping from Friday to Monday free so that I can always fly over when you feel well enough for me to do so.

The ranch sounds like everything charming and it is a joy to know that you are there and not in that terrible New York.

I am talking to Sturge[s] tonight. As a matter of fact, I think it's a good thing that you are *not* near the telephone.

All love,
Cole

P.S. I am sending you, under separate cover, a most beautiful present. My secretary, Mrs. Egan, gave it to me as she has never fallen out of love with Gracie.†

The composer also hinted at his concern for his wife in the following letter to their friend William Skipper, who had sent flowers to Linda:

---

* Cole Porter Trust. The earliest of the cases was from 8 December 1930 for the opening of *The New Yorkers*. Porter also removed a 'gold key ring with baubles attached'. Porter's collection of cigarette cases was auctioned by Parke-Bernet, New York, on 17 May 1967; see Sanka Knox, 'Cole Porter's Cigarette Cases Draw Eager Throng to Auction', *New York Times* 17 May 1967, 74.

† Linda's dog.

30 January 1949: Cole Porter to William Skipper[11]

Dear Skip: –

Your flowers for Linda arrived just when she was leaving for the train, so they have been decorating my room instead of her's. [sic] She asked me to write to you and thank you, as she is not well enough to thank you herself, and has left for Arizona.

It was very thoughtful of you to send these flowers and she deeply appreciated it.

Sincerely yours,

[signed:] Cole

Porter's periodically strained relationship with the press continued in late January, when he was quoted in an interview in the *New Yorker* as saying 'Porter is a Yale man, and the author of "Bingo" and "Bulldog," as all who witnessed a 1946 movie based (roughly) on his life know, but he regards most Yale graduates as colossal bores, exempting from the indictment only his brothers in Scroll and Key, a fashionable society.'[12] Porter wrote to correct the quotation:

2 February 1949: Cole Porter to the Editors, *The New Yorker*[13]

Brentwood, Calif.,
To the Editors, *The New Yorker*,
Sirs:

I would appreciate it very much if you would correct the statement attributed to me in your issue of January 29th. The article says, "He [meaning me] regards most Yale graduates as colossal bores."

What I said has been misconstrued, to a point of reversing my meaning. I was asked if I still keep in touch with Yale, or with Yale men, or something to that effect, and replied that when I was at Yale, I noticed that Yale men two or three years out of college became awful bores – meaning bores to the undergraduates. I intended this as an explanation of my not having gone back to New Haven often in the years since I graduated. I would not say that I have never met a Yale man who was a colossal bore, but the fact is I have

found many Yale men brilliant, and the great majority of my oldest and dearest friends are Yale graduates.
Yours very truly
Cole Porter

Meanwhile, business continued with *Kiss Me, Kate* thriving on Broadway. The next four letters provide a window into the everyday matters that a successful Broadway songwriter had to deal with. The first two concern an exchange with Patricia Morison, star of *Kiss Me, Kate*, about signed photographs; in the third, Porter graciously provides a further autographed photograph to a fan; and the fourth addresses a typical request from a friend, Jean Howard, for tickets to his hit show:

28 January 1949: Cole Porter to Patricia Morison[14]

Dearest Pat: –
In return for this horror, will you please send me a beautiful photograph of yourself?
My address is:
416 No. Rockingham Ave
West Los Angeles 24
California
I shall miss you greatly.
Love,
[signed:] Cole

19 February 1949: Cole Porter to Patricia Morison[15]

Wonderful Pat:
The photograph arrived. It is magnificent! I am having it framed quick.
I am very well. Linda is better but still suffering in Arizona.
Your writing paper is charming. What is your new address?
Love to you and Richard.
[signed:] Cole

10 February 1949: Cole Porter to Kenneth M. Browne, Bangor Maine[16]

Dear Mr. Browne:

I am sending you, under separate cover, the autographed photograph you asked for.

Thank you very much indeed for your charming letter. Letters such as yours make people such as me work harder.

Sincerely,

[signed:] Cole Porter

17 February 1949: Cole Porter to Jean Howard[17]

Dearest Jeannie:

Upon receipt of your wire I immediately telephoned to New York, to the producers' office, and got you two seats for next Friday, February 18th. I have wired you to that effect. Some day, before you die, let me know whether you ever received the seats.

Love,

[signed:] Cole

P.S. There is no hurry!

Goddard Lieberson (1911–77), who later became the President of Columbia Records, had produced the cast album of *Kiss Me, Kate* and would go on to produce the recordings of Porter's *Out of This World* and *Silk Stockings* too. Lieberson's cultural influence and social status was significant, so it is no surprise that he became friends with Porter. He wrote to the composer on 1 March to say that 'I am sure it's no simple coincidence that the moment you left the weather turned from spring to winter and I write to you from a promontory facing snow-laden buildings. That is perhaps an inept way of saying that Helen Traubel* is not yet singing, "WERE THINE THAT SPECIAL FACE." ... I suspect that someday she will sing some of your songs. These things happen slowly in the world of divas. However, that

---

* Helen Traubel (1899–1972) was an American opera singer who also appeared in Rodgers and Hammerstein's *Pipe Dream* (1955).

is not the only front (and it is an extended one) on which I am busy with the works of Cole Porter and I shall write to you whenever anything electrifying happens.' Porter responded:

5 March 1949: Cole Porter to Goddard Lieberson[18]

Dear Goddard:
 Thanks a lot for your letter of March 1st.
 I am very happy that you are still pulling for the works of Cole Porter and I hope you catch some big fish.
 All my best,
 [signed:] Cole

The same day, the *New York Times* reported that 'The seventy-five backers of "Kiss Me, Kate" have received the first payment on their $180,000 investment in the Cole Porter-Sam and Bella Spewack musical. The full investment is expected to be returned to the "angels" by the end of April.'[19]

Porter liked to keep abreast of the latest musicals. The next letter shows his collegiality: he wrote to congratulate Ray Bolger, who had starred in Porter's *Rosalie* (1937), on his performance in the newly released Warner Bros. movie *Look for the Silver Lining*:

19 March 1949: Cole Porter to Ray Bolger[20]

Dear Ray:
 I just saw you in <u>Silver Lining</u>. All my congratulations. You are magnificent!
 Sincerely yours,
 [signed:] Cole Porter

He was also sensitive in writing to his friend William Skipper, when the latter was turned down for the role of Bill in the touring production of *Kiss Me, Kate*:

2 April 1949: Cole Porter to William Skipper[21]

Dear Skip:

Your letter from Miami Beach reached me yesterday. I am very sorry the deal on the road company of Kiss Me, Kate did not work out for you, but the majority preferred Marc Platt.*

Linda is still recovering from pneumonia in Arizona and will be there for at least another month and I commute to see her every two weeks.

Don't be upset because you didn't get the "Kate" job. You have great talent and a delightful personality and somebody is bound to snap you up quick.

All my best,
[signed:] Cole

He also received the following business letter from Max Dreyfus† at the publisher Chappell. Dreyfus explains how they have been taking steps to get the songs from *Kiss Me, Kate* heard on the radio in an attempt to capitalize on the novelty of the score:

13 April 1949: Max Dreyfus to Cole Porter[22]

Dear Cole:

Thanks for your letter 8th April quoting paragraph from communication from Mr. St. Subber to you. This has to do with the exploitation of the "KISS ME KATE" music.

As you know we have been working hard, and what we think successfully, on the exploitation of "SO IN LOVE".

We are still on "WHY CAN'T YOU BEHAVE" and "ALWAYS TRUE TO YOU IN MY FASHION".

We are now preparing to work on "WUNDERBAR".

"TOO DARN HOT" has been banned by the major networks, therefore, under these circumstances, exploitation is almost impossible.

---

* Marcel Emile Gaston LePlat (1913–2014) was a dancer and actor, known for appearing as Daniel in MGM's *Seven Brides for Seven Brothers* (1954).

† Max Dreyfus (1874–1964) was president of Chappell, Porter's publisher.

FROM KISS ME, KATE TO OUT OF THIS WORLD, 1949–1950

While "WERE THINE THAT SPECIAL FACE" is a wonderful and very valuable asset to your show, we have found that this song does not lend itself to commercial exploitation.

We have tried "BIANCA" in certain spots without much favorable reaction, nevertheless, we are still on it.

It is very true that the "KISS ME KATE" and "SOUTH PACIFIC" songs are "flooding the air" and all the other writers and producers are complaining. Be assured, Cole, that we are giving all our efforts to the songs from "KISS ME KATE" and be further assured that I am on the job and in back of the boys every minute.

[Albert] Sirmay is coming along but it has been a hard pull for him.

We are well, hope you are the same and best love.

[handwritten:] as always,

Max

Buried in the *New York Times* on 22 March was a brief mention of Porter's new project, which would become *Out of This World*. Under the subheading 'Porter Plans Greece Trip', Louis Calta revealed: 'If his wife's health has sufficiently improved, Cole Porter will depart on April 15 for Greece where he would complete the score of the contemplated "Amphitryon 38" in the locale of the Jean Giraudoux play.'[23] As Calta hints, Porter was writing the score for an adaptation of S. N. Behrman's* English translation of Giraudoux's 1929 play *Amphitryon 38*. Behrman's play had been a success for Alfred Lunt and Lynn Fontanne[†] in 1938, providing a link with *Kiss Me, Kate*: Saint Subber, the latter's producer, had supposedly witnessed the Lunts' backstage squabbles during a production of *Taming of the Shrew*, thus inspiring the backstage plot of *Kiss Me, Kate*.[24] The *Amphitryon* musical would tell the exploits of Jupiter, who pursues a mortal American, Helen, much to the disdain of his wife, Juno, and with the help of his son, Mercury. Saint Subber and Ayers were to produce the show, following their success with *Kiss Me, Kate*, but it would take another twenty months before it opened on Broadway. The principal problem was the

---

* Samuel Nathaniel Behrman (1893–1973) was a celebrated writer and journalist. He was the screenwriter of Porter's *The Pirate* (1948), among many other important films and plays.

† Alfred Lunt (1892–1977) and Lynn Fontanne (1887–1983) were a beloved theatrical couple who appeared in numerous productions together.

book: on 3 April, the *New York Times* suggested Paul Osborn* might write the script, which was eventually written by Dwight Taylor.† That Porter had already apparently been working on the score indicates the difference of approach compared to his close collaboration with Spewack on *Kiss Me, Kate* (which won the first Tony Award for Best Musical on 24 April).[25]

The *New York Times* cynically reported on 8 May that 'Somewhat optimistically, Cole Porter and Dwight Taylor have reported from the coast that they expect to have the first draft of their new musical ready by Sept 1.'[26] Despite his work on the new musical, most of Porter's correspondence that survives from the first half of this year focuses on personal matters. The next two letters are trivial requests from Porter to Stark, still one of his closest friends, while the third is a rare surviving letter from Linda to Cole. Although brief, the message from wife to husband is a vivid example of their affection for and closeness to one another. Of particular interest is Linda's dismissive reaction to hearing Ezio Pinza and Mary Martin singing songs from Rodgers and Hammerstein's new show, *South Pacific*, on the radio. This musical would prove to be the main competition for *Kiss Me, Kate* throughout its Broadway run.

30 April 1949: Cole Porter to Sam Stark[27]

Dear Sam:

Will you please send to Ed Tauch,‡ from me, some of those wonderful dates which you brought up a short time ago from Palm Springs? Send the bill to me. Please put in a card saying Love from Cole.

His address is:

Room 305,

Neurological Institute of New York

Fort Washington Ave. & W. 168th St.,

New York 32, New York.

Love,

[signed:] Cole

---

* American writer Paul Osborn (1901–88) was a prolific playwright (*The Vinegar Tree*, *Morning's at Seven*) and screenwriter (*South Pacific*, *East of Eden*).

† Dwight Taylor (1903–86) wrote numerous plays, films and musicals, including Porter's *Gay Divorce* (1932).

‡ Porter's lover at the time. See McBrien, *Cole Porter*, 154–5.

FROM KISS ME, KATE TO OUT OF THIS WORLD, 1949–1950

7 May 1949: Cole Porter to Sam Stark[28]

Dear Sam:

Thank you so much for sending two more of those delightful postcards to me.

Thank you also for the note from the Hollywood Reporter, dated May 3rd, 1949, and for recommending the story in the New Yorker. Robert* read it last night and said it is delightful. I shall get to it shortly.

I found the article on Elsie† excellent.

The Yosemite trip fell through.

[signed:] Cole

[17 May 1949]: Linda Porter to Cole Porter[29]

Tues 17th

Darling: The [illegible] arrived in good condition. Ernest unpacked them and put them away in your cottage.

At nine o'clock last night I listened to the Telephone Hour with Pinza and Mary Martin.‡ My goodness! How can either music or lyrics be compared with yours? The critics are damn fools, but then I always thought they were. And who cares?

I am trying to get off the 27th or 28th – the dentist, as usual, holds me up. Jean§ is not well + must have a complete rest. Fortunately Miss Ellis can look after me.

How is Paul?¶ Dreadful after all the care he has taken, himself that this should happen. Two servants in our family with ulcers is too much. Two servants in one family with ulcers is too much.

All love, my darling

Linda

---

* Perhaps Robert Bray.
† Perhaps Elsie de Wolfe, Lady Mendl.
‡ The Bell Telephone Hour was broadcast on 16 May and focused on *South Pacific*.
§ Presumably Jean Howard, Linda's friend.
¶ Paul Sylvain, Porter's valet, who evidently had an ulcer.

Porter was also close, albeit in a contrasting sense, to Irving Berlin. They were contemporaries, and despite coming from different backgrounds (Berlin was a Jewish immigrant and never had a formal education of any kind) the pair held each other in particular regard. Not even Richard Rodgers could match them in terms of numbers of hit songs: they saw each other as peers. The next five letters are on the subject of *Miss Liberty*, Berlin's forthcoming musical. Porter had heard that Berlin had recorded some of the numbers for his private use and wrote to request a copy. He seems to have responded particularly well to the number 'Home Work' and also mentions playing the records for Mr and Mrs Fred Astaire:

27 May 1949: Cole Porter to Irving Berlin[30]

Dear Irving:

I am tired of people telling me about this wonderful album you have made, in which you sing the numbers from MISS LIBERTY. Considering the fact that I have always been your No. One Fan I am a little bit shocked that you didn't send me the first album. Will you please rectify this mistake and send me one quick, quick, to 416 North Rockingham Avenue, West Los Angeles 24.

I hear nothing but delightful reports about your new score.

Lots of love to you and Ellen [sic].*

[signed:] Cole

4 June 1949: Cole Porter to Irving Berlin[31]

Dear Irving:

The records arrived but so far I have only played one of them, which is HOME WORK. This I have played over and over again with great joy, as it is delightful and unadulterated Berlin.

I shall give all the other songs the same treatment and report to you at the finish.

---

* Berlin's wife was called Ellin.

Oh, how I wish I could be in New York for that opening. It will be something!

Thanks an awful lot, dear Irving, and love from

Your fan,

[signed:] Cole

11 June 1949: Cole Porter to Irving Berlin[32]

Dear Irving:

The Astaires* came to dinner last night and we had a great session with your recordings. The final report is that all of these songs are so wonderful that we can't pick our pets.

Thanks again for your great thoughtfulness in sending them to me.

Love,

[signed:] Cole

14 July 1949: Cole Porter to Irving Berlin[†]

LUCK AND LOVE
    COLE=

[?] July 1949: Cole Porter to Sam Stark[33]

PLEASE SEND ON THOSE MISS LIBERTY NOTICES TO FRED ASTAIRE LOVE FROM US ALL=
    =COLE=

By the end of June, *Kiss Me, Kate* had set in for a long run. There were rumours about interest from studios including MGM for the movie rights, countered by the claim that 'Porter and the Spewacks have been entertaining the idea of doing the film version themselves.'[34] But since it was selling on Broadway to capacity, there was no rush to produce a Hollywood version yet. As the *New York Times* reported on 23 June, the show had achieved its 200th

---

* Fred Astaire and his wife Phyllis.

† This was sent for the opening of *Miss Liberty*, which Porter could not attend. Irving Berlin Collection, Library of Congress.

performance the previous night, with more than $75,000 of profits already having been returned to investors. (By October, that figure hit $300,000 and because the production had settled in for a long run, the sets and costumes were 'completely refurbished'.)[35] On 20 July, Porter wrote in response to a letter from Patricia Morison, in which she apologized for comments she had been quoted as making in an interview. While the matter is trivial, Porter's response is of interest for its insights into his attitudes to the press:

20 July 1949: Cole Porter to Patricia Morison[36]

Dear Pat:

Your very sweet letter arrived. I was never upset about the interview which you were supposed to have given but I was upset by the fact that several people seemed to believe it. I have gone through life being misquoted so I am not at all surprised that you were. Don't worry, dearest Pat, as I shall always love you dearly and, as far as I go, you could do no wrong.

Lots of love,

[signed:] Cole

Over the summer, Linda's health suffered a further decline, as Porter reports in this letter to Sam Stark from August. He also mentions the casting of the upcoming *Out of This World*, which had not yet been given its final title:

16 August 1949: Cole Porter to Sam Stark[37]

Dear Sam:

I enclose The New Yorker article which you sent me. I read it with great interest. Also I enclose the letter from Majorie [sic] Gateson.* Please write to her and tell her that the part for which she would have been very good has disappeared from the script.

I haven't written you before because until very lately Linda was so ill that I did not want to spread the bad news. She is back from the hospital at last,

---

* Marjorie Gateson (1891–1977) was an American actress who had appeared in Porter's movie *You'll Never Get Rich* (1941).

and as I bought an oxygen unit for her to be next to her bed, there is no more danger of these sudden crises. She is very weak, can barely walk, and her voice trembles a great deal when she talks. It is pitiful. She has, however, great courage and a will to survive which will help her during the future. She doesn't realize how ill she is, thank God. She will never be much better.

Sturge* is here with all the gossip of the Continent and I think he has done her a lot of good.

The place is beautiful what with an excellent gardner [sic] and two very competent assistants. We have a wonderful French cook who use [sic] to work for Pat Boyer† and later for Annabella, and if Andre starts acting up when I come back to the coast I shall send for this great girl.

We lost Carol Channing‡ for the part of Juno in the new show§ and I am brokenhearted. I thought of a very good title for the show yesterday. Please write it down and see if you like it. It is -- <u>Sacred and Profane</u>.

Robert¶ can tell you more Linda news when he sees you as I talk to him twice a week and give him all the details. My arrival here from the coast was far from cheerful.

All my best to you and Allen.**

Your pal,

[signed:] Cole

The following letter to Porter's friend Roger Davis provides further details of Linda's health, as does the next one to Stark. There is a clear sense of Porter trying to carry on with his busy social and professional lives while being keenly aware of his wife's fragility:

---

* Howard Sturges.
† Perhaps the actress Pat Paterson (1910–78), wife of the actor Charles Boyer.
‡ The actress Carol Channing (1921–2019) was prominent at the time as the original star of the upcoming Broadway production of *Gentlemen Prefer Blondes* (1949).
§ *Out of This World.*
¶ Probably Robert Bray.
** Allen Walker, Stark's partner.

19–20 August 1949: Cole Porter to Roger Davis[38]

Roger –

Linda showed me your roller-skating* postcard tonight before dinner + she laughed so much that it did her more good than all the doctors.

[Howard] Sturges is here + he fills her with gossip from all the capitols [sic] of Europe, with laughs.

This is what she needs most, – to laugh.

She is far from well but she is in great form. And she is very beautiful for her hair is grey, the grey that Mona† had for a while + gave up for the brass.

We have had visitors. Hanna‡ passed through + out, several times. Wimsey appeared + disappeared, sober. He is more amusing, drunk.

Tell Sam [Stark], if you still speak to him, that I have met something here in Williamstown that defies all discription [sic].

Tell him also that I miss <u>you</u>, Mr. Davis.

Goodnight

Cole.

22 August 1949: Cole Porter to Sam Stark[39]

Dear Sam:

Thank you for your note regarding Robert§ and his dining with you. I enclose the names of three books which Linda says you must read if you have not already done so. I also enclose a clipping from the New York Times regarding a new book by Ward Morehouse¶ which I think might interest you.

---

* Stark has added 'ice-' above here.

† The socialite Mona Williams (1897–1983), who was married at the time to Harrison Williams, one of the richest men in America, and later married the grandson of German Chancellor Otto von Bismarck.

‡ Leonard Hanna, a wealthy classmate of Porter's from his Yale days.

§ Probably Robert Bray.

¶ *Matinee Tomorrow: Fifty Years of Our Theater* (1949). Ward Morehouse (1895–1966) was a theatre critic and playwright, known for writing the 'Broadway After Dark' column for the *New York Sun* for twenty-five years, moving to the *New York World-Telegram and Sun* in 1950.

Linda is slightly better but very weak. [Howard] Sturge[s] is here and he is a joy.

All my best.

[signed:] Cole

Although no new Porter musicals appeared in 1949, a new song (or at least a new lyric) was premiered. In the Katharine Hepburn-Spencer Tracy film *Adam's Rib*, the actor David Wayne* performs a song called 'Farewell, Amanda'. Porter had recycled the music from a song called 'So Long, Samoa', a trunk song from 1940, although he did not admit as much to his publisher, Max Dreyfus, at the time:

22 August 1949: Cole Porter to Max Dreyfus[40]

Dear Max:

The following is the dope on Farewell Amanda. The picture, Adam's Rib, had a sneak preview last Wednesday night at the Pacific Palisades. According to the response, this Metro picture looks like a terrific box office hit. It stars Katherine [sic] Hepburn and Spencer Tracy. In the picture, Dave Wayne sings Farewell Amanda first. In a later sequence a radio is turned on and one hears Frank Sinatra singing it.† The music of Farewell Amanda is used as background music throughout the entire picture. Everyone connected with this new film feels that Farewell Amanda looks like a palpable hit.

So my request to you now is to get Larry Spier‡ busy on the exploitation of the song. He should arrange broadcasts and recordings and quick because they expect to release the picture in six weeks. I always dread asking you to call for action from Larry Spier, but I feel very strongly in this case that he do

---

* David Wayne (1914–95) was a prolific American actor, known at that time for appearing as Og in the original Broadway production of *Finian's Rainbow* (1947).

† The Sinatra recording is brief in the film and the complete version has never been commercially released.

‡ Larry Spier, Snr. (?1901–56) had founded Memory Lane Music Group, which controlled numerous song copyrights, and was General Manager of Chappell Music.

much better than in the past what with all profits going to the Damon Runyon Cancer Fund.*

I hope you are feeling fine, dear Max. I shall call you when I come next to New York and force you to lunch with me. All my best.

Sincerely,

[unsigned]

On 4 September, Linda reported to Jean Howard that 'Cole arrives back at the Waldorf on the 7th – I shall go down to meet him and spend several days before returning to Buxton Hill.'[41] It seems the Porters were communicating separately with Howard at this point, because Cole wrote to her a day later, providing further details of his activities and of Linda's deteriorating health:

5 September 1949: Cole Porter to Jean Howard[42]

Jean –

I wrote to Bob Bray tonight + told him that you had asked <u>me</u> to tell <u>him</u> to phone <u>you</u>, any day, during the week, at noon. So please don't leave instructions with your <u>Personal Maid</u> to say, when he calls, "She says she's out!"

If you can find time, I beg you, see him, if only for a moment. He is so alone + lonely. And it is most important for him to be with a lady instead of a tramp. Do this for me.

The Linda news is far from good. Today, it was very humid here + to watch her struggle to breathe was terrifying.

[Howard] Sturges comes back next Tuesday to be here in my cottage. This will build her up more than any amount of oxygen.

I miss you, dear Jeannie. I always miss you + love you.

Your

Cole

A few days later, Porter's regular correspondence with Stark reiterates the situation with Linda's health – he was evidently trying to come to terms with

---

* The Damon Runyon Cancer Fund was established by Walter Winchell in 1946 in memory of his friend Runyon, who had died that year of throat cancer. Runyon's stories were the basis of the musical *Guys and Dolls* (1950).

her mortality – and also mentions 'Farewell, Amanda', along with a project he had turned down (a musical version of the 1939 movie *The Women*):*

9 September 1949: Cole Porter to Sam Stark[43]

Dear Sam:

There has been absolutely no letter from the manager of the Hotel La Quinta.[†] Will you please call him up and ask him what is the matter?

I enclose a professional copy of <u>Farewell Amanda</u>. It appears that it goes very well in the picture, Adam's Rib, and that the picture itself is a knockout. I believe it will be released in December.

[Howard] Sturges is back with us, consequently Linda is being constantly amused during the luncheon hour what with all his delightful stories about so many people. This is what she hungers for and I, alas, forget everybody's name. She is not improving and we have to face that.

All my best to you all.

[signed:] Cole

P.S.: I also enclose <u>The Women</u>. Max Gordon wants to make a musical of it and asked me to do the score. I have refused. Please read it and see if you don't agree with me.

C.P.

Porter's next letter to Jean Howard brings to life the everyday atmosphere of the Porter household and reinforces the importance of Howard in the Porters' social circle:

13 September 1949: Cole Porter to Jean Howard[44]

Dear Jeannie:

Your wonderful letter arrived and amused me so much that I gave it first to Essie[‡] to read and later to Linda. When I saw them at lunch time instead of

---

* *The Women* (MGM, 1939) was a highly successful comedy film directed by George Cukor.
† Porter was trying to make a booking for Linda.
‡ By 'Ess' and 'Essie', Porter probably means Sylvia Ashley.

being as enthusiastic as I was, they were furious and said with one voice, "but she never writes us letters like that!"

Robert [Bray] writes me that he is having lunch with you tomorrow and I am so glad. I can't tell you how much he wanted to be with nice people.

Ess came up, stayed the night, and for lunch the next day, and then went back to see poor Boy who, as you probably know, had an awful automobile accident.

Between you and me, Linda is not getting at all better.

I miss you a lot, dear Jeannie. Let me know when you return to town. I stay here with Linda until the end of October.

Your devoted,

[signed:] Cole

Four days later, Porter's itemized response to a letter from Stark contains various pieces of news, as well as interesting comments on F. Scott Fitzgerald, yet the comment on his wife ('But Linda is dying') reveals the emotional burden Porter was dealing with at the time. Further updates later in September mention her continuously, alongside humorous comments on everything from metal staples to the latest popular book:

17 September 1949: Cole Porter to Sam Stark[45]

Sat. night.

Sammie – I sent a dictated letter to you this afternoon. Then, this evening, your letter, dated Sept 14th arrived. I enclose this letter + answer the following numbered paragphs: [sic]

No. 1. I thank you again for tracking down the manager of the hotel at La Quinta.

No. 2. I couldn't write to Tito* for I feel, as you do, that he is dead.

3) I told Linda that you had young William Washbourne + she was delighted.

4) Write me this. I love long letters.

5) It makes me sad that Allen [Walker] also dislikes Bobby Raison. I know this is Bobby's fault.

---

* Perhaps Tito Reynaldo, a dancer in Porter's *Du Barry Was a Lady*.

1. Cole Porter, Yale yearbook photograph (1913). Porter enrolled at Yale in the autumn of 1909 and while there performed in numerous theatrical and singing groups, as well as composing songs for the Yale football team, the most famous of which is 'Bingo Eli Yale'.

2. Westleigh Farms, Cole Porter's childhood home in Indiana (2011). The house as it now survives was built c.1913; it was placed on the National Register of Historic Places in 2003.

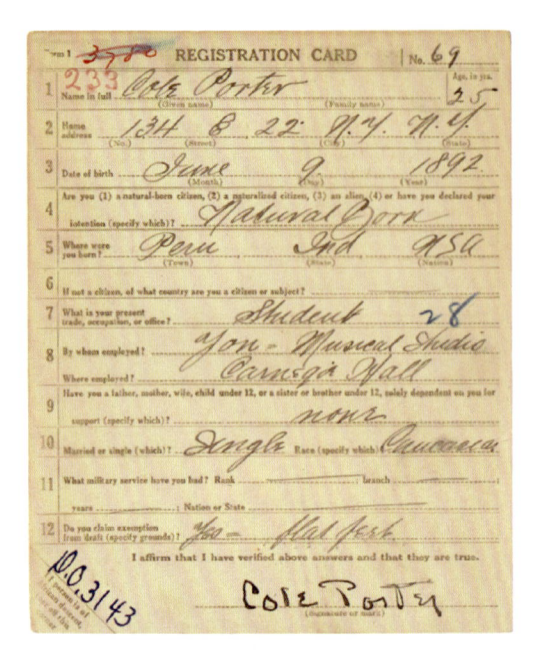

3. Cole Porter's World War I draft registration card (5 June 1917). In July he sailed to Europe on the paquebot 'Espagne', at first serving in the Duryea Relief Organization. He was discharged on 17 April 1919, at which time he was stationed with the 26th Light Infantry Battalion at Vincennes, France.

4. Linda Porter (1919). Porter first met the divorcee Linda Lee Thomas at a wedding in Paris in January 1918, while still on military duty; they married on 19 December 1919.

5. From left to right: Cole Porter, Linda Porter, Bernard Berenson and Howard Sturges in Venice (c.1923). During the 1920s, the Porters regularly spent their summers in Venice, renting a succession of palazzi on the Grand Canal. Howard Sturges was a life-long friend of Porter's from Yale; the art historian Bernard Berenson was a life-long friend of Linda Porter.

6. From left to right: Gerald Murphy, Ginny Carpenter, Cole Porter and Sara Murphy in Venice (1923). It was about the time this photograph was taken that Porter and the artist Gerald Murphy created the ballet *Within the Quota*. The Murphys were part of the Porters' social set not only in Venice but also in Paris.

7. From left to right: Serge Diaghilev, Boris Kochno, Bronislava Nijinska, Ernest Ansermet and Igor Stravinsky in Monte Carlo (1923). Porter probably met Diaghilev, already famous for his association with the composer Igor Stravinsky – in particular their production of the ballet *The Firebird* – as early as 1919.

8. Letter from Cole Porter to Boris Kochno (September 1925). Porter fell in love with Kochno in the autumn of 1925, at which time they had an affair while the Porters were travelling in Italy. While Porter was sincere in his affection, Kochno appears to have been opportunistic and to have carried on multiple affairs at the time.

9. Scene from the original stage production of *Fifty Million Frenchmen*, first given at the Lyric Theatre, New York on 27 November 1929. With a book by Herbert Fields, a frequent Porter collaborator, the show ran for a respectable 254 performances considering that it opened barely a month after the stock market crash that year.

10. Irene Bordoni, star of Porter's show *Paris* (1928). One of the great stars of early twentieth-century musical theatre, Bordoni took the role of Vivienne Rolland in Porter's show, introducing the song 'Let's Do It, Let's Fall in Love'. A sign of Porter's affection for her, she is mentioned in the lyrics to 'You're the Top' from *Anything Goes* (1934).

11. Sheet music cover for the song 'Love for Sale' from *The New Yorkers* (1930). At the time of its premiere, the *New York Herald Tribune* theatre critic wrote that 'When and if we ever get a censorship, I will give odds that it will frown upon such an honest thing' – which in fact turned out to be the case.

12. Production designer Jo Mielziner showing a set for *Jubilee* (1935). Mielziner was considered the premiere set designer on Broadway from the 1930s to the 1950s; his credits include the Gershwin musical *Of Thee I Sing* (1931) and Rodgers and Hammerstein's *Carousel* and *South Pacific* (1945 and 1949).

13. Cole Porter composing as he reclines on a couch in the Ritz Hotel during out-of-town tryouts for *Du Barry Was a Lady* (1939). Porter insisted on luxurious accommodations stocked with his favourite foods and medicines, more or less replicating his apartment at the Waldorf Towers in New York.

14. Cole and Linda Porter (c.1938). When they met in 1918, Porter wrote to his friend Monty Woolley, 'I lunch and dine with Linda Thomas every day, and between times, call her up on the telephone. She happens to be the most perfect woman in the world and I'm falling so in love with her that I'm attractively triste.'

15. Ethel Merman in the New York production of Cole Porter's *Panama Hattie* (1940). Possibly the greatest female star on Broadway from the 1930s to the 1950s, Merman had first appeared for Porter in *Anything Goes* (1934); she subsequently took leading roles in *Red, Hot and Blue!* (1936) and *Du Barry Was a Lady* (1939) before appearing in *Panama Hattie*.

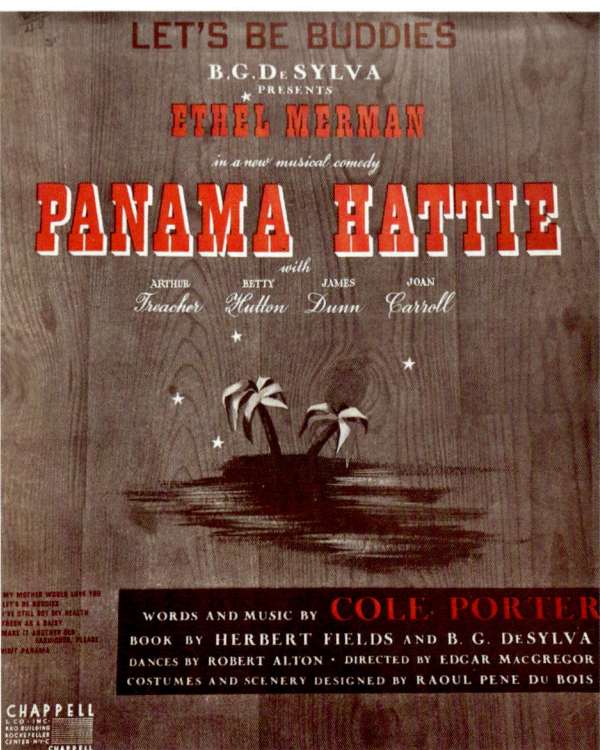

16. Sheet music cover for the song 'Let's Be Buddies' from *Panama Hattie* (1940), sung by Ethel Merman and Joan Carroll. The illustration evokes the title character's trip to Panama after reluctantly winning an essay contest with a piece entitled 'Why I Hate Panama'.

17. Draft of 'I Am Ashamed That Women Are So Simple' from *Kiss Me, Kate* (1948). It was originally intended that the character of Kate would speak much of Shakespeare's original text at the end of the show but Porter decided instead to adapt it as a song.

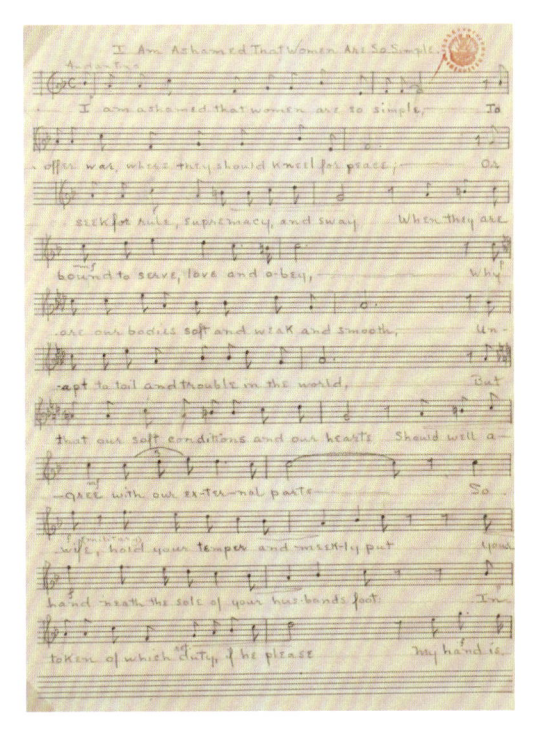

18. Monty Woolley, publicity photo (1949). Woolley was an intimate friend and collaborator of Porter's from their time together at Yale. He played himself in the 1946 Cole Porter biopic *Night and Day*.

19. Nelson Barclift rehearsing for Irving Berlin's *This is The Army* at Camp Upton (1943). Barclift, who became Porter's lover in the 1940s, appeared in Irving Berlin's *This is the Army* (1942) and later choreographed the Orson Welles–Cole Porter flop *Around the World* (1946).

20. Charlotte Greenwood in Cole Porter's *Out of This World* (1950). The actress Charlotte Greenwood got her start in vaudeville in the 1910s. Her part as Juno in *Out of This World* was one of her most successful roles. According to Grant Hayter-Menzies (*Charlotte Greenwood* [London, 2007]), she was uncomfortable in the role, feeling it was too risqué.

21. Cole Porter and Ed Sullivan discussing a two-part profile of Porter (aired on 24 February and 2 March 1952) on Sullivan's popular television show, *Toast of the Town*. Porter seems to have had little enthusiasm for the shows; in a letter of 27 January 1952 he described the idea as 'dull news'.

22 and 23. Cole Porter in advertisements for Bromo-Seltzer (c.1950) and Rheingold Beer (*Daily News*, New York, 18 May 1953). From the late 1910s on, and increasingly in the 1940s and 1950s, Porter was asked to appear in advertisements for a variety of products, including beer, cigarettes and Bromo-Seltzer, an antacid. He sometimes donated his earnings from advertisements to charity.

24. From left to right: Ann Miller, Cole Porter, producer Jack Cummings and Kathryn Grayson on the set of *Kiss Me Kate* (1953). Kathryn Grayson took the role of Lilli Vanessi/Kate and Ann Miller the role of Lois Lane/Bianca.

25. Cole Porter and Jean Howard (1954). A close friend of the Porters for many years, Jean Howard toured Europe with Cole Porter in 1955 and 1956 and later published a valuable book describing their travels (New York, 1991).

26. Scene from *Silk Stockings* (1955). Based on the Billy Wilder–Ernst Lubitsch screenplay *Ninotchka* and Porter's last stage musical, it premiered at the Imperial Theatre, New York, on 24 February 1955 and ran for 478 performances. It was produced by Cy Feuer and Ernest Martin, who two years earlier had produced Porter's *Can-Can*.

27. Cole Porter, music director Andre Previn and producer Jack Cummings working on the film *Kiss Me Kate* (1953, dropping the comma). Exceptionally, the film was shot in stereoscopic 3-D, which Porter disapproved of, writing to his lawyer John Wharton, 'To my regret, it is being done in wide screen, 3-D,' although, as he noted, 'they are also making a flat version which can be seen in theatres'.

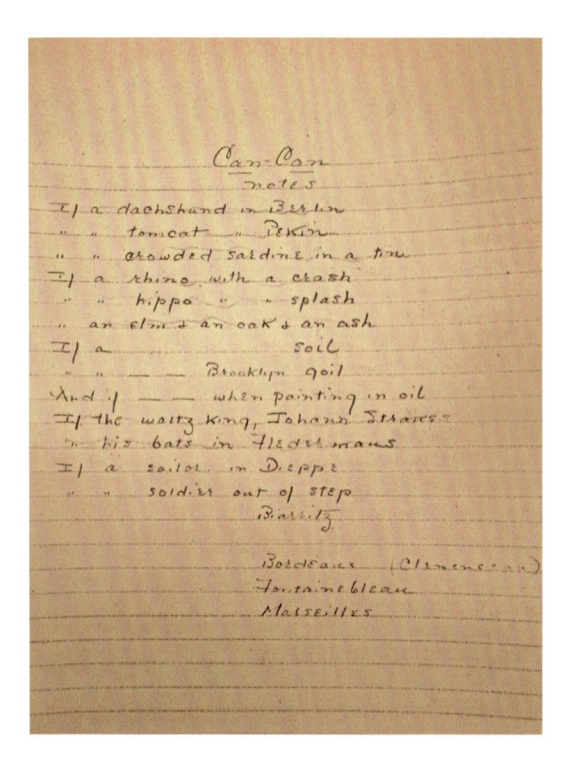

28. Cole Porter, autograph lyric sheet for the finale from *Can-Can* (1953). Numerous drafts by Porter survive for his lyrics. Frequently he conceived a series of internal and end rhymes, then revised them with additional text to fit the music. In this example, the lines 'If the waltz king, Johann Strauss / If his bats in Fledermaus' became 'If the waltz king Johann Strauss can, / It is so simple to do, / If his gals in Fledermaus can, / 'Twill be so easy for you'.

29. Sheet music cover for the song 'True Love' from the film *High Society* (1956). Like most sheet music from film musicals, the cover depicts not only the singers of any particular song – Bing Crosby and Grace Kelly for 'True Love' – but also other major stars of the film, in this case Frank Sinatra.

30. Louis Armstrong and Grace Kelly on the set of *High Society* (1956), Porter's second to last film musical (*Les Girls*, 1957 was his last). Porter was enthusiastic about Grace Kelly's rendition of 'True Love', her only song in the show (in fact a duet with Bing Crosby), writing to the composer Johnny Green, 'I can't tell you how surprised I am at the singing of Miss Grace Kelly.'

31. The last photograph of Cole Porter, taken at his home in the Waldorf Towers, New York (1964).

FROM *KISS ME, KATE* TO *OUT OF THIS WORLD*, 1949–1950

6) My Robert* has practically moved back to <u>416</u>, which makes me very happy. You can write him or phone him there + receive an answer shortly. He is entirely rid of that tramp.

7) Linda has improved lately, but not in her essential illness. I hate to think of you feeling miserable, all the time, at Laguna. Why don't you make sense + move back to a desert climate?

8) Thanks for the story on Scott Fitz G.† I knew him first when he was a most attractive cock-teaser. Later I knew him with Zelda. They were both exhibitionist drunkards + when I saw them anywhere in Paris, I always made a quick exit for I knew that if I stayed, this would implicate me in a possible police raid. They were all that is tawdry. And the dégringolade of Scott was horrible to watch as he had so much talent.

[Howard] Sturges is here in the cottage with me. The trees have begun to turn. The skies are spectacular. The cook is pure French with an ass so big that I can't understand how she keeps her balance. I'm working well, I believe. But Linda is dying.

All my love. Get hold of Robert [Bray]. He needs nice people like you + Allen [Walker]. He is so alone.

Your devoted – Cole.

18 September 1949: Cole Porter to Sam Stark[46]

Dear Sam:

Thank you very much for your wire concerning La Quinta reservations. I have not yet heard from Mr. Proves but I await his letter with interest.

Why haven't I heard from you for so long? Have you been ill?

Linda is slightly better. She has gained four pounds since she left the hospital and she has more red corpuscles, but she is far from well.

[Howard] Sturges has given up going abroad for which I thank God.

Lots of love from us all.

Your devoted,

[signed:] Cole

---

* Perhaps Robert Bray.

† F. Scott Fitzgerald (1896–1940) is best remembered for his novel *The Great Gatsby* (1925). He was married to the socialite Zelda Fitzgerald (1900–48), who was also a writer and artist.

28 September 1949: Cole Porter to Sam Stark[47]

Dear Sam:

Thanks a lot for your delightful letter of September 23. In the future, however, don't put those nasty clips in the corner of the paper. It took me years to persuade Robert [Bray] to give them up and now suddenly to be confronted with them once more is discouraging.

As I told you on the telephone Linda is all set for La Quinta, but we are awfully grateful to you for looking into the other places.

Your account of Tito [Reynaldo]'s visit made me roll on the floor.

As for your new drug, if this can be applied to Linda also it might be the secret of her improving a great deal. It is so horrible to think that there are so many cures just around the corner.

The Aspirin Age* is not an article in a magazine – it is one of the Best Sellers. It is so popular throughout the East that book shops have great difficulty in keeping it in stock. In case it might help you to trace down this obscure literary effort, it is edited by Isabel Leighton and published by a struggling new firm called Simon and Schuster.

Lots of love from Peppy and Blethe to Judy.†

[signed:] Cole

THIS IS WHAT I MEAN

[Porter draws a line from this up to the staple in the top left-hand corner, with arrows pointing to the staple and to the mention of 'nasty clips' in paragraph 1.]

5 October 1949: Cole Porter to Sam Stark[48]

Dear Sam:

Thank you a lot for the clipping about Robert.‡ He wrote me last week that she is filing suit for a divorce.

---

* A collection of twenty-two short stories about life in America between the wars, edited by Isabel Leighton.
† The names of their dogs.
‡ Perhaps Robert Bray.

The story about the Vedanta Monastery* is so fantastic that it kept me awak [sic] last night. How dreadful of all these talented young people to be taken in by that rot.

Lots of love from us both and from [Howard] Sturges.

Devotedly,

[signed:] Cole

5 October 1949: Cole Porter to Sam Stark[49]

Dear Sam: –

I started to get "The Little Sister"† for Linda but Sturge had already read it and was quite sure she wouldn't like it. She doesn't like books with four-letter words in them. I can't understand why she won't grow up.

Love,

[signed:] Cole

P.S. Thank you very much for sending me the news about Jefty's‡ death. I shall write to Bill O'Connor immediately.

Linda was also the subject of the following exchange between Porter and his favourite performer, Ethel Merman:

18 October 1949: Cole Porter to Ethel Merman[50]

Dear Ethel,

My Linda has been seriously ill for eight months. But if anything can make her well again, it is your broadcast every Sunday night at 9:30. I always listen too. You are wonderful and I sit beside her and watch her revel in your excellence. You probably know after a few years on stage that no one can equal you. This is a love letter from Linda and me to you.

My best to you all.

From your devoted

Cole

---

* Founded in 1930, the Vedanta Society of Southern California is a branch of the Ramakrishna Order.

† A novel by Raymond Chandler, published in September 1949 by Houghton Mifflin.

‡ Stark's note: 'L.A. attorney. Jefty was Bill O'Connor's son.'

Merman wrote to Linda in mid-October 'on the pretense of letting her know that I was on the air'. Porter thanked her:

22 October 1949: Cole Porter to Ethel Merman

Dearest Ethel:

Linda is being taken down by ambulance to New York on Monday, October 24th, and I can't tell you how she looks forward to listening to you sing again. You are so sweet to have notified her.

Lots of love,
Cole

In fact, Merman had written to Linda to make sure she would listen to the show on 24 October, and Linda responded with a telegram:

25 October 1949: Linda Porter to Ethel Merman

I WAS A' LISTENIN' AND IT THRILLED ME. LOVE TO YOU AND THE BABIES. LINDA

26 October 1949: Cole Porter to Ethel Merman

Dearest Ethel:

You have no idea what a great thing you did for Linda when you dedicated "You're the Top" to her on your last Monday's program. She had just come down by ambulance to New York and, for the first time, I felt that she had lost her morale due to exhaustion – but the moment your program was turned on and she heard those wonderful words you said to her it brought back all of her bravery.

You are a darling to have done this and I shall never forget it.

Lots of love,
Cole

Further letters and a telegram from Porter to Stark show the seriousness of Linda's condition. Stark had suggested certain medications that might help her but Porter explains here why the doctor had other plans for her. He

FROM KISS ME, KATE TO OUT OF THIS WORLD, 1949–1950

also mentions that the success of *Kiss Me, Kate* meant that it was easy to find backers for *Out of This World* and those who had financially supported *Kate* would be given priority:

10 October 1949: Cole Porter to Sam Stark[51]

Dear Sam:

Thank you so much for your letter concerning The Desert Clinic. I shall keep this with care. There is very little chance, however, that Linda will be able to go West as she is becoming daily worse. I have gone into it in detail with Linda's doctor in New York and the doctors for TWA.* The planes are pressurized between four thousand and eight thousand feet and even four thousand feet is too high for her. When I suggested chartering a plane and having it flown at a low altitude they refused this, maintaining that it would be too dangerous a trip. The train is absolutely out as one cannot use an oxygen tent. Dr. Jones, however, wants me to keep the reservation at La Quinta just on the chance that she might improve during November and December, but I doubt this very much.

I'm so happy that Roger† has deigned to speak to Fannie again.

Tell Allen [Walker] not to depend too much upon that cook book [sic].‡ For instance, there is one recipe recommended by Nalasha Wilson (nee Princess Paley).§ Everyone who stays with Nalasha says that she is the worst cook in history.

We are not interested in any new backers. We feel that the backers of KMK¶ should be given first chance and they are all fighting to get in on the new show. For instance, Howard Cullman who invested $15,000 in <u>Kate</u> wants to put $50,000 in the new show.

---

* Trans World Airlines.

† Perhaps Roger Davis, Porter's friend. The reference later in the letter is presumably to the same person.

‡ Presumably a cookbook consisting of favourite recipes of celebrities.

§ Natalia Pavlovna Paley (1905–81) was the wife of John C. Wilson (the director of *Kiss Me, Kate*). A Russian aristocrat, she was the daughter of Grand Duke Paul Alexandrovich of Russia and a cousin of Nicholas II. She was known as 'Natasha' but Porter's handwriting makes the given spelling of 'Nalasha' clear, which suggests it was a nickname.

¶ *Kiss Me, Kate*.

Thanks a lot for the wonderful photographs of Roger [Davis]. Thank you also for the picture of Judy* which you took with your new polaroid camera. If Judy were not sitting up it would be a much more remarkable photograph.

Love from us both.

[signed:] Cole

13 October 1949: Cole Porter to Sam Stark[52]

Dear Sam:

Dr. Jones got all the data on Ethylenedisulfanate† [sic] and finds that it would not do Linda any good, but he has high hopes that Pyribenzamine‡ may dry out her bronchial tract somewhat. She began using the latter last night so it is too soon to find out whether it will bear results or not.

She was glad to know that you had again taken up crossword puzzles.

I think that as long as we booked the La Quinta, and in all probability Linda will never be able to leave New York, that it is useless to make other reservations.

Thanks for the clipping about Frank Riddiger. I forwarded it to Robert. Thank you for the beautiful picture of Roger and Allen Vincent.

In fact, thanks, thanks, thanks, thanks.

Love,

[signed:] Cole

P.S. Please send your moccasins to me here. There is an excellent shop in Williamstown which will repair them beautifully unless they are so old that they are falling apart.

CP

Porter also sent a telegram to Stark when he heard that he was unwell with asthma:

---

* Stark's dog.

† This appears to have been a comparatively recent treatment for lung disease: see R. T. Fisk et al., 'The Experimental Use of Ethylene Disulfonate (Allergosil Brand) in the Prevention of Anaphylaxis in Guinea Pigs', *Journal of Allergy*, 15:1, 14–17.

‡ A fairly new drug at the time, used as an antihistamine. See https://www.nejm.org/doi/full/10.1056/NEJM194710022371401 for a 1947 article about its effects.

27 October 1949: Cole Porter to Sam Stark[53]

WE ARE ALL WORRIED ABOUT REPORTS REGARDING YOUR HEALTH[.] PLEASE WIRE OR WRITE ME WILLIAMSTOWN[.] I SHALL BE THERE UNTIL MONDAY 1100 AM[.] LOVE FROM LINDA[,] STURGES AND MYSELF=
COLE=

Porter's generosity is shown in the following series of letters to and from his cousin Harvey, who wrote to ask for help in obtaining tickets for himself and Porter's other cousin, Omar, for the Chicago run of *Kiss Me, Kate*:

27 October 1949: Harvey Cole to Cole Porter[54]

Dear Cole:

Omar and I and our respective spouses expect to be in Chicago on the evening of Monday, November 28, and would like very much to see your show. Your mother told Omar that if any of us were to be in Chicago you could arrange to get tickets for us. I understand that--praise be to God--the tickets are difficult to obtain. If you can see that we get some reasonably good seats, we will appreciate it and will promptly remit the cost. If by any chance they are not available on the 28th, our desire to see the show is such that we would stay over until the evening of the 29th.

All join in best regards and in the hope that Linda is improving.

Sincerely yours,

[unsigned]

5 November 1949: Harvey Cole to Cole Porter[55]

Dear Cole:

I received both your wire and your letter advising me that four tickets for Kiss Me, Kate will be waiting at the box office of the Shubert Theatre in Chicago on the evening of November 28. We all appreciate your kindness very much and are looking forward to seeing the show with a great deal of pleasure.

With best wishes for Linda's continued improvement,

Sincerely yours,

[unsigned]

30 November 1949: Harvey Cole to Cole Porter[56]

Dear Cole:

Mildred, Josephine, Omar, and I returned last evening from Chicago where we saw "Kiss Me, Kate" on Monday evening from the very best seats in the house. When I called for them, they told me that you had paid for them. I did not want or intend that you should do this and would be embarrassed at having you give us the seats after I had asked that you arrange to get them. I accordingly enclose herewith check for their approximate cost. We all enjoyed the show very much. It was the highlight of our bat.

All join me in best regards,
Sincerely yours,
[unsigned]

5 December 1949: Cole Porter to Harvey Cole[57]

Dear Harvey: –

I am very sorry but I cannot accept your check. It was a great joy to get those tickets for you, and I felt flattered that you all wanted to go to see my show.

All my best,
Sincerely,
[signed:] Cole

Although Porter did not spend vast amounts of time in Indiana, he seems to have kept regularly in touch with his family at home. The gesture described in these letters seems to be genuinely affectionate rather than a sign of Porter's indifference to money due to his wealth.

The next two letters to Stark are mainly of importance because they imply that *Out of This World* would be ready for its world premiere early in 1950. Both letters address casting issues and the first mentions the intention to move *Kiss Me, Kate* to another theatre so that the new show could take its place. There was also more optimistic news about Linda's health, suggesting Porter's earlier fears that she may die would not come true just yet:

FROM *KISS ME, KATE* TO *OUT OF THIS WORLD*, 1949–1950

1 November 1949: Cole Porter to Sam Stark[58]

Dear Sam:

Thank you for your letter of October 26. Bill Haines has already written me about your asthma trouble and we were all very worried, so it was a relief to get your letter.

In answer to the rumors which you have heard about me:

(1) I did not attend the San Francisco opening of <u>Kiss Me, Kate</u>.
(2) Fannie Brice* is not playing Alcmene.
(3) Polly Moran[†] is not playing Helen.
(4) David Wayne[‡] is in the show.
(5) The show does not open December 30. It goes into rehearsal on January 2.
(6) The show will open in New York around March 15.
(7) Alfred Drake does not go out of KMK and into Amphitryon.
(8) KMK does not go to the Winter Garden. We shall probably open the new show at the Century and move <u>Kate</u> somewhere else.

[Howard] Sturge[s] and I send our love to all of you.

[signed:] Cole

8 November 1949: Cole Porter to Sam Stark[59]

Dear Sam: –

The following letter is supposed to be a telegram:

You ask for news about Linda. A month ago I felt that she couldn't live for more than a half year more. Today, I believe she may live, and in comfort, for quite a few years. This is all due to my having had her apartment air-conditioned. What I resent is that <u>I</u> thought of this and not her Doctor. He should have thought of it years ago. But she likes him because he has one of the phoniest smiles I have ever seen on any face. What's more, he's a fashionable Doctor. You call him in desperation, and he has either gone to play golf or, in the evening is off to some big ball. But she likes him.

---

* See p. 200.
† Polly Moran (1883–1952) was, like Brice, a vaudevillian. She appeared in *Adam's Rib*.
‡ See p. 335 above.

Little Bobbie [Raison] sent me one of the funniest letters I have ever read, last week. I am so glad to hear that Bud sued the tavern keeper and won a thousand dollars. He will do so much good with it.

There is a great chance we may have Judy Holliday* in the new show. Don't miss <u>Adam's Rib</u>, if you can catch it. Maybe you know somebody at Metro who can show it to you in a projection room. It is one of the funniest pictures in years.

Good-bye, Sam. You have no idea how much we love you. Often during the day Linda and I sit together and simply repeat, over and over, "We love Sam"; and even as I sign my name, tears are dropping because you are so far away.

[signed:] Cole

It is obvious from these letters that Porter expected *Out of This World* to go into rehearsal soon. But the next letter, undated yet clearly written later in the month, revealed that it was nowhere near ready. The book writer, Dwight Taylor, was to be replaced:

[November] 1949: Cole Porter to Sam Stark[60]

Dear Sam:

This is the lowdown on my show situation. Keep it under your biggest hat.

Dwight Taylor handed in a book which I refused. It was so underwritten, lacked love interest and above all two great comedy scenes, that we decided to give the book to Betty Comden and Adolph Green† who wrote <u>On The Town</u>, <u>Billion Dollar Baby</u>,‡ <u>The Barkleys of Broadway</u>, and the book§ version

---

* Judy Holliday (1921–65) was an American actress, known for appearing to great acclaim in the stage and screen versions of both *Born Yesterday* (1946; 1950) and *Bells Are Ringing* (1956; 1960).

† Betty Comden (1917–2006) and Adolph Green (1914–2002) were prominent book writers, lyricists and performers. Their work included, as Porter points out, *On the Town* (1944), with music by Leonard Bernstein, and the recently opened MGM movie *The Barkleys of Broadway* (1949).

‡ *Billion Dollar Baby* (1945) was a modestly successful Broadway musical with music by Morton Gould.

§ Porter may mean 'film version'; clearly he intends to distinguish between the stage (1944) and screen (1949) versions of *On the Town*.

of On The Town. They are as bright as buttons and write very fast and I believe they will deliver the goods in time so that we can start rehearsals during the second week of January.

Dwight Taylor, however, is behaving like his famous little mother. He is being dramatically Irish about my not accepting his book. He is perfectly willing to sacrifice his royalties, but he wants large bills saying Book by Dwight Taylor and then in very small letters Libretto by Comden and Green. Naturally Comden and Green won't accept such billing nor would anybody else who was good. This has been pointed out to him constantly, but he goes on maintaining that he is outraged and must at least save face. We have suggested to him that the billing read Libretto by Comden and Green and then underneath, Based on Play by Dwight Taylor in the same type as the Comden-Green combination. So far he will not accept this. I am seeing him personally this week and I believe I can talk him off his silly high horse. I can easily point out to him that my score is much more popular* than the Kate score, and that a lot of the material could be used either for several pictures or for another show. I can also tell him that my income is far too big to be comfortable and that if the show falls through I shall save a lot of money. On the other hand he will lose a lot, as according to his contract he should make $1,500 a week from box office royalties. All he has to sacrifice are his subsidiary rights and only a part of these rights. I believe he needs money and will finally come through. In the meantime he is holding us up.

I like Betty Comden and Adolph Green very much. They are young Jews and in thinking over the past, I believe that Jews make the best musical comedy books. I shall keep you posted on this present upheaval which somehow doesn't upset me very much as the fun always is in writing and not in seeing what you have written produced.

A real miracle has happened to Linda due to her air conditioned apartment. She now has to go into her tent only between 2 a.m. and 7 a.m. During the day she can wander about and always breathe dry air. The result is that she is able to take a drive every day in her car and walk a bit in the park, and beginning next week she will start having guests for luncheon in her sitting room. This contact with the outside world will do her a lot of good.

---

* In other words, popular in style and therefore more commercial and portable to another context or project.

The only thing that worried me is that she is scheming very soon to go to Mainbocher's* to order a lot of new clothes. This will definitely kill her but it is a beautiful way to die I suppose. Old Mrs. Ogden Mills† died fitting a dress at Callot's in Paris, and Mrs. Hamilton Rice,‡ who was formerly married to George Widener, died fitting a hat at Reboux's. Perhaps Linda has become socially ambitious.

[Howard] Sturge[s] is here with me over this week-end and Robert§ arrives next Friday morning to stay a week with me. We shall have the weekend in Williamstown. Friday night he will go to Kiss Me, Kate, Monday night to Les Ballets de Paris, Tuesday night to Kit Cornell's opening (the play is called That Lady and I hear that it is a dud),¶ Wednesday night he goes to South Pacific, and Thursday night I am asking a few attractive people to Thanksgiving dinner at the Pavillon, after which he will fly West again. I think he needs this stimulus as he has had too many months of trying and trying to get work without success. I don't want him to give up until he is convinced that it is hopeless.

If Linda continues to recover she will, after all, be able to go to La Quinta. I still have the rooms.

My Ma arrives for her winter rest at the Waldorf with our cousin Lu Bearss on December 1. She will be in New York for at least three months as it will take her at least three months to see all the shows, concerts, operas, lectures, dressmakers and milliners which she plans to see. She is totally well again and I squirm when she picks up the New York telephone book and can read the numbers.

Goodbye Sammy. Lots of love to Allen [Walker] and yourself.

[signed:] Cole

---

* Mainbocher's was a fashion brand run by the American couturier Main Bocher (1890–1976).

† Ruth Livingston Mills (1855–1920) died in Paris.

‡ Eleanor Elkins Widener (1862–1937) was an heiress, known for establishing the Widener Library at Harvard University in memory of her son, Harry Elkins Widener, who died in the sinking of the Titanic.

§ Perhaps Robert Bray.

¶ Kate O'Brien's That Lady opened on 22 November 1949 at the Martin Beck Theatre, New York.

FROM KISS ME, KATE TO OUT OF THIS WORLD, 1949–1950

Porter continued to work hard on *Out of This World*, corresponding with the actor David Wayne about his songs. Wayne was to have played Mercury but was ultimately replaced by William Redfield:

1 November 1949: Cole Porter to David Wayne[61]

Dear David:

Please find enclosed the music and lyrics of Use Your Imagination, and corrected lyrics of They Couldn't Compare To You, and the lyrics of Midsummer Night.

Will you rehearse this number Use Your Imagination on a stage with someone and let me know what key is the best for you to sing it in. You must be sure of this because I have to make a transmission into another key for the soprano who will play the part of Helen and sing it after you.

In regard to Midsummer Night, this is sung to the tempo of a rather slow polonaise and at the finish of the vocal number the tempo will quicken and a real polonaise will take place on stage.

Dwight Taylor just handed me a completely revised First Act, and although it still lacks a great belly laugh comedy scene and a slight love scene between the bride and the bridegroom, I think this new script has great distinction and a lot of charm. It also makes your part much more attractive, and I believe you will be crazy about it.

All my best,
[signed:] Cole

Also involving Wayne (singing 'Farewell, Amanda'), the next two letters concern *Adam's Rib*, which was released on 18 November to acclaim. The note to Katharine Hepburn is amusing (it is accompanied by a drawing) – an interesting sign of Porter's new friendship with perhaps the greatest actress of Hollywood's golden age:

14 November 1949: Cole Porter to Sam Stark[62]

Dear Sam: –
Thanks a lot for the publicity sheet on "Adam's Rib".
Love,
[signed:] Cole

c.1949: Cole Porter to Katharine Hepburn[63]

Dear Kate –
   This is your tie (over)
   It should be
   Tied this way
   It looks
   Indecent
   Love
   Cole

A letter from Linda to Sam Stark in November confirmed that she was feeling much better with her new breathing apparatus.[64] The following two letters to Stark from Cole similarly confirm her improved well-being as the year came to a close – and that Comden and Green were announced as the new book writers on 19 December in the *New York Times** shows that work on *Out of This World* continued through December:†

2 December 1949: Cole Porter to Sam Stark[65]

Dear Sam: –
   Thank you very much for the flag directory. These flags interest me very much and I shall order them when I arrive in the West.
   Linda is so much better that she goes out nearly every day – and preferably to the dentist. She looks like a million bucks and she has become, once more, most amusing.
   My mother and my cousin arrived yesterday. My mother looks a bit older. She has a right to look a bit older, as she is 89 this year, instead of 88 last year . . .
   Love,
   [signed:] Cole

---

* Sam Zolotow, 'Keen Bidding Seen for Logan's Play', *New York Times*, 19 December 1949, 22.

† A column in the *New York Times* also mentioned that Mitzi Gerber – who later changed her name to Mitzi Gaynor – was heading to New York to appear in Porter's new musical, then called *Heaven and Earth*. Thomas F. Brady, 'Hartman Writing Bob Hope Comedy', *New York Times*, 7 December 1949, 42.

28 December 1949: Cole Porter to Sam Stark[66]

Dear Sammie: –

The package with all of those wonderful cocktail appetizers, etc. etc. arrived, and we both thank you from the bottom of our hearts. Linda, however, will not be able to enjoy them as I have stolen them immediately to take to the country.

I hope you had a grand Christmas.

Lots of love from us both,

[signed:] Cole

In the new year, Porter's correspondence with Stark was typically wide-ranging, including discussion of Christmas presents, movie scores and Linda's health:

7 January 1950: Cole Porter to Sam Stark[67]

Dear Li'l Sammie –

I brought up your Xmas present to Linda + me. Paul* + I undid it. Therefore I want to thank you for the mousse au foie d'oie truffe, the rolled fillets of anchovies, the sliced smoked salmon, the deviled tuna, the smoked shad, the paté of smoked Rainbow trout, the bloater paste, the Beluga caviar, the "Au Gourmet" frankfurters, the Spanish olives stuffed with fillets of anchovies, the boned goose + the charming serving tray on which it was placed. I can't wait to tackle especially the <u>boned goose</u>.

Harry Krebs is here with me + are temporarily snowbound. It's fun.

Love to Allen [Walker] + my best to you.

Cole.

11 January 1950: Cole Porter to Sam Stark[68]

Dear Sam: –

I am sending you two sides of the incidental music from <u>The Third Man</u>.†
This music has not been released yet in this country, but it has taken England

---

* Paul Sylvain, Porter's valet.

† The Third Man is a British noir film starring Orson Welles and Joseph Cotten, released in 1949. Anton Karas wrote and performed the score, all of which was played on the zither.

by storm on account of the use of the zither. You probably won't like this music much, but it will be nice to have when you hear all your friends trying to buy it, so that you can turn up your famous nose.

Love,

[signed:] Cole

17 January 1950: Cole Porter to Sam Stark[69]

Dear Sam: –

I received the Rustcraft* [sic] calendar for 1950. On the back of this there are columns concerning: (1) Flowers and birthstones by months; (2) important greeting card dates for 1950 and 1951; and (3) wedding anniversaries and their meanings. Why did you send this to me?

I received the Theatre Magazine books quite a long while ago. I am sorry not to have acknowledged this sooner.

Linda is so much better that she has been to Mainbocher's[†] once; and last week she felt so well that she lunched with her niece, Linda Lee, at her niece's apartment, in spite of the fact that her niece always has a very bad cook and Linda doesn't like her niece.

Love from us all to the Postman, and our best to you,

[signed:] Cole

[in bottom left corner:]

P.S. I know what to do with the useful calendar! And I will still know when they casually ask me, "What does one give for a Tenth Wedding Anniversary", or "Can I only give diamonds to girls born in April?" etc.

[signed:] M. Smith

Secretary

The postscript to the last letter is a reminder of the important role played by Madeline P. Smith, Porter's secretary, in his life: most of his letters from his last decade and a half appear to have been typed by her.

---

* The Rust Craft Greeting Card Company manufactured Christmas cards and calendars, as well as having a radio and television division known as Rust Card Broadcasting. It was founded in 1906 by Fred Winslow Rust and was sold off in 1980.

† The couturier's.

FROM *KISS ME, KATE* TO *OUT OF THIS WORLD*, 1949–1950

Linda's health certainly improved as 1950 wore on: in a letter of 7 February she revealed to Sam Stark that she intended to go and see *Kiss Me, Kate*, thus resuming the kinds of activities that her condition had made impossible in 1949.[70] Porter himself seems to have regained something of his former levity in the next four letters and one telegram to Stark, none of which reveals much about his activities but all of which depict his personality vividly:

9 February 1950: Cole Porter to Sam Stark[71]

Dear Sam: –

I am sending you, under separate cover, a museum piece. It is a record made in the interior of New Zealand by Lawrence C. Thaw* and, as the label indicates, it is sung by some very sweet sounding Maoris.

That's all.

[signed:] Cole

10 February 1950: Cole Porter to Sam Stark[72]

Dear Sam: –

How dare you send a chain letter to Linda and to me!

[signed:] Cole

11 February 1950: Cole Porter to Sam Stark[73]

Dear Sam –

I'm sending you a book named <u>Special Friendships</u>.† It deals with a nasty little boy in a Catholic boarding-school in La Belle France. It won a big prize. I read 135 pages because Saint Subber gave it to me, telling me how fine it was. I find it a bore.

Love to Allen [Walker],

Cole

---

* Possibly Lawrence Copley Thaw (1899–1965), described in an obituary as 'a Wall Street stockbroker, world traveler, and big-game hunter', *New York Times*, 28 June 1965, 29.

† Roger Peyrefitte's novel of 1943, which won the Prix Renaudot, a prestigious French literary award.

17 February 1950: Cole Porter to Sam Stark[74]

Dear Sam –
    I hit Brentwood, a week from tonight. I shall telephone you quick.
    Best,
    Cole.

21 February 1950: Cole Porter to Sam Stark[75]

DEAR SAM CAN YOU LUNCH WITH ME NEXT SUNDAY[,] USUAL TIME[?] PLEASE LEAVE ANSWER WITH MAX [annotation by Stark: "AYOT (Butler)"] [.] JAR OF JASMINE FLOATING SOAP JUST ARRIVED=
    COLE=

By April, there was still no completion in sight for *Out of This World*. The following letter makes it clear that it had now been postponed for another six months:

22 April 1950: Cole Porter to John Beal*[76]

Dear John:
    Thank you for your letter of April 18th, 1950.
    The book of the new show which we have in preparation is still in such a vague state that I can tell you nothing now as to whether there will be a good part for you or not, but we all remember you well and have you in mind. The present plan is to go into rehearsal on October 1st, 1950.
    Sincerely,
    [signed:] Cole

With the show on hold, Porter naturally explored other projects. The following letter to one of his lawyers is a response to a proposal that he should write the score of a musical version of *Reunion in Vienna*, a 1931 play by Robert E. Sherwood (1896–1955) (MGM had made a film version

---

* John Beal (1909–97) was an American actor, whose film career included *The Little Minister* (1934) opposite Katharine Hepburn.

starring John Barrymore in 1933). The letter also addresses the size of the orchestra in relation to a proposed move of theatre for *Kiss Me, Kate*, which was still running on Broadway:

6 May 1950: Cole Porter to Ben Schenkman (Paul, Weiss, Wharton & Garrison)[77]

Dear Ben:

Will you please communicate with Mr. James Russo* and tell him that I have read REUNION IN VIENNA very carefully and cannot see how a musical version of it could be made without destroying it? I am writing this same answer to Bob Sherwood† in England.

Will you kindly call up Dr. [Albert] Sirmay, at Chappells, with reference to the number of musicians who could be put in the pit in the Shubert Theatre? My information from him was that this pit would hold 28 musicians, but your information is quite different. I should like to have this settled before the matter comes up. At present the producers tell me that they intend to move to the Shubert Theatre in July.

After I wrote to you, suggesting that I communicate with Sam and Bella Spewack, in regard to doing a musical, I received a telephone call the following day from Saint Subber, saying that they had approached him and asked him to telephone me to find out if I would be interested in doing a musical with them sometime in the future. I replied that I would be if I felt that the subject matter would be a good spring board for me.

Sincerely,
COLE

On 9 June, Porter celebrated his fifty-ninth birthday, which Sam Stark had apparently marked with a provocative telegram:

---

* Probably James Russo (?1914–82), the stage manager of *Finian's Rainbow* (1947) and the producer of *The Last Dance* (1948), both on Broadway.

† Robert E. Sherwood (1896–1955), playwright of *Reunion in Vienna* as well as *Idiot's Delight* (1936), among many other successful plays.

THE LETTERS OF COLE PORTER

15 June 1950: Cole Porter to Sam Stark[78]

Dear Sam: –

The birthday wire arrived. You're not so damn young yourself.

[signed:] Cole

Perhaps a birthday celebration or other event brought Luella Gear* out to perform 'Mr. and Mrs. Fitch', which she had introduced in *Gay Divorce* in 1932. Porter wrote to thank her:

16 June 1950: Cole Porter to Luella Gear[79]

Dear Luella: –

I can't tell you how touched I was at your kindness in coming in and singing the melody of Mr. & Mrs. Fitch. Such kindness is mighty rare.

All my best to you,

Sincerely,

[signed:] Cole Porter

Over the next couple of months, Linda's health improved. Signs of her revived spirits can be seen in several letters of this period, for example the following telegram from Linda's dog to Sam Stark's dog:

19 June 1950: Gracie Porter to Miss Judy Stark[80]

THANKS FOR YOUR BIRTHDAY GREETINGS. YOU ARE BEAUTIFUL SO AM I LOVE. GRACE PORTER

A further letter from Linda to Stark on 11 July showed further signs that she was on the mend, and another from 1 August reiterated that her health was much better.† At the end of August, Porter wrote to Bernard Berenson,

---

* Luella Gear (1897–1980) was an American stage and screen actress whose appearances included a role in Porter's *Gay Divorce*.

† She also responded humorously to a gift from Stark of some Louis Philippe plates that were initialled 'L.P' (Linda's initials) for 'Louis Philippe': 'THE PLATES ARRIVED AND ARE PERFECTLY BEAUTIFUL[.] AM THRILLED AND SO HAPPY YOU DIDN'T SEND THEM TO LOUELLA[.] MUCH LOVE[.] MANY THANKS.' The reference to 'Louella' is to Louella Parsons, another L.P. Stanford University, Cole Porter Collection, shelfmark FE209, Correspondence: 1950 (TLS on Waldorf stationery), 1–9.

an old friend of the Porters, and again mentioned Linda's health, as well as the forthcoming rehearsals and tryouts of *Out of This World*:

31 August 1950: Cole Porter to Bernard Berenson[81]

Dear B.B.: –

Thank you very much indeed for your charming letter of August 20th. Alas, the rumor that I am coming to Italy is entirely untrue, as I have a new show going into rehearsal the beginning of October, and after the opening in New York at the end of November I shall probably have to go to Hollywood to seek more talent for a touring company.

I envy you a great deal your visit to Paris. I haven't been there since 1937 and I constantly pine for it.

I spend long week-ends with Linda in the country. Her improvement goes on and she is gaining a great deal of strength. I think that when she returns to New York at the end of October she will be able to lead a fairly normal life again after nearly two years of being so seriously ill.

We talked about you a lot and would love so to see you.

Lots of love from us both,

Your devoted

[signed:] Cole

When Porter needed to spend an extended period of time out of town with the tryouts of a new musical, preparations for his stay were elaborate. The following sequence of documents shows what seems to have been his typical requirements. First, he wrote in mid-September to the Barclay Hotel in Philadelphia to reserve several rooms:

[Undated but before 22 September 1950]: Cole Porter to Arthur T. Murray, manager of the Barclay Hotel, Philadelphia[82]

Dear Sir: –

Can you make the following reservations for me:
    AN APARTMENT FOR MYSELF WITH A
    SITTING ROOM;
    KITCHEN OR KITCHENETTE;
    2 BEDROOMS, EACH WITH BATH

This apartment should be in some spot of the hotel where I shan't bother your other guests, as I shall need a piano in my sitting-room [sic] during my whole stay in Philadelphia.

Also, as near by as possible, a ROOM AND A BATH FOR MY VALET, PAUL SYLVAIN.

I shall arrive on MONDAY, OCTOBER 30th, and will need the apartment, in all probability, until SATURDAY, NOVEMBER 25th.

Also, could I have a room and bath for my SECRETARY, MRS. MADELINE SMITH, from Tuesday Oct. 31 until Sunday, Nov. 5.

If I can make the above reservations will you also see to it that I have a very good BLACK BABY GRAND STEINWAY PIANO, in my sitting room for the duration of my stay. Two years ago, when I stopped at the Barclay, the piano was black it [sic] was also a Steinway – but it was not good; so I hope you can arrange that I get a really excellent one.

I look forward very much to being with you again.

Yours very truly,

COLE PORTER

The exchange continued with clarification of the needs of his valet:

26 September 1950: Cole Porter to Arthur T. Murray[83]

Dear Mr. Murray: –

Thank you for your letter of September 22nd, relative to room for my valet, PAUL SYLVAIN.

Rather than the arrangement of which you write, namely, servants quarters connected with my suite – my valet prefers to have the same arrangement as last time: a <u>separate regular guest bedroom</u> with bath, if possible on the same floor. I hope you may be able to make this arrangement.

Your sincerely,

COLE PORTER

On 3 October, Madeline P. Smith then wrote to the Barclay Hotel asking for an additional room and bath for Porter's 'Musical Assistant' Albert Sirmay, who was scheduled to arrive on 30 October and stay for approximately one week.[84] On 23 October, Porter informed the hotel of a list of additional requests:

[23 October 1950]: List of items to be sent to Porter at the Barclay Hotel, Philadelphia, on the morning of 30 October[85]

~~3 cans Sturgeon~~
3 Quarts Grade A Milk
~~2~~ 1 lbs. sweet Butter
COLD CUTS: ½ lb. each of: Roast Beef
                                Ham
              all   Liverwurst
              sliced   Salami
              very thin   Bologna
~~1 pint jar sour cream~~
1 box ginger (ground)
3 lbs Beef for Pot Roast
24 cans Pabst Blue Ribbon Beer
~~½ lb. white onions – medium~~
1 ~~2~~ doz. Fresh eggs
[handwritten:] ['1' changed to:] 2 White Bread Sliced*

Evidently, Porter was keen to make his hotel suite as much like home as possible.

Awaiting the opening of *Out of This World* at the end of October, Porter temporarily resumed normal life. In the following letter to Stark he outlines his recent news, including a typical jab at a journalist, Wolcott Gibbs (1902–58) of the *New Yorker*, who had written a well-received play:

5 October 1950: Cole Porter to Sam Stark[86]

Dear Sam: –

Thanks a lot for your letter of Sept. 28th. Linda's reaction to your story about Roger [Davis] taking shots which were meant only for a pregnant woman who had nausea was, "I am not at all sure that he is not a woman, and he might even be pregnant."

---

* Handwritten note at bottom: 'We will have all the items listed for Mr Cole Porter on the morning of Oct 30, 1950. Thanking you for your order we remain, / Yours very truly / M. A. Menna.'

I lunched yesterday with Orry Kelly,* who is here for a month, and he gave me all the lowdown on Hollywood, which was fun to hear.

Linda becomes better and better. I leave for the country again tomorrow to stay over the week-end.

[Howard] Sturges arrives on October 16th, and will come up immediately to Williamstown for a few days.

The best show I have seen so far is Black Chiffon.† The Wolcott Gibbs play, Season in the Sun,‡ received the most wonderful press possible. I suppose this is because all the critics felt that, one day, one of them might also write a play. But the play is a great disappointment and not worth the price.

Russell [sic] Crouse and Howard Lindsay put their new second act in Call Me Madam§ last Friday night, and it appears that it is no good. But, with an advance sale of a million dollars and an excellent first act, the show will have a fine run.

Love to the entire Coast.

[sic:] Cole

On 2 October the actress Martha Raye¶ appeared in a TV adaptation of *Anything Goes*, but it received a mixed report from the *New York Times*, as Porter informed his lawyer, Ben Schankman:

9 October 1950: Cole Porter to Ben Schankman[87]

Dear Ben: –

Thank you for your letter of October 6, 1950 with the Tribune clipping on the TV "Anything Goes".[88]

This is a very nice notice from John Crosby – but I ask you to look up the notice in the New York Times[89] about it and you will be less encouraged.

Sincerely, [unsigned]

---

* Orry Kelly (1897–1964) was an Australian-American costume designer, whose formidable credits include over 300 films and three Academy Awards.

† A British play by Lesley Storm, which had opened on 27 September.

‡ A play that had opened on Broadway on 28 September. Gibbs was known as a journalist, hence Porter's subsequent remarks.

§ Irving Berlin's new musical, which opened on Broadway on 12 October. Lindsay and Crouse had written the book, a function they also performed for Porter's *Anything Goes* and *Red, Hot and Blue!*

¶ Martha Raye (1916–94) was a popular comic actress of numerous films (including several musicals). Later, she had her own television show.

Considerably more impressive were the reviews of *Call Me Madam*, the latest show of Porter's favourite songwriter (Irving Berlin) and star (Ethel Merman). The show opened on 12 October and the following telegrams from Porter to Berlin show that he had been treated to the best seats in the house:

12 October 1950: Cole Porter to Irving Berlin[90]

DEAR IRVING. THANK YOU SO MUCH FOR MY WONDERFUL SEATS I SHALL BE THERE TO CHEER YOU TONIGHT. LOVE COLE

13 October 1950: Cole Porter to Irving Berlin[91]

DEAR IRVING. DUE TO YOUR KINDNESS JEAN FELDMAN AND I SAT IN THE FIRST ROW LAST NIGHT AND HAD A WONDERFUL TIME. YOUR SCORE IS SIMPLY DELIGHTFUL AND I CONGRATULATE YOU. ALL MY BEST COLE

Porter's own new show, *Out of This World*, was now well into rehearsal and he was cranking up his efforts to prepare for it. For example, on 16 October he wrote to the producers to ask for tickets for key music personnel:

16 October 1950: Cole Porter to Saint Subber and Lemuel Ayers[92]

Dear Saint and Lem: –

I enclose two requests from Stan Stanley, who is plugging the music from Out of This World, and also a letter from Dr. Sirmay.

I would appreciate it very much if you could grant these requests, especially as it is no longer a question of doing a favor for Chappell, but of doing one for me personally, as I am now a partner with Max Dreyfus in the publication of the present score.

Sincerely,

[unsigned]

The reference in this letter to being a partner is important: Porter had finally decided to become more closely involved in the business side of publishing his music, following in the footsteps of Berlin.

The Porters knew the show was in trouble: it had been through so many permutations and changes of book writer and personnel that it was unlikely to become an outright hit. Still, they tried to keep as upbeat as possible. On 19 October, Linda wrote to Jean Howard: 'Cole leaves Sunday for Boston [sic]* where the new show opens Friday of that week. Pray for a success.'[93] Six days later, Madeline P. Smith wrote to Sam Stark to confirm his room reservations for the opening of *Out of This World* in Boston and gave him the dates for the tryouts (which would prove inaccurate when the tryouts were extended). She commented that the show 'will, of course, be a BIG success'.[94] Contrary to Smith's optimism, Porter wrote to Berlin to report that the dress rehearsal had been disappointing:

30 October 1950: Cole Porter to Irving Berlin[95]

Dear Irving: –

I came back from a most discouraging run-through of <u>Out of This World</u> last night, to find a charming message from you saying that you like Dinah Shore's recording of <u>Nobody's Chasing Me</u>.† This was a nice finish to a discouraging day.

All my best,

[signed:] Cole

A few days later, he was able to wire Stark more positively:

4 November 1950: Cole Porter to Sam Stark[96]

SHOW OPENING TO MILD RECEPTION BUT I DON'T BELIEVE IT IS A FLOP. COLE.

Quickly, it became clear that the show had potential but drastic change would be needed. Therefore, the veteran George Abbott‡ was brought in to

---

* The Philadelphia tryout came before Boston.

† One of the songs from *Out of This World*.

‡ George Abbott (1887–1995), perhaps the most respected and prolific director of Broadway musicals of the twentieth century.

redirect the show, replacing Agnes de Mille,* and the replacement was announced in the *New York Times* on 17 November: 'Henceforth the directorial department will be supervised by George Abbott while F. Hugh Herbert[†] has been drafted to clarify the story line . . . A spokesman for Agnes de Mille said she didn't see eye to eye with the management, her casting suggestions were ignored and she wasn't given the proper cooperation. One of the conditions stipulated by Mr. Abbott was that he be permitted to make whatever cast changes deemed necessary . . . Until the Messrs. Abbott and Herbert entered the picture, no real rewriting had been accomplished, the show was speeded up by 15 minutes and some slight changes had been made in a couple of dances. When Miss de Mille's departure was announced to the company yesterday, the players were visibly affected at her departure, it was reported.'[97] As a result of the revisions, the tryouts were extended by two weeks:

10 November 1950: Cole Porter to Sam Stark[98]

OPENING OF SHOW WILL BE ON THURSDAY DECEMBER 14TH INSTEAD OF THURSDAY NOVEMBER 30TH SO PLEASE MAKE YOUR TRAIN OR PLANE RESERVATION FOR TWO WEEKS LATER COMING AND GOING. COLE

Further changes were communicated to Stark via Madeline P. Smith on 16 November, who also commented: 'The show is beautiful to look at – but they are having book and direction trouble, which they hope to iron out before getting to N.Y.'[99] Linda Porter also wrote to Stark, revealing Cole's relief that Abbott was making 'the necessary changes . . . The score is beautiful, the deco and costumes lovely, but the book let them down.'[100]

As the Broadway opening itself was finally settled for 21 December, Porter wrote again to Stark, for whom he had also arranged for tickets to six other shows, including Leonard Bernstein's *Peter Pan* and Frank Loesser's *Guys and Dolls*:

---

* Agnes de Mille (1905–93), known primarily for her enormous impact as a choreographer (such as on Rodgers and Hammerstein's *Oklahoma!* and *Carousel*) but also a prolific director.

† F. Hugh Herbert (1897–1958) was a veteran screenwriter and occasional playwright.

22 November 1950: Cole Porter to Sam Stark[101]

DEAR SAM[,] EXPECT YOU WALDORF SATURDAY MORNING DECEMBER SIXTEENTH[.] YOUR ROOM IS RESERVED UNTIL FRIDAY AFTERNOON DECEMBER TWENTY SECOND[.] YOU WILL HAVE A PAIR OF SEATS FOR SIX SHOWS BEGINNING SATURDAY MATINEE DECEMBER 16[.] IN ADDITION WE EXPECT YOU TO GO WITH US TO OUT OF THIS WORLD ON THURSDAY NIGHT DECEMBER TWENTY FIRST[.] SO HAPPY THAT YOU ARE COMING[.] LOVE FROM US BOTH. COLE

By 26 November, Porter had become philosophical about the fate of *Out of This World* ('be it a success or a flop'), as he revealed in his next letter to Stark. The reference to having organized tickets for *Call Me Madam* is of interest because although he was great friends with Berlin, he must have been jealous that the latter had another hit on his hands when *Out of This World* was so troubled:

26 November 1950: Cole Porter to Sam Stark[102]

Dear Sam: –

Mrs. Smith wrote to you about the reservations I made for you at the Waldorf. If this suits you please let me know.

Also, Linda and I expect you to go to the opening of the new show with us – be it a success or a flop.

I have applied for two seats for you for <u>Call Me Madam</u> for the night of November 29th. Are there other reservations for seats which you wish me to make?

We are so late in our rehearsals that I don't see how we can ever open in Philadelphia on time. We have a benefit on Thursday night, November 2nd, and another one on Friday night, November 3rd. We open to the public on Saturday night, November 4th.

I wish Robert* would come down and see you. Why don't you leave a message for him to ring you from 416? He is very depressed as his home life is a-shambles [sic]. I am awfully sorry for him.

---

* Perhaps Robert Bray.

Linda is back in New York and in great form. She lunches today at the Pavillon for the first time in two years.

Love from us both,

[signed:] Cole

To a good friend such as Jean Howard, Porter remained openly damning in his assessment of *Out of This World*, though perhaps Linda's revived health (mentioned in the letter to Stark above) prevented the show's fate from making him too depressed:

8 November 1950: Cole Porter to Jean Howard[103]

Dearest Jean: –

I received your two wild wires. I shall certainly keep two seats for you for the opening of <u>Out of This World</u>, which is on November 30th. But I warn you that, so far, the show is no good and that if you should, by any chance, appear in time to the seats you will be bored to death.

New York misses you.

Love to you both,

[signed:] Cole

He was a little more even (if hardly enthusiastic) in his assessment of the show to John Wharton, who had informed him of the death of the lead lawyer at the firm that represented him (Paul, Weiss, Wharton & Garrison):

25 November 1950: Cole Porter to John Wharton[104]

Dear John: –

Thank you very much for your letter of November 18, 1950. I send you my deep sympathy on the death of Louis Weiss. I can imagine what a great shock this has been to you.

The show hobbles along – not fast enough in its improvements, but at least George Abbott and Hugh Herbert are doing excellent work.

All my best,

[signed:] Cole

Not only was Porter concerned about the quality of the show, in Boston the censor demanded nine cuts to tone down the more suggestive elements of the book and lyrics, presenting a new problem to deal with.[105] Porter's concern continued in the next letter, written to Cloyd E. Small, a veteran teacher (1922–66) from the Worcester Academy, which had been the home of some of Porter's most formative years as a boy:

9 December 1950: Cole Porter to Cloyd Small, Worcester Academy[106]

Dear Mr. Small: –

Thank you a lot for your letter of December 5, 1950. It cheered me greatly, as I am still very worried about Out of this World.

Please give my regards to Mrs. Aldrich when you see her. I remember her well, and her kindness to me.

Sincerely yours,

[signed:] Cole Porter

As the first night on Broadway approached, tickets were at a premium. After all, this was the first Porter musical to open since his greatest hit, *Kiss Me, Kate*, and the public's anticipation was high. The following letter to Jack Warner, producer of *Night and Day*, hints at the pressure on Porter to provide tickets for his friends:

11 December 1950: Cole Porter to Jack Warner[107]

Dear Jack: –

Thank you for your letter of December 8th. I am still hoping that I can rescue two of the tickets which I have already given away for opening night of Out of This World for you and Ann. If I can rescue them, I prefer to hold them here until you let me know definitely whether you and Ann can use them, as I have a long waiting list of old friends.

Hoping to see you,

and with love to you both,

Sincerely

[unsigned]

Porter returned to New York from the Boston tryout of the musical on 16 December on the 1:10 plane and joined Stark and other friends at the Colony for coffee, which marked the beginning of a few days of socializing before the big night.[108]

Out of This World opened on Broadway on 21 December 1950. As always, Porter invited a formidable number of his friends, including the former King Edward VIII and Mrs Simpson, to attend:

21 December 1950: List of Cole Porter's guests for the opening night[109]

Duke & Duchess of Windsor	Mrs. Wm. Wallace
Mrs. Wm. Randolph Hearst	Mr. Andre Kostelanetz
Mr. & Mrs. Gilbert Miller	Miss Lily Pons
Mr. & Mrs. John C. Wilson	Mr. Leonard Hanna
Mrs. Kate C. Porter	Mr. Main Bocher
Mrs. Hiram Bearss	Miss Edith Fellowes Gordon
Mr. & Mrs. Lytle Hull	The Duke di Verdura
Miss Elsa Maxwell	Mr. John Pinto
Mr. Howard Sturges	Countess di Zoppola
Mr. Samuel Stark	Mr. & Mrs. Henry Colgate
Mr. Robert Bray	Mr. Harry Krebs
Miss Merle Oberon	Mr. Edward Tauch
Mrs. Jean Howard	Mrs. Wm. von Rath
Mr. Charles Feldman	Mr. & Mrs. Valentin Parera
Mr. John Royal	Mr. Jules Glaenzer

As expected, the reviews were none too enthusiastic. Brooks Atkinson's for the *New York Times* began with the condemnatory statement 'Although it is difficult to make sex a tiresome subject, "Out of This World" has very nearly succeeded.' Yet there was some acknowledgement of the quality of Porter's work, much of which had been done before the book was written: 'Some of Mr. Porter's songs are among the finest he has written, and he has the singers who can do justice to them.'[110]

CHAPTER EIGHT

FROM LIMBO TO THE WRITING OF *CAN-CAN*, 1951–1952

Having survived the mixed reception of *Out of This World*, Porter was now without work for the first time in several years. In a letter to Sam Stark of 14 January 1951, Linda reported: 'Cole is in the country, he only left yesterday as he was on Television Friday night – 'We the People' – + I am told he was excellent. The country does him great good – he rests + sleeps which is impossible in N.Y. – he got so tired, poor darling!'[1] Writing to Stark himself ten days later, Porter expressed a hunger for a new project, evidently undaunted by the experience of the previous autumn:

24 January 1951: Cole Porter to Sam Stark[2]

Dear Sam: –

Thank you a lot for your letter of Jan. 20, 1951, enclosing the new notice on Kiss me, Kate in Los Angeles. It goes into my Scrap Book quick.

I have no idea when I am coming out. At the present moment I am looking for work, which means that I am hunting for a Broadway show for next season. I have one fairly well lined up for the season following,* but I don't want to wait that long before going to work again.

You will receive shortly the album of Out of this World which is being sent to you by Columbia direct. It seems to me that it is rather good.

I received a strange card from you, advertising the Fish Shanty Restaurant.†
Why should I like the Fish Shanty Restaurant?

---

* *Can-Can*.

† A seafood restaurant in Los Angeles that opened in 1950. For more information, see http://martinostimemachine.blogspot.com/2014/06/fish-shanty-and-kooky-world-of-la.html (accessed 11 September 2018).

[Howard] Sturges just arrived back from Palm Beach. His accounts of it make me long for Los Angeles all the more.

I am sending you, under separate cover, a novel called "The Night Air",* which I want you to explain to me after you have read it. After you have finished it, please give it to Stan Musgrove, and ask him to give it to Bobbie Raison when <u>he</u> has finished it.

All of New York sends you love,

[signed:] Cole

Among the possible projects on offer to Porter was *The Sobbin' Women* (a property that later became MGM's *Seven Brides for Seven Brothers* with a score by Gene de Paul and Johnny Mercer):

24 January 1951: Cole Porter to Leland Hayward[3]

Dear Leland: –

Thank you very much for sending me "The Sobbin' Women". I shall take it to the country over the week-end, and report on my arrival back.

All my best,

Sincerely,

[signed:] Cole

He also received a suggestion of a show from Bella Spewack, who was no doubt keen to continue their collaboration after *Kiss Me, Kate*:

13 February 1951: Cole Porter to Bella Spewack[4]

Dear Bella: –

I am very sorry, but I can't possibly imagine a musical made our [sic] of <u>The Night was Young</u>.†

Best,

[signed:] Cole

---

* *The Night Air* (The Dial Press, 1950) was a recent novel by Harrison Dowd, dealing with homosexuality.

† A play that the Spewacks had written. It was registered for copyright in 1932 (renewed 1959) but seems not to have been produced.

Nothing came of either suggestion, but Porter had at least a small job to keep him occupied: providing new lyrics for the London production of *Kiss Me, Kate* to address both the needs of the censor (the Lord Chamberlain) and the need to clarify a few cultural references for the British audience:

31 January 1951: Cole Porter to Jack Hylton[*5]

Dear Jack: –

I enclose altered lyrics for the English production of Kiss me, Kate. You will note that all the lyrics which have been altered are written in red ink.

All my best – and good luck to you.

Sincerely,

[unsigned]

Apparently, the new lyrics did not arrive on the first attempt at sending, because the choreographer Hanya Holm, who was to reproduce her Broadway choreography for the London production, wrote to Porter on 4 February: 'During the first 4 days I was here, I auditioned 1400 dancers + singers . . . 20 dancers and 20 singers were picked. This is not the land of raving beauties but I did my best to combine talent with looks . . . By the end of this week, we will have the main outline of the show under control. There is nothing to worry as far as music concerns . . . Have you thought about the Bianca lyrics?'[6] Porter replied:

8 February 1951: Cole Porter to Hanya Holm, London[7]

Dearest Hanya: –

I was very surprized [sic] to read your letter of Feb. 4, 1951, saying that you had not yet received the altered lyrics for the London production of Kiss me, Kate. I am sending you herewith a copy of all alterations which I have made. These were sent to Jack Hylton, by Air Mail, over a week ago. Will you please see to it that these alterations are made during rehearsal.

All the rest of your news is wonderful, and it sounds as if we are going to have a fine show.

---

* Jack Hylton (1892–1965) was a bandleader and later a producer of musicals in London, including the West End production of *Kiss Me, Kate*.

We miss you here in New York.

Lots of love [unsigned]

[underneath:]

Dear Miss Holm:

The alterations for English production are the lines typed in <u>red</u>. Good wishes to you, and good luck – wish I were in London too.

Secretary. [Madeline Smith]

Kiss Me, Kate had also opened on the West Coast, and Sam Stark had gone to see the opening night with Robert Raison. Porter wrote to thank Stark for his report:

1 February 1951: Cole Porter to Sam Stark[8]

Dear Sam: –

Your letter dated "Sunday" arrived; I take it that it means last Sunday. I was delighted to hear that you and Bobbie [Raison] went to see the road company of <u>Kiss me, Kate</u>. I immediately notified the producers that Marc Platt's* tights were dirty and that his shoes were unshined, and their retort was that they had received long letters from Edwin Lester† and Louis Shurr‡ in Los Angeles, who had gone to the opening night of <u>Kiss me, Kate</u>, both of whom reported on the fact that the production was immaculate. Could you possibly have gone to the wrong show?

I enclose a wire from Eddie Davis,§ as I have no idea where he lives. Will you kindly call him up and thank him for his thoughtfulness?

The Barberry Room is in the Hotel Berkshire. It is rather smart and gloomy. Michael [Pearman] seems to like his job very much, but I worry for him as I am so afraid that he will insult some of the customers, as not all of them belong either in the Social Register or to Burke's Peerage.

Gracie¶ sends love,

[signed:] Cole

---

* The dancer Marc Platt played Bill in the national tour of *Kiss Me, Kate*.
† Edwin Lester (1895–1990) was a major producer of musicals on the West Coast.
‡ Louis Shurr (?–1967) was a prominent Hollywood agent, with clients including Bob Hope and Betty Grable.
§ Porter probably means the saxophonist Eddie Davis (1922–86).
¶ Linda's dog.

These letters suggest Porter was perfectly cheerful despite the critical reaction to *Out of This World*, which closed on 5 May after only 157 performances. Linda reported to Stark on 5 February that 'Cole is in the country + returns today. His week ends do him endless good – no telephones, nobody can bother him – a real Ivory Tower. [Howard] Sturges goes with him next week end; on the 23rd he flies to Paris + Cole + I will miss him terribly. No one could have a nicer companion.'[9] Without his closest friend Sturges at his side, Porter planned to fly to California, partly to see the road company of *Kiss Me, Kate*, no doubt:

13 February 1951: Cole Porter to Sam Stark[10]

CAN YOU LUNCH WITH ME SUNDAY FEBR 18 AT 416 I MAY NEED YOU FOR SATURDAY NIGHT ALSO BUT CANT TELL YET. PLEASE LEAVE ANSWER WITH MAX. COLE

The next sequence of letters provides a detailed insight into Porter's business affairs and in particular his partial lack of awareness as to his wealth and position. His lawyer, John Wharton, had taken over his business affairs in addition to his legal affairs in 1949, but Porter seemed concerned by the rise in the fee being requested:

14 February 1951: Cole Porter to John Wharton[11]

Dear John:

Correct me if I'm wrong, but I seem to recall that when we discussed the advisability of your office's managing my business affairs during the early part of 1949, that you told me the fee would be $15,000. during a "show year."

Although there was no show produced during 1949, your constant and expert advice during the building of <u>OUT OF THIS WORLD</u>, and in other business connections was invaluable, and there was no question in my mind but that you were fully entitled to the $15,000. fee. However, I do feel that the proposed fee of $25,000. for 1950 is a bit rough on me. Your explanation that the $25,000. actually costs me only 2,500. would relegate this business deduction to the top bracket and make other business deductions subject to a lesser tax deduction.

Don't feel that I am underestimating your help or Ben's . . . . but do you think you can shave the fee somewhat?

With kindest regards,

Sincerely,

[signed:] Cole

Cole Porter

Wharton replied to Porter on 15 February[12] explaining why he felt $25,000 was an appropriate fee for 1950, noting that his firm had taken on extra responsibilities – previously handled by his agent Dick Madden. But he added that after his explanation, Porter could 'name the amount' because '[c]omplete confidence between' them was his priority.

Alongside this correspondence, Porter also wrote to Wharton's firm to recommend a friend, the pianist and composer Lew Kesler. The letter, and a subsequent mention of Kesler in the letter of 7 March below, demonstrates Porter's loyalty towards his friends:

[n.d.] February 1951: Cole Porter to John Wharton[13]

Dear John:

I am writing you in reference [sic] to a friend of mine, Lew Kesler, who has discussed his situation with me carefully and he wishes to connect himself with television. Because I think so highly of his talent, I feel free to prevail upon you with a letter of recommendation.

The following resume will acquaint you with his background. He was associated in an advisory capacity on the Production Staffs of:

"Jubilee"	Mary Boland
"As Thousands Cheer"*	Marilyn Miller and Clifton Webb
"I'd Rather Be Right"†	Geo. M. Cohan
"Hot Mikado"‡	Bill Robinson

---

* Irving Berlin's Broadway musical of 1933.

† Rodgers and Hart's show of 1937.

‡ An African-American Broadway version of Gilbert and Sullivan's *The Mikado* from 1939.

"DuBarry Was A Lady"	Ethel Merman
"Panama Hattie"	Ethel Merman
"Let's Face It"	Danny Kaye
"Something for the Boys"	Ethel Merman
"Mexican Hayride"	Bobby Clark
"Up in Central Park"*	
"As The Girls Go"†	Bobby Clark

He also has to his credit two major night club shows produced in Florida which he staged and directed, featuring such personalities as – The Goldwyn Girls, Jack Cole Dancers, Jane Frohman [sic], Carmen Miranda, Ray Bolger and Joe E. Lewis.

Aside from his ability to direct, coordinate and organize, he is an accomplished pianist and musician and was associated with me on my shows for six years. If you would see him personally and talk to him, I am sure you would be convinced of his value.

Best regards

[unsigned]

Further correspondence with Wharton's colleague Ben Schankman addresses other business matters, such as a possible regional production of *Anything Goes* and a radio show:

24 February 1951: Cole Porter to Ben Schankman[14]

Dear Ben:

Gene Mann just called me up, saying that he would like to produce <u>ANYTHING GOES</u> this summer at the Greek Theatre here and later take it to San Francisco, but he says that Edwin Lester‡ has the stage rights for <u>ANYTHING GOES</u> tied up and what is even worse, Lester has decided not to do it this summer.

I cannot believe that this is true, as I have never heard of the matter. Can you enlighten me?

---

* A Broadway musical (1945) by Sigmund Romberg and Dorothy and Herbert Fields.

† A musical comedy by Jimmy McHugh and Harold Adamson (1948).

‡ Edwin Lester (1895–1990) was a director and producer of numerous productions, most notably overseeing the Los Angeles Light Opera Company for many years.

In regard to your letter of February 21, 1951, concerning the proposed Cole Porter radio program, don't you think that considering my very big income and my terrifying taxes for 1951, that it would be wiser to put this whole matter off until 1952, when in all probability my income will be much smaller?

If you agree with me about this, I still could start work on it here, although I should not like to spend more than four hours a week on it.

All my best.

Sincerely,

[signed:] Cole

Cole Porter

Porter's next letter to Schankman mentions another musical he was considering – an adaptation of the French comedy film *La Kermesse héroïque* (*Carnival in Flanders*):*

7 March 1951: Cole Porter to Ben Schankman[15]

Dear Ben:

Thank you for your letter of February 23rd, 1951, regarding Mr. Geller. I have noted its contents.

In another letter from you, dated February 23rd, 1951, I talked to George Oppenheimer† on the telephone yesterday and he promised me an outline shortly. The night before talking to him, I discussed him and Harry Kurnitz‡ with Sam Goldwyn. Sam thinks that Oppenheimer might turn in an excellent script, but as for Mr. Kurnitz, he said "He can tell a good story, but he can't write it."

I enclose copies of letters I sent to Tams-Witmark and to Dick Madden.[16]

I hope these are correct.

---

* The film – known in English as *Carnival in Flanders* – was released in 1935. In 1953 a Broadway musical adaptation appeared with a score by Johnny Burke and Jimmy Van Heusen. It was a flop at only six performances but gave rise to the standard 'Here's that Rainy Day'.

† The screenwriter George Oppenheimer's (1900–77) projects included the Marx Brothers movie *A Day at the Races* (1937).

‡ Harry Kurnitz (1908–68) was best known for writing material for Errol Flynn but also wrote the screenplay for such musicals as *Ship Ahoy* (1952) and *One Touch of Venus* (1948).

In regard to the proposed Cole Porter transcription radio program, I am at the present moment not interested, mainly because after arriving here I suddenly realized how mentally tired I was and this mental fatigue continues; but I shall keep an open mind. I also received from you the letter which Martin Poll* wrote to you regarding this radio transcription program, and I shall keep it in my files.

Have you been able to see my friend, Lew Kesler[,] yet regarding his embarking upon a television career? In case you have lost his address, it is 155 East 48th Street. His telephone number is Plaza 5-4721 and he is usually in at 11:00 A.M. or at 6:30 P.M.

Sincerely

[signed:] Cole

Various offers continued to pour in for Porter to write a musical. For example, on 13 March a young writer called Allen Keith offered to send him a synopsis of a musical play he had written called *Love or Money*, but Porter seems not to have pursued the idea.[17] On 14 March he wrote again to Ben Schankman, revealing his disappointment in the *Carnival in Flanders* material:

14 March 1951: Cole Porter to Ben Schankman[18]

Dear Ben:

In answer to your letter of March 8, 1951, in which you enclosed a letter from Martin Poll, my reaction is that perhaps I have been too quick in turning down this radio job. I might very easily be interested if you and John can assure me that you can make a deal by which I can get capital gain. Otherwise, I do not think it is practical.

In answer to your letter of March 9, 1951, I had already voted for Fred Ahlert† before receiving your letter.

In answer to your letter of March 12, 1951, I received the first draft from George Oppenheimer on Carnival in Flanders. My first reaction is that the

---

* Martin Poll (1922–2012) was a prolific producer for film and television, including *The Lion in Winter* (1968).

† Frederick Ahlert (1892–1953) was a prolific songwriter of such standards as 'Mean to Me' and 'I'm Gonna Sit Right Down and Write Myself a Letter'.

story line is clear, but that it is totally lacking in humor. I have written asking him to send me some dialogued scenes before I turn it completely down. This is a great disappointment to me.

Regarding the letter to Tams-Witmark,* I take it that you first received the copy of my letter for your own files and that later the actual letter to Tams-Witmark, care of you, arrived with the notation on the envelope "Please Forward". This was done because I did not know the address of Tams-Witmark; in fact, I don't know today what Tams-Witmark is.

Isn't there any way, beside the letter which I wrote to Dick Madden, to stop him from making future deals without consulting your office and me? Has he the legal right to do this? I can't believe that he has.

I appreciate deeply all the trouble that you have taken about my friend, Lew Kesler. I know how difficult it is to get a job for anybody. For years I have tried and for so many people, but usually without success.

All my best.
Sincerely,
[signed:] Cole
Cole Porter

P.S. the We, The People† broadcast recording arrived and I like it immensely.

The London production of *Kiss Me, Kate* opened on 8 March to mostly excellent reviews, which Porter's mother Kate was pleased to note in a letter to his secretary, Madeline Smith:

n.d. [c. March 1951]: Kate Porter to Madeline Smith[19]

Dear Mrs Smith:

Thank you so much for the clippings about the London success of 'Kiss Me Kate'. I read each and all greedily. I noticed some criticisms by sour Puss reporters but who cares? I believe they are plain jealous. I hear my son Cole shush me, and say "Ma every one has a right to his opinion"[.]

---

* The Tams-Witmark theatrical rentals company.

† Porter's appearance on *We, the People* was Season 4, Episode 2, and aired on 12 January 1951.

I know that you and Mrs. Pane are holding the fort alone and <u>gallantly</u> – and so am I, after a fashion –, for instance I have attended several little social gatherings, been to a Church Missionary Meeting (of all things!) and looked after household duties. Just <u>now</u> I am interesting in turning in my old five year car for a <u>new</u> one, that is always exciting. We still have Winter in Indiana and one Spring is [illegible]: the fields are brown and bare, I do understand there <u>has</u> been a bit of clover seed sowing –, but nothing else on account of weather conditions.

Have you heard from Mrs Bearss?* I believe she is still in New York. I miss her <u>so</u> much, she is so happy and cheerful – a great person. The house seems vacant without her, and also I miss you and all – I gained a lot while resting carefree there!

How is radiant Elise?† I am glad she is having a happy time, give her my love please and tell her I often think of that pretty little tea party at the Waldorf – it was sweet of her. And now I must hie me to the New York Herald Tribune for the late news. Take care of yourself Mrs Smith – perhaps I may hear from you again?

Affectionately K. C. Porter

But Porter seems to have missed the London opening, choosing instead to stay in California, as Linda revealed in a letter to Sam Stark: 'Cole is so happy in California – his rest has done him endless good – his only worry seems to be the loss of his excellent cook, but perhaps the new one he has engaged will turn out well – I do hope she tries.'[20]

Nor was Porter interested in further projects that came through, including the idea of turning Fields and Chodorov's‡ 1940 play and its 1942 film adaptation, *My Sister Eileen*, into a musical (it became the successful *Wonderful Town* by Bernstein, Comden and Green):

---

* Lou Bearss, an old friend of the Porter family.

† Madeline Smith's daughter.

‡ Joseph A. Fields (1895–1966) and Jerome Chodorov (1911–2004), playwrights; they won the Tony Award for writing the book for *Wonderful Town* (1953).

FROM LIMBO TO THE WRITING OF CAN-CAN, 1951–1952

11 April 1951: Cole Porter to Ben Schankman[21]

Dear Ben:

In answer to your letter of April 5, 1951, I am not interested in the production which Gloria Safier* and Irene Sharaff† propose for <u>Nymph Errant</u>.

In answer to your letter of April 4, 1951, I have read the play <u>My Sister Eileen</u> and cannot possibly see how it can be made into a musical without hurting the subject matter.

In regard to the Bing Crosby picture, I must stress the fact that no word has ever come to me from Paramount direct, and since Louis Shurr's departure, I have heard no word at all from Bing Crosby. So all of this enthusiasm may be mostly in Louis Shurr's mind. Therefore, I suggest that we wait for direct word from Paramount before talking to Paramount through Louis Shurr. Don't you think this is more dignified?

I have just received notes from ASCAP.[22] There is one paragraph entitled <u>Writer's Representation By Income Classes</u>. It then goes on to mention that there is one writer in the "more than 1,000 point classes". Under this, it mentions one writer in the "1,000 point class"; and under this, one writer in the "950 point class"; and again under this, four writers in the "900 point class". Can you tell me where I stand in this rating?

I enclose the vote which I have been asked to make by ASCAP. I have signed it, but I leave it to you to signify my vote and post it to ASCAP, as I don't know how I should vote.

Sincerely,

[signed:] Cole

Cole Porter

He also turned down the opportunity[23] to turn John Colton's 1941 movie *The Shanghai Gesture* into a musical to star Marlene Dietrich, and a proposed Bing Crosby film for Paramount mentioned in the letter of 11 April above (the movie may have been *Just For You*, which was released in 1952 with a score by Harry Warren):

---

* Gloria Safier (1921/2–85), writers' agent and representative for actors including Elaine Stritch and Mary Astor.

† Irene Sharaff (1910–93), a celebrated costume designer. She later won a Tony Award for *The King and I* in the 1952 awards ceremony.

25 April 1951: Cole Porter to Ben Schankman[24]

Dear Ben:

Will you please write to Mr. Maurice C. Brockway, whose letter I enclose, telling him that due to previous engagements, I cannot consider writing a score for the Shanghai Gesture.

All my best.
[signed:] Cole
Cole Porter

2 May 1951: Cole Porter to Louis Schurr, Savoy Hotel, London[25]

Dear Louis:

Thank you for the long cablegram. I cannot change my mind about the Crosby picture. I am sure that the script, however excellent, is not my dish.

Have a lot of fun, and please come back with a heavy British accent.

All my best to Bob Hope and to you, dear Louis.
Sincerely
[signed:] Cole
[typed:] Cole Porter

By the end of May, Porter was vexed by all the projects that had been proposed to him, as he lamented in the next three letters to Bella Spewack:

29 May 1951: Cole Porter to Bella Spewack[26]

Dear Bella: –

Thank you so much for the post card with the tinsel on it.

It was nice to hear that Sam [Spewack] is writing the new play, and I wish him great success.

Any number of people have sent me bad ideas for musicals, both for pictures and for New York. I am surprised that you have been so lax as not to have sent something brilliant by now.

All my best to you both,
Sincerely,
[signed:] Cole

FROM LIMBO TO THE WRITING OF CAN-CAN, 1951–1952

30 May 1951: Cole Porter to Bella Spewack[27]

Dear Bella: –

I am sending you, under separate cover, a copy of the play "Berkeley Square".* This was suggested to me as a possible basis for a musical. So far, I have read only one act and, with my usual lack of imagination, I can't see it – but perhaps if you and Sam would look it over, you might find something possible here.

I hope you are having a wonderful time.

All my best to you both,

[signed:] Cole

14 June 1951: Cole Porter to Bella Spewack[28]

Dear Bella:

As your letter dated June 9, 1951, though full of hysterical charm, contained so many difficult questions, I have forwarded it to Ben Schankman who will answer you direct.

After reading Berkeley Square carefully, I don't believe it has enough guts for the basis of a musical. Don't you agree?

My best to you both

Cole.

My address is always ze Waldorf.

In addition to the lack of work, Porter's fluctuating income affected his taxes, leading to an extended discussion with his advisers as to how to deal with it. He describes some of the issues in the first of the following two letters to Stark, as well as sharing gossip about the affair between the Duchess of Windsor (the former Wallis Simpson) and Jimmie Donahue, the Woolworth heir:

4 June 1951: Cole Porter to Sam Stark[29]

Sam lamb –

Endless Theatre Magazines, bound, arrived today. I hate to think of your expressage bill but I thank you.

---

* *Berkeley Square* was a play by John L. Balderston from 1926 whose Broadway (1929) and film (1933) versions both starred Leslie Howard.

Linda & I drove up here in state, last Thursday, to find first, two days of unbearable heat + since then, rain + suffocating humidity so thank heaven for the great air-conditioned indoors.

The big meeting with the lawyers, the tax experts and the accountant took place with a strange result. Instead of giving up the California house, I am practically condemned to six months of it per annum as I can write off 60% of my California expenses but only 50% of my N.Y.C. sejour. As for Williamstown, it is considered pure extravagance. Therefore, if I can make a decent deal with the Hainses, I shall take 416 for another five years after Sept. 1952.

Linda is not as well as she should be but she's a hell of a lot of fun. She says that Jimmie Donahue's* valet is quoted as having said "Mr. Jimmie's relationship with the Duchess,† I realize now, is more than a friendship. After he has been out with her, I always find lip-stick on his shorts." Linda adds "Tricks she learned in China, I presume."

Goodnight Sammie. Stay thin + don't go to Mexico for too long. I return, probably with Sturges at the end of the month. Love to y'all. Cole.

8 June 1951: Cole Porter to Sam Stark[30]

Dear Li'l Sam:

Forgive me for flooding your mail-box with letters but I hasten to thank you for the New Yorker article on wines which will help me especially on the coast.

[Howard] Sturges is due in N.Y. in a few days although he is always so intangible that we may not pin this old butterfly down for months.

I enclose a birthday greeting for your files.

Love from us,

Cole

In the background, things were more mixed than Porter had confessed. A letter from his valet Paul Sylvain to Stark reveals that both of the Porters had been suffering from health problems: '... M\mr. C.P. is in good health and spirits and his appetite has increased somehow. He will soon regain the few pounds he lost in Hollywood if he keeps up eating so much more than he used to. Mrs. C.P. I'm sorry to say is not much better. However

---

* James Donahue Jr. (1915–66) was an heir to the Woolworth fortune.
† Wallis, Duchess of Windsor.

her fighting heart is still strong and is still hanging on firmly to life.'[31] But Porter's messages to Stark continued to focus on the lack of excitement in his life (mostly occasioned by the lack of a musical to work on):

18 June 1951: Cole Porter to Sam Stark[32]

W'mst'n, Mass.
Dear Sam:

A letter + a theatre program from Guadalajara. I'll bet that zarzuela you saw was a pip!

Life is very quiet here but Linda + I are having enough fun to make up for terrible weather. After a week of endless rain, we are wilting under a stifling heat-wave. Why did God give all the good climate to California?

[Howard] Sturge[s] + I fly to L.A. on July 2nd where he will stay for two weeks only. After that I shall be entirely alone. Poor Cole, all alone + no friend in Dana Point to come up + visit him.

I envy you your trip, however, so please see everything without taking snapshots.

We send love to you, Sammie + I send my very best to Allen [Walker].
The Dull Mr. Porter.

Indeed, by the middle of June, the composer seems to have started more seriously to consider *Berkeley Square* as a property after all:

21 June 1951: Cole Porter to Bella Spewack[33]

Dear Bella: –

Thank you for your letter of June 18th. I am still scared about Berkeley Square; but I am very interested in the fact that Sam has an original idea for a musical. Please tell me more about this. I like very much the idea of Ray Bolger as a lead, with a bevy of beautiful girls. It seems to me that this is important at the present moment. A good example of the lack of colorful background is A Tree Grows in Brooklyn.* In spite of George Abbott's having engaged top artists for the sets and costumes, it is so ugly to look at.

---

* *A Tree Grows in Brooklyn* had recently opened on Broadway, with a score by Arthur Schwartz and Dorothy Fields.

My plans are to go to California for July and August, after which I shall be either here in New York or in Williamstown, Mass. – but my address is always the Waldorf.

I talked to Ben Schankman on the telephone about the matters which you mentioned, and he asked me to forward your letter on to him and he will answer you direct.

All my best to you both,
[signed:] Cole

P.S. – I have no idea whatsoever as to who has the rights for Berkeley Square, nor who would consider producing it. Frances Goldwyn* simply gave me a copy, saying that she thought it might make a good musical.

On 10 July, Porter was given the opportunity to write a musical for Mercury Records, with the idea of launching it as an album before it appeared on the stage. ('His idea is to start the music prior to its production, using the show album as more or less of a testing ground . . . He is prepared to offer you participation almost at your own price.')[34] One might have thought that kind of music-centred approach would have suited Porter, who does not seem to have particularly enjoyed engaging with book writers on the whole, and it is curious that this idea pre-dated the Lloyd Webber-Rice musicals (several of which started as albums) by nearly two decades. But even this does not appear to have tempted Porter, and the following letters to Bella Spewack and Sam Stark make it sound as if he had settled in for a quiet summer in California:

12 July 1951: Cole Porter to Bella Spewack[35]

Dear Bella:

Thank you so much for the postcard covered with tinsel. I was very amused to see that the young lady was playing a lute.†

---

* Frances Goldwyn (1903–76) was a Hollywood actress from 1925 to 1935 and became the second wife of legendary producer Samuel Goldwyn in 1925.

† A reference to *Kiss Me, Kate*.

We rented the Chateau de la Garoupe for two summers – 1921 and 1922 – and enjoyed every moment. But in those days we were considered crazy, as it was before the days anyone went to the Riviera in the summer, as the weather was considered too hot.

I shall be here at 416 North Rockingham Avenue, Los Angeles until September first, but it is better always to address me care of The Waldorf.

My best to you both.

[signed:] Cole

Cole Porter

12 July 1951: Cole Porter to Sam Stark[36]

Dear Sam:

Your notes and your theatre programs have kept me in constant touch with you. But your news of yesterday about Dud* has made me very sad indeed and I hope you will keep me posted as to his progress.

[Howard] Sturges received bad news also yesterday. A cable arrived, saying that Christos had had a terrible automobile accident. He fractured his hips in seven places and his right arm in eleven places. He is in a hospital in Bayonne.

At the present moment, [Howard] Sturges decided not to rush back, as Christos' sweetheart and her husband are both living nearby and promised to take excellent care of him. So Sturges will leave here Saturday to stay with Whitney Warren† for a bit and then spend most of August with Linda before returning to France.

We have been having a whirl here, due mostly to Sturges being with me. It is wonderful to watch him weave his magic spell upon everyone he meets. In fact, it is going to be very lonesome without him, as he – like you – has the rare genius of companionship with humor.

Even if you do come back earlier than you anticipated, I don't see how you can spend much time with me, what with Dud being so laid up. But I shall continue here in my little home until September first, notwithstanding.

---

* It has not been possible to identify Dud or Christos in this letter.

† Whitney Warren Jr. (1898–1986), son of the architect Whitney Warren (1864–1943), was a horticulturalist who lived in San Francisco.

Sturges and I both send you love and our best to Allen [Walker]. Thank you again for the programs and the letters.

[signed:] Cole
Cole Porter

18 July 1951: Cole Porter to Sam Stark[37]

Dear Sam:

Your letter dated July 18th arrived. Naturally, it alarmed me greatly, as if Allen [Walker] expects a very fine position in Mexico it will mean that you will <u>never</u> come back.

The rat movement which you started here is growing. First, <u>you</u> ratted on me. Then Sturge came and filled in all Southern California with his blythe light. Then <u>he</u> ratted on me. <u>Merle</u> [Oberon], who had intended to stay practically all summer, rats on me. She flies to Monte Carlo to do a picture. <u>Jean</u> [Howard Feldman] rats on July 16th, when she and Charley [Feldman] go to Europe.

I practically never see Robert,* as he is so busy being a father and mother to his children. Roger Davis is so angry with Fannie [sic] Brice for not leaving him a fortune, that he has a hate for everyone who loved Fannie. He is, therefore, out of my life also.

I blame all the above on you. It is wonderful, however, to hear of your having a whirl in Mexico, and I wish you many happy days and nights.

Linda's health is only fair, but you are not supposed to know this. She has cronies staying with her until August first, when Sturges goes back to stay a month. Then I appear for September and October.

It was very nice to read your letter that Dudley is improving. Please give Allen and him all my best and continue to write to me – even if you do contemplate becoming an ex-patriate.

Love,
[signed:] Cole
Cole Porter

---

* Perhaps Robert Bray.

In mid-July, still with no new musical on the horizon, Porter reacted well to the suggestion of a studio album of *Nymph Errant* (1933), an early Porter show that was not performed live in America until 1982:

25 July 1951: Cole Porter to Ben Schankman[38]

Dear Ben:

Thank you for your letter of July 20, with check enclosed from the Music Publisher Holding Co. I shall welcome the other checks as soon as you can have them sent, for you know what a great amount out of each check must go for taxes.

I return to you the letter from Stan Stanley, and I wish you would speak to him directly regarding this. I agree with you that I see no reason for having a show record album made of an unproduced musical. But I also think that it might be an excellent idea to make an album of my English show, Nymph Errant. This score is in the hands of Chappell in London. It would be a wonderful idea if we could get Mary Martin to do most of the numbers.

As for the other show, Wake Up and Dream, I don't think this score contains enough interest for an album.

All my best wishes.

Sincerely,

[signed:] Cole

By August, Porter and the Spewacks were starting to have discussions about the film version of *Kiss Me, Kate*, now that the London and national tour productions were open:

1 August 1951: Cole Porter to Bella Spewack[39]

Dear Bella:

Thank you very much for your letter of July 25, 1951. I immediately called up Rita Hayworth and asked whether she would consider the possibility of Kiss Me, Kate as a picture. Her reply immediately was that she liked it enormously, but found that the part of Kate was much too vocal for her. I asked her whether she had mentioned Kiss Me, Kate to Harry Cohn* and she said

---

* Harry Cohn (1891–1958), co-founder of Columbia Pictures.

she had not, but that she would. I have heard nothing since and from her attitude, I am afraid it is a lost cause.

Her remarks about the part being too vocal had nothing to do with the fact that the part was written for a soprano. I agree with you perfectly that it could be sung in a picture by a mezzo-soprano, or by a contralto. But if the part is to be sung at all, it must be well sung to be effective. I believe it would have been tactless of me to mention the fact that her, Rita's, voice could be dubbed.

I am sending you a play, entitled A Tailor-Made Man,* for you and Sam [Spewack] to look over as a possibility for a musical. It was sent to me by John Wharton, who thinks that it has great possibilities. I doubt these possibilities.

I arrive in New York on the night of August 31 and intend to leave for Williamstown the next morning. I plan to return to New York on September 12, to be there until September 14, but if you and Sam have any ideas as to what you want to talk to me about, I could come down to the city sooner.

All my best to you, dear Bella. I am so glad that you are enjoying Antibes so much.

Sincerely,
[signed:] Cole
Cole Porter

Porter's continued boredom is apparent from the following letter to Stark, whose return from a trip was a great relief to the composer:

1 August 1951: Cole Porter to Sam Stark[40]

Dear Sam:

Thank you very much for the alarming paragraph regarding male hormones. I immediately called up Jack Schwab,† who told me that my Creon tablets were quite harmless, and that I need not worry in the least. Aren't you the one to cause trouble!

I received also two more programs from you, which interest me a great deal, and today a letter saying that you would arrive in Dana Point around

---

* A play of 1923 by Harry James Smith, which was adapted into a film in 1931 starring William Haines (Porter's landlord in California).

† Schwab's Pharmacy was a famous drugstore where movie actors could often be found. Thanks to Ian Marshall Fisher for this observation.

FROM LIMBO TO THE WRITING OF CAN-CAN, 1951–1952

August 14. Please call me up quick upon your arrival, as I leave here on August 31.

There have been great gaps of boredome [sic] during this visit of mine here, due to your outrageous absence. But I have persuaded myself no longer to think of these gaps, but rather to revel in your hilarious rediscovery of Mexico.

Love to you from Brentwood, and my very best to Allen [Walker] and to Dudley. I am so glad that Dudley is better.

[signed:] Cole

Cole Porter

Financial pressures continued to be on his mind too. The next two letters to Ben Schankman reveal his concerns over his taxes and income:

1 August 1951: Cole Porter to Ben Schankman[41]

Dear Ben:

I enclose a letter, a most upsetting letter, which you may or may not think that you should answer. I believe I spoke to you last Winter in New York, asking you whether you thought that the present arrangement of distribution of funds from ASCAP would endure or not, and you seemed to think that it would. It is difficult for me to agree with you when I receive such a letter as the one enclosed. Or am I wrong?

I received the copy of A Tailor-Made Man and have forwarded it to the Spewacks, as they write me every now and then of the possibility of our doing a musical together. To me, this play has a charming idea and plot, but I question whether the background is colorful enough and whether the thesis regarding capitalism and labor does not date. Thank you, however, very much for sending it to me.

Thank you very much indeed for having the different publishers' checks for royalties sent to me so promptly. My accountant here, Ford Dixon, is writing you in detail about them and about what must be done to carry me through September.

Sincerely,

[signed:] Cole

Cole Porter

4 August 1951: Cole Porter to Ben Schankman[42]

Dear Ben:

In the letter which I dictated, last Wednesday, I underplayed my gratitude to you for having hurried up those royalty checks. This was because I have a gossiping secretary here and were she to have any idea of my precarious financial future, the news would spread all over town. But I am deeply grateful to you.

You will, by now, have received a letter from my accountant here, Ford Dixon[,] telling you of my total lack of funds for September. I don't see how these demands for advances can lead to anything but disasters for 1952. John [Wharton] + you both tell me not to worry but in spite of your advice, I am living in constant dread. Forgive me for not snapping out of this but I can't overcome it.

Again my gratitude, dear Ben, + all my best to you + to John.

Sincerely

Cole

Schankman appears to have made an attempt to quell Porter's concerns on 3 August and he replied more cheerfully five days later:

8 August 1951: Cole Porter to Ben Schankman[43]

Dear Ben:

Thank you very much for your letter of August 3, 1951 regarding the letter which I received from the Independent Group West Coast Writers. It calmed me greatly.

Also, thank you for your letter of August 2, 1951. It seems to me that Mr. Carlton of Mercury Records is wasting a great deal of your time, and I should not bother further with him.

All my best.

Sincerely,

[signed:] Cole

Cole Porter

Porter's lack of business acumen – which seems to have been at the heart of his general financial anxiety – also runs through the next letter to

Schankman. The rules about ASCAP royalties confused him and in the letter he seems at a total loss to understand them. He also discusses a possible broadcast of his unrevived 1935 musical *Jubilee* and makes some interesting comments about his artistic control over his work:

15 August 1951: Cole Porter to Ben Schankman[44]

Dear Ben:

Please give me your advice on the enclosed letter from The Authors League of America, Inc.* and return it to me.

I enclose also a letter from ASCAP. Does this letter mean that as I am both a composer and a writer of lyrics, that my ASCAP checks will be doubled from now on? The wording of this letter gives me this impression, though I cannot believe that it is true.

In regard to your letter of August 8, 1951, re Jubilee, as for getting a script of it, if you will telephone my secretary, Mrs. Smith, at the Waldorf, or at her home – BUTTERFIELD 8-5124 – I am practically sure that she has a script of Jubilee, which she can lend to you. If she has not, then I advise you to call up Moss Hart's office in New York and try to get one.

I don't think it is practical to buy the musical material for Jubilee, which is now held by the [Sam] Harris† estate. Apart from the music and lyrics which were published of Jubilee, the lyrics are very topical and would have to be completely re-written to apply to any revival of the show today. This would be a major job, which I should find it impossible to do. But I agree with you and Miss Rubin that $1,250.00 is a suitable price to ask for one broadcast.

As regards the clipping that you sent to me, written by Dorothy Kilgallen,‡ concerning changing of the lyrics of Down In The Depths On The Ninetieth Floor, I agree with you and not with Selma. The lyrics for his new recording have merely generalized my lyrics, so that they could be understood by anybody, whether he had ever been in New York or not. So I see no harm

---

* The Authors League was founded in 1912 to promote writers' rights, including freedom of expression and copyright.

† Sam H. Harris (1872–1941) was a prolific theatre producer whose credits included *Jubilee* (1935).

‡ Dorothy Kilgallen (1913–65) was a journalist and was a regular panellist on *What's My Line?* from 1950.

done. It does seem strange to me, however, that changes in my lyrics are often made, and even changes in the music, without anyone ever asking my permission. But perhaps, if we demanded my permission always be given, it would hold up a lot of recordings of songs which might never be revived.

Best wishes,
Sincerely,
[signed:] Cole
Cole Porter

Jubilee and *Nymph Errant* are also topics of the following letter, in which Porter appears to show enthusiasm for writing a television musical (he would eventually do so, but not for seven years):

20 August 1951: Cole Porter to Ben Schankman[45]

Dear Ben:

Thank you for your letter of August 15, 1951, regarding Miss Rubin and the license fees for Anything Goes.

Thank you for your letter of August 16, 1951, enclosing a check from Harms, Inc. and information as to future checks to which I can look forward.

In regard to one of your two letters dated August 17, 1951, thank you for clarifying the ASCAP performance income.

As for buying the musical material for Jubilee from the Sam Harris estate, I talked to Moss Hart. He said that he thought it would be very unpractical to buy the musical material. He suggested that as the fees for stock representations are so small, it would be better if we merely rent the musical material from the Sam Harris estate for each performance. He also suggested that it might be better not to make Jubilee a property for stock performances, but rather to hang on to it until there should be a demand for television, when all the television people run short of material. If you want to write to him, his address is – until October first – 522 Ocean Front, Santa Monica, Calif.*

In case Mrs. Smith does not have a book of Jubilee, Moss has one at his country place in Pennsylvania, but could not give it to you until October.

---

* Hart was in California with his film *Hans Christian Andersen*.

I note also in this letter that you have advised Miss Rubin that I am willing to accept $1,250.00 for a one-shot radio broadcast of this property.

In your second letter dated August 17, 1951, regarding Martin Poll, I should certainly be very interested in a one-shot television project. As I shall be in the country from now on until toward the end of October, perhaps it would be better to plan it for November or December, in case the deal goes through.

I have suddenly changed my plans and will be in Williamstown this coming Wednesday night, August 22. My two telephone numbers are – 742 and 385.

I just remembered that Goddard Lieberson spoke to me last winter about Columbia Recordings doing an album of <u>Nymph Errant</u>. If he could get Mary Martin to do this, it would be a wonderful album and probably much better than the one which you suggested.

Sincerely,

[signed:] Cole

Cole Porter

Porter's implicit worries throughout these letters are confirmed in the following message from Linda to Stark, in which she summarizes with concern his current mental and physical state:

25 August 1951: Linda Porter to Sam Stark[46]

Dear Sam:

A thousand thanks for the charming little basket from Mexico. I have a weakness for baskets + this one gives me much pleasure.

Cole is here, he looks thin, poor darling! + seems <u>so</u> worried. He worries about <u>every</u>thing, having no money, having no show etc etc – all of which is perfectly absurd. And he knows it. But he can't get hold of himself, sleeps badly + eats too little. It is a new Cole. I have never seen him in such a state before. However, he is happy to be at home + before long I feel I can straighten him out + rid him of all his nightmarish ideas. For he has really nothing to worry about!! We are both so anxious to have you here for a visit, and if you can possibly arrange to come, you would do him no end of good.

That it does so do let me know if there is a chance. Between us, we could work wonders.

Ever so much love, Sam

Linda

Cole wrote less than a week later to underline Linda's urgent invitation for Stark to come and stay with them to cheer him up:

31 August 1951: Cole Porter to Sam Stark[47]

Minutes have passed,
    hours " " ,
    days " " ,
but not a word from St. Sam except the article re the lonesome girl.

Oh Sam, it's rather wonderful here + not a bit too hot. And the place + the country side is so beautiful + the pool so refreshing + Linda is in grand form.

When do you hop into your motor + come to stay + stay + stay?

You will be so welcome + we shall all take such good care of you. Even Gracie* will pet you.

And Ambroisine is one of the finest cooks in the world.

Come, Sam, come. Remember the autumn? It is very poetic here in the Berkshires. And you will make it seem even poetical. So hurry, dear Sam. We want you + need you.

Lots of love from us.

Your

Cole

And my best to Allen [Walker] + to Dudley.

It appears from the mention of a painting in the following letter that Stark did indeed visit Porter in early September. But the paranoia that Linda had referred to had continued, and he flew to Paris on his doctor's instructions. Linda's account of the situation was much more explicit than Cole's:

---

* Linda's dog.

FROM LIMBO TO THE WRITING OF CAN-CAN, 1951–1952

21 September 1951: Linda Porter to Sam Stark[48]

Dear Sam:

Cole flies to Paris next Wednesday to join [Howard] Sturges for a month or six weeks; his doctor strongly advises it, says he needs a <u>complete</u> change – + I agree thoroughly. He has worn himself out with worrying and is in no condition to work at present. Cole had a complete check-up – all tests satisfactory except that he has an overactive thyroid which accounts for his sleeplessness + loss of weight. I pray God this change will put him on his feet – it is so distressing to see him in such a state.

Much love to you – in haste

Linda

21 September 1951: Cole Porter to Sam Stark[49]

Dear Sam: –

Linda has fallen so in love with the painting you brought me that she is bringing it to New York to be framed and then it will go into the front downstairs guest bedroom in Williamstown.

After all my worries on the Coast, I had a meeting with the two lawyers, the tax expert, and the accountant, and found that these worries were totally without reason and that I am in excellent financial shape. But, in the meantime, I have run myself down so much that the Doctor recommends a complete change for a few weeks. Therefore, I fly to France with Paul [Sylvain] for a few weeks, where my address will be:

c/o Morgan & Co.

Place Vendome

Paris, France

I only wish you were going along; we could have so much [sic] laughs together.

Lots of love,

[signed:] Cole

But after only a week, Porter came home with a nervous condition that required serious medical treatment, as Paul Sylvain secretly reported to Sam Stark:

7 October 1951: Paul Sylvain to Sam Stark[50]

Dear Mr. Stark:

Have news for you of the greatest urgency. However, it is Mr. C.P.'s severe order that none of his good friends be told anything. But after examining my conscience, I know, that you, being a very special friend, should be told; though it was Mr. C.P.'s thought that it would make you feel too sad! I've come to the conclusion that, were you not told now, it would grieve you the more to be told later. Naturally, little do I need to stress the point that this is strictly confidential and that not even Mr. Walker or Mr. Bray be told. For all they know, or should, or even yourself, is that Mr. C.P. and I are still abroad – in Paris, France; as indeed we were for a very short time (Sept. 28 to Oct 3).

Before we left by air, via Pan American, it was the opinion of everyone concerned – doctors and Mrs. C.P. and even myself – that a trip abroad would be excellent for his health, in as much as he had fallen into depths of dismal thinking, worrying about expenses; had developed bad nerves; and a very bad case of insomnia. After 5 days in Paris, Mr. C.P. became so depressed he was entirely broken down physically – and mentally. Talked immediately with Mr. Sturges and we decided to bring Mr. C.P. back to U.S.A. We talked to Mrs. C.P. on transatlantic phone and we decided going directly to Boston, Phillips House,* and consult Dr. Cope on thyroid, and a neurologist. The captain on the Pan American plane would have gladly dropped us at Boston, but the weather would not let him, at [?] we reserved hotels American [?], but at La Guardia flights were cancelled so we drove all the way to Boston in a car rental. Dr Cope found the thyroid, not nervous, but Dr Calf, an eminent neurologist (in fact, all doctors think he is God) helped Mr. C.P. essentially by finding the mind O.K. but suffering from distressing moods, and a change of life for a man of 60. So we came back to Waldorf, and Drs. Moorhead and Whitemore and Stevenson sent Mr. C.P. to the Doctors Hospital, where we still are, under the name of Paul Sylvain – we did all that traveling back without anyone knowing Cole Porter, the composer, was ill – and where Electric Shock Treatments were started. He's had two so far, with a shot of Kourari† [sic] for his legs, and they have done wonders. Naturally there is

---

* The General Hospital in Boston.
† Curare, a common drug treatment of the period that aided muscle relaxation.

much progress to be made – for Mr. C.P. is far from being recovered completely – but there is great hope indeed, that in two weeks or so, Mr. C.P. will be his old, vivacious, charming, witty self again. There is nothing to worry about any more.

I write Mr. Sturges every night; and talk to Mrs. C.P. every day, who is still in Williamstown until next Monday. She will be coming back to the Waldorf then. I assure you that everything is being done for Mr. C.P.'s health, as well as comfort. I spend the day at the Doctor's Hospital and sleep at the Waldorf in 41C. Mr. C.P. is not allowed any visitors as yet; we are waiting till he asks for them, which he will when he is better. Don't hesitate to ask me anything and if you want to phone me for direct inquiries and our news use our private line, which is near my bed – Plaza 5 - 8575 – I am usually home after midnight. You will realize, I'm sure, we are doing our best to keep this news from the N.Y. press and Hollywood's. News from my wife are good so far. No worries there. But delivery expected soon.

All my best to you.
Sincerely
Paul

Within weeks, Porter was able to resume his correspondence again and was also going to the theatre once more, though he pretended that the need for work rather than his health was the reason for not being able to travel to California:

1 November 1951: Cole Porter to Sam Stark[51]

Dear Little Sammie: –

Thanks a lot for your letter of Oct. 24th. I am out of the hospital and recuperating as well as can be expected. I shan't tell you the details until we meet, as it was all rather awful.

It was wonderful to read that your book is progressing so beautifully. Do you begin to see a possible finish?

There is no chance of me coming to the Coast any more this year, as I am still hunting for work. So far, everything that has been presented is impossible – but, as I have been through this before, I am not yet discouraged. In the meantime, Linda and I have our usual luncheons together and, in the evening, I am either invited out or I find a cronie. I have seen quite a few shows but nothing that I like enough. This coming Saturday night, dainty Elsa* and I go to see <u>The Four Poster</u>,† which has received excellent notices. I can't imagine, however, being diverted for the length of a whole show by a cast of two people. I shall report on this.

Please write me gossip. I need it for my convalescence.

Linda and I both send love.

Your elderly friend,

[signed:] Cole

As the year drew to a close, Porter's health had considerably improved – Paul Sylvain commented to Sam Stark that "Mr C.P. as you know is doing very well, almost completely recovered"[52] – and he even contemplated writing a musical version of the Spewacks' 1935 play *Boy Meets Girl*.

17 November 1951: Linda Porter to Sam Stark[53]

Dear Sam:

Your birthday telegram arrived – how nice of you to always remember me. I thank you so much!

Cole is in the country this week end... – he phoned last night + sounded so happy to be back in his little house. A few days away from N.Y. does him great good. Cole is so much better, he looks like himself again.

My love to you

Linda

18 December 1951: Cole Porter to Bella Spewack[54]

Dear Bella: –

I have been trying to work on all the <u>Boy Meets Girl</u> material that you left with me for quite a few days now, but I can get nowhere. I am afraid the

---

* Elsa Maxwell.

† *The Fourposter* was a play by Jan de Hertog. As Porter intimates, there were only two actors in the cast.

reason is that the subject matter, even though it may be excellent, does not appeal to me, and I must withdraw from our possible collaboration on this show.

I can't tell you how sad this makes me as I wanted so much to do another show with you and Sam. Perhaps you will come up with another idea. This would be wonderful.

A Happy Christmas to you – and my gratitude for your patience.

Love,

[signed:] Cole

P.S. – I have written also to Sam [Spewack].

While nothing came of *Boy Meets Girl*, the renewed optimism and energy that Linda noted would prepare Porter for embarking on *Can-Can*, his next musical. The show was discussed by Sam Zolotow in his *New York Times* column of 17 November, and while the librettist and star would later change, it was clear that Porter was finally back in business with a musical set in one of his favourite cities:

Except for the formality of signing contracts, everything is set for Cole Porter and F. Hugh Herbert to write the songs and book, respectively, of a new musical. Steeped in a Parisian atmosphere, it will be called "Can-Can." Next season, the show will be put on the boards by Cy Feuer and Ernest Martin, a team of producers who have dedicated themselves to the production of hits, an assertion plainly evident from their first two offerings, to wit, "Where's Charley" and "Guys and Dolls." Factors concerned agree that the leading role is eminently suited for Carol Channing, now in Chicago with the touring company of "Gentlemen Prefer Blondes." With her in mind, Mr. Herbert is writing a part designated as La Goulue, otherwise referred to as the Queen of Paris' Montmarte district. Entirely original in concept, the story of "Can-Can" will deal with the era of the famous artist Toulouse-Lautrec, an habitué of Montmartre. The painter, however, will not be included as a character.[55]

Even after Porter's discharge from hospital in October 1951, Paul Sylvain continued to keep Sam Stark secretly updated on the songwriter's health. On 7 January 1952, he informed Stark: "... You will be glad to hear that

Mr. C.P. is putting on weight. From the 124 lbs of the Doctor's Hospital days, he went up to 139. He is much more active socially ... We have just returned from a week end [sic] in Williamstown, with Mr. [Howard] Sturges, and as there was a great deal of snow, Mr. C.P. was happy to see Fairy Land in Winterland."[56] The improvement in Porter's spirits is obvious from the following letter, despite his complaints about Stark's possible move to Mexico and his boredom about appearing on Ed Sullivan's television show, *Toast of the Town*:

27 January 1952: Cole Porter to Sam Stark[57]

3rd Sunday after Epiphany

Sam –

Bobby Raison writes "Rumor has it that he (meaning <u>you</u>) + Allen* are going to Mexico City to live. That would be our loss."

Could this tragic news be true?

Please write me the truth quick.

Dull news: Ed Sullivan is doing 2 T.V. Shows on my life. I appear on the 1st one. This will be on Feb. 23rd, Sat. from 8.00 to 9.00 P.M., N.Y. time. The 2nd show will be on Mar. 1st, same time.†

Hot news: Max writes that he has found me an excellent German cook. I told him to engage her from Feb. 15th on if necessary so that she can get used to the horror of it all before I arrive during the last week in Feb.

My God, this note is so full of dates.

Harry Krebs is here for the week-end with me. He is really breaking up. He can no longer hear, see nor taste. He assures me he can still feel.

I'm waiting for [Bill] Haines‡ to send me a new lease on <u>416</u> for a five year extension beginning Oct. 1st, 1952. He agreed to my terms but the delay may mean that Jimmie [Shields] wants the house for himself.

---

* Allen Walker, Stark's partner, who was thinking of moving to Mexico for work.

† Porter signed his contract for the programmes on 18 February. Source: contract with Marlow Lewis, executive producer at CBS, for two appearances on the Ed Sullivan *Toast of the Town* show on 24 February and 2 March 1952 (it was broadcast a day after filming on each occasion). A photograph is available at https://commons.wikimedia.org/wiki/File:Ed_Sullivan_Cole_Porter_Toast_of_the_Town_1952.JPG.

‡ Porter's landlord in California.

FROM LIMBO TO THE WRITING OF CAN-CAN, 1951–1952

Goodnight, dear Sam. I pine to see you + <u>hear</u> your rollicking laughter.
My best to Allen <u>if</u> he isn't going to move you to Mexico.
Your worried
Cole.

The problems Porter mentions with his lease on the 416 North Rockingham house were resolved later in the month and he signed a four-year agreement on 1 February to rent it,[58] which he confirmed to Stark via telegram a day later:

2 February 1952: Cole Porter to Sam Stark[59]

DEAR SAM[,] MANY THANKS FOR YOUR WIRE[.] LEASE ARRIVED JUST BEFORE I LEFT NEW YORK[.] JEAN FELDMAN AND I SEND YOU OUR LOVE=COLE=

Periodically, Porter would make a point of writing to thank people who had been involved in making his productions a success. George Hirst was the conductor of the return engagement of *Kiss Me, Kate* on Broadway from 8 January, but it appears from the following letter that he was planning to leave the show early. Ever polite, Porter acknowledged his work. It is striking that the composer's correspondence was voluminous, and it must have been a daily chore to process all of his business letters every day:

23 January 1952: Cole Porter to George Hirst[60]

Dear George Hirst: –
  Thank you very much for your letter.
  I can't tell you how much I appreciate all the excellent work you did while conducting the Orchestra for <u>Kiss Me, Kate</u>, and I wish you lots of success in the future.
  Sincerely yours,
  [signed:] Cole Porter

Porter remained on the East Coast while he awaited the taping of his *Toast of the Town* television appearance, but he was impatient to return to California:

9 February 1952: Cole Porter to Sam Stark[61]

Sam, my Lamb –

Can you lunch at 416 on Sunday, Mar 2nd at 1.30 P.M. Come early if you want to swim. It's a little luncheon to meet you. [Howard] Sturges will be there + I hope, Stannie [Musgrove] + old Bob Raison.

I pray to arrive the night of Feb. 28th. I pine for the Coast + I sizzle to see you.

Love – Cole

[On reverse:] Thank you for the Nathan* article which I had not seen.

The show was successful, but one of Porter's claims in the interview section was corrected by a knowledgeable viewer, Sylvan Taplinger, who wrote to Sullivan: 'Perhaps Cole Porter has forgotten about it, but the reason "Just One of Those Things" and "Begin the Beguine" didn't hit when they first came out was this. Just after the show "Jubilee" was hitting its stride, the Warner Bros. music publishing houses failed to renew their performing licenses with the networks, with the result that much good music (including Porter's) was missing from the radio for many months. When the licenses were renewed, "Jubilee" had pretty well run its course, and there were several Warner musical pictures with good songs waiting for air plugs.'[62] Porter seems to have been pleased by the information:

18 March 1952: Cole Porter to Sylvan Taplinger[63]

Dear Mr. Taplinger:

Ed Sullivan forwarded a letter which you had written to him, explaining why JUST ONE OF THOSE THINGS and BEGIN THE BEGUINE didn't hit when they first came out. This was very interesting indeed to me as I had forgotten.

Sincerely,

[unsigned]

In addition to *Can-Can*, rumours of Porter's connection with other possible new shows continued in the press – for example, a musical

---

* Probably an article by Porter's critical nemesis, George Nathan.

adaptation of the Austin Strong play *Seventh Heaven** – but nothing came of them. He made plans to start work properly on the score of *Can-Can* when he got to California, writing to the pianist and composer Alex Steinert to hire him to come and transcribe his songs: 'Can you play two pianos with me beginning about March 2nd?'[64] *Can-Can* was mentioned again in the press in mid-March, when the Spewacks were now named as the librettists;[65] by early April their names had been dropped and no book writer had yet been hired to replace them.[66] In the background, Porter's business affairs also required regular attention, as the next two letters demonstrate:

11 March 1952: Cole Porter to John Wharton[67]

Dear John:

Thank you for your letter of March 6, 1952, enclosing the two checks.

The successor to my accountant, Miss Berleant, is Mrs. Suzanne L. Eastman. Her home address is P. O. Box 131, Greenlawn, New York. [. . .]

I also note in your letter that you have sent Ben [Schankman] away for a month's vacation and that in case I want to get in touch with you and cannot I should communicate with Mr. Robert Montgomery† in your office.

Sincerely,

[signed:] Cole

11 March 1952: Cole Porter to [Albert] Harvey Cole[68]

Dear Harvey:

Thank you very much for your letter of March 7, 1952.

I have filed, in duplicate, the papers which you forwarded, signed them on the line following the word "(signature)" and mailed them to the Collector of Internal Revenue, Indianapolis, Indiana.

All my best regards.

Sincerely,

[signed:] Cole

---

* Mentioned in Sam Zolotow, '"Seventh Heaven" Bought by Lesser', *New York Times*, 18 February 1952, 14. *Seventh Heaven* was eventually produced in 1955 with a score by Victor Young. Austin Strong (1881–1952) was an American writer of plays and films.

† Robert Montgomery (1923–2000) was an associate at Wharton's firm at the time, though he went on to become a senior partner and later became the trustee of Porter's estate.

To a fan, Porter wrote the following in response to a request for information about the origins of 'Begin the Beguine':

13 May 1952: Cole Porter to Kenneth Dirlam[69]

Dear Mr. Dirlam:

I got the idea of a Beguine from going often to a public dance hall in Paris, where many natives from the Isle of Martinique met every night and danced the Beguine. The Beguine, as a dance rhythm, originated in the Isle of Martinique.

Sincerely yours,

[unsigned]

He also wrote to the distinguished director George Cukor to offer him a copy of the novel *A Distant Summer* (1947) by Edith Saunders, a minor British author. The novel depicts Queen Victoria and Prince Albert in 1855. A great reader, Porter seems quite often to have shared books with his close friends, of whom Cukor was one; a few years later, Cukor would direct Porter's last film musical *Les Girls*:

20 May 1952: Cole Porter to George Cukor[70]

Dear George:

Under separate cover I am sending you A DISTANT SUMMER. I hope you have not read it.

When I read it last winter it seems to me that you would enjoy it also, so I ordered this copy from England for you.

All my best.

Sincerely,

[signed:] Cole

Sometime in May, Abe Burrows agreed to take over the book-writing duties (from the Spewacks) on *Can-Can*. He would be the final choice and a natural one for Cy Feuer and Ernest Martin, having co-written the book for the hit musical *Guys and Dolls* (1950), which they produced. The correspondence between Porter and Burrows for the musical is unusually rich and detailed, showing Porter's often-overlooked enthusiasm for collaboration. In the first letter, he expresses optimism for the project:

27 May 1952: Cole Porter to Abe Burrows[71]

Dear Abe:

Forgive me if I have delayed a bit in sending you lyrics and lead sheets, but I have not been at all well.

It was great seeing you out here and I really believe that you and I can do a fine show together.

Sincerely, and all my best
[signed:] Cole

Three weeks later, Burrows responded to Porter, having apparently received one of the songs from Cy Feuer:

16 June 1952: Abe Burrows to Cole Porter[72]

Dear Cole:

Sorry to hear you haven't been well. I do hope you're feeling better by the time you get this.

Cy [Feuer] played me LIVE AND LET LIVE. It sounded wonderful even the way Feuer thumped it out on the piano. And I think the philosophy that is expressed in the lyrics is just perfect for The Girl.

I am slaving away at [the] story line. Cy and I have been meeting every day and when he comes back to the Coast (he's leaving Thursday), he'll bring a flock of my notes out to you and elaborate on them. There are some interesting notions which I think will work. I am tremendously excited about the whole thing.

Please take care of yourself and keep well.
Best,
[unsigned]

Porter replied quickly, and it is obvious that he was hard at work. The letter is particularly interesting because it shows that he was more concerned about the relationship between his songs and the books of his musicals than is usually assumed:

18 June 1952: Cole Porter to Abe Burrows[73]

Dear Abe:

A very nice letter arrived from you, dated June 16, 1952, with a new address – 1161 York Avenue. Is this a permanent new address or not? The address which you gave me when you were out here was 450 E. 63rd Street, East Building, New York, New York.

I am worried about the song I wrote, titled <u>WHO SAID GAY PAREE</u>? I realize that the idea of the lyric puts you in an unfair spot but I do hope that you can fit it in to your story line as I have tried it on several experts and with such success that I feel it would be a big loss to the show if we have to throw it out. I shall send you a lead sheet of this song shortly.

Naturally, I look forward a lot to Cy's arrival with the material which he will bring from you. I continue writing and, I believe, rather well, but some of the songs I have written may very easily not apply, so the quicker I can follow your book the better for both of us.

All my best.
Sincerely,
[signed:] Cole

In the midst of these documents related to his work, the following letter provides a rare insight into the domestic lives of the Porters, as Cole instructed Linda as to how his cottage at Williamstown should be prepared for his return later in the summer:

18 June 1952: Cole Porter to Linda Porter[74]

June 18, 1952
Darling:

Paul [Sylvain] suggests the following concerning my cottage:
Kitchen walls and woodwork should be washed. Also, all the shelves.
The records in the workroom should all be removed and dusted. Also the shelves themselves.

In the sitting room, all books should be removed and dusted, including the albums around the Capehart.* All of these shelves should be dusted also.

All curtains which have not already been cleaned should be cleaned, but not put up until just before our arrival.

The stair carpet and the carpet in my bedroom should be cleaned. If a cleaning woman cannot do it then Stevens should do it.

All of my clothing should be put out in the sunshine and then put back in the closets.

Everything in the pantry and kitchen should be taken off the shelves and dusted. The shelves should then be washed before the dusted articles are put back in their proper places.

Paul says that this work is too heavy for Elsie to do and some outside woman should be engaged to do it.

We intend to arrive there toward the end of August so perhaps it is too early for all this to be done.

All love. [unsigned]

A week later, Porter wrote again to Burrows, this time with two songs for *Can-Can*. One of them, "I Love Paris," became a hit, while the other, "I Do", was dropped at some point:

24 June 1952: Cole Porter to Abe Burrows[75]

Dear Abe:

I enclose lyrics to two songs which I have written lately. Seeing merely the lyrics may be confusing to you but I shall send you lead sheets as soon as they can be properly made. Cy [Feuer] seemed to think that if I forwarded the lyrics to these songs at once they might be a help to you.

The song <u>I DO</u> is a light foxtrot, to which I can add lyrics ad libitum. It might be useful for another couple besides our two leads. On the other hand, you might feel that it would be better for the two leads during some portion of our show.

The song <u>I LOVE PARIS</u> is also a foxtrot. The first half of it is in minor and the second half in major.

---

* Porter's phonograph.

Without patting myself on the back (or am I?) Cy is very enthusiastic about these two songs.

All my best.

Sincerely,

[signed:] Cole

In his response, Burrows is diplomatically enthusiastic about the songs (bearing in mind that he only had the lyrics to read at the moment) and also makes a suggestion for a further song about the law, which Porter took up:

28 June 1952: Abe Burrows to Cole Porter[76]

Dear Cole:

Just received the two lyrics. They look very interesting. The overlapping quality of I DO has a wonderful feel. As a matter of fact, in some of the dialogue I have mapped out mentally I have planned to go for that bitten off quality. I have noticed that the French seem to talk that way, interrupting each other whenever anyone takes a breath.

I LOVE PARIS reads very charmingly, and with the musical plan you outlined, it must be a lovely thing. I think you can pat yourself on the back.

I am not yet ready to pay [sic] myself on the back, although I think the story is beginning to shape up well. I understand Cy [Feuer] has already told you about the leading man being a judge who believes in the letter of the law. This gives us a fellow who can be very righteous and proper without being unlikeable.

Incidentally, I understand Cy has spoken to you about a song possibility we discussed on the subject of the law. I'd like to expand on this a bit. It struck me that there is a certain kind of man to whom the law is a beloved thing. He thinks of it having a pure, holy beauty. As a matter of fact, I have known lawyers who have spoken of the law as though it were a beautiful woman. You know, the basic law book all over the world is CORPUS JURIS (body of the law) and some of these lawyers speak of the body of the law as though it were a body of a beautiful woman.

Therefore, I thought if our man could sing a ballad about the beauty of the law it might be effective. It may be the only way our man can sing attractively and emotionally before he falls in love with the girl. After he falls for the girl, there will be no problem with him. But there is a bit of a problem as to what a judge would sing up early in the show.

I'd like to know what you think of all this. Maybe I'll call you next week and we can talk it out more.

By the way, in reference to the two addresses I have given you, they are both correct. [. . .]

New York has been horribly hot so I just remain in my apartment. Sort of like living in an air conditioned [sic] ivory tower.

I will talk to you soon.

Best,

[unsigned]

Indeed, Burrows was so specific in his instructions about the new song that Porter seems to have been able to write it almost instantly:

1 July 1952: Cole Porter to Abe Burrows[77]

Dear Abe:

Thank you very much for your letter of June 28, 1952.

Your notes concerning the song which I have to write about the law helped me so much that the song is nearly finished. Do you know other phrases besides the body of the law, the letter of the law and the arm of the law, which would also apply to a beautiful woman? If you could send me these I could write several more lyrics. My secretary just suggested the clutches of the law and the shadow of the law, but I need more.

Your decision to make our leading man a young judge is, I think, wonderful.

I enclose the lyrics to a new song. It is for the spot where our leading lady is a cashier in a bistro. I still have to write the verse of this song, which will say that if she has done at all well it is because of a little folk song which her mother used to sing to her when she was a child. The music of this number is in three-quarter tempo and has the feeling of a French Java.* I shall send this to you as soon as a lead sheet can be made.

---

* A dance popular in France during the first half of the twentieth century.

I can't tell you how excited I am about this show and how confident I am that you will write a delightful book.

All my best.

[signed:] Cole

Porter continued to work at 'The Law' and asked Burrows to return the version he had sent him so that he could replace it with another. He also asks in this letter for advice on how another song was going to fit in the book:

5 July 1952: Cole Porter to Abe Burrows[78]

Dear Abe[,] Please return to me as soon as possible the lead sheet of the song entitled "The Law" which I sent you. I have greatly improved it. Also let me know as soon as possible the situation for an important ballad which I have written for the male lead entitled "To Think That This Could Happen To Me"[.] I don't want to write any lyrics of it until I am sure they will fit the situation. The angle which I would like to write would be the happiness of the male lead now that he has found love. I believe it would be better if this song was sung to the girl but perhaps I could write it so he could sing it either to her or alone on stage[.] All my best = Cole

Parallel to these discussions, Cy Feuer wrote to Burrows, rather discouraged by the quality of Porter's latest work:

7 July 1952: Cy Feuer to Abe Burrows[79]

Dear Abe:

As you know, Cole has been writing like hell and, in my opinion, of late not too well. I realize the importance of not stopping a guy when he's rolling, but I have come to think that one of my problems is to slow him down without actually inhibiting him – if such a thing is possible.

The LAW song, which you received, is musically clever and would probably orchestrate brilliantly. Lyrically, I'm afraid it leans a bit toward the Gilbert & Sullivan, which early in the show would establish the wrong level. I have pointed this out to Cole and he honestly doesn't understand it. Not having anything further to go on than the idea, it was difficult for me to carry the argument any further than mere disagreement. Considering that he stayed up all night (finished work at 6 A.M.) it didn't seem the proper time to put the heavy knock on the material.

I would like to point out that aside from the Gilbert & Sullivan aspect of the lyrical answers by the BOYS, the lyric itself is not too bad and could possibly be fixed to work. Cole asked me to tell you that what he meant by BOYS was whatever characters would normally be available to do the lyrical answers. He's afraid that the word "boys" has a chorus connotation that he didn't actually intend.

He has an idea for a ballad entitled TO THINK THAT THIS COULD HAPPEN TO ME, about which he is very high. He has already written the music and has decided not to write the lyric until getting further information from you. Unfortunately, I find the music very usual and not at all up to the kind of thing to be expected from Porter. Today or tomorrow I am going out to tell him so and have him try to come up with something melodically superior.

Give my love to Karen [sic]* and Ernie [Martin].† More later.

Love and kisses,

[signed:] Cy

Since he did not know of Feuer's misgivings, Porter continued to work on the score:

8 July 1952: Cole Porter to Abe Burrows[80]

Dear Abe:

After wiring you regarding the ballad I have written entitled TO THINK THAT THIS COULD HAPPEN TO ME, saying that I would not write any lyrics to it until I heard from you, I got out of hand and wrote the lyrics which I enclose. I don't see how this lyric can <u>NOT</u> be correct and, as I believe, it is the best lyric that I have written for a long time, I only pray that it will be correct, bookwise, for the important ballad of the show. Please send me your quick opinion about this.

---

* Burrows's wife was called Carin.

† Feuer's producing partner.

I enclose a first refrain of WHAT A FAIR THING IS A WOMAN. Cy Feuer mentioned to me a scene in which you show either a painter or a sculptor in the middle of his work, as he paints or sculpts a beautiful model. I could easily write three more refrains for your three other Quatz Arts* boys. Each refrain would have a surprise ending and perhaps the four boys could dance to this for a finish, as they do in La Boheme in the studio. The music of this song is a lively, faintly Viennese, waltz.

I also enclose the lyrics of MONTMARTRE, which is a spirited march. This might be useful for the finish or the closing of some scene.

My very best to you.

[signed:] Cole

Of these three titles, only 'Montmartre' would make it into the show.

Burrows continued to be both deferential and patient with Porter in his response, but it is obvious from the following letter that he wanted to encourage the composer to write the score with more consideration of its relationship to the book:

8 July 1952: Abe Burrows to Cole Porter[81]

Dear Cole:

I have just sent back the lead sheet on THE LAW, as you requested. Of course, I don't know how you plan to change it but, from what I can see offhand, the feel of the song seems to be very right, and I think it will make a wonderful number.

In your letter, you ask for some further phrases about the law. I have attached a sheet of random notes on which I have put everything that pops into my head on the subject at the moment.

In regard TO THINK THAT THIS COULD HAPPEN TO ME, I am not quite sure of the situation that will surround it, but I am fairly certain that there will be a situation that such a song would fit.

Our hero is going to fall in love with the girl and he is going to be astounded by this fact. I should think it would be a good idea if the lyrics would contain, in addition to the hero's happiness, something about the fact

---

* The Bal des Quat'z'Arts was an annual ball held in Paris between 1892 and 1966.

that he is surprised by all this. This is a fellow who never thought he would fall in love with a woman, never thought he was capable of emotions like that. He was sure that his only interest was the law.

Incidentally, I have developed a little sidelight on this fellow's character I would like to tell you about: I think the key is the fact that he is a judge at the age of, let's say, 37, certainly no more than 40. A man who becomes a judge at this age must have really worked hard. He is a sort of legal Wunderkind, and he must have had time for very little else besides the law in his life. Women would have been a distraction; normal emotions would have been a bother. Consequently, there is a whole segment missing from our hero's life, and, therefore, he has some very unFrench lack of interest in all the amenities and delights of life.

Consequently, when love hits this man, his reactions will be slightly atomic. He'll be frightened, happy, chilled, warmed, ecstatic, puzzled, upset, shocked and delighted. This sounds like the love reaction of a schoolboy, but it's my theory that our hero's emotional growth stopped temporarily the day he entered school.

Anyway, you can see from all this that TO THINK THAT THIS COULD NEVER HAPPEN TO ME is actually what our hero would say. However, I do think you are right in not wanting to rush into doing the lyrics until you know a little more about the situation.

As to whether he sings it to the girl or alone, I couldn't say anything about that either as yet. Of course, that would affect the song very much. If she is present, I guess he wouldn't expose his thrilled bewilderment as much as if he were alone.

I am plowing away at the story back here. I took some penicillin last week and now am covered with a few unsightly lumps. I don't think any disease is as dangerous as penicillin. Mankind will yet live to regret inventing it. However, I feel good and very happy about the whole project.

Best,

[unsigned]

In his parallel correspondence with Feuer, Burrows confessed that he had invited Porter to suggest song ideas for certain spots but did not want him to start writing 'until we've checked'.[82] To Porter himself, he wrote gently but critically, warning him against writing generic material:

14 July 1952: Abe Burrows to Cole Porter[83]

Dear Cole:

I got the lyrics and your note on Saturday, but I wanted to mull the stuff over a bit before answering.

It's really quite difficult for me, at this moment, to give you a valid opinion about whether or not any lyric is correct. I'm still striving for a clean overall picture, and so my individual scenic ideas are all vague or half-formed both as to action, content and character.

I hope I don't sound ponderous but I always approach these things with the intensity that one devotes to a serious play. I have always felt, and I know you agree with me, that a musical should make as much sense as anything else in the theatre.

I honestly feel that it is <u>impossible</u> for you to write a bad lyric. Your artistic instincts are too sound and true, but I do know that when I give you some more scenic meat and character content, you will be able to fatten up lyrical content (with all this talk of meat and fat, I sound like a butcher).

One of the things I always fear in a musical is a preponderance of what I call "generic songs" -- that is, songs that would fit any musical. In our case, this would refer to songs that would fit any French musical. I think the value of our show will be its uniqueness and this uniqueness can only be obtained by a complete unity of characters, scenes and songs.

Now, on the other hand, I know that important ballads must have universal meaning and shouldn't be overly restricted, otherwise [sic] you'd have no scope. When a fellow or a girl fall in love, their feelings are of a universal character and I guess love talk is pretty much the same in any language. However, I think even love ballads can be tailored to the level and uniqueness of our particular show.

For instance, in a song like TO THINK THIS COULD HAPPEN TO ME, it would seem to me that the fact that the man is a staid judge, in love for the first time, would make it obligatory for the song to represent an explosion of emotion. I really feel the judge would take the whole thing very big, much bigger than the lyric suggests. Of course, it may be possible that we want to show the judge in two stages of his emotional development: In one stage he is vaguely loved and titillated and, in the next stage, he bursts forth.

I think this is open to discussion. If you have any ideas on this, I'd love to hear them.

Any notions you have about any of the characters would be of enormous help to me. For instance, I am working on a secondary story line which uses one of the Quatre Arts boys and one of the laundresses. Tentatively, he is a sculptor very modern and unsuccessful. At present, he is engaged in making an enormous statue. His stuff is always enormous and unsaleable, but she loves him and she supports him. However, he loves other women for the beauty and symmetry of their bodies, and he cheats on her in the completely unguilty fashion of the French, especially the bohemian French. She accepts his cheating ungrudgingly because she doesn't want to be thought bourgeois. I wonder if you have any song ideas that might fit into this or that might give the relationship a character twist.

Another item: Cy has told you about the fact that I'm trying to get a duel scene into the second act. It would obviously be treated tongue-in-cheek. I am sure it would use the Quatre Arts boys and our hero and, probably, Senator Marceaux, who is the man chiefly responsible for the growth of censorship in Paris. I think you and I agree that duels are rather silly things which are taken fairly seriously by the participants. Duels solve nothing except they just vaguely save someone's honor. Honor in this case is a very pompous and bumptious word. I wonder if you have any ideas for expressing the character of such a duel musically. There might be a funny notion here. The duel proper will be between our hero and the senator. The Quatre Arts boys will be seconds of our hero. Other people present might be a doctor, spectators, etc. There might be a spot for a song at the beginning of the scene if the Quatre Arts boys arrive before the principals. Let me know what you think.

WHAT A FAIR THING IS A WOMAN looks like a very funny idea. However, here again I am not exactly certain of the situation, although I am sure the basic notion will fit.

This has been a very long, verbose letter. I do hope it makes some sense. I think the most important thing I'd like to see happen is for us to have a steady exchange of rough ideas. I will not plunge into any scenes until I check with you and I hope you will send me any rough ideas you have. I think this will save us both a lot of work.

I feel quite diffident about writing this letter. I do hope I haven't sounded critical. I haven't meant to. It's a great thing for me to be working with you and all I want to do is to get complete synchronization between us.

Please write me soon.

Best,

[unsigned]

Porter does not seem to have been pleased to have 'To Think That This Could Happen To Me', his favourite new song, critiqued by Feuer (he had not yet received Burrows's letter of 14 July), but little could undo his enthusiasm at being at work once more on a musical:

15 July 1952: Cole Porter to Abe Burrows[84]

Dear Abe:

Thank you very much indeed for your letter of July 8, 1952.

I have noted the details about our leading man and when I start writing another ballad for him to sing I shall try to follow them closely. At the moment Cy Feuer doesn't think TO THINK THAT THIS COULD HAPPEN TO ME is an important enough song. Personally, I do, but we may both change our minds.

I hope your penicillin is much better.

All my best.

Sincerely,

[signed:] Cole

Two letters from Porter to his lawyer John Wharton show his ongoing business affairs, including a possible movie version of *Jubilee*;* the second is especially amusing:

---

* See also the letter of 11 October 1952 from John Wharton to Irving Lazar (CPT, Correspondence 1952): Wharton writes to Lazar concerning the possibility of a movie version of *Jubilee*. Lazar wanted to act as Porter's agent in Hollywood for the project, but Wharton wanted to be sure that none of the people who represented Porter at the time of the Broadway show would want to add commission. Nothing came of the project.

15 July 1952: Cole Porter to John Wharton[85]

Dear John:

Will you please answer the enclosed letter from Ray Stark?* I don't like this fellow, Ray Stark. Twice in the past he has put me in a most embarrassing position with Paramount, so if you allow him to represent me on this deal concerning JUBILEE I should not be put in an embarrassing position again.

I also enclose a letter from an old friend of mind [sic], Edward R. Tauch, Jr., 250 East 49th Street, New York, New York. Would you kindly look into the two matters which he mentions in his letter?

All my best.

Sincerely,

[signed:] Cole

22 July 1952: Cole Porter to John Wharton[86]

Dear John:

Thank you very much for your letter of July 19, 1952.

Please tell Jane Rubin that I should be very interested in working on a musical version of THE BARRETTS OF WIMPOLE STREET† if she can guarantee me a singing dog.‡

All my best.

[unsigned]

Another important event from July was the announcement that MGM had bought the screen rights to *Kiss Me, Kate*, with a view to making it in the coming months.[87]

The *Can-Can* correspondence resumes with a letter from Porter to Burrows in which he announces that he has replaced 'To Think That This Could Happen to Me' with a new song and asks for advice on another song:

---

* Ray Stark (1915–2004) was one of the most successful movie producers of the twentieth century, with important titles including *West Side Story* (1961), *Lolita* (1962), and *Funny Girl* (1968).

† *The Barretts of Wimpole Street* (1930) is a play by Rudolf Besier. It was later turned into a musical, *Robert and Elizabeth* (1964), with a score by Ron Grainer.

‡ The cocker spaniel Flush plays a major part in the plot of the film.

22 July 1952: Cole Porter to Abe Burrows[88]

Dear Abe:

Your very interesting letter of July 14th arrived.

I now agree with you and Cy [Feuer] about the number called TO THINK THAT THIS COULD HAPPEN TO ME and I have written a new song, titled I AM IN LOVE, the lyrics to which I enclose herewith. I have been working on this new song so hard that I haven't had time to work on anything else but I hope to begin on your idea about the sculptor song shortly. In your letter, however, is [sic] isn't clear to me whether you want the sculptor to sing it or his laundress girlfriend. Please let me know about this.

I also enclose the complete lyrics of WHAT A FAIR THING IS A WOMAN.

All my very best to you, dear Abe, and thank you again for your letter.

[signed:] Cole

P.S. I have just played and sang (with my beautiful voice) I AM IN LOVE to Cy and he thinks that both the music and lyrics are right for the spot. In fact he is very enthusiastic about it and this makes me happy, as it was such a tough job to solve.

Without waiting for a reply, Porter carried on working and wrote two telegrams in quick succession, informing Burrows of decisions he had made about the lyrics:

23 July 1952: Cole Porter to Abe Burrows*

I WROTE YOU YESTERDAY REGARDING THE SONG YOU MENTIONED FOR EITHER THE SCULPTOR OF [SIC] HIS TOLERANT GIRLFRIEND. I HOPE THAT THIS SONG CAN BE SUNG BY THE TOLERANT GIRLFRIEND AND NOT THE SCULPTOR AS I HAVE NEARLY FINISHED A SONG ENTITLED QUOTE YOU WILL ONE DAY RETURN TO ME UNQUOTE. THIS IS A LIGHT COMEDY SONG IN WHICH SHE SAYS THAT HE CAN

---

* CPT, Correspondence 1952. On 23 July it was also announced that Lilo, 'a French entertainer', would play the role originally designed for Carol Channing in *Can-Can*. See Sam Zolotow, '"I Am a Camera" Will Not Reopen', *New York Times*, 23 July 1952, 20.

PLAY AROUND AS MUCH AS HE WISHES WITH AS MANY GIRLS AS HE LIKES BECAUSE SHE KNOWS THAT ONE DAY HE WILL RETURN TO HER. MAY I GO ON WITH THIS? ALL MY BEST = COLE

23 July 1952: Cole Porter to Abe Burrows[89]

DEAR ABE SINCE MY FORMER TELEGRAM TO YOU TODAY I HAVE CHANGED THE TITLE OF THE NEW SONG TO "YOU WILL ONE DAY PREFER ME" BEST=COLE

Burrows's reply has not survived but the next letter from Porter, written from Peru, Indiana, reveals the sad news that his mother was dying:

28 July 1952: Cole Porter to Abe Burrows[90]

Dear Abe:

I enclose four lyrics to a new song which I hope can be sung by one of our Quatz' Arts boys. The tune is a lively fox-trot + it sounds like a hit as the melody is easy + the rhythm makes it good to dance to.

I write from here as my mother had a serious stroke and is quickly dying. As soon as this is over, I shall return to the coast. Until then, my phone number is Peru, Indiana, 5872. My address is on the back of this envelope.

Best,
Cole

On 31 July, Paul Sylvain wrote to Sam Stark to inform him that 'Mrs. K.C. is still alive ... she has lost her reflexes and cannot take any feeding ... we are waiting for the end to come ... As for the boss he is behaving very well under the circumstances.'[91] But two days later, Mrs Porter died, aged ninety:

3 August 1952: Cole Porter to Madeline P. Smith[92]

DEAR MRS. SMITH: THE GREAT KATIE DIED LAST NIGHT AUGUST 2. AFTER HER STROKE SHE SUFFERED NO PAIN. I THOUGHT YOU WOULD WANT TO KNOW. PLEASE NO FLOWERS. MY BEST REGARDS=COLE PORTER

Considering Porter was so close to his mother, it is perhaps surprising that he resumed work on *Can-Can* so quickly. In the next letter he sends Burrows what must have been the lyrics to the title song:

12 August 1952: Cole Porter to Abe Burrows[93]

Dear Abe:

I am enclosing the lyrics to a new song which could easily be the most important in the Show. As far as numbers go, this song could be sung by a solist [sic] alone on stage or to several other people on stage. It need not be danced to immediately after the vocal is finished, but could be used as a dance number later in the Show. This is a real Can-Can in its tempo and in its feeling. I shall send you the music to this shortly.

I am already working on two other sets of lyrics which will become the fourth and fifth refrains. I hope to write even more lyrics, as this song can easily become a national game, such as was "<u>Your</u> [sic] <u>The Top</u>" and "<u>Let's Do It</u>".

Ci [sic, Cy Feuer] has asked me not to write any more, but merely to clear up what I have written so far. This I shall do so as not to encumber your book any more.

All my best –
Sincerely
[signed:] Cole

On 23 August, Michael Kidd (of Feuer and Martin's *Guys and Dolls*) was signed to choreograph *Can-Can*, but the show is only occasionally mentioned in the extant correspondence of the rest of 1952. For example, Porter wrote the following note to Feuer and Martin about rehearsal pianists for the production, providing an insight into his musical sensitivity towards his choice of collaborators:

10 September 1952: Cole Porter to Cy Feuer and Ernest Martin[94]

Dear Cy and Ernie: –

I enclose the addresses of the two best pianists I know for rehearsal, to teach singers. I prefer Alan Moran to Irving Schlein but I have worked with them both and they are excellent.

Sincerely,
[signed:] Cole
<u>Alan Moran</u>
111 Adams St.
Sea Cliff, L.I.
<u>Irving Schlein</u>
266 Lenox Road
Brooklyn 26, N.Y.

But the majority of the other letters to the end of 1952 deal with personal or business issues. For example, this letter unexpectedly reveals the marriage of Sam Stark:

21 August 1952: Cole Porter to Sam Stark[95]

Sammy –

When you said on the phone "Oh Cole, I'm going to be so happy" I began to bawl like a baby for your happiness is vital to mine. I can't tell you how delighted I am at this beautiful news, dear Sam.

My love to your bride.

Your devoted

Cole

On 3 September it was agreed that Knopf would publish the libretto of *Kiss Me, Kate*; the agreement was signed in November.[96] Then on 13 September, Porter started to deal with issues related to his mother's estate, for example forwarding a bill for flowers to his cousin Harvey to pay from Kate's money:

13 September 1952: Cole Porter to [Albert] Harvey Cole[97]

Dear Al: –

This should be paid from my Mother's estate, under the item of "funeral expenses."

Best,

[signed:] Cole

In another update to Stark, Porter reveals his lively social life, which he resumed after the hard work of writing the score for *Can-Can*. He seems not to have been entirely enthusiastic about Stark's engagement at this point:

17 September 1952: Cole Porter to Sam Stark[98]

Dear Sam: –

I died laughing at your letter from Palm Springs. I am more convinced than ever that the sooner you can get out of that tie-up gracefully, and the sooner you can stop kidding the Pope, the happier you will be. During all of your latter visits to me before I left, I felt that you had been drugged, and I think you owe it to everyone, especially Allen [Walker], to become your old delightful self again.

You ask me what I am doing. I continue to give small dinners in my little apartment here at the Waldorf. Last night, I had Charlie Chaplin and Harry Crocker* (Oona was ill),† the Bob Sherwoods‡ and the Bill Paleys;§ and we had a wonderful time, as Chaplin took the stage and went on and on. You would have liked it.

Tonight, Niki de Gunzberg¶ [sic] and I go to see the Balinese Dancers, who opened only last night.** The papers are full of rave notices.

By the way, Noel Coward's play†† for the Lunts is one of the biggest hits of his life, and they all believe that it will continue for quite a few years, but it opened last night in London to unanimous panning by the London critics.

---

* Harry Crocker (1893–1958) was a journalist for the *Los Angeles Examiner*, but earlier in his life he had appeared in a number of Hollywood films, including Charlie Chaplin's *The Circus* (1928). He was also Chaplin's assistant for a period.

† Charlie Chaplin's fourth wife.

‡ i.e. Mr and Mrs Robert Sherwood.

§ William S. Paley (1901–90) was the chief executive of CBS and one of Porter's closest friends. His wife, Barbara Cushing (1915–78), known as Babe, was a socialite and fashion icon who worked for *Vogue* for a period before her marriage.

¶ Baron Nicolas de Gunzburg (1904–81) was a French-born magazine editor of publications such as *Town and Country*, *Vogue* and *Harper's Bazaar*.

** A troupe of Balinese dancers played New York's Fulton Theatre from September 1952. John Martin in the *New York Times* described it as 'a perfectly beautiful show'. John Martin, 'Balinese Troupe Shows its Wares at the Fulton', *New York Times*, 17 September 1952, 34.

†† *Quadrille*, which opened in London on 12 September 1952 and played Broadway in 1955.

FROM LIMBO TO THE WRITING OF *CAN-CAN*, 1951–1952

The play, however, is so strong that it can survive and do beautifully.

Thank you so much for sending me the article from the New Yorker on the Saucers.[99] For some reason, I had missed it and shall read it with great interest over the week-end. I sent you Hedda Hopper's book.[100] It is entertaining. I also ordered for you, to be sent as soon as it comes out, Tallulah Bankhead's book.[101] I have an advance copy. It is synthetic trash and I believe Dick Maney* must have written most of it.

[Howard] Sturges and Brother Warren are both up with Linda, and I return on Friday, as usual.

Love,

[signed:] Cole

The next letter from Porter was written in acknowledgement of a present from Stark of *Hammond's Nature Atlas of America*, a hardcover atlas by E. L. Jordan, which contained 320 colour plates:

30 September 1952: Cole Porter to Sam Stark[102]

Dear Sam: –

Hammond's Nature Atlas of America just arrived. What a beauty! This will give me years of pleasure, and I thank you so much.

Also, I thank you for the clipping from your old pet, Durling.†

I just motored down from the country with [Howard] Sturges. Jean Feldman [Howard] was there with us too, and we had a lovely time, as Linda seemed slightly better. The leaves become more beautiful every week-end and I only wish that you were a free man so that you could hop on a plane and come to stay with us until we close the house.

Love,

[signed:] Cole

Although most of the score of *Can-Can* had been completed over the summer, the next letter shows that Burrows and Porter were still corresponding about it:

---

* The famous press agent, Richard Maney.
† Perhaps the film journalist E. V. Durling (1893–1957).

3 November 1952: Abe Burrows to Cole Porter[103]

Dear Cole:

Here are some possible content for the special material section of the "If You Loved Me Truly" sequence:

CLAUDINE

Dancing makes her happy.

Dancing makes her feel like a bird.

Dancing makes her feel like a queen.

Dancing makes her feel beautiful.

Dancing makes her feel loved.

BORIS

When a woman has a man she should think of nothing else but him.

Her career should be secondary to his.

She should be happy to die for him, if necessary.

She should be a sweetheart and a mother.

Other great artists' sweethearts have always looked after them.

Rembrandt's girl wasn't a dancer.

Beethoven's girl looked after him.

Dancing is not an art -- it is just something to do with your feet.

Boris can refer to Claudine as "My dear Mademoiselle Premiere Ballerina."

GABRIELLE AND/OR CELESTINE

She agrees with Claudine.

Maybe a girl can get famous and rich from dancing.

She can have a mansion with a chaise longue _and_ a bed.

Maybe a girl can meet rich men.

Maybe she can become a mistress of a member of the Ministry.

Maybe she can become attached to a handsome attache.

Maybe she can meet a banker, American or Swiss.

Maybe one can have a bathtub of one's own.

All the above male things can be used interchangeably for Boris or the Quatz' Arts boys and similar things can be used interchangeably by the girls except that Claudine is the only one who should not have lines about other men, etc.

I think it will be a good idea if the three other girls and the Quatz' Arts boys are brought into the song through the fact that they "butt in" on the discussion between Boris and Claudine.

I am enclosing the last section of Scene 3 which follows what you have and which leads up to the "If You Loved Me Truly" sequence. You will notice that the last two lines of dialogue establish the "you do not love me" business. I thought from here you would go into the special material argument, then into your verse and song, but the fact that the argument came out of the "you do not love me" construction means that your two lines of dialogue provide a headline which makes a solid unit out of the whole sequence.

I'll be home all day tomorrow, Tuesday. Will you call me as soon as you have a chance to digest this.

Best,

[unsigned]

The final letter of 1952 shows Porter bringing Stark up to date with his social life, though he also mentions that he is still working hard on *Can-Can*:

11 November 1952: Cole Porter to Sam* Stark[104]

Dear Sam: –

Mrs. [Madeline P.] Smith thanks you infinitely for the stickers which you sent to make her life easier,* and I add my gratitude.

Thank you for the clippings from your pet, Durling.*

Thank you very much for the vintage chart of French wines, with the calendar on the back.

I was distressed to hear the news about Paula Holmes and I shall write her a note at once.

You sound very happy indeed in your letter and this is, as you know, what I always want most for you. The only time I see red is when you let me know that you are not happy.

I am working very hard over every week-end, and leading a wild life in New York. I've taken up cocktail parties. I never thought that I should sink that low. Tonight, [Howard] Sturges, Helen Hull,† Fulco‡ and I go to the City Center Ballet, and we shall miss you.

---

* Perhaps E. V. Durling.

† Probably Helen Huntington Hull (1893–1976), arts patron, who was on the board of directors of the New York City Ballet.

‡ The Duke of Verdura.

Love to all the gang, and especially to Allen [Walker]. Tell Allen that I have sent a book to Stanley Musgrove, asking him to forward it to Allen after he has finished reading it. I believe it will interest Allen a great deal. It's [sic] title is <u>Look Down in Mercy</u>.*

Love,

[signed:] Cole

P.S. – Linda has a new neck piece of the four most beautiful and fattest sables I have ever seen, and it has made her radiant. After all it's the little things that count.

----

* I do. Cleverest and useful-est idea that has come my way in a long time. [signed:] M.P.S.†

---

* Walter Baxter's best-selling novel *Look Down in Mercy*, dealing with the experiences of a British army officer in Burma during World War II, was published in New York in 1951.

† Madeline P. Smith.

CHAPTER NINE

TWO LAST BROADWAY HITS, *CAN-CAN* AND *SILK STOCKINGS*, 1953–1954

The first two letters of 1953 address business matters regarding ASCAP royalties and a legal case (valued at $150 million) being developed by ASCAP composers led by Arthur Schwartz against an alleged radio-television-record label monopoly, including the licensing agency BMI:*

8 January 1953: Cole Porter to John Wharton[1]

Dear John: –

I enclose two pages from the anniversary issue of <u>Variety</u>.

1. Why doesn't Chappell mention Buxton Hill† in its list of publishing companies?
2. Is Irving Berlin also giving 5% of his ASCAP earnings to which I am asked to subscribe my 5%?

The reason I ask about this second item is not because I doubt your advice, but because more and more demands seem to be made upon me and I begin to worry about having adequate cash on hand in the future.

Best,

[signed:] Cole

---

* The $150 million anti-trust suit was announced on the front page of the *New York Times*. See Val Adams, 'Composers Sue for $150,000,000; Allege Radio-TV-Record Monopoly', *New York Times*, 10 November 1953, 1.

† Porter's publishing company, named after his Williamstown address.

15 January 1953: Arthur Schwartz to Cole Porter[2]

Dear Cole,

I want to thank you for your check. We are rapidly reaching our goal, and your contribution is a most substantial help.

Some day I'd like to tell you what we are doing. The conspiracy against all ASCAP writers is shocking.

Sincerely,
Arthur

In these matters, Porter was eager to be recompensed appropriately for his work, but equally he recognized the need to participate fully in issues affecting Broadway composers, of which he was one of the two or three most prominent. Nevertheless, business was not his milieu and a letter from Cy Feuer, regarding the actress Gwen Verdon's (ultimately successful) audition for *Can-Can*, must have been of much more interest to him: 'I have made arrangements for Gwen Verdon to fly into New York, arriving Saturday, the 24th. She'll be ready to audition for us on Sunday, the 25th, at the 46th Street Theatre at 3 o'clock. It was necessary to make this arrangement because Miss Verdon has to leave here Sunday night to be back at 20th Century Fox Monday morning. Will you please make arrangements to be at the theatre at that time.'[3] The correspondence of late January also suggests the possibility of a new musical. A letter from Fred Lounsberry to Porter of 28 January suggests that Lounsberry would produce and Norman Corwin* would direct and write the show, with a score by Porter. The titles mentioned are 'The Undecided Molecule'† and 'Descent of the Gods'.[4] Porter wrote to John Wharton to keep him informed:

---

* Screenwriter Norman Corwin's (1910–2011) work includes the screenplays for *The Blue Veil* (1951), *Lust for Life* (1956) and *The Story of Ruth* (1961). He was particularly active during the golden age of radio.

† Corwin's *The Undecided Molecule* was a fantasy radio play originally broadcast in 1945. See http://www.radiodramarevival.com/episode-173-norman-corwins-undecided-molecule/ (accessed 19 September 2018). *Descent of the Gods* had earlier been broadcast, again on radio, in 1941: https://www.oldtimeradiodownloads.com/drama/columbia-workshop/columbia-workshop-41-10-19-023-descent-of-the-gods (accessed 19 September 2018).

TWO LAST BROADWAY HITS, *CAN-CAN* AND *SILK STOCKINGS*, 1953–1954

30 January 1953: Cole Porter to John Wharton[5]

Dear John: –

When Fred Lounsberry was here last week and saw me in regard to his book on my lyrics, he asked me whether I would be interested in writing an original musical score for television, with a book by Norman Corwin, and with him (Lounsberry) and his partner, Ray Wander, as co-producers. I said that I would be interested.

By the copy of the letter which I have just received from him, copy of which I enclose, you will see how far he has gone. I simply want you to be au courant about all this.

Best,

[signed:] Cole

The following letter to Sam Stark summarizes Porter's activities over the Christmas period, including his continuing work on *Can-Can*, and also reveals a recent ailment:

31 January 1953: Cole Porter to Sam Stark[6]

Dear Sam: –

Thank you so much for your letter marked "Thursday".

The Christmas holidays were a riot of cocktail parties, dinners and wonderful balls. But, finally, the gods caught up with me and gave me a strange skin disease* which has now been solved, but which is maddening as it is an itch, due to iodine poisoning. Luckily, I am at least in the hands of a great dermatologist who found the secret of my trouble, and by persistent injections of arsenic I shall either get well or go to my grave.

I continue writing for the show.† It looks as if I should never finish. The dancers go into rehearsal on Feb. 16th, and everybody else a week later. Then, after four weeks, we open in Philadelphia for a month's run, and then to the critics of New

---

* McBrien, *Cole Porter* (338), cites a letter from Linda Porter to Bernard Berenson in which she reveals details of this: 'The Porters have started the New Year badly. Cole has some mysterious skin infection which itches constantly & almost drives him crazy . . . and I have been confined to my apartment for days with bursitis in my right arm (a new disease for me) and a rather alarming cough. I hope to get out for some air next week. I have so few activities that I miss them terribly when they are taken away.'

† *Can-Can*.

York. It looks as if I should come West during the last week of April and oh, how I shall welcome it. What a joy it will be to sit in my little back yard again by the pool. I have an added reason for longing for this, as somebody gave me a bird whistle for Christmas. By means of this whistle, I can imitate the songs of all the different birds and attract them to my side. The only thing left for me to do is to be converted into the Catholic church and become another Saint Francis of Assisi.*

It was grand to hear that your book is beginning to take shape and to please you. I don't agree with you that everybody else is bored with this book. I think it will be a "must", and I can't wait to buy a copy.

Love,

[signed:] Cole.

4 February 1953: Cole Porter to Sam Stark[7]

Dear Sam: –

The Reader's Encyclopedia just arrived, and I thank you very much indeed. It looks to me like an excellent reference book and I wouldn't think of letting Linda even touch it.

Forgive me if I don't write at length, but I am harassed with work. Everybody here is fine; in fact, Linda is so well that often I invite people to my sitting-room for dinner instead of to the Pavillon, so that Linda can dine with us – and its [sic] so much more pleasant thus.

We both send love.

[signed:] Cole

While being harassed to complete *Can-Can*, Porter also received an offer of a further (unknown) project, which did not prove tempting:

4 February 1953: Cole Porter to Robert Montgomery[8]

Dear Bob: –

I am returning to you the synopsis which Jack Hylton[†] asked me to read. It seems to me that it is beneath contempt.

Best

[unsigned]

---

* St Francis of Assisi (1181/2–1226), the patron saint of animals.
† Hylton was the producer of the London production of *Kiss Me, Kate*.

TWO LAST BROADWAY HITS, CAN-CAN AND SILK STOCKINGS, 1953–1954

Other matters had to be attended to as well. He received the first draft of the screenplay of *Kiss Me Kate* (the movie dropped the comma from the title) on 12 February in order to approve the addition of an opening scene in which Porter himself was depicted as a character. Then on 9 March he also received a request from RCA to have his own performance of 'You're the Top' included on an album to accompany a book called *Show Biz* by Abel Green and Joe Laurie.[9]

On 1 March, Sam Zolotow made an announcement in the *New York Times*:

> Acting on the entirely laudable theory that no one should permit Cole Porter to be idle for too long, the firm of Cy Feuer and Ernest Martin disclosed the other day that they had reached an agreement with Mr. Porter to compose a score for a musical to be offered sometime next season. Just what the subject will be, the gentlemen who sponsored "Where's Charley?" and "Guys and Dolls" would not say. It will, however, be modern in concept as compared with their currently rehearsing "Can-Can," which is set in the Paris of the Nineties and for which Mr. Porter provided the words and notes to a book by Abe Burrows . . . In any event, this is the schedule for Mr. Porter: He will, of course, be present hereabouts until the opening of "Can-Can" at the Shubert on April 23. Following that he heads for Hollywood to attend the filming of "Kiss Me, Kate," the musical he wrote with Bella and Samuel Spewack.* The chore completed, he will put on his composer's cap and begin picking out the melodies for the contemplated musical.[10]

Evidently Porter's relationship with Feuer and Martin was so strong that they already had further plans to work together, but first they had to see *Can-Can* through to its Broadway opening. Madeline P. Smith wrote ahead to Porter's preferred hotel in Philadelphia to ask them to make preparations for his visit:

---

* On 6 April 1953, Robert H. Montgomery informed Porter that instead of writing three additional songs for the film of *Kiss Me, Kate* (at $7,500 each), MGM would like to use 'From This Moment On' and would pay $7,500. Since the song was cut from *Out of This World*, there were no contractual obligations with producers or authors of that show. CPT, Correspondence 1953.

6 March 1953: Madeline P. Smith to Barclay Hotel, Philadelphia

ROOM SERVICE CAPTAIN(S)
　Mr Arthur Pieri ~~– or successor~~ (and associates)
　BARCLAY HOTEL
　Philadelphia, PA

Dear Sir: –

　Herewith enclosed is a list of Mr. Cole Porter's needs in his suite during his stay at the Barclay Hotel while his new show ("Can-Can") is playing in Philadelphia.

　He will greatly appreciate it if you will kindly see that these supplies are on hand at the time of his arrival: Tuesday, March 17th, 1953.

　Thanking you in anticipation of your usual excellent service,

　Yours very truly,

　[unsigned]

　Secretary to COLE PORTER

TO BE PUT IN <u>PANTRY</u> OF COLE PORTER'S SUITE
2 Ice buckets filled with ice cubes (to be put in bottom of ice box)
1 Dinner Table – (put in second bedroom)
1 breakfast table " " " "
1 breakfast bed tray
2 large serving trays
2 dozen linen napkins
6 coffee cups & saucers
6 dessert plates
6 fish plates
6 Dinner plates
6 bread & butter plates
6 finger bowls
6 demi-tasse cups & saucers
12 white wine glasses (long stems)
12 High ball glasses
12 cocktail glasses
6 old fashioned glasses
3 sherry wine glasses

TWO LAST BROADWAY HITS, *CAN-CAN* AND *SILK STOCKINGS*, 1953–1954

    10 dessert spoons
    10 coffee spoons
    10 dinner knives
    10 dinner forks
    10 fish forks
    6 butter knives
    6 serving spoons
    6 demi-tasse spoons
    10 glass tumblers
    6 cereal bowls
    10 Tall, slim beer glasses
    1 12-inch silver platter
    6 cordial liqueur glasses

In addition, Madeline Smith wrote to the Libros Apothecary in Philadelphia with a list of items to be placed in Porter's suite in time for his arrival:

    2 large bottles Witch Hazel
    3 Bromo Selzer Dispenser
    2 Large Eno Fruit Salts
    2 large Phillips Milk of Magnesia
    1 large Nivea Skin Oil
    2 1-lb Anhydrous Lanolin
    2 4-oz Noxema Shaving Cream
    6 Aromettes – assorted scents
    1 carton pocket Kleenex
    2 Tubes Toilet Lanolin
    ~~12 pkgs Dr. Scholl's Calous Pads – K 31~~
    1 Carter's Little Liver Powder
    2 Roger Gallet White Pomade
    1 Carton Gillette Red Razor Blades – 20 pkg. size
    1 pint Alcohol – 90% proof
    1 pint Hydrogen Peroxide
    2 Pkgs. EOETS
    1 4-oz Boric Acid Solution
    2 Small PRIVINE
    12 large KLEENEX

In the middle of the tryouts of *Can-Can,* Porter wrote to his friend Gerald Murphy to thank him for sending some records of the music of J. S. Bach, a reminder of Porter's interest in a range of musical genres. In return, he sent Murphy a copy of Bob Merrill's 'How Much Is That Doggie in the Window?' that had been released in January in a hit recording by Patti Page (it reached No. 1 in the charts):

Cole Porter to Gerald Murphy, 1 April 1953*

Dear Gerald: –

I played the Bach recordings over and over again. They are very beautiful. I also had great difficulty understanding what the crowd was singing when they sang "Tais-toi". Could they possibly have been addressing God? And, if so, why?

I am sending you, from Liberty Music Shop, the most popular record in the country, titled "Doggie in the Window". To me, this is the most repulsive song that has ever been written. Please send me your comment.

Love to you both,

[signed:] Cole

The first performance of *Can-Can* in Philadelphia at the Shubert Theatre took place on 23 March and Porter's initial reaction by telegram to Sam Stark was positive:

25 March 1953: Cole Porter to Sam Stark[11]

MANY THANKS FOR WIRE EVERYTHING IS GRAND LOVE=
    COLE=

In the event, the tryouts of *Can-Can* were extended, for reasons Porter later disclosed to his friend Jean Howard:

---

* Yale University, Beinecke Rare Book and Manuscript Library, shelfmark YCAL MSS 468 (TLS).

TWO LAST BROADWAY HITS, CAN-CAN AND SILK STOCKINGS, 1953–1954

9 April 1953: Cole Porter to Jean Howard[12]

Dearest Jean: –

Thank you for your letter dated "Sunday" – which Sunday?

Please plan to stay longer in California. At present, it looks as if I would hit the Coast around the 10th of May, as I believe Can-Can will be put off another week before opening in New York. We are going through constant re-writing in Philadelphia, and cutting. On the opening night in Philadelphia, the show was 45 minutes too long, and it is very tough to take 45 minutes out of a show and still have a show left. In any case, we are all working very well together and I am devoted to Abe Burrows and the two producers.

I took Linda out for a drive last Sunday, as it was such a glorious day here. I took her up to Harlem to see the Easter hats on parade, and suddenly she began to suffocate. I got her back here as soon as possible, and she went into her oxygen tent. By evening her temperature was three degrees over normal, and the nurses had to be called again, to be there around the clock. This is most discouraging for her as it looked as if she had entirely recovered two weeks ago, after having been seriously ill since February 1st. I wonder constantly at her great courage.

I have no idea why [Howard] Sturges hung up so suddenly when I called you the other night from Williamstown. Perhaps it was because I hadn't warned him that I was calling you and he was already too sleepy to make sense. He flew off to Switzerland last Sunday, to be met by Christos, who drove him immediately to Cannes. This proves once again what Linda and I have always maintained, which is that he hates Paris and always devises some means of being elsewhere.

I pine to see you and I do hope that when I arrive you will give me a little of your precious time.

My love to you both,

Your fan,

[signed:] Cole

Despite the problems with the length of the show, it contained several hits, including 'I Love Paris,' 'C'est Magnifique' and 'It's All Right With Me'. As always, Stark requested copies of the sheet music for his collection from Porter, who wrote back, teasing him about it:

7 April 1953: Cole Porter to Sam Stark[13]

Dear Sam: –

Your gay little letter of March 31st arrived and it was nice to hear from you. I have notified Dr. Sirmay, at Chappell's, to send you the sheet music. I have already sent this music to several people, and I hesitated to send it to you until you mentioned it, as I thought that probably by now you were only interested in Gregorian chants.

Love,

[signed:] Cole

While *Can-Can* was still undergoing changes, Porter also had to accept changes to some of his lyrics for the screen version of *Kiss Me, Kate* due to the censor's office:

10 April 1953: Saul Chaplin to Cole Porter[14]

Dear Cole Porter:

In the song WE OPEN IN VENICE, it was necessary to change the reference to L. B. Mayer. We are using the following lines:

"... A group of strolling players are we.

Shakespearean portrayers are we ..."

The rest of the lyrics remain intact.

In the song I HATE MEN, the censors objected to certain lines. We are using therefor: [sic]

"... I Hate Men.

They should be kept like piggies in a pen.

Don't wed a traveling salesman,

Though a tempting Tom he may be.

For on your wedding night he may be off to far Araby.

While he's away in Mandalay,

It's thee who'll have the baby.

Oh, I Hate Men.

"If Thou shouldst wed a businessman,

Be wary, oh, be wary.

He'll tell you he's detained in town on business necessary.

His business is the business with his pretty secretary.
Oh, I Hate Men..."

The above lyrics are acceptable to the censors. We will, of course, welcome any suggestions or improvements. [...]

13 April 1953: Cole Porter to Saul Chaplin[15]

Dear Mr. Saul Chaplin: –

Thank you for your letter of April 10, 1953, which contained the revision on the <u>Kiss Me, Kate</u> lyrics. I congratulate whoever did them, and I highly approve.

One day I want to give a big party and invite nothing but Censors, to find out how their minds work.

Yours

[unsigned]

Another aspect of the screen adaptation of *Kiss Me, Kate* was the decision to interpolate 'From This Moment On', which had been cut from *Out of This World* in 1950, into the score, rather than having Porter write three new songs (which had originally been agreed). John Wharton wrote to Porter to explain a hitch with the plan:

21 April 1953: John Wharton to Cole Porter[16]

Dear Cole:

I wanted to explain the following rather complicated matter to you in person, but Mrs. Smith says that you may not be in New York until next week. Consequently, I shall try to make it clear in this letter.

As you of course know, Metro has offered to pay you $7500 for the right to use "From This Moment On" in KISS ME KATE and terminate your obligation to write from one to three additional songs for the picture. Max Dreyfus feels that Buxton Hill should receive a synchronization fee of $2500 from Metro for this use. He has, I think, a legal right to ask for a synchronization fee.

However, Metro has taken the position that they will not pay any synchronization fee to Buxton Hill. They have also hinted that, if the $7500 is not accepted, they will stand on the contract and request you to write additional songs.

It seems to me that, in this situation, we can act in one of three ways:

1. We could refuse to permit the use of the song unless Metro pays the synchronization fee to Buxton Hill. If they are not willing to pay it, we would notify them that you are prepared to write the additional songs. At that point, Metro might break down and pay the synchronization fee, but, of course, we cannot be sure of that. You should weigh the adoption of this course of action against the inconvenience which would be caused to you if they did not back down and, instead, request you to write the additional songs. I am inclined to think that it is not worth the risk and do not recommend this course.

2. We could ask Max not to demand a synchronization fee for Buxton Hill. Max has already offered to do this. I do not think it would be wise to accept Max's offer. As I said above, I think Max has a legal right to ask this fee and I don't think we should put ourselves in the position of asking him to do you a monetary favor. I want Max to feel that you grant whatever favors are to be granted.

3. The third alternative is to accept $7500 as full payment, with the provision that $5,000 is to be paid directly to you and $2500 is to be paid as a synchronization fee to Buxton Hill. I know that at first glance it appears that you would lose $2500 under this plan. Actually, however, the loss is insignificant and, indeed, there may even be some minor tax advantages in diverting $2500 of the income to Buxton Hill. Of the $2500 synchronization fee, you would receive $1250 as your royalty payment from Buxton Hill. Because of your 50% stock ownership of Buxton Hill you will ultimately get the benefit of one-half of the remaining $1250. Because corporation tax rates are lower than your highest bracket, you may actually receive more this way, after taxes, than in any other way.

In any event, there is no substantial difference in income (after taxes) between the second and third courses of action. The third does have the affirmative effect of making Max feel that you are a composer who stands by him and, hence, one he must always do <u>his</u> best for. For this reason, I suggest that we adopt it.

I will be interested to hear your reaction to this above. I hope I have made the entire situation clear to you, but if I have not, please call me.

Sincerely,
[unsigned]
John F. Wharton.

The matter was resolved on 5 May.[17] Porter had obviously not received this message when he wrote the following to Wharton; the mention of a revival of *Anything Goes* is interesting because of Porter's objection to having a director-choreographer (Jerome Robbins, of Rodgers and Hammerstein's *The King and I*) in charge, after his bad experience on *Out of This World* with Agnes de Mille:

24 April 1953: Cole Porter to John Wharton[18]

Dear John: –

Will you please get hold of the April 22nd issue of VARIETY. Turn to page 56, right upper corner, Show Finances, Call Me Madam. This illustrates the profit distribution on Call Me Madam, and you will note that Irving Berlin gets a certain profit distribution. Why can't I get the same thing with future shows?

The only tie-up I don't like in the Anything Goes revival is the idea of having Jerome Robbins as a director. If I were you, I should talk with Russel Crouse and Howard Lindsay regarding this also. I don't believe any dance director is capable of directing a whole show, especially after my fatal experience with Agnes de Mille.*

Please tell Bob Montgomery that I received his check for $214.28 from the Haresfoot Club† of the University of Wisconsin.

Best regards,
[unsigned]

In preparation for the premiere of *Can-Can* on Broadway, Porter invited several of his old friends, including Elsa Maxwell:

---

* A reference to de Mille's disastrous direction of *Out of This World*.
† A drama society that ran for sixty-five years, closing in 1964.

THE LETTERS OF COLE PORTER

24 April 1953: Cole Porter to Elsa Maxwell[19]

Dear Elsa: –

Do you want to go with me to the Opening of Can-Can May 7th?

Leave word with my secretary, Mrs. Madeline Smith, Apt. 41-C, Waldorf Towers.

I have also asked my cousins, Omar and Josephine Cole, Helen and Lytle Hull, Countess di Zoppola, Millicent Hearst, Duc di Verdura and Baron de Gunzburg.

I hope you can, and if "Yes", please be at my apartment – 41C – at 6:30 for a snack. The curtain will go up promptly at 7:30.

Love,
COLE

On 4 May 1953, Porter's secretary Madeline P. Smith wrote to Sam Stark with advance clippings of *Can-Can* and commented: 'On Thursday, this week, the SHOW GOES ON, and we are agog with excitement over it.'[20] Meanwhile, Porter was preparing to fly straight to California after the opening of the show:

[May 1953]: Cole Porter to Sam Stark[21]

DELIGHTED TO DINE WITH YOU PERINOS* MONDAY MAY ELEVENTH[.] MAY I BRING ALONG EITH[ER] ROBERT [RAISON?] OR STANLEY [MUSGROVE]? LOVE=COLE=

[May 1953]: Cole Porter to Sam Stark[22]

PLEASE LET ME OFF DINING WITH YOU MONDAY NIGHT MAY ELEVENTH[.] I CANT [sic] FACE CAROUSEL[.]† I WILL CALL YOU WHEN I ARRIVW [SIC] AND WE CAN EASILY MAKE ANOTHER ENGAGEMENT[.] LOVE=COLE=

---

* A restaurant on Wilshire Boulevard in Los Angeles that opened in 1932. It closed in 1986 and was demolished in 2005.

† Rodgers and Hammerstein's *Carousel* (1945), which was enjoying a brief revival at City Center from 6 March to 27 June.

TWO LAST BROADWAY HITS, CAN-CAN AND SILK STOCKINGS, 1953–1954

Just before the opening of *Can-Can* on Broadway, the *New York Times* ran an extensive feature on the show. Seymour Peck's article contains some brief but revealing remarks from Porter: "'I hate to have the New York curtain go up,' he said. 'Then the show is on, and the whole thing's over for me.' Porter smiled a faintly melancholy smile. 'I lose a friend,' he said quietly."[23] The show opened on Broadway on 7 May. Porter reported the reception to Jean Howard:

8 May 1953: Cole Porter to Jean Howard[24]

DEAR JEANNIE SHOW WENT WONDERFULLY LAST NIGHT AND PUBLIC ATE IT UP[.] SOME NOTICES NOT GOOD ENOUGH BUT MAJORITY VERY NICE INDEED. LOVE=COLE=

Brooks Atkinson's review was a little dismissive of Porter's contribution: 'Nor is the score one of Mr. Porter's most original works, for there are some recognisable clichés in both the music and the lyrics. But the music is gayer than the book. Mr. Porter has composed it in several styles from good hurdy-gurdy music to Parisian balladeering, with some joyful part singing in the Arthur Sullivan style.'[25] Nevertheless, the score was well received by other reviewers and plans were made to record the songs:

13 May 1953: Cole Porter to Capitol Records, Inc.[26]

Gentlemen:

I am the author of the music and lyrics of the play CAN-CAN and I am advised that you have agreed to make a musical recording of the play with the original Broadway cast.

This will serve as my consent and permission to you to use and publicize my name, signature and likeness as composer and lyricist for advertising and trade purposes in connection with the said album, subject, however, to such billing provisions as are contained in my agreement with Feuer & Martin.

Very truly yours,
[signed:] Cole Porter
Cole Porter.

Although the album was released by his rivals Capitol rather than his company Columbia, Goddard Lieberson wrote to praise Porter's efforts: 'I just wanted to tell you that you have written a beautiful score "à la manière Français", with at least three lovely, and in my opinion, permanent songs. I think I have some experience in the matter of show-music. I do not think that the critics have. Some of the songs from "Can-Can" will be praised by them, nostalgically, several years hence when they will conveniently have forgotten what they once said.'[27] As ever, though, the show's greatest fan was Irving Berlin, Porter's most constant admirer among the Broadway community, who wrote the following flattering words after he finally saw the show in late July:

30 July 1953: Irving Berlin to Cole Porter[28]

Dear Cole:

Elizabeth (my youngest) and I went to see "Can-Can" last night and along with a packed house of satisfied customers, we loved it.

It's a swell show and I still say, to paraphrase an old bar-room ballad, "anything I can do, you can do better".*

Love,

[signed:] Irving

From within the production, too, there was enormous affection and admiration, as the following two letters from Burrows to Porter show:

5 June 1953: Abe Burrows to Cole Porter[29]

Dear Cole:

I had to write you today because I spent most of last night talking about you. I had dinner with Gar and Ruth Kanin.† We ate at a charming little bistro on the Left Bank. In Paris today "a charming little bistro" means a place where you can eat for less than 9,000 francs. Anyway, we spent a good deal of the evening

---

* A reference to 'Anything You Can Do' from Berlin's *Annie Get Your Gun* (1946).

† Writer and director Garson Kanin (1912–99) and actress Ruth Gordon (1896–1985) were a legendary theatrical and Hollywood couple.

TWO LAST BROADWAY HITS, CAN-CAN AND SILK STOCKINGS, 1953–1954

discussing you. It seems we all love you. This fact, of course, makes for pretty dull conversation because things never get interesting at the dinner table unless people are knocking someone, but we managed to have a good time.

We are going to stay here until June 10th and then we go back to London. We'll stay in London until June 30th and then we sail for home on the LIBERTE.*

As you may have heard, GUYS AND DOLLS went very well in London. Incidentally, thanks for your opening night wire. It was very thoughtful.

The reports I get on CAN-CAN sound very good and, of course, the Rodgers and Hammerstein notices† made ours sound wonderful. I'm still gathering together my thoughts on our show. It's interesting to be able to do it from a distance. I think about things that I did wrong, things that I did right, things that I left undone – but, all in all, I guess we all did the best we could. Doing a show is not unlike bringing up a child. The child develops a life of its own. The parents do their best but certain things remain immutable, and the child is what he is – cantankerous, attractive, disobedient, intelligent, annoying – but still your child. Anyway, now that it's over, it seems to me that it was a very happy experience, and it was wonderful working with you.

I will be here until June 10th and after that I can be reached at the Savoy in London. I'd love to hear from you. I hope you're well and happy. Let me know how "Kate"‡ is going.

Carin sends her love.

Love,

[signed:] Abe

6 June 1953: Abe Burrows to Cole Porter[30]

Dear Cole:

I wrote you yesterday. You must have the letter by now. In that letter I forgot something. What I forgot was to apologize for forgetting something else.

---

* The SS *Europa* was a high-speed German ocean liner that worked the transatlantic route. It was built in 1929 and renamed the SS *Liberté* in August 1950. The ship was scrapped in 1963.

† Rodgers and Hammerstein's *Me and Juliet* had opened to lukewarm reviews on 28 May 1953.

‡ A reference to MGM's film *Kiss Me Kate*.

I suddenly realized, to my horror, that, in the excitement of opening night and the madhouse preparations for my trip to Europe, I never really said anything to you about the magnificent painting you sent me. It was one of the greatest moments of my life. When the picture came and I unwrapped it, I just stared at it. I was numb. Nothing like that had ever happened to me. The thrill of having a beautiful work of art, the subject of which was personal to me. When I think of the trouble you must have gone to in order to arrange it and the thought that it took, I'm flabbergasted. Perhaps that's why it took me so long to really thank you properly for it. Sometimes, a gesture is so big and so great that the recipient unconsciously feels that there is no way he can say "Thanks" sufficiently. However, let's forget all these philosophical and psychological nuances and let's just say that I was a louse not to have thanked you sooner.

The weather has turned lovely in Paris. For a few days, it was cold and raining and miserable, but now it's warm and delightful. As I told you, we will be here until June 10th. On June 9th, we are attending Edward Molyneux'* first exhibition and we are looking forward to that.

I'll write you again from London.

Love,

[signed:] Abe

In June, Porter was in California, where he was involved in the filming of *Kiss Me Kate*. He wrote to John Wharton to share his feelings on it:

8 June 1953: Cole Porter to John Wharton[31]

Dear John:

Thank you a lot for your letter of June 5th. I am enjoying this place tremendously, what with the perfect weather and a lot of old friends.

KISS ME, KATE of Metro seems to be progressing quickly and from the rushes that I have seen I believe we can expect a good picture but, of course, that new economy move on everywhere might make the final results look a bit skimpy. To my regret, it is being done in wide screen, 3-D but they are also making a flat version which can be seen in theatres which do not have

---

* Edward Molyneux (1891–1974) was a British fashion designer.

the new equipment. The silence elsewhere on the great lot of MGM is a bit terrifying!
All my best.
Sincerely,
[signed:] Cole

Also in June, Porter sent his usual regular messages to the Starks, including two telegrams of thanks, the second of which is especially unusual:

10 June 1953: Cole Porter to Sam and Harriette Stark[32]

MANY MANY THANKS FOR THE MAGNIFICENT FLOWERS FOR THE GEMINI CARD AND FOR THE CLIPPINGS LOVE==COLE

[n.d.] 1953: Cole Porter to Sam and Harriette Stark[33]

DEAR HARRIETT [sic] AND SAM THE BEAUTIFUL TOILET SEAT ARRIVED AND I HAVE INSTALLED IT AT THE POOL IT WILL GIVE JOY TO MANY ALL MY GRATITUDE AND LOVE=COLE=

A further message from Saul Chaplin (of MGM's music department) shows Porter's participation in the adaptation of his score of *Kiss Me, Kate* for the screen:

18 June 1953: Saul Chaplin to Cole Porter[34]

Dear Cole Porter:
We tried to reach you by telephone yesterday, but found that you were out of town.
We are doing "Always True To You In My Fashion" as a duet between Bianca and Bill. Following are the lyrics:
[lyrics reproduced in letter]
Of course we shall welcome any suggestions, and will give you a call Friday.
[signed:] Sincerely,
Saul Chaplin

In the following letter to the singer George Byron (who married Jerome Kern's widow), Porter answers questions about the inspiration for eight of his songs:

30 June 1953: Cole Porter to George Byron[35]

Dear George:

Under separate cover, by Registered mail, I return the sheet music which you so kindly sent to me. The following are the stories which I can remember concerning the numbers included, and most of these stories are very dull.

    1. <u>HOT HOUSE ROSE</u>. Fanny Brice visited Venice in 1926, when my wife and I were living in the Palazzo Rezzonico. At this time in my life I had given up all hope of ever being successful on Broadway and had taken up painting but Fannie, [sic] whom we grew to know very well, asked me to write a song for her. This was the reason for HOT HOUSE ROSE. When I finished it I invited her to the Rezzonico to hear it and afterwards she always told friends how wonderfully incongruous it was, that I should have demonstrated to her this song about a poor little factory girl as she sat beside me while I sang and played it to her on a grand piano that looked lost in our ballroom, whose walls were entirely decorated by Tiepolo paintings and was so big that if we gave a Ball for less than one thousand people in this room they seemed to be entirely lost. She never sang the song.

    2. <u>IT'S BAD FOR ME</u>. This I wrote for Gertrude Lawrence. The name of the show was Nymph Errant; book by Romney Brent. I did the music and lyrics and it was produced by C. B. Cochran in 1933 in London but never played New York, although it was a great success. Gertie sang this song in a train compartment to a Parisian producer who had made her acquaintance when she boarded the train in Zurich, on her way to England from a Swiss Ladies Finishing School. Gertie was supposed to have reached home by June 20th. She did reach home June 20th but a year later, due to the advice that she received from her Science teacher, who sang to all the girls as they were graduating the song, Experiment.

    3. <u>EXPERIMENT</u>. This has been explained above.

TWO LAST BROADWAY HITS, CAN-CAN AND SILK STOCKINGS, 1953–1954

4. GIVE HIM THE OO LA LA. This song was written at the last moment in Boston during the tryout of DU BARRY WAS A LADY, when we all suddenly realized that Ethel Merman didn't have quite enough material, as she was so great in this show. This show was also interesting for the fact that it was the first time Betty Grable played Broadway, and she made an instantaneous hit.

5. AFTER YOU. I shall always be grateful to AFTER YOU because I had been engaged by Dwight Wiman for Gay Divorce. Our great hope was to persuade Fred Astaire to play the lead. We were living in Paris at the time and I asked Fred over to the house to hear what I had written so far. Once I had played AFTER YOU he decided to do the show.

6. LOOKING AT YOU. I wrote LOOKING AT YOU for Clifton Webb, when I was doing a review at Les Ambassadeurs in Paris in 1927. Clifton did it so well that in 1929 I put it in the score of WAKE UP AND DREAM in London, where it was sung by Sonny Hale. Later, when Jack Buchanan starred in WAKE UP AND DREAM on Broadway he sang this song.

7. OURS. I wrote OURS for the motion picture BORN TO DANCE in 1936. It was thrown out. I put it in the score of RED, HOT AND BLUE, a Broadway show starring Ethel Merman, Jimmy Durante and Bob Hope. It was thrown out.

8. WALTZ DOWN THE AISLE. I wrote WALTZ DOWN THE AISLE for a Broadway show named ANYTHING GOES. It was thrown out, so the next year I put it in the score of JUBILEE. It was thrown out.

Let me congratulate you on all three albums. I played the Kern Album and the Gershwin Album* over and over and they are delightful.

My best to you both.

Sincerely,

[unsigned]

In the middle of a positive period of work, with *Can-Can* set in for a long run and the *Kiss Me Kate* film in the middle of production, Porter wrote to his friend and copyist Dr Albert Sirmay and mentioned his next Broadway project:

---

* Both Byron's Gershwin and Kern albums were released on Atlantic Records in 1952.

9 July 1953: Cole Porter to Albert Sirmay[36]

Dear Doctor:

Thank you very much for your letter of June 30th. I don't like any of Mr. Kassern's French lyrics enough. If you think I should pay him something for his effort I should be delighted to do so and then, if later I change my mind and use the lyrics, I shall naturally pay him whatever he would ask. For the time being, however, get me out of this tactfully.

I don't see why you continue giving flattering offers to the people connected with Kismet* as Frank Loesser tells me that he is publishing the score.

In answer to your letter of July 3rd, regarding your bet that we would receive unanimously favorable notices for CAN-CAN. You simply use as a weapon one notice from Variety. This was made before the weekly magazines appeared with their blasts, so you will have to dine with me at Le Pavillon when I return and we shall discuss this matter in detail – over a big souffle. It does seem, however, as if the unfavorable notices have done little harm as Cy Feuer, who is here, assures me that we shall be sold out over the dog-days.

Keep this under your old Hungarian hat, but Cy came out to see me regarding doing a new show with him and Ernie [Martin], and brought along an excellent script written by George S. Kaufman and his wife.† It is based upon NINOTCHKA but it is much funnier, with an excellent love story. I have decided to do it so I go back into slavery on August 1st, scared but happy. Thank you very much for the new sheet music cover for MY HEART BELONGS TO DADDY.

Lots of love,

[signed:] Cole

Porter also mentioned the *Ninotchka* musical – based on the famous Greta Garbo film of 1939 – to his lawyer, John Wharton, who by now was

---

* Robert Wright (1914–2005) and George Forrest (1915–99) were the composer-lyricists of the forthcoming *Kismet* (1953).

† Kaufman's wife was Leueen MacGrath (1914–92), who played Clara Eynsford-Hill in the 1938 movie version of *Pygmalion*. With Kaufman, she wrote the unsuccessful plays *The Small Hours* (1951) and *Fancy Meeting You Again* (1952). They divorced in 1957.

TWO LAST BROADWAY HITS, CAN-CAN AND SILK STOCKINGS, 1953–1954

managing all his business affairs. The show would become *Silk Stockings* (1955). The letter furthermore discusses a possible revival of *Nymph Errant*, which had been produced in London by Charles Cochran in 1933:

9 July 1953: Cole Porter to John Wharton[37]

Dear John:

I enclose a letter from one of my dearest friends, L. C. Hanna, Jr. He was in my class in college and he is now a very big shot in Cleveland. Will you please look into the contents of his letter and answer him direct?

I don't see how you can possibly get all the rights to do this show,* without infinite work, and I wonder if it is worth it. As you probably remember, Charlie Cochran died about two years ago and I imagine his estate is in the hands of his wife, Evelyn, who has been drunk for years. In any case, try to answer Len Hanna as tactfully as possible.

Keep it under your hat, but it looks as if I was going to do a new show for Feuer and Martin. They have come up with an excellent script.

All my best.
Sincerely,
[signed:] Cole

Wharton replied in July to say that he believed the materials were lost.[38]

Also in mid-July Porter replied to Burrows's letters from June, because he had not had the writer's address while he was abroad. The most interesting part of his reply is his initial reaction to *Kiss Me Kate* on the screen (four months before its official release), with a mixture of feelings about the use of technology:

14 July 1953: Cole Porter to Abe Burrows[39]

Dear Abe:

I haven't written you before because I attempted to send you a birthday cable and the news came back that you had left your Paris hotel, leaving no forwarding address. I don't believe this.

---

* *Nymph Errant.*

Now that I know you are safe in New York again I want to thank you so much for the two great letters you sent me. Your paragraph in one letter, describing the show as having all the attributes of a child, is so true that I have put it in my scrapbook. In your other letter you wrote me how much you liked the painting by Vertes. I can't tell you how happy I am that it pleased you.

I have been watching KISS ME, KATE at Metro. Unfortunately, it has been shot in that silly 3D (how I hate those glasses!) and it has also been shot in "flat". In both versions there is a wide screen. Metro has a new color process called Ansco* which is very superior to Technicolor and the picture is extraordinarily beautiful to look at. I don't know the pace of the picture yet as there was [sic] always long pauses between each reel. The revelation of the picture, however, is the performance of Howard Keel,† who is an excellent Petruchio. He is everything that one would NOT expect – flamboyant and romantic. Also, his diction is perhaps even better than Alfred Drake's.

I spend a lot of time here going out in the evenings, and it is so much fun to loll in somebody's sitting room and see an unreleased picture every night – although I still think it is unfair to the picture to be plied with Martinies and New York Cut and then have all the lights go out.

Cy and Posey [Feuer] have been here and it was a joy to see them.

Isn't it nice that our little CAN-CAN is doing so well!

My love to you and Carin and, again, my gratitude for those two wonderful letters.

Love,

[signed:] Cole

In July, Noël Coward wrote to Porter to ask for permission to perform his own lyrics for 'Let's Do It' during his cabaret residency in Las Vegas. In his response Porter mentions Linda's health, which had only recently recovered from problems over the winter:

---

* Ansco color was originally a German process called Agfacolor. Although it was only used in Hollywood from the late 1940s, it was introduced in Germany in 1932.

† Howard Keel (1919–2004) was one of MGM's most beloved leading men and the star of films including *Annie Get Your Gun* (1950) and *Kismet* (1955).

TWO LAST BROADWAY HITS, CAN-CAN AND SILK STOCKINGS, 1953–1954

14 July 1953: Cole Porter to Noël Coward[40]

Dear Noley:

Thanks a lot for your letter of June 11th, explaining the lyrics of LET'S DO IT.

I hear nothing but great reports about your different efforts.

We are having a heat wave here and I am in a constant rage. The reason I always come to this place for the summer is to avoid the horror of our east coast.

Linda is at our house in the Berkshires and having a ball. After being seriously ill most of the winter she is entirely well again and it makes me so happy every time we talk on the telephone. Her guests now are Mainbocher* and his friend, Pollard. They stay through July and then Natascha [Wilson] and Nickie come up, so she is well taken care of while I gad about with the Goetzes.†

Love,

[signed:] Cole

At the end of June, the *New York Times* had revealed that Porter's mother left $551,550 in her estate, most of it to Cole.[41] It is noticeable that he complains of his finances much less often in the letters from 1953. Perhaps Porter's recent inheritance was behind his decision to raise his secretary's salary in July:

15 July 1953: Cole Porter to Madeline P. Smith[42]

Dear Mrs. Smith:

Ever since arriving here I have been conscious of doing you an injustice, as you do so much work for me while I am away. Therefore I have arranged with Ford Dixon today to send you your full salary, retrospective to the last half of May. You will be on full salary throughout the year and, if circumstances permit, we will continue this arrangement in the future but the time might arise when I could no longer afford this and would have to put you on half-salary again in my absence.

---

* Mainbocher (1890–1976) was a celebrated fashion designer. His long-time companion, Douglas Pollard, was a fashion artist.

† William and Edie Goetz.

Please send the Arthur Fiedler Boston Pops record of CAN-CAN* to all the original list. Each of these records should have an adaptor placed in it's [sic] center before sending. The company from whom you order these will understand what I mean.

Also, please send to me here one MGM album (33 speed) of THE BAND WAGON.† Send me two Jan August recordings of ALLEZ-VOUS EN.‡

Sincerely,

[signed:] Cole Porter

In the 1950s the nature of celebrity shifted with the expansion of television. At the same time, the mature Porter had started to realize, thanks to the guidance of Wharton and his colleagues, that his name was a brand that could be significantly commercialized. The next two letters show an approach, and Porter's uncertain response to it, from Old Angus scotch, who wanted to use his name in their advertising:

21 July 1953: Lawrence Fertig & Company to Cole Porter[43]

Dear Mr. Porter:

It is the most difficult thing in the world, I think, to come to an artist (and a sophisticated one at that!) with anything remotely resembling a business endeavor! But come to you I must for I have the conviction that you would be perfect for the following endeavor and will not, of course, be satisfied until I learn your pleasure.

One of this advertising agency's clients, the Old Angus scotch people, have a yearly campaign featuring four celebrities of various realms, celebrities who will have an appeal to the men who are ostensibly their audience – men who are metropolitan in ways, well-read, dignified in their behavior and who have reached a point in life where they can afford to enjoy the work of those celebrities. In the past, we have featured Bennett Cerf, Peter Arno, Ogden

---

* Issued by RCA Victor (ERA 151).

† The soundtrack to MGM's recent film of the same name, starring Fred Astaire (Porter's long-term friend).

‡ An EP of the song from *Can-Can* with pop singer Jan August accompanied by Richard Hayman and his Orchestra (Mercury 1-3084).

TWO LAST BROADWAY HITS, CAN-CAN AND SILK STOCKINGS, 1953–1954

Nash, Sir Cedric Hardwicke, Arthur Fiedler and Maurice Evans,* and I have just concluded successful negotiations for S. J. Perelman for this year's campaign. I would, of course, like to maintain this pattern, and, of course, enhance it. It is for this very reason that I come to you (as a matter of fact, it is with an enormous amount of restraint that I remain this objective – having the personal idolatry I do for your music!).

Our advertising is done almost entirely in The New Yorker, Time and Esquire magazines and we offer (other than a television set or like piece of furniture, or the client's product or a check in the amount of $500 – really more a gratuity than an enticement!) the opportunity of a credit line (in your case, I would imagine your record albums would be your choice) which would benefit by an audience of the width and kind of this campaign.

Would you be good enough to let me know what your decision is and if you should wish any other particulars, I shall be happy to oblige. I am enclosing a tear sheet of one of the past ads for your information.

Thank you for your courtesy.

Cordially yours,

[signed]

Patricia Bunker

23 July 1953: Cole Porter to Robert Montgomery[44]

Dear Bob:

Will you please look into the enclosed from the Lawrence Fertig Advertising agency? If, without much trouble, I could get $500.00 for the Runyan [sic] Cancer Fund for this ad it might be wise for me to do it. On the other hand, in the past I have received much more than this for lending my name and photograph to products and maybe it would be a bad precedent to come down suddenly to $500.00. As I remember, I received either $2,500.00 or $2,000.00. Whatever you decide will be O.K. with me.

Best regards,

Sincerely,

[signed:] Cole

---

* Bennett Cerf (1898–1971), founder of Random House publishing house; Peter Arno (1904–68), cartoonist; Ogden Nash (1902–71), American poet; Cedric Hardwicke (1893–1964), British actor; Arthur Fiedler (1894–1979), conductor of the Boston Pops; Maurice Evans (1901–89), British actor.

By early August, Porter was hard at work on the musical based on *Ninotchka*, which would eventually become *Silk Stockings*. The subject of the show had been announced in the *New York Times* on 26 July: '[The] department ferret now brings to light the fact that the musical Mr. Porter will do is "Ninotchka". George S. Kaufman and his wife, Leueen McGrath [sic], are well along in their task of fashioning the book based on Melchior Lengyel's* satire of Soviet life ... Probably only the basic idea will remain and, indeed, the title is bound to go the morning someone gets an inspiration either in the shower or while shaving.'[45] The following letter to Ernest Martin, co-producer of the show with Cy Feuer, suggests Porter was looking for material that he could use in the song 'Paris Loves Lovers':

5 August 1953: Cole Porter to Ernest Martin[46]

Dear Ernie:

Could you put your Research Department on the following:

Phrases, nouns, verbs, adjectives and adverbs which are most commonly used by Soviet Russia?

The first adjective that comes to my mind is "capitalistic". These phrases, etc., should be pro-communistic and anti-communistic.

Love to you and Pem Davenport.†

[signed:] Co e [sic]

Two weeks later, Porter had also drafted the song 'All of You', then titled 'Of You' in a letter to Cy Feuer:

21 August 1953: Cole Porter to Cy Feuer[47]

Dear Cy:

Please find enclosed the newest lyric to OF YOU, which I also consider the best. Please destroy the other two lyrics which you have. I have a series of substitute lines for this song which we can use in case the enclosed lyric doesn't apply.

---

* Melchior Lengyel (1880–1974), Hungarian writer.
† The musical director of *Kiss Me, Kate*.

TWO LAST BROADWAY HITS, CAN-CAN AND SILK STOCKINGS, 1953–1954

Tell Ernie [Martin] that his niece, Ann, came to lunch with me yesterday and has started the research on the current Russian cliches. I found her very attractive and as bright as a button. She explained that she had been employed by Ernie and you to do this work, so that I no longer felt embarrassed about asking for favors. Thank you both a lot for helping me in this research.

Haven't you a spare script of Ninotchka around that you could send to me? Even though it is not yet correct, by reading it over and over again I could perhaps get some good ideas.

All my best.

Sincerely,

[signed:] Cole

In August, Porter wrote a typically eclectic letter to Sam Stark, though he did not mention *Silk Stockings*. The comments on two other famous musicals – Rodgers and Hart's *Pal Joey* and Wright and Forrest's *Kismet* – are intriguing:

21 August 1953: Cole Porter to Sam Stark[48]

Dear Sammy:

Your charming letter, full of treasure, appeared and I thank you.

As for the Boston Pops recording* – throw it in the sea!

I have examined the photographs of you in detail and I will NOT take this alibi about your fatness keeping you from coming up for lunch one Sunday. Why don't you be honest and simply say that you don't <u>want</u> to come to lunch? You write that a cousin of Harriet's [sic] arrives on Sunday. Cousins of Harriet's [sic] are always arriving. How many are there?

I saw KISMET† last night and a lot of it is excellent. It is corn but, after all, you prefer corn. I don't think, however, you will like it as much as the Student Prince.‡

---

* The Arthur Fiedler recording mentioned above.

† Wright and Forrest's *Kismet* was in its pre-Broadway tryout on the West Coast.

‡ Romberg's *The Student Prince* (1924) was the quintessential Broadway operetta. The movie version, produced by MGM, opened in June 1954.

You cannot lure me to dine with you at Perino's on Tuesday, September first, and go to see Pal Joey* with you. I hate dining early and I hate Pal Joey, but I would love nothing better than to have you both come up and dine with me one night, without cousins. That is, if this is not too long a trek for you, since after dinner there is no way in which I could provide a Broadway production...

Love to you both.

Your former friend,

[signed:] Cole

Another project that came up at this time was a request from John C. Wilson, director of the original *Kiss Me, Kate* in 1948, to use some of Porter's trunk songs in a play:

13 August 1953: John C. Wilson to Cole Porter[49]

Dear, dear Cole --

This is again to thank you for your sweetness and hospitality to me in California but, secondarily, to bring to your attention another proposition for LIFE BY ME.

It was never my intention to make this into a musical comedy. I hoped to duplicate a sort of GAY DIVORCE without a chorus and even without (although I think they are in the script) ballet sequences. I think it ought to be a straight play as it was when it was written, with 6 or 8 or at the limit 10 interpolated numbers. I know that you are doing NINOTCHKA, but it occurred to me that you might have in the files a sufficient number of songs that you might permit me to use at my discretion, if you were not available, to integrate and interpolate into the script. There are two that I know about, for every good reason, which are naturals, and they are WE WILL NEVER BE YOUNGER and IT WAS GREAT FUN THE FIRST TIME.† There are probably

---

* The 1952 Broadway revival of *Pal Joey* went on tour after it closed in New York in April 1953.

† These songs had been cut from the score of *Kiss Me, Kate* before it opened on Broadway, but Wilson (as director) remembered them.

a great many others in your files which you could dig up and send to me without any necessity of creating new material. Will you give this matter serious consideration.

Let me emphasize again this is not to be a musical comedy but that if you could spare a series of songs that could be suited to the story line you could do NINOTCHKA as well, and without any additional effort, provide the musical background for what I believe is an intelligent and worthwhile script.

Natasha* had a wonderful week-end with Linda – says she is in fine form and they giggled and laughed their way through the week-end with great happiness all around.

My nicest memories of Hollywood are those I spent with you and I thank you again --

[unsigned]

Porter replied politely, implying he intended to help further down the line:

18 August 1953: Cole Porter to John C. Wilson[50]

Dear Jack:

Thanks for your letter of August 13, 1953.

I am at present making an album of all my songs that have been thrown out of productions in the past, so when i come east in the early part of October this album will be completed. If John Wharton agrees, we can look over the whole lot and find out if anything is suitable to you, but I can't give you the total number now as this is quite a job.

Love you to you both.

Your devoted

[signed:] Cole

Yet in a letter to John Wharton, Porter revealed that he was not at all keen on the prospect:

---

* Wilson's wife.

1 September 1953: Cole Porter to John Wharton[51]

Dear John:

Thank you for your letter of August 29, 1953, enclosing a nice, big check from KISS ME, KATE performances.

Regarding Jack Wilson and his idea of using old songs of mine for his show BIOGRAPHY, I have told him that I would talk it over with him when I arrive back in New York in the first week of October, but I don't like the idea of giving up all these old songs to him a bit, and I hope in some way you can take the rap and get me out of it. These old songs are awfully useful to keep, as now and then I should be able to throw some of them into different pictures.

It is very strange that neither Howard Seitz nor Bob Montgomery ever received my answer to your letter of July 14th, in which you made a suggestion for the re-draft of my will. I am sure I answered this letter immediately upon its receipt, asking that you not rush this re-draft but continue to clear all the difficulties before sending me out a copy to sign. I even went so far as to suggest that it be sent to Ed O'Conner, my attorney out here, and he has been waiting for it ever since.

Since you approve of the Lounsberry idea of putting my lyrics on cocktail napkins I also say ok by me.*

Irving Lazar will arrive shortly to talk to you about the new Metro contract. It looks as though it were definitely going through as even Dore Schary telephoned me a few days ago to say how enthusiastic he was about it and that he felt sure it could all be arranged financially.

I arrive in New York on the evening of Monday, October 5th. I would like to get up to Williamstown to be with Linda as quickly as possible so, unless there are very pressing matters, perhaps I could arrange to come down the following week to see you.

All my best, dear John, and I am so glad you had a good vacation.

Sincerely,

[signed:] Cole

---

* Porter's friend Fred Lounsberry had proposed this as another opportunity to commercialize the Porter brand.

TWO LAST BROADWAY HITS, *CAN-CAN* AND *SILK STOCKINGS*, 1953–1954

In his reply, Wharton promised to help Porter with Wilson's request, showing how invaluable his firm had become to managing his career at this time; a separate letter from around the same time reveals Robert Montgomery's attempts to retrieve the script and score of *Nymph Errant* from Charles B. Cochran's papers for a possible revival. Wharton's two letters below also mention another important project of this period that almost came to pass: an MGM film using Porter's back catalogue in the context of a new story, in the vein of *Singin' in the Rain* and *An American in Paris*. Eventually it would be called *Wonderland* and was abandoned before being shot, but in the initial stages it was referred to as the 'Porter Cavalcade':[52]

8 September 1953: John Wharton to Cole Porter[53]

Dear Cole:

Thanks for your nice letter of September 1st. I have written Jack Wilson the enclosed letter and will try to keep him as happy as possible when I next see him. By the way, Jack thought the only thing standing in the way was some kind of a record album which was being issued this fall. Is there such an album in process?

We have ransacked our files and could find no record of an answer to my letter of July 14. In any event, we are going ahead with the re-draft and you will hear from us shortly in this connection.

The most immediate matter involves a luncheon I had today with Howard Reinheimer.* Howard was under the impression that you had decided to cancel the Metro deal and to go into an arrangement for a Cole Porter Cavalcade picture with Feuer and Martin, Abe Burrows and Fred Astaire. Cy Feuer also called me about this just before I left town last weekend.

Howard Reinheimer seemed to think that the advantages of the proposed combination were so great that you should unquestionably give up the Metro deal. I told him that I was extremely dubious. In the first place, while there is great excitement about it now, either Feuer or Martin, or Abe Burrows, or Fred Astaire could easily become more interested in something else later on.

---

* The lawyer Howard Reinheimer (1899–1970). His clients included Rodgers and Hammerstein, Alan Jay Lerner and Moss Hart.

In the second place, even if they get to the point of signing contracts, they still have to make a deal with one of the coast studios and that could fall through.

In the third place, I do not, as yet, see where there are any <u>certain</u> great financial advantages to you. Howard says that he <u>thinks</u> there would be financial advantages but obviously could not guarantee them. His main point was that he thought it would be much more satisfactory for you to be a co-owner than simply to get a payment from Metro.

If there were no Metro deal in the wind, I would certainly want to explore Feuer and Martin's proposition, but to give up something which has reached the stage where even the Studio Head is telephoning you for what seems to be a nebulous hope is something I cannot recommend. In fact, I told Howard that I thought it possible that negotiations with Metro had gone so far that it would be extremely embarrassing not to pursue them to the finish. It is my opinion that we should pursue the Metro negotiations to the finish and consider the Feuer and Martin idea only if the terms offered by Metro turn out to be unsatisfactory in the end.

Of course, you must make the ultimate decision. I understand that Irving Lazar is planning to come to New York next week and if you really are thinking of cancelling the Metro deal, you should, of course, let him know immediately. Perhaps you would like to telephone me. I have to be in New Haven Wednesday night and Thursday but you can reach me any time on Friday.

Sincerely,
[unsigned]
John F. Wharton

12 September 1953: John Wharton to Cole Porter[54]

Dear Cole:

First let me clear up the mystery in my telegram. On Wednesday, Cy [Feuer] and Ernie [Martin] came to my office and assured me that if they could get the songs they needed, they could work out a deal to make this picture the first Cinerama* musical, – which would have tremendous publicity and a <u>really</u> good chance of capital gains. They were so insistent, and seemed

---

* A widescreen process.

so certain that the Metro deal was still entirely nebulous, that I said I would communicate with you further, and, as they wish to try to keep the Cinerama angle a secret, I said I would wire you and arrange to talk to you. Hence the somewhat mysterious wire, since they did not want the word Cinerama mentioned in a telegram. You very sensibly had Irving [Lazar] call me first and this was followed by a call from Ken MacKenna.* Ken gave me the full facts; I reported these to Cy and Ernie and told them they should accept them and drop any further talk or they might prejudice the NINOTCHKA† deal, for which the contracts have not yet been <u>signed</u>. They quickly agreed; I phoned Ken back, also told Irving that Cy and Ernie had misunderstood the facts about the status of the Metro deal, and I trust all is now back on the track.

A few other matters.

I hope to send you a complete copy of the new will before you leave, but I should much prefer to have it executed in New York. Maybe you can take twenty minutes for this on the day of your arrival, before you leave for Williamstown. Do you expect to come by plane or train?

On July 28, Bob Montgomery wrote you and enclosed three copies of a document to be signed and go to RCA-Victor in connection with the "Abel Green" album. Apparently you mislaid these. Will you look for them and if you find them, sign them and send them to me? If they are lost, let me know and I will send a new set.

I had a nice talk with Max [Dreyfus] about your Buxton Hill contract. He was in a very loquacious mood, – for Max. I asked him who was going to run Chappell when he passed out of the picture, and he smiled and said, "That's a very proper question, John. Other people, such as Dick and Oscar,‡ are asking it too. Well, this is a big business and I assure you somebody competent to run a big business will be here. We have a man in mind, now." I suggested, however, that we would prefer a shorter contract and he readily agreed, saying to make it two or three years as we chose.

---

* Kenneth MacKenna (1899–1962) was an actor, director, patron of the arts, and story editor and department head at MGM. He was the brother of Jo Mielziner, who designed *Can-Can*. His final movie appearance was as Judge Kenneth Norris in *Judgment at Nuremberg* (1962).

† The *Ninotchka* deal was presumably the rights to turn the movie *Ninotchka* into a stage musical – an unusual reversal of the normal situation, since films were not generally adapted into Broadway shows in this period.

‡ Richard Rodgers and Oscar Hammerstein II.

I recommend that you let me tell Max now that we will renew for two years. At the end of that period we should have a clearer preview of the future. Moreover, if we ever do decide to look elsewhere, I would be dead against it at a time when you are about to start work on a new score.

Bob Montgomery, who got no vacation last year, is off to Europe for five weeks. I have to be in Chicago most of the week of September 20th, but otherwise expect to be at the office regularly. In Chicago you can always reach me by calling Field Enterprises Inc., 211 West Wacker Drive, Randolph 6 8554.

Looking forward to seeing you in October I am,

As always,

[unsigned]

John F. Wharton

As Wharton hints, Feuer and Martin were enthusiastic to move forward with *Silk Stockings* as soon as possible, but Porter felt that it was unrealistic and unwise to rush ahead:

3 September 1953: Cole Porter to Cy Feuer[55]

Dear Cy:

Thank you for your letter of September 1st, 1953. I am very glad to hear that the weekend with the Kaufmans* was successful and await the detailed results with impatience!

With regard to bending every effort to get the show into rehearsal on February 1st, I don't see how we can possibly do a decent job in that short a time.

I arrive in New York Monday evening, Octob er [sic] 5th. I can't come earlier than that because I have to be in Indiana on Tuesday, Septemb er [sic] 29th, to sign a lot of papers about my mother's estate. Both the family lawyer and my cousin, who has a great deal to do with my affairs, will be away on vacation until that date.

On arrival in New York I should like to get up to the country and be with Linda as quickly and as much as possible, as she closes the Williamstown big

---

* George S. Kaufman and his wife Leueen MacGrath, the writers of the book for *Silk Stockings*.

TWO LAST BROADWAY HITS, CAN-CAN AND SILK STOCKINGS, 1953–1954

house on October 23rd. Of course, from there I can always commute once a week to see you or Ernie regarding the new show.

Please keep me posted.

Best regards.

[signed:] Cole

As for the film based on his back catalogue – the *Cavalcade* – Porter pursued the idea with Feuer too:

19 September 1953: Cole Porter to Cy Feuer[56]

Dear Cy:

I enclose the list of tunes which Metro intends to use for my Cavalcade picture, but this is subject to change.

Best regards,

[signed:] Cole

LIST:
WHAT IS THIS THING CALLED LOVE
NIGHT AND DAY
I GET A KICK OUT OF YOU
BEGIN THE BEGUINE
RIDIN' HIGH
MY HEART BELONGS TO DADDY
FRIENDSHIP
DON'T FENCE ME IN
BLOW, GABRIEL, BLOW
WHY SHOULDN'T I?
YOU DO SOMETHING TO ME
LET'S DO IT
KATY WENT TO HAITI
DE LOVELY
JUST ONE OF THOSE THINGS

Three letters of 18 September (not reproduced here) to John Wharton from Irving Lazar, who acted on Porter's behalf in his Hollywood business, hint at other opportunities that came Porter's way. One letter contains an offer from 20th Century Fox to write a musical of *Daddy Long Legs* for Fred Astaire; they were prepared to wait for Porter. The other two letters ask whether Lazar can represent Porter in the negotiations to turn *Can-Can* into a movie, in which there was considerable interest.[57] But *Daddy Long Legs* went to Johnny Mercer (it was released in 1955), and it would be several years before *Can-Can* reached the screen. Porter's entire attention was on *Silk Stockings*, and the following letter to Sam Stark shows that not even a flattering article could prevent his nerves about the new musical:

26 September 1953: Cole Porter to Sam Stark[58]

Dear Sam:

Thanks a lot for the clipping, which would have given me a rather swelled head except that I have started work on a new show and, as usual, am scared to death.

Forgive me for not having called you but I have been racing around so in the daytime and going out every night to dinner.

I am off for the east Monday.

Love to all,

[signed:] Cole

On 5 November, MGM's *Kiss Me Kate* opened at the Radio City Music Hall. Bosley Crother's enthusiastic review for the *New York Times* described it as 'a beautifully staged, adroitly acted and really superbly sung affair – better, indeed, if one may say so, than the same frolic was on the stage'.[59] The same month, Porter instructed his lawyers to write to Sam and Bella Spewack to object to the introduction they had written to the published script of *Kiss Me, Kate*, no doubt scheduled to coincide with the opening of the movie. He was particularly unhappy about two references to his working process, which had been included without discussion with him. The Spewacks immediately wrote to him to say they were 'astonished' to receive the threatening letter and reassuring him that they meant no insult: 'Although we deprecate our own contribution to "Kiss Me, Kate" – as witness the references to the New Art Form – it seems to us

TWO LAST BROADWAY HITS, CAN-CAN AND SILK STOCKINGS, 1953–1954

that we pay full tribute to you and to your score. For example, we wrote "For both, (i.e., "Kiss Me, Kate" and "Leave It to Me") Cole Porter provided wonderful music and lyrics." ... We are distressed to hear that we have offended you. We have no desire to hurt you, even unwittingly."[60] Porter responded:

23 November 1953: Cole Porter to Sam and Bella Spewack[61]

Dear Sam and Bella: –

I have your letter of November 18, 1953. Naturally, I accept your word that you had no desire to hurt me. I still can't understand why you did not show me this material before it was published.

I assume that you will instruct Knopf that no other edition of the book will be published without my approval of any reference to me.

Sincerely,

[signed:] Cole Porter

On 24 November, the Spewacks wrote again to confirm that they had instructed Knopf not to print further editions of the book without Porter's approval, but all further relations between them were strained.[62]

Throughout the autumn, Irving Lazar negotiated with MGM about the 'catalogue' movie they were to make. For example, in a letter of 2 October, the financial deal was laid out, including a list of songs they wanted to use,[63] and when there had been no progress by 1 December, Lazar gave MGM a deadline.[64] The deal was signed with the Arthur Freed Unit on 8 December for fifteen songs to be used and Porter agreed to write two new songs. He was to be paid $100,000 for the picture. He was not allowed to give another studio permission to make a catalogue movie, but he was allowed to sell the screen rights to a full stage musical or to write a new movie score.[65] The movie was announced in the *New York Times* as Gene Kelly's next project, with Betty Comden and Adolph Green to write the screenplay.[66] Vera-Ellen was later announced as Kelly's co-star.[67]

On 1 December, Porter wrote to Jean Howard, who had been ill, and brought her up to date on his plans for the coming days, which included spending time with royalty – another reminder of Porter's remarkable social position:

1 December 1953: Cole Porter to Jean Howard[68]

Dearest Jeanie:

Such a sweet letter arrived from you yesterday, and cheered us. I am so glad that things are better for you, but I realize that for a while you must have gone through hell.

Two days after Linda arrived in New York from Williamstown, she suddenly had a terrible pain in her back. This turned out to be a disc pressing upon the nerve, and not until this last week did we find anybody who could help her. He is an orthopedic specialist named Patterson, and he is sure that he can cure her. This is being done by exercises that will strengthen the muscles in her back. A woman comes and gives her these exercises daily. She is still in great pain, but at last she has hope. For a while I was very worried about her, but her come-back is delightful.

New York is hectic. This afternoon I go to Fulco's* private showing of his miniatures. I've seen most of them, and they are incredible in their dexterity. Tonight I dine with the Moss Harts. Tomorrow night I dine with Elsa [Maxwell] at the Metropolitan [Opera] and then see the new version of "Faust",† which sounds awfully interesting, as the period has been transposed to the 19th Century and Mephistopheles wears the tails. The King and Queen of Greece‡ will be there too, and afterwards we are invited to Millicent Hearst's§ new apartment to meet the King and Queen, at a small supper party. After that I go to a dance given by Irene Selznick¶ in honor of your friends Bill and Edie

---

* The Duke of Verdura.

† Peter Brook's production of Gounod's *Faust* opened on 16 November 1953, with a cast including Jussi Björling and Victoria de los Ángeles. Pierre Monteux was the conductor: http://archives.metoperafamily.org/archives/scripts/cgiip.exe/WService=BibSpeed/full-cit.w?xCID=164000&limit=2500&xBranch=ALL&xsdate=&xedate=&theterm=1953-54&x-=0&xhomepath=&xhome= (accessed 4 July 2018).

‡ Paul of Greece (1901–64) was king from 1947 to his death. He married his wife, Frederica of Hanover (1917–81), in 1938.

§ Millicent Hearst (1882–1974) was the wife of media tycoon William Randolph Hearst (of the *New York Journal*), the inspiration for the title character in *Citizen Kane*. Millicent was a vaudeville performer earlier in her life. The pair divorced in 1951.

¶ Irene Selznick (1907–90) was the daughter of movie producer Louis B. Mayer. She produced the plays *A Streetcar Named Desire* (1947), *Bell, Book and Candle* (1950) and *The Chalk Garden* (1955) on Broadway.

TWO LAST BROADWAY HITS, CAN-CAN AND SILK STOCKINGS, 1953–1954

Goetz. The night after, I go to the opening of "Kismet",* and afterwards to a party given by Jolie Gabor† in honor of her three daughters.

There are several excellent shows to see, and I do hope when you hit New York you will be able to stay a bit.

Don't forget that we think of you constantly and we are so relieved that things are better for you. Lots of love to you and Charlie,‡

Your devoted,

[signed:] Cole

The following letter from 14 December relates the attempt to use Porter's songs without seeking advance permission:

14 December 1953: Robert Montgomery to Cole Porter[69]

Dear Cole:

On Friday afternoon CBS telephoned me, requesting permission to present on STUDIO ONE on Monday, December 21st, a story entitled "Cinderella 53". The script contains approximately ten of your songs, at least half of which are used dramatically, i.e., they are integrated into the script. In effect, they are presenting a Cole Porter musical.

It seems incredible to me that they should seek a clearance on this material one week before they plan to present the show. In any event, I am sending to you herewith the script. If you do not like it, we can kill it right away. If you do like the script, or if you have no active objection to their presenting the show, I will turn the matter over to Herman Starr (since most of the songs are Harms§ songs) to make a deal with CBS.

Can you telephone me as soon as you have read the script.

Sincerely yours,

[unsigned]

Robert H. Montgomery

---

* Wright and Forrest's *Kismet* opened on Broadway on 3 December.

† Jolie Gabor (1896–1997) was a Hungarian-born socialite, best remembered today as the mother of actresses Magda, Zsa Zsa and Eva. She owned a successful costume jewellery business.

‡ Although Jean Howard divorced Charles Feldman in 1948, the pair lived together until he died in 1968.

§ The music publishing house.

A pencil note on the bottom reads: 'Cole Porter telephoned on 12/15 to say that he had no objection to script being used on Studio One. RHM, Jnr.'*

Arthur Schwartz's continued efforts to bring legal action against BMI, which Porter had donated funds towards in January 1953, brought a further request for money in December:

23 December 1953: Cole Porter to Arthur Schwartz[70]

Dear Arthur: –

Thank you for your nice letter of Dec. 21, 1953. I am delighted that you feel that the Songwriters' suit against B.M.I.[71] is progressing well. I have forwarded your letter to John Wharton and will follow, naturally, whatever advice he gives me as to my sending the same check for the coming year.

All my best,
Sincerely,
[signed:] Cole

At the year's close, Porter wrote to Stark and Burrows to thank them for Christmas gifts:

30 December 1953: Cole Porter to Carin and Abe Burrows[72]

Dear Carin and Abe: –

A magnificent magnum of Bollinger '45 arrived from you at Christmas time, and I am very grateful. It will add greatly to my drinking future.

Love,
[signed:] Cole

31 December 1953: Cole Porter to Sam Stark[73]

Dear Sam: –

The beautiful <u>Can-Can</u> can filled with English walnuts – nuts – nuts† arrived and will provide me with sustenance for years. Thank you very much indeed.

---

* It was broadcast by CBS on 21 December 1953 as *Cinderella '53*.

† A joke in reference to the title song from *Can-Can*, in which Porter uses the phrase 'can can-can'.

And A HAPPY NEW YEAR to you both.
Your chum,
[signed:] Cole

He also wrote again to Jean Howard, conveying to her his travel plans and reporting on Linda's health:

31 December 1953: Cole Porter to Jean Howard[74]

Dearest Jeannie: –

This is to wish you a HAPPY NEW YEAR. [Howard] Sturges has probably written you that we have planned to arrive in St. Moritz March 2nd, and you will probably be in Cold Water Canyon. But if you could possibly wait over a bit and become our guide, we would be most grateful.

Linda's health varies so much from day to day that it is difficult to report about her. Her night nurse, however, who was absent for two weeks, has returned, and tells me that she finds that in that time Linda has lost ground. The most disturbing fact is that her heart has begun to act up. She has had two slight attacks, during which her pulse was much too high. To rectify this, her Doctor is giving her Digitalis. The sum-total of her maladies is so great that I wonder she has any courage left at all; and just before Christmas she broke a rib from coughing too hard.

My life here is as usual, – I work hard* in the daytime and go to a show or an opera or a party at night. Strangely enough, the new production of Tannhauser† at the Met. is the best presentation of it I have seen since I was a child, in Munich.

We think about you both and talk about you constantly; and, by the way, Linda and Sturges and I have decided that you write the best letters in the world. Where did you get this beautiful literary style?

Lots of love,
[signed:] Cole

---

* On *Silk Stockings*. The title of the show was announced on 20 November in the *New York Times*. See Sam Zolotow, "'Gimmick' Plotted by Producing Pair", *New York Times*, 20.

† Herbert Graf's new production of Wagner's *Tannhäuser* opened at the Metropolitan Opera on 26 December 1953, with a cast including Ramon Vinay, Astrid Varnay and George London, conducted by George Szell.

Early in the new year, Porter wrote to advise Sam Stark to avoid Rodgers and Hammerstein's latest musical – an interesting sign of his animosity towards the great Broadway writers:

5 January 1954: Cole Porter to Sam Stark[75]

Dear Sam: –

Thank you for your letter of December 28th. I suggest that you see Murray Anderson's ALMANAC* instead of that gloomy "Me and Juliet". The sketches are very funny.

Give me a ring when you get here if you have time.

Best,

[signed:] Cole

He also wrote to his regular Hollywood agent Irving Lazar to thank him for his efforts, perhaps in trying to get a film agreement for *Can-Can*:

19 January 1954: Cole Porter to Irving Lazar[76]

Dear Irving: –

Thank you for your letter of Jan. 13, 1954. Again I congratulate you on your patience in trying to put over that Metro deal for me.

I shall await any further news from you with great interest.

Best regards,

[signed:] Cole

On 17 February, the great composer and producer Jule Styne wrote to Porter to report on progress with a television version of *Anything Goes* that was to be aired on 1 March, starring the original Reno Sweeney, Ethel Merman: 'I am terribly excited, sitting here with Leland, only wishing that you were here to see what is going to be done with "Anything Goes" with Ethel, Bert Lahr, and Frank Sinatra. It's a pretty good score.' Styne wanted

---

* The revue *John Murray Anderson's Almanac* ran from 10 December 1953 to 26 June 1954. Rodgers and Hammerstein's *Me and Juliet* ran from 28 May 1953 to 3 April 1954 – a disappointing run compared to the team's earlier musicals together (e.g. the five-year run of *Oklahoma!* from 1943).

permission to add new lyrics for some of Porter's songs for use in the commercial breaks so that other music would not be heard in the middle of the show.[77] Initially Porter was willing to allow this but changed his mind.[78] Nonetheless, Styne's production of the show was a triumph, with one reviewer commenting: 'To hear Miss Merman run through "You're The Top," "I Get A Kick Out of You," "Blow, Gabriel, Blow" and the title song was to have the best in Broadway musicals right in the home.'[79]

Porter wrote to Sam Stark in late February with his usual miscellany of topics:

26 February 1954: Cole Porter to Sam Stark[80]

Dear Sam: –

Thanks for your letter dated "St. Valentine's Day". Do you realize that there were two St. Valentines?

Thank you for the book by Aldous Huxley, "The Doors of Perception".* I had already read it, so I shall give the copy you sent to me to the Old Sailors Home.

As for the wine, "Camp Vallon", try the following man: E. Des Baillets, 2008 Whitney Avenue, Hollywood 28; Telephone, Hollywood 4-5098. I believe that we used to get that wine from him. In any case, he is the best man I know for all wines, as he really knows about them. Don't forget the delicious white wine from the River Loire, "Sancerre". It is very light and very dry.

I arrive on the Coast during the second week in April.

Love to you both,

[signed:] Cole

In March, Porter flew to Switzerland, staying at the Badrutt's Palace Hotel, where he encountered the actress Paulette Goddard (1910–90) and her future husband, the German novelist Erich Maria Remarque (1898–1970) of *All Quiet on the Western Front* (1928) fame:

---

* The book (New York, 1954) details Huxley's (1894–1963) taking the psychedelic drug mescaline in May 1953.

15 March 1954: Cole Porter to Paulette Goddard[81]

Dear Paulette – you were sweet to send the charming carnations. They do a lot toward neutralizing the horror of this early Badruttian sitting-room.

We missed you + Eric in the grill tonight. Your table was occupied by a dull-looking gentleman + a lady who looked like quite a good horse.

Otherwise the grill was empty as the Cadoval-Niarkos* [sic] gang was throwing a big dinner in the bowling alley. This same gang danced until 9 A.M. this morning when the orchestra left as it's [sic] contract with the hotel was over. Cadoval + Niarkos [sic] caught them at the Italian frontier + bought [sic] the orchestra back to stay on until the gang collapsed.

Don't forget, when you hit N.Y., I live in those li'l ole Waldorf Towers.

It was a joy seeing you both + Mr. Sturges + I send you our love.

Cole No-Mind.

Porter planned to return to California in April to resume work on *Silk Stockings*:

22 March 1954: Cole Porter to Sam Stark[82]

Dear Sam: –

The wonderful "Southern Artichoke Relish" which you sent Linda must have found an artichoke in the East – as it never arrived. I look forward to my own wonderful souvenir "Artichoke Relish", which you say will be waiting for me in the wilds of Rockingham.†

Why did you send me the enclosed clipping with the ring around "Hey, nonny, nonny?"

I hit the Coast on the night of April 6th, and I hope that during the Summer, in spite of the fact that I am a good hard-shelled Baptist, you won't treat me like a leper.

Love to all,

[signed:] Cole

---

* A reference to the Portuguese Duke of Cadaval and the Greek shipping Niarchos family. Porter later went on two cruises on Stavros Niarchos's boat.

† Porter's house in California.

TWO LAST BROADWAY HITS, *CAN-CAN* AND *SILK STOCKINGS*, 1953–1954

Porter also wrote to the choreographer Jerome Robbins to say he was pleased that Robbins had been put in charge of the dances of *Silk Stockings*:

26 March 1954: Cole Porter to Jerome Robbins*[83]

Dear Jerry: –

One of the nicest things that happened to me while I was abroad was the cable from Cy Feuer telling me you would be with us on SILK STOCKINGS. I can't tell you how happy I am about this.

Please look me up when you come to the Coast. My address is 416 No. Rockingham Ave., Los Angeles 49, California; and my telephone (it is private, God knows why) is Arizona 9-3246.

All my best wishes to you on your present venture,†

[signed:] Cole

In the event, Robbins was replaced by Eugene Loring,‡ but according to Deborah Jowitt, he came in to help with the show during its troubled tryouts in early 1955.[84]

Porter often shared his music with other composers and was delighted when they did the same. The following letter to Noël Coward thanks the British songwriter for some recent sheet music:

29 March 1954: Cole Porter to Noël Coward[85]

Dear Noley: –

Four numbers from AFTER THE BALL§ appeared. They have given me great pleasure, and I congratulate you on your beautiful job.

It seems to me that you have two new standards in Sweet Day and I Knew That You Would Be My Love.

---

* Jerome Robbins (1918–98) was one of the most prolific directors and choreographers of the twentieth century, both on Broadway and in the ballet world.

† *Peter Pan*.

‡ Eugene Loring (1911–82), choreographer for Broadway and especially Hollywood, whose films included *Funny Face* (1957).

§ Coward's *After the Ball* was an adaptation of Oscar Wilde's *Lady Windermere's Fan*, set to open on 10 June 1954.

It was a joy to see you at Ina's.*

Linda must have been confused. She expected you for tea on the Friday before you left. She was all dressed up for you, and so disappointed that you didn't arrive. When you have time, please write her a little note.

Love,

[signed:] Cole

By early May, Silk Stockings was in the advanced stage of preparation, with actors Don Ameche[†] and Hildegard Neff[‡] signed to play the lead roles. Porter wrote to John Wharton about choosing the right record company for the cast album:

5 May 1954: Cole Porter to John Wharton[86]

Dear John:

Thank you for your note of March 20th, 1954, which you had sent to Switzerland.[§]

Thank you, also, for your letter of May 3rd, 1954. In regard to the show album of SILK STOCKINGS, it seems to me that if RCA will give us as good a deal as Capitol offered[,] RCA would be preferable, as there might be an angle by which we could get free advertisements through RCA tieups with NBC and NBT.[¶] I leave the whole matter, as from now on, in your hands.

I agree with you and the producers that it would be stupid to produce CAN CAN in London in the very near future and that it would definitely be wrong to arrange any other foreign productions before the British production.

---

* Ina Claire (1893–1985) was a prolific actress whose roles included the Grand Duchess in Ninotchka (1939), which became the basis of Porter's next musical, Silk Stockings.

† Don Ameche (1908–93) was a popular actor on film and radio. He won the Academy Award for Best Supporting Actor for Cocoon (1985).

‡ Hildegard Neff (1925–2002) was a German performer and writer who starred in over fifty films and also made records and wrote several volumes.

§ Porter's letter is addressed from California.

¶ The radio and television broadcasting arms of RCA.

TWO LAST BROADWAY HITS, CAN-CAN AND SILK STOCKINGS, 1953–1954

A man called Richard G. Hubler,* who has written articles on quite a lot of people for the Saturday Evening Post, is anxious to do one on me. He has talked to the head man of the Post, who now wants to know how much money I would ask for this. I told Hubler I must write to you for your advice. He asked me to remind you that this article would come out at about the time SILK STOCKINGS is opened in New York, just before, and would have great publicity value. Naturally, he had in mind that on account of this you should advise me to take less than would be expected. Please let me know about this.

Sincerely,

[signed:] Cole

On 8 May the MGM Porter cavalcade was postponed as Comden and Green had come up with the idea for the movie that became *It's Always Fair Weather* instead; Arthur Freed agreed they would return to the Porter project afterwards.[87] Then on 17 May, Porter wired Jean Howard to inform her of unexpected and alarming news:

17 May 1954: Cole Porter to Jean Howard[88]

DEAR JEANNIE AND CHARLIE[,] THANK HEAVEN I GOT HERE IN TIME BUT LINDA IS VERY CRITICALLY ILL[.] LOVE=COLE=

Linda's emphysema had taken a turn for the worse. Three days later, she died at home in her apartment at the Waldorf Towers, aged seventy:

20 May 1954: Cole Porter to Abe and Carin Burrows[89]

DEAR ABE AND CARIN[,] LINDA DIED TODAY. PLEASE NO FLOWERS: COLE

---

* Richard G. Hubler (1912–81) was a prolific biographer, known for ghostwriting Ronald Reagan's autobiography (1965). Of note, he published *The Cole Porter Story, as Told to Richard G. Hubler* (1965).

Linda's sudden death took her friends by surprise. The next few letters show how Porter's inner circle was supportive with their company, messages and gifts:

22 May 1954: Cole Porter to Sam and Harriette Stark[90]

Dear Sam and Hariette: – [sic]
 Thank you so much for your sympathy; I appreciate it deeply. Will see you soon.
 Love,
 [signed:] Cole

26 May 1954: Cole Porter to Harriette and Sam Stark[91]

Dear Harriet[te] and Sammy:
 Thank you for the three bottles of Neuchatel 1950, with the monkeys crawling over them. They are very beautiful!
 Love,
 [signed:] Cole

8 June 1954: Cole Porter to Jean Howard[92]

Dear Jean:
 Thank you so much for the lovely flowers you sent for Linda's burial.
 Love,
 [signed:] Cole

12 June 1954: Cole Porter to Hedda Hopper[93]

Dear Hedda:
 Thanks a lot for your letter of condolence. It did great good.
 Love always,
 [signed:] Cole

20 June 1954: Cole Porter to Hedda Hopper[94]

DEAR HEDDA YOU WERE SO NICE TO INVITE US TO YOUR DELIGHTFUL PARTY. WE HAD A GRAND TIME AND WE SEND YOU OUR LOVE=COLE PORTER AND HOWARD STURGES

26 June 1954: Cole Porter to Sam Stark[95]

Dear little Sam:

I am having such fun with the Rand McNally World Guide.* It makes for charming reading while waiting for people who are late!

My love to you both.

Your chum

[signed:] Cole

30 June 1954: Cole Porter to Harriette and Sam Stark[96]

Dear Harriet[te] and Sam:

The very interesting book, written by the English lady on her trip to Mexico, arrived this morning. I have already started it and it fascinates me. Thank you both so much.

Your devoted,

[signed:] Cole

Porter's business affairs had to continue through his bereavement, of course, and he mentioned Linda a little wistfully in the following letter to Wharton:

6 July 1954: Cole Porter to John Wharton[97]

Dear John:

Thank you for your detailed letter concerning reinvestments which you want to make on my stocks and bonds. When you arrive here you will have

---

* Rand McNally's *World Guide* was published in 1953. It was arranged by continent and included excerpts from the *Columbia Lippincott Gazetteer of the World*.

to give me a little time and try to explain all of this, as I understand none of it! Perhaps, also, I should take lessons when I get back to New York so that I won't be such an idiot regarding my own estate.

I am ashamed – when I think of Linda, who was taught very carefully by John J. Milburn so that she knew exactly what she owned and why constant changes were made in her investments.

Sincerely,

[signed:] Cole

P.S. I enclose a letter from Fred Lounsberry. I have wired him that I am forwarding this letter to you and you will advise him your decision as to his "Gillettes do it" idea.*

Stark continued to keep Porter updated on the latest books and gossip in July and August:

16 July 1954: Cole Porter to Sam Stark[98]

Dear Sam:

You were very thoughtful to send me word of the new Britannica World Language Dictionary. I had already ordered it, but the title I asked for was incorrect, so now I shall get it very shortly from Mrs. Smith – in spite of the fact that I have no desire at all to improve my Yiddish.

Love to you both.

[signed:] Cole

---

* On 4 July 1954, Fred Lounsberry had written to Cole Porter about the possible use of 'Let's Do It' with new words in a Gillette commercial (CPT, Correspondence 1954): 'Dear Cole, I am moving soon to Detroit, to enter advertising as a writer and idea man. There are many fine opportunities there, one of them being the chance to write advertising for Gillette razors ... This is a new slogan, quite clearly connected with one of your song titles. The idea is that however rough a shaving job may be ... Gillettes do it ... This would be embroidered into ... Gillettes do it, / So let's do it ... / Let's get Gillettes.'

TWO LAST BROADWAY HITS, CAN-CAN AND SILK STOCKINGS, 1953–1954

12 August 1954: Cole Porter to Sam Stark[99]

Dear Sam:

I was amused at your quoted note from Allen [Walker].* It is true that we knew Chato Elizaga† for years in Paris. He was a very attractive young man and we were all so fond of him. Later, when I went to Mexico with [Bill] Haines and Company he and his wife entertained us. I didn't like her at all. She seemed to feel very superior to Mexicans, as I believe she is partly Spanish. She is not your dish.

Love to you both.

[signed:] Cole

Silk Stockings was now expected to open on Broadway at the end of December, and work continued over the summer as the cast was slowly assembled.[100] Meanwhile, Cy Feuer and Ernest Martin had opened up offers for Hollywood to buy the screen rights to Can-Can for $750,000, but nobody came forward.[101] Other business matters, including a television adaptation of Panama Hattie with Ethel Merman, are discussed in the next letter to John Wharton:

24 August 1954: Cole Porter to John Wharton[102]

Dear John:

I received two letters on August 19th, one from Bob Montgomery, which I hereby acknowledge.

In regard to Mr. Roger Pryor and his desire to have my approval to use WUNDERBAR to exploit a food product, I have forwarded his request to Max Dreyfus, plus the recording which he sent me, suggesting to Max that I disapproved of this highly but if Max wants it very much I will agree.

I enclose the four signed copies of the contract for televising PANAMA HATTIE.

Best regards.

Sincerely,

[signed:] Cole

---

* Stark's former partner.

† Chato Elizaga (dates unknown) was at one time engaged to the soprano Grace Moore. He later married the Spanish movie actress María Luisa Pérez-Caballero Moltó (1923–95).

To his friend and former collaborator on *Jubilee*, Moss Hart, Porter wrote the following letter, mentioning Hart's recent heart attack:

25 August 1954: Cole Porter to Moss Hart[103]

Dear Moss:

I was so distressed to hear about the suffering you have been through for much too long and it was reassuring to hear from Kitty [Carlisle Hart] that you are better now and will go home shortly.

In spite of having two producers* here, constantly on my neck, I have managed to go out a great deal this summer and see all of your friends. Last Sunday, for instance, I went to a party which Jimmy McHugh† gave to unveil Louella Parsons's‡ new face. Louella just returned from London, where Dr. Gillis did the job. Dr. Gillis did a very bad job indeed, as the face seems quite the same while the neck, which used to be rather full and nice, looks now like the Duchess of Windsor's.

You remember that in Hollywood people only give dinners <u>for</u> someone. Therefore, there is a great onslaught of them next week when Jean Vanderbilt arrives to stay with the Luther Davises.§ When they first arrived the constant menace was to meet "the Rodgers and Hammersteins" but since they stayed a bit no one entertains for them at all and it is rather sad.

I have seen a great deal of Edie and Bill [Goetz] this summer and my new discoveries, Jack Pressman and Claudette [Colbert],¶ and I love all four of them dearly.

---

* Feuer and Martin.

† Jimmy McHugh (1894–1969) was the composer of over 500 popular songs, including 'I Can't Give You Anything But Love' and 'On the Sunny Side of the Street'.

‡ Louella Parsons (1881–1972) was a pioneering early movie columnist, known as the 'Queen of Hollywood'.

§ Writer Luther Davis's (1916–2008) work included the book for *Kismet* (1953), for which he won a Tony Award in 1954.

¶ Claudette Colbert (1903–96) was a major Hollywood star, with appearances including *It Happened One Night* (1934), for which she won an Academy Award. She was married for thirty-three years to Dr Joel Pressman, a surgeon at UCLA.

I am the only man in town who hasn't seen A STAR IS BORN* but I congratulate you heartily because everybody says it is terrific and that your script is a thing of beauty and a joy forever.

I arrive in New York on the night of Labor Day, September 6th, and until I go into rehearsal on October 18th I shall be commuting between New York and Williamstown, closing the big house – which is a major operation.†

Silk Stockings has a fine script and it seems to me that I have done a good job on the music and lyrics, although one never knows. Certainly it has been a stimulating job and I rather look forward to that strange existence that one leads in Philadelphia for a month after an opening.

Lots of love to you and Kitty and I do hope you are better, dear Moss.

Your devoted

[signed:] Cole

P. S. Irving Berlin called me up this morning and talked to me for half an hour, telling me how GREAT the pictures White Christmas and No Business Like Show Business are.‡ His final line was "Cole, I only called you to tell you I love you".

While working, Porter continued to keep up to date with the latest musicals, such as MGM's *Seven Brides for Seven Brothers*, which was produced by Jack Cummings (who had also produced *Kiss Me Kate* on the screen):

14 September 1954: Cole Porter to Jack Cummings[104]

DEAR JACK[,] I SAW YOUR GREAT JOB SEVEN BRIDES LAST NIGHT AT A PACKED RADIO CITY. ALL MY CONGRATULATIONS=COLE PORTER=

A further brief message to Sam Stark comments on a recent fire at Perino's restaurant, a favourite of Porter's in California:§

---

* *A Star is Born*, Judy Garland's most famous post-MGM film, had a screenplay by Moss Hart.

† Porter planned to close up and destroy Linda's house and move his cottage from its original plot in the grounds into the space left by her house.

‡ Berlin's latest movies, *White Christmas* and *There's No Business Like Show Business*, were both released in 1954.

§ The fire took place on 10 September 1954. See https://calisphere.org/item/3642800c3431e31f8c561f6918778e5d (accessed 4 July 2018) for an image.

17 September 1954: Cole Porter to Sam Stark[105]

Dear Sammie: –

Thank you a lot for sending me the clipping about the Perino fire. I am distressed for him.

Love to you both,

[signed:] Cole

He also attended the opening night of *Reclining Figure*, a new play by Harry Kurnitz that Abe Burrows had directed, and later attended dinner at the Burrowses':

5 October 1954: Cole Porter to Abe Burrows[106]

Dear Abe: –

Your magnificent gift arrived this morning, and we shall be sitting in A 2 and 4, promptly at 8:00 P.M. on Thursday night. What a thoughtful person you are.

Love to you and Carin,

Your old friend,

[signed:] Cole

21 October 1954: Cole Porter to Carin Burrows[107]

Dear Carin: –

Last night was a joy, and I thank you so much.

As I told Abe, I am sending you Music and Musicians, which is practically my bible. There is a section titled "Plots of Operas", which you will find in the latter part of the book, which is the most complete that I know.

Love to you both – and again, my thanks.

Your devoted

[signed:] Cole

The following letter shows his reaction to the unexpected interest of 20th Century Fox in *Jubilee*:

TWO LAST BROADWAY HITS, CAN-CAN AND SILK STOCKINGS, 1953-1954

8 November 1954: Cole Porter to Irving Lazar[108]

Dear Irving: –

Thank you for your letter of Nov. 4, 1954, concerning the sale of Jubilee to Twentieth Century Fox. I am surprised that any studio is interested in it if it can not use Begin the Beguine.

I have forwarded your letter of [sic] John Wharton, and he will write to you.

Yours sincerely.

[signed:] Cole

Silk Stockings was nearing its opening date in Philadelphia but it was in deep trouble, as Porter confides to his friend Robert Raison in the next letter. He also mentions his move to a new apartment in the Waldorf and the planned demolition of the main house in Williamstown so that his cottage could be moved in its spot, following Linda's death:

9 November 1954: Cole Porter to Robert Raison[109]

Dear Bobbie: –

Thank you for your letter of Oct. 26, 1954. I am sorry that your deal with Nat Goldstone* has not come off – but perhaps it will. In the meantime, you know that you are an excellent agent and are bound to get ahead.

You say that you hope my show is going along beautifully. It is not going along beautifully. It looks disastrous; slow, gloomy, and most of the numbers very badly done. We shall, however, see.

I have only seen Colin Fox once, but I thought he was delightful. Everyone who knows him is devoted to him. This includes Merle Oberon.

[Howard] Sturges arrives on Monday, November 15th, to go with me to Philadelphia and protect me during those awful weeks which I always have to face after an out of town Opening. He's always a blessing to have along because he never talks show business. He only talks about nice, rich, fashionable people and it's such a lovely contrast.

---

* Nat C. Goldstone (1903–66), Broadway producer. He founded a Hollywood talent agency with his brothers Charles and Jules.

My new apartment at the Waldorf is going to be a dream of beauty. And my little cottage in Williamstown, moved to the site of the main house, will look pretty. They start ripping the main house apart as soon as I have taken out of it whatever furniture I need for the New York Waldorf apartment. Everything else in it will be stored as I could never afford to buy what is there again.

I hope your trip with Stannie [Musgrove] to San Francisco howls with excitement.

Gracie sends love to John.

[signed:] Cole

He even found time to respond politely and helpfully to a French actress, who had written to him mistakenly believing him to be an agent:

10 November 1954: Cole Porter to Micheline Bardin, Théâtre National de l'Opéra, Paris, France[110]

Dear Miss Bardin: –

I have received your letter and the separate package containing photographs and publicity material.

As for your mentioning that I produce shows: it is incorrect: I merely write music and lyrics for shows.

You give the impression in your letter that you would like to have an agent in New York. I highly recommend the following agent:

LESTER SHURR
Paramount Building
1501 Broadway
New York 36, New York
Telephone:
Chickering 4-8240

I cannot assure you that he can get you work in this country, but I can vouch for his complete honesty, besides which he has a brother, Louis Shurr, in Hollywood, who is completely reputable; and this makes a very good tie-up with both centers of entertainment: New York City, N.Y. and Los Angeles, California.

I have forwarded your letter and your photographs and publicity to Lester Shurr. You will undoubtedly hear from him. This is all I can do for you – but I hope this little bit helps.

Sincerely yours,

[signed:] Cole Porter

On 10 November, Ethel Merman starred in an hour-long colour television adaptation of Porter's *Panama Hattie*, which she had originated on the stage. A reviewer felt that Merman 'brought what sense she could to the occasion', but the score had been both trimmed and augmented with famous songs from other shows, so it did not prove to be a triumph for Porter.[111] In the following letter to Stark, Porter pokes fun at Elsa Maxwell's recently published autobiography *R.S.V.P.* in which she made the remark, 'I have been attracted by two men in my life – Cole Porter and Aly Khan – but I was much too old when I met them to consider an attachment'.[112]

11 November 1954: Cole Porter to Sam Stark[113]

Dear Old Theatre and Minstrel Items: –*

Thank you for your letter of November 5, 1954.

The most interesting thing about Elsa's new book is that none of it is true. Noel Coward and I actually confronted her with the famous lie which she has revived in this book, namely that she was born in a box in Keokuk, Iowa, during a performance of Mignon.† She finally admitted that the noise of a mother's labor pains during a performance would be slightly disturbing for members of the cast. And when I asked her whether there was a Doctor in the house, she broke down and said that maybe it was all untrue but that was what her mother had told her. I also had my spies check on the Opera House in Keokuk, Iowa, and it doesn't exist and, therefore, neither did the box.

I could go on endlessly about the number of elaborate false words in this book, but luckily for Elsa, most of the people about whom she tells these fairy tales are conveniently dead.

---

* Stark had set up a business selling theatre collectables.

† *Mignon* (1866), an opera by Ambroise Thomas (1811–96).

Silk Stockings is going through major operations, and our Opening in Philadelphia has been put off until November 26th. At the present moment it all looks like a howling flop.

I am so sorry you are finishing your book. What can you do then?

Love to you both,

[signed:] Cole

A further letter to Robert Raison shows again Porter's excitement about his new apartment at the Waldorf Towers:

15 November 1954: Cole Porter to Robert Raison[114]

Dear Bobbie: –

I couldn't be happier about your closing the deal with Nat Goldstone – but I shan't believe it for about six months . . .

You ask me what color is your room in my new apartment. As a matter of fact, I shall have a guest room, but I wouldn't ask you to stay in it for anything in the world because you bring strange people in and run up outlandish bills. I shall be delighted, however, to have nice, civilized Stannie [Musgrove].

Love,

[signed:] Cole

The tryout of Silk Stockings opened in Philadelphia on 26 November. Porter wrote twice to the Starks, implying it was a success:

27 November 1954: Cole Porter to Sam and Harriette Stark[115]

SMASH HIT=COLE=

29 November 1954: Cole Porter to Sam Stark[116]

Dear Sam: –

Thank you so much for the Exchange Computer. I am going abroad the end of February and will be traveling so much it will be invaluable.

TWO LAST BROADWAY HITS, CAN-CAN AND SILK STOCKINGS, 1953–1954

I know you will be delighted to hear that at least a hundred people wired me: "May your Silk Stockings run forever."

Love to you both,

[signed:] Cole

He reiterated this impression in the following letter to Irving Lazar about the film of *Silk Stockings*:

1 December 1954: Cole Porter to Irving Lazar[117]

Dear Irving: –

Thanks for your wire to Philadelphia. When I wired you last I had forgotten that the producers had already made a picture deal with Metro, so there is nothing to be done. It seems too bad now because the property looks so valuable.

All my best,

[signed:] Cole Porter

But the initial reaction did not cover up the fact that the show was in trouble. On 2 December, the *New York Times* contained a column in which the Kaufmans admitted that they would spend two days in their hotel room rewriting the book. The show would now stay in Philadelphia until 1 January 1955, move to Boston for two weeks, and then open on Broadway on 21 January. This would allow the actress Yvonne Adair to join the show in the secondary female role, following an operation.[118] Abe Burrows was also brought in to take over the direction from Kaufman. Among Porter's chores during this extended tryout was the addition of the song 'Siberia'. Kaufman sent him two notes with some suggestions:

[n.d.] George S. Kaufman to Cole Porter[119]

Monday

Dear Cole:

Here is the revised scene leading to the song for the three boys. And here are at least some subjects for the Siberia song:

There is good skating all year round. You can out figure eights and your throat.

You meet all the best people there. Nicer than the ones you meet in the rest of Russia.

Something about electric blankets and how wonderful they are.

You get rid of your in-laws.

You never get that letter from your dentist, saying "Come in and see me." You never get any mail at all, not even the ones asking for money. And so you never have to write answers.

You don't get phone calls saying "Guess who this is!" Or wrong numbers either, in the middle of the night. There are no phones at all.

There are wonderful hockey games.

Take along plenty of anti-freeze.

Wonderful cold drinks.

No traffic problem.

You never burn your tongue on the soup, because it is always cold.

Beautiful mountains to climb – bracing air.

Our love,

[unsigned]

[Handwritten note below:] Where all day the sun shines bright
And I'm also told that it shines all night.

[n.d.] George S. Kaufman to Cole Porter

Tuesday

Dear Cole:

Two more minuscule notions for "Siberia."

You never run out of ice at your cocktail parties.

Your relatives do not drop in on you.

And Vladivostok is up there some place. Sounds like a good word, that's all.

Anything about sighing for Siberia?

I'd better keep my mouth shut.

Love,

[signed:] George

But Porter struggled to come up with enough lyrics. An old friend came to his assistance:

23 December 1954: Cole Porter to Noël Coward[120]

Dear Noley: –

How grand it was of you to take all that trouble about sending me more lyrics for "Siberia." I shall take them along when I return to Philadelphia, and I am sure that some of them will come in most handy.

At the present moment, I am in exile, as I have nothing to do until more changes have been made in the libretto. We are having very great trouble about filling the role of the Hollywood actress. The girl who was going to take the understudy's part turned out to be so unreliable that we gave up and got another girl, named Marilyn Ross. Never in your future theatrical career get Marilyn Ross. She looked like a saucy little pony, with platinum locks and a bobbed nose; and during rehearsals let out a voice that could only be equalled by [Ethel] Merman. Then she went into the show. Every good quality she had completely disappeared the moment she was on stage, including the voice. So – we are hunting for another girl. Today, it was decided that the show is in such bad condition that we shall stay in Boston for a month instead of two weeks, and open in New York on Feb. 3rd. My impression is that the producers are terrified, due to their past record, to bring in anything that isn't a smash hit, which I must say is a very high standard.

Our troubles, however, are as nothing to those of "The House of Flowers".* A week ago Friday, Miss Pearl Bailey, due to anger from another girl in the cast having been given a song which registered, pretended to be ill and retired to her dressing room during a performance. Then Saint Subber received a note from her Doctor saying she was too ill to work for the Saturday matinee or the Saturday night performance. That same Saturday night she was seen in a night club in New York, feeling very well indeed. She repeated this little gesture again this last Tuesday night. And Natasha told me yesterday that Peter Brook† had left the show. In the meantime, they have

---

* Harold Arlen and Truman Capote's *House of Flowers* opened on Broadway on 30 December 1954.

† Peter Brook (1925–) is one of the greatest living British directors for stage and screen and a multiple award winner.

fired [George] Balanchine* and have a new dance director named [Herbert] Ross,† from Hollywood. There is a constant rumour that "The House of Flowers" may never come to New York, but I cannot vouch for this.

Your little Elsa [Maxwell] telephoned me earlier to say that she has a wonderful new game in her column once a week. From now on, she will rave about the sartorial splendour of the Duke of Windsor and never once mention the Duchess' clothes. Isn't that a dull little game.

Good-bye, dear Noley, and again my gratitude for the lyrics. You are a wonderful friend, and I wish you great happiness for Christmas and New Year.

Your fan,

[signed:] Cole

The last surviving letter of the year shows that Porter turned down the opportunity to write new material for a screen adaptation of *Anything Goes*:

27 December 1954: Cole Porter to Irving Lazar[121]

Dear Irving: –

Thank you for your letter of Dec. 24, 1954.

I hate to let people down, but I am in no position to do any work on "Anything Goes" at all. In the first place, Cy feuer [sic] just telephoned from Philadelphia saying that George Kaufman and Leueen have definitely retired from the show, due to George's health. It appears that this constant re-writing has put him in such a state of worry that his sleeping pills no longer work; besides which, his blood pressure has gone way up. I feel sure that somebody else will be brought in to rewrite, although this has not been mentioned to me as yet. But I must keep my calendar open so, in case the rewrite job calls for definite numbers from me, I shall be on hand to do them. The

---

* George Balanchine (1904–83), one of the most prolific and influential choreographers of the twentieth century.

† Around this time Herbert Ross (1927–2001) had choreographed *A Tree Grows in Brooklyn* (1951) and *Three Wishes for Jamie* (1953) on Broadway and later choreographed and/or directed films such as *Funny Girl* (1968) and *Pennies from Heaven* (1981), among many others.

TWO LAST BROADWAY HITS, *CAN-CAN* AND *SILK STOCKINGS*, 1953–1954

opening in New York has already been put off till February 3rd, and I shouldn't be a bit surprised if it were put off to a later date.

My plans are to fly to Switzerland on February 20th, and then go on quite a long trip with friends. I have been working on Silk Stockings for over a year and a half, and the brain is frankly tired. I want to go to work on a new show in the middle of June, 1955 for Feuer & Martin, and it seems to me that this vacation will prepare me better than anything else.

I can't tell you how sorry I am not to be more help in "Anything Goes".

All my best to you, dear Irving, and thanks for your constant kindness.

[signed:] Cole

P.S. – I would like to telephone Edie Goetz on New Year's day. Where will she be then? If still in Palm Springs, would you let me know how I can track her down.

CHAPTER TEN

PORTER'S LAST MUSICALS, 1955–1957

Over Christmas 1954, Nunnally Johnson* had signed a contract to produce, write and direct the screen adaptation of *Can-Can* for 20th Century Fox.[1] It was natural that he would turn to Abe Burrows, writer of the Broadway version of the book, for help. In his reply, Burrows shares some ideas for *Can-Can* that he had had to drop when writing the stage version and reports on the current state of *Silk Stockings*, then in its Boston tryout:

15 January 1955: Abe Burrows to Nunnally Johnson[2]

Dear Nunnally:

Your letter was forwarded to me up here in Boston. I am here to help out on Silk Stockings (the Ninotchka musical). George Kaufman got ill what with the strain of directing and writing and he had to go back to New York – so they asked me to jump in and I'm up here to do what I can.

The show is not in bad shape. There are just a lot of little things that George wasn't able to get to because of his physical condition. We are doing terrific business in Boston – sold out for the whole four weeks – and then we go to Detroit for three weeks and it looks as though we will be sold out there too. I'm delighted to have the opportunity to go to Detroit. It's a wonderful place to spend February in.

In order to send you the additional stuff on Can-Can, I'll have to get back to New York and dig it out. I hope you're in no rush for it. Basically, what it involved was a character named Senator Beauvallon, who was based on an

---

* Nunnally Johnson (1897–1977) was a writer, director and producer of movies, including *The Grapes of Wrath* (1940), for which he was nominated for an Academy Award for Best Screenplay.

actual fellow named Senator Rene Berenger* who was an odd kind of sophisticated blue nose in Paris in the '90s. He actually was backed by a group called The League Against Sidewalk Licentiousness which is mentioned in the present play. He led the first raid against the Quat'z Arts Ball.

In my original opening courtroom scene I had Senator Beauvallon come on and demand drastic punishment for the girls. Later, I used him to furnish some pressure on the hero and in the final courtroom scene the hero and heroine's victory was a defeat for him. That's what the thing generally amounted to.

When I get back to New York, I'll send it on to you for what it's worth. If, from my brief resume, you decide that you can't use it, just let me know and I won't bother sending it.

It's snowing in Boston.

Aside from Burrows's impressive collegiality in sharing his ideas for something he would not be actively involved in, the letter shows that *Silk Stockings* was well on the way to becoming a success. Porter himself seems to have spent most of his time in New York rather than being permanently on the road, perhaps for reasons that he revealed to his cousin Omar Cole and his friend Sam Stark on 17 January:

17 January 1955: Cole Porter to Omar Cole[3]

Dear Omar: –

I am really ashamed of this show, "Silk Stockings". The opening in New York has now been put off till February 24th. I shall not be here as I am flying to Switzerland on February 20th – but if you and Jo want to come, everything will be arranged for your comfort, with an apartment here at the hotel, opening night seats, seats for any other show you wish to see, and the use of my limousine and chauffeur. It would be a joy if you came.

Four new scenes go into the first act tonight in Boston, but as new scenes are always badly played when they first go into a show, I am waiting till the latter part of the week to go there and see them; also, I have a new song going in tonight.

---

* René Bérenger (1830–1915) was a French judge and politician.

Thank you for the Jouett check – and love to you all,
[unsigned]

17 January 1955: Cole Porter to Sam Stark[4]

Dear Sam: –

I have ordered <u>The Searchers</u>.*

The great dramatic moment in "Anastasia"[†] is in the second act when the Grand Duchess recognizes Anastasia as her true granddaughter.

When you call Harriette[‡] "Har", how do you pronounce it? Do you pronounce it as if it were "Har", or do you pronounce it as if it were "Hair"? I find both the abbreviations unattractive.

I did receive your history of the Keokuk Opera House, but I still maintain that little Elsa [Maxwell] was never born in one of those boxes.

Love to all,
[signed:] Cole

P.S. – If you have not read "The Wilder Shores of Love", by Lesley Blanch,[§] get it quick. Don't let Harriette read it though, because it might give her ideas.

Porter's irritation at seeing another preview of *Silk Stockings* is palpable in the following terse letter to one of the show's producers, Cy Feuer, about its secondary female star, Yvonne Adair:[¶]

27 January 1955: Cole Porter to Cy Feuer[5]

Dear Cy: –

Adair sings "Where she rose to reach the highest peak" (in JOSEPHINE).

---

* Alan Le May's *The Searchers* is a Western novel (New York, 1954). A movie version, starring John Wayne, was released in 1956.

† Marcel Maurette's play *Anastasia* opened on Broadway in December 1954.

‡ Stark's wife.

§ The novel was published in 1954. It tells the story of a group of women travelling to the East in search of love and adventure, hence Porter's joking reference in the following sentence.

¶ Yvonne Adair (?1922–?2001), Broadway actress. She originated the role of Dorothy Shaw in *Gentlemen Prefer Blondes* (1949). She was replaced in *Silk Stockings* by Gretchen Wyler before it reached Broadway.

This does not make sense. The line should be:
"Yet she rose to reach the highest peak."
Later on in the number, she sings: "But other good points as well."
The line should be: "Plus other good points as well."
Best,
[unsigned]

Rather than waiting for the opening of *Silk Stockings*, Porter, Robert Bray and Jean Howard departed for Switzerland, from where the composer wrote to his friend George Eells (according to McBrien,[6] 'Richard' is a reference to Porter's masseur in New York):

24 February 1955: Cole Porter to George Eells[7]

Dear George –

[Howard] Sturges went to bed, Jean Howard went to bed & I'm sitting here all alone with a whisky & soda worrying about Richard. What does one do about all the Richards in our great country? I don't mean the Richard whom I know & for whom I have a strange affection. I mean all the Richards all over the U.S.A., beautiful, sweet as hell but with, instead of schooling, television sets. It scares me. Please try to keep track of this victim of the atomic age. I'm sure that the equivalent of the contemporary Richard was much better equipped for the future, before Noah's flood.

Jean, Sturges & I have become very Swiss since our Zurich season started what with falling into German with all the local servants.

Last night we were practically quoting Goethe in a little German restaurant here which nothing but the old aristocracy knows when in walked a sad-looking little man with bad teeth and so lonely. We had had several drinks and so we decided to take pity on him and asked him to join us.

He turned out to be . . . [over]

Darryl Zanuck.*

Best –

Cole

---

* Darryl F. Zanuck (1902–79) was a prolific film producer and studio executive at 20th Century Fox. The story is significant because Fox was to produce the film of *Can-Can*.

Meanwhile, far away in Boston there was considerable tension behind the scenes at *Silk Stockings*. An unusually explicit news item appeared in the *New York Times*:

> Herewith a telegram sent from Boston yesterday by George S. Kaufman and his wife Leueen MacGrath, authors of "Silk Stockings", the impending musical with songs by Cole Porter: "It has been mutually decided that the areas of disagreement between ourselves and the producers [Cy Feuer and Ernest Martin] are too great to be bridged. Accordingly, we have withdrawn and the show is now in the hands of Mr. Feuer as director, with Abe Burrows working on the book. It is our wish that Mr. Burrows be billed as co-author." Astonishment was expressed by Mr. Martin when the contents of the joint wire were relayed to him in Boston, where "Silk Stockings" is being whipped into shape for its delayed premiere on Feb. 24 at the Imperial. After regaining his poise, Mr. Martin said, "The Kaufmans are in complete disagreement with all those in charge of the show." [. . .] Lately, the Kaufmans have been collaborating on changes with Mr. Burrows, who was invited to step in during the emergency. The first act is "much improved," it was said by Mr. Martin, who added that second-act revisions will be inserted this week.*

Burrows's work continued through February and the show was ready to open as planned. The *New York Times* ran an interview feature with Porter, in which he commented on his work:

> [Porter] will attend the opening but not the opening-night party. Nor will he wait up for the notices. "The next morning," he said recently in his suite at the Waldorf Towers, "this valet, Paul [Sylvain], I've had for twenty years will wake me up and either nod or shake his head. I cannot wait until I begin the next one. I begin in June. I'd rather write than do anything on earth." [. . .]
>
> He has no helpful hints for aspiring songwriters. "I haven't the faintest notion how one writes hits," he said. "I don't know of anybody who sits

---

* Sam Zolotow, 'Run of "Festival" Will Be Extended', *New York Times*, 24 January 1955, 20.

down to write a hit, with the exception of Irving Berlin who can't help writing hits. I certainly don't know how. It never enters one of our heads when I sit down to write. 'My Heart Belongs to Daddy' was a hit. It was written simply to fill in a stage wait in 'Leave it to Me.' 'I Love Paris' in 'Can-Can' was written because Jo Mielziner had designed such a beautiful set. I once wrote a song called 'Rosalie' for a picture called 'Rosalie.' I'd written about six of that title. I handed in the sixth and played it for Louis B. Mayer. 'Forget Nelson Eddy,' he said. 'Go home and write a honky-tonk tune.' It was a hit. I don't like it. The one he threw out was better." [. . .]

Obviously stirred by the breeze of some recollection or other, Porter tacked. "I've been accused most of my life of being remote," he said. "But that's not so. I've been working. It's awful to tell people things like that. I've done lots of work at dinner, sitting between two bores. I can feign listening beautifully and work. That's the reason I like to go out. I have no hours. I can work anywhere. I work very well when I'm shaving or when I'm in a taxi. When this horse fell on me, I was too stunned to be conscious of great pain, but until help came I worked on the lyrics for the songs for 'You Never Know,' a song called 'At Long Last Love' in particular. When are you going to ask me which comes first, the music or the lyrics? I don't work at a piano.

"My sole inspiration is a telephone call from a producer. If Feuer and Martin phoned me today and asked me to write a new song for a spot, I'd just begin thinking. First, I think of the idea and then I fit it to a title. Then I go to work on the melody, spotting the title at certain moments in the melody, and then I write the lyric – the end first – that way, it has a strong finish. It's important for a song to have a strong finish. I do the lyrics like I'd do a crossword puzzle. I try to give myself a meter which will make the lyric as easy as possible to write without being banal. On top of the meter, I try to pick for my rhyme words of which there is a long list with the same ending.

"I'm becoming less and less interested in tricky rhymes. I think I used to go overboard on them. In Yale, I was rhyme-crazy. (He wrote 'Bingo' and 'Bulldog' at school.) That was due to the fact that I was Gilbert and Sullivan crazy. They had a big influence on my life. My songs are easier than they used to be, musically and lyrically. I've never been able to get complete simplicity the way Berlin does. Sometimes, I'll take twenty-five minutes to write a song, sometimes two days. I can tell a bad line by watching audiences. The minute they look at a program, I know the line's got to be thrown out. Pretty often, though, you've got to have a bad line so the next one'll look good. It's planting, you know."

Porter thought that musical comedies were much more "musicianly" than they used to be, and, just like anybody else, that Rodgers and Hammerstein were principally responsible for the phenomenon. "The librettos are much better," he said, "and the scores are much closer to the librettos than they used to be. Those two made it much harder for everybody else." [...]

The winds of memory stepped up his pace. "I think the greatest surprise I ever had," Porter went on at a great rate, "was in Zanzibar in 1935. We went to a little hotel with a patio. All these ivory dealers from East Africa were sitting around in their burnouses and listening to 'Night and Day' being played on an ancient phonograph.

"That was a shock. People like to think composers get great pleasure out of hearing their songs played. I suppose some do. I don't, particularly. And when you tell them you don't, their faces fall and they say, 'You must get very little out of life.' They're entirely wrong. I get a hell of a lot out of life. I've had two great women in my life – my mother, who thought I had this talent, and my wife, who kept goading me along, in spite of that general feeling that I couldn't appeal to the general public."[8]

The interview was well received – indeed, one distinguished reader wrote a letter to the *New York Times* about it:

> I cannot refrain from writing and congratulating Gilbert Millstein for his wonderful article, "Words Anent Music By Cole Porter" (Feb. 20). Mr Millstein's admirable style was even more enhanced by the subject matter chosen.
>
> If Mr. Porter has, as he suggested in talking to Mr. Millstein, written anything but "hit" songs, I have never heard them.
>
> As modest as he is prolific, Mr. Porter says that his "sole inspiration is a telephone call from a producer." How inspired, I wonder, would he be

as a result of a telephone call from a coloratura? An opera by Cole Porter? What a divine idea!

LILY PONS*

New York.

Despite what he claimed in the interview about attending the opening of *Silk Stockings* on Broadway on 24 February, Porter in fact was away in Europe for it. Albert Sirmay wired him the reaction of the critics:

25 February 1955: Albert Sirmay to Cole Porter[9]

OPENING GIGANTIC SUCCESS[.] BROOKS ATKINSON RAVING ESPECIALLY ABOUT WORDS AND MUSIC[.] ALL OTHER PAPERS SIMPLY WONDERFUL[.] ABE BURROWS AND CY [FEUER] HAVE ACHIEVED A THEATRICAL MIRACLE[.] AUDIENCE MOST ELEGANT IN YEARS[.] GRETCHEN WYLER† STOPPED SHOW TWICE WITH JOSEPHINE AND STEREOPHONIC[.] YOU HAVE EVERY REASON TO BE HAPPY AND PROUD[.] LOVE AND KISSES=SIRMAY

As Sirmay reported, Brooks Atkinson's review was especially glowing: 'Everything about "Silk Stockings", which opened at the Imperial last evening, represents the best in the American musical comedy emporium.' He also said it was 'on a level with' *Guys and Dolls* and remarked that the subject matter had put Porter 'back in his best form'.[10] Evidently the composer was boosted by the news: his valet Paul Sylvain wrote to Sam Stark from St Moritz on 2 March to report that 'Mr. C.P. is in good health and spirits . . .'[11] A day later, Porter's secretary, Mrs Smith, also reported to Stark that *Silk Stockings* was 'a great hit'.[12] Porter himself wrote to Stark on 6 March, with sarcastic comments on a relation's reaction to the show:

---

* Lily Pons (1898–1976) was one of the foremost American opera singers of the twentieth century, specializing in the Italian coloratura repertoire.

† Gretchen Wyler (1932–2007) was a veteran Broadway actress who appeared in the original productions of *Guys and Dolls*, *Silk Stockings* and *Bye Bye Birdie*, among others. She played Janice Dayton in *Silk Stockings*, replacing Yvonne Adair.

6 March 1955: Cole Porter to Sam Stark[13]

Dear Sam,

Thanks for your letter of February 25th. I was awfully amused to read in your letter about one member of your family in Philadelphia who hadn't been to the theater since My Maryland* played there.

I also was delighted with your relative who liked Stereophonic Sound and Yvonne Adair. She must have excellent ears and wonderful eyesight as Yvonne Adair did not go into the show until Boston and Stereophonic Sound made its first appearance in Detroit.

How awful that Johnny Smithson is returning to Los Angeles to live. That means that Stannie [Musgrove] will begin fighting with me as soon as I arrive to persuade me to invite Smithson for Sunday lunch.

Love to you and Harriet[te].

[signed:] Cole

(Cole)

Stark responded defensively: 'According to my Phila program of Silk Stockings Yvonne Adair sang Satin + Silk and a number "There's a Hollywood That's Good".'[14]

Business continued too. Porter wrote to his lawyer Robert Montgomery from St Moritz:

8 March 1955: Cole Porter to Robert Montgomery

Dear Bob,

Thanks a lot for your letter of March 4th, 1955.

I shall keep strict notes on our trip to Greece and its beautiful islands and see to it that you get them.

What is the cable-address of:

PAUL, WEISS, RIFKIND, WHARTON & GARRISON?

If there is none please invent one!

Best

[signed]: Cole

Cole

---

* A musical by Sigmund Romberg from 1927.

He received a detailed letter from his other lawyer, John Wharton, about the film adaptation of *Can-Can*. The show was still running on Broadway and would not close until 25 June before going on a national tour:

11 March 1955: John Wharton to Cole Porter[15]

Dear Cole:

This is in the nature of a progress report on the history of the CAN-CAN motion picture contract. The story of this contract is getting as long as War and Peace; only most of it is war. Mr. Moscowitz* is still being as difficult as ever but I think we may be able to finish it when [Darryl] Zanuck returns from his vacation.

Irving Lazar, Bob [Montgomery] and I have, of course, been patiently but persistently insisting on the clauses that are necessary for your protection. We have been getting them conceded one by one and there are now only two left, which I think Moscowitz will give in on in the near future.

There is one other clause, affecting both you and the producers, but primarily their problem, which has become the subject of great dispute. That is the clause which covers the release date of the picture. We have felt all along that Moscowitz was trying to get an unwarranted early date, but we felt we should let Cy [Feuer] and Ernie [Martin] make the final decision, since it rested on their judgement as to how long they could tour the production. As you know, prior to the opening of SILK STOCKINGS, Cy and Ernie were sending messages to me that they were willing to concede anything to get the contract signed and they even criticized me to you for any delay occasioned by my insistence on getting proper protective clauses for you. However, since the opening of SILK STOCKINGS, Cy and Ernie have become much more aggressive about the whole contract and indicate that they want to make a fight about the clause on the release date. This is all right with me but I do disagree with their proposed method. As usual, with their abounding energy, their first suggestion was for Irving Lazar to fly to Europe and break in on Zanuck and work the deal out right there. Irving feels that this might irritate Zanuck immensely and the proper thing to do is to wait until his return. When Irving took this position their next suggestion was to call up

---

* Joseph Moskowitz, an executive at 20th Century Fox.

Moscowitz, tell him that the deal was off and that they were bringing suit against Fox immediately. We pointed out that they could not sue Fox; any suit would have to be brought by you and Abe Burrows; and that we were certainly not going to get you into any lawsuits, particularly one in which they could give no basis that would afford a hope of winning.

I feel we should follow Irving's advice. Ever since we retained him on the original KISS ME KATE negotiations* we have gotten everything we wanted if we allowed Irving to negotiate it in his own way and on his own time schedule. Therefore I am going to continue to follow Irving's advice. He may fail this time, but I see no reason to think that he will fail if he is left alone, and by the way, with the money that will come in now from SILK STOCKINGS, it will make very little difference to you after taxes whether the CAN-CAN contract goes through or not. But of course we shall do everything to put that contract through. In the meantime, if Cy or Ernie want to fly to Europe and see Zanuck that is their privilege. They should not, however, try to get Irving to do this, particularly since he is not their agent and is getting no payment from them.

Do not bother to answer this letter unless you feel that you want to overrule my decision to follow Irving's advice in this matter. As I said in the beginning, it is merely a progress report on facts which you should have before you.

Hope the vacation continues to go as well as the run of SILK STOCKINGS. I have suddenly been swamped with work again but I am feeling in pretty good shape.

As ever,
[unsigned]
John F. Wharton

22 March 1955: Cole Porter to John Wharton[16]

Dear John,

Thank you for your letter of March 11th, 1955.

I read with great interest the progress of the Can-Can Motion picture contract. I do hope that it can be worked out, if only for the sake of Cy and Ernie.

---

* For the MGM film version.

We are having a wonderful time in ideal weather. I have fallen in love again with Europe and I want to come back every year.

All my best,

Sincerely,

[signed:] Cole

COLE PORTER

In March, Porter's trip to Switzerland extended into a tour of Europe, including Spain, Italy, Portugal and Greece. Much of the journey was recorded in diaries by Porter's friend Jean Howard and by Porter himself; they were also joined by Robert Bray and Paul Sylvain, and Howard Sturges and Charles Feldman (Jean Howard's ex-husband) came on parts of the trip. On 14 March, Howard wrote: 'Cole and Sturges return [from Paris, where they went for a few days when the rest of us got sick] tomorrow in time to depart for Monte Carlo.'[17] The tour was packed with activity: for example, in Milan, they saw Maria Callas at La Scala in Bellini's opera *La Sonnambula*, conducted by Leonard Bernstein. In another entry, Howard remarks: 'I don't mean to make Cole out to be inhuman, although there were many times that I did think just that . . .'[18]

Porter continued to write to friends such as George Eells during his journey:

15 March 1955: Cole Porter to George Eells[19]

Dear George. I'm very grateful for your letter dated Mar 1st telling me the details of Those Old Silk Stockings. By the way, nine anonymous bitches sent me the Hawkins notice, blasting the whole show.*

We're well organized for our trek to the West (Portugal). For touring, there is the 1955 red-leather lined Cadillac. (I suddenly realized, day before yesterday that I had ordered it red-leather lined because when Pep and Berthe [Porter's dogs] make spots from their privates, it's so easy to wash the leather. But Pep isn't here, nor is Berthe.) There is also a Pontiac station wagon. In this goes the luggage, so far 37 pieces – with Luigi & Paul [Sylvain]

---

* Richard Hawkins's review of *Silk Stockings* in the *World Telegram and Sun* was the only negative notice the show received.

on the front seat. On the top of the Cadillac, there is a super-rack for extra luggage & it's a super, super-rack because it's held on by suction. This means that when one arrives somewhere & doesn't want one's Cadillac to have a super-rack, one presses a button, there's no more suction & everything is respectable again, no more rack. I don't understand this.

To continue, in the trunk of the Cadillac is my collapsible wheel-chair. This means, what with the aid of Luigi, the chauffeur, Paul & Bob Bray, I can be carried up & down all the stair-cases & then be wheeled around & around. The result is, as we have been sight-seeing every day, that Luigi, Paul & Robert all come back to the hotel exhausted wrecks. I'm still fresh & rarin' to go.

This Luigi is a great chauffeur from Rome & highly recommended but when I first saw him, I was shocked by his clothes and also because he looked so much like Jackie Gleason.* Sturges & I took him to a chauffeur's shop to get him the proper outfit to the last detail. He still looks like Jackie Gleason.

Today, we drove to Bergamo, the magic city on the hill & tomorrow we lunch in Turin where I shall be carried up-stairs & down-stairs & wheeled around & around again to see the beautiful treasures. I believe you would like seeing all these treasures. They're all so far from Fleur Cowles.[†]

Maybe when I arrive at Monte Carlo I shall have news from you about Richard.[‡] I have great affection for him. I also believe he has exciting possibilities but he's so disorganized & un-equipped to buck this cruel world. I'd like to help him but mere money isn't the answer. He needs a great nurse – a John Foster Dulles,[§] or perhaps a Marlene Dietrich[¶] to do this. How can we save him?

Goodnight George. Forgive me for the longest letter I have written in years but I miss your companionship. One day, we should take a trip together & see beautiful things, inanimate & animate.

Best --
Cole.

---

* Jackie Gleason (1916–97) was a comedian, writer, actor and television presenter. Porter is making a joke about his physical stature.

† Cowles was Eells's editor at *Look* magazine; see Howard, *Travels with Cole Porter*, 31.

‡ Porter's masseur, according to McBrien.

§ John Foster Dulles (1888–1959) was an American politician. At that point, he was U.S. Secretary of State under President Eisenhower.

¶ Marlene Dietrich (1901–92), the German-born Hollywood movie star.

Jean Howard continued to be sick, so the party did not leave for Monte Carlo until 17 March.[20] Her diary notes that on 24 March, 'We lunched with Cole's friend Bebino (Bepi) Salinas,* near Les Beau. We spent the night at Montpellier.'[21] The following day: 'First night in S'Agaro, a lovely place on the Costa Brava, at the Hostal de la Gavina, a heavenly spot. Lovely walk along the sea – white beaches, small, with dark green pine trees. [Salvador] Dali has a place about an hour away. We were not stopped very long at the border. On the Spanish side, one of the soldiers came out with Cole's passport in his hand, looked in the car, and said, "Cole Porter . . . Begin the Beguine!" and kissed his fingers to the air, and began to sing the song. Cole's music is known everywhere we go – even in remote spots.' On 26 March, Howard wrote: 'Tonight the village folk came up and entertained us with melodies and dances called the *sardanas* – it is said that they date from the time the Greeks were in Spain. All this was arranged for Cole. He was most gracious.'[22]

The following letter reflects Porter's apparent immersion in the local music he encountered during his travels (also evidenced in transcriptions of folk melodies in his papers at the Cole Porter Trust). The package of seven discs seems to represent some form of research:

30 March 1955: José Ensesa Gubert in Barcelona to Cole Porter at the Hotel Fenix, Madrid[23]

Dear Mr. Porter:

I hope you had a good trip to Madrid and that in your arrival at the hotels of Zaragoza and Madrid you were fully attended as you deserve.

I send you to-day to the Fenix Hotel, by "recardero", which means a firm that takes messages and parcels from one town to another, (a more sure and quicker way than the State Railways or Post Offices), 7 discs in which are recorded 36 sardanas of various authors, old and modern.

The oldes, whose melodies takes us, people of the sixties, back to our youth, and perhaps for this motive gives us a greater thrill, together with Morera and Garreta, who all died long ago.

---

* A photograph of Bebino di Salina (dates unknown) at a masquerade ball with Porter resides at Yale University in the Natalie Paley photograph albums (call number: GEN MSS 574). This suggests Salina was a friend from Porter's European days.

I could not find the sardana "Marinada"* which was played twice in S'Agaró, but I will continue my search and I hope to discover some disc of that melody. If you are still at Madrid I will send it to you to the Fenix Hotel and if not I hope I shall have the opportunity to hand it to you when you come again to Barcelona on your journey to Italy and Greece.

I wish you every enjoyment during your visit to Spain and please remember me as

Yours truly,

[signed:] José Ensesa Gubert[†]

[Handwritten by Porter at bottom of page:]

Show me this when I return, please.

Howard notes that in Spain the party encountered Edgar Neville (1899–1967), the Spanish playwright and director: 'Neville gave a dinner for Cole, but Cole was ill and couldn't (simply wouldn't) go. Poor Neville – the dinner was an awful bust... The fact was that Cole had had enough of Edgar Neville, who was trying *too* hard to please.' She also claims: 'It was somewhere along here (between Barcelona and Madrid, I believe) that Cole looked back from the front seat and hummed the melody of "True Love". I told him that I thought that song would be one of his biggest hits. He said, "You're crazy." '[24] Howard's ex-husband, Charles Feldman, joined them in Spain.

On 9 April they arrived in Lisbon,[25] and on 10 April they dined with José Ferrer.[26] Two days later, Howard reports: 'Lunched with Cole and Bob Bray. Later went sightseeing... Enjoyed Cole today more than any time since we started out.'[27] A Fado party, focusing on the local music of Lisbon from the nineteenth century, took place on 15 April in Porter's honour, and he dined with Eddie Fisher,[‡] Debbie Reynolds[§] and her mother, Fisher's piano accom-

---

* A Catalan dance.

† José Ensesa Gubert (1892–1981) was the proprietor of the Hostal de la Gavina on the Costa Brava. See Catherine Reynolds, 'Sedate Splendor on the Costa Brava', *New York Times*, 17 July 1994.

‡ Eddie Fisher (1928–2010) was a hugely successful popular singer and the husband of Debbie Reynolds. He later married Elizabeth Taylor and then Connie Stevens. He had his own television show and had seventeen Top Ten hits during the 1950s.

§ Debbie Reynolds (1932–2016) was one of MGM's most popular actresses, notably appearing in *Singin' in the Rain* (1952), *Tammy and the Bachelor* (1957) and *The Unsinkable Molly Brown* (1964).

panist, and his agent. Howard also notes: 'After dinner the ex-king of Italy, Umberto,* came to greet Cole.'[28]

On 16 April, Porter visited Bussaco,† from where he wrote some instructions to his secretary Mrs Smith in New York:

17 April 1955: Cole Porter to Madeline Smith[29]

Dear Mrs S – up here to see some treasures we missed before we went to Lisbon.

Please get book & keep for me, <u>Napoleon III</u> by Albert Guerard, pub. Knopf.‡

Since I hit Milan have had only one-half day of rain & that was on the day I hit Milan.

I can't tell you how happy I am that you like your new office so much.§

All well – Paul [Sylvain] is a wonderful traveller. He has such fun with my 37 bags.

Best,
C.P

Howard's diary entries continued to comment on Porter's personality. For example, on 20 April she noted: 'Dinner with Cole. He is making an effort to be gay. He's good at it.'[30] She added: 'I was alone in Madrid. I was waiting for Cole to return so I could tell him that I was thinking of going to Sevilla for a few days of the *feria* . . . When Cole and Bob [Bray] got back to Madrid, I told Cole that I was going to Sevilla, not knowing that Bob was returning to California to take a part in the movie *Bus Stop*.¶ When I did tell Cole my plans, he decided to fly to Paris because [Howard] Sturges was

---

* Umberto II (1902–83) was the last King of Italy, reigning for thirty-four days from 9 May to 12 June 1946. Italy became a republic and Umberto moved to Cascais in Portugal for the rest of his life.

† Howard's diary notes that Robert Bray and Henry May went with him.

‡ The book *Napoleon III: A Great Life in Brief* was published in New York in 1947.

§ A reference to Porter's new apartment in the Waldorf Towers, which had been lavishly refurbished.

¶ *Bus Stop* (1956), a film directed by Joshua Logan and starring Marilyn Monroe. He played Carl in the movie.

there. Cole felt that I had let him down, and I was in a state of confusion. On April 21 Cole left for Paris . . .'

From Paris, Porter wrote more instructions to Mrs Smith (the identities of the people he refers to are unknown):

23 April 1955: Cole Porter to Madeline Smith[31]

Dear Mrs. Smith,

. . . Please show me the enclosed letter from Lorna McIntosh on my return to New York.

Please send to Miss Margaret Frickelton, 153 Rue Legendre, Paris, 17e, a box of pencils. The make which she wishes is Venus Velvet 3557, No. 2. This is a present.

Best,

[signed:] Cole Porter

Cole Porter.

P.S. Please put in my Wheeldex in my address book, the enclosed card, under Secretary, Paris.

Enclosure

[annotation:] Paul [Sylvain] is suddenly laid up with an infected foot. This delays our departure for Rome.

Porter remained in Paris until 29 April,* where Jean Howard joined him on the 26th. The next day, her diary reads: 'Lunched with Cole at the Berkeley. He looks very well indeed. Paris has done him a world of good . . . Later dined with Cole, Charlie [Feldman, Howard's ex-husband], and Christos [Bellos].' On 28 April, she 'Lunched with Cole at Coc Hardy – beautiful! Really enjoyed Cole today. He was relaxed and good company.'[32]

Howard joined Porter in Rome on 30 April: 'Left Paris for Rome today . . . Dined tonight with Sturges, Cole, and Carla Boncompani. She is charming. [Jean] Cocteau† is here in Rome. Charming as always. After

---

* On 29 April 1955, Howard's diary (*Travels with Cole Porter*, 50) notes: 'Cole left for Rome. I hope to feel well enough to meet him there tomorrow.'

† Jean Cocteau (1889–1963) was the prolific writer of novels such as *Les Enfants Terribles* (1929) and director of films like *Beauty and the Beast* (1946) and *Orpheus* (1949).

dinner drove to the fountains of Rome – beautiful night. Cole seems to love it.'[33] They dined with the Princess Pallavicini* on 3 May and with the Baroness Lo Monaco on 4 May: 'She has an apartment in some great palace – huge rooms – just beginning to enjoy myself when at 12 o'clock Cole wanted to go. Came back to hotel and talked to Cole until 2 a.m.!'[34]

On 6 May, Porter sent a postcard of Rome to Sam Stark, reporting his plans to return to California:

6 May 1955: Cole Porter to Sam Stark (postcard from Rome)[35]

Dear Sam – I don't see why the Pope doesn't move here. It's so bang-up.
  Love to you both,
  Cole
I hit Hollywood around the 15th of June + stay as long as I can bear Bobbie Raison.

He also wrote that day to Mrs Smith, who had made a blunder with a gift for one of the producers of *Silk Stockings*:

6 May 1955: Cole Porter to Madeline Smith[36]

Dear Mrs S–
  By your letter of May 3rd I note that you gave Ernie Martin the wrong picture, if you gave him the picture on the north-west wall of 41C. This is a maquette of a ballet, – it shows a girl standing in a doorway (Diaghileff gave it to me). The Utrillo is the picture that was on the West wall south of the air-conditioner. It is a scene of the streets of Paris with the dome of Sacré [sic] Coeur in the background. Give him the Utrillo + get the maquette back quick. Shame!!
  Best
  C.P.

On 9 May, the party left for Athens. 'Cole and Sturges on tenterhooks with each other,' notes Howard. 'Funny to see Sturges dump a whole tomato

---

* Princess Elvina Pallavicini (1914–2004) was a member of the so-called Black Nobility in Rome who supported Pope Pius IX after the overthrowing of the Papacy in 1870.

and cucumber salad *almost* into Cole's lap.'[37] Porter wrote twice to his increasingly close friend George Eells from Athens:

11 May 1955: Cole Porter to George Eells[38]

Dear George –

We spent ten days in Rome & all my pet princesses were most angry about an article which appeared in Look* saying that all Italians had negro blood in them. One of them showed me a Rome newspaper headline "So the U.S.A. calls us "Niggers." Tell Fleur [Cowles], & I'm sure you will do it gracefully, that if she wants to get Clare's (or is it Claire's?)† job, this is an ineffective bit of propoganda [sic] for Fleur.

I may have told you before that [Howard] Sturges & I hit N.Y. on June 7th. Please call me up. I pine for the prose that emanates from your entrails.

Love & Kisses

KΩΛH ← fuck it, it's

Cole

14 May 1955: Cole Porter to George Eells[39]

Dear George –

I have no idea if you are in London or Timbucktoo but I enclose a new letter from our problem child, Richard.‡ I'm constantly delighted by the fact that he + his family never make sense yet they seem to be so much more benign than you + I who do make sense.

We sail tonight, after a too-big dinner, on our beautiful Eros.§

All my best

Cole

Porter started his own diary in Greece, outlining the major stopping points and activities:[40]

---

* *Look* magazine, for which Eells wrote articles. Fleur Cowles was its editor.
† Clare Boothe Luce (1903–87), the conservative politician and author. At that point she was ambassador to Italy.
‡ Richard, Porter's masseur.
§ Stavros Niarchos's yacht.

14 May 1955

Dinner at our pet taverna, 'The Old Phoenix'; then the Eros. At once a feeling of comfort and great taste.

15 May 1955

At dawn, terrific noise. Then, for breakfast, to sit on this pretty craft and look up at the Temple of Poseidon, Sunion [Cape Sounion].

16 May 1955

Nauplia – automobiles to Tiryns, Argos (theatre built out of solid rock), Mycenae (Lion's Gate), graveyards where gold masks and jewels were found, the prize of the Athens Museum, Tomb of Agamemnon (bee-hive). We set for Mykonos. Rough weather.

17 May 1955

Mykonos, a town entirely whitewashed. A donkey. I sit side-saddle and wander through enchanting streets, 360 churches here, each offered by a sailor to his saint if he would return safe from the sea, the big shock, no noise because no cars, no telephone, the ladies all weave, the gentlemen all fish, a former top whore who is now a top bootblack, bang-up lunch at a bang-up 'moderne' hotel, the local museum with our delightful guide who suddenly made Greek vases interesting by explaining the profess of their decoration, the village idiot on the quai, the boat that moved in and killed our view, the constant joy of this incredible gift from Stavros [Niarchos, Porter's host].

18 May 1955

Delos. Again on a donkey, vast ruins covering acres, first the sacred part with its temples and statues, seven beautiful lions looking Syrian, phallic symbols for the Temple of Dionysus, the museum with some local archaic statues, then the actual city, floors in mosaic, better mosaic than in Pompeii, a theatre holding 4,000 people. In the afternoon, Tenos with its church containing a miracle-working ikon and many gold and silver votive offerings.

19 May 1955

Santorini (Venetian name), Thira (Greek name). In port beside an unreachable cliff. Then all of us on donkeys by triangular zig-zag pavements to the summit to find not only a fairy-tale town with fascinating vistas in every street but also a view down to the sea on the other side, everything green and accessible and, as against the cliffside, strangely uninhabited. The museum with two Egyptian torsos and a lovely fresco from Crete. Then a visit to the Vulcan hotel to meet the proprietress, who gave us local wine and cakes and exhausting French truisms. Down by donkey to harbor to board the Chris Craft to examine a nearby volcanic island, which rose from the sea only in the early 1920s. As we skirted the shores of this already cool mass of land, I felt the beginnings of the earth and the terrors of hell.

20 May 1955
A shock to wake up in the harbor of Rhodes to see on the left a big medieval chateau fort, on the right a church that recalled the church in Verona and a campanile, in front of us a Turkish-looking building and in the background, infinite greenery. Later, in motors, first to the Hospital of the Knights of St. John and its museums, then through the Street of the Knights to the Palace of the Greet Masters (mosaics from island of Kos), surrounded by three rows of outer walls with two moats. In the evening, folk dances in the public square. Greek airmen in uniform suddenly joined the girl dancers in their traditional costumes and the contrast of today and long-ago was touching.

21 May 1955
Rhodes. By car to the top of Mount Philerimos, next to ruins at Kamiros (2nd century B.C.), then to Valley of Butterflies for a big lunch by a brook. Afterwards, nap and tea at Hotel des Roses.

22 May 1955
Motored to Lindos. Arrived to find remnants of the fourth century B.C. and a vast medieval castle on top of a great hill by the sea. Terrific heat so we all decide not to make the trip. Good lunch in a cool restaurant. Nearby a table of Americans, the men drinking quantities of martinis and straight whiskeys. They decided not to make the climb either. The blessed [yacht] Eros rounded the point and we boarded her to find a cool breeze.

23 May 1955
A glorious morning, whitecaps and the Eros under full sail. Heraclion, Crete. Left late afternoon, motored to Phaestos, countryside very hilly and fertile. Ruins at Phaestos disappointing what with only the foundations left to see.

PORTER'S LAST MUSICALS, 1955–1957

24 May 1955

Heraclion, Crete. Motored to Knossos. Great ruins of palace partially and excellently restored. Then to museum at Heraclion; fascinating treasures, golden and precious stone jewels, jar sculptures and frescoes in many colors. The high spots – a sculptured bull's head and a profile fresco of a very dressy lady with painted lips known as "La Parisienne."

25 May 1955

En route to Katacolon, port near Olympia. A wonderful day, brisk day, jib and foresail up. In late A.M. passed Cythera where Aphrodite was born, then up west coast of Peloponnesus.

26 May 1955

Katacolon. Short drive to Olympia. We went all over the ruins, the most notable feature, the great size of the sections of the columns of the Temple of Zeus. In the museum, the east and west pediments of this temple and the Hermes of Praxiteles in Parian marble.

27 May 1955

Itea (port near Delphi). Cars up into the hills passing through groves of olive trees. The museum with friezes from Temple of Apollo and bronze charioteer. Then a hard donkey ride to site of the oracle and the surrounding ruins, a wonderful view, very melodramatic.
Off across the gulf, arriving evening at port of Corinth.

28 May 1955

By car to museum. Corinthian vases whose decoration shows strong oriental influence. Temple of Zeus [Apollo], 700 B.C., a few columns standing, then the ruins of a big agora. Far above us, on a great hill, the Acrocorinth, where the prostitutes lived in the days of Corinth's glory. In the afternoon, through the Corinth Canal, arriving in the evening at Epidaurus.

From Epidaurus, with the trip coming to a close, Porter wrote to Robert Montgomery, asking for advice on how to repay his friend Stavros Niarchos, who had loaned the party his yacht *Eros* for the cruise:

29 May 1955: Cole Porter to Robert Montgomery

Dear Bob – Please begin looking up some charity organization which would help Greece and which the U.S. government would recognize as deductible.

I figure that this cruise would have cost me about $10,000 if it hadn't been a present from Stavros Niarchos + the only way I can repay him is by a gift which would benefit his people as he is a great patriot. And the sooner I give this present, the better.

Can you + John [Wharton] lunch with me, 1.00 P.M. Thursday, June 9th? Please leave word with Mrs. Smith.

Best –

Cole

The matter was still lingering in late July:

31 July 1955: Cole Porter to Robert Montgomery[41]

Dear Bob:

Whatever happened to the $10,000.00 charity I was going to give for Greece?

Sincerely,

[signed:] Cole

The matter was resolved when Niarchos himself suggested that Porter donate the money to the charity branch of the Greek Merchant Navy Schools.[42]

Porter's diary in Greece continues:

29 May 1955

Drove to theatre, 350 B.C., holding 15.000 people.

30 May 1955

Aegina. A car to the temple of Aphaea on the top of the island in its very center, looking over the sea on every side. To Piraeus after lunch aboard with toasts from + to the crew. The dream is over.

Jean Howard's diaries on the trip conclude: 'After the cruise we returned to Athens, where we stayed two or three days. Cole and [Howard] Sturge then left for Switzerland and I left for Rome...'[43]

Back in America, Porter made plans to have a rose named in Linda's memory. John Wharton managed the affair through the famous Bobbink and Atkins plant nursery, who replied: '... One thought occurs to us, and it is this, that, perhaps, the rose should not be called THE LINDA PORTER ROSE (MRS. COLE PORTER). In alphabetical listing of roses, this rose will then appear under the letter "T". We would therefore suggest that we amend this just slightly and say, "LINDA PORTER" and then underneath it, (MRS COLE PORTER). It will then appear in all catalogues in this style, and under the letter "L" instead of under the letter "T". We trust that Mr. Porter and your good self will see the wisdom of doing this . . . Inasmuch as there will be good rose flowers in September from original stock plants, and the finest June blooms are now already gone, we plan to have a number of photographs taken in bloom in September, and Mr. Cole Porter will probably be very interested in picking out the one he likes best to have color plates made in ample time for use in Fall of 1956 and Spring of 1957.'[44] Later in June, Porter wrote to Robert Montgomery to ask for his advice on a proposed television show:

25 June 1955: Cole Porter to Robert Montgomery[45]

Dear Bob:

I enclose a suggestion for a TV program based upon my music. I know nothing whatever about Mary Markham but you may find it interesting. It looks to me like an impossible program to arrange, as I don't believe any of these artists mentioned would consider being on it for less than formidable money.

As you will see by my letter to Stanley Musgrove, who deals in publicity out here and who is an old friend of mine, I say that either you or John [Wharton] will take care of the whole matter. I do not want Bob Raison, who is mentioned in the Musgrove letter, to have anything to do with this, in spite of the fact that he is a good friend of mine. I would rather have the whole thing done by you or John.

Sincerely,
[signed:] Cole

Also in June, Porter turned down the opportunity to work again with the Spewacks, perhaps because of the tensions over the publication of the script for *Kiss Me, Kate* (though he was also preparing to work on *High Society*):

25 June 1955: Cole Porter to Bella Spewack[46]

Dear Bella:

I hope this letter will be forwarded to you abroad.

I don't feel like working at the present moment, on a show, but maybe later we could get together.

I hope you both have a wonderful trip.

All my best,

[signed:] Cole

Jean Howard's diary notes that by July, Porter was back in California writing the score for *High Society*, though news of his participation in this musical adaptation of *The Philadelphia Story* only appeared in the press in late August.[47] According to Howard, 'Cole was happy and feeling well, as indeed was I – of course our recent travels were a topic of conversation ... Just as I had suggested the first journey, Cole suddenly said, "Let's do it again!" I laughed and replied, "Why not!" '[48]

On 21 August, Porter wrote to Sam Stark about a recent gift of a washing machine:

21 August 1955: Cole Porter to Sam Stark[49]

Dear Sam:

The Wash and Dry arrived and it is sensational! Last Tuesday night I had people for dinner and everybody who hadn't heard of it proceeded to experiment, with the greatest enthusiasm. It was most thoughtful of you to send it to me.

Thank you also for the clipping about my song being sung in the Kansas City Starlight.

Love to you and Harriette.

[signed:] Cole

PORTER'S LAST MUSICALS, 1955–1957

A telegram to Katharine Hepburn, by now a good friend, expressed appreciation for her recent film appearance:

28 August 1955: Cole Porter to Katharine Hepburn[50]

KATHERINE [sic] HEPBURN
HER MAJESTY THEATRE MELBOURNE
DEAR KATE[,] I JUST SAW YOUR MOST MAGNIFICENT PERFORMANCE IN SUMMERTIME[.]* ALL MY CONGRATULATIONS AND LOVE + COLE PORTER +

The next letter is significant only for its mention of one of Porter's favourite hobbies – listening to the radio show *Stella Dallas*, which ran from October 1937 to December 1955:

10 September 1955: Cole Porter to George Eells[51]

Dear George:

Thank you very much for your letter, part of which I have already answered.

Thank you also for the story on Stella. I am in despair about Stella, as I have been told that NBC is cutting out all its soap operas. What does the future hold for me?

I am delighted you are coming out. It will be a joy to see you.

All my best,

[signed:] Cole

Porter's next letter to John Wharton not only asked him to do a favour for a friend, it also commented on the possibility of Porter receiving an honorary doctorate from Yale:

12 September 1955: Cole Porter to John Wharton[52]

Dear John:

Thank you very much for your letter. I am so glad that Colorado was so successful. I enclose a letter from the son of one of my good friends

---

* *Summertime*, starring Katharine Hepburn and Rossano Brazzi, was directed by David Lean. It is based on Arthur Laurents's play *The Time of the Cuckoo*.

in Yale.* I have asked him to telephone to you, after having written him to say that I have asked you to do everything possible to clear that BEGIN THE BEGUINE difficulty in his revue. I should appreciate your helping him.

Regarding your sending a four page biography of me to Dean Atchison, in regard to the Yale Honorary Degree, I see no objection to this nor to a short statement about my music, written by Alex Steinert, but I must say it all sounds a little bit cold-blooded.

All my best.
Sincerely
[signed:] Cole

The correspondence about the degree continued twelve days later:

24 September 1955: Cole Porter to John Wharton[53]

Dear John:

Thank you for your nice letter of September 19th, 1955.

I have gone over the biography in detail and enclose herewith a corrected version. It is always strange to me how many fables are connected with the facts of anyone's life. For years I have been haunted by being credited with having been given the Croix de Guerre. This never happened.

Also, many biographies speak about Linda and me running a night club in Venice. This must stem from the fact that I had a huge barge converted into a dance floor. I imported a negro band from London and once a week this barge was towed around the lagoons of Venice. The membership consisted of about one hundred of our friends, who paid a certain amount for the privilege of belonging to this club. All the proceeds were given to a local charity. So much for the night club!

Best.
Sincerely,
[signed:] Cole

---

* Thomas Noyes and Lyn Austin were to produce *Joyce Grenfell Requests the Pleasure* . . . at the Bijou Theatre in New York from 10 October. Most of the music was by Richard Addinsell but the choreographer had prepared a routine to Porter's 'Begin the Beguine' and Noyes was unsure who to ask permission to include the music. Thomas Noyes's father, Newbold, was one of Porter's classmates at Yale. See the letter of 8 September 1955 from Noyes to Porter, CPT, Correspondence 1955.

On 1 October, John Wharton wrote to Porter to confirm that his regular amanuensis and arranger Alex Steinert had written the biography for Porter's degree application. He also commented on Porter's plan to reuse a song from *Around the World* in a new project. The composer replied:

3 October 1955: Cole Porter to John Wharton[54]

Dear John:

Thank you for your letter of October 1st, 1955.

I read the article written by Alex Steinert and find it very good but I suggest that you get also a letter from Dr. Sirmay, as his point of view will be more professional and less personal. He also might mention how much my music is played all over the world.

I read with horror about the song I wanted to use from AROUND THE WORLD. I shall have to completely re-write what I have just written so that there can be no legal objections.

My best.

[signed:] Cole

It would be several years before Porter received the degree.

Jean Howard had assembled a photograph album of her trip to the Greek islands with Porter, which delighted him when it arrived, paving the way for their next holiday the following year:

19 September 1955: Cole Porter to Jean Howard[55]

Dearest Jeannie:

When I talked to you on the telephone the beautiful album of our Greek cruise had not yet arrived. You say that this is not a work of art, but to me it definitely is and I shall always treasure it!

I miss you dreadfully.

My love to you both.*

[signed:] Cole

---

* i.e. to both Howard and Charles Feldman, her ex-husband.

Porter's *Out of This World* received a brief revival off-Broadway at the Actor's Playhouse from 12 October, directed by Rick Besoyan, who went on to write the book, music and lyrics for the successful musical *Little Mary Sunshine* (1959).[56] A review in the *New York Times* commented that *Out of This World* had appeared 'sporadically dull' on Broadway but now seemed 'rather charming in a Greenwich Village basement', adding that it contained 'some of Mr. Porter's best songs'.[57] But Porter's attention was on *High Society*. It was announced on 28 November that Grace Kelly,* Bing Crosby and Frank Sinatra would star in the film, which would be directed by Charles Walters and be filmed in January 1956.[58] Porter had done most of his job by this point, but a particularly rich body of correspondence survives from this period on the latter stages of preparing the music for the film. He wrote to the movie's producer, Sol C. Siegel, and to the associated music director, Saul Chaplin, on 10 November about a song that was ultimately abandoned:

10 November 1955: Cole Porter to Sol Siegel[59]

Dear Sol: –

Find enclosed a copy of double number ("SO WHAT?"). This should be sung sentimentally by Mike – and rather sarcastically by Dexter.

Best,

[unsigned]

P.S. – I enclose a note for Saul Chaplin.

10 November 1955: Cole Porter to Saul Chaplin[60]

Dear Saul: –

Please study this <u>SO WHAT</u>? number before you play it for Sol Siegel.

Please note that the first two measures are legato; the second two measures are staccato and hot; the third two, legato; the fourth two, staccato and hot; continuing until measure fourteen, when all the notes are staccato except for slurs. This should be observed not only instrumentally, but vocally.

All my best,

[unsigned]

---

* Grace Kelly (1929–82) was one of Hollywood's biggest stars of the 1950s, appearing in *Dial M for Murder* (1954), *Rear Window* (1954) and *To Catch a Thief* (1955) among many others, before marrying Prince Rainier III of Monaco (1923–2005) in April 1956.

He wrote again to Siegel later in the month:

23 November 1955: Cole Porter to Sol Siegel[61]

Dear Sol: –

I enclose a verse to Who Wants to be a Millionaire? I know you don't want it for the picture, but we need it for published copies. Therefor, [sic] will you kindly have this verse joined to the refrain and have the usual number of copies sent to Chappell, and three copies sent to me personally.

Best,

[signed:] Cole

Siegel gave the letter to Johnny Green, one of the film's two musical directors, who responded with the copies on 9 December and asked him to 'address such purely musico-mechanical matters as this directly to [him]' in the future.[62]

Porter responded on 12 December:

12 December 1955: Cole Porter to Johnny Green

Dear Johnny: –

Thank you very much for your note of December 9, 1955, enclosing the copies which I requested of Who Wants To Be a Millionaire?

In the future, I shall take your advice and address all musical-mechanical matters to your department directly. Thanks for the tip.

Yours sincerely,

[signed:] Cole

(Cole Porter)

Nevertheless, Porter continued to correspond with Siegel:

14 December 1955: Cole Porter to Sol Segal [sic][63]

Dear Sol: –

In regard to the French lyric and the refrain of Little One, I called Dr. Sirmay at Chappell asking him to have the head of the Chappell Publishing

House in Paris find a French lyracist [sic] to make a French lyric of this song, and the type of lyric which would be commercially valuable when the numbers from High Society are published in France. I should receive this shortly, and will forward it to you. Naturally, if there is any expense connected with this, it will be my own expense.

I can't tell you how happy your telephone call made me. Writers all like an occasional tap on the back, and yours was so welcome.

Best,

[unsigned]

He also continued to send music to Chaplin for preparations for the movie:

15 December 1955: Cole Porter to Saul Chaplan [sic][64]

Dear Saul: –

I am sending with this note, an ink copy of the extra refrain of Now You Has Jazz. The reason is because I wish you would get to know it well before Sol Siegel receives his copy of the same. I am not sending his copy until Saturday.

Best,

[unsigned]

The following letter to Siegel is typical of Porter's advocacy for charitable causes:

17 December 1955: Cole Porter to Sol Segal [sic][65]

Dear Sol: –

I realize the following is perhaps far too early a request:

A very old and very dear friend of mine, Mrs. Lytle Hull, is the head of an organization named the HOSPITALIZED VETERANS SERVICE. What she would like to do is get a Preview of High Society as a Benefit for this organization.

I have always been interested in this organization myself, and contributed to it for years. It is part of the Musicians Emergency Fund. I enclose the descriptive leaflet which may interest you.

Will you be good enough to communicate with Mrs. Hull directly concerning this? Her address is:

MRS. LYTLE HULL
860 Fifth Avenue
New York, N.Y.
Best,
[unsigned]

Johnny Green wrote to Porter again on 22 December, commenting that 'Only in the last ten days have my decks been cleared for action on "HIGH SOCIETY", which means that only in the last ten days have I had a chance to get really familiar with the score. It is perfectly <u>wonderful</u>!! In my view, it is really top drawer Porter! Each of the songs is so right for its spot that it is difficult for me to pick a favorite or favorites. I <u>can</u> tell you that I just <u>love</u> "Samantha". It has that hauntingly special quality that is yours and I'm just crazy about it!'[66] Green was working with Saul Chaplin on the musical direction of the film and Chaplin had written at length on 17 December to describe how the score was being treated. Chaplin reported that Siegel and the film's director Charles Walters 'love' 'High Society Calypso' and 'I Love You, Samantha' and liked his new lyrics to 'Well, Did You Evah?' They all felt that 'Calypso' was 'one verse too long' so they eliminated one; 'We also found that staging-wise we could get more fun out of the number by repeating the chorus . . .' he continued. He additionally made a suggestion for a second verse of 'Well, Did You Evah?' He concluded: 'As you know, Johnny Green is going to conduct the score. I had a long meeting with him yesterday during which time I went through all the music with him, explaining your intentions regarding each song. One of the important points I made was simplicity of orchestrations.'[67] The composer responded with comments on minor changes to the lyrics:

21 December 1955: Cole Porter to Saul Chaplin[68]

Dear Saul: –

Your letter of December 17, 1955, made me very happy indeed, and I am so glad that you are determined that I shall see <u>High Society</u> without any surprises.

I understand perfectly why you cut the lyric in the CALYPSO song. Thank Heaven, it was too long rather than too short.

As far as <u>WELL, DID YOU EVAH?</u> goes, I think your lyric:
HAVE YOU HEARD THE STORY OF
A BOY, A GIRL, UNREQUITED LOVE?
is difficult to understand unless Crosby pauses after "Boy" and after "Girl". How would you like this line?:
HAVE YOU HEARD THE STORY OF
DEXTER BOY'S UNREQUITED LOVE?
If everyone prefers your line, it's O.K. with me.*

I am so sorry you didn't get that extra week here, but maybe one day I shall get another job at Metro and can wangle a longer visit for you in the wilds of New York.

A happy Christmas to you.

All my best,

[signed:] Cole

At the end of the year, Porter wrote to Irving Lazar, his agent in Hollywood, to update him on current projects. Although Cy Feuer and Ernest Martin were keen on a further collaboration, Sol Siegel was willing to offer Porter another movie after *High Society*, called *Les Girls*:

31 December 1955: Cole Porter to Irving Lazar[69]

Dear Irving: –

Thank you for your letter of Dec. 28, 1955. I am not an idiot child. I do not call Sol "Saul", nor do I call Saul "Sol". These are two different people. There is a producer named Sol Siegel – and an assistant producer name Saul Chaplin. Sol sent Saul to be with me here for ten days while I wrote new material. This was done in order that I make no mistakes as to what was required in detail. Since Saul (not Sol) returned to Culver City, I have received charming telephone calls from Sol, and a most enthusiastic letter from Saul.

---

* Chaplin's version was used in the film.

Feuer & Martin are changing ideas every day about our new show. I cannot say yet that I shan't do whatever they find, but I am very tempted to tell them, in case this goes on, that I have decided to accept a commitment from Sol Siegel. This would solve my working life perfectly, as I go abroad toward the end of February, will be back in New York on June 1st, and plan to start the usual summer in California at 416 North Rockingham Ave. What you write about Les Girls sounds most interesting, and I do hope you can come up with more detailed news about this.

This letter may be forwarded to you in Moscow. Answer me when you have time.

A very Happy New Year to you.

Your devoted,

[unsigned]

Two further letters from Porter to Chaplin reveal additional discussion on the adaptation of 'Well, Did You Evah?', an old Porter song from *Du Barry Was a Lady*, for *High Society*:

31 December 1955: Cole Porter to Saul Chaplin[70]

Dear Saul: –

I tried to telephone you a few nights ago to wish you a happy New Year. I was up in the country and did not have your 'phone number, so I telephoned to Mary Kidd, who quickly gave me a wrong number. Then I telephoned her back, got your correct number and you were out. This is merely to register the fact that I wish you a HAPPY NEW YEAR.

In reference to your letter or [sic] December 23, 1955, I don't understand your routine in Well, Did You Evah? You write: "We timed it and found it ran two minutes and thirty seconds, which is long as picture numbers go, but it is such fun that it feels short. As a result we are doing something bold: At the end of the number the boys walk out into the ball room (at Uncle Willie's party), look at all the squares dancing, go right back into the library and do a planned encore which runs about another minute." What does this mean? Do they repeat the lyrics they have already used, or do you need new lyrics?

My lawyer received a very heavy letter from the head office of Metro, mentioning certain names and asking whether they were based upon live

people or not, – for instance, Professor Munch, Countess Krupp and Mimsey Starr. I answered that, as far as I knew, these people were my own invention.*
I don't think you will get into any trouble about these names, except possibly Mimsey Starr. Perhaps it is dangerous to use a Christian and a family name together – in which case, I suggest "Grandma Starr". I wouldn't think of causing MGM any extra expense.

The only thing that terrifies me about your letter is that you register such a tidal wave of happiness as you start to work with the different actors. I have always found that when this happened during rehearsals of a show, the moment the show opens all the actors hate one another's guts.

All my best,
[signed:] Cole

11 January 1956: Cole Porter to Saul Chaplin[71]

Dear Saul: –

Your detailed letter explaining the encore of <u>Well, Did You Evah?</u> arrived, and calmed me.

As for <u>Now You Has Jazz</u>, it sounds wonderful; I can't wait to hear the recording. Please continue to keep me posted. Your letters give me great joy.

All my best,
[signed:] Cole

Porter wrote again to Lazar on 11 January to ask his advice:

11 January 1956: Cole Porter to Irving Lazar[72]

Dear Irving:

How can the following be solved without my coming to Hollywood:

Sol Siegel telephoned me last week asking if I couldn't go out to have publicity pictures taken with the cast. It would be most difficult for me to come out, as I am very busy here now trying to settle a show with Feuer & Martin.

So many people have spoken to me about the lack of publicity I am getting on <u>High Society</u>. Everyone else connected with it gets almost daily

---

* Porter's letter to Robert Montgomery is in CPT, Correspondence 1955. He writes: 'Thanks for your letter of Dec 21, 1955. As for "Professor Munch", "Countess Krupp", and "Mimsey Starr", they are, as far as I know, entirely fictitious people.'

publicity, including Sol Siegel. Maybe you have some Irving Lazar method by which this could be solved?

Feuer & Martin are being very nice, so that if Sol Siegel comes through with a picture in June, I can do both the picture for Sol and the show for Feuer & Martin.

I am so glad you are not going to Moscow. It's much better that you stay at home and make lots and lots of money.

Love,

[unsigned]

Curiously, it appears that rights for the use of 'Well, Did You Evah?' had not formally been cleared with Max Dreyfus at Porter's publisher Chappell, and the composer was concerned that this might affect his current negotiations with Siegel and MGM to write *Les Girls*:

13 January 1956: Cole Porter to Irving Lazar[73]

Dear Irving: –

Your letter of Jan. 10, 1956 arrived with my breakfast. I can't tell you how happy I am that this new [Sol C.] Siegel deal looks so posible. I waited at 4:30 yesterday afternoon for your call in regard to [Well,] Did You Evah? rights. Before that I had called Bob Montgomery at Wharton's office, to ask him to talk to you, and telling him that Max Dreyfus' insistence upon his being paid might endanger my next picture deal with Metro. I hope this has been settled. It is a slight worry to me.

I am off on February 19th with my same travelers, Jean Howard and Bob Bray. We plan to be back in New York the first week of June. Say nothing – but there is a possibility that Yale will give me an honorary degree this Summer, in which case I could not be in Hollywood until around the middle of June. But this honorary degree may easily not be forthcoming.

I was shocked that you weren't at the opening of The Great Sebastians.*
You would have looked so lovely in your fur coat.

Love,

[unsigned]

---

* *The Great Sebastians* by Howard Lindsay and Russel Crouse (librettists of Porter's *Anything Goes*) had opened on 4 January. It starred Alfred Lunt and Lynn Fontanne.

A further letter to Chaplin mentions the recent engagement of *High Society*'s star Grace Kelly to Prince Rainier III of Monaco:

19 January 1956: Cole Porter to Saul Chaplin[74]

Dear Saul: –

Thank you very much for your detailed letter of January 12, 1956 – and I was delighted to read how well Grace Kelly is turning out. What God-given publicity!

Please keep me posted when you have time. I deeply appreciate your thoughtfulness.

Best,

[signed:] Cole

Porter heard again from Johnny Green on 28 January, his letter also enclosing the pre-recordings of all the songs from *High Society* apart from 'True Love', which had not yet been recorded. Green advised: 'I wish to call to your attention that these recordings are standard groove 78 rpm. Please, dear Cole, play them on a real good up-to-date machine. We're all kinda proud of them and would like to feel that you are listening to them under fine acoustico-electronic conditions.'[75] Porter responded:

2 February 1956: Cole Porter to Johnny Green[76]

Dear Johnny: –

When you can, will you please send me the instrumental recordings from High Society also, – I mean those that are used for Montage, etc.

This is a pest request, – would you please send to Fred Astaire (1129 Summit Drive, Beverly Hills) the recording of Now You Has Jazz, as it was entirely due to his taking me to Norman Granz'* Jazz at the Philharmonic that started the idea of this number.

Once more, let me thank you for those wonderful records.

My best to you both,

[signed:] Cole

---

* Norman Granz (1918–2001) was a jazz record label owner and producer. His labels included Verve, and his Jazz at the Philharmonic concerts ran from 1945 to 1957.

Green fulfilled Porter's request on 14 February by sending him three more recordings from the film – the French version of 'Little One', Louis Armstrong's band's version of 'Samantha' and the jazz version of the Wedding March – and confirmed that 'Now You Has Jazz' had been sent to Astaire.[77] A day later, he wrote again to Porter, asking permission to make a small change: 'We humbly submit to you that the melody as included in the <u>first</u> ending on page 5 of the enclosed copy should not exist, and that the melody on "one gal guy" as it appears in the second ending should be the <u>only</u> melody for the ending of the refrain. In other words, the trick of the word "gal" on the two notes E and D going up to the G on the second line for the last note is something real special and characteristic, and should be the only way in which the last phrase of the tune is ever heard. You will note that we took the liberty of so proceeding in our recording with Crosby . . .'[78] Porter replied to these letters:

17 February 1956: Cole Porter to Johnny Green[79]

Dear Johnny: –

Thank you for your letter of Feb. 14, 1956. The recordings of <u>LITTLE ONE</u>, <u>I LOVE YOU</u>, <u>SAMANTHA</u>, and <u>WEDDING MARCH</u> arrived, and I thank you very much.

Although I am off for Europe on Sunday, I would appreciate it if you would send the recording of <u>TRUE LOVE</u> to me at the Waldorf, attention of Mrs. Smith, my secretary, to await my return.*

Thank you very much for sending <u>NOW YOU HAS JAZZ</u> to Fred Astaire.

If, in the normal course of things at Metro, you do not make discs for distribution of background scoring, nevermind [sic] making them for me.

All my best, and thank you again very much for your thoughtfulness.

Sincerely,

[signed:] Cole

---

* Green sent the recording of 'True Love' on 1 March, commenting: 'In the event that you should find the tempo a little slower than perhaps you would have liked, let me point out that this was most carefully considered and that the requirements of the scene dictated what we have done tempo and mood-wise.' Letter of 1 March 1956 from Green to Porter. Madeline P. Smith replied on 5 March to acknowledge receipt of the recording. Sources: USC, MGM Music Department collection. Box PR-31A.

18 February 1956: Cole Porter to Johnny Green[80]

Dear Johnny: –

Thank you for your letter of Feb 15, 1956, concerning the ending of I Love You, Samantha. I'm ahead of you: Quite a while ago I realized that the first ending of the refrain was dull and I have already arranged with Chappell that both the first and the second refrain end with the notes E and D, going up to G.

I am glad we agree about this.

All my best.

Sincerely,

[signed:] Cole

While Porter was engaged with the final preparations for *High Society*, on 16 February it was announced that *Silk Stockings* – still running on Broadway – would be filmed by the Arthur Freed unit at MGM.[81] And later in February, an old wound was scratched when Robert Montgomery wired Porter about the forthcoming revival of *Kiss Me, Kate* at New York's City Center. It appears that the tension between Porter and Bella Spewack following the publication of the script of *Kiss Me, Kate* had not been forgotten:

21 February 1956: Robert Montgomery to Cole Porter[82]

IN CITY CENTRE PRODUCTION OF KATE, SPEWACKS REQUEST SAME SIZE BILLING AS YOU. UNDER ORIGINAL CONTRACT THEY GET THREE-FOURTHS. WILL YOU CONSENT? CABLE ANSWER "LONGSIGHT". MONTGOMERY

22 February 1956: Cole Porter to Robert Montgomery

NEVER CONCESSIONS TO SPEWACKS=COLE

Earlier in the month, in preparation for a tour of Europe and the Holy Land, Porter had sent Jean Howard the following telegram:

3 February 1956: Cole Porter to Jean Howard[83]

I HAVE GOT CERTIFICATE FROM RECTOR ST. BARTHOLOMEW'S SAYING YOU ARE CHRISTIAN THIS WILL SUFFICE. COLE

Howard explains: 'I knew that Cole had some anxiety about safely traveling in certain parts of the Holy Land, but I was surprised when I received the following cable prior to our leaving for this trip ... I suppose he was concerned about the name Feldman, on my passport, being Jewish. At the time I thought it silly; today it seems clairvoyant.'[84] Porter flew from America to Switzerland on 19 February and his diary begins on 29 February:

29 February 1956[85]
Flew from St Moritz to Madrid in [Stavros] Niarchos' DC3, a four-and-a-half hour flight. Spring!

1 March 1956
Dined with Albas* in completely restored Palacio de Liria.

2 March 1956
Arrived Cordova.

3 March 1956
Cordova Mosque. Afternoon, arrived Sevilla.

4 March 1956
Sevilla, El Alcazar.

5 March 1956
Sevilla Cathedral. At 7:00 p.m., a concert in my honor at orphanage – boys 7 to 14, singing sacred and regional songs. Expert singing and touching experience.

6 March 1956
Left Sevilla. At 1:00 p.m. arrived Xerez de la Fronteira. [sic][†] To Gonzales-Biass sherry winery. A lot of local students there in choir-boy robes, the robes trimmed in long ribbons, each from a different girl. They elected

---

* Porter's long-term friends, the Duke and Duchess of Alba.
† Porter means Jerez de la Frontera.

Jean Howard their "Queen," then they all took off their robes to make a beautifully soft dance floor. Surrounding Jean in a circle, they persuaded her to dance on their robes as they sang and played their mandolins and guitars. Jean became suddenly Spanish and danced like a lovely gypsy. Arrived Algeciras at 7:00 p.m. Hotel Reina Cristina. A strange kick to look out the window and see the rock [sic] of Gibraltar – and an unexpected shock to find a hot coal fire in my sitting-room after dinner, arranged by Robert [Bray]. Nice surprise!

7 March 1956
Lunch at Hotel Rock, Gibraltar. Gibraltar so big and so British. In the late afternoon, Fuengirola on the Mediterranean. Hotel Malhamar. Customers here mostly British and Scandinavian. The British have been coming to this Costa del Sol for years. Thus, dull food as against the rest of Spain. Hotel Malhamar run by a brilliant young Spanish girl. "Papa always in Madrid." She could run the Chase National Bank.

8 March 1956
Drove for lunch to Ronda – remarkable bridge and house of the Moorish king.

9 March 1956
Evening, Granada. Alhambra Palace Hotel, after driving through beautiful mountains covered with blooming fruit trees. The road wonderful.

10 March 1956
The Alhambra. At night a great gypsy song-and-dance show in a cave.

11 March 1956
The Royal Chapel with the tombs of Ferdinand and Isabella, Joana, The Mad, and Phillip, The Fair.

12 March 1956
The Generalife.

13 March 1956
Murcia.

14 March 1956
Valencia, after a picnic by the sea.

15 March 1956
Barcelona. A wonderful bistro, Los Caracoles.*

17 March 1956
Monte Carlo.

18 March 1956
Monte Carlo. Lunch at La Reserve, Beaulieu. Henry May, also. Dinner, Salle Privee, Julie Thompson.

19 March 1956
Lunch with Bertha Michelham. Tea with Daisy Fellowes. Dinner with Pierre de Monaco at his villa.

20 March 1956
Gave a dinner at Le Snack, excellent Italian restaurant, for all the friends.

24 March 1956
Lunched at Valeria Litta's; and dined at Marina Cicogna's.

25 March 1956
Flew to Palermo, Palace Hotel, Mondello.

26 March 1956
Monday. La Favorita, charming Chinese royal villa, Capella Palatina, Bagheria, Palagonia villa with monster statues, tombs of Norman and Hohenstaufen royalties in cathedral.

27 March 1956
La Martorana, San Giovanni degli Eremiti – and after lunch, the beautiful Monreale. On the way home, horrible catacombs full of half-preserved hanging bodies under a Capucine monastery. We had lunch with Conchita (Contessa d'Assaro) in the family's Mazzarini Palazzo. After, a tour of the palazzo; one room full of exquisite porcelaine [sic] table services, including Compagnie des Indes, Vienna, Spode, and a huge service of Ginori.

Porter's correspondence was irregular during this trip, but the following letter to George Eells brings his friend up to date. He does not, however, mention the release of the new film adaptation of *Anything Goes* on

---

* The entry for 16 March is blank.

21 March, nor his fortieth anniversary as a Broadway composer on 28 March (mentioned in the *New York Times*):*

27 March 1956: Cole Porter to George Eells[86]

George – your letter of Mar 19th hit me here today, a bit slow as there are airplanes. But the letter was so full of the news I love to hear that it all sounded like this morning's Winchell.† I'm so happy about <u>My Fair Lady</u>‡ + <u>The Most Happy Fella</u>,§ sorry about <u>Mr. Wonderful</u>¶ + infinitely sad about Jack Wilson** being thrown out of <u>Strip For Action</u>.†† I knew he would be thrown out, but now that it has happened, I worry about my dear friend, Natasha,‡‡ who will have to cope with more + more hysterics.

Sicily is The Dream. Southern Spain had constant sunshine but it was <u>not</u> warm. Here in Palermo, it makes me remember a remark of my grandfather, years ago. It was "Cole, there's nothing like Spring in Peru, Indiana."

Your letter makes me worry about Richard§§ but I can't solve his life though, as you know, I have great affection for him.

Stan Musgrove writes that Bobbie [Raison] + dere Vere have moved from Malibu to West Hollywood. Where is West Hollywood?

I love your story re April, the child + the finger, – the clean finger. I told it to Sicilians today at lunch at the Palazzo Mazzarini. There people are <u>very</u>

---

* The *New York Times* review of the film was headed 'Cole Porter Music Still Fresh'. A. H. Weiler, *New York Times*, 22 March 1956, 38. The *Times* carried a mention of Porter's fortieth anniversary on 28 March 1956, 26, though he had a song performed on Broadway in 1915 before his full debut in 1916.

† Walter Winchell (1897–1972) was a famous journalist, known for siding with Joseph McCarthy against Communism in his gossipy reportage.

‡ Lerner and Loewe's *My Fair Lady* opened on 15 March.

§ Frank Loesser's *The Most Happy Fella* opened on 3 May. Eells must have seen the pre-Broadway tryout.

¶ Jerry Bock, Larry Holofcener and George David Weiss's *Mr. Wonderful* opened on 22 March. Sammy Davis Jr. was the star. Porter's 'It's All Right With Me' was interpolated.

** Porter's old friend, John C. Wilson, director of *Kiss Me, Kate*.

†† *Strip For Action*, by Jimmy McHugh and Harold Adamson, was due to open in April but was postponed until September.

‡‡ Wilson's wife.

§§ Porter's masseur (see McBrien, *Cole Porter*, 363).

grand, and probably the greatest family in Sicily. Luckily for me, they all understand English perfectly. When I told them this story at the luncheon – 20 of us, the luncheon became a riot + they suddenly were crazy for me.

Best + thanks

Cole

28 March 1956: Cole Porter's diary

Segesta and its great Doric temple, so alone in the mountains. A drink with my beloved Gabriella (now Principessa Gardinelli) at her palazzo, a vast sixteenth-century palace in the slums. I hadn't seen her for 28 years. She was so lovely in our Venice days, when she was married to Andy Robilant. In fact, they were the best-looking young couple I have ever seen. And what delightful parties they gave in their two, but connecting, Mocenigo palazzi. Gabriella is still very pretty with her slightly gray hair, and evidently supremely happy with her big brute of a husband. She was so touched when I told her I had sent a little St. Cloud box to Carlino, her younger son and Linda's god-child.

29 March 1956

Lunch at Castelvetrano. Afterwards to Selinunte (Selinus) to see the most vast ruin in Europe, on a hilltop overlooking the sea. This was a great Greek city, 7th Century B.C., destroyed by the Carthaginians at the beginning of the 5th Century B.C. Only one fragment of a temple is still standing but acres and acres of huge sections of temples lying on the ground. A breath-taking sight.

In the evening, Agrigento and the Hotel Grande-Bretagne and Gellia. Huge crowds in the streets, and very narrow streets. This hotel has all been so recently redone that nothing works as yet, but a very good dinner and a smiling staff. Most Sicilians are little and ugly but with great humor.

From Sicily, Porter wrote to Albert Sirmay:

March 1956: Cole Porter to Albert Sirmay[87]

Sicily is a dream that I remember so well when Linda and I honeymooned here years ago, and this Palermo has so many beautiful examples of so many civilizations that one could see and see for months and months. *En plus* very warm sun, every tree in bloom outside my window as I write you a full moon over the gentle Mediterranean. True Love, High Society, Cole.

30 March 1956: Cole Porter's diary

Extraordinary Good Friday morning procession. After lunch, more vast ruins like those of Selinunte but more has been left standing. This destruction, same period as Selinunte, also by Carthaginians.

31 March 1956

Drove to Siracusa.

A postcard from Porter to Eells reads:

31 March 1956: Cole Porter to George Eells[88]

Dear George –

We saw this villa* built by the Prince of Palagonia in the 18th Century. He was so ugly that he engaged top sculptors to make monsters all around the house so that his wife could look at him without vomiting.

What a great idea.

Best + love to Richard.

Cole.

1 April 1956: Cole Porter's diary

The Ear of Dionysus, Greek theatre, Roman theatre.

2 April 1956

Easter Monday. Drove through laughing crowds to Hotel San Domenico, Taormina.

From Taormina, Porter wrote to the director John Fearnley,† who was interested in helming a revival of *Nymph Errant*:

---

* The Villa Palagonia is located in Bagheria, near Palermo in Sicily. It was built in 1715 by the architect Tommaso Napoli.

† John Fearnley (1914–94) was a casting director for the Rodgers and Hammerstein Organization from 1945 to 1955 and also directed numerous productions at the New York City Center Civic Light Opera and Jones Beach Marine Theater.

PORTER'S LAST MUSICALS, 1955–1957

3 April 1956: Cole Porter to John Fearnley[89]

Dear John – NY

Your note dated Mar 26 was here when I arrived.

When Nymph Errant opened in Manchester, the press was so good, due to Douglas Fairbanks Jr. arriving to pose with Gertie Lawrence in all the publicity shots, that even Charley Cochran was fooled. The shocking thing was that, in spite of the weak last scene of Act I – I wrote a new song for the 1st Act curtain named Nymph Errant – only fairly effective – and in spite of a very weak next-to-last scene in Act II, Romney Brent who was essentially a ham + was stunned by the papers, got permission from Cochran to leave + went to Egypt. From then on, we wandered through several towns + finally opened with great éclat in London. But the weak spots killed the high spots in spite of Gertie Lawrence + we lasted only 5 or 6 months.

As I think of the lyrics, – I forget many of them – but I remember <u>Solomon</u>. This was a show-stopper sung by a great negress, Elizabeth Welch. But these lyrics date.

I recommend my cousin, Ted Fetter. He could do a fine job for you. He just did the revised lyrics for my songs in the new – and I hear dull – picture out of Paramount, <u>Anything Goes</u>. He no longer writes lyrics. He sold his soul to T.V. + I believe he now is one of Bill Paley's powers. But he might do this job for you. And he won't rob you.

His name is –
Theodore H. Fetter
Home: 142 E 18th St.
Phone, Al. 4, 3385
Work: C.B.S. Television
485 Madison Ave.
Phone – Pl. 12345.

If you want to write to me in the future, call my secretary, Mrs Madeline Smith at my apartment at – The Waldorf Towers. She will always forward your letters. If she doesn't answer, call her at her flat, – BU 85124.

Best – Cole

P.S. I worry about you on this venture. It was a charming show but it lacked guts when it needed them.

P.P.S. Ted Fetter also did several jobs adapting my lyrics for London when I was too busy elsewhere to do the job myself. He failed as a lyricist because he never had the spark. But he had everything else. Given an idea, he was great. Don't tell him this. And if you aren't interested, don't call him up.

This Taormina is of such beauty that it scares me.

Again, best

Cole

3 April 1956: Cole Porter's diary
Roman (Graeco-Roman) theatre, drive way up to the village Castel Mola; later, Public Gardens.

4 April 1956
Rest and clean.

5 April 1956
From Messina by boat to Cosenza. Calabria lovely, mountainous but fertile country. All peasant women in bright red skirts with black bustles.

6 April 1956
Drove through strange Trulli region. Trulli are cone-shaped stone houses with white tops and curious designs on their fronts. Drove through terrible hailstorm, arriving for lunch, Bari – bitter cold and awful wind. In p.m. saw Cathedral of San Nicolas and San Gregorio, also Frederick II castle.

8 April 1956
Sunday. Still bitter cold. Molfetta, Duomo Vecchio; . . . Trani, beautiful Romanesque cathedral, lunch, then [to] Barletta, San Sepolcro (thirteenth century), nearby ugly Colossus of A.D. fourth century. Motored by battlefield of Cannae where Hannibal defeated Romans in 216 B.C. Castel del Monte, magnificent, thirteenth century. Castle of Frederick II on hilltop. The whole countryside nearly covered with snow. We found a nearby bar and drank coffee and homemade liqueurs. Back to Bari, still so cold, and the cyclonic wind goes on.

9 April 1956
Drove over Apennine mountains to Naples and Warm sunshine. The dear Hotel Excelsior, a beautiful suite overlooking the bay. Henry May waiting in the bar.

10 April 1956
Pompeii.

11 April 1956

The great palace of Caserta, beautiful architecture, fountains and gardens. Also, fascinating eighteenth-century and Napoleonic (Murat) interiors. In the evening to San Carlo* to hear [Rossini's] *Guglielmo Tell*. [Renata] Tebaldi[†] magnificent but the opera is a dud. Museo della Floridiana – porcelain.

12 April 1956
Posillipo.

13 April 1956
Rest and clean.

14 April 1956
National Museum – frescoes, mosaics, and sculptures from Pompeii and Herculaneum. Also frescoes from Paestum.

15 April 1956
Sunday Church and Museo di San Martino

Porter wrote again to George Eells from Rome:

15 April 1956: Cole Porter to George Eells[90]

Rome – 2 A.M. Thursday, April 19, '56

Dear George –

Mrs. Smith will phone you re The Observer. It's one of those mysteries which only the oracle at Delphi in ancient Greece could have solved. My Xmas present to you was a year's subscription to The Listener, a great English weekly.[‡]

Your letter of April 8th arrived. Richard[§] news is always interesting news to me. Oh how, oh how, can his life be solved? Why, instead of a second-hand Cadillac, doesn't he buy a first-hand bicycle?

---

* The famous opera house in Naples.

† Renata Tebaldi (1922–2004) was (with Maria Callas) one of the two greatest sopranos of Italian opera of her generation.

‡ It appears that Porter had ordered a subscription to *The Listener* as a Christmas present to Eells, but he had received *The Observer* instead.

§ Presumably Porter's masseur, as identified in McBrien, *Cole Porter*, 363.

As for Mark Richards, break him in. He has only that value & that value should not be wasted.

It will be a relief to leave Rome. Rome, to me, means merely a series of luncheons, dinners & balls. I can't escape this here as all the parties are given by old friends who still think that the only song I ever wrote was <u>Night & Day</u>.

A letter came from [Robert] Raison. What a snob! He explained that they had moved to Schuyler Road in North Hollywood. He also wrote that like my house in Brentwood, surrounded by the lower middle-class, their new house in North Hollywood had even more distinction. It is surrounded by peasants. Poor dere Vere. It all must upset, so much, her kosher standards.

Frank Loesser's job* in sheet music arrived. As usual, excellent lyrics & the tunes, – I believe, better.

As for <u>Fair Lady</u>, what wonderful work! I pine to see it.

Good night, dear George. Give the enclosed bill for 10,0000 lire to Richard. It's worth about sixteen bucks.

My love to you & Mark

Everybody's pal –

Cole

In Porter's absence, Sam Stark wrote to *Variety* to correct an article they had printed on the composer in late March. The notion that Porter had nothing but flops in the 1940s before *Kiss Me, Kate* remains a common misconception:

9 April 1956: Sam Stark to *Variety*[†]

Dear VARIETY:

That was a nice tribute to Cole Porter on page 1 in your March 28th issue, however, there were a few errors. Mr. Porter really made his Broadway bow

---

* *The Most Happy Fella.*

† A draft copy of the letter also includes the following: [handwritten:] 'The flops' [typed:] 'In 1943 Mexican Hayride had a run of 167 performances. The only flops were Seven Lively Arts in 1944 with 183 performances and Around the World in Eighty Days in 1946 with 75 performances.' On Stark's headed stationery: 'Sam Stark, collector, photographs, lithographs, books, scrap books, biographical data of stage and screen personalities.' Stanford University, Cole Porter Collection, shelfmark FE209, Correspondence: 1955 (on Waldorf stationery), 1–17.

PORTER'S LAST MUSICALS, 1955–1957

in 1915. He had a number called, "Two Big Eyes" in a show MISS INFORMATION starring Elsie Janie and Irene Bordoni, at the George M. Cohan Theatre, that opened October 15, 1915.

Reading further along in the article:

"During that time, from around 1940–48, Porter turned out a series of flops."

That is not correct. The list below could not be called flops.

1940. Panama Hattie. 501 perf.

1941. Let's Face It. 547 perf.

1942. Something for the Boys. 422 perf.

Most sincerely,

[signed:] Sam Stark

Stark omits the successful run of *Mexican Hayride* (1944) at 481 performances. Around the same time as this letter Porter sent a postcard to Stark:

18 April 1956: Cole Porter to Sam Stark[91]

Dear Sam – Thanks a lot for Missia [sic] Sert's book.* I shall read it with joy on my return.

Rome lovely but too many parties. It will be a relief to get to Egypt + meet only an occasional cobra.

Love to you both

Cole

Porter's diary continues:

16–19 April 1956: Cole Porter's diary
Rome, hectic.

A business matter disturbed Porter in Rome:

---

* Misia Sert's memoirs, *Misia and the Muses: The Memoirs of Misia Sert*, were published in English in 1953, with an introduction by Jean Cocteau.

17 April 1956: Cole Porter to Robert Montgomery[92]

Rome, Tues. April 17th 56

Dear Bob –

I hope you won't ask me to do this often. It wrecked an entire morning for me when I might have been looking at Michelangelo + I have only 2 full days here. Why can't you start a big movement to do away with, at least notaries public + all consulates?

Rome is full of sunshine + too many friends. I pine for Luxor + the peace of meeting only occasional cobras.

My best to you + to John [Wharton]

Cole.

From Cairo, Porter wrote to his masseur, Richard,[93] the following comical letter:

20 April 1956: Cole Porter to Richard [?]

Dear Richard –

Why don't you give up your faded Cadillac + buy yourself a Vespa? Rome abounds in Vespas. I'm sure you would be much happier on a Vespa than in a Cadillac for, 1) a Vespa can go just as fast as a Cadillac, 2) a Vespa makes much more noise and 3) it is infinitely more dangerous. So think of this when a rich chick wants to give you a gift.

This afternoon we fly to Egypt, our longest flight – six hours.

On your Easter card you wrote "Letter will follow." If you still have a complex about writing the English language, dictate to one of George [Eells]'s secretaries. I want your news.

My best to your family + to you. Thank Heaven I'm leaving Rome. My Italian masseur is much too violent. Perhaps he is too young.

C.P.

20 April 1956: Cole Porter's diary
Seven-hour flight to Cairo and Mena House.

21 April 1956
Saturday. Cairo. Pyramids, Sphinx, Mosque of Sultan Hassan, Mosque of Mohammad Ali (all alabaster).

22 April 1956

Sunday. Memphis and its lying-down Colossus. Sakkara, the great underground tombs of the sacred bulls, the step pyramid earlier than all.

23 April 1956

The Cairo Museum, the early Egypt, the middle and the late – the late beginning with Akhenaton, then to Tutankhamen and incredible loot from Tutankhamen's tomb in Luxor, discovered in 1922 by Carnarvon and Howard Carter. Everything in top condition and of extreme beauty.

24 April 1956

For dinner, a beautiful tent in the desert, under the full moon. We looked at the pyramids from the opposite side and the light on them was enchanting. After dinner, an Arab orchestra, two belly dancers, two male Sudanese comedians, and a beautiful Arabian horse, the only horse I have ever seen who could dance, even without his rider, in perfect tempo. On the way home, the usual stop to look at the Sphinx who has been there watching for five thousand years.

25 April 1956

Back to the Museum.

25 April 1956: Postcard of the Sphinx from Cole Porter to Sam Stark[94]

Still won't talk.
    Love
    Cole

27 April 1956: Cole Porter's diary

Friday. By plane to Beirut, Lebanon. Hotel Excelsior, excellent. Beirut beautiful and as against Cairo, not even one fly.

29 April 1956

Sunday. Drove to Byblos and saw ruins of so many civilizations, unluckily not beautiful. Up through magnificent country to a sad little patch of Lebanon cedars, some of them very old. The night in Tripoli, a run-down town. The hotel a remnant of Turkish domination. Terrible cozy corners but bang-up food.

30 April 1956

To the Krak des Chevaliers, a magnificent fortress originally built by the Kurds and later enlarged to become the finest example of what the crusaders could build. It is on top of a mountain and looks like a big walled city. Once inside, one goes up and up on a rather wide road designed for horsemen, until finally the summit.

I was carried up and then down by Paul [Sylvain], the Lebanese guide, and the two chauffeurs. They were exhausted and I felt sorry for them. But the Krak (Turkish for fortress) is one of the world's greatest wonders.

On to Baalbek and the charming Hotel Palmyra, with its delightful patron and patroness.

1 May 1956

Tuesday. In the morning to the most beautiful Roman ruins, the Temple of Jupiter with its very high columns, the Temple of Bacchus, on a smaller scale but nearly complete. Great restoration is being done here. A glimpse at the Temple of Venus, very little left. On to Damascus, seeing only the new city, to the Hotel Omayyad.

2 May 1956

Damascus. St Paul's window from which he escaped, Ananias's* house, underground (now a chapel), where he hid before his escape. (This Ananias was not the liar.) The Azzim Palace, a fine example of eighteenth-century aristocratic living, Saladin's tomb, the huge Omayyad Mosque, and the *souks* (bazaars) for miles and miles, so colorful. For a finish, the lovely Tequiha Mosque.

3 May 1956

Lunch at Amman in Jordan. On the way, women working on the road in constantly different costume. It seems that each village has its own costume. Camels grazing and many of them. Sheep in huge flocks and beautiful black goats. Bedouin tents scattered on the hillsides. The Allenby bridge over the little, muddy, fast-flowing Jordan. We passed the Mount of Temptation where Satan tempted Christ, also the Inn of the Good Samaritan. We stopped at Jericho, a lovely oasis and then the beau-

---

* Ananias of Damascus was one of Jesus's disciples at Damascus, mentioned in the Acts of the Apostles in the Bible. Ananias and his wife Sapphira were characters who lied about money in chapter 5.

tiful Dead Sea, with its Mount Nebo looking at us, where Moses was buried and Joshua took over and brought the Jews back to the Promised Land. All these stories of the Old and the New Testaments, what with two excellent guides, bring back my days in Sunday School when they were such good stories. Being here, they are even more, they are very moving. Jerusalem Friday.

4 May 1956

Jerusalem. Mount of Olives (ascension), Pater Noster church where Christ gave Lord's prayer to disciples for second time. Garden of Gethsemane, Church of Agony with its rock where Christ prayed, High Priest Caiaphas' house, where he and scribes decided to have Christ crucified and to spare Barabas and where Peter denied Christ. Underneath, prison where Christ was put. Pretorium of the Romans, Ecce Homo gate where Pilate showed Christ to populace. Ecce Homo house where Christ was mocked, scourged, and given crown of thorns. The Via Dolorosa to Church of Holy Sepulchre near Calvary, in a sedan chair.

5 May 1956

By chartered DC3 to Ma'an, drive in cars to a police station where horses and donkeys are waiting to take us to Petra. Finally to a great gorge, very high and very narrow where, after a long ride, suddenly everything opened and we were in a vast mysterious city carved out of solid rock and the rock multicolored. It was originally built by the Nabateans, enlarged by the Hellenistic Greeks, and elaborated by the Romans. There is a Roman aqueduct from the beginning of the gorge to the city, and in the city, a big Roman theatre (where did they get the actors?), on every side lovely palaces, temples, and tombs, carved in the solid rock; and even up in the mountains above, all of these becoming more colored by the setting sun. We each had a text. A good dinner, to which I invited Miss Kirk-Bride, an English archaeologist who is digging here and has found arrows, etc., from the Stone Age. After diner, Bedouin singers and dancers. Then to Miss Kirk-Bride's big cave where she has been living for months. She has her own stove, a cook, a maid, and many books.

6 May 1956

Sunday. After lunch, back to Jerusalem and on the way, constant evidences of the Arab League, of whom many are British, the whole outfit formed and still trained by the British. They wear British uniforms, very smart, but Arab headdresses (the *caipha* or scarf and the *egal* or double cord to keep the *caipha* on). We all wore these headdresses, beginning with our ride to Petra. They are most practical in the desert as they can be adjusted in any number of ways to protect one against the wind, cold, heat, dust, and flies.

7 May 1956

Bethlehem and the Church of the Nativity. The extraordinary thing about this "Holy Land" is not the spots, as most of the spots are mere conjecture. The moving part of it all is the Christians who have come from the entire world to worship.

8 May 1956

Plane to Beirut. Most of the plane occupied by very old Greek Orthodox peasants returning to their homes in Australia after having visited Jerusalem to pray. Two of them could barely walk. They all must have spent their life savings for this pilgrimage.

9 May 1956

Arrive Istanbul and Horrible Hilton. Outrageous invasion of press and photographers.*

10 May 1956

St. Sophia, Blue Mosque, Suleiman Mosque, former sultans' palace, to see jewels (fabulous and hideous).

11 May 1956

A drive to the Black Sea along the Bosphorus. One villa after another, each one more repulsive than the other, but the Bosphorus beautiful, looking very much like the Hudson. Back to the palace of the sultans, to see a huge collection of porcelain, most of it very valuable and very ugly. To the seven walls, to see the prison where people's heads were cut off and dropped in a hole to float or sink in the Sea of Marmora.

---

* Jean Howard notes: 'Cole wanted to avoid the press as much as possible. He turned against the Hilton hotel in Istanbul because hotel officials allowed them in – all the way in – the press actually walked straight in and found Cole in his bathtub. He was furious. The hotel did make the newspeople turn over the negatives, which Cole destroyed, but he didn't calm down.' *Travels with Cole Porter*, 184.

12 May 1956

Athens, bless it, and the charming Grande-Bretagne.

Back in Athens, Porter wrote to George Eells of his journey:

12 May 1956: Cole Porter to George Eells[95]

Dear George,

Thanks a lot for your letter dated May 1st.

Our trip through the Near, or if you prefer, the Middle East was continually another Arabian Night, mostly in the day-time.

The hotels everywhere were charming. Then we hit Istanbul + the Istanbul Hilton. This is an interesting hotel in that it has probably the most breathtaking site of any hotel in the world. It is wonderfully planned + beautifully built + it is the God-damnedest worst hotel on this Earth.

I can't tell you what a joy it is to be in Athens again + this excellent Grande Bretagne. (Hotels are important to tourists.)

On Monday, the 14th, we start our cruise on the beautiful [Stavros] Niarchos yacht to see islands of which I have dreamed for years.

I hit N.Y. on June 5th. Please warn Richard* I have written him to phone me but he easily may have forgotten where I live.

The show news in N.Y. is very exciting. I shudder when I read about Shangri-La† + The Ziegfeld Follies‡ + I can't wait to see My Fair Lady + Frank Loesser's [The Most] Happy Fella.

I shall ring you when I arrive to "date" you. It will be a joy to see you.

Best

Cole

His diaries continued:

---

* Porter's masseur. See McBrien, *Cole Porter*, 363.

† Harry Warren's Broadway musical *Shangri-La* opened on Broadway on 13 June and ran for only twenty-one performances.

‡ *The Ziegfeld Follies of 1956*, with a cast including Bea Arthur and Tallulah Bankhead, closed in Boston during its pre-Broadway tryout.

13 May 1956: Cole Porter's diary

Dined with Spiros Harocopos* in his beautiful apartment, the walls lined with fine Byzantine ikons. Among the guests, Paxinou,† the actress.

15 May 1956

Tuesday. Lunch aboard Eros; same charming crew. First stop, Hydra, a peaceful island. Visited late Byzantine church with lovely ikons.

16 May 1956

Parso, famous for marble quarries. Visited eleventh-century church, Byzantine, full of charming, simple carvings on varied marbles. At sunset, passed Naxos.

17 May 1956

Cos (or Kos). The fortress of the Crusaders, facing the east of Turkey, the huge plane tree under which Hippocrates is supposed to have first taught hygiene and curing (don't believe it). Hippocrates was born in Cos; the Asclepieion, the first spa in history, supposedly founded by Hippocrates, recently very restored by the Greek government.

In the evening, after a beautiful sail, arrived Patmos and its enchanting harbor.

18 May 1956

Friday. Patmos. We were taken in a truck by a terrifying road to a mountaintop to the Monastery of St. John the Divine, founded in the eleventh century. An old monk suddenly spoke to me in good English. He had been born on Patmos, went to the U.S.A., hated the bustle so much that he had come back here and had become a monk in a monastery "to find God and Eternal Peace." On the way down, to St. John's cave, where he lived after having been exiled from Rome by Domitian and where he wrote the Revelation.

19 May 1956

Samos. A drive to vast ruin of Temple of Hera, facing nearby coast of Turkey. Temple made of blue Samion marble, one huge column left standing.

In the evening, we arrive Chios, a sheltered harbor. Most of our crew comes from Chios. The captain's wife and two daughters, our chief steward, Niko's wife, daughter, and mother come aboard. These women are all

---

* Probably a Greek film producer.
† Katina Paxinou (1900–73) was a Greek actress of stage and screen.

beautiful, still retaining the widely separated eyes, the fine noses, and the small mouths of the classic Greek sculptures. We all drink and have hors d'oeuvres together, smiling and not being able to exchange one word.

20 May 1956

By car and then by donkey to Nea Moni (New Monastery), eleventh century, to see fine Byzantine mosaics comparable to those of Osias Lukas* and Daphne. Our departure from monastery (now a nunnery) delayed by Mother Superior who gave us a fig liqueur and *loukoum* made of rose petals. Both great. Lunch in a lovely spot under big plane trees. Later, dinner by the sea, and a terrible orchestra, but always top food.

All these people on the islands are alike in their simplicity, their dignity, and their happiness.

21 May 1956

Lesbos (Mytilene). A drive through mountainous but very fertile country to Ayassos, where ugly church contains beautiful small ikons, some of them resembling Persian miniatures.

22 May 1956

Thasos (looking like the mountains of New Hampshire). We had a private bus to see ruins of 450 B.C. city and the museum containing a strange archaic statue of Apollo, practically Egyptian. Also beautiful horses' heads and a sculpture of Venus without her upper half riding a delightful dolphin. Thasos honey was brought aboard, the most powerful honey in Greece. Many bees on deck though we were moored far from the shore. Slightly to the north, the coast of Macedonia.†

23 May 1956

Mt. Athos. We skirted the southern and the western coasts all morning looking through binoculars at numerous monasteries, some on the shore, others high on the mountainside. These monasteries are so big they look like villages; some of them are occupied by Greek monks, others by Bulgarian, Russian, or Serbian monks. Many monks, however, prefer to live in groups of two or three while the most ascetic of all live completely alone in caves or eagles' nests.

---

* A walled monastery in Boeotia, Greece.

† Jean Howard notes: 'Cole arranged to have some of the honey sent to New York – it was great.' Howard, *Travels with Cole Porter*, 191.

After lunch we first visited Dochiarion monastery near the shore. The interior of the church is entirely painted in the eleventh-century Byzantine style, though done in the sixteenth century. Beautiful. We met several monks, all old except one young man named Innocent who, in spite of his mustache and beard and long hair, looked like Audrey Hepburn.

Farther along the coast, Monastery of Dionysiou high on a cliff. Service was going on in the dusk of the church here, the monks all sitting in choir stalls around the edges and those participating in the service wearing black veils. Each monk seemed to be chanting a different chant, the whole effect nearly terrifying. After service, we were taken into a small sitting room to be given anisette, loukoum, and coffee, while an old monk who had spent eight years in the U.S.A. talked to us in fluent broken English about Atlanta, Georgia; Houston "good town," Texas; New York City ("too cold"); Chicago ("too cold"), and Los Angeles ("warm"). What he liked best in the U.S.A. was the Automat.

We didn't attempt to go to the monastery of Grand Lavra, though to get there one no longer has to be lifted up to it in a basket as there is a new steep road. But to get to the road one must go for many hours, mule-back.

The monasteries of Mt. Athos used to have 40,000 monks. Now there are only 2,000, and very few young men want to come here and become monks. The ones who are here do no good for the world. This has always been true. They have merely retired from life. The ones I met today seemed to be happy but nearly infantile. They all pray at least eight hours a day. Some in the less strict monasteries till small plots of land, which they own. Others sit around and live on the income of the monasteries into which they have retired, the income derived from properties the monasteries own on many nearby islands and lands. It is a strange experience to have been here, and fascinating, but it reeks of rot. (Look up Meteora monasteries of Thessaly.)

24 May 1956

Thursday. Skiros (Northern Sporades). Drove to town of Skiros, highly picturesque, rather like Mykonos but much higher and more dramatic. Saw memorial statue to Rupert Brooke* with inscription, 'To Rupert

---

* Rupert Brooke (1887–1915), the British First World War poet.

Brooke and Immortal Poetry." In museum, pottery of Cretan and Mycenaean civilizations mostly discovered by University of California archaeologist Dorothy Hanson.

25 May 1956
Skopelos (near Skiros), another peaceful isle. We didn't land. At sunset, Skiathos, a port full of fishing boats and no automobiles. When the Germans had to leave this port at the end of World War II, they bombed the town and set it afire. It has been charmingly rebuilt.

26 May 1956
Saturday. Cruised to another part of Skiathos and moored off a lovely sandy beach backed by huge pines. Then on to the gulf that separates northern Greece from Euboea. On our right we saw Mt. Olympus and, farther south, the mountain beyond, which is the pass of Thermopylae. In the evening we laid anchor at Chalkis. To the right is Tanagra.

27 May 1956
Sunday. Chalkis, farther on. From the bay here, the Greek fleet sailed for the Trojan War. Drove first to museum to see fine archaic sculptures from Eretria, then to Eretria, destroyed by Persians in 490 B.C. A few foundations left.

28 May 1956
Proceeded towards Petali. On our right, the plain of Marathon, Mt. Pentelikon, and, farther still, Mt. Hymettus. Anchored off Petali, island owned by Embericos* family. In the evening, a completely calm sea, the stars nearly on our hands, and silence.

29 May 1956
Had breakfast, as usual, on the deck. Arrived at Piraeus and the beautiful cruise is over. On the way to the Grande-Bretagne, we stopped to see the Mycenaean gold, which is once more exposed at the museum.

In the evening to the Benaki Museum, which was specially opened for us, after hours, to see fascinating Greek regional costume and jewelry, plus a fine collection of ikons.

---

* The Embericos family were world leaders in shipping, founded by Epameinondas C. Embericos (1858–1924), a founder of the Hellenic Steamship Navigation Company, Minister of Shipping, and co-founder of the Bank of Athens.

In *Travels with Cole Porter*, Jean Howard notes: 'Cole didn't say good-bye that May in Athens. The day after our return he left this note for me at our hotel':[96]

30 May 1956: Cole Porter to Jean Howard[97]

Dear Jean –

Robert [Bray] has to stand by in Rome to find out when he must hit Hollywood + I'm going along for the ride.

So goodbye, have fun + my love to you both.*

Cole.

On 1 June, Madeline P. Smith informed Sam Stark: 'Mr. P. comes home Tues, June 5.'[98] There was much for Porter to deal with on his return. For example, Cy Feuer and Ernest Martin hoped to tempt him with a musical adaptation of *The Shop Around the Corner*.† He also had *High Society* to catch up with:

6 June 1956: Cole Porter to Johnny Green[99]

Dear Johnny: –

I came back to find the sound track recording of TRUE LOVE waiting for me, and I can't tell you how surprised I am at the singing of Miss Grace Kelly.

I also found waiting the HIGH SOCIETY Overture,‡ which could easily resurrect the dead.

You can understand why I am coming back on June 18th to become again the slave of MGM, after the beautiful treatment given my efforts by Sol Siegel and by you and your great Music Department.

All my best to you, dear Johnny,

[signed:] Cole

---

* i.e. Howard and her ex-husband, Charles Feldman.

† They abandoned the project; much later, it became Bock and Harnick's *She Loves Me*, 1963. For the announcement of the possible musical, see Sam Zolotow, 'Audrey Christie Gets Stage Role', *New York Times*, 8 June 1956, 20.

‡ During Porter's holiday, Green had sent him a copy of the theatre-style overture to the film, which was to be 'played in deluxe houses before the picture itself goes on' and differed from the overture heard on the soundtrack album. Letter of 16 May 1956 from Johnny Mercer to Cole Porter. USC, MGM Music Department collection. Box PR-31A.

The latter paragraph refers to the composition of *Les Girls*, which would turn out to be Porter's final movie score. His regular business correspondence with Robert Montgomery continued:

23 June 1956: Cole Porter to Robert Montgomery[100]

Dear Bob:

Should I join the Composers and Lyricists Guild of America or do I already belong to this? Will you please attend to this matter?

I enclose your letter regarding the Lockheed airplane endorsement. I would be perfectly willing to fly Lufthansa, Air France or LAI but NOT TWA, so ask the Lockheed people to get hold of me and I will pose prettily.

Sincerely,
Cole

He also had several months' worth of the latest Broadway musicals to see. Alan Jay Lerner and Frederick Loewe's *My Fair Lady* had opened on Broadway on 15 March and when Porter finally saw it in June, he loved it. Over the coming months he became good friends with Lerner, who arranged for him to have regular seats for the show on Wednesday nights from the autumn:

2 July 1956: Alan Jay Lerner to Cole Porter[101]

Dear Cole:

I enjoyed seeing you so very much the other night. Your enthusiasm for the show means more to me than I can possibly say. I am naturally always pleased when people like it, but especially so when some do, and I cant [sic] think of anybody to whom that applies more than you.

I'll have your seats for you in the fall and I do hope we'll be able to have an evening together while you're here.

Have a wonderful summer.

Best regards,
[unsigned]

P.S. Crest Toothpaste is dazzling. I bought a tube the next morning. Best thing since French pastry.

7 July 1956: Cole Porter to Alan Jay Lerner

Dear Alan:

Thanks a lot for your letter of July 2nd. I can't tell you how happy I am about those seats in the fall.

According to the papers, you and your wife are coming out here for the summer but suddenly Dr. [Albert] Sirmay tells me that you have taken a house on Long Island. I am sorry, as I looked forward to seeing you this summer, but we can meet in the autumn.

All my best.

Sincerely,

[signed:] Cole

The next two letters give an insight into the role played by Madeline P. Smith in managing Porter's personal and business affairs. By July, Porter was in his house in California:

7 July 1956: Cole Porter to Madeline Smith[102]

Dear Mrs. Smith:

Please send to Romain Gary,* Esq., 1919 Outpost Drive, Los Angeles, Calif., the following book: HISTORY OF THE BYZANTINE EMPIRE by VASILIEV, Publisher: University of Wisconsin Press, with a card saying "Best regards from Cole Porter".

Please send two dozen each, size 8 x 10, reprints of the photograph and also the picture I use for fan mail.

Please keep the enclosed book from Dr. Shepard Krech and give it to me when I return to New York.

Please send me the English book THIN ICE by Compton Mackenzie, published by Chatto & Windus.

Please get two copies each of the following books, 1 set for the New York apartment and the other for Williamstown. If it is impossible to get all of

---

* Romain Gary (1914–80) was a French novelist and diplomat. He also wrote the screenplay for *The Longest Day* (1962) and directed two films.

these let me know and I shall bring them back from here, as I need them in all three places:

RIMARIO LETTERARIO DELLA LINQUA [sic] ITALIANA A CURADI GIOVANNI MONGELLI HAPLI-MILANO

JUAN DE PENALVER DICCIONARIO DE LA RIMA NUEVA EDICION CUIDAOSAMENTE [sic] CORREGIDA Y ALFABETTIZADA [sic] EDITORIAL SOPENA ARGENTINA SRL

P. H. MARTINON DICTIONNAIRE METHODIQUE ET PRATIQUE DES RIMES FRANCAISES LA ROUSSE [sic] – PARIS VIe

Best.

[unsigned]

14 July 1956: Cole Porter to Madeline P. Smith[103]

Dear Mrs. Smith:

Please order for me two copies of the book THE RHYMERS LEXICON (some later editions are named the Rhymers Dictionary) by Andrew Loring, published in London by George Routledge & Sons, Ltd., and in New York by E. P. Dutton & Company. This is probably out of print but I should be delighted even to have second hand [sic] copies. I need two of these as mine are falling apart. Don't, in desperation, take the copy which I have at the Waldorf.

Please steal and send a big box of the plastic toothpicks which I use at the Waldorf to:

Mrs. Leland Hayward
243 South Mapleton
Beverly Hills, California
with a card saying, "Sent by Cole Porter."
The enclosed list is for my bathroom at the Waldorf.
All my best.
[signed:] C. P.

After his long holiday, Porter was back in the game, writing what would become his final movie score for MGM, *Les Girls*, to star Gene Kelly. As with *High Society*, Sol Siegel was the producer. Porter mentions the project in passing in the following letter to Sam Stark, as well as teasing him about his habit of hoarding newspaper clippings:

29 July 1956: Cole Porter to Sam Stark[104]

Dear Sam:

Thanks a lot for your brief note of July 16th.

Why do you keep all the copies of the Variety, Saturday Review, Town and Country, Theatre Arts, Time and Life? This worries me as I am so afraid that you will end up like those two brothers that were found dead in Harlem, smothered by old magazines. As for my wanting to see anything in these magazines, one can get them in the smallest village in any country in Europe, in Africa or the Near East.

Please tell George Kelly* that I can't read his plays yet. I have a long list to read first but I appreciate very much your sending them to me.

I am awfully sorry that our date for Sunday had to be cancelled but I am under Sol Siegel's command!

Love to you both.

[signed:] Cole

On 9 August, *High Society* was released in cinemas. The reviews were surprisingly mixed, given the all-star cast – Bosley Crowther's review savagely refers to 'tedious stretches'[105] – but Porter himself was full of praise for director Charles Walters's work:

4 August 1956: Cole Porter to Charles Walters[106]

Dear Chuck:

This is a typed record of my congratulations to you for your great job on High Society.

All my best, dear Chuck.

[signed:] Cole

Indeed, Bosley Crowther's dismissive *New York Times* review of *High Society* was in turn criticized by one of Porter's colleagues, who wrote a letter to the newspaper:

---

* Presumably Porter means playwright George Kelly (1887–1974), winner of the Pulitzer Prize for *Craig's Wife* (1925).

Criticism is a grand and essential art, but criticism of criticism – even though a sort of cannibalism – is legitimate, too.

Take Mr. Crowther's review of "High Society," now at the Radio City Music Hall, for example. He makes a kindly reference to one of the songs sung by Bing Crosby, "I Love You, Samantha," and then he adds in parenthesis "(whoever she is)".

But the dialogue makes it quite clear who she is. She is Tracy Lord, played by Grace Kelly. Frank Sinatra mentions her distinctly as "Tracy Samantha Lord." Bing Crosby calls her "Sam" again and again through the picture. Wasn't Mr. Crowther listening?

Again, he refers to Louis Armstrong and his band "beating out some catchy tunes that have been borrowed from old Cole Porter albums or especially written by him for this show." The fact is that eight of the nine songs in "High Society" were written by Mr. Porter "for this show." The one exception, "Well, Did You Evah?", is not played by the Armstrong band, nor do they play anything else from "old Cole Porter albums."

This seems rather hit-or-miss criticism, with the accent strongly on the "miss." It's not like Mr. Crowther, who is usually alert and accurate. And it is not fair to his readers.

HOWARD DIETZ

Vice President in Charge of Advertising and Publicity, Metro-Goldwyn-Mayer, Inc., New York

Aside from his role at MGM, Dietz (1896–1983) was, of course, a distinguished lyricist in his own right, with musicals including *The Band Wagon*.

In response to a request to allow a Cole Porter Songbook to be published, Porter wrote:

19 August 1956: Cole Porter to John Wharton[107]

Dear John:

Thank you for your letter of August 19th, 1956. [...]

As for a Cole Porter song book being published by Simon and Schuster. This should be done, I believe, only if Simon and Schuster can publish it in such a way that it is possible to put it on a piano rack and be able to play it without the book falling off the rack. This was the great trouble with the Rodgers and Hart book.[108]

I look forward to seeing you a great deal in early October.

Best –

[signed:] Cole

He also continued to engage with charitable causes:

25 August 1956: Cole Porter to John Wharton[109]

Dear John:

I want very much to send $1,000.00 to help the Greek Islands which have lately been so injured by an earthquake.* In fact, my favorite island Santorini (Thera) has almost been wiped out.

Will you please let me know to whom the check should be made and how it can be made a tax deductible item?

Best.

[signed:] Cole

Porter planned to return to New York for the autumn:

29 September 1956: Cole Porter to Sam Stark[110]

Dear Sam:

Thank you so much for your letter of September 25th.

I hope we shall meet in New York before you sail. I arrive there on the night of October 8th.

Love to Y'all

[signed:] Cole

The first important event of the autumn was a ninety-minute colour television tribute to Porter on the 'Ford Star Jubilee', with performers including Shirley Jones, Gordon MacRae, Louis Armstrong and Dolores Gray. Porter wrote an article in anticipation of the broadcast on 6 October:[111]

---

* On 9 July 1956 the Greek island of Amorgas was hit by the largest known earthquake in the history of Greece.

30 September 1956: Cole Porter in the *New York Herald Tribune*:*
Now I Get A Kick Out Of TV
By Cole Porter

Television has undergone a great transformation, show-wise, in the last few years. I've been watching it happen. For a long while television was afraid to seem too polished. She stayed nice and folksy, trying to find that nonexisting group, the "average audience." When she reached the point where even the folksiest of us were saying, "Poor drab creature," then suddenly television peeked out of her poke bonnet and wondered if she might try on something just a little bit elegant. She slipped into a sleek and stylish format a few times and she hasn't been the same since. Now she's got class!

If the suggestion of a Cole Porter musical revue on television had been made four seasons ago, I doubt that it would have stirred my enthusiasm a while. But after watching the medium grow to combine, wisely, the best Broadway and Hollywood production ideas with fresh and clever television experiments, the idea of working on a hour-and-one-half musical was like the old station house fire gong. If there's anything I love, it's the planning, the concentration, the panic and the crises of getting ready an opening night – when you think you've really got a good show. Ours is set for this Saturday at 9:30 p.m., the "Ford Star Jubilee" premiere of the season on CBS Television, and we think it's worth all the excitement.

My only stipulation at the contract-signing was the same one that has applied to all my Broadway shows, that I be allowed to approve the staging. This may sound overbearing, but it's a matter of personal pride and affection. I have been in love with every show I've written, and it hurts and irritates me to hear one of my tunes mistreated – as it would to participate in a formal marriage ceremony while "The Wedding March" is played to a rock-and-roll beat.

I love the people that have made my shows and songs popular, and we have always worked together in rehearsal to make the numbers express

---

* The article (on p. G4) is accompanied on pp. 1–2 by pictures of Dolores Gray, Gordon MacRae, Shirley Jones, Dorothy Dandridge, and a group shot with Porter 'checking' the score. Caption: 'They'll star in the Cole Porter salute.' Also a p. 3 picture of Sally Forrest and George Chakiris rehearsing 'a number set for the Porter "spectacular"'. On p. 4, 'Dolores Gray, under the watchful eye of Cole Porter, zips through a song'.

the same feeling, whether snippy or sentimental, that is intended – and to make both the singer and the song the most effective.

We have hand-picked our television cast as carefully as for a Broadway revue. For the romantic ballads we're working with Shirley Jones and Gordon MacRae. They're studying – and I mean studying – such numbers as "In the Still of the Night," "I've Got You Under My Skin" and "So in Love." The galvanic Dolores Gray belts out "I Get a Kick Out of You," "Why Can't You Behave," "Just One of Those Things" and "Make It Another Old Fashioned" in a way that make my ears ring with delight. Louis "Satchmo" Armstrong, one of my all-time favorites, raises the ceiling with "Blow, Gabriel, Blow" and teams with Gordon MacRae for the "High Society" duet of "Now You Has Jazz." The gorgeous, sultry Dorothy Dandridge makes such a slinky Calypso sensation out of "You Do Something to Me" that I've asked her to try a number that I never thought could be duplicated, Mary Martin's "My Heart Belongs to Daddy."

My old friend George Sanders was asked to join us and give the audience a sampling of the comic personality he usually reveals only in singing at parties. He's agreed to render my variable "Let's Do It" as well as some comedy specials we're working on.

We had to have a team for such bouncy numbers as "Friendship" and "Be A Clown," and what better luck than to be able to nab Peter Lind Hayes and Mary Healy between Las Vegas engagements! "Night and Day" and "Begin the Beguine" are given the works with none other than the petite blonde actress Sally Forrest set to surprise everyone in her television dancing debut.

Can you imagine a show like this a few years ago? I couldn't. Then, when I saw a few hour-and-one-half television musicals appear on the horizon, with original scores, top performers, brilliant direction, then television came of age for me.

It has the added incentive of a one-time audience of millions. It had them all along. But it was first getting used to whirling out some 18 hours of entertainment a day, and I think there just wasn't time enough to sit back and really consider what enormous possibilities lay ahead. When television got past her baby steps, her brat stages and her self-conscious gawkiness, she decided to grow up all of a sudden. She's a lady now and should be treated as one. She can look good in blue jeans all the time. Let her wear her mink now and then, too. We'd like to show her off just as smartly as she can, so we're giving her the "class" treatment this Saturday.

Porter himself made a brief appearance in the finale of the show. Another important project at this time was the MGM film version of *Silk Stockings*. For the screen adaptation, as with *Kiss Me, Kate*, some of the racier lyrics had to be toned down. The censor had various objections to some of the 'unacceptably vulgar'[112] lines and Porter dutifully provided MGM with replacements:

29 September 1956: Cole Porter to Arthur Freed[113]

Dear Arthur: –

In answer to your letter of September 20th, 1956, including a copy of the letter to Dore Schary by Geoffrey M. Shurlock, these are the changes requested:

STEREOPHONIC SOUND: Instead of the lines,*
"If Zanuck's Latest Picture were the good old-fashioned kind,
There'd be no one in front to look at Marilyn's behind"
CHANGE TO:
"If folks today could witness Valentino in "The Shiek",
They never would appreciate that lover-boy's technique,"

STEREOPHONIC SOUND: Instead of the lines,
"Unless her lips are scarlet and her bosoms five feet wide"
CHANGE TO:
"Unless her lips are scarlet and her chest is five feet wide"
OR:
"Unless her lips are scarlet and her head is five feet wide"

SATIN AND SILK: Instead of the line,
"She can shake like hell and spell success"†
CHANGE TO:
"Any demoiselle can spell success"

---

* The two lines from 'Stereophonic Sound' were specifically described as 'unacceptably vulgar' in Shurlock's letter.

† Shurlock writes: 'The following line is unacceptable'.

JOSEPHINE: Instead of the word "Bum"* use "crumb"
Sincerely yours,
[unsigned]

There were other day-to-day questions to answer too. On 3 October, Fred Lounsberry wrote to Cole Porter, asking him to read and approve an article he had written about Porter's lyrics for *Playboy* magazine.[114] The document is thirty-five pages long and is headed: 'THE COMEDY OF COLE PORTER / A guided tour of his funniest and spiciest songs / Conducted by Fred Lounsberry / Editor of the Random House book / "103 Lyrics of Cole Porter". Porter responded:

7 October 1956: Cole Porter to Fred Lounsberry[115]

Dear Fred:

I am delighted with your copy of the PLAYBOY article. I have only one correction to make. On page six instead of "To this scurvy wench?" the line should be changed to "To this curvy wench?"

I wish you great success with this article.

Sincerely,

[unsigned]

Porter's regular Wednesday night seats for *My Fair Lady* arrived when he returned to New York. He wrote to Alan Jay Lerner to thank him:

26 October 1956: Cole Porter to Alan Jay Lerner[116]

Dear Alan: –

My "subscription" seats for MY FAIR LADY arrived, and I can't tell you how deeply I appreciate it.

From now on, any time you happen to be in your theatre and want a companion between the acts, I shall be there (on Wednesday nights).

---

* Shurlock notes: 'The word "Bum" ... has too vulgar a meaning to be approved. May we suggest that the word "crumb" be substituted.' The letter also notes that in "All of You" the lines "I'd love to make a tour of you. / The arms the eyes the mouth of you, / The east, west, north <u>and</u> the south of you" 'must be delivered in a non-suggestive manner'. Similarly, the 'acceptability' of 'Satin and Silk' 'will depend primarily on the manner in which it is sung'.

If there are other people whom I should thank, please let me know.
My very best to you both,
[signed:] Cole

Porter also wired the songwriter Johnny Mercer on the opening of the latter's musical *Li'l Abner* on Broadway:

14 November 1956: Cole Porter to Johnny Mercer[117]

DEAR JOHNNY[,] I WISH YOU EVERYTHING GOOD TONIGHT[.] I HAVE BEEN A FAN OF YOURS FOR MANY YEARS[.] ALL MY BEST=COLE PORTER=

Porter himself was out of town working 'so hard on a film',[118] according to a letter from Madeline Smith to Bella Spewack in late November. This was presumably a reference to *Les Girls*, because on 5 December he sent a copy of the title song to Sol Siegel and another to Albert Sirmay for publication purposes:

5 December 1956: Cole Porter to Sol Siegel[119]

Dear Sol: –
I enclose a copy of a refrain of the song, Les Girls, entirely in English, as you requested.
I hope all goes well with you and Bing.
My best,
[unsigned]

5 December 1956: Cole Porter to Albert Sirmay[120]

Dear Doctor: –
Find enclosed copy of a refrain of Les Girls, from the film Les Girls.
Please notice that it is entirely in English, as against the other refrains. Perhaps this might be useful to you later on in case of publication of the number.
In any case, put it in your files (and in the files of "Easily Accessible.")
Love,
[unsigned]

Back in New York in December, Porter wrote brief notes to Sam Stark, this time about travel conditions and Christmas presents:

7 December 1956: Cole Porter to Sam Stark[121]

Dear Sam: –

I believe this is the address that you gave me for forwarding any letters to you.

I have received several postcards with joy – and a note from San Sebastian. Please write me as you travel on: About the gasoline conditions you meet, and about heat in hotels – as it will affect me if I go abroad.

My love to you both,
[signed:] Cole

28 December 1956: Cole Porter to Sam and Harriette Stark[122]

Dear Harriet[te] and Sam: –

The perfect present arrived from you. I have kept lists of lunch and dinner guests, together with the menu and the service used, on nasty little pads before – but now, this beautiful book will fill the bill to perfection.

Please try to find out the low-down on gasoline and oil for a car in Italy, and let me know.

Love to you both,
[signed:] Cole

Early in the new year, Porter was unwell. On 17 January 1957, Madeline P. Smith wrote to Sam and Harriette Stark: "Mr. Porter bids me . . . to let you know about his being hospitalized. They operated on him for a large gastric ulcer on January 8th, and he is still languishing up there at Harkness Pavilion – though he will probably be back in his apartment in a week or two. The doctors say that he will eventually "be better than ever", though he is on a soft diet at the moment . . . Mr. Porter can take little walks down the hall, even though they tired him, as he is still weak."[123] Similarly, Mrs Smith wrote to Porter's friend George Eells:

14 January 195[7]: Madeline Smith to George Eells[124]

Dear Mr. Eells: –

As Mr. Porter cannot yet carry on any of his affairs, he bids me thank you so very much for the lovely geraniums. I <u>know</u> he is enjoying these, because Paul [Sylvain] called and said to be on the look-out for more to replace these when they were gone!

But – can I find geraniums? No! "They're out of season." How can you – a mere man – find geraniums when <u>I</u> can't?!

Well, anyway – Paul says that Mr. P. walks about a little during the day, which tires him enough to make him fall asleep when they put him back to bed. And he can have some soft foods, instead of those awful intravenous injections. But – no visitors.

He will probably be hospitalized a couple of more weeks, at least. He sends his most appreciative thanks.

Yours sincerely,
[signed:] Madeline P. Smith
Mrs. Madeline P. Smith
Secretary to COLE PORTER

In his own letter to the Starks a week later, Porter barely mentions the event:

24 January 1957: Cole Porter to Harriette and Sam Stark[125]

Dear Harriet[te] and Sam: –

Your words from Cannes arrived, and I am so happy that you are enjoying it.

If you happen to move on during your stay in the Riviera, don't forget the blessed Hotel de Paris of Monte Carlo, as it is one of the great hotels of the world, and there are beautiful suites overlooking the square and the sea; usually the square is wonderfully planted with flowers. Another thing about this hotel is the restaurant, which is excellent. There are quite a few other restaurants in Monaco that you would like, especially one little Italian restaurant, the name of which I forget, but where we went often and where I even gave parties as it was so charming and the food was so good.

If you have enough gasoline for your car, I recommend that you take a trip slightly inland in the mountains to see a spectacular chateau called

"Gourdon". This was once owned and occupied by an American woman whom we knew, named Miss May Morris, but she went broke doing it over and buying all the land around it so that her view would not be spoiled. I have no idea who occupies it today – but it is really something to see.

Keep me posted, and my love to you both.

I am back from the hospital, convalescing.

[signed:] Cole

A month later, Porter had planned two holidays to help him recover from his surgery:

19 February 1957: Cole Porter to Harriette and Sam Stark[126]

Dear Harriet[te] and Sam: –

Thank you very much for your Christmas card from Spain, the letter from Rome, and postcards from Naples, Pompeii and Taorinina [sic].

I do hope that when you had your audience with the Pope that he didn't have to say to you, as he did to Clare Luce,* "But I am a Catholic".†

I am off to Jamaica on February 22nd for a month, and then toward the end of April I hope to go abroad for a month. But these latter plans are still vague.

It will be such fun to talk to you both about your trip when we next meet again, as you have visited so many of the places that I like most in the world.

Lots of love,

[signed:] Cole

After his Jamaican holiday, he wrote to Mary Lee Fairbanks (wife of Douglas Jr.) and mentioned further travel plans:

---

* Clare Boothe Luce, American ambassador to Italy.

† A popular joke of the time, whereby the Pope supposedly responded in this way to Luce's attempts to persuade him to be tougher on communism.

2 April 1957: Cole Porter to Mary Lee Fairbanks[127]

Dear Mary Lee: –

Thank you so much for your letter. That operation of mine belongs to the forgotten past, and I am becoming well again.

I, too, am so sorry that I missed you both when you were here.

Alas, I cannot accept your invitation to the Ball on June 18th as I shall be in the wilds of California. I plan to leave in two weeks for Italy and motor about for a month, ending up in Monte Carlo and returning to the USA via Nice.

I know you will be delighted to hear that Bruno [Pagliai]* gave Merle [Oberon] a smashing diamond as an engagement ring. It is pear-shaped and blue-white – part of the great Jaeger Winston diamond. And it is adjusted so that when it becomes too heavy for her finger, she can wear it on a chain around her beautiful neck.

They don't talk about the date of their marriage but they did mention taking a yacht for a cruise in the Aegean Sea during the summer. Also, Bruno is building a guest house connected with his place in Cuernavaca. So, I believe it will go through shortly. Merle has decided not to sell her house in Bel Air, so everything seems to be booming.

Lots of love to you both and, again I thank you for that dear letter.

Your devoted

[signed:] Cole

From Italy, Porter wrote a wry message about the weather to Jean Howard, referencing 'The Rain in Spain' from *My Fair Lady*:

30 April 1957: Cole Porter to Jean Howard[128]

The rain in Italy stays mainly in Bologna.

Love

[signed:] Cole

Back in America in June, Porter wrote to Montgomery to turn down a project:

---

* The Italian-born industrialist Bruno Pagliai (dates unknown) married the actress Merle Oberon in 1957. They lived together in Mexico and were divorced in 1973.

14 June 1957: Cole Porter to Robert Montgomery[129]

Dear Bob: –

Will you please tell the lawyers for Phil Langner and Tom Ewell* that I shall have to return "Comfort Me With Apples" when I get to the Coast, as lately I have been bombarded with scripts which had to be examined, before you gave me this book.

All my best,
[signed:] Cole

Charity was again on his mind in his next letter to Montgomery:

22 June 1957: Cole Porter to Robert Montgomery[130]

Dear Bob:

Thank you for your letter of June 17th, 1957, regarding an offer from Rheingold Beer of $2,000.00, which I would give to the Damon Runyon Cancer Fund.

I should like to arrange this for late in the summer and it would be very nice if Rheingold would pay me more than $2,000.00 because I like to give as much as possible to the Damon Runyon Cancer Fund.

Best wishes,
[signed:] Cole

13 July 1957: Cole Porter to Robert Montgomery[131]

Dear Bob:

Thank you very much for your letter of July 10th. I am definitely interested in the Rheingold peoples' offer of $2,500.00 to photograph me and let me give this sum to the charity of my choice but I want to do it much later in the summer. In fact, early September would be ideal. Will they agree to that?

---

* Philip Langner (1926–) is an American film and theatre producer. The actor Tom Ewell (1909–94) appeared in several dozen Hollywood movies, including the screen adaptation of *The Seven Year Itch* (1955), in which he had also appeared onstage.

I also received your letter of July 3rd, in regard to Bella Spewack. I suppose she will continue to bother us for the rest of our lives!

Will you please read the enclosed and answer it? I don't understand it.

Best –

[signed:] Cole

He continued to struggle to find a new musical to work on:

13 July 1957: Cole Porter to John Wharton[132]

Dear John:

Thank you for your letter of July 10th.

So far I have found no work that I like. [Irving] Lazar can find me nothing in the way of a picture and the only people who are pressing me about a show are Feuer and Martin. They are lunching with me this coming Tuesday, but this is a heavy project with no fun in it so I am really not enthusiastic about it.

As for my health, I feel better but not well enough, but it is a bad rumor to spread so I am keeping it very quiet. I have a trainer-masseur every day and I swim, but so far the energy has not returned and I am tired of being patient.

Best –

[signed:] Cole

On 18 July the movie version of *Silk Stockings* opened at the Radio City Music Hall. The reviews were enthusiastic, with Bosley Crowther calling it 'delightful and entertaining' and even suggesting that a national holiday should be declared so that everyone had the chance to see it.[133] And Porter wrote to John Wharton about another possibility of bringing *Nymph Errant* to New York:

20 July 1957: Cole Porter to John Wharton[134]

Dear John:

I enclose a letter from Bob Montgomery who, it appears, is on vacation and a letter from Albert Da Silva regarding an off-Broadway production of NYMPH ERRANT. I have no objection to an off-Broadway production of this show if you don't think it might hurt any possibility of an important Broadway production being made of it, or 20th Century Fox, who has the rights to it, adapting it for a musical picture.

I feel that this is a very good score of mine but the actual book would have to be entirely re-written to be suitable for today. I must leave it to your judgment to decide on this matter.

My best to you.

[signed:] Cole

A further possibility of work came up a few days later:

27 July 1957: Cole Porter to John Wharton[135]

Dear John:

In regard to Bob Montgomery's letter of July 12th, about ALL ABOUT EVE* being made into a musical play, strangely enough it had just been suggested to me by an agent here as a possible motion picture and Charles Brackett has offered to run it. I told Irving Lazar about this and he and I are going to 20th Century Fox to see it one day, although Lazar thinks it would be no good either as a musical play or as a motion picture.†

I received your telegram in regard to José Ferrer directing a production of CAPTAIN'S PARADISE.‡ This does not interest me at the present moment as I don't want to embark on any show yet.

Irving Lazar has a very good idea for me, which is to collaborate with S. J. Perelman§ on a television show based upon Aladdin's Lamp. Perelman is coming out here in about ten days with an outline, after which I could make up my mind. If I like the outline and decide to do it it does not mean a rush job and will be just the amount of work that I feel up to at the moment. I shall keep you informed about this.

All my best –

[signed:] Cole

---

* The celebrated film of 1950.

† In 1970, Lauren Bacall appeared in *Applause*, a Broadway musical based on *All About Eve*.

‡ It became *Oh, Captain!* (1958) with a score by Jay Livingston and Ray Evans, based on the 1953 film *The Captain's Paradise*.

§ S. J. Perelman (1904–79) was the screenwriter of the recent Academy Award-winning *Around the World in 80 Days* (1956).

In the event, Porter was less than impressed with Perelman's initial work on *Aladdin*:

10 August 1957: Cole Porter to John Wharton[136]

Dear John:

Thank you for your letter of July 30th, 1957.

Your criticism of Perelman, I am afraid, is right! He has sent me a treatment for the "Aladdin" television Spectacular and it strikes me as being dead and heavy. I have sent it to Irving Lazar to read, in the hope that he may find some saving grace, as I definitely want to work and nothing else is in the offing.

I enclose a letter from ASCAP. I never received the letter referred to. Will you kindly answer this for me?

Sincerely,
[signed:] Cole

Lazar must indeed have found a 'saving grace' because Porter took the job on *Aladdin*. It would be his final score.

Back in January, a feature in the *New York Times* on the new roses for the coming season had mentioned the Linda Porter rose: 'Linda Porter was personally selected by composer Cole Porter as the one rose he considered worthy of being named for his wife. The plant is vigorous and healthy. It produces good stems. The beautiful clear China pink flowers are delightfully flagrant.'[137] Porter sent two to Jean Howard:

17 August 1957: Cole Porter to Jean Howard[138]

Dear Jeannie:

I have ordered from the east two Linda Porter rose bushes sent to you. It may take some time before they arrive, but when they do arrive don't be surprised.

Love –
[signed:] Cole

7 September 1957: Cole Porter to Jean Howard[139]

Dear Jean:

I enclose a copy of the order from the people who will ship you the two Linda Porter rose bushes. They inform me that they will probably be shipped in December.

I miss you awfully and I wish you would come back quick. Nice dinners continue rather often. For the first time I went to the Buddy Adlers* for dinner. It was extraordinary – such a beautiful house and food for the Gods. Perhaps the dinner wasn't big enough for you – there were only nineteen – but, of course, I am a simple boy from Indiana who likes quiet evenings.

Lots of love –

[signed:] Cole

But the main news of August was that Porter was to compose an original musical for television. On 5 August it was announced that Porter 'had been signed to write the music and lyrics for "Aladdin", which will be based on the "Arabian Nights" tale about a young man and his magic lamp'. The script was to be written by S. J. Perelman for CBS, with an anticipated broadcast date of 21 February.[140] The show was to be produced by Richard Lewine, who met with Perelman and Porter in California in August to make plans. The following sequence of letters charts their collaboration, starting with the following from Richard Lewine to Porter:

27 August 1957: Richard Lewine to Cole Porter[141]

Dear Cole:

I have sent you today the Osbert Sitwell† book, ESCAPE WITH ME!, that Sid [Perelman] mentioned when we saw you. Only the second half of the book deals with Peking, but this half contains a lot of useful information

---

* E. Maurice Adler (1906–60) was a producer for 20th Century Fox, the studio that held the rights to Porter's *Can-Can*. Among his most important films were *From Here to Eternity* (1953), *Love is a Many-Splendored Thing* (1955) and *Bus Stop* (1956). His wife Anita Louise (1915–70) was an actress, appearing in several dozen films from her childhood (*Down to the Sea in Ships*, 1922) through to adulthood (her last film was *Retreat, Hell!*, 1952).

† Sir Francis Osbert Sitwell (1892–1969) was a prolific literary figure and part of the famous Sitwell family. *Escape with Me!* was Sitwell's account of his tour of Asia, published in 1939.

about the market place. You might look at pages 164–168, 205–209, 269, 307–312. Pages 251–252 list names of various sections of the Imperial Palace.

I will shortly be sending you further material as promised. This will include a description of the then known world for use in the Emperor's song; a list of the stars for the Astrologer; and as much detail as we can get about life at the Palace for the song at the tradesmen's entrance. I will enclose with this letter other information about the market place that had already been researched.

The city, Peking, was called by this name, but from 1421 onward.

I want also to send thanks from both Sid and myself for your cordiality to us. We feel that a great deal was accomplished in our meetings and we're both very excited about the prospect of working with you. Be sure to let me know as you discover other information that we can dig up for you, and I will send you progress reports from time to time. From both of us again, many thanks for everything.

[signed:] Dick

Evidently, the research that had gone into Porter's scores for *Can-Can* and *Silk Stockings* was to be repeated for *Aladdin*:

31 August 1957: Cole Porter to Richard Lewine[142]

Dear Dick:

Your letter with its detailed information, together with the book by Osbert Sitwell, arrived last night and I shall study it with great care, and thank you and Sid very much.

I have been working on the MAKE WAY FOR THE EMPEROR number and on the ballad which Aladdin first sings. As usual, when I start a job, I am having a dreadful time, not only with the music but with the lyrics, so I beg you – be patient.

Could you and Sid [Perelman] find a spot anywhere in the story where the Princess could sing about having met Aladdin, being in love with him and wanting him to be in love with her? This song would be a counterpart to Aladdin's song about her. I have written this song with the title ALADDIN, which might greatly help our product. The song is very simple and has, I think, a haunting and slightly sad melody. I enclose a lyric of the refrain to give you an idea of what I mean.

I can't tell you how nice it was to see you and Sid when you were here and I look forward to our next meeting very much indeed.

All my best –

Sincerely,

[signed:] Cole

Lewine continued to send him research materials:

4 September 1957: Richard Lewine to Cole Porter[143]

Dear Cole:

I have your letter which was written before our telephone conversation. As you know, I am delighted with the Aladdin song and as soon as I get your final version, we can start on specific plans for early exploitation.

I'm sending herewith additional research as follows:

1. Extent of the then-known world for possible use in the Emperor's song.
2. List of the stars as then known for the Astrologer.
3. General material which might be helpful in describing life at the palace.

Hope the above is of some help to you and again, the new song sounds wonderful. Let me know if there's anything I can do.

Best regards,

[signed:] Dick

In his reply, Porter reveals his progress on the score:

7 September 1957: Cole Porter to Richard Lewine[144]

Dear Dick:

Thank you for your letter of September 4th, including additional research. I have not been able to look at this, as yet, as I am working very hard on the song MAKE WAY FOR THE EMPEROR and the song THE SUPER MARKET IN OLD PEKING. On the MAKE WAY FOR THE EMPEROR song there is one lyric line which I cannot get and it is driving me crazy. In the THE SUPER MARKET IN OLD PEKING song I am progressing beautifully and am trying to write two sets of lyrics, in case the song can stand a repetition in its one spot. The lyrics to this song will have to be sung by somebody with excellent diction. Otherwise, it will lay an old Chinese egg.

I enclose the corrected lyric for the refrain of ALADDIN. I believe this is as well as I can do.

All my best to you and Sid.

Sincerely,

[signed:] Cole

Later letters suggest Porter was struggling with his work:

14 September 1957: Cole Porter to Richard Lewine[145]

Dear Dick:

Thank you for your letter of September 12th, 1957. I was most interested to read that Sid [Perelman] has finished more than half the script. At present I expect to return to New York on October 15th and I don't know, as yet, whether it will be wise to send me the new script or not, as my progress is not as speedy as I had hoped.

The Supermarket song is practically finished and I hope you will both like it, but the song about the constellations worries me greatly as I think very few people know anything about the constellations. In fact, most people even think that planets are stars. I am trying to write a song based upon the title TRUST YOUR DESTINY TO THE SKIES, as I refuse to rhyme "stars" with "Mars." It has been done far too often. My problem is to work out this refrain so that the words be general instead of specific but, as yet, I cannot solve it.

I have written a song with the far from startling title of I ADORE YOU, to be used as a duet for Aladdin and the Princess. I hope you will like it.

And I also hope you get Cyril Ritchard.*

All my best –

[signed:] Cole

---

* Cyril Ritchard (1898–1977) was a veteran Australian actor, especially popular in that period for his appearance in the Mary Martin version of *Peter Pan* (1954). Lewine and Porter wanted the actor to play The Magician in *Aladdin*.

Of course, work rarely prevented Porter from maintaining his social life, as the following note to the writer Clifford Odets* shows:

21 September 1957: Cole Porter to Clifford Odets[146]

Dear Clifford:
Thanks so much for your charming painting of naive flowers.
It was a joy having you for dinner the other night.
All my best –
[signed:] Cole

The arrival of Alex Steinert, whom Porter had been using as his musical assistant for a number of years, signalled that the score was at an advanced stage of completion:

21 September 1957: Cole Porter to Richard Lewine[147]

Dear Dick:
I enclose two lyrics on the Marketplace song and I don't believe I can write any more on this subject. I also don't believe that it needs a verse as it is a 48 bar song, written in a fairly leisurely swing tempo. The first section of each refrain is 12 bars long. Also the second section. The third section is the release and is 8 bars long, and the final section is 16 bars long.

I hope you will approve of this lyric, because if you don't I will take an overdose of ant poison.

Alex Steinert has arrived and we start on Monday to write out the tunes I have written, which consists of five. This will be slow work as I want every detail to be correct.

I have nearly finished the NO WONDER TAXES ARE HIGH song but I am still having trouble with lyrics. This is another long song – in fact each refrain, of which I hope to write three, has 60 bars of music, but this NO WONDER TAXES ARE HIGH song is in a quicker tempo than the Market song.

---

* Clifford Odets (1906–63) was the writer of such plays as *Paradise Lost* (1935), *Golden Boy* (1937), *The Russian People* (adaptation, 1942) and *The Country Girl* (1950). He was also a director and the screenwriter of films such as *Sweet Smell of Success* (1957).

My best to you and Syd [Perelman]. [sic]

[signed:] Cole

A week later, Porter wrote again to Lewine with further updates on *Aladdin*. This is the last extant letter from Porter to a collaborator while writing a musical:

28 September 1957: Cole Porter to Richard Lewine[148]

Dear Dick:

When I sent you two blueprints of the song <u>ALADDIN</u> I also sent one blueprint and the onion skin to Dr. Sirmay at Chappell, so that you can get as many copies as you wish.

Today I am sending you two blueprints of COME TO THE SUPERMARKET IN OLD PEKING and to Dr. Sirmay one blueprint and the onion skin. At first you may find the rhythm of the bass in SUPERMARKET song a bit complicated, but if you play it often enough it will become easy for you. I think that this bass will be most effective when orchestrated. I have written half of MAKE WAY, which is the song introducing the procession of the Emperor and the Princess. When you receive it don't be upset by the fact that the vocal part goes up to a G. Perhaps it should be put in even a higher key, as it should be sung by a first tenor with a very nasal voice. This trick, as you undoubtedly know, was used in LE COQ D'OR* in the sorcerer's part and is most outstanding. The whole number, which is not long, sounds completely Chinese until the finish – when I shall probably cheat a bit.

I am also writing down <u>I ADORE YOU</u>. You will receive two versions of this song, in the hope that Aladdin can first sing it, either to or about the Princess, and that later Aladdin and the Princess can sing it as a duet.

I believe I have solved the difficulty of the song about the stars. This is a slow waltz and the title is TRUST YOUR DESTINY TO YOUR STAR. If you wish, I can write a verse mentioning some of the stars of the greatest magnitude and then mention the fact that Aladdin should choose one of these stars.

---

* A reference to Rimsky-Korsakov's opera *The Golden Cockerel*, which was premiered posthumously in 1909.

Don't forget also that I shall write two verses for the song ALADDIN by which Aladdin can sing it, first, in thinking about the Princess and, later, the Princess can sing it to, or about, Aladdin. These two verses will be entirely different, not only musically but lyrically, the one from the other.

I return to New York on October 15th to stay.

Get Cyril Ritchard. Get Cyril Ritchard. Get Cyril Ritchard! He could also sing beautifully the TAXES ARE HIGH number, of which I have finished the lyric but not the music.

All my best to you and Sid –

[signed:] Cole

A month later, he remained too busy with *Aladdin* to consider projects that had been offered to him by the producer Leland Hayward and the screenwriter Howard Emmett Rogers:

22 October 1957: Cole Porter to Leland Hayward[149]

Dear Leland: –

I thought I could read the Lady from Colorado* immediately, but I find I have a lot to do on the spectacular which I am doing for CBS. So, please be patient.

Best,

[signed:] Cole

22 October 1957: Cole Porter to Robert Montgomery[150]

Dear Bob: –

I am returning to you the copy of THE GUARDSMAN, as I cannot consider a Broadway show at the present moment. I am too busy on the CBS spectacular.

---

* Homer Croy's *The Lady from Colorado* was published in July 1957 by Duell, Sloan and Pearce. It is based on the story of Katie Lawder.

Please thank Mr. Emmett Rogers* for thinking of me.
Best,
[signed:] Cole

Les Girls had its world premiere at the Radio City Music Hall on 3 October. One reviewer called it a 'joy and delight' and Porter came out of it well: his music was described as 'excellent' as well as 'agreeably mischievous and daring'.[151] Porter's friend and record producer Goddard Lieberson was also an admirer: on 24 October he wrote to the composer to compliment him on one of his new songs – 'I have not seen "Les Girls" yet, but this song is enough to get me there' – and Porter responded:

29 October 1957: Cole Porter to Goddard Lieberson[152]

Dear Goddard: –
Thank you so much for your letter about "Ca C'est L'amour". I am so happy that you like it.
All my best,
[signed:] Cole

Meanwhile, work continued on *Aladdin*. On 29 November, Lewine wrote to Porter to report that the team had '[come] up with a much better ending for the story. I won't try to describe it here, but it keeps the suspense alive until the very last moment and is generally much better story construction.'[153] Lewine also sent Porter a copy of a recording of the actress who was to play the Princess in the production:

---

* Howard Emmett Rogers (1890–1971) was a prolific screenwriter whose work included *Billy the Kid* (1941) and *Calling Bulldog Drummond* (1951). *The Guardsman* (1931) was a film starring Alfred Lunt and Lynn Fontanne.

3 December 1957: Cole Porter to Richard Lewine[154]

Dear Dick: –

Thank you so much for sending me the Anna Maria Alberghetti* album. I played it and enjoyed it very much. But we must get her down. I heard her on another TV program a few nights ago, and she didn't go up in the clouds until her finish number, which was most pleasant; and she looked very beautiful.

I shall await with expectation the new script.

I am delighted that Irene Sharaff and Bob Markell are already at work. It looks most promising.

Quite a few people have heard the private recording and liked it very much indeed.

All my best. I hope you are enjoying California.

Sincerely,

[unsigned]

The last letter of 1957 is Porter's typical post-Christmas message to the Starks, thanking them for their Christmas gift:

27 December 1957: Cole Porter to Harriette and Sam Stark[155]

Dear Harriette and Sam: –

The beautiful red leather book to record my luncheons and dinners arrived. It is so practical and lovely, and I thank you both so much.

It arrived this morning, Dec. 27th, with a sticker on the outside, "Do Not Open Till Christmas", but I decided not to wait until next Christmas and broke the instructions.

I think of you so often and do hope that we shall meet next summer and have a lot of laughs.

Love,

[signed:] Cole

---

* Anna Maria Alberghetti (1936–) is an Italian singer and actress who won the Tony Award in 1962 for appearing on Broadway in the Bob Merrill musical *Carnival!* Capitol Records released an album of hers titled *I Can't Resist You*, which included Porter's 'I Concentrate on You', in 1957. She played Princess Ming Chou in Porter's television musical *Aladdin* in 1958.

CHAPTER ELEVEN

THE FINAL YEARS, 1958–1964

On 18 February 1958, Paul Sylvain wrote to Sam Stark: 'Mr. C.P. has been here since Jan 14th last, for an operation on his right leg. It was very successful, and the doctor predicts that Mr. C.P. will eventually be feeling much better generally. This morning, he will have another operation performed, on the same right leg – a minor thing, a sort of continuation of the first operation, to expedite the healing up process.'[1] Porter's hospitalization was also reported in the *New York Times*: 'Cole Porter has undergone another operation, one of many, on his right leg, which he injured in a horseback riding accident in 1937. He is a patient at Harkness Pavilion, Columbia-Presbyterian Medical Center.'[2] As the days wore on, Mrs Smith kept Porter's friends up to date on his progress. On 21 February she wrote to Bella Spewack: 'Porter has been in the hospital more than five weeks, but the doctors think he can come home in early March. It is his old leg trouble.'[3] Four days later, Mrs Smith wrote to the Starks:

25 February 1958: Madeline P. Smith to Sam and Harriette Stark[4]

Dear Mr. and Mrs. Stark: –

Mr. Porter asks me to thank you for your good telegram to him at the hospital. He was happy to hear from you.

We are hoping that he can come home in a week or two – but are keeping our fingers crossed. It has been such a long time now: 6 weeks today that he has been at Harkness Pavilion.

He hopes you are both well and happy, and sends his love.

Yours sincerely,

[signed:] Madeline P. Smith

(Secretary)

But two weeks later, he had not been moved:

10 March 1958: Madeline P. Smith to Sam and Harriet[te] Stark[5]

Dear Mr. Stark: –

As Mr. Porter is still in the hospital (8 weeks tomorrow), he has asked me to thank you for him for the Los Angeles Times clipping re ALADDIN.[6] What an excellent one it is – and will grace our Scrap Book.

Poor Mr. P. is getting discouraged after this long hospitalization, but I am sure they will have conquered the leg infection before long.

With best regards,

Yours sincerely,

[signed:] Madeline P. Smith

(Secretary)

Mrs Smith's letter makes reference to a review of *Aladdin*, which had been broadcast on 21 February to a generally negative reception. 'Cole Porter and S. J. Perelman should send out for the genie,' wrote the *New York Times*. 'Their attempts to make a musical out of "Aladdin", the imperishable "Arabian Nights" story of the boy with the magic lamp, ran headlong into sustained disaster. The ninety minutes on the du Pont monthly show over Channel 2 were a pretentious ordeal.'[7] It was a sad debut for Porter's last musical.

But *Aladdin* was the least of his problems. As the weeks wore on, it was clear that the situation with his leg was serious. Finally, a decision had to be made – so drastic that it was announced in the newspapers: 'Cole Porter's right leg was amputated yesterday at the Harkness Pavilion, Columbia-Presbyterian Medical Center. The 64-year-old composer's condition was described as "excellent" by hospital authorities. The hospital said that the operation had been necessitated by chronic osteomyelitis, a bone disease. In 1937 Mr. Porter suffered fractures of both legs in a horseback riding accident.'[8] It was the end of Porter's creative life, though that was not yet clear. Friends sent him messages and gifts in hospital:

THE FINAL YEARS, 1958–1964

7 April 1958: Madeline Smith to Leland Hayward[9]

Dear Mr. and Mrs. Hayward: –

Mr. Porter was so touched with the beautiful pink Azalea plant that came to him from you for Easter. He asks me to send you his grateful thanks and to tell you how much he enjoys having it in his room, to remind him of what kind friends you are.

He sends you both his love.

Yours sincerely,

[signed:] Madeline P. Smith

Secretary.

In April, Sam Stark was involved in a car accident, but it was decided not to inform Porter yet because of his own condition. Mrs Smith wrote to Stark:

15 April 1958: Madeline P. Smith to Sam Stark[10]

[...] Mr. Porter was happy to hear from you via your pencilled letter; and we have not yet told him about your accident, as you ask, for we keep every possible worry away from him. I am happy to say that yesterday and today have been his first good days. He was plagued with hic-cups [sic] after the operation, which have stopped only two days ago (they were intermittent hic-cups [sic]). He has also had trouble keeping his food down, but that too has abated somewhat. The pain is gone – and that is a great thing, for he had been suffering with it for so long. It is 13 weeks today since he went to the hospital, and we only hope he can get out of there before too long – and as soon as he can, I am sure he will want to go to sunny California, and then you will see him. They get him up for a few minutes daily, and have him take a few steps with the help of some kind of a walker. It will be slow – but, when we look ahead to the future, I am sure it will all be for the best. [...]

You have one advantage over Mr. Porter that I can think of: You have a fine wife to help you get well. Mr. P. seems so alone – friends and admirers by the thousands, but no <u>immediate</u> family. I take little black "Pep" home with me every week-end, as he is the only other creature – except Paul [Sylvain] – who lives in this beautiful apartment ...

Two weeks later, Mrs Smith sent a further update to Stark on Porter's health. From this point to the end of Porter's life, Smith was the main source of information for Stark on the composer's health and activities, and most of the letters in this chapter are therefore from her rather than Porter:

30 April 1958: Madeline P. Smith to Sam Stark[11]

Dear Mr. Stark: –

Mr. Porter has asked me to thank you for your card from Texas, which he appreciated receiving. I have not yet told him of your misfortune, as we do not like to give him any worries at all if we can help it. He is now doing so nicely, that we want to keep him improving and hasten the day when he can leave the hospital.

It has now been 3 ½ months that he has been at Harkness Pavilion. He has only just begun to have visitors – one a day – to get him accustomed to the world of activity again, and, fortunately, they all give good reports of how Mr. Porter looks and seems. He is tanned (sun lamp and visits to the hospital garden), gets regular exercise in the hospital gym, eats better than he did (is on hospital diet now) – and he is anxious "to get back to work", which of course is a very good sign. He really hopes to get to California in June, but we must wait and see about that.

He had his first ride last week, and got into his car by himself. We sent "Pep" up to go riding with him – first time he has seen his little black dog since January. The osteo-myelitis is all gone, which means that all the pain is also gone. So, we must not feel too badly for him, as he is going to be much better, eventually. [. . .]

The correspondence between Mrs Smith and Sam Stark continued in mid-May, because Porter was still unable to write letters (and still in hospital):

16 May 1958: Madeline P. Smith to Sam Stark[12]

[. . .] Mr. Porter asks me to thank you, too, for your letter and clipping (which I return herewith). He was glad to hear from you, and sends you his best. He had wanted to get out to California by June, but he is still at Harkness Pavilion, trying hard to master the new leg – which, he says, "weighs eight tons". Poor man – what a fearful winter he has had. We all hope he can get back to normal living before many more months have elapsed.

We are having a small elevator put into his 416 No. Rockingham house, which will be a help. And I shall have "Pep" all polished and perfumed for Mr. P's homecoming. [. . .]

A week later, Smith was able to write more optimistically to another of Porter's concerned friends, Leland Hayward:

22 May 1958: Madeline Smith to Leland Hayward[13]

Dear Mr. Hayward: –

Mr. Porter has asked me to thank you for your thoughtfulness in calling the hospital; and also for your card from Europe earlier this year.

I am happy to add that Mr. Porter is finally leaving Harkness – after 4 ½ months there – next Monday, the 26th, and is returning to his New York apartment at long last, although he will have to make intermittent hospital visits before he finally takes off for California for the summer.

He sends his love to you and Mrs. Hayward.

Yours sincerely,

[signed:] Madeline P. Smith Secretary

Porter was able to pass his birthday (9 June) at home at the Waldorf Towers. Mrs Smith finally informed him of Stark's accident, which the composer alludes to in this brief note to his friend (it was perhaps the first letter he wrote upon returning home):

11 June 1958: Cole Porter to Harriette and Sam Stark[14]

Dear Harriette and Sam: –

Thank you so much for your birthday card.

I do hope you have fully recovered, Sam, from your unfortunate accident of last Winter.

Lots of love,

[signed:] Cole

Porter had to remain in New York for his follow-up visits to the Pavilion, and Stark resumed his old habit of sending his friend new books of interest (in this case, Eric Bentley's compendium of George Bernard Shaw's music-themed essays):

26 July 1958: Cole Porter to Sam Stark[15]

Dear Sam:

The book SHAW ON MUSIC[16] arrived and I shall read it with great joy. I realize that he was a music critic even before being a drama critic and I know that every page will be full of interest.

My love to you and Harriet[te] and please ring me when you get back from San Francisco.

[signed:] Cole

Remarkably, Porter started to seek out a new project, indicating that he had not yet abandoned his career. A newspaper article revealed on 8 August: 'An intensive search for a plot worthy of Cole Porter's ministrations as composer-lyricist has ended. Cy Feuer and Ernest Martin, producers of Mr. Porter's most recent shows, "Can-Can" and "Silk Stockings", believe the desirable qualities are inherent in Rip Van Ronkel's* "The Rascal and the Bride", which might be called "Baldzare", for the leading character. Mr. Porter concurs in their opinion, too. All agree the material should emerge as a comic operetta for the 1959–60 season. This would be a departure from the sophisticated product dispensed by Mr. Porter as well as his favorite purveyors.'[17] And in August, Porter returned to California. But although the operation had been successful, his mood continued to be a concern, as excerpts from two letters from Stark written on the same day reveal:

31 October 1958: Sam Stark to Cole Porter[18]

[. . .] Harriette and I had such a grand time and such a wonderful dinner last Tuesday night, with the particular joy of seeing you again. I worry so about you, and I hope you can keep your same good spirits up and enjoy life once

---

* Alford Van Ronkel (1908–65) was a writer and actor, known for *Destination Moon* (1950).

again. You were always so full of life and interested in everything and everyone that I hate to see you depressed. [...]

31 October 1958: Sam Stark to Madeline P. Smith[19]

[...] My wife and I have dined several times with Mr. Porter. We were there last Tuesday night. Confidentially I am very worried about him as he seems very depressed. Of course I never have a chance to be alone with him and have a heart to heart talk. His mind seems to be far away and although he is always the usual gracious host, I know him too well for him to fool me. I do hope and pray that he comes out of this. [...]

Porter did not comment on Stark's concerns in his reply:

1 November 1958: Cole Porter to Sam Stark[20]

Dear Sam:

Thank you so much for your letter of October 31st. I am sending you the autographed photograph for Miss Murial Fulton.*

It was a joy to see you and Harriette and I do hope you can come up another night before I go back east.

Love to you both –

[signed:] Cole

Madeline P. Smith, however, was deeply worried. She wrote to Stark: '... It is sad to note how depressed "The Little Boss" continues to be. And I understand only too well how almost impossible it is to strike a responsive note, or to reach him at all. I regret so much that he has not the strength, that comes in time of need, of a bolstering religion. Even a Buddhist, a Seven [sic] Day Adventist, a Jehova's Witness, <u>any</u> thing to take the place of "just nothing". Without faith – one is like a stained glass window in the dark. But how to read his particular darkness is the enigma. Maybe when you come to New York in the interest of your new book (and congratulations!) you will have the opportunity to speak deeply with him. I hope so...'[21]

---

* Presumably a friend of Stark's.

Perhaps the broadcast on 20 November of a television version of *Kiss Me, Kate*, starring the Broadway leads (Alfred Drake and Patricia Morison, with Julie Wilson replacing Lisa Kirk as Lois), inspired its librettist, Bella Spewack, to write to Porter (who returned to New York that month) and suggest they might work together again. But Porter's reply makes it clear that that would not be physically possible for him at that time, which no doubt also explains why there had been no more discussion of the new Feuer-Martin musical:

26 November 1958: Cole Porter to Bella Spewack[22]

Dear Bella: –

Thank you for your note of Nov. 15th.

If you have a good idea for a show I would like nothing better than to work with you and Sam again – but I am not ready for it yet as I still have a lot of pain.

I thought <u>Kiss Me, Kate</u> was wonderful on TV.

My love to you both,

[signed:] Cole

Porter spent the winter in New York. He continued to turn down offers of work:

27 January 1959: Cole Porter to Robert Montgomery[23]

Dear Bob: –

I am returning your script from Alice Jones, as I am not up to any musical comedies at the present moment.

Sincerely,

[signed:] Cole

P. S. – I am also enclosing a letter from Orry Kelly, which I would be glad if you would answer.

On 19 February 1959, Paul Sylvain – who had himself undergone medical treatment for a malignant growth in the summer of 1958[24] – reported to Sam Stark that 'Mr. C.P. is getting on as well as can be expected.'[25] Mrs Smith's update to Stark on 31 March (delayed because she had been off work with a dislocated shoulder and pneumonia) reported more candidly: 'He is getting on slowly, has days of ups and downs; goes to the country each weekend from Friday noon to Monday afternoon, always taking one guest with him. But he seldom goes out anywhere, having no confidence in his artificial leg. However, we all do hope that, with the passage of more time, he will gain more confidence and more interest in everything in general. He still goes each afternoon to the Institute for training in walking.'[26] In reply, Stark commented that 'I am so concerned about him, as no one on the coast seems to know how he is doing.'[27]

Mrs Smith's message inspired Stark to write to Porter: 'I have felt so unhappy lately about you. Stanley Musgrove and Roger Davis were down to see us and neither of them had had any word of you. I sometimes feel we are lost to one another because of the great silence. It would be so good for you and it would make me happy if I were to hear that you are working again on a new show, and that you are back to being your old fun-loving Rover boy again.'[28] The composer replied briefly:

7 April 1959: Cole Porter to Sam Stark[29]

Dear Sam: –

Thank you for your letter of April 3rd.

I do hope that your book works out without too much cutting, as I realize the years of work you have put into it.

My improvement is very slight and my artificial leg is no good – in fact, a man has to come from Virginia tomorrow to examine it.

Love to you and Harriette,

[signed:] Cole

Porter's message seemed to close down discussion, but Mrs Smith and Sam Stark continued to keep in touch secretly about the composer's health. On 13 April, Smith explained: 'Mr. Porter should be back from Williamstown any minute, with Paul [Sylvain] who must go to the hospital again tomorrow for more check-ups. We are certainly a decrepit lot here at the Waldorf apartment this winter – even Pep* spent time at the Vet's – and when I get

---

* Porter's dog.

sick, then I know we must be falling to pieces.'[30] Porter's ill health prevented him from writing new material for the movie version of *Can-Can*:

7 April 1959: Cole Porter to Irving Lazar[31]

Dear Irving: –

You will have to arrange some way by which any added numbers in CAN CAN, as a picture, will be either other songs of mine or songs written by somebody else. I realize that MGM has my catalog, but maybe you can wangle something.

The reason for this is because I am living in torture and it doesn't seem to decrease.

I am so sorry that I missed you when you were here last.

Love,

[signed:] Cole

Despite his pain, Porter did occasionally go to the theatre* and kept up with his formal correspondence for a while. In April he received the foreword by his friend and former collaborator Moss Hart to a new, lavish *Cole Porter Songbook*. He was delighted with it and also shared a story about 'Begin the Beguine' from Hart and Porter's *Jubilee*:

23 April 1959: Cole Porter to Moss Hart[32]

Dear Moss: –

Henry Simon sent me the foreword that you wrote for the Cole Porter Song Book. I couldn't like it more, although I find it perhaps too flattering. But thank you so much.

My love to you and Kitty,

[signed:] Cole

P. S. – If you wish to augment the part about the "Beguine", I wrote it in New Guinea, having gotten the idea from a night club in Paris, where they played

---

* For example, his presence was noted at the opening of the Bolshoi Ballet's production of *Romeo and Juliet* at the Metropolitan Opera on 16 April. See Anon., 'Bolshoi Opening Hailed by Crowd', *New York Times*, 17 April 1959, 1.

beguines all evening and all the clientele came from Martinique. The beguine in Martinique is a folk dance.

To Stark, Porter remained brief and to the point, rarely sharing anything personal about his health or mood:

28 April 1959: Cole Porter to Sam Stark[33]

Dear Sam: –
Thank you for your delightful letter of April 21st. I love your stories about the Grand Canyon and Virginia City.
Love to you both,
[signed:] Cole

29 April 1959: Cole Porter to Sam and Harriette Stark[34]

Dear Harriette and Sam: –
Thank you so much for the beautiful bow ties, which arrived in the most charming box.
I think of you both constantly.
Love,
[signed:] Cole

At the end of May, Stark wrote to Porter, tempting him to Europe on a trip with him and Harriette,[35] but he resisted by ignoring that part of the message:

2 June 1959: Cole Porter to Sam Stark[36]

Dear Sam: –
I expect to arrive in California around June 16th or 17th.
I know you will have a beautiful time abroad, but I shall miss both of you very much during the summer.
Love,
[signed:] Cole

The same month, Paul Sylvain – Porter's trusted valet – was diagnosed with terminal cancer.[37] Stark wrote in concern: 'Such good news that you are arriving around June 16. Perhaps we can see you before we leave on the 26th ... I heard dreadful news about Paul and I cannot get Laura on the 'phone. Please write me it is all untrue.'[38] The composer responded:

16 June 1959: Cole Porter to Sam Stark[39]

Dear Sam: –
    Alas, it is true about Paul. He is dying. I have made no plans yet.*
    Love to you both,
    [signed:] Cole

On 26 June, Mrs Smith reported to Stark that 'Mr. Porter left for California yesterday, via jet plane, taking his chauffeur and two valets with him (both excellent men). And I have just sent Pep† out about a half hour ago; he goes by Air Cargo. So now I am alone here – and will hold the fort all summer, except for my holiday to British Columbia later on.' She continued: 'Paul is very low at the hospital and we are keeping in touch with him. He has bad days and good days, but sooner or later, he will have no days. It has been hard on Mr. Porter – just waiting – and everyone has been urging him to go to the Coast.'[40] Only occasional business letters survive from the summer. For example, Porter wrote to the gossip columnist Walter Winchell to thank him for drawing attention to the ongoing issues with ASCAP royalties:

4 July 1959: Cole Porter to Walter Winchell, *New York Mirror*

Dear Walter:
    Stanley Adams, of ASCAP, forwarded me the column you had written about Public Domain. This is most thoughtful of you and I hope it will do some good – although I doubt it.
    All my best -
    [unsigned]

---

* i.e. for a replacement.
† Porter's dog.

He also wrote to approve Saul Chaplin's revised lyrics for the film adaptation of *Can-Can*, which was at last, after many years of setbacks, in production at 20th Century Fox:

4 July 1959: Cole Porter to Saul Chaplin[41]

Dear Solley:

I received the script and your letter, for which I thank you very much. I think your lyric changes are excellent and the script looks very good to me indeed.

I hope that in a short time you can come out and have dinner with me.

All my best –

[signed:] Cole

Although his personal correspondence slowed down, a note to his old friend Stanley Musgrove shows that he was part of Porter's otherwise imploding social circle:

11 July 1959: Cole Porter to Stanley Musgrove[42]

Dear Stan:

Your letter of July 9th arrived, with its beautiful photograph, and I thank you so much.

I am delighted that my biography is being written by Jimmy Shields and Harriett[e] Stark!

Could you come out here and have dinner with me, in your oldest slacks, on either July 21st or July 23rd?

Best –

[signed:] Cole

Porter's former travel partner, Jean Howard, also remained one of his correspondents, though the messages were now very brief:

11 July 1959: Cole Porter to Jean Howard[43]

Dearest Jean:

It was such a joy to get a letter from you. You are missing a terrible heat wave here that has everybody crushed!

Give my love to any friends of mine that you see, but keep a great deal for yourself because I miss you. Please change your mind and come out here after Europe.

Your devoted –

[signed:] Cole

Porter was also brief in response to Bella Spewack's suggestion that they should write a musical version of *Tovarich*, a 1933 French play that had been performed on Broadway in 1936 in a well-received English translation by Robert E. Sherwood:

25 July 1959: Cole Porter to Bella Spewack[44]

Dear Bella:

I have forwarded your letter to John Wharton.

As to the last two items, I do not want to do TOVARICH. It has often been offered to me but it doesn't seem to ring the bell that is necessary.

I should think a revival of LEAVE IT TO ME would be excellent but I must get the advice of John Wharton.

All my best –

[signed:] Cole

The revival of *Leave it to Me!* went ahead in a revised version by Spewack at the Margo Jones Theatre in Dallas at the end of October.[45]

Porter remained positive about new projects related to his work that did not require him to contribute anything new:

25 July 1959: Cole Porter to Robert Montgomery[46]

Dear Bob:

I should think it would be a good idea to have a one-shot television show covering my life as a composer but of course I could not be present.

All my best –

[signed:] Cole

8 August 1959: Cole Porter to Robert Montgomery[47]

Dear Bob:

Thank you for your letter of August 5th regarding an off-Broadway production of GAY DIVORCE, produced by Gus Schirmer, Jr. I would be interested!

Sincerely,

[signed:] Cole

Paul Sylvain died on 21 July and Mrs Smith wrote to Sam Stark: 'Just to be sure that you know about Paul – I thought I should drop you this line, to tell you he died at long, long last, after many weeks of hospitalization and suffering. It must have been a welcome release – and I am sure Mr. Porter will feel less tension, in spite of his sorrow. While in Los. A. I found Mr. Porter looking remarkably well, but still shaky and too little confidence in himself. We all hope that next year will be a better one.'[48] In fact, Porter was back in hospital for a brief stay early in August:

8 August 1959: Cole Porter to Jean Howard[49]

Dearest Jean:

I have just come back from the hospital, where I had intestinal trouble, and found two postcards from you.

Paul [Sylvain] died on July 21st. It had to be but I shall never cease to miss him. Wasn't he wonderful?

Love -

[signed:] Cole

Porter continued to pay Sylvain's wages after his death to his widow, Laura – a sign of his esteem for his late valet as well as his generosity generally.[50]

Saul Chaplin made further tweaks to the lyrics of *Can-Can* for the screen but Porter was remarkably passive in his response:

19 September 1959: Cole Porter to Saul Chaplin[51]

Dear Solly:

I received the lyrics and find them very amusing. Of course, I can't follow them as I don't know how they fit the music.

All my best wishes to you.

[signed:] Cole

By the winter, Porter's correspondence had slowed down. The Starks were two of the only people he wrote to and even these letters tend to be brief notes acknowledging gifts:

28 December 1959: Cole Porter to Harriette and Sam Stark[52]

Dearest Harriette and Sam: –

The beautiful bottle of brandy with a glass attached to it arrived, and I thank you both so much.

Love,

[signed:] Cole

28 December 1959: Cole Porter to Sam Stark[53]

Dear Sam: –

Your Christmas card arrived and inside the ad. from VARIETY about your anthology. Congratulations.

Love to you both,

[signed] Cole

8 January 1960: Cole Porter to Sam Stark[54]

Dear Sam: –

I was charmed to receive your letter, written on the new writing paper showing you in the lower left-hand corner.

My love to you both,

[signed:] Cole

Things seemed to have improved by 15 January 1960, when Madeline P. Smith was able to write to Stark: 'Mr. Porter, I am happy to say, has taken to walking with two canes, instead of with one and holding onto the arm of one of his valets. This is progress – as he depends on his own powers this way. Also, he does a bit more reading now, and listening to music – but he does not touch the piano, or go anywhere except to the country. But we feel encouraged.'[55] Porter was unable to attend 20th Century Fox's long-awaited film adaptation of his stage musical *Can-Can*, but the following letters show the studio's keen attempts to lure him along:

4 February 1960: Cole Porter to Charles Einfeld (V.P., 20th Century Fox)[56]

Dear Mr. Einfeld: –

Thank you very much indeed for your kind telegram of February 3rd. I would indeed be happy to have the tickets for the advance showing of CAN CAN [sic] that you suggest.

Could the dates be as follows:
Sunday, March 6 – 4 pairs tickets
Monday "   7 – 4   "   "
Tuesday "   7 – 4   "   "

How thoughtful of you, and all at 20th Century Fox, to remember me for this new film. I hope it will be a great "smash".

With kindest regards,
Yours sincerely,
[unsigned]

9 February 1960: Cole Porter to Charles Einfeld[57]

Dear Mr. Einfeld: –

Thank you so much for your charming letter and the newspaper article. Unfortunately for me, inspite of your kind invitation, I am not well enough to personally attend the gala premiere of CAN-CAN. I only wish I could – and I appreciate very much your thoughtfulness. I am hoping that members of my staff can attend the previews.

With every good wish,
Yours sincerely,
[unsigned]

16 February 1960: Cole Porter to [?] Weiss[58]

Dear Mr. Weiss: –

My secretary has told me of your visit today, leaving the tickets for the previews of CAN CAN. [sic] Again, my most appreciative thanks.

She has also told me of your reiteration of the invitation for me to make my appearance at CAN CAN. I regret very much that I am not able to do this, but I greatly appreciate your kind thought.

As for the suggestion re tickets for the producers of CAN CAN, as well as the writer, I think it would be a splendid gesture to send them tickets. The names and addresses are:

MR. CY. FEUER
158 East 63 St.
New York 21, N.Y.

MR. ERNEST MARTIN
219 East 62 St.
New York 21, N.Y.

MR. ABE BURROWS
1 West 81 St.
New York 24, N.Y.
Yours very sincerely,
[unsigned]

As always, the Starks periodically wrote to Porter, and he always responded politely but without disclosing details of his health or activities:

19 April 1960: Cole Porter to Harriette and Sam Stark[59]

Dear Harriette and Sam: –
Thank you very much for the post card [sic] from Tucson.
I hope you both will come and dine with me often during the Summer.
Love,
[signed:] Cole

There are no signs that Porter did any work during his winter in New York. The lack of detail in the few surviving letters discloses nothing of his professional life. In June he planned to make his annual trip to California:

THE FINAL YEARS, 1958-1964

8 June 1960: Cole Porter to Robert Raison[60]

Dear Bobbie: –

I arrive Wednesday, June 15th. If it is convenient, please meet the plane and stay to dinner with me. I hope you can dine with me practically every night and be with me all day every Sunday for lunch and dinner.

Telephone to Max* re June 15th, and say that you are coming.

Love

[signed:] Cole

A day after writing this letter, on his sixty-ninth birthday, Porter was visited at home for the award of an honorary degree by his alma mater, Yale University. The address read:

Cole Porter:

As an undergraduate, you first won acclaim for writing the words and music of two of Yale's perennial football songs. Since then you have achieved reputation as a towering figure in the American musical theater. Master of the deft phrase, the delectable rhyme, the distinctive melody, you are, in your own words and in your own field, the top. Confident that your graceful, impudent, inimitable songs will be played and sung as long as footlights burn and curtains go up, your Alma Mater confers upon you the degree of Doctor of Humane Letters.[61]

The Starks were thrilled by the award:

14 June 1960: Harriette and Sam Stark to Cole Porter[62]

Congratulations on your doctorate. That puts you right up there with Dr. Rockwell, Dr. I.Q., Dr Jekyll, Dr. Cronkhite, Dr. Crippen, Dr. Spock, and Dr. Kildare. Love and welcome home.

Harriette and Sam.

---

* Porter's butler in California.

18 June 1960: Cole Porter to Sam and Harriette Stark[63]

Dear Sam and Harriet[te]:

Thank you so much for the beautiful book on Paris and for your wire about my getting a Degree from Yale.

Love –

[signed:] Cole

Porter also wrote to Goddard Lieberson of Columbia Records, who had helped to form the special collections at Yale University devoted to musical theatre and who had been instrumental in the degree being awarded to Porter:

25 June 1960: Cole Porter to Goddard Lieberson[64]

Dear Goddard:

I received your 'phone call but I didn't call you back as I have not been feeling very well lately. I hope the next time you will call me and come out and have dinner with me.

You were awfully nice to send me the letter to you from Yale University regarding Yale giving me a degree. I know how much you must have done to push this into a climax and I appreciate it awfully.

All my best to you both –

[signed:] Cole

In August there was interest in a revival of *Paris*, Porter's first successful Broadway musical:

13 August 1960: Cole Porter to Robert Montgomery[65]

Dear Bob:

Mr. Gable has written me about producing PARIS and I have answered that he contact you.

All my best –

[signed:] Cole

And in September there was a similar approach to revive *Out of This World*:

24 September 1960: Cole Porter to Robert Montgomery[66]

Dear Bob:

Regarding Mr. Douglas Crawford's interest in producing OUT OF THIS WORLD in England. I should be delighted, if I don't have to do any more work on it myself.

All my best –

[signed:] Cole

Porter's correspondence for the rest of the year remained perfunctory, as the following two letters to the Starks demonstrate:

30 July 1960: Cole Porter to Harriette and Sam Stark[67]

Dear Harriett[e] and Sam:

Thank you so much for the beautiful postcard from San Francisco. I hope you are having a wonderful time.

I would love to see you. Some day when you aren't too busy please Telephone me around 2:00 P.M.

Lots of love –

[signed:] Cole

1 November 1960: Cole Porter to Sam and Harriette Stark[68]

Dear Sam and Harriett[e]: –

Thank you so much for the record which Max has sent on to me. I do appreciate your thoughtfulness.

It is nice to be back in New York, but I do miss California too.

Love,

[signed:] Cole

The following letter from Mrs Smith to Stark hints at why there had not been more letters:

18 November 1960: Madeline P. Smith to Sam Stark[69]

Dear Mr. Stark: –

I am going to take the liberty of acknowledging your letter of Nov. 11th to Mr. Porter, as he has not been well at all of late – eats hardly anything, and is weak. As a matter of fact, we have finally got him to agree to go to the hospital next week for a complete check-up. He left for Williamstown, as usual, today.

He has been passing up answering his mail and that is why you do not hear from him direct, although he read your letter and commented on your change of address (which I will note in our files). [. . .]

Stark responded: 'I appreciated your letter of November 18 although it was a sad one for me to receive, even though I have been expecting news like this. In my own happiness I had neglected seeing Mr. Porter, but mainly because I could not face seeing him in the state he has reached. I had a letter from Fred Astaire several weeks ago expressing concern about Mr. Porter's health and state of mind.'[70] Mrs Smith's reply confirms Stark's suspicions about Porter's condition: 'Mr. Porter is at Harkness Pavilion, where they are trying to build him up a bit. He has eaten so very little of late, and become thinner; so we finally, at long last, persuaded him to have the Doctor and finally go up to the hospital (but very grudgingly, I can assure you.) They want to get him a little stronger before they take further tests, etc., so we are hoping that the stay there will really do him good.'[71]

In fact, Porter's stay at the Pavilion lasted over seven months. His Christmas telegram to the Starks was sent from the hospital:

21 December 1960: Cole Porter to Sam and Harriette Stark[72]

HAPPY CHRISTMAS AND LOVE=COLE.

Early in the New Near, Mrs Smith reported to Stark: 'The Doctor tells me that Mr. P. has improved a great deal; is no longer anemic; much more alive, willing to talk and participate; and there is absolutely no TB or cancer. So, this sounds encouraging – even though the nurses tell me that Mr. P. still eats far too little. They have begun exercises, both arm and leg – hoping to get him physically underway. He has even asked for several visitors – one at a time.'[73] One such visitor was Alan Jay Lerner, the lyricist of *My Fair Lady*:

17 February 1961: Madeline P. Smith to Alan Jay Lerner[74]

Dear Mr. Lerner: –
Mr. Porter has asked me to thank you for him for your good letter from Paris. He was pleased to hear from you, and hopes that you (alone, or with Mrs. Lerner) can find time to drop in to see him at Harkness Pavilion when you return. He has been getting along very well there, but still finds difficulty in using his artificial leg. He sends his best to you both.
Yours sincerely,
[signed:] Madeline P. Smith
(Secretary to COLE PORTER)

If Porter's behaviour appeared to have become more regular in these letters, the next one from Mrs Smith to Stark painted a darker picture. By the end of February, Porter had not yet opened his Christmas presents:

27 February 1961: Madeline P. Smith to Sam Stark[75]

Oh. Mr. Stark – I am so conscience smitten about Mr. Porter's Christmas presents! Believe it or not, they are piled up just outside my door awaiting his return from the hospital. I tried several suggestions to get him to look at them at the hospital, such as asking if we should not send them one at a time, etc. – but his instructions were: "NO. Just keep them there until I get back, so I can have the pleasure of opening them myself." So, nothing to do but await his return, and that <u>may</u> be the end of this week. I sent tentative acknowledgements to people whose name was on the outside of the package, but mostly there must be cards inside – and I did not feel at liberty to open Mr. P's own packages (much as I would like to.) So, it won't be long now before you hear from The Little Boss himself.

You can't imagine how he has improved: gain of 20 pounds or more; looks perfectly fine; is cheerful; and, in fact, I think he <u>likes</u> being up there at Harkness Pavilion, for he does not rebel at all, and seems only mildly interested in any date of release. I only hope we can <u>keep</u> him in this improved condition when he does get home. It was three months yesterday since he went up to the hospital. He has been having one visitor a day, at 5:30 each afternoon, for quite some time. His two valets alternate going up and wheeling him to the Solarium, making the drinks and canapes, etc. – so it is fairly pleasant for him. He has taken to watching the late, late T.V. shows also, so this brings his sleeping hours far into the morning. However, he seems to thrive on it all. (Could it be the nurses??!)

All is well at the Waldorf apartment. Pep* is now nearly 15 years old, and still going pretty strong, though he spends most of his time sleeping and gets up on his feet in a rather lumbering fashion – unless it is his dinner that is forthcoming.

We have been snowed in most of the Winter. I don't suppose you ever have much winter in San F.

My best to you and Mrs. Stark,

Sincerely,

[signed:] Madeline P. Smith

Porter did not change his mind about the presents until mid-March:

17 March 1961: Cole Porter to Sam Stark[76]

Dear Sam: –

At long last I have allowed my Christmas presents to be brought up to the hospital, one at a time, and have just had your beautiful package opened, to find the great bottle of "Courvoisier" and the beautiful long-stemmed glasses, all superbly packed in the carrying case. What a handsome present!

I hope you will forgive me for this long delay in acknowledging, and will accept my most grateful thanks.

I had no idea I would be here at Harkness Pavilion such a long time – but I do not expect to have to stay much longer. They tell me I am "fine" now.

Love to you and Harriette,

[signed:] Cole

But the composer's optimism about being discharged was sadly ill-founded:

---

* Porter's dog.

29 May 1961: Madeline P. Smith to Sam Stark[77]

Dear Mr. Stark: –

Believe it or not, Mr. Porter is <u>still</u> in the hospital. He complains a bit about bursitis in his shoulder, but otherwise, has been getting on famously, but just doesn't come out of the hospital!

This morning I find a large envelope on my desk with a note from him, saying "Keep these photographs, and thank Mr. Stark very much for them. I enjoyed seeing them a lot. And send them my love."

So, that's it.

Sincerely,

[signed:] Madeline P. Smith

[handwritten note at bottom:] and what a BEAUTIFUL abode you have! (with the million-$ view.)

The date of 9 June marked Porter's seventieth birthday but it was not marked formally or publicly because he believed his birth year to have been 1892 rather than 1891. As usual, though, the Starks remembered it was his birthday:

12 June 1961: Cole Porter to Sam and Harriette Stark[78]

Dear Sam and Harriette: –

How wonderful of you both to remember my birthday and send me the beautiful flowers. I have been enjoying them so much, and send you my most appreciative thanks,

and love,

[signed:] Cole

In July, Porter was finally released from the hospital:

3 July 1961: Madeline P. Smith to Sam Stark[79]

Dear Mr. Stark: –

Mr. Porter asks me to send you and Mrs. Stark his thanks for the "Cosmic View" book. This will give him something to think about!

By the time this letter reaches you, Mr. Porter will be back in his Waldorf apartment – after seven months and eight days at Harkness Pavilion. He returns here tomorrow afternoon, and leaves on Thursday, the 6th, for California. He is greatly improved, but we wish he were even better, for he still has very little appetite, and is not inclined to do any work, in spite of the many manuscripts offered him. We do hope the California sun, the swimming pool, and some outdoor life will be a telling factor out there.

He sends you his love - - and perhaps you will hear from him personally after he gets settled for the summer. He has not been taking on his dictation jobs yet – just notes in brief for me to augment.

Best personal regards,

Sincerely,

[signed:] Madeline P. Smith*

Mrs Smith elaborated on Porter's condition just over a week later, to both Bella Spewack† and in more detail to the Starks:[80]

. . . Mr. Porter, at long, long last (7 months and 8 days), came home to his apartment, stayed only 2 nights and then took off for California a week ago today. He <u>looked</u> splendid, but I note that he is still nervous and eats very little. Last summer he had hardly any guests at all, and came back to New York looking so thin and listless - - I hope it won't be like that this year. If only he would take it into his super-talented mind to work, it would be his salvation – but nothing and no one has so far been able to stir him into action.

I might add that, in the course of the somewhat sparse conversation, he mentioned those fine photographs of your San Francisco home. They must have made an impression, as indeed they would on anybody who sees them . . .

---

* On the reverse there is a handwritten note from Stark: '. . . Thank you for letting me know about Mr. Porter. Sometimes I wake up in the middle of the night worrying about him. I think of our past happy times together + his many + great kindnesses to me . . .'

† Letter of 17 July 1961 from Madeline Smith to Bella Spewack (Spewack Papers, Columbia University). Smith reveals that Porter spent only two nights in New York before returning to California. She refers to an eight-foot 'Embrassez-moi Caterine' (*Kiss Me, Kate*) poster spread out on the sofa and says Porter seemed 'fine' but 'still nervous' with a 'bird-sized appetite'.

THE FINAL YEARS, 1958–1964

P.S. – He took his "Cosmic View" book with him to the Coast (no doubt, to confound his friends). The sister-in-law of the author of the introduction is an old Washington friend of mine.

The composer himself confirmed to Robert Montgomery that he had made it to California:

15 July 1961: Cole Porter to Robert Montgomery[81]

Dear Bob:

I don't want to see Freddie Brisson.* I am not well enough to contemplate a new project. I hope you can get me out of this tactfully.

The trip out was very easy – five hours and fifteen minutes. I complained to Shadforth before I left that it was too long and he said "Be patient. In a short time you will go to the coast via rocket and it will only take an hour."

All my best.
Sincerely,
[signed:] Cole

Porter wrote briefly from California to another of his close friends:

22 July 1961: Cole Porter to George Eells[82]

Dear George:

I was astounded to get your postcard from Peru† and especially from the Bearss Hotel.[83] This hotel belongs to a distant cousin of mine and my grandfather, in his old age, used to sit in the big window with all his pals and watch the world go by.

I hope you are coming out and I know you do too.

All my best –
[signed:] Cole

---

* Frederick Brisson (1912–84), prolific theatre producer and husband of the celebrated actress Rosalind Russell.

† Peru, Indiana.

Madeline P. Smith's correspondence to Sam Stark had become flagrantly indiscreet by this point and she wrote to him about Porter yet again in late July: '... I forgot to mention one item that I meant to include in my last letter: The only thing that Mr. Porter asked to have taken to the Coast with them when they left earlier this month, was that beautiful bottle of Corvoisier that you sent him for Christmas. He really did appreciate it so much – just wanted you to know. And we have little hanging vines growing in the tall, long-stemmed glasses that accompanied the C: one on each side of the sofa. I continue to get cheerful little notes from Mr. P., so all seems to be peaceful and happy there this year. May it continue so. He goes every afternoon to the U.C.L.A. clinic for walking exercises...'[84] This cheerfulness continued into a brief note from Porter to Albert Sirmay, the composer's former arranger, in August:

12 August 1961: Cole Porter to Albert Sirmay[85]

Dear Doctor:

A postcard from Boston made me think of the happy days at the Ritz-Carlton there. How I should love to go back with a brand new show but, alas, there is nothing in the offing.

Thank you also for sending me the clippings, the program and the sheet music of Noel's new show.*

Love –

[signed:] Cole

In October, Porter returned as normal to New York for the winter. He continued to hear occasionally from old friends, on this occasion from Richard Lewine, the producer of *Aladdin*, who had (with Alfred Simon) just published a catalogue of songs written for the theatre:

---

* Noël Coward's *Sail Away*, which opened on 3 October 1961 at the Broadhurst Theatre in Manhattan.

22 November 1961: Cole Porter to Richard Lewine[86]

Dear Dick: –

Thank you so much for sending me the ENCYCLOPEDIA OF THEATRE MUSIC[87] – and please also thank Mr. Simon. How kind of you to be so thoughtful.

All my best,

[signed:] Cole

The composer continued to manage his business affairs where necessary, such as in this letter about George S. Kaufman:

28 November 1961: Cole Porter to Robert Montgomery[88]

Dear Bob: –

I agree with you that, on account of George Kaufman's wishes, we had better not negotiate for the presentation of SILK STOCKINGS in Germany.*

All my best,

[signed:] Cole

Again, we rely on Madeline Smith's letters to Stark to fill in the gaps in Porter's activities leading up to Christmas. She wrote on 14 December: 'You will probably like a report on Mr. Porter: Genius is still dormant, alas; but he is much better than he was this time last year. Some days he seems very good, and then again on other days he is not so good – eats little, not very interested, rather difficult to talk to, etc. We try to talk him into taking a nice boat trip, but do not succeed. He goes to the country every week-end on Fridays, and returns on Monday, taking one guest with him; this week it is Lew Kesler, who has just returned from his "Gypsy"† tour.'[89] Kesler, who had been a rehearsal pianist and arranger for Porter in the 1940s (including on *Mexican Hayride*), also wrote to the Starks on 15 December to confirm that 'Mr. P. is fine and sends his love . . .'[90]

---

* Presumably, Kaufman held anti-German sentiments after the Second World War.

† Presumably Styne and Sondheim's *Gypsy*, which ran from March to December 1961.

Porter remained stable through most of the winter – on 26 January 1962 Mrs Smith reported that 'Mr. Porter is about the same'[91] – and on 9 June his seventieth birthday was publicly celebrated, a year late. For example, Alan Jay Lerner wired him:

8 June 1962: Alan Jay Lerner to Cole Porter[92]

DEAREST COLE: WITH ALL MY HEART I SEND YOU BIRTHDAY GREETINGS. PLEASE COME BACK TO US SOON. LIFE IS A LOT LESS GAY WHEN YOU'RE NOT WRITING. AFFECTIONATELY, ALAN

Mrs Smith wrote to the Starks about the celebrations:

20 June 1962: Madeline P. Smith to Sam Stark[93]

[. . .] I thought you might be interested in a couple of the clippings re Mr. Porter's birthday, June 9th. Everybody but Mr. Porter celebrated! He spent the weekend quietly in the country.

He is now in California, having arrived there with his two valets (Henry and Eric), leaving the chauffeur here to have a two-months vacation (which he merits, having had none for a long, long time). Bentley (chauffeur) had a heart attack out there last summer, and has to be rather careful. The cook had one this year, so they have been going the rounds to find a new good cook. Even "Pep", whom I am sure you remember – our little dog, now 16 years old – had a heart attack about a month ago, but a good vet, brought him back to alertness in good shape, so I sent him off to California all by himself two days before Mr. P.

We still have no prospects of a new musical in the offing – or any compositions of any kind. However, "The Little Boss" looks fine and is in pretty good health, though very slowed down in any activity – especially walking. [. . .]

Sam Stark continued to write to Porter directly on a regular basis, and Porter always replied affectionately, albeit in no detail:

4 August 1962: Cole Porter to Sam Stark[94]

Dear Sam:

Thank you so much for sending me the clipping about Frank Sinatra, Jr.* I am glad he was singing Cole Porter songs.

My love to Harriette and to you, dear boy.

[signed:] Cole

On 24 August, Mrs Smith wrote to Sam Stark to comment that 'Notes from Mr. Porter all sound cheerful, I am glad to say. He returns Oct. 15th.'[95] But his West Coast secretary Tully (Margaret Egan) was more sober in her message to the Starks a day later: 'Cole seems so much better but he is still seeing only Bobbie [Raison], George Eells, George Cukor, Fred Astaire – goes for a drive every day at 5:30 when he puts on his artificial leg. I don't think he walks around much on it. He always speaks so fondly of you both – I don't know why he didn't come to the telephone when you called. I think this withdrawal from all his friends will pass as he gains more strength. His hands don't shake this year and he seems to be so much STRONGER – not tired and listless. How sad if this talent dies out and he writes no more.'[96]

Porter certainly had the opportunity to work but he always turned down such approaches. The following letter to Anita Loos, written just before his return to New York for the winter, implies he has seriously considered an idea she had suggested but knew his health prevented it:

13 October 1962: Cole Porter to Anita Loos[97]

Dear Anita:

I have read the first act of Edouard Bourdet's† play and enjoyed it very much. I am returning it to you as I couldn't consider working on it at the present as I have too much phantom pain.

I look forward to seeing you a lot.

Love-

[signed:] Cole

---

* Frank Sinatra, Jr. (1944–2016) was the son of the more famous Frank Sinatra (1915–98) and, like his father, was a singer and actor.

† Edouard Bourdet (1887–1945) was a French playwright. It is unclear which of his plays had been offered to Porter.

In October, Porter bequeathed his Williamstown home (but not its contents) to nearby Williams College (which sold it in 1966):

30 October 1962: Cole Porter to John Wharton and Robert Montgomery[98]

Dear John and Bob: –

Please ask that all objects d'Art and framed photographs be removed from my cottage in Williamstown before it is given to Williams College.

All my best,
Sincerely
[signed:] Cole
(Cole Porter)

The following Christmas message confirms that the veteran director George Cukor – of Porter's *Les Girls* – was one of the few people with whom he regularly communicated:

11 December 1962: Cole Porter to George Cukor[99]

Dear George: –

Thank you so much for the beautiful Christmas card.
All my best,
[signed:] Cole

Yet the composer remained indolent when it came to work, as Mrs Smith wrote on Christmas Eve to Sam Stark: '. . . Mr. P. is really considerably better this year – but he just won't be pushed into doing anything at all; so, we accept him as he is and try to make his life as pleasant as possible . . .'[100] Early in 1963, Porter and Mrs Smith helped Stark with an exhibition of theatre memorabilia he was curating at Stanford University; Porter lent him a manuscript from his Yale days and another from *See America First*.[101] But by April, another letter from Smith to Stark begins: 'I write instead of Mr. Porter, as he is again in the Hospital (Harkness Pavilion) after a set-back.'[102] A month later, she wrote again to Stark: '. . . I shall see Mr. Porter at Harkness Pavilion this afternoon and I do hope to find him EATING – but I know I won't because nobody, but nobody, can make him eat enough. However, he does not seem to mind being in the hospital; I suppose he feels secure there and knows that all his affairs will be loyally taken care of, so he will probably be there until he goes to California. "Pep" has already gone to the Coast . . .'[103] She wrote again on 27 May from the Harkness Pavilion:

27 May 1963: Madeline P. Smith to Sam Stark[104]

Dear Mr. Stark: –

Mr. Porter dictated the enclosed letter at the hospital. He does very little dictating, so you are evidently one of the chosen few.

I meant to mention previously that the Performing Arts society of San Francisco honoured Mr. Porter – and he was "delighted to accept". He no doubt has you to thank for this.

I am sad to say that our little "Pep" died last week at 416 in California. His heart just gave out. However, he had had such a long, good life.

Best,

[signed:] M.P.S.

From hospital Porter wrote to congratulate Irving Berlin on his seventy-fifth birthday, and thanked Sam Stark for sending an article on the same subject:

9 May 1963: Cole Porter to Irving Berlin[105]

Dear Irving,

Birthday greetings to you, young fella!*

I recently heard about this "vintage Berlin" folio† you're planning and I just wanted to tell you that I hope it will include some of my long time favorites such as "Play a Simple Melody," "International Rag," "I Love a Piano," and "A Pretty Girl is Like a Melody." After all, Irving, your copyrights aren't staying as young as you are.

Again, happy birthday.

Cole

---

* Berlin's birthday was 23 May.

† A songbook. It does not appear that such a volume was published in the end. Porter lists Berlin's song hits from the 1910s and 1920s.

27 May 1963: Cole Porter to Sam Stark[106]

Dear Sam: –

Thank you so much for the article on Irving Berlin.

Love to you and Harriette,

[signed:] Cole

But his stay in hospital continued:

3 June 1963: Madeline P. Smith to Sam Stark[107]

Dear Mr. Stark: –

I am returning herewith the Frank Scully article, which I read to Mr. Porter at the hospital, to his great interest. (And I, too, was fascinated as I read along). I looked for the May 15th VARIETY among the magazines that Mr. P. always has, so I could include an extra copy of this article, but alas, it had been thrown out.

Personally, I was particularly interested to learn how your research collection had come down through the generations. People don't realize how much of one's "life's blood" goes into these things.

I shall see Mr. P. this afternoon; he seemed rather downhearted last Friday when I was there. I hope I find him more cheerful today. He seemed to think he could get off to the Coast about the 21st of June – but that really remains to be seen.

Yours sincerely,

[signed:] Madeline P. Smith

By the time Porter wrote to Jean Howard in early July, he was still in hospital:

8 July 1963: Cole Porter to Jean Howard

Dearest Jean: –

The balloon arrived and changed my dreary room into a big Fourth of July celebration. Thank you so much.

Things are going slowly here but I hope to get out one day.

Lots of love,

[signed:] Cole

Nor had he been released by 2 August, when Tully Egan wrote to the Starks: '... Thank you so much for the birthday card. As Cole says, it cheered me. He is still in New York, in the hospital. Mrs Smith probably wrote you about it. He wasn't eating this spring and they finally put him in the hospital and fed him through a nose tube. When he was about to leave he had to have a minor operation so he is still there...'[108] Porter made it to California for the end of the summer and then returned to New York in the second week of November. He appeared to be improving, according to Mrs Smith's postscript to the following letter from Porter to Stark:

19 November 1963: Cole Porter to Sam Stark[109]

Dear Sam: –

I was very interested in the Gleeson Library Association card telling me about the First Edition of More's Utopia,* with your note attached.

Love to you and Harriette.

[signed:] Cole

P.S. from M.P.S. – Mr. Porter has been back from California just a week looking remarkably well, and seemingly much, much better than he has been for a long time. I hope it will last.

My regards,

[signed:] M. P. Smith

By this point, Mrs Smith had practically become a friend of Sam Stark's in her own right, and in a letter from 5 January 1964 she remarked on Porter's attitudes towards faith: '... I was happy to read your remarks about Mr. Porter saying his prayers on the trips with you in earlier days. He told me he did not believe in a hereafter, which made me sad, for I knew if he had more faith and a little more of spiritual values he would have been a happier man, and a stronger one, better equipped to handle his ailments. But he was not receptive to discussions on this subject, though his cousin, Mrs. Bearss, tried many times to interest him. I'm sure his

---

* Harriette Stark donated the precious volume to the library. See https://crl.acrl.org/index.php/crl/article/viewFile/11656/13102 (accessed 20 September 2018).

early youth was directed in the right direction, but perhaps the materialistic world in which he later travelled led him astray. Though he mentioned more than once during his late illnesses, "How am I going to meet my God?"..."[110]

On 28 January, Porter was the subject of a special episode of the *Bell Telephone Hour* – an hour of television devoted to his music, hosted by and starring Ethel Merman:

29 January 1964: Cole Porter to Harriette and Sam Stark[111]

Dear Harriette and Sam: –
    Thank you so much for the wire regarding the Bell Telephone Hour. It was most thoughtful of you.
    Love,
    [signed:] Cole

But Porter himself did not participate in the show and his work as a songwriter had finished more than six years earlier. Ironically, on 17 March, Irving Berlin wrote to inform Porter that the two of them continued to head the list of the 'top ten ASCAP writers', based on performance income, despite no new Porter songs having appeared for some time.[112] Berlin remained a close friend through Porter's final days and on 11 March, Berlin sent him a copy of the new songs for his projected new MGM film musical *Say It With Music* (it went unproduced). The previous night the Berlins had dined with Porter – 'I don't have to tell you, Cole, how wonderful it was for me and Ellin to be with you'[113] – and Porter was delighted by both the scores and the ASCAP news:

11 March 1964: Cole Porter to Irving Berlin[114]

Dear Irving: –
    Thank you so much for sending me the new songs that you have written for "Say It With Music". I shall always treasure these.
    It was a joy to see you and Ellin last night.
    Love,
    [signed:] Cole

19 March 1964: Cole Porter to Irving Berlin

Dear Irving: –

Thank you so much for sending me the list of the Top Ten writers in ASCAP. It is most interesting.

Love,

[signed:] Cole

On 19 June, Mrs Smith wrote to Stark with news of yet another setback in Porter's health (the reference to *Kiss Me, Kate* is probably regarding a BBC television adaptation starring Howard Keel and Patricia Morison, which had been broadcast in colour on 20 April and designed to launch BBC2):

19 June 1964: Madeline P. Smith to Sam Stark[115]

Mr. Porter asks me to send you his very appreciative thanks for all the good clippings. We shall put them in our K.m.K. Scrap Book. It was most thoughtful of you to send them.

Now, I am sorry to have to report that, alas, Mr.P. is again in the hospital – Harkness Pavilion. A few days ago – just before he was to take off, with his retinue, for California – he fell in the bathroom and fractured his right hip. The valet had gone out of the room, so C.P. was there alone at that moment. He never wants to go to the hospital, so we had to use subterfuge, pretending to start off for the country (as it was Friday) but just going on to his "old stamping ground". What would Columbia Medical Center do without Cole Porter - - or, we might add, "What would Cole Porter do without the hospital."

Well, anyway, it is getting discouraging. However, having put his hip in a splint, they can, at least, feed him intravenously to offset his predisposition to eat next to nothing. When recovered enough, I am sure he will go directly to the Coast, where poor Max keeps having the stop and go sign for summer cooks, always a problem.

Smith updated the concerned Starks again just five days later:

24 June 1964: Madeline P. Smith to Sam Stark[116]

Dear Mr. Stark:

Yesterday I was at the Hospital and found Mr. Porter somewhat brighter than previously. He asked me to send you his thanks for the additional K.m.K.clippings. All for the Scrap Book.

He thought he would be at Harkness only about "a week longer" – but I don't know whether or not this is wishful thinking. Time will tell.

Best,

[Signed:] Madeline P. Smith

A few days later, he was back at the Waldorf:

29 June 1964: Cole Porter to Jean Howard[117]

Dearest Jean: –

Thank you so much for your note. I hope you will come to the West Coast during the Summer.

Love,

[signed:] Cole

[Annotation in Madeline P. Smith's hand:]
Dear Mrs. H. –

He is back now in 33-A – but weak. He really plans on going to Calif. this Saturday.

Best,

M.P.S.

In her next letter to Stark, Madeline Smith not only summarizes Porter's current health but also comments on his letter-writing (or lack of it):

8 July 1964: Madeline P. Smith to Sam Stark[118]

Dear Mr. Stark: –

Thank you for your July 3rd letter. It is always nice to hear from you.

Mr. Porter did not have to stay too long at the hospital, thank Goodness. It was an "impacted* hip-fracture" which did not have to be operated on. So, he was able to leave on July 4th for California – taking with him two valets, 1 chauffeur and wife, and others to meet him at the West Coast end. He could not wear his artificial leg as it hurt him, and, while he looked very well in the face, he is thin and quite introspective. I think, on the Coast, he seldom sees his old-time friends, alas.

How nice of you to think of something for him that he can use. I'm sure the flashlight will be most useful. If it arrives here, I will see that it is forwarded to California.

If only he <u>would</u> show even a little interest in doing any of his special work at all, and especially in doing MY AUNT MAXINE* – but, as you surmise, this is a lost cause now. I have had to return every script that has been sent to him since his amputation – "with regrets". (And with those "one-liners" that he always dictates these days.) He never wrote long letters, but now they are less than short. I am always glad when he will even <u>dictate</u> his own replies.

All good wishes to you and Mrs. Stark,
Sincerely,
[signed:] Madeline P. Smith

*One in which one fragment is driven into the other so as to be held fast.
 - Gould's Medical Dictionary.

Porter continued to write briefly only to his closest friends, such as Jean Howard and Sam Stark, from California in July:

12 July 1964: Cole Porter to Jean Howard[119]

Dearest Jean:
Your letter of July 6th, from London, arrived and made me very happy. I do hope you will come to California later and, if possible, with Michael.
Lots of love,
[signed:] Cole

---

* Diana Forbes-Elliott's memoir of her aunt, the actress Maxine Elliott (1868–1940), was published by Viking in 1964. Elliott was a friend of Porter's in the 1920s and 1930s.

18 July 1964: Cole Porter to Harriette and Sam Stark[120]

Dear Harriette and Sam:

Thank you so much for the beautiful flashlight and holder. This made my birthday worth while [sic].

Love to you both.

[signed:] Cole

Mrs Smith, too, only received brief notes from him while he was away at his other residence: '... I don't know whether or not I have given you any late report on Mr. Porter – but, inasmuch as I, too, get only one-line notes, I asked him right out – in my subtle way – recently, how his hip was progressing. He wrote back that it was "infinitely better", so I hope he is really much better; he never says unless I ask. He will probably stay a little later this year, as he left late for the Coast (July 4th).'[121] More forthcoming was Tully, his secretary in California: '... I asked Cole to loan me $1,000.00, assuring him I can pay him back by the first of the year (I get a nice bonus at Christmas) and he was so darn sweet and told Ford to make me out a check right away. He said "Tully, don't be embarrassed. I've asked for a loan many times." What a darling he is and so understanding. I sometimes feel he is living in another plane but he understood this situation. I have to be practical and make arrangements for a burial plot and services because something might happen to [Tully's mother] at any time . . . Cole is simply marvelous – very talkative and seems to feel so much better. That was terrible thing that he had to fall – on his stump yet – but the hip seems better and I notice his left does not throb from the phantom pain. He is now seeing people for the first time in a long time – I mean people like Vivian Leigh* etc. She was over for dinner the other night . . .'[122]

But within weeks, he was back in hospital, this time in California. He declined rapidly and on 14 October, Stanley Musgrove reported that 'Cole is very low this afternoon, so the situation is touch and go.'[123] The following night, he died:

---

* Vivien Leigh (1913–67), the celebrated actress perhaps best remembered for her landmark appearances in MGM's *Gone With the Wind* (1939) and *A Streetcar Named Desire* (1951).

16 October 1964: Madeline P. Smith to Sam and Harriette Stark (9:54 AM)[124]

JUST TO LET YOU GOOD FRIENDS KNOW COLE PORTER DIED LAST NIGHT PRIVATE FUNERAL IN PERU INDIANA NO FLOWERS PLEASE MADELINE SMITH

A week later, Mrs Smith wrote to one of Porter's closest friends, Jean Howard, to describe his death and funeral:

23 October 1964: Madeline P. Smith to Jean Howard[125]

Dear Mrs. Howard: –

Out of a stack of letters awaiting a reply, I will give your's [sic] precedence, for I know how much you will want to know details. Your letter arrived in this morning's mail. I sent Sylvia (la Princesse) a wire immediately upon Mr. P's death, asking her to inform you (as I did not have your London address, but I knew you often see her). Am so glad you put your current address inside your letter, as the one on the envelope was almost illegible, owing to the postmark all over it.

Our "Little Boss" died at 11.05 Thursday night, Oct. 15 – the day he should have been returning to New York. They took him to St. John's Hospital in Santa Monica on Sept. 22; he was desperately ill the week before he died and did not recognize anyone. They hoped not to have to operate for the removal of a kidney stone, but eventually found they had to. But, his weakened body could not take it, uremic poison set in and he lapsed away. Bobbie Raison leaned over him shortly before he was gone and asked Mr. P if he knew him; Mr. P smiled but could not talk. Stanley Musgrove was also there that night. Our peculiar and secretive valets said all along, "it is nothing serious" but Max and Helene, Tully, Mr. Jules Omar Cole and [Robert] Raison kept me informed and we knew from their reports that it was almost the end. I had everything ready, names, addresses, telegrams, etc. (remembering all we did for Mrs. Porter's funeral) – but to no avail! They sealed the Waldorf apartment immediately (midnight) and we could not get in. So I did all I could from home, luckily having an address book that I used for Mr. P. on occasion while at home.

The body was flown directly to Peru, Indiana, where the funeral was held on Sunday, Oct. 18 at 2:30 in the afternoon, with only "the relatives and a few close friends" present (this was stipulated in the Will). It was a dreary, drizzly day – even the skies were weeping. And, alas, another tragedy had taken place: the 23-year-old Grandson of Jules Omar Cole was killed in an automobile accident the same day Mr. P died. So there were two funerals. It is all so sad. I will save assorted clippings for you to read, if you like.

I am glad you agree with me that we must not grieve for our friend, for he will never have to suffer again. This is the end of an Era. Three great and good men have left the Waldorf now: General MacArthur, Cole Porter, and Herbert Hoover, this year.

They are retaining me probably until the estate is settled, along with Mr. P's accountant, Frances Kingston (two truly honest souls). It will probably take a long time before everything is settled. I have been there the longest of anybody now – 17 years. I might mention that he left his Meissen china to you.

The leg amputation was really the beginning of the end – and all we could do was sit and see the downward trend – for, no matter what anyone on the outside says, he was not a man to be lead [sic] around in any way, try as one might; it only worried him to be "pushed".

His cousin, Mrs. Bearss, is still in Peru, but I shall hear her news when she returns. Jules Omar Cole (Mr. P's first cousin, and only 19 days younger than C.P.) is the Executor and has charge of everything along with our lawyers. All will be worked out in due time – but how I shall miss that beautiful apartment (and how I miss my desk and my stuff NOW while I am locked out! The Law, you know.)

SO many friends have been perfectly darling – not knowing any of his relatives, they have written to me or telephoned, and I will tell the Peru Coles, but they will not know the people as I do. It is a great comfort thus hearing from Mr. P's many friends.

I hope you are having a happy time in London. Elise (daughter) spent several days with Sylvia in her lovely 15 Audley St. house before going on a cruise around the Grecian Islands. Give Sylvia my love when you see her.

Thank you for your letter, and I hope this one will ease your mind a bit.
With my love,
[signed:] Madeline P. Smith.

ENDNOTES

ABBREVIATIONS

ALS: autograph letter signed
TL: typed letter
TLS: typed letter signed

ARCHIVES

AHC: American Heritage Center, University of Wyoming, Laramie, Wyoming
CPT: Cole Porter Musical and Literary Property Trusts, New York
LC: Library of Congress, Washington
NYPL: New York Public Library
SOA: The Shubert Archive, Shubert Organization, New York
UCLA: University of California, Los Angeles
USC: University of Southern California, Los Angeles

1 FROM PERU, INDIANA, TO BROADWAY, 1891–1919

1. Richard Hubler, *The Cole Porter Story, as Told to Richard G. Hubler* (Cleveland, 1965), 5.
2. William McBrien, *Cole Porter* (New York, 1998), 4.
3. We are grateful to Frank Callahan for this information.
4. https://www.worcesteracademy.org/page/about
5. Source: Worcester Academy. Abercrombie's letters to Kate Porter are given here in extract only.
6. *Peru Republican*, 20 July 1906, 1.
7. *Peru Republican*, 14 September 1906, 4.
8. Robert Kimball, *The Complete Lyrics of Cole Porter* (New York, 1992), xxvii.
9. Letter of 22 February 1916: Abercrombie to Meylert B. Mullin.
10. A copy of Porter's 'scholarship record' at Yale survives at Yale University, Irving S. Gilmore Music Library, MSS 131, William McBrien Papers, Series IV, Box 5, folder 162.
11. Hubler, *The Cole Porter Story*, 11.
12. See Kimball, *The Complete Lyrics of Cole Porter*, 4–9.
13. Source: Yale University, Irving S. Gilmore Music Library, Cole Porter Collection, Series 2, Box 49, folder 295 (transcription at CPT, Correspondence 1912). For the texts to *The Pot of Gold*, see Kimball, *The Complete Lyrics of Cole Porter*, 18–24.
14. *Yale Alumni Weekly* 23 (1913–14), 166: '166 Alumni Associations . . . The second meeting of the Boston Yale Club and the first regular dinner of the year was held on the evening of October 22 at the Boston City Club . . . One of the features of the evening was the general singing, as well as solos by Cole Porter, '13, which Professor Phelps characterized as the best singing he had ever heard at any alumni dinner.'

15. *Yale Alumni Weekly* 23 (1913–14), 715: 'The New York Alumni Dinner. Well over a thousand alumni from New York and more remote places filled nearly one hundred and fifty tables which were crowded into the grand ballroom, the two balconies, and a room adjoining, of the Waldorf-Astoria Hotel, New York, on the evening of March 13 ... Features of the cabaret show were solos by Herbert Witherspoon, '95, and Ericsson Bushnell of New Haven, selections by a sextette from the University Mandolin Club, a melodramatic burlesque by graduates and undergraduates, several vaudeville sketches by Yale talent, and a pianologue by Cole Porter, '13.'
16. The book for *Paranoia* survives at Yale University, Beinecke Rare Books and Manuscript Library, Miscellaneous Manuscripts Collection P-R, Polymnia Literary Society, Group 352, Series VII, Box 46.
17. *Yale Alumni Weekly* 23 (1913–14), 1,023.
18. Kimball and Gill, *Cole*, 24 (facsimile; source location not given).
19. *New York Daily News*, 4 November 1939; see McBrien, *Cole Porter*, 51.
20. Source: facsimile in Kimball and Gill, *Cole*, 30 (telegram).
21. Ibid.
22. Source: facsimile in Kimball and Gill, *Cole*, 30 (TLS).
23. Source: facsimile in Kimball and Gill, *Cole*, 31.
24. Ibid, 27.
25. The following telegrams are reproduced from facsimiles in Kimball and Gill, *Cole*, 31–2.
26. See the *New York Times* for 1 April 1906, 10; 16 June 1911, 2; 8 October 1911, 12; 17 December 1912, 14; and 30 May 1916, 8.
27. *Evening World*, 29 March 1916, and *Evening Sun*, 29 March 1916; see McBrien, *Cole Porter*, 54–5.
28. *History of the Class of Nineteen Hundred and Ten Yale College* (New Haven, 1917), ii, 245.
29. *New York Daily News*, 8 November 1953; see McBrien, *Cole Porter*, 56.
30. *The Paint and Varnish Record*, 15 February 1917, 6.
31. The song is not mentioned in Kimball, *The Complete Lyrics of Cole Porter*.
32. *New York Times*, 1 February 1917.
33. *Yale Alumni Weekly* 26 (1916–1917), 10 November 1916, 202.
34. http://myall.bangordailynews.com/2016/10/07/home/cole-porter-and-cannon-fire-a-brunswick-franco-american-in-ww1/
35. *Peru Republican*, 5 October 1917.
36. See McBrien, *Cole Porter*, 59.
37. Yale University, Irving S. Gilmore Music Library, Cole Porter Collection MSS 82, Box 87 (AL but not signed).
38. George Eells, *The Life that Late He Led: A Biography of Cole Porter* (New York, 1967), 53.
39. Ibid, 53–4.

2 COLE PORTER IN EUROPE, 1918–1928

1. https://www.ebay.com/itm/PORTER-COLE-PORTER-B-autographed-letter-GREAT-CONTENT-GOLDENAGE-ESSENTIALS/182832251530?hash=item2a91a6c28a:g:PIQ AAOSw76JZ4zf3 (TLS on stationery of the American Embassy, Paris; accessed 31 October 2017).
2. McBrien, *Cole Porter*, 70.
3. See *New York Times*, 31 December 1921, 6: 'Five liners sail today for Europe carrying numbers of prominent Americans who are going to spend the Winter in the South of France, Algeria and Egypt and a few of the passengers have expressed their intention of going over the newly opened route from Cairo to Cape Town in February. The list of more than 600 first cabin passengers on the White Star liner Olympic for Cherbourg and Southampton includes ... Mr. and Mrs. Cole Porter.'
4. Yale University, Irving S. Gilmore Music Library, Cole Porter Collection MSS 82, Box 87.
5. *New York Times*, 31 December 1922, 15.
6. Kimball, *The Complete Lyrics of Cole Porter*, 133–4.

7. They are not listed in ibid, or mentioned in McBrien, *Cole Porter*.
8. Kimball, *The Complete Lyrics of Cole Porter*, 85.
9. Robert Craft, *Stravinsky: Selected Correspondence. Volume 1* (New York, 1981), 75.
10. Wilfried Van den Brande, 'Cole Porter, European', in Don M. Randel, Matthew Shaftel and Susan Forscher Weiss, eds, *A Cole Porter Companion* (Urbana, 2016), 44.
11. Evergreen Museum, Johns Hopkins University, Alice Garrett Papers.
12. Kimball and Gill, *Cole*, 50.
13. See Kimball and Gill, *The Complete Lyrics of Cole Porter*, 131.
14. *The Times*, 20 September 1920, 8.
15. *The Times*, 10 March 1922, 10.
16. McBrien, *Cole Porter*, 89.
17. Darius Milhaud, *Notes Without Music* (New York, 1953), 153.
18. *New York Herald Tribune (European Edition)*, 26 October 1923, 1 and 4.
19. Only the text survives for 'Oh So Soon', which may have been intended for Raymond Hitchcock's *Hitchy-Koo of 1919*; see Kimball, *The Complete Lyrics of Cole Porter*, 67.
20. Gilbert Seldes, *The Seven Lively Arts* (New York, 1924), 92–4.
21. Yale University, Irving S. Gilmore Music Library, Cole Porter Collection MSS 82, Box 87.
22. Archives of American Art, Smithsonian Institution, Charles Green Shaw Papers, Box 1. The date of this postcard cannot be read with certainty but it is likely, given that it was sent from Morocco, to be the 1925 North Africa trip.
23. Yale University, Irving S. Gilmore Music Library, Cole Porter Collection MSS 82, Box 87.
24. Archives of American Art, Smithsonian Institution, Charles Green Shaw Papers, Box 1.
25. Yale University, Irving S. Gilmore Music Library, Cole Porter Collection MSS 82, Box 87.
26. Archives of American Art, Smithsonian Institution, Charles Green Shaw Papers, Box 1. Although Kate Porter's letter is undated, the envelope in which it was sent is postmarked Peru, 22 April 1920.
27. All of these letters survive in Archives of American Art, Smithsonian Institution, Charles Green Shaw Papers, Box 1.
28. On stationery of 'The Travellers', 25 avenue des Champs-Elysées, Paris.
29. Ibid.
30. Ibid.
31. Postcard from Madeira; the postmark is difficult to read: it could be 1928 or 1929.
32. Archives of American Art, Smithsonian Institution, Charles Green Shaw Papers, Box 1.
33. *New York Herald Tribune (European Edition)*, 1 August 1925, 4.
34. Richard Buckle, *Diaghilev* (New York, 1979), 458–9.
35. NYPL, *ZBD-162, Diaghilev Correspondence: 'Cher Monsieur Diaghileff. Voulez vous venir diner Dimanche soir a 8½. Nous aurons in[v]ité Tante Winne & je crois qu'elle pourra venir. S'ils pourront, nous serions tres [sic] hereux [sic] d'avoir Lifar & Riete. Boris a déja [sic] accepté . . . Sincerely, Cole Porter.'
36. Kimball and Gill, *Cole*, 72 and 75.
37. McBrien, *Cole Porter*, 106–7.
38. CPT, Correspondence 1953 (TLS on stationery of 416 N. Rockingham).
39. Kimball and Gill, *Cole,* 70.
40. Kimball, *The Complete Lyrics of Cole Porter*, 87.
41. *New York Times*, 22 May 1927, 30.
42. Helen Josephy and Mary Margaret McBride, *Paris Is a Woman's Town* (New York, 1929), 17–18.
43. https://www.ebay.com/itm/COLE-PORTER-TYPED-LETTER-SIGNED-02-09/372121421108?hash=item56a42a4534:g:FxgAAOSwLdBZ944V (accessed 31 October 2017).
44. *New Yorker*, 20 October 1928, 27.
45. *New York Times*, 15 April 1928, 34.
46. *New York Times*, 19 February 1928, 114.
47. *L'Intransigeant*, 21 May 1928, 5.

48. Victor Glover, 'Paris Theatres', *New York Herald Tribune (European Edition)*, 15 May 1928, 8.
49. http://www.icollector.com/Cole-Porter_i27095675 (ALS on stationery of Carlton Hotel, Lyon, accessed 3 April 2018). The date derives from the postmark.

3 PORTER'S RETURN TO THE UNITED STATES, 1928–1937

1. CPT, Correspondence 1928 (TLS).
2. *Vanity Fair* 29/4 (1928), 71.
3. *New York Herald Tribune*, 28 November 1929, 14.
4. *New York Herald Tribune (European Edition)*, 17 July 1929, 11.
5. *New York Herald Tribune (European Edition)*, 23 July 1932, 3.
6. http://www.lionheartautographs.com/autograph/19790-PORTER,-COLE-Composer-Cole-Porter-Writing-About-Tax-Issues-on-Black-Tuesday-1929. ALS on stationery of the Ritz-Carlton Hotel, New York.
7. McBrien, *Cole Porter*, 134.
8. Yale University, Irving S. Gilmore Music Library, Cole Porter Collection MSS 82, Box 87.
9. *New York Times*, 9 December 1930, 34.
10. Richard J. Madden to Cole Porter, 13 rue de Monsieur. Source: Indiana Historical Society (image: http://images.indianahistory.org/cdm/ref/collection/V0002/id/3792).
11. CPT, Correspondence 1931.
12. Ibid.
13. *New York Times*, 30 November 1932, 23.
14. Yale University, Irving S. Gilmore Music Library, Cole Porter Collection MSS 82, Box 49, folder 298.
15. Kimball and Gill, *Cole*, 110 (facsimile).
16. McBrien, *Cole Porter*, 157. (AQ)
17. *Manchester Guardian*, 29 September 1933, 11.
18. *The Times*, 7 October 1933, 10.
19. CPT, Correspondence 1933.
20. For an account of the disaster and rescue attempts, see *New York Times*, 9 September 1934, 25.
21. *Time Magazine*, 3 December 1934.
22. *New York Times*, 22 November 1934, 26.
23. *New York Herald Tribune*, 22 November 1934, 14.
24. Yale University, Gilmore Library, Cole Porter Collection MSS 82, Box 49, folder 299.
25. Yale University, Irving S. Gilmore Music Library, Cole Porter Collection MSS 82, Box 49, folder 299.
26. Worcester Academy, Massachusetts.
27. According to McBrien, *Cole Porter*, 176, the Porters sailed on 12 January. If Porter's letter is correct, then they sailed on the evening of 11 January.
28. Heritage Music & Entertainment Memorabilia. Signature Auction #616, 8 October 2005, Dallas, Texas, lot 20286.
29. Swann Galleries, sale 2367, 20 November 2014, lot 240.
30. CPT, Correspondence 1935 (TLS on Waldorf stationery).
31. *Theatre World* 23/24 (London, September 1935), 107.
32. https://www.ebay.com/itm/COLE-PORTER-Songwriter-Composer-SIGNED-AUTOGRAPH-Letter-To-MONTY-WOOLLEY-2Noms-/112716526332?nma=true&si=t%252BtgdvxAkP7jUBilBOyLSPtOHjU%253D&orig_cvip=true&rt=nc&_trksid=p2047675.l2557_ (ALS on stationery of the Beverly Wilshire apartment-hotels, Beverly Hills).
33. *New York Times*, 5 December 1936; *Variety*, 31 December 1936.
34. *Variety*, 2 and 9 December 1936.
35. *New York Times*, 14 October 1935, 20.
36. *New York Herald Tribune*, 30 October 1936, 22.

37. *Time Magazine,* 9 November 1936.
38. Kimball and Gill, *Cole,* 145.
39. TLS from 501 Sunset Boulevard, Beverly Hills. https://www.ebay.com/itm/Cole-PORTER-Songwriter-Typed-Letter-Signed-to-Monty-WOOLLEY-at-Christmastime/382323054085?hash=item59043ad605:g:suYAAOSwCtJaRSFk (Schubertiade Music & Arts, accessed 12 February 2018).
40. *New York Herald Tribune,* 20 December 1936, F2.

4 SETTLED – AND INJURED – IN NEW YORK, 1937–1944

1. Irving Berlin Collection, Library of Congress.
2. Source: Princeton University, Seeley G. Mudd Manuscript Library, Brooks Bowman Papers (AC #165), Box 9, folder 5.
3. *New York Times,* 20 July 1937, 19 and 14 August 1937, 39.
4. Swann Galleries, New York, sale 2367, 20 November 2014, lot 241; Schubertiademusic.com, spring 2015 catalog, lot 152; TLS on stationery of North Country Community Hospital, Glen Cove, New York.
5. Goldberg Auctions, sale 24, lot 444, http://images.goldbergauctions.com/php/lot_auc.php?site=1&sale=24&lot=444&lang=1. TLS on stationery of Doctors Hospital, New York.
6. We have not seen the original of this document but it is reproduced in David Grafton, *Red, Hot & Rich! An Oral History of Cole Porter* (New York, 1987), 114–16.
7. Present location unknown; auctioned on 18 June 2014 at http://www.rrauction.com/bidtracker_detail.cfm?IN=629 (accessed 16 June 2014). It is not out of the question that the song may also have been intended for *Greek to Me,* or possibly whichever of the two shows would eventually be produced.
8. SOA, Show Series, Box 85, folder 7.
9. SOA, Show Series, Box 85, folder 7.
10. Florence, Villa I Tatti.
11. USC, Eells Collection, folder 5.
12. Florence, Villa I Tatti.
13. Jean Howard, *Travels with Cole Porter* (New York, 1991), 15.
14. McBrien, *Cole Porter,* 225.
15. *New York Herald Tribune,* 7 December 1939, 26.
16. *New York Times,* 7 December 1939, 34.
17. McBrien, *Cole Porter,* 235.
18. Howard, *Travels with Cole Porter,* 14.
19. McBrien, *Cole Porter,* 236.
20. Howard, *Travels with Cole Porter,* 16.
21. Ibid. Linda Porter's letter is dated only 'Saturday'; since *Panama Hattie* had opened on Tuesday 8 October, the date of Linda Porter's letter is almost certainly 12 October.
22. https://www.ebay.com/itm/COLE-PORTER-TYPED-LETTER-SIGNED-10-29-1940/282714518487?hash=item41d31933d7:g:pD0AAOSwCPdZ9430 (accessed 31 October 2017). TLS on Waldorf stationery.
23. *New York Herald Tribune,* 31 October 1940; *New York Sun,* 31 October 1940; *New York Times,* 31 October 1940.
24. Howard, *Travels with Cole Porter,* 17.
25. Swann Galleries, sale 2367, 20 November 2014, lot 239.
26. *New York Journal-American,* 30 October 1941; *New York Times,* 30 October 1941.
27. Howard, *Travels with Cole Porter,* 17; Linda Porter's letter is postmarked 21 December.
28. Yale University, Irving S. Gilmore Music Library, Cole Porter Collection MSS 82, Box 87. Porter wrote the song 'What Am I to Do' for the film.
29. Georgia State University, Johnny Mercer Papers, shelfmark M001.
30. Yale University, Irving S. Gilmore Music Library, Cole Porter Collection, MSS 82, Box 49, folder 300.

31. Ibid.
32. See the *New York Times* for 22 July 1942, 22.
33. Bonhams, 26 June 2011, sale 19045, lot 2021.
34. NYPL, William Skipper Papers, (S)*MGZMD 185, Box 3.
35. CPT, Correspondence 1942.
36. *New Yorker*, 19 September 1942, 2.
37. Yale University, Irving S. Gilmore Music Library, Cole Porter Collection, MSS 82, Box 49, folder 300.
38. NYPL, William Skipper Papers, (S)*MGZMD 185, Box 3 (TLS on Waldorf stationery).
39. Ibid.
40. CPT, Correspondence 1943. The story recounted by Glazer appears to have been first reported in *The Cambridge Chronicle* for 1854 as 'Father Abbey's Will. To which is now added, a Letter of Courtship to his virtuous and amiable Widow. Cambridge, December 1730'. See Evert A. Duyckinck and George L. Duyckinck, *Cyclopaedia of American Literature* (New York, 1856), vol. 1, 126–7.
41. CPT, Correspondence 1942 (copy).
42. NYPL, William Skipper Papers, (S)*MGZMD 185, Box 3 (written on Waldorf stationery but sent from 416 N. Rockingham).
43. CPT, Correspondence 1943.
44. USC, Jack Warner Collection, Box 26, folder 'Mississippi Belle'.
45. CPT, Correspondence 1954. Robert Buckner (1906–89), screenwriter.
46. CPT, Correspondence 1943.
47. Yale University, Irving S. Gilmore Music Library, William McBrien Papers, Series IV, Box 4, folder 105.
48. Stanford University, Cole Porter Collection, shelfmark FE209, Correspondence: 1943–5 (handwritten postcard).
49. Ibid. August was the only month in 1943 when the 14th fell on a Saturday.
50. https://www.baumanrarebooks.com/rare-books/porter-cole/autograph-letter-signed/102278.aspx, seen 22 April 2017. ALS on Waldorf stationery.
51. American Heritage Center, Jean Howard Papers, Box 6 (handwritten postcard).
52. Howard, *Travels with Cole Porter*, 18.
53. Stanford University, Cole Porter Collection, shelfmark FE209, Correspondence: 1943–5 (TLS on Waldorf stationery).
54. CPT, Correspondence 1943.
55. Ibid.
56. Ibid.
57. Stanford University, Cole Porter Collection, shelfmark FE209, Correspondence: 1943–5 (handwritten postcard).
58. CPT, Correspondence 1943.
59. Copy at ibid.
60. Stanford University, Cole Porter Collection, shelfmark FE209, Correspondence: 1943–5 (ALS written at Williamstown).
61. https://www.ebay.co.uk/itm/382428581841?ul_noapp=true (TLS on Waldorf stationery).
62. Stanford (TLS on Waldorf stationery).
63. Ibid.
64. Stanford University, Cole Porter Collection, shelfmark FE209, Correspondence: 1943–5 (TLS on Waldorf stationery).
65. Stanford University, Cole Porter Collection, shelfmark FE209, Correspondence: 1943–5.
66. CPT, Correspondence 1944.
67. CPT, Correspondence 1944 (telegram).
68. Stanford University, Cole Porter Collection, shelfmark FE209, Correspondence: 1943–5 (TLS on Waldorf stationery).
69. Stanford University, Cole Porter Collection, shelfmark FE209, Correspondence: 1943–5 (telegram).
70. *New York Herald Tribune*, 29 January 1944, 8A.

71. *New York Times*, 29 January 1944, 9.
72. Porter Collection, Library of Congress.
73. CPT, Correspondence 1944 (telegram).
74. Yale University, Irving S. Gilmore Music Library, Cole Porter Collection, MSS 82, Box 49, folder 300.
75. Ibid.
76. CPT, Correspondence 1944.
77. Ibid.
78. Ibid.
79. Yale University, Irving S. Gilmore Music Library, Cole Porter Collection, MSS 82, Box 49, folder 300.
80. CPT, Correspondence 1944.
81. Ibid.
82. Stanford University, Cole Porter Collection, shelfmark FE209, Correspondence: 1943–5 (TLS on Waldorf stationery).
83. NYPL, William Skipper Papers, (S)*MGZMD 185, Box 3 (on Waldorf stationery).
84. CPT, Correspondence 1944.
85. 18 August 1944. CPT, Correspondence 1944.
86. CPT, Correspondence 1944.
87. Ibid.
88. Ibid.
89. Ibid.
90. Ibid.
91. Stanford University, Cole Porter Collection, shelfmark FE209, Correspondence: 1943–5 (TLS on Waldorf stationery).
92. CPT, Correspondence 1944.
93. Ibid.
94. Howard, *Travels with Cole Porter*, 19.
95. Stanford University, Cole Porter Collection, shelfmark FE209, Correspondence: 1943–5 (telegram).
96. CPT, Correspondence 1944.
97. Ibid.
98. Ibid.
99. NYPL, William Skipper Papers.
100. American Heritage Center, Jean Howard Papers, Box 6.
101. CPT, Correspondence 1944.
102. Ibid.
103. NYPL, JPB 82-75, no. 10.
104. Ira & Larry Goldberg Auctioneers, sale 6, lot 796.
105. Swann Galleries, sale 2244, 21 April 2011, lot 295.
106. Yale University, Irving S. Gilmore Music Library, Cole Porter Collection, MSS 82, Box 49, folder 301.
107. http://www.schulsonautographs.com/pages/books/2452/cole-porter/typed-letter-signed-4to-on-the-barclay-hotel-stationery-philadelphia-nov-29-1944. TLS on stationery of the Barclay Hotel, Philadelphia.
108. CPT, Correspondence 1944.
109. American Heritage Center, Jean Howard Papers, Box 6.
110. Letter of 1 December 1944. Yale University, Irving S. Gilmore Music Library, Cole Porter Collection, MSS 82, Box 49, folder 304.
111. Howard, *Travels with Cole Porter*, 20.
112. CPT, Correspondence 1944 (copy).
113. CPT, Correspondence 1944 (unsigned copy).
114. CPT, Correspondence 1944.
115. Ibid.

5 A PORTER BIOPIC AND TWO FLOPS, 1945–1947

1. CPT, Correspondence 1945.
2. Ibid.
3. *Variety*, 31 January 1945, 26.
4. CPT, Correspondence 1945 (unsigned copy).
5. Herrick Library, Hedda Hopper Collection, Box 2648 (telegram).
6. CPT, Correspondence 1945.
7. Stanford University, Cole Porter Collection, shelfmark FE209, Correspondence: 1943–1945 (handwritten note on index card).
8. NYPL, William Skipper Papers, (S)*MGZMD 185, Box 3.
9. Letter of 14 February. CPT, Correspondence 1945.
10. CPT, Correspondence 1945.
11. Stanford University, Cole Porter Collection, shelfmark FE209, Correspondence: 1943–1945 (TLS on Waldorf stationery).
12. *Variety*, 24 March 1945, 1 and 55.
13. CPT, Correspondence 1945.
14. Ibid.
15. See 'How to Beget a Musical Comedy by Cole Porter as told to Richard G. Hubler', Stanford University, Cole Porter Collection, shelfmark FE209, 2-9, Manuscripts, 8.
16. Kimball, *The Complete Lyrics of Cole Porter*, 208.
17. CPT, Correspondence 1945.
18. Yale University, Irving S. Gilmore Music Library, Cole Porter Collection MSS 82, Box 48, folder 300 (ALS).
19. Yale University, Beinecke Rare Book and Manuscript Library, shelfmark YCAL MSS 468 (TL).
20. Yale University, Irving S. Gilmore Music Library, Cole Porter Collection, MSS 82, Box 49, folder 300.
21. Ibid.
22. CPT, Correspondence 1945 (copy).
23. Washington, Library of Congress.
24. NYPL, William Skipper Papers, (S)*MGZMD 185, Box 3.
25. CPT, Correspondence 1945.
26. Ibid.
27. Indiana, The Lilly Library.
28. CPT, Correspondence 1945.
29. Stanford University, Cole Porter Collection, shelfmark FE209, Correspondence: 1943–5 (ALS on 'NO TRESPASSING' stationery).
30. Stanford University, Cole Porter Collection, shelfmark FE209, Correspondence: 1946 (TLS on Waldorf stationery).
31. Stanford University, Cole Porter Collection, shelfmark FE209, Correspondence: 1946.
32. Stanford University, Cole Porter Collection, shelfmark FE209, Correspondence: 1946 (TLS on Waldorf stationery).
33. CPT, Correspondence 1946.
34. Ibid.
35. Ibid (probably a transcription of a telegram).
36. Both contracts are in CPT, 014 Around the World.
37. Herrick Library, Hedda Hopper Collection, Box 2648 (telegram).
38. *Daily Boston Globe*, 29 April 1946, 8.
39. *Daily Boston Globe*, 28 April 1946, 30A.
40. Stanford University, Cole Porter Collection, shelfmark FE209, Correspondence: 1946 (TLS on Waldorf stationery).
41. Ibid.
42. CPT, Correspondence 1946 (transcription of a telegram).
43. Both letters in CPT, Correspondence 1946.

44. Arthur Schwartz Collection, LC.
45. Howard, *Travels with Cole Porter*, 21. Although Linda Porter's letter is dated only 'Monday 13 1946' the month must be May, the only month in 1946 when Monday fell on the 13th.
46. Stanford University, Cole Porter Collection, shelfmark FE209, Correspondence: 1946 (telegram).
47. Ibid. The date suggested by Stanford may be incorrect. Porter writes as if he had seen the finished film, which was not released until 11 June 1948.
48. Indiana, The Lilly Library.
49. *Variety*, 10 July 1946, 8.
50. *New York Herald Tribune*, 4 August 1946, C1.
51. *New Yorker*, 27 July 1946, 48–9.
52. CPT, Correspondence 1946.
53. CPT, Correspondence 1946.
54. http://www.historyforsale.com/html/prodetails.asp?documentid=278890&start=1
55. Stanford University, Cole Porter Collection, shelfmark FE209, Correspondence: 1947 (TLS on Waldorf stationery).
56. Stanford University, Cole Porter Collection, shelfmark FE209, Correspondence: 1947 (ALS on Waldorf notepaper).
57. Ibid.
58. Stanford University, Cole Porter Collection, shelfmark FE209, Correspondence: 1947 (TLS on Waldorf stationery).
59. NYPL, Harburg Collection.
60. Stanford University, Cole Porter Collection, shelfmark FE209, Correspondence: 1947 (ALS on Waldorf notepaper).
61. Stanford University, Cole Porter Collection, shelfmark FE209, Correspondence: 1947 (ALS on 'No Trespassing' stationery).
62. Stanford University, Cole Porter Collection, shelfmark FE209, Correspondence: 1947 (ALS on Waldorf notepaper).
63. Ibid.
64. Stanford University, Cole Porter Collection, shelfmark FE209, Correspondence: 1947 (ALS on 'NO TRESPASSING' stationery).
65. USC, Freed Collection, Box 56, folder "The Pirate".
66. Ibid.
67. McBrien, *Cole Porter*, 302.
68. Irving Berlin Collection, LC (postcard). Dated '1 April' at LC, the postmark is difficult to read and may be '19 April'.
69. Yale University, Irving S. Gilmore Music Library, Cole Porter Collection MSS 82, Box 87. The letter itself is not dated; the envelope in which it was sent is postmarked 29 May 1947.
70. http://weissauctions.hibid.com/lot/6312148/cole-porter-letter-signed-to-monty-woolley.
71. USC, Freed Collection, Box 38, folder 6 (TL).
72. See 'How to Beget a Musical Comedy by Cole Porter as told to Richard G. Hubler', Stanford University, Cole Porter Collection, shelfmark FE209, 2-9, Manuscripts, 5.
73. Stanford University (Sam Stark Collection; written from Williamstown).
74. *The Montreal Gazette*, 24 September 1947, 9.
75. Boston University, Howard Gottlieb Archival Research Center, Douglas Fairbanks, Jr. Papers, shelfmark B. 157, Scrapbook II (TLS).
76. Boston University, Howard Gottlieb Archival Research Center, Douglas Fairbanks, Jr. Papers, shelfmark B. 157, Scrapbook II (ALS).
77. Stanford University, Cole Porter Collection, shelfmark FE209, Correspondence: 1947 (TLS on Waldorf stationery).
78. Ibid.

6 KISS ME, KATE, 1948

1. Stanford University, Cole Porter Collection, shelfmark FE209, Correspondence: 1948 (TLS on Waldorf stationery), 1-6.
2. Letter is annotated with a handwritten note at the bottom, possibly not Porter: 'I am ill with the'.
3. Stanford University, Cole Porter Collection, shelfmark FE209, Correspondence: 1948 (TLS on Waldorf stationery), 1-6.
4. Scan from historyforsale.com.
5. Letter of 25 February 1948 from Cole Porter to Harvey Cole. Yale University, Irving S. Gilmore Music Library, Cole Porter Collection MSS 82, Box 49, folder 299. The letter is on Waldorf stationery.
6. Yale University, Irving S. Gilmore Music Library, Cole Porter Collection, Box 49, folder 299.
7. Ibid.
8. Louis Calta, 'Coward's Revival Leaves Saturday', *New York Times*, 9 March 1948, 27.
9. Stanford University, Cole Porter Collection, shelfmark FE209, Correspondence: 1948 (TLS on Waldorf stationery), 1-6.
10. *New York Times*, 14 March 1948, p. 31. A further *Times* article of 21 March 1948 (X1) also mentions the casting of Novotna and Ferrer.
11. Stanford University, Cole Porter Collection, shelfmark FE209, Correspondence: 1948 (TLS on Waldorf stationery).
12. 'Bray' has been added by Stark above the word 'Robert'.
13. Stanford University, Cole Porter Collection, shelfmark FE209, Correspondence: 1948 (TLS on Waldorf stationery).
14. Note by Stark in margin: 'my nephew S.S.'.
15. A copy of Porter's contract is in the Bella Spewack Papers at Columbia University. Curiously, three other documents are also signed by Sam Spewack, who is not named as a co-author of the script on the drafts of the book until October 1948.
16. A copy of the rider is at the Cole Porter Trust, New York.
17. Stanford University, Cole Porter Collection, shelfmark FE209, Correspondence: 1948 (TLS on Waldorf stationery).
18. Ibid.
19. Ibid.
20. Marginal annotation by Stark: 'I kept it S.S.'
21. *New York Times*, 2 May 1948, 81.
22. Stanford University, Cole Porter Collection, shelfmark FE209, Correspondence: 1948 (TLS on Waldorf stationery).
23. Anon. 'Of Local Origin,' *New York Times*, 20 May 1948, 35.
24. Thomas M. Pryor, 'Marxism Can Be Fun Too', *New York Times*, 23 May 1948, X1.
25. Ibid.
26. *New York Times*, 31 May 1948, p. 13.
27. CPT, Correspondence 1948.
28. Spewack Papers, Columbia University.
29. Cole Porter Trust.
30. Columbia, Spewack Collection, Catalogued Correspondence: Cole Porter. Transcription.
31. Columbia, Spewack Collection, Catalogued Correspondence: Cole Porter.
32. Of tangential interest: on 22 June, the *New York Times* reported that Porter ('of musical comedy fame') was represented in an exhibition of publications of former students of John M. Berdan, Professor Emeritus of Literature at Yale University.
33. Columbia, Spewack Collection, Catalogued Correspondence: Cole Porter.
34. *New York Times*, 29 June 1948, p. 20.
35. *New York Times*, 17 July 1948, p. 7.
36. *New York Times*, 25 July 1948, p. X3.

37. 30 August 1948: Telegram from Arnold St Subber to Hanya Holm: he is interested in engaging her for *KMK* (Hanya Holm Papers, NYPL, *MGZMD, Box 136, folder 497). Contract: dated 30 September, Holm Papers, NYPL, Box 136, folder 498.
38. Stanford University, Cole Porter Collection, shelfmark FE209, Correspondence: 1948 (TLS on Waldorf stationery). Marginal note by Sam Stark refers to 'The whole trip: Motor trip with Bob Bray from Los Angeles to North Dakota + Chicago'.
39. Stanford University, Cole Porter Collection, shelfmark FE209, Correspondence: 1948 (TLS on Waldorf stationery).
40. Ibid.
41. Sam Zolotow, 'News of the Rialto', *New York Times*, 2 October 1948, 11.
42. Hanya Holm Papers, NYPL, *MGZMD, Box 136, folder 498.
43. Stanford University, Cole Porter Collection, shelfmark FE209, Correspondence: 1948 (TLS on Waldorf stationery).
44. Announcement of audition on 7 October 1948 for backers is found in the Holm Papers, NYPL, *MGZMD, Box 136, folder 498.
45. 8 October 1948: telegram from Arnold St Subber to Hanya Holm, 'first call for singers and dancers will be this Thursday [=?] at the Majestic Theater, Equity only' (NYPL, *MGZMD, Box 136, folder 497). 11 October 1948: telegram from Arnold St Subber to Hanya Holm, auditions for 'special singers and dancers – the ones I have a list for, set for Friday [=?] at Majestic Theater'.
46. *New York Times*, 16 October 1948, p. 9: 'No contracts have been signed yet, but according to certain parties Patricia Morison is set for one of the leading stints in "Kiss Me, Kate", the Cole Porter-Sam and Bella Spewack musical, which is due here on Dec. 29 under the banner of Lemuel Ayers and Arnold Saint Subber. Miss Morison, say the scouts, will sign the necessary papers over the week-end.'
47. Yale University, Irving S. Gilmore Music Library, Robert Shaw Papers, Box 285, folder 55 (on Waldorf stationery).
48. *New York Times*, 28 October 1948, p. 36.
49. Stanford University, Cole Porter Collection, shelfmark FE209, Correspondence: 1948 (on Waldorf note card).
50. Ibid (on Waldorf stationery).
51. *New York Times*, 23 November 1948, p. 36.
52. Stanford University, Cole Porter Collection, shelfmark FE209, Correspondence: 1948 (TLS on Waldorf stationery), 1–6.
53. Ibid.
54. Ibid.
55. Ibid.
56. American Heritage Center, Jean Howard Papers, Box 6.
57. Stanford University, Cole Porter Collection, shelfmark FE209, Correspondence: 1948 (telegram), 1–7.
58. Letter of 30 December 1948 from Alfred Drake to Cole Porter (CPT).

7 FROM *KISS ME, KATE* TO *OUT OF THIS WORLD*, 1949–1950

1. Telegram from Irving Berlin to Cole Porter, 4 January 1949. Cole Porter Collection, Library of Congress.
2. Howard Taubman, 'Cole Porter is "The Top" Again', *New York Times*, 16 January 1949, SM20.
3. Columbia University, Spewack Collection, E Catalogued Correspondence: Cole Porter.
4. Stanford University, Cole Porter Collection, shelfmark FE209, Correspondence: 1949 (TLS on Waldorf stationery), 1–7.
5. Ibid.
6. Ibid.
7. 'The Professional Amateur', profile, *Time* magazine, 31 January 1949, 44.

8. Stanford University, Cole Porter Collection, shelfmark FE209, Correspondence: 1949 (TLS on Waldorf stationery), 1–7.
9. Yale University, Irving S. Gilmore Music Library, William McBrien Papers, Series IV, Box 5, folder 158.
10. Quoted in Eells, *The Life that Late He Led*, 256 (the original copy of the letter is lost). It is possible, of course, that Eells's transcription is altered or censored in some way, but other letters that he quotes for which the original has been obtainable suggest he is generally reliable in representing sources.
11. NYPL, William Skipper Papers, (S)*MGZMD 185, Box 3.
12. See *New Yorker*, 29 January 1949, 18.
13. See *New Yorker*, 12 February 1949, 83.
14. Cole Porter Papers, Indiana Historical Society (on Waldorf stationery).
15. Ibid.
16. The identity of Kenneth M. Browne is unknown: https://www.liveauctioneers.com/item/446104_cole-porter
17. American Heritage Center, Jean Howard Papers, Box 6.
18. Goddard Lieberson Papers, Correspondence, Yale University.
19. Louis Calta, '600 Stage Artists Set for ANTA Show', *New York Times*, 5 March 1949, 10.
20. Copy sold on eBay.
21. NYPL, William Skipper Papers, (S)*MGZMD 185, Box 3.
22. CPT, Correspondence 1949 (written on Chappell Music stationery).
23. Louis Calta, 'Webster to Tour Straw-Hat Circuit', *New York Times*, 22 March 1949, 31.
24. See McBrien, *Cole Porter*, 303.
25. Anon, ' "Salesman", "Kate" Win Perry Awards', *New York Times*, 24 April 1949, 19.
26. Lewis Funke, 'Gossip of the Rialto', *New York Times*, 8 May 1949, X1.
27. Stanford University, Cole Porter Collection, shelfmark FE209, Correspondence: 1949 (TLS on Waldorf stationery), 1–7.
28. Ibid.
29. Ibid, 1–8 (handwritten and undated).
30. Irving Berlin Collection, Library of Congress.
31. Ibid.
32. Ibid.
33. Stanford University, Cole Porter Collection, shelfmark FE209, Correspondence: 1949 (TLS on Waldorf stationery), 1–7.
34. A. H. Weiler, 'By Way Of Report', *New York Times*, 8 May 1949, X5.
35. Louis Calta, 'Abbott's Musical Will Bow Tonight', *New York Times*, 13 October 1949, 33.
36. Cole Porter Papers, Indiana Historical Society (on Waldorf stationery).
37. Stanford University, Cole Porter Collection, shelfmark FE209, Correspondence: 1949 (TLS on Waldorf stationery), 1–7.
38. Ibid. Handwritten on 'NO TRESPASSING' notepaper. The recipient's surname is not given but Porter salutes 'Mr. Davis' at the end of his letter. Davis is depicted in a photograph of a group of friends in McBrien, *Cole Porter*, 268.
39. Stanford University, Cole Porter Collection, shelfmark FE209, Correspondence: 1949 (TLS on Waldorf stationery), 1–7. Letter written from Williamstown.
40. Copy sold on eBay.
41. Quoted in Howard, *Travels with Cole Porter*, 22.
42. Howard Papers, AHC, Box 6 (handwritten on 'No Trespassing' stationery).
43. Stanford University, Cole Porter Collection, shelfmark FE209, Correspondence: 1949 (TLS on Waldorf stationery), 1–7.
44. Howard Papers, AHC, Box 6.
45. Stanford University, Cole Porter Collection, shelfmark FE209, Correspondence: 1949, 1–7 (handwritten on 'No Trespassing' stationery).
46. Stanford University, Cole Porter Collection, shelfmark FE209, Correspondence: 1949 (TLS on Waldorf stationery), 1–7. Addressed from Williamstown.

47. Ibid.
48. Ibid.
49. Stanford University, Cole Porter Collection, shelfmark FE209, Correspondence: 1949 (TLS on Waldorf stationery), 1–7.
50. The source for this and the next two letters: Ethel Merman and George Eells, *Merman: An Autobiography* (New York: Simon and Schuster, 1978), 153–4.
51. Stanford University, Cole Porter Collection, shelfmark FE209, Correspondence: 1949 (TLS on Waldorf stationery), 1–7.
52. Ibid.
53. Ibid.
54. Sold at historyforsale.com
55. Ibid.
56. Ibid.
57. Ibid.
58. Stanford University, Cole Porter Collection, shelfmark FE209, Correspondence: 1949 (TLS on Waldorf stationery), 1–7.
59. Ibid.
60. Ibid. Undated.
61. Kent State University archive, David Wayne Papers.
62. Stanford University, Cole Porter Collection, shelfmark FE209, Correspondence: 1949 (TLS on Waldorf stationery), 1–7.
63. Handwritten card, Margaret Herrick Library, Katharine Hepburn Collection, Folder 1140 'P-Miscellaneous'.
64. Undated letter from 11/1949: Linda Porter to Sam Stark. Stanford University, Cole Porter Collection, shelfmark FE209, Correspondence: 1949 (TLS on Waldorf stationery), 1–8.
65. Stanford University, Cole Porter Collection, shelfmark FE209, Correspondence: 1949 (TLS on Waldorf stationery), 1–7.
66. Ibid, 1–8.
67. Ibid, 1–9 (handwritten on 'No Trespassing' stationery).
68. Ibid.
69. Stanford University, Cole Porter Collection, shelfmark FE209, Correspondence: 1950 (TLS on Waldorf stationery), 1–9.
70. Ibid. Letter from Linda Porter to Sam Stark, 7 February 1950.
71. Stanford University, Cole Porter Collection, shelfmark FE209, Correspondence: 1950 (TLS on Waldorf stationery), 1–9.
72. Ibid.
73. Ibid (handwritten on 'No Trespassing' stationery).
74. Ibid.
75. Stanford University, Cole Porter Collection, shelfmark FE209, Correspondence: 1950 (TLS on Waldorf stationery), 1–9.
76. CPT, Correspondence 1950.
77. Ibid.
78. Stanford University, Cole Porter Collection, shelfmark FE209, Correspondence: 1950 (TLS on Waldorf stationery), 1–9.
79. Swann Galleries, sale 2351, lot 175.
80. Stanford University, Cole Porter Collection, shelfmark FE209, Correspondence: 1950 (TLS on Waldorf stationery), 1–9.
81. Florence, Villa I Tatti.
82. CPT, Correspondence 1950.
83. Ibid.
84. Ibid.
85. Ibid.
86. Stanford University, Cole Porter Collection, shelfmark FE209, Correspondence: 1950 (TLS on Waldorf stationery), 1–9.

87. CPT, Correspondence 1950.
88. See John Crosby, 'Exuberant, Funny and Tuneful', *New York Herald Tribune*, 6 October 1950, 25.
89. See Jack Gould, ' "Anything Goes" Revived on Video', *New York Times*, 3 October 1950, 44.
90. Irving Berlin Collection, Library of Congress.
91. Ibid.
92. Cole Porter Collection, Library of Congress.
93. Jean Howard, *Travels with Cole Porter*, 22.
94. Stanford University, Cole Porter Collection, shelfmark FE209, Correspondence: 1950 (TLS on Waldorf stationery), 1–9.
95. Irving Berlin Collection, Library of Congress.
96. Stanford University, Cole Porter Collection, shelfmark FE209, Correspondence: 1950 (TLS on Waldorf stationery), 1–9.
97. Sam Zolotow, 'Crabtree's Play in Debut Tonight', 17 November 1950, *New York Times*, 43.
98. Stanford University, Cole Porter Collection, shelfmark FE209, Correspondence: 1950 (TLS on Waldorf stationery), 1–9.
99. Ibid; letter of 16 November 1950 from Smith to Stark.
100. Stanford University, Cole Porter Collection, shelfmark FE209, Correspondence: 1950 (TLS on Waldorf stationery), 1–9; undated handwritten letter from Linda Porter to Stark.
101. Stanford University, Cole Porter Collection, shelfmark FE209, Correspondence: 1950 (TLS on Waldorf stationery), 1–9.
102. Ibid.
103. Howard Papers, AHC, Box 6.
104. CPT, Correspondence 1950.
105. Anon, 'Boston Censors Musical', *New York Times*, 1 December 1950, 38.
106. Worcester Academy (on Waldorf stationery).
107. Cole Porter Collection, Library of Congress.
108. Memo of plans for Stark from 16 December 1950, including a postscript about coffee at the Colony. Stanford University, Cole Porter Collection, shelfmark FE209, Correspondence: 1946 (TLS on Waldorf stationery), 1–10.
109. Stanford University, Cole Porter Collection, shelfmark FE209, Correspondence: 1950 (TLS on Waldorf stationery), 1–10.
110. Brooks Atkinson, 'At the Theatre', *New York Times*, 22 December 1950, 17.

8 FROM LIMBO TO THE WRITING OF *CAN-CAN*, 1951–1952

1. Stanford University, Cole Porter Collection, shelfmark FE209, Correspondence: 1951 (TLS on Waldorf stationery), 1–12.
2. Ibid.
3. NYPL *T-Mss 1971-002, Series III, Subseries 1, Box 199.
4. Columbia University, Spewack Collection, Catalogued Correspondence: Cole Porter.
5. CPT, Correspondence 1951.
6. Ibid.
7. Photocopy; CPT, Correspondence 1951.
8. Stanford University, Cole Porter Collection, shelfmark FE209, Correspondence: 1951 (TLS on Waldorf stationery), 1–12.
9. Ibid. Letter of 5 February 1951 from Linda Porter to Sam Stark.
10. Stanford University, Cole Porter Collection, shelfmark FE209, Correspondence: 1951 (TLS on Waldorf stationery), 1–12.
11. CPT, Correspondence 1951 (on Waldorf stationery).
12. CPT, Correspondence 1951.
13. Ibid (copy).
14. Sent from 416 N. Rockingham. CPT, Correspondence 1951.

15. Ibid.
16. These letters apparently do not survive.
17. Letter of 13 March 1951 from Allen Keith to Cole Porter, offering via Ben Schankman a synopsis of *Love or Money* if interested. CPT, Correspondence 1951.
18. Sent from 416 N. Rockingham. CPT, Correspondence 1951.
19. Yale University, Irving S. Gilmore Music Library, Cole Porter Collection MSS 82, Box 49, folder 301. Handwritten on stationery of Westleigh Farm, Peru, Indiana.
20. Letter of 31 March 1951 from Linda Porter to Sam Stark. Stanford University, Cole Porter Collection, shelfmark FE209, Correspondence: 1951 (TLS on Waldorf stationery), 1–12.
21. Sent from 416 N. Rockingham. CPT, Correspondence 1951.
22. The ASCAP papers can be viewed at NYPL. See http://archives.nypl.org/mus/22936 (accessed 11 September 2018).
23. Letter of 18 April 1951 from Maurice C. Brockway to Cole Porter. CPT, Correspondence 1951, photocopy.
24. Sent from 416 N. Rockingham. CPT, Correspondence 1951.
25. TLS, from 416 N. Rockingham. https://www.ebay.com/itm/COLE-PORTER-TYPED-LETTER-SIGNED-05-02-1951/302016979237?hash=item46519d6125:g:3BkAAOSwMsVXjBBH; accessed 31 October 2017.
26. Columbia University, Spewack Collection, Catalogued Correspondence: Cole Porter.
27. Ibid.
28. Ibid.
29. Stanford University, Cole Porter Collection, shelfmark FE209, Correspondence: 1951 (TLS on Waldorf stationery), 1–10 (handwritten on Buxton Hill paper).
30. Ibid, 1–12.
31. Letter of 11 June 1951 from Paul Sylvain to Sam Stark. Stanford University, Cole Porter Collection, shelfmark FE209, Correspondence: 1951 (TLS on Waldorf stationery), 1–12 (handwritten on Buxton Hill paper).
32. Ibid.
33. Columbia University, Spewack Collection, Catalogued Correspondence: Cole Porter.
34. Letter of 10 July 1951 from Stan Stanley, Chappell & Co. to Cole Porter. CPT, Correspondence 1951.
35. Columbia University, Spewack Collection, Catalogued Correspondence: Cole Porter.
36. Sent from 415 in L.A. to Stark in Mexico. Stanford University, Cole Porter Collection, shelfmark FE209, Correspondence: 1951 (TLS on Waldorf stationery), 1–12.
37. Ibid.
38. CPT, Correspondence 1951.
39. Columbia University, Spewack Collection, Catalogued Correspondence: Cole Porter.
40. Sent from 416 N. Rockingham to Mexico. Stanford University, Cole Porter Collection, shelfmark FE209, Correspondence: 1951 (TLS on Waldorf stationery), 1–12.
41. Sent from 416 N. Rockingham; CPT, Correspondence 1951.
42. Handwritten, CPT, Correspondence 1951.
43. Letter written from California; CPT, Correspondence 1951.
44. Sent from 416 N. Rockingham; CPT, Correspondence 1951.
45. Ibid.
46. Stanford University, Cole Porter Collection, shelfmark FE209, Correspondence: 1951 (handwritten on Buxton Hill stationery), 1–12.
47. Stanford University, Cole Porter Collection, shelfmark FE209, Correspondence: 1951 (handwritten on 'No Trespassing' stationery), 1–12.
48. Stanford University, Cole Porter Collection, shelfmark FE209, Correspondence: 1951, 1–12.
49. Stanford University, Cole Porter Collection, shelfmark FE209, Correspondence: 1951 (handwritten on Waldorf stationery), 1–12.
50. Ibid.

51. Ibid.
52. Ibid.
53. Ibid.
54. Columbia University, Spewack Collection, Catalogued Correspondence: Cole Porter.
55. Sam Zolotow, 'F. Hugh Herbert, Porter Doing Show', *New York Times*, 17 November 1951, 22.
56. Letter of 7 January 1952 from Paul Sylvain to Sam Stark. Stanford University, Cole Porter Collection, shelfmark FE209, Correspondence: 1952 (handwritten on Waldorf stationery), 1–13.
57. Stanford University, Cole Porter Collection, shelfmark FE209, Correspondence: 1952 (handwritten on 'No Trespassing' stationery), 1–13.
58. CPT, Correspondence 1952.
59. Stanford University, Cole Porter Collection, shelfmark FE209, Correspondence: 1952 (handwritten on 'No Trespassing' stationery), 1–13.
60. Typed letter on Waldorf stationery: https://www.ebay.com/itm/PORTER-COLE-Typed-Letter-Signed-to-musical-director-George-Hirst-Lot-187/202076470638?hash=item2f0cb23d6e:g:HxIAAOSwyjJZ2nwj; accessed 31 October 2017.
61. Stanford University, Cole Porter Collection, shelfmark FE209, Correspondence: 1952 (handwritten on 'No Trespassing' stationery), 1–13.
62. CPT, Correspondence 1952 (copy).
63. CPT, Correspondence 1952.
64. Original not found. Quoted in McBrien, *Cole Porter*, 333.
65. Sam Zolotow, 'Burr and Pearson Split On "Willows"', *New York Times*, 17 March 1952, 16.
66. Sam Zolotow, 'Delay in Staging "The Baker's Wife"', *New York Times*, 9 April 1952, 26.
67. CPT, Correspondence 1952.
68. Yale University, Irving S. Gilmore Music Library, Cole Porter Collection MSS 82, Box 49, folder 299.
69. CPT, Correspondence 1952 (copy).
70. Margaret Herrick Library, George Cukor Collection, Box 854.
71. CPT, Burrows file.
72. Ibid.
73. Ibid.
74. Yale University, Irving S. Gilmore Music Library, Cole Porter Collection MSS 82, Box 49, folder 301. Typewritten letter; carbon copy.
75. CPT, Burrows file.
76. Ibid.
77. NYPL, Abe Burrows Papers, *T-Mss 2000-006, Box 13, folder 19.
78. CPT, *Can-Can* binder.
79. NYPL, Abe Burrows Papers, *T-Mss 2000-006, Box 8, folder 3.
80. CPT, Correspondence 1952.
81. Ibid.
82. Letter of 14 July 1952 from Abe Burrows to Cy Feuer. CPT, Burrows file.
83. CPT, Correspondence 1952.
84. Ibid.
85. Ibid.
86. Ibid.
87. Anon., 'Metro to Do Film of "Kiss Me, Kate"', *New York Times*, 9 July 1952, 23.
88. CPT, Correspondence 1952.
89. Ibid.
90. Ibid. Handwritten letter.
91. Letter from Paul Sylvain to Sam Stark, dated 31 July 1952. Stanford University, Cole Porter Collection, shelfmark FE209, Correspondence: 1952 (handwritten on Westleigh Farm, Peru, Indiana notepaper), 1–13.
92. George Eells Collection, Porter research, folder 5, USC.
93. CPT, Correspondence 1952; scan.

94. Stanford University, Cole Porter Collection, shelfmark FE209, Correspondence: 1952, 1–14.
95. Stanford University, Cole Porter Collection, shelfmark FE209, Correspondence: 1952 (handwritten on 'COLE PORTER' stationery), 1–13.
96. Letter of 3 September 1952 from Alfred A. Knopf to Bella Spewack. CPT, Correspondence 1952. Letter of 17 November 1952: agreement between Porter, the Spewacks and Knopf. Columbia University, Ms Coll Spewack. See also letter of 30 October 1952 from John Wharton to Cole Porter (CPT, Correspondence 1952), informing Porter that contracts have been submitted to Knopf.
97. TLS on Waldorf stationery to Peru, Indiana. Seen online at http://www.historyforsale.com/html/prodetails.asp?documentid=278887&start=16&page=104, accessed 19 May 2016. In response, Harvey Cole wrote on 17 September 1952: 'I have your letter of September 13, 1952 including Bill Miller's flower bill which I have sent to Joe Huber for payment along with other funeral expenses': http://www.historyforsale.com/html/prodetails.asp?documentid=278887&start=16&page=104, accessed 19 May 2016.
98. Stanford University, Cole Porter Collection, shelfmark FE209, Correspondence: 1952 (handwritten on Waldorf stationery), 1–13.
99. Daniel Lang, 'A Reporter at Large: Something in the Sky', *New Yorker*, 6 September 1952, 62–82.
100. *From Under My Hat* (Boston and New York, 1952), Hopper's memoir.
101. *Tallulah: My Autobiography* (New York, 1952).
102. Stanford University, Cole Porter Collection, shelfmark FE209, Correspondence: 1952 (handwritten on Waldorf stationery), 1–13.
103. CPT, Correspondence 1952; scan.
104. Stanford University, Cole Porter Collection, shelfmark FE209, Correspondence: 1952 (handwritten on Waldorf stationery), 1–13.

9 TWO LAST BROADWAY HITS, *CAN-CAN* AND *SILK STOCKINGS*, 1953–1954

1. Stanford University, Cole Porter Collection, shelfmark FE209, Correspondence: 1953.
2. CPT, Correspondence 1953 (handwritten; year not included).
3. Letter of 16 January 1953 from Feuer to Porter and Burrows. NYPL, Abe Burrows Papers, *T-Mss 2000-006, Box 8, folder 5.
4. Fred Lounsberry to Cole Porter, 28 January 1953. CPT, Correspondence 1953.
5. CPT, correspondence 1953.
6. Stanford University, Cole Porter Collection, shelfmark FE209, Correspondence: 1953 (on Waldorf stationery), 1–14.
7. Ditto.
8. CPT, Correspondence 1953.
9. Letter of 12 February 1953 from Jack Cummings (MGM) to John Wharton, sending the first forty-eight pages of a temporary screenplay for *Kiss Me, Kate* (CPT, Correspondence 1953). Letter of 9 March 1953 from Steven R. Carlin (RCA) to Cole Porter (CPT, Correspondence 1953). Of note, Porter is not shown as having a physical disability in the film.
10. Sam Zolotow, 'Porter Agrees to Do Another Musical for Feuer and Martin', *New York Times*, 1 March 1953, X1.
11. Stanford University, Cole Porter Collection, shelfmark FE209, Correspondence: 1953, 1–14.
12. Jean Howard Papers, AHC, Box 6.
13. Stanford University, Cole Porter Collection, shelfmark FE209, Correspondence: 1953 (on Waldorf stationery), 1–14.
14. CPT, Correspondence 1953.
15. Ibid.
16. Ibid.

17. 5 May 1953: Thomas Robinson (MGM) to Robert Montgomery (CPT, Correspondence 1953): letters of agreement for $7,500 (for 'From This Moment On') and release of prior agreement of 12 September 1952 for three additional songs, and licence with Buxton Hill Music for use of 'From This Moment On' in *KMK* film.
18. CPT, Correspondence 1953.
19. Ibid. Maxwell is not named in the source but it is obvious that she is the recipient.
20. Stanford University, Cole Porter Collection, shelfmark FE209, Correspondence: 1953 (on Waldorf stationery), 1–14.
21. Ibid.
22. Ibid.
23. Seymour Peck, 'Can-Can from Old Montmartre', *New York Times*, 3 May 1953, X1.
24. Jean Howard Papers, AHC, Box 6.
25. Brooks Atkinson, 'First Night at the Theatre', *New York Times*, 8 May 1953, 28.
26. CPT, Correspondence 1953.
27. Handwritten letter of 17 May 1953 from Goddard Lieberson to Cole Porter; Yale University, Irving S. Gilmore Music Library, Cole Porter Collection MSS 82, Box 49, folder 303.
28. Reproduced in *You're Sensational: Cole Porter in the '20s, '40s and '50s* (Indianapolis: Indiana Historical Society, 1999), 68.
29. Written on stationery of the Hotel Windsor Etoile, Paris. Yale University, Irving S. Gilmore Music Library, Cole Porter Collection MSS 82, Box 49, folder 302.
30. Ibid.
31. CPT, Correspondence 1955 [sic].
32. Stanford University, Cole Porter Collection, shelfmark FE209, Correspondence: 1953 (on Waldorf stationery), 1–14.
33. Ibid.
34. CPT, Correspondence 1953.
35. Ibid. Written from California.
36. ebay: http://www.ebay.co.uk/itm/331622594951 (accessed 2017).
37. CPT, Correspondence 1953.
38. Letter of 16 July 1953 from John Wharton to Mr L. C. Hanna. CPT, Correspondence 1953.
39. CPT, Correspondence 1953.
40. Noël Coward Foundation.
41. Anon, '$551,550 Left to Cole Porter', *New York Times*, 28 June 1953, 32.
42. CPT, Correspondence 1953.
43. Ibid.
44. Ibid.
45. Lewis Funke, 'News and Gossip of the Rialto', *New York Times*, 26 July 1953, X1.
46. https://www.ebay.co.uk/itm/391990441648?ul_noapp=true (accessed 2 March 2018).
47. https://www.bonhams.com/auctions/24254/lot/1088 (accessed 8 August 2018).
48. Stanford University, Cole Porter Collection, shelfmark FE209, Correspondence: 1953 (on Waldorf stationery), 1–14.
49. CPT, Correspondence 1953.
50. Ibid.
51. Ibid.
52. Letter of 2 September 1953 from Robert Montgomery to B.A.T. Productions Ltd., London. CPT, Correspondence 1953.
53. CPT, Correspondence 1953.
54. Ibid.
55. http://universityarchives.com/Cole_Porter-ITEM63505.aspx (accessed 8 August 2018).
56. http://universityarchives.com/Cole_Porter-ITEM63506.aspx (accessed 8 August 2018).
57. Three letters of 18 September 1953 from Irving Lazar to John F. Wharton. CPT, Correspondence 1953.

58. Stanford University, Cole Porter Collection, shelfmark FE209, Correspondence: 1953 (on Waldorf stationery), 1–14.
59. Bosley Crowther, 'The Screen in Review', *New York Times*, 6 November 1953, 23.
60. Letter of 18 November 1953 from Sam Spewack to Porter. CPT, Correspondence 1953.
61. CPT, Correspondence 1953.
62. Letter of 24 November 1953 from Sam and Bella Spewack to Cole Porter. CPT, Correspondence 1953.
63. Letter of 2 October 1953 from Irving Lazar to John F. Wharton. CPT, Correspondence 1953.
64. Letter of 1 December 1953 from Irving Lazar to Robert Montgomery. CPT, Correspondence 1953.
65. 8 December 1953: Deal with MGM (Arthur Freed Unit) for the Porter Cavalcade. CPT, Correspondence 1953.
66. Thomas M. Pryor, 'Porter's Music in Metro Plans', *New York Times*, 28 December 1953, 28. Gene Kelly (1912–96), actor, singer and movie star.
67. Thomas M. Pryor, 'Charlton Heston to Portray Moses', *New York Times*, 16 February 1954, 29. The actress Vera-Ellen (1921–81) is best remembered for her appearance in the movie *White Christmas* (1954).
68. Jean Howard Papers, AHC, Box 6. Annotated at top: 'I was ill in Switzerland.'
69. CPT, Correspondence 1953.
70. On Waldorf stationery. Many thanks to Paul Schwartz for sharing this letter.
71. More information is given here: https://www.encyclopedia.com/social-sciences-and-law/economics-business-and-labor/businesses-and-occupations/broadcast-music-inc (accessed 11 September 2018).
72. CPT, Burrows file.
73. Stanford University, Cole Porter Collection, shelfmark FE209, Correspondence: 1953 (on Waldorf stationery), 1–14.
74. Jean Howard Papers, AHC, Box 6.
75. Stanford University, Cole Porter Collection, shelfmark FE209, Correspondence: 1954 (on Waldorf stationery), 1–15.
76. Cole Porter Collection, Library of Congress.
77. Letter of 17 February 1954, Jule Styne to Cole Porter. CPT, Correspondence 1954.
78. Letter of 19 February 1954, Cole Porter to Pete Barnum, NBC. CPT, Correspondence 1954.
79. Jack Gould, 'Television in Review: Song Magic', *New York Times*, 3 March 1954, 35.
80. Stanford University, Cole Porter Collection, shelfmark FE209, Correspondence: 1954 (on Waldorf stationery), 1–15.
81. Handwritten on stationery of the Palace Hotel, St Moritz. NYU, Fales Library, Erich Maria Remarque Papers, Series 12, Subseries A, Box 2, folder 9. Headed: 'Monday night, Mar 15 '54'.
82. Stanford University, Cole Porter Collection, shelfmark FE209, Correspondence: 1954 (on Waldorf stationery), 1–15.
83. Jerome Robbins Papers, NYPL.
84. See Deborah Jowitt, *Jerome Robbins: His Life, His Theater, His Dance* (New York: Simon and Schuster, 2004), 250.
85. Noël Coward Foundation.
86. CPT, Correspondence 1954.
87. Thomas M. Pryor, 'Warners to Team Sinatra and Day', *New York Times*, 8 May 1954, 15. *It's Always Fair Weather* was released on 1 September 1955, starring Gene Kelly.
88. Jean Howard Papers, AHC, Box 6.
89. CPT, Burrows file.
90. Stanford University, Cole Porter Collection, shelfmark FE209, Correspondence: 1954 (on Waldorf stationery), 1–15.
91. Ibid.
92. Jean Howard Papers, AHC, Box 6.

93. Margaret Herrick Library, Hedda Hopper Collection, Box 2648.
94. Ibid.
95. Stanford University, Cole Porter Collection, shelfmark FE209, Correspondence: 1954 (on Waldorf stationery), 1–15.
96. Ibid.
97. CPT, Correspondence 1954.
98. Stanford University, Cole Porter Collection, shelfmark FE209, Correspondence: 1954 (on Waldorf stationery), 1–15.
99. Written from 416 N. Rockingham, California. Stanford University, Cole Porter Collection, shelfmark FE209, Correspondence: 1954 (on Waldorf stationery), 1–15.
100. Sam Zolotow, 'New Team Seeks Schulberg's Play', *New York Times*, 9 July 1954, 22.
101. Anon., 'Metro Will Film Anderson Drama', *New York Times*, 20 July 1954, 16.
102. CPT, Correspondence 1954.
103. Ibid.
104. Margaret Herrick Library, Jack Cummings Collection, Box 60, folder 'Seven Brides for Seven Brothers Correspondence'.
105. Stanford University, Cole Porter Collection, shelfmark FE209, Correspondence: 1954 (on Waldorf stationery), 1–15.
106. CPT, Burrows file.
107. Ibid.
108. Cole Porter Collection, Library of Congress.
109. Yale University, Irving S. Gilmore Music Library, Cole Porter Collection MSS 82, Box 87 (on Waldorf stationery).
110. On Waldorf stationery. Swann Galleries, sale 2413, 5 May 2016, lot 248. http://catalogue.swanngalleries.com/asp/fullCatalogue.asp?salelot=2413+++++248+&refno=++712675&saletype=.
111. Jack Gould, 'Television in Review', *New York Times*, 12 November 1954, 29.
112. Quoted in the *New York Times* review of the book by Cleveland Amory, 24 October 1954, BR6.
113. Stanford University, Cole Porter Collection, shelfmark FE209, Correspondence: 1954 (on Waldorf stationery), 1–17.
114. Yale University, Irving S. Gilmore Music Library, Cole Porter Collection MSS 82, Box 87 (on Waldorf stationery).
115. Stanford University, Cole Porter Collection, shelfmark FE209, Correspondence: 1954 (on Waldorf stationery), 1–15.
116. Ibid.
117. Cole Porter Collection, Library of Congress.
118. Louis Calta, 'Irra Petina Stars in "Hit the Trail"', *New York Times*, 2 December 1954, 40.
119. Cole Porter Collection, Library of Congress.
120. Noël Coward Foundation.
121. Gershwin Fund Collection, Library of Congress.

10 PORTER'S LAST MUSICALS, 1955–1957

1. Thomas M. Pryor, 'Sinatra to Star in Musical Film', *New York Times*, 17 December 1954, 36.
2. NYPL, Abe Burrows Papers, *T-Mss 2000-006, Box 9, folder 25.
3. Cole Porter Collection, Library of Congress, Box 25, folder 7.
4. Stanford University, Cole Porter Collection, shelfmark FE209, Correspondence: 1955 (on Waldorf stationery), 1–16.
5. Cole Porter Collection, Library of Congress, Box 24, folder 2.
6. See McBrien, *Cole Porter*, 363.
7. Handwritten on stationery of Baur au Lac, Zurich. Yale University, Irving S. Gilmore Music Library, Cole Porter Collection, MSS 82, Box 49, folder 30.

NOTES to pp. 500–518

8. Quoted in Gilbert Millstein, 'Words Anent Music by Cole Porter,' *New York Times*, 20 February 1955, SM16.
9. Howard, *Travels with Cole Porter*, 30.
10. Brooks Atkinson, 'Satire on the Soviet', *New York Times*, 25 February 1955, 17.
11. Handwritten letter of 2 March 1955 from Paul Sylvain to the Starks (Palace Hotel, St Moritz stationery). Stanford University, Cole Porter Collection, shelfmark FE209, Correspondence: 1955 (on Waldorf stationery), 1–16.
12. Letter of 3 March 1955 from Madeline P. Smith to Sam Stark. Ibid.
13. Letter from the Palace Hotel, St Moritz. Ibid.
14. Handwritten note from Stark to Porter. Ibid, 1–18.
15. CPT, Correspondence 1955.
16. Ibid.
17. Howard, *Travels with Cole Porter*, 32.
18. Ibid, 51.
19. Yale University, Irving S. Gilmore Music Library, Cole Porter Collection, MSS 82, Box 49, folder 301.
20. Howard, *Travels with Cole Porter*, 31.
21. Ibid, 34.
22. Ibid, 36.
23. https://www.baumanrarebooks.com/rare-books/porter-cole/autograph-letter-signed/103877.aspx (accessed 17 April 2017).
24. Howard, *Travels with Cole Porter*, 36.
25. Ibid.
26. Ibid, 38.
27. Ibid.
28. Ibid.
29. On stationery of the Palace Hotel, Bussaco; Swann Galleries, sale 2367, 20 November 2014, lot 247.
30. Howard, *Travels with Cole Porter*, 40.
31. A facsimile of the letter appears in Grafton, *Red, Hot & Rich!*, between pp. 122 and 123.
32. Howard, *Travels with Cole Porter*, 50.
33. Ibid, 51.
34. Ibid.
35. Stanford University, Cole Porter Collection, shelfmark FE209, Correspondence: 1955 (on Waldorf stationery), 1–18.
36. Handwritten note on stationery of Grand Hotel, Rome. https://www.ebay.com/itm/COLE-PORTER-AUTOGRAPH-LETTER-SIGNED-05-06-1955/302507487599?hash=item466ed9f16f:g:6bYAAOSwHUhZ94wN (accessed 31 October 2017).
37. Howard, *Travels with Cole Porter*, 55.
38. Yale University, Irving S. Gilmore Music Library, Cole Porter Collection, MSS 82, Box 49, folder 301.
39. Yale University, Eells Papers.
40. Source for all Porter's diaries from this trip: CPT, Correspondence 1955.
41. Ibid.
42. Letter of 25 July 1955 from A. Capparis to John F. Wharton, CPT, Correspondence 1955. Capparis comments: 'These schools educate and train the future Deck and Engine Officers of the Greek Merchant Marine, which is actually the backbone of the Greek national economy.'
43. Howard, *Travels with Cole Porter*, 104.
44. Letter of 16 June 1955 from Bobbink and Atkins to John F. Wharton. CPT, Correspondence 1955.
45. CPT, Correspondence 1955.
46. Columbia University, Spewack Collection, Catalogued Correspondence: Cole Porter.

47. See Thomas Pryor, 'Hollywood Scene', *New York Times*, 28 August 1955, X5.
48. Howard, *Travels with Cole Porter*, 111.
49. Stanford University, Cole Porter Collection, shelfmark FE209, Correspondence: 1955 (on Waldorf stationery), 1–16.
50. Margaret Herrick Library, Katharine Hepburn Collection, Box 166, 'Correspondence 1954 – Summertime'.
51. Yale University, Eells Papers.
52. CPT, Correspondence 1955.
53. [no address] CPT, Correspondence 1955.
54. Ibid.
55. Jean Howard Papers, AHC, Box 6.
56. Anon, 'Cole Porter Revival', *New York Times*, 1 October 1955, 11.
57. A.G., 'Musical in the Village', *New York Times*, 10 November 1955, 44.
58. Thomas M. Pryor, 'M-G-M Signs Trio for "High Society"', *New York Times*, 28 November 1955, 27.
59. CPT, Correspondence 1955.
60. Ibid.
61. USC, MGM Music Department collection. Box PR-31A.
62. Letter of 9 December 1955 from Johnny Green to Cole Porter. USC, MGM Music Department collection. Box PR-31A.
63. CPT, Correspondence 1955.
64. Ibid.
65. Ibid.
66. Letter of 22 December 1955 from Johnny Green to Cole Porter. USC, MGM Music Department collection. Box PR-31A.
67. CPT, Correspondence 1955.
68. Saul Chaplin Papers, AHC, Box 4.
69. CPT, Correspondence 1955.
70. Saul Chaplin Papers, AHC, Box 4.
71. Ibid.
72. CPT, Correspondence 1956.
73. Ibid.
74. Saul Chaplin Papers, AHC, Box 4.
75. Letter of 28 January 1956 from Johnny Green to Cole Porter. USC, MGM Music Department collection. Box PR-31A.
76. Ibid.
77. Letter of 14 February 1956 from Johnny Green to Cole Porter. Ibid.
78. Letter of 15 February 1956 from Johnny Green to Cole Porter. Ibid.
79. Letter of 18 February 1956 from Cole Porter to Johnny Green. Ibid.
80. Ibid.
81. Thomas M. Pryor, 'MGM Will Film "Silk Stockings"', *New York Times*, 16 February 1956, 25.
82. CPT, Correspondence 1956.
83. Howard, *Travels with Cole Porter*, 171.
84. Ibid.
85. The diary entries for this trip are transcribed from the document titled '1956 TRIP' at CPT in a folder marked 'Cole Porter Diaries'. The entries are also reproduced in Jean Howard, *Travels with Cole Porter*, p. 114ff.
86. Yale University, Eells Papers (handwritten).
87. Quoted in Howard, *Travels with Cole Porter*, 136.
88. Yale University, Irving S. Gilmore Music Library, Cole Porter Collection MSS 82.
89. Gershwin Fund Collection, Library of Congress (handwritten).
90. Yale University, Irving S. Gilmore Music Library, Cole Porter Collection MSS 82, Box 49, folder 301 (handwritten).

91. Stanford University, Cole Porter Collection, shelfmark FE209, Correspondence: 1956 (on Waldorf stationery), 1–17.
92. CPT, Correspondence 1956 (handwritten on small note-size paper).
93. McBrien specifically identifies the Richard in this letter as Porter's masseur. See McBrien, *Cole Porter*, 363.
94. Stanford University, Cole Porter Collection, shelfmark FE209, Correspondence: 1956 (on Waldorf stationery), 1–17.
95. Yale University, Irving S. Gilmore Music Library, Cole Porter Collection MSS 82, Box 49, folder 301 (handwritten).
96. Howard, *Travels*, 208.
97. Howard papers, AHC, Box 6 (handwritten).
98. Letter of 1 June 1956 from Madeline P. Smith to Sam Stark. Stanford University, Cole Porter Collection, shelfmark FE209, Correspondence: 1956 (on Waldorf stationery), 1–17.
99. USC, MGM Music Department collection. Box PR-31A.
100. CPT, Correspondence 1956.
101. Quoted in Dominic McHugh, *Alan Jay Lerner: A Lyricist's Letters* (New York: Oxford University Press, 2014).
102. Yale University, Irving S. Gilmore Music Library, Cole Porter Collection MSS 82, Box 49, folder 301 (typewritten copy).
103. George Eells Collection, USC, folder 5.
104. Stanford University, Cole Porter Collection, shelfmark FE209, Correspondence: 1956 (on Waldorf stationery), 1–17.
105. Bosley Crowther, 'No "Philadelphia Story"', *New York Times*, 10 August 1956, 9.
106. USC Cinematic Arts Library, Charles Walters Collection, 'High Society' (bound script), Box 2:3. Letter sent from N. Rockingham Avenue to Walters in Beverly Hills.
107. CPT, Correspondence 1956.
108. *The Rodgers and Hart Songbook* (ed. Albert Sirmay) (New York: Simon & Schuster, 1951).
109. CPT, Correspondence 1956.
110. Stanford University, Cole Porter Collection, shelfmark FE209, Correspondence: 1956 (on Waldorf stationery), 1–17.
111. Much of the show can be viewed at https://archive.org/details/FordStarJubilee-ColePorter (accessed 11 July 2018).
112. Copy of a letter from Geoffrey Shurlock (censor) to Dore Schary (MGM) on 7 May 1956. Cole Porter Collection, Library of Congress.
113. Cole Porter Collection, Library of Congress (carbon copy).
114. George Eells Collection, USC, folder 5, Cole Porter research.
115. Ibid.
116. Liz Roberton.
117. Johnny Mercer Papers, Georgia State University.
118. Letter of 22 November 1956 from Madeline P. Smith to Bella Spewack (Spewack Papers, Columbia).
119. Cole Porter Collection, Library of Congress (carbon copy).
120. Ibid.
121. Stanford University, Cole Porter Collection, shelfmark FE209, Correspondence: 1956 (on Waldorf stationery), 1–17.
122. Ibid.
123. Letter from Smith to the Starks. Stanford University, Cole Porter Collection, shelfmark FE209, Correspondence: 1956 (on Waldorf stationery), 1–17.
124. Yale University, Irving S. Gilmore Music Library, Cole Porter Collection MSS 82, Box 49, folder 301. Typewritten on 'The Towers' stationery. The letter is dated 1956 but the content clearly belongs to 1957.

125. Stanford University, Cole Porter Collection, shelfmark FE209, Correspondence: 1957 (on Waldorf stationery), 1–17.
126. Ibid.
127. Douglas Fairbanks Jr. Papers, Howard Gottlieb Archival Research Center, Boston University.
128. Quoted in Howard, *Travels with Cole Porter*, 210.
129. CPT, Correspondence 1957 (on Waldorf stationery).
130. Ibid.
131. CPT, Correspondence 1957 (on N. Rockingham stationery).
132. Ibid.
133. Bosley Crowther, 'The Screen: "Silk Stockings" Arrives', *New York Times*, 19 July 1957, 11.
134. Yale University, Irving S. Gilmore Music Library, William McBrien Papers, Series IV, Box 4, folder 108 (typewritten, from 416 N. Rockingham).
135. CPT, Correspondence 1957 (on 416 N. Rockingham stationery).
136. [no address] CPT, Correspondence 1957.
137. R. C. Allen, Director, Kingwood Center, Mansfield, Ohio, 'Rose Abundance: The New Arrivals Have An Age-Old Appeal', *New York Times*, 27 January 1957, X43.
138. Howard Papers, AHC, Box 6.
139. Ibid.
140. Val Adams, 'Cole Porter Signs for Musical on TV', *New York Times* (5 August 1957), 32.
141. Porter Papers, Yale University, Box 49, folder 305.
142. Richard Lewine Papers, NYPL, *T-Mss 2006-008, Box 1.
143. Yale University, Irving S. Gilmore Music Library, Cole Porter Collection MSS 82, Box 49, folder 305.
144. Richard Lewine Papers, NYPL, *T-Mss 2006-008, Box 1.
145. Ibid.
146. The Lilly Library, Indiana.
147. Richard Lewine Papers, NYPL, *T-Mss 2006-008, Box 1.
148. Ibid.
149. Leland Hayward Papers, NYPL, *T-Mss 1971-002, Series III, Subseries 1, Box 199.
150. CPT, Correspondence 1957 (on Waldorf stationery).
151. Bosley Crowther, 'Screen: "Les Girls"', *New York Times*, 4 October 1957, 27.
152. Source for both letters: Yale University, Lieberson Papers, Correspondence. Porter's is on Waldorf stationery.
153. CPT, Correspondence 1957.
154. Ibid.
155. Stanford University, Cole Porter Collection, shelfmark FE209, Correspondence: 1957 (on Waldorf stationery), 1–17.

11 THE FINAL YEARS, 1958–1964

1. Letter of 18 February 1958 from Paul Sylvain to Sam Stark (on stationery of Harkness Pavilion, Washington Avenue, New York). Stanford University, Cole Porter Collection, shelfmark FE209, Correspondence: 1958, 1–18.
2. Sam Zolotow, '"Stay Away Joe" to Be a Musical', *New York Times*, 29 January 1958, 32.
3. Letter of 21 February 1958 from Madeline Smith to Bella Spewack (Spewack Papers, Columbia).
4. Stanford University, Cole Porter Collection, shelfmark FE209, Correspondence: 1958 (on Waldorf stationery), 1–17.
5. Ibid.
6. Probably Cecil Smith's review, headed '"Aladdin" Was a TV Miracle', *Los Angeles Times*, 24 February 1958, 34.

7. Jack Gould, 'TV Review: Aladdin is Offered on du Pont Show', *New York Times*, 22 February 1958, 33.
8. Anon., 'Cole Porter's Leg Amputated', *New York Times*, 4 April 1958, 17.
9. Leland Hayward Papers. NYPL, *T-Mss 1971-002, Series III, Subseries 1, Box 199.
10. Stanford University, Cole Porter Collection, shelfmark FE209, Correspondence: 1958 (on Waldorf stationery), 1–17.
11. Ibid.
12. Ibid.
13. Leland Hayward Papers. NYPL, *T-Mss 1971-002, Series III, Subseries 1, Box 199.
14. Stanford University, Cole Porter Collection, shelfmark FE209, Correspondence: 1958 (on Waldorf stationery), 1–17.
15. Ibid.
16. Eric Bentley (ed.), *Shaw on Music* (New York: Applause, 1955).
17. Sam Zolotow, 'Cole Porter Gets Stage Assignment', *New York Times*, 8 August 1958, 11.
18. Stanford University, Cole Porter Collection, shelfmark FE209, Correspondence: 1958 (on Waldorf stationery), 1–17.
19. Ibid.
20. Ibid.
21. Letter of 3 November 1958: Madeline P. Smith to Sam Stark. Stanford University, Cole Porter Collection, shelfmark FE209, Correspondence: 1958 (on Waldorf stationery), 1–17.
22. Columbia, Spewack Collection, Catalogued Correspondence: Cole Porter.
23. CPT, Correspondence 1959 (on Waldorf stationery).
24. See Eells, *The Life that Late He Led*, 312.
25. Letter of 19 February 1959 from Sylvain to Stark. Stanford University, Cole Porter Collection, shelfmark FE209, Correspondence: 1959, 1–18.
26. Stanford University, Cole Porter Collection, shelfmark FE209, Correspondence: 1959 (on Waldorf stationery), 1–17.
27. Ibid.
28. Letter of 3 April 1959 from Sam Stark to Cole Porter. Stanford University, Cole Porter Collection, shelfmark FE209, Correspondence: 1959 (on Waldorf stationery), 1–17.
29. Stanford University, Cole Porter Collection, shelfmark FE209, Correspondence: 1959 (on Waldorf stationery), 1–17.
30. Letter of 13 April 1959 from Madeline P. Smith to Sam Stark. Stanford University, Cole Porter Collection, shelfmark FE209, Correspondence: 1959 (on Waldorf stationery), 1–17.
31. Gershwin Fund Collection, LC.
32. CPT, Correspondence 1959.
33. Stanford University, Cole Porter Collection, shelfmark FE209, Correspondence: 1959 (on Waldorf stationery), 1–17.
34. Ibid.
35. Letter from Stark to Porter, 28 May 1959. Stanford University, Cole Porter Collection, shelfmark FE209, Correspondence: 1959 (on Waldorf stationery), 1–18.
36. Stanford University, Cole Porter Collection, shelfmark FE209, Correspondence: 1959 (on Waldorf stationery), 1–17.
37. Eells outlines the situation in *The Life that Late He Led*, 313.
38. Letter of 10 June 1959 from Sam Stark to Cole Porter. Stanford University, Cole Porter Collection, shelfmark FE209, Correspondence: 1959 (on Waldorf stationery), 1–17.
39. Stanford University, Cole Porter Collection, shelfmark FE209, Correspondence: 1959 (on Waldorf stationery), 1–17.
40. Letter of 26 June 1959 from Madeline P. Smith to Sam and Harriette Stark. Stanford University, Cole Porter Collection, shelfmark FE209, Correspondence: 1959 (on Waldorf stationery), 1–18.
41. Saul Chaplin Papers, AHC, Box 4.

42. George Eells Collection, Cole Porter research, folder 5, USC.
43. Jean Howard Papers, AHC, Box 6.
44. Columbia, Spewack Collection, Catalogued Correspondence: Cole Porter.
45. Arthur Gelb, 'Two Irish Plays Will Be Staged', *New York Times*, 15 August 1959, 9.
46. CPT, Correspondence 1959 (on N. Rockingham stationery).
47. Ibid.
48. Letter of 4 August 1959 from Madeline P. Smith to Sam Stark. Stanford University, Cole Porter Collection, shelfmark FE209, Correspondence: 1959 (on Waldorf stationery), 1–20.
49. Jean Howard Papers, AHC, Box 6.
50. Letter of 18 October 1959 from Laura Sylvain to Sam Stark. Stanford University, Cole Porter Collection, shelfmark FE209, Correspondence: 1959, 1–18.
51. Photocopy; Margaret Herrick Library, Jack Cummings Collection, Box 13.
52. Stanford University, Cole Porter Collection, shelfmark FE209, Correspondence: 1959 (on Waldorf stationery), 1–20.
53. Ibid.
54. Stanford University, Cole Porter Collection, shelfmark FE209, Correspondence: 1960 (on Waldorf stationery), 1–20.
55. Letter of 15 January 1960 from Smith to Stark. Stanford University, Cole Porter Collection, shelfmark FE209, Correspondence: 1960 (on Waldorf stationery), 1–20.
56. Porter Collection, LC.
57. Ibid.
58. Ibid.
59. Stanford University, Cole Porter Collection, shelfmark FE209, Correspondence: 1960 (on Waldorf stationery), 1–20.
60. Yale University, Irving S. Gilmore Music Library, Cole Porter Collection MSS 82, Box 87. On Waldorf stationery.
61. Reproduced in Eells, *The Life that Late He Led*, 314.
62. Marked 'Night Letter'. Stanford University, Cole Porter Collection, shelfmark FE209, Correspondence: 1960 (on Waldorf stationery), 1–20.
63. Ibid (on 416 N. Rockingham stationery).
64. Lieberson Papers, Yale University.
65. CPT, Correspondence 1960. Written from N. Rockingham.
66. Ibid.
67. Stanford University, Cole Porter Collection, shelfmark FE209, Correspondence: 1960 (on 416 N. Rockingham stationery), 1–20.
68. Stanford University, Cole Porter Collection, shelfmark FE209, Correspondence: 1960 (on Waldorf stationery), 1–20.
69. Ibid.
70. Letter of 26 November 1960 from Sam Stark to Madeline P. Smith. Stanford University, Cole Porter Collection, shelfmark FE209, Correspondence: 1960, 1–20.
71. Letter of 1 December 1960 from Madeline P. Smith to Sam Stark. Stanford University, Cole Porter Collection, shelfmark FE209, Correspondence: 1960 (on Waldorf stationery), 1–20.
72. Stanford University, Cole Porter Collection, shelfmark FE209, Correspondence: 1960 (on Waldorf stationery), 1–20.
73. Letter of 6 January 1961 from Madeline P. Smith to Sam Stark. Stanford University, Cole Porter Collection, shelfmark FE209, Correspondence: 1961 (on Waldorf stationery), 1–21.
74. CPT, Correspondence 1961.
75. Stanford University, Cole Porter Collection, shelfmark FE209, Correspondence: 1961 (on Waldorf stationery), 1–21.
76. Ibid.
77. Ibid.
78. Ibid.

79. Ibid.
80. Letter of 13 July 1961 from Madeline P. Smith to Harriette and Sam Stark. Stanford University, Cole Porter Collection, shelfmark FE209, Correspondence: 1961 (on Waldorf stationery), 1–21.
81. CPT, Correspondence 1961.
82. George Eells Collection, USC, folder 5, Cole Porter research.
83. The Bearss family connection is discussed in chapter 1. A photograph of the hotel can be seen at https://indianaalbum.pastperfectonline.com/photo/3868198B-3D63-46D7-9805-549618767485 (accessed 11 September 2018).
84. Letter of 28 July 1961 from Madeline P. Smith to Sam Stark. Stanford University, Cole Porter Collection, shelfmark FE209, Correspondence: 1961, 1–21.
85. Schubertiade music. https://www.schubertiademusic.com/items/details/14466-porter-cole-four-short-typed-letters-signed-to-doc-sirmay (accessed 8 August 2018).
86. Richard Lewine Papers, NYPL, *T-Mss 2006-008, Box 1.
87. Richard Lewine and Alfred Simon, *Encyclopedia of Theatre Music* (New York, 1961).
88. CPT, Correspondence 1961.
89. Letter of 14 December 1961 from Madeline P. Smith to Sam and Harriette Stark. Stanford University, Cole Porter Collection, shelfmark FE209, Correspondence: 1961, 1–20.
90. Letter of 15 December 1961 from Lew Kesler to Harriette and Sam Stark (Buxton Hill stationery). Stanford University, Cole Porter Collection, shelfmark FE209, Correspondence: 1961, 1–21.
91. Letter of 26 January 1962 from Madeline P. Smith to Sam Stark. Stanford University, Cole Porter Collection, shelfmark FE209, Correspondence: 1962, 1–22.
92. Copy in a private collection.
93. Stanford University, Cole Porter Collection, shelfmark FE209, Correspondence: 1962, 1–22.
94. Ibid.
95. Letter of 24 August 1962 from Madeline P. Smith to Harriette and Sam Stark. Stanford University, Cole Porter Collection, shelfmark FE209, Correspondence: 1962 (on Waldorf stationery), 1–22.
96. Letter of 25 August 1962 from Margaret Egan to Harriette and Sam Stark. Stanford University, Cole Porter Collection, shelfmark FE209, Correspondence: 1962, 1–22.
97. Sent from 416 N. Rockingham, LA. https://www.ebay.com/itm/COLE-PORTER-TYPED-LETTER-SIGNED-10-13-1962/282714521873?hash=item41d3194111:g:v9AA AOSwXaRZ947e (accessed 31 October 2017).
98. CPT, Correspondence 1962.
99. Margaret Herrick Library, George Cukor Collection, Box 854 (on Waldorf stationery).
100. Letter of 24 December 1962 from Madeline P. Smith to Harriette and Sam Stark. Stanford University, Cole Porter Collection, shelfmark FE209, Correspondence: 1962, 1–22.
101. Letter of 4 January 1963 from Madeline P. Smith to Sam Stark. Stanford University, Cole Porter Collection, shelfmark FE209, Correspondence: 1963, 1–23.
102. Letter of 11 April 1963 from Madeline P. Smith to Sam Stark. Stanford University, Cole Porter Collection, shelfmark FE209, Correspondence: 1963, 1–23.
103. Letter of 10 May 1963 from Madeline P. Smith to Sam Stark. Ibid.
104. Stanford University, Cole Porter Collection, shelfmark FE209, Correspondence: 1963, 1–23.
105. Irving Berlin Collection, LC (handwritten on Waldorf stationery).
106. Stanford University, Cole Porter Collection, shelfmark FE209, Correspondence: 1963, 1–23.
107. Ibid.
108. Letter of 2 August 1963 from Margaret Egan to Sam and Harriette Stark. Stanford University, Cole Porter Collection, shelfmark FE209, Correspondence: 1963, 1–23.

109. Stanford University, Cole Porter Collection, shelfmark FE209, Correspondence: 1963, 1–23.
110. Letter of 5 January 1964 from Smith to Stark. Stanford University, Cole Porter Collection, shelfmark FE209, Correspondence: 1964, 1–23.
111. Stanford University, Cole Porter Collection, shelfmark FE209, Correspondence: 1964, 1–23.
112. Letter of 17 March 1964 from Irving Berlin to Porter. CPT, Correspondence 1964.
113. Letter of 11 March 1964 from Irving Berlin to Cole Porter. Irving Berlin Collection, LC.
114. Source (both letters): Berlin Collection, LC.
115. Stanford University, Cole Porter Collection, shelfmark FE209, Correspondence: 1964, 1–23.
116. Ibid.
117. Jean Howard Papers, AHC, Box 6.
118. Stanford University, Cole Porter Collection, shelfmark FE209, Correspondence: 1964, 1–23.
119. Jean Howard Papers, AHC, Box 6.
120. Stanford University, Cole Porter Collection, shelfmark FE209, Correspondence: 1964, 1–23 (carbon copy).
121. Letter of 20 August 1964 from Madeline P. Smith to Sam Stark. Stanford University, Cole Porter Collection, shelfmark FE209, Correspondence: 1964 (on Waldorf stationery), 1–23.
122. Letter of 25 August 1964: Margaret Egan to Harriette and Sam Stark. Stanford University, Cole Porter Collection, shelfmark FE209, Correspondence: 1964, 1–23.
123. Letter of 14 October 1964 from Stanley Musgrove to Sam Stark. Ibid.
124. Stanford University, Cole Porter Collection, shelfmark FE209, Correspondence: 1964, 1–23.
125. Jean Howard Papers, AHC, Box 6.

SELECTED BIBLIOGRAPHY

Block, Geoffrey. *Enchanted Evenings: The Broadway Musical from "Show Boat" to Sondheim and Lloyd Weber*, second edition (New York: Oxford University Press, 2009)
Citron, Stephen. *Noel & Cole: The Sophisticates* (New York: Oxford University Press, 1993)
Eells, George. *The Life that Late He Led: A Biography of Cole Porter* (New York: G. P. Putnam's Sons, 1967)
Ewen, David. *The Cole Porter Story* (New York: Holt, Rinehart and Winston, 1965)
Furia, Philip. *The Poets of Tin Pan Alley: A History of America's Great Lyricists* (New York: Oxford University Press, 1992)
Gill, Brendan. *Cole: A Biographical Essay* (London: Joseph, 1972)
Grafton, David. *Red, Hot & Rich!: An Oral History of Cole Porter* (New York: Stein and Day, 1987)
Hischak, Thomas S. *The Oxford Companion to the American Musical* (New York: Oxford University Press, 2008)
Howard, Jean. *Travels with Cole Porter* (New York: Abrams, 1991)
Hubler, Richard G. *The Cole Porter Story, as Told to Richard G. Hubler* (Cleveland: World Publishing Co., 1965)
Kimball, Robert. *The Complete Lyrics of Cole Porter* (New York: Alfred A. Knopf, 1983)
Kimball, Robert. "Cole Porter". *You're the Top: Cole Porter in the 1930s* (Indianapolis: Indiana Historical Society, 1992)
Kimball, Robert and Brendan Gill. *Cole* (New York: Dell, 1971)
Krasker, Tommy and Robert Kimball. *Catalog of the American Musical: Musicals of Irving Berlin, George and Ira Gershwin, Cole Porter, Richard Rodgers and Lorenz Hart* (Washington, DC: National Institute for Opera and Musical Theater, 1988)
McBrien, William. *Cole Porter: A Definitive Biography* (New York: Alfred A. Knopf, 1998)
Morella, Joe and George Mazzei. *Genius and Lust: The Creativity and Sexuality of Cole Porter and Noel Coward* (London: Robson Books, 1996)
Randel, Don M., Matthew Shaftel and Susan Forscher Weiss, eds. *A Cole Porter Companion* (Urbana: University of Illinois Press, 2016)
Rimler, Walter. *A Cole Porter Discography* (San Francisco: Sylvan, 1995)
Salsini, Paul. *Cole Porter: Twentieth Century Composer of Popular Songs* (Charlotteville, NY: SamHar Press, 1972)
Schwartz, Charles. *Cole Porter: A Biography* (New York: Da Capo Press, 1977)
Wilder, Alec. *American Popular Song: The Great Innovators 1900–1950* (New York: Oxford University Press, 1972)

INDEX

1-2-3 Club, 172, 271

Abbott, George, 154, 365, 367, 385
Abercrombie, Dr Daniel Webster, 2, 3, 5–9
Abravanel, Maurice, 216–17
Academy Awards, 131, 154, 169, 293, 298, 362, 476, 482, 494, 572
Acheson, Dean, 15
Adair, Yvonne, 489, 496, 501, 502
Adam's Rib, 335–7, 347, 348, 351
Adios Argentina, 88, 108, 225, 229, 236
Aladdin, 572–82, 584, 610
Alba, Duke of, 29, 32, 77, 283, 533
Alberghetti, Anna Maria, 582
Alfonso XIII, King of Spain, 29
All About Eve, 130, 318, 572
'All of You', 456
Ameche, Don, 222, 476
Anderson, John Murray, 310, 472
Anderson Galleries, 36
Anything Goes
  Broadway show (1934 and revivals), 86, 88, 97–102, 108, 109, 121, 127, 139, 140, 142, 154, 164, 165, 200, 212, 260, 292, 376, 394, 441, 449, 529,
  movie (1956), 492–3, 535, 539
  television version (1950), 361
  television version (1954), 472–3
Armstrong, Louis, 531, 559, 560, 562
Armstrong, Paul, 181, 186, 188, 203, 205
Armstrong, Roger, 189
Around the World (Porter musical), 167, 195, 247, 251, 253, 255, 256, 258, 259, 264, 281, 521, 542
Around the World in Eighty Days (movie), 572
Ashley, Sylvia, 168, 183, 195, 241, 261, 287, 337

Astaire, Fred, 94, 95, 99, 110, 122, 160, 164, 165, 207, 211, 212, 217, 218, 226, 232, 234, 244, 266, 283, 330, 331, 449, 454, 461, 466, 530, 531, 604, 613
Astaire, Phyllis, 283, 330, 331
Astor, Alice, 82, 272
Astor, Mary, 381
Astor, Vincent, 181, 272, 276
As Thousands Cheer, 114, 139, 375
Atkinson, Brooks, 117, 155, 162, 166, 316, 368, 443, 501
'At Long Last Love', 153, 499
Ayers, Lemuel, 292, 293, 296, 305, 309, 312, 320, 327, 362

Bacall, Lauren, 180, 572
Baker, Phil, 114
Ball, Lucille, 133, 169
Ballets Russes, 33, 35, 37, 53, 69, 70
Ballets Suédois, 40
Bankhead, Tallulah, 425, 549
Barclift, Nelson, 48, 167–9, 172, 184, 193–4, 198–9, 205, 241, 242, 243, 247, 251, 260, 261, 270
Barrymore, John, 47
Baz, Ben, 168, 221
'Be a Clown', 281, 284
'Bearded Lady', 8
Bearss, Lou, 349, 368, 380, 617, 624
Beebe, Lucius, 160
'Begin the Beguine', 139, 159, 225, 226, 227, 237, 238, 318, 404, 406, 465, 485, 507, 520, 562, 592
Behrman, S. N., 327
Benchley, Bob, 225, 226
Bennett, Robert Russell, 200, 217, 305
Benson, Sir Rex, 28
Berenson, Bernard, 32, 154, 156, 161, 296, 358–9, 431

654

INDEX

Berkeley Square, 383, 385, 386
Berlin, Ellin, 187, 317, 330, 618
Berlin, Irving, 39, 45, 75, 95, 102, 114, 139, 147, 167, 169, 170, 175, 187, 230, 245, 249, 250, 262, 272, 279, 317, 330, 331, 362, 363, 364, 375, 441, 444, 483, 499, 500, 615, 616, 618, 619
Bernstein, Leonard, 200, 348, 365, 380, 505
'Bianca', 327, 372
Bismarck, Otto, 334
'Blow, Gabriel, Blow', 248, 249, 465, 473, 562
Bocher, Main *see* Mainbocher
Boland, Mary, 119, 139, 375
Bolger, Ray, 325, 376, 385
Bolton, Guy, 97, 190
Bordoni, Irene, 80–1, 87, 234, 239, 543
Born to Dance, 88, 103, 108, 109, 110–38, 449
Boston, 140, 142, 156, 162, 172, 177, 188, 189, 190, 206, 253, 256, 258, 259, 275, 307, 308, 310, 363, 367, 368, 398, 449, 489, 491, 494, 495, 498, 502, 449, 610
Boston Pops Orchestra, 454, 455, 457
Boy Meets Girl, 112, 400–1
Bray, Robert, 246, 252, 258, 263, 287, 294, 295, 297, 298, 307, 308, 314, 329, 333, 334, 336, 338, 339, 340, 350, 366, 369, 388, 398, 497, 505, 506, 508, 509, 529, 534, 554
Brent, Romney, 448, 539
Brice, Fanny, 75, 76, 200, 241, 347, 388, 448
Bricktop (Ada Smith), 72–3, 106
Broadway Melody of 1940, 100, 118, 160
Broadway Theatre, New York, 91
Browning, Elizabeth Barrett, 73
Browning, Robert, 73, 74
Bruce, Carol, 300
Bruce, Virginia, 123, 127, 131, 136
'Brush Up Your Shakespeare', 302, 303, 316
Buchanan, Jack, 88, 148, 449
'Bull Dog', 10
Burke, Joe, 227
Burke, Johnny, 377
Burrows, Abe, 104, 406, 407–22, 424–6, 433, 437, 444–5, 451, 461, 470, 477, 484, 489, 494–5, 498, 501, 504, 600
'But in the Morning, No', 161
Buxton Hill, Williamstown, 161, 167, 183, 184, 205, 263, 336
Buxton Hill (publishing company), 429, 439–40, 463
Byron, George, 76

'Ça, c'est l'amour', 581
Caesar and Cleopatra, 36

Can-Can, 292, 370, 401, 404, 405–27, 430–8, 442–4, 449, 450, 452, 454, 463, 466, 460, 472, 481, 494, 497, 549, 503–5, 574–5, 588, 592, 595, 597–9
Capehart, 168, 193, 408
Carnarvon, Lord, 33, 545
CBS, 200, 276, 402, 424, 469, 470, 561, 574, 580
censors, 92, 248, 319, 368, 372, 417, 438–9, 563
Cerf, Bennett, 454–5
'C'est Magnifique', 437
Chanel, Coco, 203
Chaplin, Charles, 84, 92, 130, 196, 424
Chaplin, Michael, 241
Chaplin, Saul, 438–9, 447, 522, 524, 525–8, 530, 595, 597–8
Chappell (music publisher), 91, 95, 143, 154, 176, 185, 197, 204, 223, 225, 245, 326, 335, 357, 363, 389, 429, 438, 463, 523, 529, 532, 579
Chappell, George, 37
Chicago, 2, 138, 196, 206, 215, 245, 299, 307, 345, 401, 464, 552
Chicago Lyric Opera, 217
Cinderella (fairytale), 177
Cinderella '53, 469–70
circus, 1, 256, 276
Clark, Bobby, 191, 376
Cochran, Charles B., 38–9, 86–8, 95, 98, 99, 448, 451, 461, 539
Cocteau, Jean, 40, 510, 543
Colbert, Claudette, 482
Colby, Frank, 237
Cole, Albert Harvey, 79, 80, 86, 87, 91, 93, 94, 96, 102, 108, 109, 267, 288, 289, 290, 345, 346, 405, 423
Cole, James Omar, 1, 2
Cole, Jules Omar, 623–4
Cole, Kate, 2, 244
Cole, Omar, 162, 244, 288, 289, 345, 442, 495
Cole Porter Songbook, 559, 592
Collier, Constance, 301, 304–5
Comden, Betty, 348, 349, 352, 380, 467, 477
'Come to the Supermarket in Old Peking', 577, 579
Cooper, Lady Diana, 75
Cooper, Duff, 75
Cooper, Gary, 194
Copland, Aaron, 198
Coward, Noël, 40, 74, 75, 86, 87, 204, 424, 452, 453, 475, 487, 491, 610
Crawford, Douglas, 603

Crawford, Joan, 133
Crawford, Kathryn, 92
La Création du Monde, 40, 42
Crosby, Bing, 103, 124, 198, 250, 381–2, 522, 526, 531, 559
Crosby, John, 362
Crouse, Russel, 97, 139, 141, 148, 362, 441, 529
Cukor, George, 241, 337, 406, 613, 614
Curtiz, Michael, 207–9, 215, 233, 240, 244, 259, 260, 264

Dali, Salvador, 193, 507
Damn Yankees, 154
Davis, Betty, 234
Davis, Eddie, 190, 373
Davis, Luther, 482
Davis, Roger, 192, 205, 261, 333, 334, 343, 361, 388, 591
Davis, Sammy Jr., 536
De Gunzborg, Baron Nicholas [Niki], 424, 442
De Mille, Agnes, 365, 441
De Polignac, Princesse Edmond [Winaretta Singer], 38, 40, 70, 71
De Sylva, Buddy, 118–19, 160, 200
Detroit, 196, 480, 494, 502
De Wolfe, Elsie, 18, 34, 76, 78, 194, 329
Diaghilev, Serge, 33, 35, 37, 53, 58, 69–71, 74, 511
Dietrich, Marlene, 193, 223, 381, 506
Dietz, Howard, 148, 561
Di San Faustino, Princess Jane, 69, 73
Di Zoppola, Countess Edith, 148, 368, 442
'Do I Love You?', 160, 161
Donahue, Jimmy Jr., 383–4
'Don't Fence Me In', 224, 225, 227, 229, 230, 235, 236, 237, 244, 267
'Down in the Depths on the Nineitieth Floor', 140, 143, 393
Drake, Alfred, 298, 300, 309, 311, 316, 318, 347, 452, 590
Dreyfus, Max, 185, 225, 326, 335, 364, 399, 463, 481, 529
Du Barry Was a Lady, 160–1, 164, 166, 169, 173, 175, 177, 199, 200, 212, 292, 338, 449, 527
Du Bois, Raoul Pène, 200
Duke, Vernon, 118, 213
Durante, Jimmy, 91, 99, 139–40, 143, 144, 207, 449

'Easy to Love', 127, 128, 138
Eddy, Nelson, 108, 145, 262, 499

Eells, George, 497, 505, 506, 512, 519, 535, 536, 538, 541, 544, 549, 566, 567, 609, 613
Egan, Margaret (Tully), 320, 321, 413, 617, 622, 623
Egypt, 539, 543, 544–5, 551
'Experiment', 198

Fairbanks, Douglas Jr., 261, 280, 282–3, 305–6, 539, 568
Fairbanks, Mary Lee, 283, 568–9
'Farming', 165, 166, 207
Feldman, Charlie, 162, 368, 388, 469, 505, 508, 510, 521, 554
Feldman, Jean *see* Jean Howard
Fetter, Ted, 539
Feuer, Cy, 220, 401, 406, 407, 409, 410, 412–15, 418, 420, 422, 430, 433, 443, 450–2, 456, 461–5, 475, 481, 482, 492–3, 496, 498, 499, 501, 503, 526, 527–9, 554, 571, 588, 590, 600
'Fi, Fi, Fifi', 8
Fields, Dorothy, 175, 195, 376, 385
Fields, Herbert, 160, 175, 195, 375
Fields, Joseph, 380
Fields, Lew, 19
Fifty Million Frenchmen, 88, 89, 93, 94
Fisher, Eddie, 508
Fontanne, Lynn, 301, 327, 529, 581
Franconia, 103, 139
Freedley, Vinton, 111, 139, 142, 157, 160, 165, 166, 173, 211
'Friendship', 212, 465, 562
'From This Moment On', 439

Gabin, Jean, 193
Gable, Clark, 111, 112, 149, 168, 287
Gabor, Jolie, 469
Gainsborough, Thomas, 45
Garbo, Greta, 99, 214–16, 450
Gardiner, Reginald, 241
Gardner, Isabella, 32
Garland, Judy, 123, 281, 284, 300, 482
Gaxton, William, 97–8, 195
Gay Divorce, 88, 94–7, 103, 147, 148, 154, 159, 164, 200, 218, 328, 358, 449, 458, 597
Gaynor, Mitzi, 352
Gear, Luella, 94, 358
Gershwin, George, 39–40, 45, 46, 53, 70, 81, 85, 95, 122, 160, 266, 449
Gershwin, Ira, 118, 122
Gibbs, Wolcott, 155, 361, 362
Gilbert and Sullivan, 202, 375, 499

INDEX

Goetz, E. Ray, 81
Goetz, Edie, 453, 469, 482, 493
Goetz, Harry, 171, 172
Goetz, William, 453, 469, 482
Goldwyn, Frances, 386
Goldwyn, Sam, 101, 234, 280, 377
Gone With the Wind, 622
'Goodbye, Little Dream, Goodbye', 124, 140
Gordon, Max, 100, 118, 121, 123, 125, 127, 225, 337
Grable, Betty, 177, 373, 449
Grant, Cary, 179, 192, 198, 226, 232, 233, 239, 244, 247, 260, 264, 265, 280
Gray, Dolores, 560–2
Greece, 282, 327, 468, 502, 505, 508, 512–16, 541, 551, 553, 560
Green, Adolph, 348, 349, 352, 380, 467, 477
Green, Johnny, 523, 525, 530–2, 554
Guys and Dolls, 336, 365, 401, 406, 422, 433, 445, 501

Haines, Bill, 181, 186, 189, 191, 194, 203, 205–6, 241, 267, 268, 274, 285, 295, 307, 308, 309, 346, 390, 402, 481
Hammerstein, Oscar II, 76, 186, 212, 270, 286, 298, 309, 324, 328, 336, 441, 442, 445, 461, 463, 472, 482, 500, 538
Hanna, Leonard, 150, 161, 172, 203, 246, 274, 334, 368, 451
Hans Christian Andersen, 394
Harburg, E. Y., 190, 270, 271
Harms, T. B., 77, 91, 92, 245, 394, 469
Hart, Kitty Carlisle, 468, 482
Hart, Lorenz, 74, 83, 126, 159, 200, 306, 375, 457, 560
Hart, Moss, 102, 103, 105, 106–7, 114, 139, 160, 195, 225, 237, 238–9, 393, 394, 461, 468, 481, 482, 592
Harvard, 15, 17, 18, 20, 178, 350
Hays Code, 210, 248
Hearst, Millicent, 269, 368, 442, 468
Hearst, William Randolph, 257, 269, 368
Hepburn, Audrey, 552
Hepburn, Katharine, 335, 351–2, 356, 518, 519
Herbert, F. Hugh, 365, 367, 401
High Society, 517, 518, 522, 523, 524, 525, 526, 527, 528, 529, 530, 531, 532, 538, 554, 557, 558, 559, 562
Hitchcock, Alfred, 223
Hitchcock, Raymond, 32, 44
Hitchy-Koo of 1919, 32, 44
Hitchy-Koo of 1922, 38
Holm, Hanya, 306, 312, 372

Holman, Libby, 155
Hoover, Herbert, 92, 624
Hope, Bob, 98, 176, 373, 382, 449
Hopper, Hedda, 231, 256, 425, 478, 479
Hot Mikado, The, 375
Howard [Feldman], Jean, 156, 161, 162, 165, 166, 167, 168, 182–3, 184, 213, 215, 216, 222, 224–5, 241, 245, 263, 269, 315, 323, 324, 336, 337, 338, 364, 365, 367, 369, 388, 403, 425, 436, 437, 443, 467, 468, 469, 471, 477, 478, 497, 505, 507, 510, 516, 518, 521, 529, 532, 533, 534, 548, 551, 554, 569, 573–4, 595, 597, 616, 620, 621, 623
Hubler, Richard, 1, 97, 238, 477, 478
Hughes, Herbert, 178
Hull, Helen, 181, 272, 368, 427, 442, 524–5
Hull, Lytle, 181, 272, 368, 442
Hutton, Barbara, 104
Hutton, Betty, 176, 196, 207, 211, 222

'I Concentrate on You', 582
'I Get a Kick out of You', 140, 164, 248, 249, 260, 465, 473, 562
'I Love Paris', 409–10, 437, 499
'I Love You', 191
'I Love You, Samantha', 525, 531, 532, 559
'In the Still of the Night', 208–9, 562
'It's All Right With Me', 437, 536
'It Was Great Fun the First Time', 311, 458
'I've Got You Under My Skin', 127–8, 129, 131, 138, 260, 562

Jamaica, 568
Jenks, Almet, 10–12
Jennings, Oliver, 168, 183, 184, 221, 297
Jolson, Al, 46, 190, 290–1
'Josephine', 496–7, 501, 564
Jubilee, 88, 102, 105, 106–7, 108, 119, 139, 140, 159, 173, 175, 211, 225, 237, 245, 260, 318, 343, 375, 393, 394, 404, 418, 419, 449, 481, 484, 485, 592
'Just One of Those Things', 245, 404, 465, 562

Kanin, Garson, 444
Kaufman, George S., 104, 160, 450, 456, 464, 489, 490, 492, 494, 498, 611
Kaye, Danny, 166, 207, 211, 234, 376
Kaye, Sylvia Fine, 166, 207
Kelly, Gene, 157, 169, 193, 284, 300, 467, 557
Kelly, George, 558
Kelly, Grace, 245, 522, 530, 554, 559

657

INDEX

Kelly, Orry, 363, 590
Kelly, Ray, 158, 185
Kern, Betty, 113
Kern, Eva, 76
Kern, Jerome, 45, 76, 95, 113, 121, 133, 315, 448, 449
Kesler, Lew, 171, 375, 378, 379, 611
Kidd, Michael, 422
Kilgallen, Dorothy, 239, 393
Kimball, Robert, 81, 223, 238
King and I, The, 130, 381, 441
Kirk, Lisa, 309, 311, 590
Kirsten, Dorothy, 301–2
Kiss Me, Kate
  film version, 113, 389, 419, 433, 438–9, 445, 446–7, 449, 451–2, 456, 466–7, 483, 504, 536, 542, 563
  stage versions, 34, 112, 288, 292, 293–4, 296, 298, 300, 301–16, 317–20, 323–4, 327–8, 331, 342, 343, 345, 346, 347, 350, 354, 356, 367, 370, 371–3, 374, 379, 386, 389, 403, 432, 458, 460, 517, 532, 608
  television versions, 590, 619
Knight, June, 157, 212
Knopf, Alfred, 423, 467, 509
Kochno, Boris, 33, 48, 53–71, 280
Koechlin, Charles, 41–4
Korda, Alexander, 195, 248

Lahr, Bert, 160, 161, 164, 198–9, 207, 209, 472
Lamarr, Hedy, 133, 148, 240
Lane, Burton, 190, 270, 271
Lang, Harold, 306, 309
Langford, Frances, 103, 123–5, 128, 129, 131, 134, 234
Lawrence, Gertrude, 95–6, 448, 539
Lazar, Irving, 418, 460, 462, 463, 465, 466, 467, 472, 485, 489, 492, 503, 526, 528, 529, 571, 572, 573, 592
Leave it to Me!, 142, 156–9, 200, 212, 213, 234, 300, 492, 499, 596
Leigh, Vivien, 622
Lerner, Alan Jay, 300, 310, 461, 536, 555, 556, 564, 605, 612
Les Girls, 406, 526, 527, 529, 555, 557, 565, 581, 614
'Let's Do It', 23, 81, 88, 89, 212, 234, 239, 422, 452, 453, 465, 480, 562
Let's Face It!, 19, 142, 165, 166, 173, 175, 176, 200, 211, 376, 543
Lewine, Richard, 574–9, 581–2, 610, 611
Liberty Music Shop, 436

Lieberson, Goddard, 324–5, 395, 444, 581, 602
Liebman, Max, 166
Lifar, Serge, 57, 58, 71
Lillie, Beatrice, 199, 200, 202, 209, 214, 269
Lilo, 420
Lindsay, Howard, 97, 139, 141, 148, 362, 441, 529
'Live and Let Live', 407
Loesser, Frank, 218, 365, 450, 536, 542, 549
Loewe, Frederick, 300, 536, 555
Logan, Joshua, 509
Loos, Anita, 241, 613
Loring, Eugene, 475
'Love For Sale', 92, 210, 212
'Love of My Life', 263, 278
Lubitsch, Ernst, 241
Luce, Claire, 95,
Luce, Clare Boothe, 276, 512, 568
Lunt, Alfred, 301, 327, 424, 529, 581
Lyons, Arthur, 122, 124, 133, 137, 179, 180, 184, 184, 196, 284, 290

MacGrath, Leueen, 104, 450, 456, 464, 489, 492, 498
Madden, Richard, 91–3, 109, 222, 375, 377, 379
Mainbocher, 349, 353, 368, 452
'Make It Another Old-Fashioned Please', 562
Marbury, Elizabeth, 18–20
Markova, Alicia, 199
Martin, Ernest, 401, 406, 413, 422, 433, 443, 450, 451, 456, 457, 461–2, 464, 481, 482, 493, 498, 499, 503, 511, 526–9, 554, 588, 590, 600
Martin, John, 424
Martin, Mary, 157, 159, 207, 211, 226, 234, 328, 329, 389, 395, 562, 571, 577
Maxwell, Elsa, 23, 47, 72, 92, 104, 161, 163, 201, 269, 284, 369, 400, 441, 442, 468, 487, 492, 496
Mayer, Louis B., 113–14, 136, 138, 148, 262, 267, 438, 468, 499
Mayfair and Montmartre, 38–9
McCarthy, Joseph, 536
Mendl, Sir Charles, 34, 47, 78
Mercer, Johnny, 118, 166–7, 371, 466, 554, 565
Mercer, Mabel, 106
Merman, Ethel, 98, 139–40, 141–2, 160–1, 162–3, 164, 171, 175–6, 195, 198, 212, 213, 292, 341–2, 363, 376, 449, 472, 473, 481, 487, 491, 618

Mexican Hayride, 19, 175, 180, 181, 186, 188, 189–91, 195, 200, 209, 235, 253, 278, 542, 543, 611
MGM, 108, 110–38, 144, 145, 148, 160, 169, 185, 196, 207, 218, 226, 231, 256, 263, 277, 278, 281, 300, 326, 331, 335, 337, 348, 356, 371, 419, 433, 439–40, 445, 446, 447, 452, 454, 457, 460, 461, 462, 463, 465, 466, 467, 472, 477, 482, 483, 489, 504, 508, 526, 527, 528, 529, 531, 532, 554, 557, 559, 563, 592, 618, 622
Mielziner, Jo, 463, 499
Milan, 57–9, 505, 509
Milhaud, Darius, 38, 40–3
Miller, Gilbert, 86, 245, 275, 310, 369
Miller, Kitty, 272, 273, 276, 369
Miller, Marilyn, 375
Mississippi Belle, 173, 176, 178, 180, 190, 193, 196, 197, 200, 206, 247
'Miss Otis Regrets', 109, 212
'Mister and Missus Fitch', 94, 358
Molnar, Ferenc, 76, 245
Monroe, Marilyn, 509
Montgomery, Robert, 405, 432, 433, 441, 455, 460, 461, 463, 464, 469, 481, 502, 503, 515–17, 528–9, 532, 544, 555, 569, 570, 571, 572, 580, 590, 596, 597, 602, 603, 609, 611, 614
Moore, Grace, 275, 481
Moore, Margaret, 163, 194, 215, 230, 247, 253, 259
Moore, Victor, 98, 156
Morison, Patricia, 301, 312, 318, 323, 332, 590, 619
Moses, Grandma, 219, 220, 224, 231, 272
Mountbatten, Philip (Duke of Edinburgh), 282
Murphy, Gerald, 34, 40–4, 241, 242, 436
Musgrove, Stanley, 157, 220, 263, 269, 275, 276, 282, 287, 324, 371, 404, 428, 486, 488, 502, 517, 536, 591, 595, 622, 623
My Fair Lady, 306, 536, 549, 555, 564, 569, 605
'My Heart Belongs to Daddy', 157, 159, 212, 213, 220, 234, 248, 249, 450, 465, 499, 562

Nathan, George Jean, 318, 404
Neff, Hildegard, 476
Niarchos, Stavros, 474, 512, 513, 515, 516, 533, 549
Nichols, Lewis, 175
'Night and Day' (song), 94, 95, 96, 110, 159, 164, 228, 465, 500, 562

Night and Day (film), 179, 180, 184, 188, 191–2, 198, 201, 206, 207, 208, 210, 211–12, 213–14, 215–18, 225, 226, 227, 229, 231–5, 239, 240, 244, 248, 250, 254, 255, 259–60, 264, 265, 266, 267, 271, 289, 290, 291, 368
Ninotchka, 450, 456, 457, 458, 459, 463, 476, 494
Novotna, Jarmila, 293
'Now You Has Jazz,' 524, 528, 530, 531, 562
Nymph Errant, 86, 94, 95, 96, 198, 381, 389, 394, 395, 448, 451, 461, 538, 539, 571

Oberon, Merle, 141, 195, 248, 283, 369, 388, 485, 569
Obolensky, Prince Sergei, 82, 272
Oelrichs, Dorothy, 51, 91, 105, 107
Oelrichs, Herman, 51, 71
Oklahoma!, 186, 212, 292, 298, 305, 365, 472
One Touch of Venus, 157, 216–17, 377
opera, 33, 70, 181, 216, 258, 261, 275, 293, 301, 302, 324, 350, 468, 471, 485, 501, 505, 541, 579, 592
Out of This World, 292, 312, 320, 324, 327, 332, 343, 346, 348, 351, 352, 356, 359, 361, 363, 364, 367–9, 370, 374, 439, 441, 522, 602–3

Paley [Wilson], Natalia [Natasha], 205, 343, 459, 491, 507, 536
Paley, William S., 276, 424, 539
Panama Hattie, 98, 154, 162, 173, 175, 176, 200, 202, 218, 292, 376, 481, 487, 543
Paris, 23, 24, 27, 28, 32, 38, 41, 43–51, 53–9, 62, 63–5, 69–74, 76–85, 88–93, 147–9, 161, 167, 169, 187, 206, 237, 282, 295, 339, 350, 359, 374, 396, 397, 398, 406, 414, 433, 437, 444, 446, 449, 451, 481, 495, 505, 509–10, 511, 524, 592, 602, 605
Paris (musical), 80–1, 86, 212, 239
Parsons, Humphrey, 14
Parsons, Louella, 126, 266, 274, 285, 358, 482
Pearman, Michael, 189, 286, 287, 292, 373
Perelman, S. J., 455, 572–5, 577, 579, 584
Peru (Indiana), 1, 2, 4, 10, 24, 31–2, 80, 155, 158, 165, 208–9, 279, 421, 536, 609, 623–4
Pirate, The, 232, 263, 277, 279, 280, 281, 284, 300, 327
Pons, Lily, 502–3

Porter, Cole
  and advertising, 22–3, 454–5, 482, 570
  aptitude for music and music lessons, 2–3, 8, 18, 37–8, 70
  and art, 35–6, 205, 219–20, 224, 446, 511
  casting singers/actors, 157, 199–200, 202, 207, 212–13, 217, 234–5, 239–40, 301–4, 390, 452, 491, 582
  and censorship, 210–12, 368, 374, 438–9
  and charity, 282–4, 515–16, 520, 524, 570
  compositional process/working methods/text revision, 10–14, 85, 98–102, 106, 110–38, 163–4, 174–5, 177–8, 197–8, 208–12, 237–9, 248–9, 256, 262, 278–9, 408, 411–14, 419, 426, 456, 489, 496–7, 498–500, 507–8, 523–4, 526, 563–4, 575–80
  exploitation of songs, 230, 326–7, 335–6, 482, 523–4
  finances, 79–80, 76–87, 91–4, 96, 102, 109, 124, 139, 148, 169, 188–9, 195, 247, 255, 286, 289–91, 296, 374–5, 377, 383, 391–5, 429–30, 439–40, 453, 461–2, 467, 479–81
  health, 4–5, 71, 148–52, 154, 166, 231–3, 242–3, 288, 299, 386, 395–401, 501, 566–7, 583–7, 589–92, 597, 604–8, 613–17, 619–24
  ideas about/conception of musical comedy, 254, 303–4, 348, 422
  interviews/writings (other than letters), 109–10, 141–4, 145–6, 158–9, 257, 266, 317–18, 498–500, 561–3
  performance practice, 218–19, 351, 357, 409, 522
  politics, 158
  residence in Paris (13, rue Monsieur), 46, 89–90, 160
  travels (outside USA and Europe), 29, 47–8, 50, 105–8, 161, 182–3, 473, 505–18, 533–4, 468–9
  war-time activities, 24–6, 33–4
Porter, Kate (mother), 1–8, 18–21, 24–5, 48, 76, 79, 87, 149, 155, 162, 209, 244, 249, 279, 288–91, 294, 297, 299, 308, 346, 350, 352, 369, 379, 421–3, 453, 464, 500
Porter, Linda (wife), 18, 23, 28–30, 32–3, 35, 38, 49–50, 52–4, 57–8, 62, 65–6, 74–5, 77, 79, 89–91, 93, 95, 105, 108, 110, 126, 133, 135, 149, 154, 156–7, 161–2, 165–6, 170, 179, 181–3, 193–5, 199, 203–6, 210, 214–15, 221, 231, 233, 235, 244, 246, 251, 253, 259–61, 263, 270–5, 277, 280, 283, 296–300, 308, 310, 313–15, 318–23, 326, 328–9, 332, 334–51, 353–6, 359–60, 362, 365–8, 370, 373–4, 380, 384–5, 387–8, 395–7, 399–401, 408, 425, 428, 431–2, 437, 452–3, 459–60, 464, 468, 471, 474, 476–80, 483, 485, 516–17, 520, 537, 573–4
Porter, Samuel (father), 1–2, 244
Pot of Gold, The, 10–14
Powell, Edward B., 130, 131, 134, 135
Powell, Eleanor, 108, 118, 121, 123, 125, 134, 135, 136, 138, 145, 160
Powell, William, 105, 161

Raison, Robert, 205, 252, 269, 271, 273, 288, 307, 308, 309, 319, 320, 338, 348, 371, 373, 402, 404, 485, 488, 511, 517, 536, 542, 601, 613, 623
Red, Hot and Blue!, 88, 97, 98, 123, 124, 127, 139, 140, 141, 142, 145, 167, 292, 362, 449, 525
La Revue des Ambassadeurs, 82, 83, 85, 86
Reynaldo, Tito, 173, 271, 338, 340
Reynolds, Debbie, 508
Rezzonico (Venice), 52, 53, 70, 73, 74, 76, 448
'Ridin' High', 140, 465
Riggs, T. Lawrason, 15–17, 21, 29–30, 149
Rimsky-Korsakov, Nikolai, 579
Ritchard, Cyril, 577, 580
Robbins, Adele, 302
Robbins, Jerome, 441, 475
Rodgers, Richard, 74, 75, 76, 83, 95, 126, 157, 186, 200, 212, 270, 286, 298, 306, 309, 317, 324, 328, 330, 365, 375, 441, 442, 445, 457, 461, 463, 472, 482, 500, 538, 560
Romberg, Sigmund, 376, 457, 502
Rome, 31, 37, 50, 61, 62, 63, 76, 77, 274, 506, 510, 511, 512, 516, 541, 542, 543, 544, 550, 554, 568, 592
Roosevelt, Franklin D., 189, 276
Roosevelt Hotel, 194
Rosalie, 88, 108, 118, 138, 144, 145, 203, 262, 325, 499
Rose, Billy, 198, 199, 200, 201, 202, 204, 206, 209, 212, 213, 217, 222, 225, 226

Sadie Thompson, 213
Schankman, Ben, 363, 378, 379, 380, 383, 384, 385, 388, 391, 393–6, 407
Schwartz, Arthur, 103, 148, 160, 175, 179, 190, 191–3, 197–8, 201, 206–15, 217,

218, 224–7, 230, 232, 235, 239, 244, 248, 249, 260, 280, 385, 429–30, 470
See America First, 15–23, 32, 83, 85, 239, 264, 614
Seldes, Gilbert, 45, 46
Seven Lively Arts, 198, 199, 200–2, 206, 209, 212, 216, 217–18, 221–3, 225, 230, 310, 542
Shakespeare, William, 111, 292, 301, 309, 311
Sharaff, Irene, 381, 582
Shaw, Artie, 159, 316
Shaw, Charles Green, 47–52, 57
Shaw, George Bernard, 36, 588
Shaw, Robert, 312
Short, Hassard, 175, 222, 225
Show Boat, 121, 128, 300
Shurr, Louis, 195, 373, 381, 486
Silk Stockings
  film version, 534, 565, 573
  stage version, 104, 292, 324, 451, 456, 457, 463, 464, 466, 471, 474, 475, 476, 477, 481, 483, 485, 488, 489, 493, 494, 495, 496, 497, 498–502, 503–5, 511, 575, 588, 611
Silvers, Sidney, 110, 111, 113, 114, 115, 116, 117, 118, 119, 120, 121, 123, 125, 127, 128, 129, 130, 131, 132, 134, 136
Simpson, Wallis, 271, 369, 383, 384, 482, 492
Sinatra, Frank, 335, 472, 522, 559,
Sinatra Jr., Frank, 613
Sirmay, Dr Albert, 95, 165, 176, 204, 223, 240, 327, 357, 360, 363, 438, 449, 450, 501, 521, 523, 537–8, 565, 579, 610
Smith, Alexis, 179, 244, 260
Smith, Kate, 235–6
Smith, Madeline P., 300, 354, 360, 364, 365, 367, 373, 379, 380, 393, 394, 421, 427, 428, 433–5, 439, 442, 453, 480, 501, 509–11, 516, 531, 539, 541, 554, 556, 557, 565, 566, 567, 583, 584, 585, 586, 587, 589, 590, 591, 594, 597, 598, 603–16, 617–24
Smithson, John, 296, 502
'So in Love', 311, 316, 326, 562
Something for the Boys, 19, 154, 174–7, 193, 195, 196, 200, 253, 270, 292, 376, 543
Something to Shout About, 169
South Pacific, 157, 305, 327, 328, 329, 350
Spewack, Bella, 34, 112, 156, 292–6, 298, 300–2, 303–4, 305, 313, 318, 325, 357, 371, 382–3, 385, 386, 389–90, 400, 433, 466, 467, 518, 532, 565, 571, 583, 590, 596, 608

Spewack, Sam, 112, 156, 300–2, 357, 433, 466, 467, 532
Stanley, Edward, 168
Stark, Harriette, 447, 478, 479, 488, 496, 566–8, 582, 583, 587, 588, 589, 591, 593, 598, 600, 601–7, 613, 616–23
Stark, Ray, 419
Stark, Sam, 180–91, 202–3, 204–6, 210, 213–14, 232–3, 235, 251–4, 257–9, 263, 266, 267, 268–77, 279, 281–2, 284–5, 286–8, 292–3, 294–300, 307–10, 312–16, 319–20, 328, 329, 331–5, 336–41, 342, 343–4, 346–8, 351, 352–8, 361–2, 364–7, 369, 370, 373–4, 380, 383–8, 390, 395, 396–404, 421, 423, 424, 425, 427, 431–2, 436–7, 438, 442, 447, 457, 466, 470, 472–4, 478–81, 483–4, 487–9, 495–6, 501–2, 511, 518, 542–3, 545, 554, 557–8, 560, 566, 567, 568, 582, 583–91, 593–5, 597–8, 600–8, 610–23
Stearns, Roger, 161, 172, 241
Steinert, Alex, 405, 520, 521, 578
'Stereophonic Sound', 502, 563
Stewart, James, 108, 123, 129
Stewart, William Rhinelander, 31, 163
Stravinsky, Igor, 37, 38, 70, 71, 199, 216, 217
Sturges, Howard, 31, 105, 158, 165, 167–8, 182–3, 184, 246, 276, 282, 285, 295, 310, 314, 333–4, 337, 339, 362, 369, 371, 374, 384, 387–8, 398–9, 402, 425, 437, 485, 505, 509, 511–12
Subber, Arnold Saint, 292, 293, 296, 305, 306, 309, 312, 318, 320, 326, 327, 355, 357, 363, 491
Sullivan, Sir Arthur, 20, 202, 375, 412, 413, 443, 499
Sullivan, Ed, 402, 404
'Swingin' the Jinx Away', 131, 132
Sylvain, Paul, 158, 276, 282, 295, 329, 353, 360, 384, 397–9, 400, 401, 408, 421, 498, 501, 505, 509, 510, 546, 567, 583, 585, 590, 591, 594, 597

Taft, William, 16, 21
Tauch, Ed, 296, 297, 328, 369, 419
Taylor, Dwight, 328, 348–9, 351
Taylor, Elizabeth, 195, 253, 508
Taylor, Laurette, 23
television, 370, 375, 378, 394, 395, 402, 403, 429, 431, 454, 455, 472, 476, 481, 487, 497, 506, 517, 539, 560–3, 572, 573, 574, 582, 590, 596, 618, 619

INDEX

Tennyson, Lord Alfred, 221
Thalberg, Irving, 136–7
Theatre Arts, 155, 558
This is the Army, 167
Time magazine, 558
Todd, Mike, 175, 195, 196, 209, 253
'Too Darn Hot', 311, 316, 319–20, 326
Tovarich, 596
'True Love', 508, 530, 531, 554
'Trust Your Destiny to Your Star', 577, 579
Tucker, Sophie, 157, 207, 243, 279

Valentino, Rudolph, 563
Velez, Lupe, 155
Venice, 48, 50, 52, 53, 54, 56, 57, 58, 61, 63, 65, 69–76, 78, 87, 91, 284, 311, 448, 520, 537
Verdon, Gwen, 430
Verdura, Duke of, 203, 204, 369, 427, 442, 468
Vidal, Gore, 284, 286
Vogue, 46, 205, 424

Wake Up and Dream, 86–8, 260, 389, 449
Walker, Allen, 186, 253, 269, 270, 272, 274, 276, 277, 282, 288, 308, 333, 338, 339, 343, 350, 353, 355, 385, 388, 391, 396, 402, 403, 424, 428, 480
Walters, Charles, 522, 525, 558
Walters, Louis, 223
Waring, Fred, 84, 85, 245
Warner, Ann, 184, 241, 245, 269
Warner, Harry M., 227
Warner, Jack, 179, 184, 190, 191, 192, 201, 207, 208, 213, 215, 227, 229, 230, 231, 232, 233, 234, 245, 250, 251, 254, 255, 256, 264, 266, 267, 368
Warner Bros. (studio), 110, 112, 130, 166, 173, 175, 176, 178, 180, 184, 185, 188, 189, 191, 197, 227, 229, 230, 233, 236, 239, 240, 244, 245, 254, 260, 266, 284, 323, 404
Warren, Harry, 170, 381, 549
Warren, Whitney Jr., 387
Warwick, Ruth, 299
Webb, Clifton, 34, 83, 84, 85, 103, 105, 148, 155, 163, 275, 375, 449
Weill, Kurt, 38, 157, 167, 200, 216, 300, 310, 312
Welch, Elizabeth, 539
'Well, Did You Evah?', 525–9, 559
Welles, Orson, 167, 247, 248, 251, 253, 255, 256, 257, 258, 264, 353

'We Open in Venice', 311, 316, 438
We're All Dressed Up and We Don't Know Huerto Go, 17
'Were Thine That Special Face', 302, 303, 324, 327
'We Shall [Will] Never Be Younger', 458
West, Mae, 157, 160
Wharton, Edith, 184
Wharton, John, 206, 357, 367, 374, 375, 376, 390, 392, 405, 418, 419, 429, 430, 431, 439–41, 446, 450, 451, 454, 459–64, 465, 470, 476, 479–80, 481, 485, 502, 503, 504, 516, 517, 519–21, 529, 544, 559–60, 571–2, 596, 614
'What Is this Thing Called Love?', 88, 225, 226, 465
Where's Charley?, 401, 433
Williams College, 614
Wilson, John C., 292, 293, 296, 301, 303, 304, 305, 311, 343, 369, 458, 459, 460, 461, 536
Wilson, Julie, 590
Wiman, Dwight Deere, 103, 126, 147, 172, 449
Winchell, Walter, 235, 236, 277, 336, 536, 594
Windsor, Duchess of, *see* Wallis Simpson
Windsor, Duke of, 77, 271, 369, 492
Within the Quota, 34, 40–4, 46, 47, 53, 70, 71
Wodehouse, P. G., 97, 100, 101, 153
Wonderful Town, 200, 382
Woolley, Monty, 17, 26, 27, 28, 32, 33, 34, 35, 37, 47, 48, 51, 75, 91, 105, 108, 126, 144, 148, 149, 150, 166, 186, 194, 201, 212, 221, 222, 226, 234, 238–9, 244, 252, 264, 279, 280
Worcester Academy, 2–9, 103, 368
Wyler, Gretchen, 496, 501

Yale, 7–11, 14–17, 19, 20, 23, 26, 27, 29, 30, 31, 32, 36, 37, 42, 44, 48, 88, 150, 201, 208, 221, 264, 265, 322–3, 334, 499, 507, 519, 520, 529, 601, 602, 614
You'll Never Get Rich, 165, 332
You Never Know, 83, 148, 153–6, 499
'You're the Top', 97, 98–9, 110, 166, 212, 260, 342, 433, 473

Zanuck, Daryl F., 244, 497, 503, 504, 563
Ziegfeld Follies, 218
Ziegfeld Follies of 1936, 118, 200
Ziegfeld Follies of 1956, 549